WHITE MALICE

WHITE MALICE

THE CIA AND THE COVERT RECOLONIZATION OF AFRICA

SUSAN WILLIAMS

PUBLICAFFAIRS

New York

PublicAffairs
Hachette Book Group
1290 Avenue of the Americas, New York, NY 10104
www.publicaffairsbooks.com
@Public_Affairs

Printed in the United States of America

First Edition: August 2021

Published by PublicAffairs, an imprint of Perseus Books, LLC, a subsidiary of Hachette Book Group, Inc. The PublicAffairs name and logo is a trademark of the Hachette Book Group.

The Hachette Speakers Bureau provides a wide range of authors for speaking events. To find out more, go to www.hachettespeakersbureau.com or call (866) 376-6591.

The publisher is not responsible for websites (or their content) that are not owned by the publisher.

Library of Congress Control Number: 2021938151

ISBNs: 978-1-5417-6829-1 (hardcover), 978-1-5417-6828-4 (e-book)

LSC-C

Printing 1, 2021

For Gervase

CONTENTS

Photo section appears between pages 266 and 267

The activities of the C.I.A. no longer surprise us. . . . Further examples of C.I.A. activity . . . in Africa could be given. They would provide material for a book of their own.

KWAME NKRUMAH,
Dark Days in Ghana (1968)

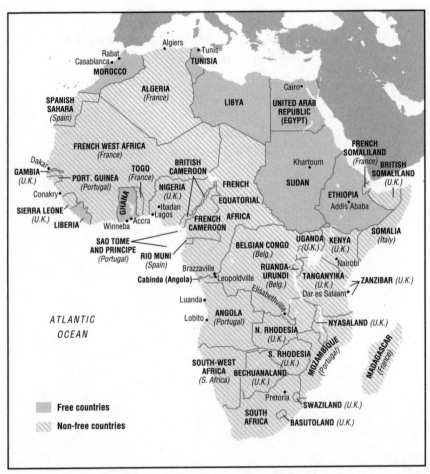

Africa in January 1958, when most territories were occupied by a European colonial power or were under white supremacist rule.

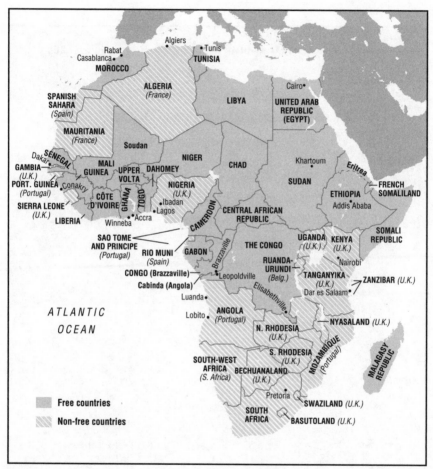

Africa in September 1960, when sixteen newly independent African states were admitted to the United Nations. The map shows the rapid pace of decolonisation since 1958.

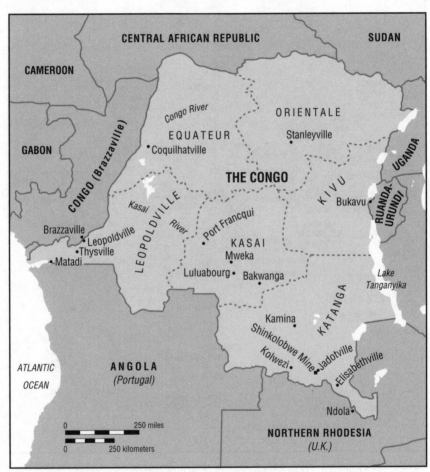

The Congo at independence from Belgium, 30 June 1960.

THE UNITED STATES OF AFRICA

Freedom at Midnight

THE HOURS OF THE DAY had been hot and charged with thunder. As darkness fell, the humid atmosphere in Accra felt explosive. Even so, the crowds had swelled along the coast, and the streets were heaving. Suddenly, the newly built Arch of Independence was floodlit against the blackness of the sea. The monument was inscribed with a short but powerful message: 'Freedom and Justice. A.D. 1957'. It stood on the spot where three unarmed men had been shot dead nine years earlier, when a British police officer had ordered his men to fire at a peaceful deputation from the African Ex-Servicemen's Union. Now, it marked the start of a new era. Fireworks soared into the sky above the arch.[1]

At the stroke of midnight, bells pealed loudly. Then the Union Jack flying above Parliament House was hauled down, and the new flag of Ghana was solemnly raised up, for the first time. As it reached the top of the pole, it fluttered slowly in the night air—red, gold and green, with the black lodestar of Africa at its centre. Cries of happiness rang out, and people danced and sang in jubilation. Over and over, people cheered and shouted out at the top of their voices: 'Freedom! Ghana! Nkrumah!'

Prime Minister Kwame Nkrumah was carried shoulder high to a dais in the Old Polo Ground, close to the roaring surf of the Atlantic Ocean. Under a flood of lights, Nkrumah's open face and large, steady eyes looked out at the thousands in front of him. Forty-eight years old, he had spent much of his life working for this moment, as had so many others. He wore a cotton smock from the north of Ghana and a Gandhi-type prison cap, marked with the initials PG, standing for 'prison graduate'. It was a badge of honour worn with pride by many Ghanaians, in remembrance of their unjust imprisonment by the British.

The noise of the crowd was deafening. Then Dr Nkrumah held out his arm to command attention, with solemn authority. He called for a minute's silence to give thanks to God. Then he asked everyone to remove their hats, as the police band played the new national anthem, 'Ghana Arise!' Tears streamed down his face, and many in the crowds were sobbing. Unmistakably, on 6 March 1957, the people of Ghana were free. The British colony of the Gold Coast was no more, and Ghana had become the first Black-majority country to obtain independence from colonialism, blazing a trail for the African continent.

'At long last', proclaimed Nkrumah, 'the battle has ended and Ghana, our beloved country, is free for ever'. Then, choked with emotion, he fell silent. It was an unforgettable moment for Cameron Duodu, a young cub reporter. 'Just sixteen words—no more', he wrote later. 'But no-one who heard them would ever be able to forget them. The cheers that greeted those sixteen words were, of course, out of this world'.[2] The iconography of Ghana's independence ceremony followed the pattern set by India on 15 August 1947, ten years earlier. Then, too, the Union Jack had been lowered and replaced by the new Indian flag at midnight.

But Ghana was not copying India for dramatic effect. It was following India's clear commitment to international nonalignment, led by Prime Minister Jawaharlal Nehru. This commitment had been a major theme of the Bandung Conference of African-Asian states in 1955, in which the Gold Coast participated. There, led by Nehru, Indonesia's Sukarno, and Egypt's Gamal Abdel Nasser, twenty-nine emergent nations across Africa and Asia had sought to lay the foundations of a nonaligned 'third force', to resist the pressures from the West and from the East in the context of the Cold War.

Not only in Ghana's capital Accra, but also in Kumasi, Tamale, Sekondi-Takoradi, and Cape Coast, similar ceremonies took place, where the Union Jack was replaced with the new flag. Families in the churches and the mosques sent prayers to God. In the night-clubs, exuberant throngs danced to the 'Highlife'—a popular fusion of Ghanaian musical traditions with Western instruments.[3]

The Reverend Martin Luther King Jr and his wife, Coretta Scott King, who had come from America to celebrate Ghana's freedom, were a part of the crowd in Accra. These young civil rights campaigners—Dr King was just twenty-eight years old—were profoundly moved. 'Before I knew it', declared Dr King in a sermon the following month to his congregation in Montgomery, Alabama, 'I started weeping. I was crying for joy. And I knew about all of the struggles, and all of the pain, and all of the agony that these people had gone through for this moment'.[4]

* * *

AT THE OPENING OF the first session of the Parliament of Ghana, Sir Charles Arden-Clarke was sworn in as governor general, as the representative of the British crown; before independence, he had been the governor, representing not only Queen Elizabeth II but the powers of the British government in its colonial territory. He made a brief personal statement, in which he declared his 'unqualified pride at his association with "colonialism"' and referred to the 'continuity of purpose of British colonial policy'. Britain's high commissioner, who attended the session, reported to London that he delivered this statement with a smile which evoked 'an appreciative response' from members of Parliament.[5] No doubt Ghana's MPs felt obliged to be polite to their guest. But it was a strange thing to say, since the struggle against colonialism had been fierce—against, as Nkrumah put it, 'the limitations on our freedom, the crimes against our dignity as human beings'.[6]

It was true that in comparison with many other territories in Africa occupied by European powers, Ghana had escaped the large invasions of white settlers, which had wrecked the lives of so many millions of people in territories such as Kenya, Southern Rhodesia (now Zimbabwe), Mozambique, and South Africa.

But there were profound and brutal forms of injustice in Ghana under British rule. Seven hospitals in the country catered for fewer than three thousand 'Europeans'—the colonisers' word for any person with white skin—leaving thirty-six hospitals for about four million Ghanaians.[7] This inequity based on skin colour was mirrored in all public services, including education. It was also manifest in the crude physical segregation of people. 'When I first went to the Gold Coast', recalled Erica Powell, who went to work for Sir Charles Arden-Clarke as his private secretary in 1952, 'there existed between the so-called elite of the Europeans and the Africans in whose country they lived a racial barrier as apparent as the Mason-Dixon Line'. She was shocked at the racism of most whites, who 'were unanimous in declaring that the Africans were nowhere near being capable of taking over the government of the country'.[8]

Powell was among those impressed by Nkrumah's charisma and magnetism. They slowly became friends, and she learnt from him a different way of looking at colonisation, which challenged her assumption that British rule was benevolent and had brought some kind of superior civilisation. One day, when she expressed ignorance of what self-government meant, Nkrumah spent more than two hours explaining it to her. 'I was held spellbound—at times horrified—by what he had to say', wrote Powell years later. It was 'not a sob story', she said, but a lesson in colonial history, politics and economics, which 'shattered into tiny little pieces my schoolgirl illusions about Britain's big-hearted give-all-and-take-naught attitude towards her colonies'. At the end, she could find nothing worthwhile to justify Britain's presence in Africa.[9]

Because of her friendship with Nkrumah, Powell was ostracised by the British community and was asked by the governor to leave the colony. Instead, she left the colonial service. In 1955, she became Nkrumah's devoted and loyal private secretary, who was as much concerned by what he ate—and didn't eat—as by his files and appointments.[10] A hard-working and conscientious woman, who wore plain clothes and a tidy hairstyle, she was thoroughly professional in her affect. Nonetheless, many of the British expatriate community regarded her as the Jezebel of Accra; they spread prurient rumours that reflected their loathing of interracial relationships. There was no evidence to suggest that Powell and Nkrumah were having a sexual relationship. Nkrumah had a number of friendships with women, rooted in shared intellectual and political interests, as well as companionship.

On the last day of 1957, Nkrumah married Fathia Halim Ritzk, a twenty-five-year old Egyptian.[11] Ritzk, a former student at the University of Cairo, was a quiet and dignified woman with dark eyes and a bright smile. When she agreed to the marriage, she had not met Nkrumah; nor had she been to Ghana. She had been identified as a possible wife by a friend of Nkrumah's, and they were shown photographs of each other.

President Nasser met with Ritzk before the marriage. He was not against the plan, he said, but wanted her to be aware of the challenges ahead. Her response was adamant: 'I would like to go and marry this anti-colonial leader. I read his autobiography, I know of his trials and tribulations, of his struggles during his student days in America and Britain, and of his spearheading the anti-colonial struggle upon his return to his homeland'.

For Ritzk, Nkrumah was an anticolonial hero, like Nasser. She wished to make her own contribution to Africa's struggle for freedom.

Their first child, born in 1959, was named Gamal, after Nasser. 'It was not meant to be a marriage made in heaven', commented Gamal Nkrumah when an adult. 'It was a political union between Mediterranean-oriented North Africa and the rest of the continent'.[12]

* * *

THE YEARS LEADING UP to Ghana's independence were a time of suffering and oppression. The killing in 1948 of three men of the African Ex-Servicemen's Union had triggered bitter and widespread violence, which transformed the political scene of the colony. The situation became so tense that in 1950, Governor Arden-Clarke declared a state of emergency and imposed a curfew, during which Nkrumah was arrested on the charge of inciting an unofficial strike. In 1951, large-scale elections to the Legislative Assembly took place. This produced a victory for the Convention People's Party (CPP), led by Nkrumah, which forced the colonial government to release him from prison. He was driven among cheering crowds to party headquarters, and the next day he was invited by the governor to form a government.

For the first time, Ghanaians had a majority in the Assembly and in the Executive Council. But the ex-officio members nominated by Arden-Clarke held the real reins of power, through their control of defence, external affairs, finance and justice. This was 'a Government largely in name', argued Nkrumah, 'with ultimate power residing in the Governor of the Gold Coast, who really represented the Colonial Office on the spot'.[13]

It was not until 1956 that a popular election was held in order to deliver a national government, in which a majority of the seats were won by the Convention People's Party.

* * *

As the outgoing power in 1957, the British selected many of the official guests to the independence celebrations of Ghana. President Nasser, president of the United Arab Republic, a political union of Egypt and Syria that had been formed in 1958, was not invited, because of the rupture in diplomatic relations between the UK and Egypt following the fiasco of the Suez crisis in 1956.

The most important guest from the point of view of the British government was Princess Marina, Duchess of Kent, who came as the representative of Queen Elizabeth II. She presided over a busy royal programme, including a meeting at the race course—a popular event in colonial circles. Reports sent to London by British officials praised the duchess's warm engagement with the celebrations, as well as her haute couture and glittering jewels.[14]

More than fifty foreign governments were invited and sent special representatives; some two hundred members of the press and media came too.[15] In the words of one press officer, 'The world had come to Accra'.[16]

The largest delegations came from the USSR, the US, and the People's Republic of China, which sent parties of twenty or more, creating logistical challenges for the new nation. The Ambassador Hotel, specially built for independence to offer modern and luxurious accommodation, was not very large and had to house all the important guests.

The American delegation, led by Vice President Richard M Nixon and his wife, Pat, and accompanied by a second plane packed with American newsmen, were put up in the Ambassador Hotel, along with the Soviets. One headline in the US noted, 'ACCRA BILLETS NIXON WITH REDS'.[17]

At a state banquet, 'all was pomp and protocol'—except that the seating plan had been drawn up alphabetically. This meant that the leader of the Soviet delegation, the handsome I A Benedictov, minister of state farming, sat at the top table, and Vice President Nixon, because his name began with the letter 'N', was placed farther down the room. Nixon was furious. Headlines in the US the following day made the most of it: 'NIXON SLIGHTED AS COMMIE HEADS TABLE; NIXON SLIGHTED ON TRIP, AIDES MIFFED; NIXON SNUB SHOWS HOW LITTLE PRESTIGE US BILLIONS HAVE BOUGHT'.[18]

A British official working for the colonial public relations service enjoyed his contact with the Russian journalists. At the airport, he found 'two solemn men standing smoking silently'. The correspondent from *Pravda* gave him a Russian cigarette and introduced him to the cameraman. Back at the hotel, he recorded, 'the two Russians became our politest guests. They sat in the lounge at night, dispensing Russian cigarettes and occasional shots of vodka that they had with them, and refused to be rattled by the political questions thrown at them by the other correspondents'. The official observed with wry amusement that they filed long stories on the social and economic aspects of life in Ghana, 'but seemed only slightly interested in what the Duchess of Kent was doing'.[19]

Visiting African dignitaries included leaders such as Habib Bourguiba, the president of Tunisia, which had achieved independence from France in 1956; William Tolbert, the vice president of Liberia; Sylvanus Olympio from Togo; and the son of Haile Selassie, the emperor of Ethiopia. From France came the minister of justice, François Mitterrand, and from the Vatican, Archbishop Know.

Dr Ralph Bunche, senior advisor to Dag Hammarskjöld, the UN secretary general, was also present. Bunche, an American, had been awarded the Nobel Peace Prize for his mediating role in the Arab-Israeli war of 1948–1949 and was the first Black person ever to be honoured in this way. At the time of Ghana's independence, Bunche was embroiled in the ongoing Suez problem and, exhausted by the pace and by constant bouts of dysentery, welcomed the respite offered by the visit to Ghana. He brought a special message from Hammarskjöld, congratulating Ghana on becoming the eighty-first member of the UN.[20]

A large number of guests came at the personal invitation of Prime Minister Nkrumah. At the top of his list were George Padmore, the Trinidadian Pan-Africanist, and his wife, Dorothy Pizer, firm friends of Nkrumah from his days in the UK. Their vision of the future of Africa meshed perfectly with his: not only free of colonial rule, but also not aligned to either the East or the West. 'We do not', stated Padmore firmly, 'intend to be like Russia, the United States, or anyone else'.[21]

With open arms, Nkrumah invited freedom fighters from all over the world, such as Cheddi Jagan from British Guiana and Norman Manley from British-ruled Jamaica. From South Africa came the Reverend Michael Scott, an Anglican priest, and the peace activist Homer Jack.

From Kenya came Mbiyu Koinange, a prominent member of the Kenya African Union and the brother-in-law of Jomo Kenyatta, its leader, who was in prison serving a seven-year sentence handed down by the British colonial administration for the alleged organisation of the Land and Freedom Movement, dubbed 'Mau Mau' by the colonisers. The British government were responsible in the 1950s for a terrible campaign of systematic and brutal torture and abuse—killing, castration and rape—of Kenyan freedom fighters.

From the US came civil rights campaigners such as Dr Martin Luther King, Mrs Coretta Scott King, Asa Philip Randolph and Adam Clayton Powell. Shirley Graham came without her eighty-nine-year-old husband, the renowned African American scholar and founding father of the National Association for the Advancement of Colored People (NAACP), Dr W E B Du Bois. He had been blocked from travelling abroad by the US government. Also from the US came distinguished academics, including Horace Mann Bond, the president of Lincoln University. Nkrumah had spent ten years studying in the US, first at Lincoln University and then at the University of Pennsylvania.

Nkrumah's landlady in London, Mrs Florence Manley, came with her daughter.[22] Mrs Manley had supported Nkrumah's political work in London and had been mentioned in intelligence reports on Nkrumah by the spies and informers of the UK's Special Branch and MI5, who speculated, wrongly, that Nkrumah and Mrs Manley were on intimate terms and planning to marry.[23] Rumours about their alleged relationship were spread by the colonial government in 1948 in a deliberate effort to discredit him.[24] They, too, were strange, prurient imaginings.

* * *

ERICA POWELL WAS CONCERNED that Nkrumah barely slept during the week of the independence celebrations. 'When he wasn't attending official functions or receiving foreign guests in private audience', she recorded, 'he was sought after by his own ministers, his party colleagues and the masses of ordinary men and women'. But her concern was unfounded: for no matter at what hour he met his guests, 'he was fresh, alert, dynamic, listening avidly to what each had to say and handling any subject with equal ability and enthusiasm'.[25]

But one challenge almost defeated him. When told he was expected to lead the dancing at the state ball, he was appalled, saying that he knew only the Highlife.

He was rescued by Lucille Armstrong, who taught him the basic steps of the waltz, foxtrot and quickstep.[26] He had met Mrs Armstrong the year before, when she had come to Ghana with her husband, Louis Armstrong, the famous American jazz trumpeter.

Armstrong was unable to go back to Ghana to celebrate independence, but Lucille flew there with a copy of *Satchmo the Great*, a new US Information Service film of Armstrong's earlier visit. The film showed Armstrong dedicating to Prime Minister Nkrumah the protest anthem from the 1920s '(What Did I Do to Be So) Black and Blue', composed by the jazz musician Fats Waller. The last lines of the song—painfully and powerfully—convey the injustice of discrimination against Black people because of the colour of skin. 'My only sin', goes the song, 'is in my skin'. One of its most heart-wrenching lines includes the words 'wished I was dead'. It asks, 'How would it end?' *Satchmo the Great* captured Nkrumah's emotional response to the song, as he listened intently to the words.[27]

The state ball during the independence celebrations was a far more formal affair than the jazz concerts the previous year. One of the guests was Genoveva Marais, a South African woman in her twenties who had arrived in Ghana the month before to work as an Inspector of Schools. She was excited to be a fully fledged Black citizen in Ghana and no longer a victim of apartheid in her own country. Her father had felt great happiness at the independence of Ghana, and 'the thrill he felt', she wrote later in a memoir, 'was translated to me'.

When the invitation to the ball arrived, Marais was 'in the heights of delight'. Beautiful, vivacious and sophisticated, she was quickly noticed by Nkrumah, who sent an officer to request her company at his table. She had noticed Nkrumah's 'easy air' as he walked around the room chatting with different people, but all the same she felt 'dizzy and nervous'.

Her unease swiftly disappeared as they joked and laughed together. They had much in common: Marais, like Nkrumah, had studied in the US—at Columbia University in New York—after her education at Fort Hare and Rhodes University in South Africa. She quickly sensed that Nkrumah was physically attracted to her, which was confirmed when the prime minister invited her to State House the following morning.

Before long, he asked her to marry him, but she refused. She noted with approval that Nkrumah 'created a new dimension for African womanhood. There were even female Members of Parliament and a judge!' But, she said, 'I was not ready for marriage and I was far too critical and independent'.

This did not prevent the development of their relationship. 'Veva', as Nkrumah called Marais, believed that she learnt 'to know and understand Kwame Nkrumah as no one else ever could'.[28] They became close companions, and it was widely rumoured that she was his lover.[29]

* * *

As the Reverend Martin Luther King witnessed the birth of Ghana, he realised its wider significance. 'This event', he believed, 'will give impetus to oppressed peoples all over the world. I think it will have worldwide implications and repercussions—not only for Asia and Africa, but also for America'. It renewed his conviction, he said in a radio interview in Accra, 'in the ultimate triumph of justice. And it seems to me that this is fit testimony to the fact that eventually the forces of justice triumph in the universe, and somehow the universe itself is on the side of freedom and justice. So that this gives new hope to me in the struggle for freedom'.[30]

The independence celebrations led King to compare African liberation with African American civil rights struggles. 'At bottom', commented King, 'both segregation in America and colonialism in Africa are based on the same thing—white supremacy and contempt for life'.[31]

King also met Vice President Nixon for the first time in Ghana. Back in America, Nixon, along with the US president, Dwight D Eisenhower, had been asked by African Americans living in the southern states to visit them, to see for themselves the ugliness of Jim Crow and the laws enforcing racial segregation. The vice president had managed to evade those requests. But soon after arriving in Accra, King attended a reception where he encountered Nixon. He used it as an opportunity to press him to visit the South. 'Mr Vice President, I'm very glad to meet you here', King told Nixon, 'but I want you to come visit us down in Alabama where we are seeking the same kind of freedom the Gold Coast is celebrating'.[32]

Generally, Nixon was in his element on the trip. When he was met at the airport by a group of ministers, he cut away from the official party and headed for the airport fence. He had spotted a crowd lining the rails and, followed by his wife, he shook hands with everybody and patted heads. According to a press officer, 'He smiled, smiled all the time'. The Ghanaian ministers, 'themselves experienced politicians, watched Nixon's technique admiringly', while an American reporter commented dryly that Nixon was 'campaigning already' for the forthcoming US election.[33]

Newsreels captured Nixon grinning broadly and wielding his movie camera throughout the visit. Echoing the euphoria of his Ghanaian hosts, he went up to one man in jovial good humour.

Slapping him on the shoulder, he asked him how it felt to be free. 'I wouldn't know, Sir', came the reply. 'I'm from Alabama'.[34]

* * *

FOR NKRUMAH, FREEDOM FOR Ghana had a significance beyond even the liberation of the nation. He set this out clearly in his speech at the Old Polo Ground. 'Our independence', he insisted, 'is meaningless unless it is linked up with the total liberation of the African continent'. Liberation would stretch from north to south. 'The Sahara no longer divides us', he said firmly. 'It unites us'.

The only way forward for Africa, Nkrumah believed, was the creation of a federation of nations—a United States of Africa. He was applying the lessons of freedom from the history of America, where thirteen colonies had revolted in 1776 against the British, and together had issued the Declaration of Independence. The colonies formed a union, eventually constituting the fifty states of the United States of America.

Nkrumah wanted Africa to achieve the same union of states, declared his friend and disciple Kofi Batsa, a Ghanaian political activist. The states would aim to serve each other with 'all the necessary economic conditions of labour, of skills, of capital, of minerals, of energy reserves—to provide a self-contained and self-development economy'. Within Africa, added Batsa, Nkrumah saw there were 'enormous skills, enormous assets and great potential' to achieve this vision.

African unity, therefore, was 'the strategy of the total liberation and complete independence of Africa'.[35] It was a bold, visionary goal, full of idealism and pragmatism.

2

'My Home Is Over Jordan'

N KRUMAH HAD BEEN A STUDENT in America for ten years, between 1935 and 1945. His experience had a profound influence on the development of his thinking and his politics. But it is extraordinary that he went to the US at all. For one thing, he came from a poor family. His father, a goldsmith, had died when he was seventeen; his mother, Elizabeth Nyaniba, with whom he had lived as a child in the village of Nkroful in Nzima in the extreme southwest of the Gold Coast, was a local trader in cigarettes and rice.[1] He left his homeland with very little money and knew that he would suffer hardship. It was also painful to go so far away from his mother, especially as he was her only child. 'It cannot be helped', she said. 'May God and your ancestors guide you'.

Most Ghanaians hoping to study abroad looked to British universities, especially if they wished to establish themselves in a profession such as law. But Nkrumah was different: his aim was not to secure a career, but to find a way of ending the colonisation of the Gold Coast. He was therefore inspired by the speeches and newspaper articles of Nnamdi Azikiwe, a Nigerian nationalist who had recently returned to Africa from his studies in the US. Azikiwe went on to become the first president of Nigeria in 1963. In the 1930s, he fired the imaginations of those who longed for freedom from the European colonisers. He urged African intellectuals to go to the US and 'to come back with the Golden Fleece'. Nkrumah was among the first to take Azikiwe's advice.

After boarding ship to the US, Nkrumah 'felt desperately alone and sat on my bunk close to tears'. But beside him he found a telegram from Azikiwe: 'Goodbye. Remember to trust in God and in yourself'.[2] This gave him the courage he needed to face the journey.

Once he had arrived in the US, Nkrumah managed to enrol at Lincoln University, in Pennsylvania. Lincoln, the alma mater of Azikiwe, was widely regarded as the Princeton of African American universities; in 1854, it had become the first institution anywhere in the world to grant degrees to Black students. At Lincoln, Nkrumah 'soared through examinations', notes his biographer Basil Davidson. He earned both a bachelor of arts in 1939 and a bachelor of theology in 1942, when he graduated at the top of his class. Then, again following in the path of Azikiwe, he went to the University of Pennsylvania, where he obtained two MA degrees.

In 1945, Nkrumah attracted the attention of the FBI, which sent a 'special agent' to investigate his behaviour on campus. The agent reported that 'while the subject had lacked leadership on the campus and had not shown initiative, he was considered loyal and honest. He knew of no radical tendencies on the part of the subject'. Nkrumah was 'not an independent thinker', added the agent.[3] Judging by its several reports on Nkrumah, the FBI gained no real sense at that time of the man who would lead his nation to freedom and take a key role on the world stage.

Nkrumah learned the art of preaching in the US and on many Sundays gave sermons at Baptist and Presbyterian churches in Philadelphia and in New York. 'When he preached it was about Africa. He was a good but quiet speaker', according to one source.[4]

Nkrumah was an intellectual of the first order; he read and studied incessantly.[5] But he learnt as much from the struggles of American daily life, he believed, as he did at institutions or libraries. These struggles included poverty and hunger. Though his way of life was simple and abstemious—he was always teetotal and did not smoke—he found it difficult to get by. He relied for survival on menial jobs, such as selling fish from a cart in Harlem in New York City. For a period he worked from midnight to eight am in all weathers in a shipbuilding yard in Pennsylvania. When not living in university accommodation, he found it hard at times to find lodging available to nonwhites and was forced to sleep on a park bench or in a doorway. In New York, he sometimes bought a subway ticket and spent the whole night travelling back and forth between Brooklyn and Harlem.[6]

He also suffered the brutal injustice of racism. In his *Autobiography*, published in 1957, the chapter on his years in America is titled 'Hard Times'. He describes a journey by bus involving a stop in Baltimore. In the refreshment room at the bus terminal, Nkrumah asked the white waiter for a drink of water:

> He frowned and looked down his nose at me as if I was something unclean. 'The place for you, my man, is the spittoon outside', he declared as he dismissed me from his sight. I was so shocked that I could not move.
>
> I just stood and stared at him.

Nkrumah had already experienced racial segregation in American buses and restaurants and other public places. But, he said, 'I could not bring myself to believe that one could refuse a man a drink of water because his skin happened to be a different colour'.[7]

A similar racist insult was suffered in the US by Komla A Gbedemah, Ghana's minister of finance, a few months after independence. The waitress at a Howard Johnson's restaurant in Delaware refused to seat him in the restaurant, because 'colored people are not allowed to eat in here'. Gbedemah, who had entertained Vice President Nixon earlier that year, was outraged. 'If the Vice President of the US can have a meal in my house when he is in Ghana', said Gbedemah, 'then I cannot understand why I must receive this treatment at a roadside restaurant in America'.

Gbedemah gave a report of the event to the press, and the episode came to the attention of President Eisenhower, who issued an official apology. 'I believe the United States as a government, if it is going to be true to its founding documents', said Eisenhower, 'does have the job of working hard toward that time when there is no discrimination made on such [an] inconsequential reason as race, color, or religion'.

Eisenhower invited Gbedemah to breakfast with himself and Nixon at the White House, demonstrating his readiness to sit at table with a person who was Black. Meanwhile, the executives at Howard Johnson's gave new instructions to the Delaware restaurant manager: from then on, he was to serve 'anybody who comes to our doors'.[8] Gbedemah, by calling out the moral wrong of American segregation, had contributed in a powerful and public way to the civil rights movement.

* * *

IN JULY 1958, DR Nkrumah returned to America. Influential figures were eager to meet the rising star of West Africa, including Eisenhower, who hosted a luncheon for him in Washington.[9]

It was a stark contrast to his first years in the country. An important stop on his 1958 tour was Harlem, where he had spent his summers as a student, looking for work in the day and sleeping in the subways at night.[10] Here, at a packed reception, Ralph Bunche spoke of Ghana's independence a year earlier, setting out the significance of Nkrumah's achievements for African Americans: 'We salute you, Kwame Nkrumah, not only because you are the Prime Minister of Ghana. . . . We salute you because you are a true and living representation of our best hopes and ideals: of the determination we have to be accepted fully as equal beings, of the pride we have held and nurtured in our African origin'. Bunche added with emphasis, 'But above all, Mr Prime Minister, we embrace you because you and your people and we are brothers—brothers of the skin and beneath the skin'.[11]

On the evening following the Harlem reception, African American organisations including the NAACP sponsored a huge dinner in Nkrumah's honour at the Waldorf Astoria, with one thousand guests.[12] Nkrumah took this opportunity to invite interested and qualified Americans to come to Ghana as teachers and technicians.[13]

Before leaving the US, Nkrumah flew to Chicago. His secretary, Erica Powell, who was travelling with him, was astonished to see that practically the whole of the route from the airport to the centre of town was lined with African Americans. 'It was like being back in Africa', she recorded in her memoir. The reception the Black community gave to Nkrumah, she said, 'was truly from their hearts. Many of them, particularly the older ones, were unashamedly weeping. Others stood as if stunned, unable to believe in miracles, that they would ever live to witness such honour bestowed on one of their own colour'.[14]

* * *

AMONG THE WEEPING CITIZENS who lined the streets to welcome Nkrumah to Chicago were many with a direct link with Africa: they were descended from ancestors taken forcibly as slaves from its shores. The link was officially remembered in the Year of Return in 2019, when the state of Ghana invited 'the Global African family, home and abroad, to mark 400 years of the arrival of the first enslaved Africans in Jamestown, Virginia'. The Year of Return was organised to mark 'the cumulative resilience of all the victims of the Trans Atlantic Slave Trade'.[15] It was followed by Beyond the Return, a ten-year project directed at 'the people of African descent, wherever they may currently be living'.[16]

In the fifteenth century, Portuguese traders had gone to West Africa to 'tap into the systems of mining and trading gold that were deeply entrenched in the region', explains K James Myers, a historian of Africa and the diaspora.[17] But by the sixteenth century, their greed had shifted to a trade in human beings. Thus began the savage removal of people from Africa to North America, South America and the Caribbean (a small percentage of people were taken to Europe or other locations, including the Atlantic Islands, such as Madeira and the Canaries). The profits to be made from the sale of human life brought in traders from other nations, too: British, French, Dutch, Spanish, Danish, Swedish, German and, in due course, American.

It has been extremely difficult to collect accurate data regarding the numbers of men, women and children who were forcibly carried away from Africa in the long centuries of the Atlantic slave trade. However, recent authoritative research for a major database estimates that more than twelve and a half million captive individuals were forced to leave Africa between 1501 and 1875.[18] Nearly two million of those people are estimated to have perished during the horrors of the journeys; many died through disease or ill treatment, and others, in despair or defiance, jumped overboard.

This crossing is often referred to as the Middle Passage, on the grounds that it was the middle leg of a triangular route from Europe to Africa (with goods that would be sold in return for captured people), then to the Americas (to sell the captives and buy sugar, tobacco and other produce), and finally back to Europe— before embarking on yet another triangular voyage. However, voyages frequently did not follow the triangular pattern, especially in the South Atlantic. For instance, journeys from Brazil to Africa, and then back, were common.

Close to eleven million people disembarked in the Americas to be sold into slavery.[19] Often, Myers states, people were disembarked only to be reshipped to another location; frequently, there were multiple legs and sales in these journeys. At the time of sale, it was common for children to be taken away from their parents and for members of partnered couples to be separated from each other.[20]

Portugal, Brazil and Britain accounted for about 70 per cent of all Africans transported to the Americas.[21] Portuguese and (from a later date) Brazilian vessels between 1501 and 1875 carried nearly six million people; vessels from England (from 1603, Great Britain) between 1551 and 1825 carried well over three million.[22]

The earliest known slave voyage direct from Africa to the Americas sailed in 1525;[23] it left with an estimated 359 slaves and lost 72 of them to death, arriving finally with 287. In 1776, the year of the US Declaration of Independence, nearly 90,000 people were taken from Africa; nearly 80,000 people arrived.[24] Those who were taken to the US did not benefit from the best-known words of the Declaration: 'We hold these truths to be self-evident, that all men are created equal, that they are endowed by their Creator with certain unalienable Rights, that among these are Life, Liberty and the pursuit of Happiness'. The principal author of the Declaration was Thomas Jefferson, who owned over a hundred slaves in 1776.[25] Jefferson subsequently served as the third president of the United States.

The lives of enslaved people were brutal, punitive and pitiless: working from sunup to sundown in plantations, farms and domestic homes, with inadequate food and the lash of the whip. Slaveholders had the right to rape the women they owned. In 1807, President Jefferson signed into law an act prohibiting the importation of African slaves into the US. In the same year, the British Parliament banned the involvement of Britons in the slave trade.

At the start of 1863, President Abraham Lincoln's Emancipation Proclamation became law, freeing some three million enslaved people. But the practise of chattel slavery was not abolished officially in the US until 1865, at the end of the Civil War, with the passage of the Thirteenth Amendment. Even now, the process of abolition is not complete: slavery as a punishment for crimes is still legal in the US under the terms of that same amendment.[26]

Slavery went on long after 1865, as did the trade. 'American ships flying false flags and fitted out as slavers were soon found at Cape Coast Castle [in what is now Ghana]', records the historian William St Clair. In 1881, he adds, 'an American slaving vessel was discovered, allegedly from Brazil, calling itself provocatively by the contemptuous racist Americanism *The Spade*'.[27]

* * *

To FACILITATE THE TRANSATLANTIC slave trade, more than fifty castles and forts were built along the 260 miles of the Gold Coast by the various slave-trading nations. Through these bleak fortifications passed people captured within what is now Ghana and in surrounding territories.[28]

An important centre was Christiansborg Castle in what is now Accra, which juts out from a rocky cliff overhanging the sea, about a mile and a half along the coast from the Old Polo Ground. The castle was built from stone brought from Denmark, with carved stone crowns and inscriptions celebrating the kings who lived in the other, original Christiansborg Castle in Copenhagen.[29] 'White, vast, standing at the edge of the Atlantic', observed the African American writer Richard Wright, the grandson of slaves, who visited the Gold Coast in 1953, 'it dominates the tropic, sandy, palm-treed landscape'.[30]

The fetid, dark dungeons where the slaves were kept lie in the depths of the castle down winding, narrow steps; men and women were kept in separate spaces. When the time came for their enforced departure from their land, the slaves were led in chains through the Door of No Return, which opened onto the white sand of the beach facing the green-blue waves. Small boats took them to the horror of the slave ships. Wright, sickened by his visit to the castle, imagined the seizing of a woman's arm, as she 'was led toward those narrow, dank steps that guided her to the tunnel that directed her feet to the waiting ship that would bear her across the heaving, mist-shrouded Atlantic'.[31] Yet further horrors awaited her: the terrible journey and then, if she survived, to be sold into a life of total servitude.

'No one will ever know the number or identity of the black men, women, and children who passed through these walls', noted Wright sadly.[32] Recent research does include information about Christiansborg Castle,[33] but it should be regarded as a bare minimum because of the problem of undocumented voyages, for which the data are missing altogether. Bearing that absence in mind, it appears that Christiansborg Castle is likely to have housed most of the slaves in voyages that, at a minimum, took away over 16,084 people. Of these individuals, it can be estimated—given the pattern of loss at sea on the slave voyages—that over 3,000 people perished at sea, and that about 13,000 reached the ships' destinations in the Americas.[34]

The numbers of individuals traded through Christiansborg Castle are shocking; however, they are substantially less than the numbers of people traded through many other centres on the Gold Coast. For example, over 115,000 people were traded through Cape Coast Castle; of these individuals, about 15,000 perished at sea, and over 100,000 arrived at the first destination of the ship on which they were carried.[35] Nearly 95,000 people were traded through Elmina Castle; of these individuals, about 13,000 people perished at sea, and over 80,000 arrived at the ship's first destination.[36]

When in 1874 the Gold Coast was declared a British crown colony, it was governed from Christiansborg Castle. An image of the castle featured prominently on Gold Coast postage stamps, revealing a shocking lack of sensitivity on the part of the colonial rulers. For nearly a hundred years, the castle—with its Union Jack flying over the white walls—was the symbol to Ghanaians of occupation by a foreign power. The horrors of slavery seemed to linger in the walls of the structure. Arden-Clarke, the last governor of the colony, woke one night to hear a persistent knocking in his bedroom. Although a down-to-earth man who did not believe in ghosts and the supernatural, he was unnerved and slept thereafter in a different room.[37]

After Ghana's freedom from British rule, Christiansborg Castle was renamed Government House, and Nkrumah's new government moved in. Only if the Ghanaian government reclaimed the former colonial edifice, Nkrumah believed, would the people of the nation grasp fully that the British were no longer in charge. 'Of all the acts symbolizing the transfer of power', observed a sympathetic British official at the time, 'none had more significance'. The installation of the new government in the castle 'must have finally brought it home to [Ghanaians], as nothing else could, that at long last the foreigner had gone forever from the country'.[38]

But the unease about the castle persisted. The cook and stewards were too frightened to stay overnight and had to be accommodated outside. Nkrumah's devoted dog, which never left his side, woke his master one night with a piercing yelp; when Nkrumah put on the light, he saw that the dog was so terrified that its fur was standing on end. The dog refused to enter the room ever again.[39]

Today the structure has been renamed Osu Castle. The new name no longer evokes the history of Denmark, but refers simply to the neighbourhood of Accra in which the castle is located. But still it symbolises the evil of the slave trade, from every corner. 'The aroma of blood, sweat and breath', said Dorothy Hunton, an American civil rights campaigner who visited the castle in the late 1950s, 'does not escape the nostrils of a sensitive soul, despite the fragrant flowers in the castle's well-kept garden'.[40]

* * *

GHANA'S INDEPENDENCE SHONE A powerful spotlight on the tragic link between the US and Africa: the centuries-long history of the slave trade and slavery. This, coupled with Nkrumah's visionary language of Pan-Africanism, drew a number of African Americans to the country's shores. 'At the height of the civil rights movement, from the late 1950s to 1966', records Kevin K Gaines in *American Africans in Ghana*, scores of African Americans went to Ghana, including intellectuals, technicians, teachers, artists, professionals, entrepreneurs and trade unionists. 'Ghana was a haven', he adds, 'for a range of activists working at the intersection of anticolonial, civil rights, leftist, and pacifist movements'.

Many of these expatriates, notes Gaines, were doubly estranged in the country in which they had been born: first, because their skin was black, and second, because they held political opinions that 'exceeded the limits of the Cold War American nation'. Among the Americans who moved to Ghana after independence were political refugees, not unlike the South African freedom fighters driven into exile by apartheid; these included W E B Du Bois; Shirley Graham; William Alphaeus and Dorothy Hunton; and Julian Mayfield, the novelist, actor and journalist.[41]

The American writer and civil rights activist Maya Angelou arrived in 1962 and was full of praise. 'Ghana was flourishing', she wrote later in *All God's Children Need Travelling Shoes*. 'People stopped in the street', she recalled with pleasure, 'and said to passersby, "Oh, but life is sweet, oh, and the air is cool on my skin like fresh water"'. The 'shared joy', she said, 'was traceable to President Nkrumah. . . . We shadowed Nkrumah's every move, and read carefully his speeches, committing the more eloquent passages to memory'.

Describing herself and other African Americans in Ghana as 'Revolutionist Returnees', she recorded how they 'danced the High Life at the Lido, throwing our hips from side to side as if we would have no further use for them'. Or, she said, 'we would sit together over Club beer discussing how we could better serve Ghana, its revolution and President Nkrumah'.[42]

Angelou's book ends with a deeply moving account of her visit to Keta, a Ghanaian village that had been hit hard by the slave trade. Some of the women she met in Keta market were shocked to recognise Angelou as someone who resembled themselves, in her looks and even in the tone of her voice. They believed she was descended from their 'stolen mothers and fathers'. They wept, seeing their history in her face; they mourned 'for their lost people'. Angelou wept with them. But she wept, she wrote, with 'a curious joy': 'Although separated from our languages, our families and customs, we had dared to continue to live. . . .We had crossed the unknowable oceans in chains and had written its mystery into "Deep River, my home is over Jordan". Through the centuries of despair and dislocation, we had been creative, because we faced down death by daring to hope'.[43]

3

The Challenge of the Congo

G HANA ACHIEVED ITS LIBERATION FROM British occupation in 1957. But Nkrumah believed that the freedom struggle had to embrace the whole of Africa, including those places where violence and rampant exploitation were still permitted and unchecked. One of the worst was the Congo. Here, argued Kwame Nkrumah, the purpose of Belgian rule had been 'not to suppress slavery, but to change its nature . . . to make slavery more profitable by employing the slave in the Congo and thus avoid the difficulties caused by the international abolition of the trade in its old-fashioned form'. That this had been possible, he added, was due in large part to the imperial rivalry between the European powers.[1]

In 1884–1885, a conference was held in Berlin, where the European powers partitioned Africa among themselves. The conference formalised the process known as the 'scramble for Africa', in which nations including Britain, France and Germany sought to colonise more and more African territory in order to acquire natural resources to feed their growing industries, and also to build global markets for these industries. One outcome of the Berlin Conference, as it became known, was the awarding of the Congo to King Leopold II of Belgium.

Leopold II's first objective on possessing the Congo, declared many Belgians over subsequent years, was to suppress the slave trade. In 1778 alone, according to the 1959 *Handbook of the Congo* published by the Belgian Government, 104,000 slaves had been exported from Africa, of whom one-third came from the Congo and Angola.[2]

26

But from 1885, Leopold II had 'owned' the Congo as his personal possession—a territory that was bigger than all of Western Europe and nearly eighty times the size of Belgium. He made a huge fortune out of this possession, known as the Congo Free State, without ever visiting it.[3]

Vast profits were generated from the forced labour of the Congolese in the collection of wild rubber and the killing of elephants for their tusks. Villages unwilling or unable to meet the assigned daily quotas 'were subject to rape, arson, bodily mutilation and murder', writes Georges Nzongola-Ntalaja, a preeminent Congolese political scientist and professor of African and global studies at the University of North Carolina at Chapel Hill, who has written seminal works on his nation's history. The lashing of people with a chicotte—a whip made of sun-dried hippopotamus hide with razor-sharp edges—was widely practised.[4] A hundred lashes of the chicotte could be fatal, records Adam Hochschild, the author of *King Leopold's Ghost*.[5]

Leopold II invited several hundred Protestant missionaries into the territory. Most of them made no protest, but some were appalled by the atrocities carried out by the Force Publique, Leopold's paramilitary army, and at the conditions in which the Congolese people were forced to live. These critics directed attention in America and Europe to the horrors they had seen: 'Africans whipped to death, rivers full of corpses, and—a detail that quickly seared itself into the world's imagination—piles of severed hands'.[6] 'Each time the corporal goes out to get rubber', explained an American missionary in the Congo in 1899, 'cartridges are given to him. He must bring back all not used; and for every one used, he must bring back a right hand! . . . [A State official] informed me that in six months they, the State, on the Momboyo River had used some 6,000 cartridges, which means that 6,000 people are killed or mutilated'. In fact, he added, the number was more than six thousand, for he had been told repeatedly that soldiers killed children with the butts of their guns.[7]

Some regions of the Congo, said one observer, were 'veritable hells on earth'.[8] Hochschild records that in the twenty-three years of King Leopold II's rule, an estimated ten million people died as a consequence of brutality and executions; this amounted to about 50 per cent of the population.[9] Nzongola-Ntalaja notes that although this violence does not meet the specific definition of 'genocide' in international law as 'acts committed with intent to destroy, in whole or in part, a national, ethnic, racial or religious group', it resulted in 'a death toll of holocaust proportions'.[10]

The Congo Free State lasted until 1908, when Leopold was forced to cede control to the Belgian government. The transfer of power mitigated the very worst excesses of the treatment of the Congolese people, but it by no means ended their pitiless exploitation.[11]

The territory was open for business to entrepreneurs. One of these was the British industrialist Lord Leverhulme, who created huge palm-oil plantations in the region of north Kasai in 1911. Leverhulme was widely celebrated as a benefactor in Britain, but his philanthropic spirit was by no means manifest in the Congo, where he made his vast wealth. In *Lord Leverhulme's Ghosts: Colonial Exploitation in the Congo*, Jules Marchal shows in careful detail that Leverhulme set up his own private kingdom, reliant on the ruthless cruelty of the forced labour system.

During World War II, Congolese workers were forced to labour at everything, 'from the railways to rubber plantations to the heavily guarded uranium mine of Shinkolobwe', records Adam Hochschild.[12] The mines producing raw materials for the Allies, he adds, worked day and night. Between 1938 and 1944, the workforce employed by Union Minière du Haut Katanga, a Belgian multinational with huge mining interests in the province of Katanga, almost doubled, increasing from twenty-five thousand to forty-nine thousand; so too did the number of fatal accidents at Union Minière plants.[13]

The injustice of Belgian occupation did not stop with the end of the war. Between 1946 and 1960, records Jules Marchal, forcible recruitment continued; those who failed to undertake the compulsory cultivation of crops were made to serve a prison sentence. The workers in the palm groves were treated abusively, in the push to produce palm-oil products for the factories of the Lever Brothers, the company founded by Leverhulme.

In 1958, the Sûreté, the security police, reported that a Belgian employee on a coffee plantation had 'tied a native, suspected of stealing coffee, behind his van and dragged him through the plantation'. The whipping of Congolese people with a chicotte had been officially banned in 1951, but it was still used and was legal in prisons.[14] The Congolese workforce, 'whether it liked it or not', comments Marchal, continued to be put 'at the disposal of European employers'.[15]

The ruling Belgians carefully segregated the Congolese majority away from themselves. In the capital city of Leopoldville (now Kinshasa), a neutral zone was established to separate the affluent district where the whites lived, known as *la ville*, from the Congolese townships, known as *la cité indigène* or, simply, *la cité*. The zone was originally planned as a *cordon sanitaire*—keeping the Congolese, who were perceived as diseased and infectious, away from the Belgians.

The deeply racist structure was strengthened in the 1930s. The physical separation, notes Mwana Mboka, an expert on the history of Kinshasa, 'was reinforced by regulation, a requirement that all Africans leave the European city at night, unless they were an employee (i.e. house help) or had a pass'.[16] Such lawful segregation, explicitly based on the colour of a person's skin, was practised widely in Africa at the time—in European colonies and in South Africa—forcefully demarcating the difference between people with black skin and people with white skin.

* * *

MANY AMERICANS IN THE 1950s knew little about the Congo or, indeed, about Africa generally. Aside from Liberia, an American settlement created for black people which declared its independence in 1847, the African continent had been seen as functioning within the European sphere of influence, with little relevance to the US.

In fact, though, Africa had been of central importance to the US in World War II. When Nazi Germany occupied North Africa in 1940, there was a fear that major parts of Africa could be invaded, leading to subsequent attacks on the Brazilian coast. To prevent this, the US Army constructed air bases in strategic areas of Africa. The Nazi occupation of North Africa was defeated, but most of the air bases remained.

An Africa Section was created in America's new intelligence service, the Office of Strategic Services (OSS), the forerunner of the Central Intelligence Agency. From OSS headquarters in Washington, the Africa Section ran three field bases: Accra in the Gold Coast; Cape Town in South Africa; and Addis Ababa in Ethiopia. The OSS station in Accra, which was established in November 1942, served as the headquarters for three separate territories: the Gold Coast itself, the Republic of Liberia, and the Belgian Congo.

The Africa Section of OSS grew rapidly. By the end of the war, it had placed a total of ninety-three agents in Africa, of whom forty-five were covert personnel, thirty-six were semicovert, and twelve were overt.[17] The section was supported by the Research and Analysis division, where Ralph Bunche worked as an analyst—one of the few Black personnel in OSS. Bunche and William Bascom, an anthropologist, wrote *A Pocket Guide to West Africa* for military personnel, advising them to leave white American racial prejudices at home when they travelled to Africa.[18]

The OSS station in the Belgian Congo had a unique, top-secret mission: to protect the export of uranium from the Congo to America and to keep it out of enemy hands.[19] Congolese ore was essential for the Manhattan Project, which produced the world's first atomic weapons and was led by the United States, with some assistance from Britain and Canada. This uranium was used to build the first atomic bomb to be tested: the Trinity test in New Mexico, in July 1945, which launched the atomic age. It was also used to build the atomic bombs that devastated Hiroshima and Nagasaki the following month—on 6 August and 9 August, respectively.

The source of the ore was the Shinkolobwe mine in Katanga, the southern province of the Congo. Shinkolobwe produced uranium that was far richer than any other uranium in the world: it assayed as high as 75 per cent uranium oxide, with an average of 65 per cent. By contrast, ores of marketable quality from the Colorado Plateau in the US and from Canada contained two-tenths of 1 per cent uranium oxide, while ores derived from South African gold mines had a uranium oxide content on the order of 0.03 per cent.[20]

The unique value of Shinkolobwe's uranium is straightforward, explains Lars Öhrström, professor of inorganic chemistry at Chalmers University in Gothenburg, Sweden. 'The reason', he says, 'is simply that the higher the concentration of the desired element in an ore, the easier it is to extract. It is both about the chemical processes that need to be developed and about the associated costs'. A high concentration also means fewer other elements to separate it from.[21]

'The Belgian Congo', wrote a senior chemical engineer involved in the work of the Manhattan Project in 1943 to L R Groves, the director of the project, 'offers natural resources of extreme importance to our domestic economy. Its known resources of uranium, which are the world's largest, are vital to the welfare of the United States'. The correspondence noted, too, that in addition to uranium, 'the reserves of copper, industrial diamonds, cobalt and probably tantalite are among the world's largest'. The report concluded, 'Definite steps should be taken to insure access to the resources for the United States'.[22]

The role of Congolese uranium in the Manhattan Project was shrouded in secrecy. In order to deflect attention away from the Congo, attempts were made to sow the idea that the uranium used to build the first atomic bombs had been sourced from Canada.[23]

But some people knew better. One of these was Nkrumah's friend George Padmore, who was aware of the activities of Union Minière du Haut Katanga, the Belgian multinational which owned the Shinkolobwe mine. Only a few weeks after the tragedies of Hiroshima and Nagasaki, Padmore published an article titled 'Africa Holds Key to Atomic Future: World's Uranium Supply Is There' in the *Chicago Defender*, a newspaper serving the African American community. The uranium deposits in the Belgian Congo, he reported, 'are being closely guarded by specially trained Congolese soldiers who supervise the native miners as they produce the uranium ores, the most valuable mineral in the world today'. These miners, he added with undisguised disapproval, 'receive an average wage of 25 cents per day plus rations and a hut provided by the company. Once they enter the mining compound they are never allowed to return to their villages'.[24]

The miners were vulnerable to many adverse health effects caused by uranium, explains Jean Bele, a Congolese nuclear physicist at MIT's Laboratory for Nuclear Science. He points to a spectrum of such effects, 'ranging from renal failure and diminished bone growth to damage to DNA'. The effects of low-level radioactivity, he adds, 'include cancer, shortening of life, and subtle changes in fertility or viability of offspring, as determined from both animal studies and data on Hiroshima and Chernobyl survivors'. The dust from the sites and the water used for dust control 'contain long-lived radioisotopes' that spread into the surrounding areas: 'Low radioactive effects can be delayed for decades . . . and are not detected in short-term toxicology studies. In the atmosphere, radon decays into the radioactive solids polonium, bismuth, and lead, which enter water, crops, trees, soil, and animals, including humans'.[25]

* * *

THE POSSESSION OF ATOMIC weapons gave the US a unique global advantage in the early years of the Cold War. But in 1949, to the shock of the West, the Soviet Union tested its own atomic bomb— and American president Harry S Truman had to announce to the American public that the Soviets, too, had the bomb.

The US was now even more determined to obtain all the Congolese uranium available and to prevent Soviet access to the Shinkolobwe mine. In 1951, the office of the Special Assistant to the Secretary of State summarised efforts to maintain the security of the Belgian Congo. 'The Shinkolobwe Mine', it stated, 'is of capital importance to the free world' and was vulnerable to various security risks. There was a threat, it added, of 'Western Europe being overrun by the Soviets and a collaborationist Belgian government being established which would attempt to cut off the United States from Congolese uranium'. In such a case, it would be necessary to seize critical areas of the Belgian Congo by force. It was proposed that the director of the CIA, as soon as practicable, 'should initiate plans and preparations for covert counter-sabotage to improve the military security of the Belgian Congo and particularly that of the Shinkolobwe Mine'.[26]

Security around the mine and the adjacent processing plant was massively increased. It was a fortress that kept out Alain Gheerbrant, an intrepid French explorer and writer. 'I am going to Elisabethville [the provincial capital of Katanga] tomorrow', he wrote in the mid-1950s in *Congo Noir et Blanc*, 'but I would not go to Shinkolobwe, the forbidden holy city of the Gods of combat'.[27]

The US was hoping that South Africa would take over from the Belgian Congo as the leading supplier of uranium. This led to an alliance between America and apartheid South Africa, which is scrutinized by Thomas Borstelmann in *Apartheid's Reluctant Uncle*. Official Washington, observes Borstelmann, looked upon the white authorities, 'oppressive as they may have been, as the guarantors of that availability'. To the US government, even a disciplined and peaceful Black liberation struggle was a threat to American mineral access in South Africa.[28]

As it turned out, South African uranium ore was disappointing. But uranium was now being found in many other parts of the world. Furthermore, as the 1950s wore on, increasingly sophisticated methods of fission were developed that were less dependent on the richness of the Shinkolobwe ore. Even so, the US continued to import large amounts of Congolese uranium.

The American government financed two major capital investment programmes at Shinkolobwe in the 1950s, in order to expand the mine and develop the plant. The first programme was completed in 1953; arrangements for the second were made in 1956–1957. The total investment was close to $25 million.[29] A secret agreement was reached in 1956 between the Combined Development Agency (a purchasing authority established by the US with the UK) and the African Metals Corporation, known as Afrimet (the commercial arm of Union Minière, headquartered in New York), whereby uranium from the Belgian Congo would be provided until the end of 1959, possibly until the end of 1960.[30]

Shinkolobwe's uranium underpinned the value of the Congo to the US through the 1950s. However, it was not the sole reason:

there were other valuable and strategic minerals in different regions of the territory. By 1959, about 9 per cent of the world's copper, 49 percent of cobalt (rising to 54 percent in 1960), 69 percent of industrial diamonds, and 6.5 percent of tin came from the Congo.[31]

* * *

IN ADDITION TO AFRICA's abundance of valuable minerals, many geographic areas of the continent were of strategic importance. There was a sense, said Frank C Carlucci III, an American diplomat who worked in the US embassies in South Africa, the Congo and Zanzibar (and was appointed deputy director of the CIA in 1978), 'that Africa was becoming a major player on the world political scene, that the cold war was extending its reach into Africa and we needed to pay more attention to it'.[32] Cape Town, for example, played a crucial role in keeping open the Cape Route, which was seen as essential in order to defend NATO, the military alliance between North American and European countries, against Soviet incursion. 'American interests in the future are so great', said Nixon in 1957 to the Senate Foreign Relations Committee, 'as to justify us in not hesitating even to assist the departure of the colonial powers from Africa'.[33]

In August 1958, a Bureau of African Affairs was created in the State Department. Joseph C Satterthwaite, a career diplomat who had previously served as US ambassador to Sri Lanka and then Burma, was appointed the Assistant Secretary for African Affairs.[34] In November 1959, a dedicated Africa Division was created by the CIA in its Directorate of Plans, the branch of the agency that was responsible for clandestine operations and the recruitment of foreign agents. Bronson Tweedy, who had served as CIA chief of station in Vienna and then London, was its first chief.[35]

Kwame Nkrumah understood that the Congo was at the centre of America's interest in Africa. He explained his reasons in *Challenge of the Congo*, which was published in 1967. It is thick with factual detail and careful argument. 'Geographically, strategically and politically', he wrote, the Congo 'is the most vital region of Africa. Military control of the Congo by any foreign power would give it easy access to most of the continent south of the Sahara'. The region owed its importance, he argued, not only to its central position, 'but to its vast area and tremendous resources'.[36] He was aware of the importance of the Shinkolobwe mine, which he identified by name. He referred explicitly in his writings to the mining of Congolese uranium by Union Minière, and its role in the Manhattan Project.[37]

'Foreign powers', noted Nkrumah, 'clearly regard the Congo as the key to the military control of Africa'. This was the significance, he added, 'of the aid which Belgium received from her allies to build great military bases at Kitona in the West and Kamina in the East of the Congo. This is the reason why there are eight international airports, thirty principal and over a hundred secondary and local airports in the Congo'.

The Congo, he argued, was the buffer state between independent Africa in the North and the lands beset by colonialism and white supremacy in the South: 'Northwards stands free Africa determined on a free continent: Southwards, Angola begins and stretches to the stronghold of colonial and racial oppression, the Republic of South Africa'.

'The degree of the Congo's independence', Nkrumah declared, 'will substantially determine the ultimate fate of the whole Continent of Africa'.[38]

4

'Hands off Africa!'

IN THE EARLY MORNING OF Monday, 8 December 1958, the white-painted Accra Community Centre was electric with anticipation. In the sunlit courtyard, overlooking the sea, people were greeting each other and chatting excitedly. The heat was already baking, and the slow turning of the fans in the large auditorium did little to cool the air. But by nine am, the room was already filling up with people waiting for the start of the All African People's Conference (AAPC)—the first time in history that Africans from across the continent would assemble together. The conference would begin officially at 10.30, with the arrival of Prime Minister Nkrumah to give the opening speech.

The heads of delegations sat on a platform behind the rostrum at the end of the hall. Behind them was an immense banner, on which was portrayed a flaming torch painted in black on a map of Africa. Above the rostrum, stretching from wall to wall in letters three feet high, were the words 'Hands Off Africa! Africa Must Be Free!'

The theme 'Hands Off Africa!' was directly influenced by a speech Nkrumah had made eight months earlier, at the closing of the Conference of Independent African States, which had been held in Accra.[1] It had been attended by the eight independent states of Africa—Ethiopia, Ghana, Liberia, Libya, Morocco, Sudan, Tunisia, and the United Arab Republic (Syria and Egypt). It was decided at this meeting to hold an All African People's Conference later that year, as a way of bringing together the freedom movements of every part of Africa—'to put meat on the bones'.[2]

Notices were rushed out to call people to the conference: 'Peoples of Africa, Unite! You have nothing to lose but your chains! You have a continent to regain! You have freedom and human dignity to attain!'[3]

More than three hundred political and trade union leaders responded.[4] They represented some sixty-five organisations from twenty-eight African territories, including colonies ruled by Britain, France, Belgium, Portugal and Spain. Fraternal delegates and observers also came, including visitors from Canada, the People's Republic of China, India, Indonesia, the Soviet Union, Czechoslovakia, the USA, Britain and other European countries.[5]

The delegates started to arrive in Accra on Friday 5 December. So too did 'an army' of local and overseas journalists and cameramen.[6] These were 'heady days', remembers Cameron Duodu, who was working at the time for the newsroom of Radio Ghana. 'The atmosphere in our part of Africa was quite intoxicating'. Apart from Independence Day the year before, he cannot recall a day that excited Ghanaians more than the day the All African People's Conference opened.[7] Signs at bus stops offered slogans of encouragement: 'Ever forward, never backward'.[8]

Once the delegates had signed in at the secretariat and received their 'freedom badges', they gathered on the terrace.[9] Many of them knew each other, at least by reputation, and the attendance has been described as a 'Who's Who of African nationalism'.[10] 'You name it', commented Maida Springer, an American labour activist at the conference, 'they were there. From everywhere'.[11]

One man was unknown to most of the delegates—Patrice Emery Lumumba, from the Belgian Congo. Lumumba, thirty-three years old, was distinctive: tall and very thin, with an earnest, bespectacled face and a slight beard. He was the president of the newly established Mouvement National Congolais (MNC) and had come to Accra with two other members of his party.

Cameron Duodu met Lumumba at the airport. Duodu, who was on an assignment to report on the arrival of the delegates, was impressed.[12] 'I remember Lumumba', he recollected many years later, 'because of his goatee beard and his glasses, which gave him the look of an intellectual. My French was not up to scratch, but with the help of an official of the Ministry of Foreign Affairs, I was able to talk to him for a while before he was whisked away by an official car'. Lumumba spoke of his wish to seek inspiration from Ghana and to exchange ideas with other freedom fighters.[13]

* * *

NKRUMAH WAS A STICKLER for punctuality; he arrived at the centre in his black Rolls Royce right on time, escorted by police outriders. Outside, a crowd of about two thousand people had been waiting for the prime minister in the morning sunshine for almost two hours. People lined the side of the road carrying placards in English and French, bearing slogans such as 'Ne Touchez Pas l'Afrique' and 'Welcome Africa's freedom fighters'. On either side of the road were the flags of the nine independent countries in Africa.

As Nkrumah's car swung into view, the crowd burst into 'thunderous cheering', reported Accra's *Daily Graphic*, and there were shouts of 'Freedom!' A smiling Nkrumah waved to them all with a white handkerchief.

Dressed in a richly coloured kente cloth and a cool white shirt, Nkrumah climbed out of his car. He was greeted by a small group of men led by Tom Mboya, a prominent Kenyan trade unionist who would chair the conference. Mboya slowly ushered Nkrumah into the centre, with his arm resting in a comradely manner on Nkrumah's shoulder; as they walked, they spoke quietly to each other, nodding their heads. They entered the hall, and immediately the buzz of conversation faded away; people rose to their feet, beaming and cheering, and there was vigorous clapping. Then Mboya led Nkrumah to the rostrum.

Mboya spoke first. 'This is a historic occasion', he observed solemnly. 'I am sure that all who are here will recognise the significance of it'. He himself was deeply conscious of its importance. He also felt keenly the honour accorded to him by the conference committee when they appointed him as chairman. The day he arrived in Ghana, when he was greeted with this unexpected news, he wrote later, was 'the proudest day of my life'.[14]

As he looked out at the packed rows of expectant faces, Mboya put aside his prepared address. Instead, the *New York Times* reported, he 'made a speech during which one could have heard a pin drop in the pauses between bursts of cheering and clapping'.[15] He said he had 'no doubt' that the two hundred million people of Africa were represented in that room. Then he drew a contrast between the conference that was just beginning and a conference that had taken place seventy-four years earlier and thousands of miles away: the Berlin Conference of 1884–1885, where European nations had met to decide how to partition Africa. That meeting, he said, was known as the 'scramble for Africa'. But today, he declared firmly, those same powers 'will now decide to scram from Africa'.[16]

This statement was heard with rapt attention by the audience. It was seized on by the foreign journalists, and the words 'Scram from Africa' soon blazed across the headlines of newspapers around the world.

Then Mboya formally called on Kwame Nkrumah to open the conference.

'Fellow African Freedom Fighters, Ladies and Gentlemen', began Nkrumah. Then he stopped. 'My pride', he went on slowly, 'overflows at the sight of so large a number of African comrades-in-arms who, imbued with the fervent desire to see Africa free, unfettered, and united, have gathered here together on African soil for the first time in the history of our continent'. He observed that the assembly in front of him marked 'the opening of a new epoch' in the history of Africa. 'Never before', he said, 'has it been possible for so representative a gathering of African freedom fighters not only to come together, but to assemble in a free independent African state for the purpose of planning for a final assault upon imperialism and colonialism'.

Then he set out his vision of the liberation and unity of the African continent. 'This coming together', he said, 'will evolve eventually into a Union of African States just as the original thirteen American Colonies have now developed into the 49 states constituting the American community'.[17]

He praised the practice of Gandhi, who had led the campaign of peaceful civil disobedience in India. This focus on struggle through nonviolence had been emphasised in the earliest plans for the conference. The cause was just, Nkrumah pointed out, and 'wholly in consonance with the principles enunciated in the Charter of the United Nations'.

But Nkrumah also included a warning: 'Do not let us also forget that colonialism and imperialism may come to us yet in a different guise—not necessarily from Europe'. This was heard in different ways by members of the audience. 'Everyone here knows that he means America', said the representative of the New China News Agency confidently.[18] Many Americans and Britons were equally convinced that Nkrumah was warning against Soviet, Chinese or Egyptian designs.

After forty minutes, Nkrumah brought his address to a close on an emphatic note. 'All Africa shall be free in this, our lifetime', he assured the audience. 'This decade is the decade of African independence. Forward then to independence'. He spoke clearly and firmly: 'To Independence Now. Tomorrow, the United States of Africa. I salute you!'[19]

There was thunderous applause. Joshua Nkomo, a freedom fighter from Southern Rhodesia, was profoundly moved. Nkrumah, he said, was 'one of the most inspiring orators' he had ever heard.[20] Ezekiel Mphahlele, a South African delegate who had been forced into exile and was now a lecturer at the Department of Extra-Mural Studies at the University College, Ibadan in Nigeria, was exhilarated. He noted that Nkrumah spoke 'with restrained impetuosity', as he warned the imperial powers 'to pack up voluntarily rather than be forced out'.[21]

* * *

AFTER NKRUMAH'S OPENING SPEECH, messages were read aloud from Nikita Khrushchev, the leader of the Soviet Union; from Chou En-lai, the premier of the People's Republic of China; and from leaders in East Germany, Bulgaria, North Korea, Yugoslavia and North Vietnam.

There was also a message from Lord Listowel, the newly appointed British governor general of Ghana, who in any case was sitting in the front row of the hall. No one would have guessed that for the past few months, civil servants in Whitehall had been communicating feverishly in cipher with the British colonial administrations in Africa, concerned about the prospect of the 'embarrassing political and security consequences in our territories' that might result from this 'subversive' conference. There was brief consideration of a plan to prevent attendance by delegates from British colonies, but the idea was rejected in case it gave the impression that Britain was 'unsympathetic to African advance'.[22]

No greeting arrived from the White House.[23] This disappointed many of the delegates, who were expecting American support not only because the US itself had struggled to overthrow colonial rule, but also because it had taken the side of Egypt against France, Britain and Israel during the Suez crisis.

After Nkrumah's address, the conference agenda was presented. Public plenary sessions would be held in the mornings, at which the heads of delegations would speak; these would be followed in the afternoons by closed committee sessions. Five committees were appointed, with the task of studying special topics such as racism and discrimination.

The organising spirit of the conference was George Padmore, whose mark was on everything 'from the conference programme . . . to the format of the programme and resolutions'.[24] After independence the year before, Nkrumah had asked Padmore to come to Ghana as his advisor on African affairs and to coordinate the activities in Ghana of Africa's freedom fighters. It proved a wise decision, in the judgement of Cameron Duodu, since 'Padmore knew everyone who was anyone in Africa, or knew someone who knew them'.[25]

Just after the end of the Second World War, Padmore, in partnership with Nkrumah, had organised the fifth International Conference of the Pan-African Congress in the city of Manchester in Britain. That congress had put a spotlight on the fact that although the war had been fought in the name of freedom, millions of people still lived under the yoke of colonial rule.

But the AAPC in Accra was different because, for the very first time, it took place *in* Africa. In the words of one Kenyan involved in the proceedings, it 'brought Pan-Africanism home'.[26] To make it clear that a new tradition had started, Nkrumah insisted on changing the label 'Pan-African' to 'All African'.[27]

Many of the African delegates faced obstacles getting to the conference, noted Maida Springer; she helped them 'with information, and doing whatever I was asked to do'. Some of them, she recalled years later, 'were there with a price on their head. You know, we had somehow sneaked them out of the country'. What was significant, she thought, 'was that Africans from east, west, north, and south were meeting for the first time! Some of them could have culture shock. They were so different from other Africans in terms of the approach, in terms of their language, in terms of attitudes. But the common denominator was that they were meeting in an African country'.[28]

Some people had been contacted. But many, recalled T Ras Makonnen, a Guyanese-born Pan-Africanist who had moved to Ghana when it became independent, 'just came'. People arrived from Nyasaland (now Malawi) by the Congo route and from all over: 'We would be rung up by the police at the frontier and told that some fellows had arrived; they would have no passports, and they would say simply: "We've got no documents, because this is our country; this is our land. What's all this about needing a passport?" It was overwhelming, and it meant that we needed enlightened policemen on the frontiers who would know not to enforce the regulations too strictly'. Makonnen continued, 'The message of independence had gone out. The call had gone to near and far, and the various groups had just set out to come to "Rome"'.

When they arrived, Makonnen took care of them, arranging clothes when necessary and a place to sleep. For West Africans, he wrote in a later memoir, it was relatively straightforward to find their way to Accra. 'But a number of the southern African delegations', he found, 'had to be aided. Our couriers had to go to places like Lesotho and Zambia [then the British protectorate of Northern Rhodesia] to help with passports'.[29]

Among the delegates were prominent leaders of the resistance movement against the hated Central African Federation (also known as the Federation of Rhodesia and Nyasaland), which had been created by the British in 1953 as a way to preserve white settler rule in central Africa. They included Kenneth Kaunda of Northern Rhodesia, who went on to become the founding president of independent Zambia in 1964; Hastings Banda of Nyasaland, who became the premier of independent Malawi in the same year; Kanyama Chiume of Nyasaland, who became foreign minister in Malawi's first independent government; and Joshua Nkomo of Southern Rhodesia, who served as vice president of Zimbabwe from 1990, following majority rule in 1980.

'The arrangements for the conference were perfect', observed Chiume, 'and it was amazing to see how everything had been geared to increase our sense of unity and common purpose. . . . Ghana seemed to be the political Mecca of Africa'. There was an atmosphere of 'free and fearless talk', he added, 'in which we argued, exchanged experience and compared notes'.[30]

Other freedom fighters included Dr Félix-Roland Moumié of French-ruled Cameroon who was the president of the Union of the Peoples of Cameroon (UPC); A R Mohamed Babu of the British Protectorate of Zanzibar; and Frantz Omar Fanon, a psychiatrist born on the French-ruled island of Martinique, who was the great-grandson of a slave. Fanon led a delegation of the National Liberation Front (FLN), which was fighting a bitter war for freedom in Algeria against its French colonisers; the FLN had set up a government in exile in Cairo just a few months before.

Eslanda Robeson, the wife of the world-famous bass baritone singer and actor Paul Robeson, was there too; she was ecstatic to be in Accra. 'Africa', she exclaimed, 'is on her way'.[31] Her only regret was that Paul, now on a concert tour, could not be with her. The Robesons, who were close friends of Nkrumah, identified closely and actively with Africa. Paul Robeson's father had been born into slavery on a plantation in North Carolina and traced his heritage to

Nigeria. 'In my music, my plays, my films', declared Paul Robeson, 'I want to carry always this central idea; to be African'. He spent time learning 'Swahili, Twi and other African dialects'.[32]

Robeson sent a telegram with 'warmest greetings' to the AAPC, explaining that he was 'deeply disappointed to miss this historic conference'. But soon, he said, he hoped to be 'on the soil of my beloved Africa'. For now, he sent his heartfelt hopes for the success of the conference's deliberations, 'for the glorious future of the African peoples'.[33]

The Soviet Union sent a team of observers, led by Pigam A Azimov, the principal of Turkmen State University.[34] It included Ivan I Potekhin, a scholar of African affairs, who had previously spent time in Ghana and was warmly welcomed back.[35]

A large delegation from the United Arab Republic was led by Fouad Galal, the vice president of the Egyptian National Assembly, who was described by a journalist at the conference as 'a squat, powerful man' who 'was everywhere—consulting, interpreting'.[36]

There was a busy programme of social events, including cocktail parties by individual delegations, official receptions, a visit to a tobacco factory, a Ghana-Guinea football game, film screenings and traditional dances. The United States Information Agency arranged a concert by Camilla Williams, a celebrated soprano on a tour of Africa. In 1946 she had been the first African American soprano to sing with a major opera company when she made her debut with the New York City Opera, performing the lead in *Madame Butterfly*.[37]

These social events were ideal opportunities for the delegates to mingle and meet each other, and Nkrumah was the ideal host. Although he himself was teetotal, he readily accepted a glass with alcohol, occasionally raising it to his lips, so that few people realised he was not drinking. Nkrumah's life was austere and disciplined: he fasted once a week and meditated daily. But he always sought to ensure that this side of his personality did not make others feel uncomfortable.

For Lumumba, the conference was a previously undreamed-of opportunity to meet the key thinkers from all over Africa. He was frequently in the company of the medical doctors Fanon and Moumié, with whom he spoke in French.[38]

Many of the participants were impressed by Lumumba's energy and enthusiasm for the Pan-African ideal; he rapidly became 'one of the stars of the conference'.[39] For George Houser, of the American Committee on Africa (ACOA), an organisation that had been founded in 1953 to support the liberation of Africa, his meeting with Lumumba was memorable. 'We had a session with Lumumba about what his situation was at that time', he noted in a report for his organisation. 'He was a very live person . . . a real activist . . . a striking personality'.[40]

Joshua Nkomo commented that Lumumba was 'an endless talker, passionate about his own country'. But, he added somewhat resentfully, 'he seemed completely uninterested in the rest of Africa'.[41]

* * *

IN THE PLENARY SESSION on the morning of Tuesday 9 December, it was Shirley Graham's turn to take the floor and to read out the speech of her husband, Dr W E B Du Bois. He was too infirm to travel and had remained in the USSR, where they now lived.[42]

Graham was one of only eight official women delegates. The small number bitterly disappointed Eslanda Robeson.[43] But, noticed Maida Springer with pleasure, 'the women, particularly the French-speaking women, were on fire!' They talked about the social problems faced by women: 'They were burning questions, and these women raised them all. Education, employment, religious and marriage customs. . . . And they annoyed some of the African men'. There were some men, she added, 'who just couldn't quite cope with the articulateness of the women'; in a couple of the small committee meetings, they tried to shout the women down.[44]

Marthe Ouandié, who represented the Kamerun Women's Democratic Union, gave a speech in which she traced the struggle of women for independence and for their own rights.[45] She was followed by Fanon, who was scheduled to speak on behalf of the FLN. Fanon walked slowly to the rostrum, dressed in a sombre, pale-coloured suit with a bright white shirt; he wore dark glasses as a shield against the glare of the sun streaming through the windows. He had resolved to use his speech at the AAPC as an opportunity, for the very first time in public, to make the case for using violence to resist colonialism. This would challenge the commitment to Gandhian nonviolence, which so far had been the hallmark of the conference.

Usually, Fanon—thin and ascetic—spoke in a dispassionate and intellectual manner. But on this occasion, he gripped both sides of the lectern and leaned forward towards the audience. However regrettable the use of violence, he insisted with emotion, it had to remain an option. He gave a disturbing account of the atrocities carried out against Algerians by the French, arguing that freedom fighters in Africa could not rely on peaceful negotiations alone. Algeria, he stated firmly, was not a part of France.[46] This brought the audience to its feet. 'He does not mince words', mused Ezekiel Mphahlele. 'What FLN man can afford the luxury anyway? Algerians have no other recourse but fight back, he says, and the FLN means to go through with it'.[47]

Some of those who did not speak French struggled to follow parts of Fanon's speech. The conference had not been able to organise simultaneous translation because of the shortage of funds, so people were interpreting from the platform.[48] Even so, Fanon's speech took the conference by storm: he got the loudest and longest ovation of all the speakers.[49] In effect, noted one delegate, Fanon succeeded in changing the theme of the conference: from 'nonviolent' liberation struggle to struggle 'by any means'.[50]

In a two-hour press conference after Fanon's speech, Tom Mboya, in his role as chairman, was interrogated by journalists about his reaction.[51] Mboya replied carefully. He said that the Algerian situation was 'one of the most important matters to be considered by the conference'. There were scenarios, he suggested, in which it was necessary to retaliate. 'African leaders at this Conference are not pledged to any pacific policies', he pointed out. 'They are not pacifists. If you hit them, they might hit back'.[52]

Fanon's speech had electrified the conference. Then, on the same day, there was another dramatic development, of a different kind.[53]

Alfred Hutchinson, a leader of the African National Congress of South Africa, suddenly—and unexpectedly—turned up. He had been one of the 156 accused of high treason by the apartheid state in the infamous Treason Trial; Nelson Mandela was another. When charges were dropped against Hutchinson, he resolved to leave South Africa immediately, without a passport, and to make his way to Ghana. He assumed the identity of a migrant mineworker from Nyasaland, travelling home. After a harrowing journey of two months, covering almost three thousand miles and passing through colonial territories supportive of apartheid, he finally arrived in Accra.

The conference delegates were overjoyed. Hutchinson stalked up the aisle, 'six feet of him', recorded Mphahlele, 'just like one of those outlaws on the screen who come to tame and civilize a noisy, lawless town of the Wild West'. Mphahlele, who was on the platform at the time, rushed down to embrace the new arrival, 'beside myself with excitement'.[54]

The next day, Wednesday 10 December, the Kenyan academic and politician Julius Gikonyo Kiano went up to the rostrum. As he walked, many in the audience lifted banners: 'Free Kenyatta now!'[55] Kiano demanded the immediate release of anticolonial leader Jomo Kenyatta and the removal from Kenya of Sir Evelyn Baring, the brutal British governor.[56] As Kiano came to the end of his speech, the audience rose to its feet with loud cries of support.

In the morning of Thursday 11 December, it was the turn of Anthony Enahoro, the leader of the Western Nigerian delegation, to speak. He changed the tone somewhat, the first real sign of a chink in the consensus. It would not be realistic, he said, to expect support for a United States of Africa from every African nation.[57] The Liberians also preached caution. 'Bowler-hatted and cigared', noted one journalist, they 'spoke in a strong American accent'.[58]

* * *

WHEN PATRICE LUMUMBA ADDRESSED the conference, he spoke without notes, as was his habit.[59] 'The fundamental aim of our movement', he declared, 'is to free the Congolese people from the colonialist regime and earn them their independence'.

As Nkrumah had done in his speech, Lumumba drew on the United Nations as a moral and global authority. 'We base our action', he said, 'on the Universal Declaration of Human Rights—rights guaranteed to each and every citizen of humanity by the United Nations Charter—and we are of the opinion that the Congo, as a human society, has the right to join the ranks of free peoples'. The current injustices, he argued, 'and the stupid superiority complex that the colonialists make such a display of, are the causes of the drama of the West in Africa'.

Lumumba expressed his gratitude to the conference for putting him and the other delegates 'in contact with experienced political figures from all the African countries and from all over the world'. Above all, said Lumumba, the conference 'reveals one thing to us'— that despite the boundaries separating people in Africa from each other and despite ethnic differences, 'we have the same awareness, the same soul plunged day and night in anguish, the same anxious desire to make this African continent a free and happy continent that has rid itself of unrest and of fear and of any sort of colonialist domination'.[60]

* * *

THERE WAS NO PLENARY session on Friday 12 December. Instead, the committees met early in the morning to complete the resolutions. Their work went on until three o'clock the next morning, by which time many of the participants were exhausted. But they successfully produced five lengthy resolutions, ready for consideration by the steering committee, which adopted them unanimously at its final meeting on Saturday morning.[61]

The closing assembly began at eleven am, bringing all the delegates and observers together for the last time. On the platform were Mboya, Nkrumah and other members of the planning committee. Patrice Lumumba was there too, indicating the high degree of respect that he had earned during the conference.

Mboya read out the resolutions. One of them tackled neatly the controversy over the use of violence, which had been the focus of debate ever since Fanon's speech. This resolution took a pragmatic approach, declaring its full support to all fighters for freedom in

Africa: 'to all those who resort to peaceful means of non-violence and civil disobedience, as well as to all those who are compelled to retaliate against violence to attain national independence and freedom for the people. Where such retaliation becomes necessary, the Conference condemns all legislations which consider those who fight for their independence and freedom as ordinary criminals'.

'Fanon's victory in Accra had been total', Cameron Duodu assessed years later. 'He had liberated the minds of all African freedom fighters who had previously entertained qualms about the use of violence to liberate their countries'.[62]

A key resolution of the conference was to establish a permanent secretariat, which would be based in Accra. Lumumba was one of the delegates elected to the secretariat, which would endorse the position of nonalignment and positive neutrality. 'We are not inclined to the East nor the West', said Mboya to cheers. 'Africa must be friendly but always maintaining and safeguarding her independence'.[63] It was agreed that an All African People's Conference would take place annually, and that the 1959 conference would meet in Tunis.

Nkrumah gave the final speech. To those who had come from beyond Africa's shores—and especially African Americans from the United States and the Caribbean—he expressed his heartfelt appreciation. 'We must never forget', he said, 'that they are part of us. These sons and daughters of Africa were taken away from our shores and despite all the centuries which have separated us, they have not forgotten their ancestral links. Many of them have made no small contribution to the struggle for African freedom'.

He concluded with his vision of the future: 'We shall, from now on, march forward in solid phalanx, united in the spirit of brotherhood and solidarity, so formidable in our strength that all the forces ranged against us shall not prevail'.[64] He was thunderously cheered.[65]

Then one of the organisers asked the audience to sing 'Nkosi Sikelel'i' ('God Bless Africa') and 'Morena Boloka Sechaba' ('God Bless Our Country'). Pointing to the map of Africa on the wall, he asked them to respond 'Mayibuye!'—'Bring back Africa!'[66]

* * *

THE CONFERENCE ENDED ON a note of euphoria.[67] 'To young Africans like myself at the time', said Bereket Habte Selassie, a representative of the Ethiopian National Patriotic Association, 'it was a moment at once defining and awe-inspiring'.[68] Fanon was also elated. He was convinced that almost sixty million Africans would be free 'by 1960'.[69]

'The African Revolution', observed Nkrumah with solemn satisfaction, 'had started in earnest'.[70]

PART II

THE CIA

5

Infiltration into Africa

THE ABSENCE OF A GOODWILL communiqué from America to the All African People's Conference in Accra had been noted with regret by the delegates. Then, just before the final session, a message arrived from Vice President Nixon. He had been advised of the bad impression created by America's silence and was seeking to put this right.[1] Even so, one of the American delegates described the telegram as 'a lukewarm statement quite out of keeping with the spirit of the Conference'.[2] In any case, his telegram arrived too late: the hardworking committees did not have time to read it out.

However, the US had, in fact, been well represented throughout the conference—in covert and unforeseen ways.

* * *

NEARLY FORTY AMERICANS WENT to Accra in December 1958— African Americans and white Americans in fairly equal numbers. Some of them attended as individuals in their own right, such as the civil rights activist Congressman Charles Diggs Jr of Detroit. Others represented nongovernmental organisations (NGOs), such as the African-American Institute, the American Society of African Culture, the Harlem-based United African Nationalist Movement, the Quaker organisation known as the American Friends Service Committee, the American Committee on Africa (ACOA), the American Federation of Labor and Congress of Industrial Organizations (AFL-CIO) and the Associated Negro Press.[3] Although they all shared an interest in Africa, they came from varied backgrounds and had different political points of view.

Many of those who were Nkrumah's personal friends had a history of involvement in the Council on African Affairs, which had been created in 1937 in the US as a way of supporting the struggle against colonialism and racism in Africa. Its headquarters were in Harlem in New York City. The first executive director was Max Yergan, an American intellectual who had been among the first Black YMCA missionaries in South Africa. Horrified by the racism of South Africa, he had eschewed the more mainstream civil rights organisations in favour of communism. In the council, he worked closely with Paul Robeson. Other members included Eslanda Robeson, W E B Du Bois, Shirley Graham, Adam Clayton Powell Jr, Ralph Bunche and William Alphaeus Hunton Jr, a former professor at Howard University.

The council published the monthly bulletin *New Africa*, which shone a spotlight on injustices in Africa with articles by scholars including Du Bois and Hunton. The council created a successful public profile and organised mass meetings, including rallies attended by tens of thousands in Madison Square Garden and at the Abyssinian Baptist Church in Harlem.[4] Nkrumah participated in a conference in 1944, organised by the council to project an international programme for the postwar liberation of Africa.[5]

Yergan was ousted as executive director in 1948. He had become openly anticommunist and from 1952 started to collaborate with the FBI against the council. By then, the council had become a casualty of the Cold War: the House Un-American Activities Committee (HUAC) accused members of the council of being communist and pointed to the fact that some, like Paul Robeson, had visited the Soviet Union. In 1954, Executive Director Hunton was subpoenaed to appear before a grand jury and was forced to surrender all the council's documents relating to their communications with the African National Congress of South Africa. The council, effectively crippled by the investigations of the HUAC, was dissolved in 1955.[6] Meanwhile, Hunton served six months in prison for refusing to reveal the names of the contributors to the Civil Rights Bail Fund.[7]

In May 1952, Yergan was named as a communist by a former staffer of the National Negro Congress and called to appear before the House Un-American Activities Committee. There, he disowned his earlier political convictions, vigorously denying any willing association with communism.[8] His biographer, David Henry Anthony III, refers to the 'relentless, still largely secret pressures to which he and his family were subjected by the intelligence community'. Only Yergan himself and those who convinced him to 'turn' knew what forced his hand. 'It is not to be found in the Yergan papers', observes Anthony. 'It is hinted at in his FBI file, however, where among bowdlerized and redacted documents lie the traces of betrayal or vengeance or other emotionally laden acts by which sensitive material was leaked to the Bureau'. It is likely, adds Anthony, that Yergan feared not only for himself but also for his children, for whom 'he was willing to sacrifice anything and everything'.[9]

* * *

WHEN THE COUNCIL ON African Affairs was dissolved, it left a substantial and significant gap in American society that, from the point of view of the CIA, needed to be filled safely by individuals who were not susceptible to communism.

The Council on African Affairs had taken a position of active political and practical support for African liberation, a stance not adopted by the African-American Institute (AAI), which sent members to the All African People's Conference in Accra in 1958. The AAI had been established in 1953 by a multiracial group of academics and businessmen with powerful mining interests in central Africa. The academics included Horace Mann Bond, who had been president of Lincoln University, Nkrumah's alma mater; in 1951, six years after Nkrumah had left the US for Britain, Bond conferred on him the honorary degree of doctor of laws. Bond went to Accra for Ghana's independence ceremony, and he also attended the AAPC the following year. By then he was the dean of Atlanta University; he had been forced to resign from Lincoln University in 1957 because of concerns about his management.

The stated aim of the AAI was to establish closer bonds between the peoples of Africa and the United States; it organised scholarship programs, teacher placements in Africa and a variety of lecture, information and visitors' services. The AAI headquarters were in New

York City, where it had plush offices at 345 East 46th Street, only a four-minute walk from the United Nations General Assembly, which facilitated access to UN delegates and events. It also had an office in Washington, centrally located at 1234 Twentieth Street, and an office in Accra. It published a monthly magazine titled *Africa Special Report* (later *Africa Report*), which was edited by Bob Keith.

But the AAI was not what it seemed. This fact emerged in February 1967, when the *New York Times* published a series of articles revealing that a number of American organisations were fronts created by the CIA and were funded secretly through an array of 'pass-through' channels and foundations.[10] The starting pistol for the articles was fired by the underground magazine *Ramparts*.[11]

An earlier series of articles about the CIA had appeared in the *New York Times* in 1966, without much impact. But now, the story took off. 'Like electricians tracing out the underground wiring of complicated circuits', reported one journalist in 1969, newsmen dug deeper and 'examined hundreds of foundation tax records and grant lists. Again and again, to their amazement they succeeded in making connections between a labyrinth of non-profit organisations and a hidden generator. This generator was demonstrably the CIA'.[12]

Eventually, more than 225 different organisations—operating in many parts of the world including Africa—were identified as direct or indirect recipients of CIA funds. Some of them were specially created by the CIA, while others had been set up independently from the agency and were then sponsored and funded by it. One of the CIA fronts, revealed the *Washington Post* on 26 February 1966, was the AAI.[13]

Bob Keith, the chief editor of the AAI journal, *Africa Special Report*, was registered at the AAPC in Accra as an American press correspondent.[14] In a dramatic moment, Keith was found hiding in the Accra Community Centre during a closed session of the conference, which was off-limits to the press. He was arrested by Ghanaian police, who discovered recording equipment on his person. Keith tried to justify why he was there; he said he had entered the building in order to obtain photographs from the centre's official photographer. Several decades later, Kojo Botsio, Ghana's minister of foreign affairs at the time of the AAPC, was asked about Keith's secretive behaviour. Botsio laughed as he remembered the occasion: 'Yes, Yes I think he was a journalist who wanted to get [to] the place, where he could record everything, he had a recording machine on him, at that time it was a very silly thing to do'.[15]

The AAI had put down roots in Accra before the AAPC. In 1957, it had established its West African office there, under the leadership of Emmett Jefferson 'Pat' Murphy, a historian of Africa who was the AAI's executive vice president.[16] On the evening of Monday 8 December 1958, the AAI held a reception for AAPC delegates in Murphy's family home. This was an ideal opportunity for the AAI to network and build contacts with the future leaders of Africa.

* * *

ANOTHER CIA FRONT THAT sent representatives to the AAPC was the American Society of African Culture. Known as AMSAC, its links with the CIA were exposed by the *New York Times* on 17 February 1967. It had been established in 1957 as a kind of American version of the Société Africaine de Culture (SAC), which was based in Paris.[17] The SAC, led by Alioune Diop, a Senegalese philosopher who also attended the AAPC, had been publishing literature on *Négritude* since the founding of its magazine *Présence Africaine* in 1947; the Négritude movement had been started by Francophone intellectuals in the 1930s as a celebration of African culture.

When AMSAC was first set up, its New York headquarters at 16 East 40th Street were shared with the Council on Race and Caste in World Affairs (CORAC), which was yet another front organisation established by the CIA. CORAC claimed to examine 'the extent to which the communists were capitalising on racial conflicts globally'.[18] In 1958, CORAC and AMSAC merged.[19]

The professed aim of AMSAC was to expose African Americans to their African heritage, and the organisation was 'explicitly anti-Communist, albeit avowedly apolitical'.[20] As well as offices in Paris and New York City, it had an apartment on Fifth Avenue to host guests.[21] It gave scholarships to African students and published its own journal, *African Forum*. It also had an ambitious cultural and educational program; in 1961 it organised a music festival in Lagos, Nigeria, which lasted two days and nights and featured the cream of African American musical talent, including Nina Simone.[22] Because of its abundant resources, AMSAC was dubbed by some as 'Uncle Moneybags'.[23] But the artists benefiting from AMSAC's largesse at that time did not know it was a covert CIA front.

AMSAC sent three representatives to the AAPC. One of these was its president, Horace Mann Bond, who was also representing the AAI. Another representative was Will Mercer Cook, a scholar of francophone literature; he was on the faculty of Howard University but lived in Paris.[24] The third AMSAC delegate was John Aubrey Davis, who was the executive director of AMSAC and a political scientist at City College, New York (CUNY); he was also a commissioner in the New York State Commission against Discrimination. All three were among the group of five African Americans who had founded AMSAC.

Davis sent AMSAC at least two detailed reports on the speakers and events at the AAPC, with careful analysis. They gave an account not only of the African delegates, but also of the other Americans who were at the conference. To one of the reports he attached various Ghanaian newspapers, which listed the names of the conference delegates with their pictures.[25]

These reports were sent to James Theodore 'Ted' Harris Jr, who was the assistant executive director of AMSAC and had been the National Student Association's second president in the late 1940s. In 1967, it was revealed that the National Student Association had been covertly used by the CIA; Harris had operated as an embedded CIA agent. According to the *New Yorker*, the National Student Association 'functioned as a glove that concealed the American government's hand and allowed it to do business with people who would never knowingly have done business with the American government. These people thought that they were dealing with a student group that was independent of the government. They had no idea that the NSA was a front'.[26]

After the exposure of covert financing by the CIA, AMSAC's funding apparatus was dismantled.[27] This left the organisation scrabbling about, looking for money. Membership declined sharply; people believed they had been fed lies and that their goodwill had been abused.

The leaders of AMSAC claimed to have been the victims of official deception, but this is contradicted by evidence analysed by Hugh Wilford in *The Mighty Wurlitzer: How the CIA Played America*. Wilford records that Adelaide M Cromwell, a sociologist at Boston University and a cofounder of its African Studies Center, was a member of AMSAC's executive council. In February 1967 she wrote a memorandum to the other members which suggests, notes Wilford, 'a widespread state of wittingness within AMSAC'. The memo stated, 'I remember the exact time and place almost eight years ago when such a possibility was first confided in me and by whom. Several years later further and more detailed confirmation was given me by another friend. Around the edges were frequent innuendoes and asides. None of this was documented, understandably so'.[28]

Wilford also refers to an illuminating report by Yvonne Walker, the managing director of AMSAC. One day, according to this report, two members of the CIA 'showed up for an appointment with Dr. Davis. I didn't know who they were at the time, but they . . . called me into the office and explained to me what was going down, and that they would require me to take an oath'.

Subsequently, Walker and other officers of AMSAC met with their CIA case officers in hotel rooms, usually in New York, but also in Washington. 'They [the CIA officers] were kept fully informed . . . by Dr. Davis on everything that was going on', she recalled, 'and I'm sure that they helped to steer some of the plans'.[29]

Wayne Urban, the biographer of Horace Mann Bond, tackles the issue of whether his subject was witting or unwitting—whether or not he knew that the AAI and AMSAC were CIA fronts. 'There is ample evidence', he writes, 'for concluding that, if he did not know, he did not want to know'. And if Bond did not know of these links, he adds, 'he should have known'. Urban also points to a letter from Bond to Nkrumah in which Bond asked for an invitation to the AAPC for AMSAC members and described the organisation as 'concerned with intellectual studies and artistic attainment. It is not a political organisation'. This was not candid, argues Urban, since a 'distinct part of AMSAC's agenda was the pursuit of the political goals of American foreign policy'.[30]

* * *

ANOTHER OF THE MANY American organisations exposed as CIA fronts in the 1960s was the Congress for Cultural Freedom (CCF), which was founded in 1950 and based at 104 Boulevard Haussmann in Paris—a handsome nineteenth-century building in the centre of the city. The CCF was the brainchild of Cord Meyer Jr, who headed a branch of the CIA called the International Organizations Division. Michael Josselson, a gifted polyglot who was the executive director of the CCF and managed it in Paris, was a salaried CIA officer. Only a selected few of those who benefited from the congress's sponsorship were told where its funds came from.

The CCF functioned as an international group of liberal intellectuals and at its height was active on five continents, with offices in more than thirty countries.[31] Among many other projects in different parts of the world, it ran an Africa programme, of which the US academic Mercer Cook was director from 1960 to June 1961; the South African exile Ezekiel Mphahlele then took over the helm.

The CCF's core aim was to mobilise left-wing thinkers who were noncommunist, according to Frances Stonor Saunders, the author of *Who Paid the Piper?*, a detailed study of the CIA and the cultural Cold War. These figures were designated as a group— the Non-Communist Left (NCL)—in State Department and intelligence circles.[32] In Latin America, where the Congress for Cultural Freedom subsidised conferences, magazines and books from 1954, its dominant ethos 'resembled that of Western European social democracy, with strong anti-Communism attached to moderate social reform in a democratic context'.[33]

'We all felt that democratic socialism was the most effective bulwark against totalitarianism', recalled the historian Arthur M Schlesinger Jr some years later. Schlesinger knew the CIA origins of the congress from the outset, explains Stonor Saunders, although he was not an employee of the agency himself.[34] Indeed, a number of CCF members were aware of the CIA connection.[35]

In 1966, the budget for the CCF topped $2 million, equivalent to nearly $16.5 million in 2020.[36] In April of that year, a team of correspondents at the *New York Times* wrote a series of five articles on the covert methods of the CIA. (These articles received little of the public attention that met the revelations published less than a year later, in February 1967.) The third article of the series, which started on the front page on 27 April, identified the relationship between the agency and the Congress for Cultural Freedom.[37] There was swift rebuttal. The CCF's leading intellectuals—Robert Oppenheimer, John K Galbraith and Arthur M Schlesinger—insisted that it was a completely independent organisation; still, they did not discuss the source of its funds.

Then, in 1967, Thomas Braden, the first head of the International Organizations Division of the CIA, acknowledged the truth of the revelations in a *Saturday Evening Post* article titled 'I'm Glad the CIA Is "Immoral"'.[38] Michael Josselson, the executive director of the CCF, admitted that CIA subsidies had been received from 1950 to 1966.[39]

The CIA had funded the inaugural convention of the congress in West Berlin in June 1950. The event brought together more than a hundred American and European intellectual celebrities, including Arthur Koestler, the author of *Darkness at Noon*, for four days; the open-air closing ceremonies were attended by some fifteen thousand West Berliners. The CCF financed numerous cultural events and some twenty well-known and highbrow periodicals, including *Encounter* in London, *Der Monat* in Berlin, *Preuves* in Paris, *Forum* in Vienna, and *Tempo Presente* in Rome.[40]

The CIA and the congress worked closely with selected publishers to support the publication of book titles. In the US, its regular partner was Frederick A Praeger, which by the mid-1950s published between 100 and 150 CIA titles a year. Over a thousand books were published by Praeger in association with the CIA during the 1950s and 1960s. 'Through these and other maneuvers', observes David

Price in an article on the CIA's book-publishing operations, 'the US government secretly corrupted scholarship and warped academic freedom in ways that left the American public uninformed'.[41]

In Mexico, the publishing house of Bartolomeu Costa Amic flourished with CIA support. '[It was the] best deal I ever had', Costa Amic is reported to have said. 'The CIA pays for all the printing, and then they buy all the copies!'[42] There is 'rich irony', Price observes, 'that the secret police of American capitalism had to covertly prop-up works that could not survive the free market that the Agency was fighting to protect'.[43]

The CIA's International Organizations Division, which over-saw the CCF, arranged the congress's funding via 'pass-through' fronts. One of these was the Farfield Foundation, which Josselson's boss at the CIA, Lawrence de Neufville, sometimes referred to as the 'Far-Fetched Foundation', as it was so obviously a front. 'Everybody knew who was behind it', he told Stonor Saunders. 'It was ridiculous'.[44]

Tom Braden explained to Stonor Saunders the functioning of such foundations:

> The Farfield Foundation was a CIA foundation and there were many such foundations. We used the names of foundations for many purposes but the foundation *didn't exist* except on paper. We would go to somebody in New York who was a well known rich person and we would say, 'We want to set up a foundation', and we would tell him what we were trying to do, and pledge him to secrecy and he would say, 'Of course I'll do it'. And then you would publish a letterhead and his name would be on it, and there would be a foundation. It was really a pretty simple device.[45]

This masquerade was successful. One of the many writers who were misled in this way was Richard Wright, who was funded by the CCF to attend the Bandung Conference in 1955. It supported him in other ways, too: three CCF magazines published excerpts from his book *Black Power* (1954), which includes an account of his visit to the Gold Coast in 1953 and his observations on Pan-Africanism;

and four Congress magazines published excerpts from *The Color Curtain*, Wright's account of the Bandung conference.[46]

Wright was therefore funded—without his knowledge—by the CIA. At the same time, he was 'being spied on by multiple acquaintances in multiple agencies', observes Joel Whitney in *Finks: How the CIA Tricked the World's Best Writers*. Wright realised, as did James Baldwin, 'that officials were spying on him. They penetrated groups he was part of, using both the FBI and the CIA to keep tabs, manage, rein in, bribe, and publicize. The dual role that the CIA played by (likely) spying on and (definitely) funnelling money to figures like Wright and Baldwin was positively schizophrenic'.[47]

* * *

IT HAS BEEN SUGGESTED that the journal *Contact* in South Africa, which was the organ of the Liberal Party, and edited by Patrick Duncan, benefited from funding by the CIA, since its publisher was associated with the Farfield Foundation.[48] No proof has been seen, however, of a direct link between Duncan and the CIA. He was one of the delegates at the AAPC and described it as the 'nearest thing to Utopia I have seen'; three pages of *Contact* were devoted to the conference.[49] Duncan's position was closer to that of AMSAC and the AAI, rather than the Council on African Affairs; the journal declared that it was 'proud to be anti-communist'.[50] Duncan was frequently in disagreement with the Reverend Michael Scott, who was also at the AAPC. In 1952, Scott had set up the Africa Bureau in London, to support Africans who wished to use constitutional means to challenge political decisions affecting their lives in the colonies of Africa. A historian has established that a 'no-strings grant of £3,000 a year to the Africa Bureau' came from the Farfield Foundation.[51]

CIA funding was provided not only via pass-through fronts such as the Farfield Foundation, but also via legitimate and established organisations such as the Ford Foundation, the Rockefeller Foundation and the Carnegie Foundation.[52] In 1954, it was agreed at the Ford Foundation headquarters to formulate a standard policy for how to handle such government-sponsored projects.[53] By the early 1960s, reports Stonor Saunders, Ford had funnelled about $7 million to the Congress for Cultural Freedom.[54] A CIA study in 1966 argued that this was 'particularly effective for democratically run membership organisations, which need to assure their own unwitting members and collaborators, as well as their hostile critics, that they have genuine, respectable, private sources of income'.[55]

Wole Soyinka, the Nigerian writer and future Nobel laureate, was shocked to learn in 1967 that the CCF was a CIA front and that he had unknowingly received some funds from America's foreign intelligence service. He was bitterly disappointed in Melvin Lasky, one of the intellectual leaders of the CCF and the editor of *Encounter*, who did not deny direct knowledge of the agency's involvement. 'Soon enough', exclaimed Soyinka, 'we would discover that we had been dining, and with relish, with the original of that serpentine incarnation, the Devil himself, romping in our postcolonial Garden of Eden and gorging on the fruits of the Tree of Knowledge!'[56]

It has been suggested that some of the African authors who were funded indirectly by the CIA were aware of the process.[57] But there was no apparent reason for African writers to mistrust the organisations offering assistance or to suspect the dystopic reality: that the US government, which loudly articulated its support for the freedom of Africa, would use its foreign intelligence service in this covert way.

The US was not alone on the Cold War axis in its patronage of artists and writers in Africa. At the other end of the axis, Soyinka has recalled, were 'rival jostlers'. In Nigeria, 'utilities' were a routine form of patronage: 'state of the art printing presses from the Soviet Union and/or via China in disguised crates formed steady contributions to the cause of intellection, creativity and general literary empowerment'. Within the Soviet Union itself, publications produced in Africa were 'pirated by the Soviet state publishing machine to the tune of a million print runs on a single title'. Those mills, adds Soyinka, 'were fertile engines, rolling out Third World Literature for internal consumption and sometimes, even export!'[58]

A frustrating aspect of Soviet patronage was the neglect of contracts and royalties. This neglect was challenged by some authors, which led to a handful receiving notices to report to the Soviet embassy and collect 'our modest windfall'. Soyinka was one of the handful: 'I banked my cheque before someone in the Kremlin or wherever chose to change his mind. Later—or perhaps it was already operational policy—the satellite states would follow suit. Hardly ever was permission sought, no contracts negotiated'. On occasion an East European nation would assign royalties, which had to be spent within its borders. 'It was actually not a bad feeling', comments Soyinka, drily, 'to know you were a millionaire somewhere in Eastern European currency'.[59]

Socialist Cuba, too, supported artists and writers, and paid for them to attend Cuban festivals. Here Soyinka confronted 'very real race issues'. There was a problem, as well, because the US prohibited its citizens from visiting Cuba, and some African governments, including Nigeria, followed suit. Cuba handled this where necessary by planting an entry stamp on a piece of paper, instead of on a passport.[60]

* * *

THROUGH ITS SECRET REPRESENTATIVES at the AAPC in Accra, the CIA was watching developments carefully. It took note that Paul Robeson sent warm greetings to the conference.[61] It also produced a report on Eslanda Robeson's attendance, with details of an interview she gave shortly afterwards in which she drew links between the freedom struggle in Africa and the civil rights movement in the US. 'The question of Africa', she said, 'is one of colonialism and the American Negro too is held in a colonial position. Its solution in Africa is bound to have repercussions in America'.

She noted that Daniel Ahmling Chapman, Ghana's first ambassador to the United Nations, had said in his maiden speech that his country's independence would be of service to African Americans. Then she added, 'Many of our people in New York crowd into public benches at the UNO just to see the African delegates sitting there on equal terms with the White nations. Even American Whites are being affected. They dare not behave towards Negroes as they used to because they cannot be sure if it is an Ambassador or a hall porter they are pushing around!'[62] Mrs Robeson had no doubt that the CIA attended the AAPC in some form. There had been rumours at the conference of a split between Nkrumah and Egypt's President Nasser, which Mrs Robeson believed were overblown—if not altogether made up. There was other gossip, too, including the claim that Cairo and Moscow wanted to take over the conference. This, she thought, was untrue and deliberately concocted.[63]

6

'Africa Has Become the Real Battleground'

PRIME MINISTER Nkrumah remained quietly within Christiansborg Castle for much of the All African People's Conference.[1] Even so, he was exerting a powerful influence through his meetings with delegates.[2]

He was introduced to Patrice Lumumba at the start of the week by George Padmore. Nkrumah had a strong sense of the significance of this meeting and wanted a photograph taken to record the event. 'I was waiting at Nkrumah's headquarters', recorded George Houser, a delegate from the American Committee on Africa, 'when someone asked if the photographer was present. Apparently he was not, but I had my camera on my shoulder and offered to take the picture that Nkrumah wanted taken with himself and Lumumba'.[3] From that moment on, 'the two men took to each other', and Nkrumah spent more time with Lumumba than with any other delegate.[4]

It was not an obvious partnership: they did not have a shared language, and Nkrumah—less than a year away from fifty—was fifteen years older than Lumumba. But they were similar in spirit: they were both hardworking, disciplined and purposeful. Like Nkrumah, Lumumba was not a drinker and smoked rarely, and, again like Nkrumah, he had 'a sharp sense of humour' and 'laughed loudly, with a spontaneity'. Lumumba had not had the opportunity to go to university, unlike Nkrumah, but he loved to read and study. According to a close friend, the 'shelves of his very small room swelled with books which themselves were filled with annotations, indicative of his thirst for education'.[5]

Nkrumah liked and admired Lumumba. He was also supportive of Lumumba's strong commitment to the development of the Congo as a 'multiethnic state', which mirrored his own commitment to nontribalism.[6]

But his primary motive for befriending the younger man was his conviction that the Belgian Congo would be at the centre of the Pan-Africanist struggle for the freedom of Africa.

* * *

BEFORE GOING TO ACCRA, Lumumba had been wholly unknown outside the Belgian Congo. The Mouvement National Congolais (MNC) had been set up just two months before the AAPC, in October 1958, and was unknown to the conference-planning committee. The committee had sent an official invitation to Joseph Kasavubu, an established Congolese politician. The stocky Kasavubu was the leader of the political party known as the Abako—the Alliance des Bakongo—which had been founded in 1950 principally to promote the language of the Kongo people, but had evolved into a determined opponent of Belgian colonial rule.[7]

The plan for Lumumba to attend the Accra conference had been last minute and almost accidental. A team representing the Pan-African Freedom Movement of East and Central Africa (PAFMECA)—including Tom Mboya, A R Mohamed Babu and Kanyama Chiume—were on their way to Accra in December 1958 when their plane made a stopover in Leopoldville. While there, a staff member at the hotel where they were staying, who spoke Kiswahili, took them to meet Lumumba. They were impressed by him and determined to bring him to Accra, together with fellow members of the MNC Gaston Diomi and Joseph Ngalua. Funds were provided by PAFMECA and also through the assistance of Bill Sutherland, an American pacifist who had been living in Ghana since 1953. Sutherland informed a fellow peace activist, the Belgian Jean Van Lierde, who helped with funds and logistics; Van Lierde was to become a loyal friend to Lumumba.[8]

When Kasavubu arrived at Leopoldville's Ndjili airport, en route to Accra, he was not allowed to proceed. The customs service told him that his inoculation certificates were not in order—evidently a strategy to prevent him from attending the conference. The Belgian government of the Congo had been furious about a powerful speech given earlier by Kasavubu, criticising colonial rule.[9]

But Lumumba and his fellow members of the MNC were allowed to go. The colonial administration of the Congo had been opposed to allowing anyone to go to Accra but, on advice from Brussels, Hendrik Cornelis, the governor general, gave permission.[10] In any case, Cornelis had no reason to suspect that Lumumba would be a troublemaker, for he knew nothing about him.

From the point of view of Lumumba and the MNC, it was a huge advantage that Kasavubu was forced to remain behind. For if he *had* attended the conference, it would have been far more difficult for Lumumba to assert himself and his new party as the voice of the Congolese people. Up to this point, Nkrumah's link with the Belgian Congo had been Kasavubu, and Ghana, wishing to support the Congolese struggle for freedom, had been sending funds to the Abako. But now, as Nkrumah recorded later, Ghana's support for the Congo 'took a new turn with the consolidation of the new and more dynamic party, the Mouvement National Congolais led by Patrice Lumumba'.[11] This was a new kind of political party in the Congo, because—as indicated by its name—it sought to strike a 'national chord' and to resist regional separation.[12] Up to that time, political parties, like the Abako, had represented local interests.

* * *

LUMUMBA'S POLITICAL VIEWS WERE transformed over the course of 1958, culminating in the Accra conference. In his early adult years, he had regarded colonialism as a positive force that would bring Western civilisation to the Congolese people.

Like Nkrumah, Lumumba grew up in a poor family. He was from the village of Onalua in Kasai—the same province in which the American John Stockwell spent his childhood. Stockwell was a CIA officer who was the chief of the agency's base in Katanga in the late 1960s; in 1975, he led the CIA's 'task force' in Angola. The following year, Stockwell became a whistleblower, exposing what he regarded as unacceptable clandestine operations. He supported the intelligence mission of the CIA, he explained in his memoir, *In Search of Enemies*, but objected to the agency's covert action interventions all over the globe. Faced with a choice between 'my loyalty to the CIA or my responsibilities to the United States' Constitution', he wrote, 'I chose the latter'.[13]

In the 1930s, Lumumba was baptised into the Methodist church and attended a Methodist mission school, while Stockwell, the son of an American Presbyterian engineer, attended the Presbyterian school in the same province. 'The two church communities overlapped', writes Stockwell. Lumumba, he adds, 'was a member of the missionary community in which my parents had spent most of their adult lives, and in which I grew up'.[14]

Lumumba continued his primary education at a Catholic mission school and then took a post as a clerk. He worked hard to educate himself and to qualify as an *évolué*—a Belgian term meaning 'evolved', which was used to specify Africans who were seen to be 'civilised' and capable of sharing in European society.[15] 'I once asked my parents what this meant', said Julienne Lumumba, Patrice's daughter. 'It was a deeply humiliating process. You would be given a test, someone would come to the house and see if you had an inside toilet, if your children wore pyjamas, if you ate with a knife and fork—only then would you be given the accreditation "évolué".'[16] The accreditation qualified Lumumba to join the tiny elite of Congolese who were given special privileges, such as being allowed to enter cafés reserved for Europeans and to take up some skilled positions.

Alongside his ambition to be an évolué, however, Lumumba had a keen sense of the injustice that supported the Belgian colony. This sense grew powerfully after a visit in 1947 to Brazzaville, the capital of French Equatorial Africa, a federation of French colonial territories.

Lumumba had taken the ferry across the deep Congo River to Brazzaville, which directly faced the Belgian Congo's capital of Leopoldville. Walking around Brazzaville in the baking heat, he became thirsty and lingered near a bar. He then stopped near a hedge which separated the avenue from the bar. But he did not enter, because only whites were seated at the tables in the garden. If he dared to enter a similar café in the Belgian Congo, he would have been severely punished. But a white woman invited him into the garden and told him to sit where he liked. This terrified Lumumba.

'Patrice's throat tightened', recorded Lumumba's friend, Pierre Clément. 'Into what trap had he fallen?' He became increasingly concerned when the owner of the bar herself brought him a glass of water—and not just any glass of water, but a glass of mineral water. 'Patrice was very uneasy', added Clément. 'He managed to pay for the drink and left as quickly as possible, without having swallowed a drop of it'.[17] But he saw that the racial practices in the French colony were different from those in the Belgian colony on his own side of the river. This opened Lumumba's eyes in a powerful way to the real possibility of change.

In 1944 Lumumba moved to Stanleyville (now Kisangani), where he joined the postal service and threw himself into professional training; he became editor of the quarterly review of postal workers. He put considerable energy into the association of évolués in the city and became increasingly involved in politics; he was vice president of the Belgian Liberal Party's Congolese branch as well as secretary general of a union for civil servants. Lumumba remained 'committed to his vocation as a dedicated autodidact', notes Nzongola-Ntalaja. 'He was able to acquire a university-level education by learning from home, through reading and correspondence'.[18]

He married Pauline Opango Ono Samba in 1951, with whom he had four children: Patrice, Julienne, Roland and Marie-Christine (who died within a few months). By an earlier relationship he had a son, François; and by a relationship beginning in 1960 he had a son, Guy, who was born after his death. An earnest champion of the value of education, he regarded the poor education of the women he loved as a shortcoming; he wished, as he saw it, to raise them up. This led to resentment at times by the women themselves.[19]

Lumumba hoped to attend the newly established Lovanium University, in Leopoldville, but was turned down on the grounds that he was married; only bachelors could be admitted. He was bitterly disappointed.[20] But in 1956, he became one of only a handful of Congolese to visit Belgium, when selected for a study tour.[21]

That same year, Lumumba was arrested for embezzling funds from the post office. He admitted to the theft, which he had already started to repay before he was caught. He was condemned to serve two years in prison, but the sentence was commuted to twelve months after the évolués of Stanleyville collected funds to pay back the rest of the sum. They understood his need for money; though he was doing the same work as whites, he was not earning the same salary.[22] Lumumba wasted no time while in prison. He wrote *Le Congo, terre d'avenir, est-il menacé?* (Congo, My Country), which was published in Brussels posthumously.[23] The book opposed racial discrimination, but from a position of support for the 'civilising mission' claimed by Belgium. This viewpoint was 'diametrically opposed' to the discourse he developed over the next few years.[24]

In 1957 he moved to Leopoldville, where he worked for the brewery Bracongo, which made Polar beer. When he took on the job of publicity director, he travelled around the country promoting the beer, which triggered a rivalry with Bralima, the brewery that made the beer Primus. During this 'beer war', writes Nzongola-Ntalaja, 'Lumumba honed the public speaking skills that would serve him so well in political rallies and meetings'.[25]

Lumumba's growing hopes for political change were nourished by a speech given in Brazzaville on 24 August 1958 by Charles de Gaulle, the prime minister of France, in which he declared his support for the self-determination of the French colonies: 'Whoever desires independence can immediately obtain it'.[26] Across the Congo River in the Belgian Congo, writes the historian David Van Reybrouck, Belgian families 'choked on their coffee' when they heard the speech on the radio. But in the cité, a cheer went up.[27]

If this could happen in French-ruled Africa, thought Lumumba and many other Congolese, why not in Belgian-ruled Africa? Two days later, a group of évolués in Leopoldville delivered a signed petition to Hendrik Cornelis, the governor general, denouncing the 'anachronistic political regime' of the Congo and demanding a date for 'complete independence'.[28] A few weeks later, some of the individuals who had signed the petition established a new political party, the Mouvement National Congolais.[29] The chairman was Lumumba.

On 28 September 1958, De Gaulle called a referendum in all the French-ruled territories in Africa, asking them if they wanted to remain as members of the French community of peoples; the alternative was self-government. The vote, they were assured, was a free one.

Lumumba believed that De Gaulle spoke in good faith. He was therefore appalled by the reaction of the French when Guinea voted against remaining in the French community and in favour of self-government—the only French colony in Africa to do so. The colony became an independent state on 2 October 1958. French nationals living in Guinea, enraged, withdrew en masse. Since few members of the Guinean population had been trained in the skills necessary to run the country, Guinea was left without administrators and technicians. It also lacked necessary equipment, since the French took away every piece of equipment they could possibly carry, including typewriters. 'France was furious', said an American general services officer working later at the US Embassy in Guinea:

> They pulled out all of their people. They ripped out the electrical wires for the street lighting, for the apartment buildings and offices, broke the generators of the local hospital, tore up the streets, I mean everything you can think of, they did. It was horrible. They broke the elevator to the one skyscraper, which was just mean and vicious, and it was ugly and the country had not been able to overcome that.
>
> It was readily apparent. I mean holes in the streets, broken down lights. . . . They broke things and the cranes. . . . I mean you just name it, they broke it. I mean they were determined to teach that country a lesson and they did.[30]

It was a savage response to the referendum slogan of the first president of Guinea, Ahmed Sékou Touré: 'Guinea prefers poverty in freedom to riches in slavery'.[31]

. Sékou Touré was faced with a colossal challenge. Nkrumah invited him to Accra in November 1958 for discussions to find a way forward. Touré returned to Conakry, Guinea's capital, strengthened by an agreement of unity with Ghana and a loan equivalent to US$28 million.[32]

There was overwhelming sympathy for Guinea among the AAPC delegates, and while the conference was in session, Ghana's Parliament approved a formal union between the two countries. This was a complex arrangement: Guinea was in the franc zone and its official language was French, whereas Ghana was in the sterling area and its official language was English. Still, Nkrumah and Touré were determined to build a Pan-African community, despite the obstacles left by colonialism.

* * *

NKRUMAH TOOK NOTICE OF Lumumba at the All African People's Conference. But it was not only Ghana's prime minister who noticed Lumumba. So, too, did the CIA.

Lumumba was on his guard against spies working for the Belgian Congo colonial government. En route to Accra, he and his fellow members of the MNC were concerned to see a fourth Congolese man on their flight to Accra, one who spoke English. They suspected he was a spy from the Sûreté and kept well away from him.[33]

It did not occur to Lumumba to suspect anyone who was neither Congolese nor Belgian. So when a friendly French speaker approached him after his arrival and offered to act as his informal interpreter, he accepted the offer gratefully. Lumumba did not speak English and was eager to understand as much as possible and to communicate with the other delegates.

Many years later, Nkrumah learned that Lumumba's interpreter at the AAPC was a CIA agent. The interpreter facilitated a friendly introduction between Lumumba and the Americans at the conference, according to Thomas Kanza, a Congolese graduate of Louvain University in Belgium and of Harvard University in the US. 'Even at the meeting between Lumumba and Nkrumah', said Kanza, many years later, 'the American was translating, and also at the meeting with the Soviets. There he appeared to be French, because they were speaking in French, and for him to be accepted as an interpreter he couldn't say he was an American'.[34]

In Kanza's judgement, Lumumba may have told the interpreter 'more than was advisable'. In private meetings with people from Western and Eastern countries alike, explained Kanza, 'Lumumba vented his anti-colonialist and anti-Belgian feelings in a way he had never been able to express to his Belgian friends'.[35]

Kanza could not recall the name of the interpreter. In fact, two Americans who were fluent in French claimed after the conference to have interpreted for Lumumba. One of them was John A Marcum, a white political scientist at Colgate University in New York, who attended the conference as part of the delegation of the American Committee on Africa. Marcum, who made the claim in a book many years later, was the recipient of a Ford Foundation grant that enabled him to travel to West Africa. He was in neighbouring Ivory Coast towards the end of 1958 and flew to Accra for the AAPC.[36]

It is not possible to establish whether the Ford Foundation grant given to Marcum came from the CIA—or, if it did, whether Marcum was aware of this. While it is the case that Marcum wrote frequently for the AAI journal *Africa Special Report*, which was financed by the CIA, few of the journal's authors knew about its funding source. The same applies to *New Leader*, a magazine that was covertly subsidised by the CIA and for which Marcum wrote a number of feature articles.[37] His article 'The Challenge of Africa', which appeared in *New Leader* in February 1960, was published with an introduction by Tom Mboya.

Whether or not Marcum was aware of the CIA's role as a source of funding for his travels, research and publications, he was increasingly involved with the Angolan politician Holden Roberto—who, as many suspected, was in the pay of America. Roberto, like Marcum, was a delegate at the All African People's Conference in Accra (registered under the pseudonym 'Rui Ventura'). He was the leader of the União das Populações de Angola (UPA), which aimed to liberate Angola from Portuguese occupation. A country summary produced in the late 1960s by the State Department's Bureau of Intelligence and Research (INR) noted that the 'CIA has had a relationship with Roberto since 1955'.[38]

George Padmore was deeply suspicious of Roberto. 'With his sharp, experienced eye', observed the Ghanaian journalist Cameron Duodu, 'Padmore easily saw through guys like Roberto, who, despite their rhetoric, had a penchant for fine clothes and designer dark glasses'.[39]

* * *

THE OTHER MAN WHO claimed to have translated for Lumumba at the AAPC was a white American trade unionist named Irving Brown, who held a senior position in the American Federation of Labor and Congress of Industrial Organizations (AFL-CIO). Brown was known as an anticolonialist; he was also known for his instrumental role in fighting communist unions in Europe and setting up anticommunist unions. He stated in an interview with the historian Richard D Mahoney, the author of *JFK: Ordeal in Africa*, that he had provided general help with interpreting at the AAPC and had given individual assistance to Lumumba.[40] A *New York Times* article covering the conference reported that Brown had been pressed into service as a simultaneous translator and that he had stood at the microphone on the conference platform all day.[41]

Brown's help with translation was open and transparent. It is unlikely, therefore, that Brown was the secret interpreter referred to by Kanza. It is more likely to have been Marcum. Nevertheless, Irving Brown's role at the AAPC was significant, since the AFL-CIO, which had been formed in 1955, was penetrating energetically into Africa. Importantly, it was CIA-backed and funded; British diplomats in the know, notes one expert on the history of the CIA, mockingly referred to it as the 'AFL-CIA'.[42] Led by its president, George Meany, the organisation was obsessed with eliminating communism and played an active role in Europe and Africa. In 1949, it had split from the World Federation of Trade Unions (WFTU) to form and to be part of—with its affiliate, the British Trades Union Congress (TUC)— the International Confederation of Free Trade Unions, known as the ICFTU. The reason for the split was that the WFTU was seen as sympathetic to communism and the Soviet Union.

'Irving was never a CIA agent', said Cord Meyer, the head of the International Organizations Division of the CIA. 'The very notion is laughable. He was as independent as you could get, and very strong-willed. What the CIA did was to help him finance his major projects when they were crucial to the Western cause. But in his operations he was totally on his own'.[43]

Irving Brown's superior was the good-looking Jay Lovestone, who would serve in the 1960s as the director of the Department of International Affairs for the AFL-CIO and has been described as 'one of the Central Intelligence Agency's most important men'.[44] He shared Brown's concern to keep communism out of Africa once decolonisation got under way. In 1957, Lovestone told George Meany that 'Africa has become the real battleground and the next field of the big test of strength—not only for the free world and the communist world but for our own country and our Allies who are colonialist powers'.[45]

* * *

EVEN IF LUMUMBA HAD not made an impact at the All African People's Conference, it was inevitable that he would be noticed by the CIA, because of the friendship that he quickly developed with Frantz Fanon. The agency had first become interested in Fanon in the late 1950s, according to the CIA agent C Oliver Iselin, whose cover was being a member of the diplomatic corps in North Africa. In 2016, Iselin gave an interview to Thomas Meaney, an American historian, in which he spoke of CIA interest in Fanon. 'We tried to keep control of, keep up to date on, what was happening in the GPRA [Provisional Government of the Algerian Republic] and whatnot', Iselin told Meaney, 'so we knew about Fanon. . . . We knew he had been a medical assistant in Blida with the French army. As he said, why cure these people when you're just gonna—anyway, so that's why he defected. I even read some of his literature and books'.[46]

The Algerians, said Iselin, 'were a very tough nut to crack'. But in 1957, Senator John F Kennedy made a controversial speech in the US Senate in which he argued against American support for French colonialism. Such support, he warned, would convert Algerian moderate nationalists into communists and conflate the process of decolonisation with the Cold War. Kennedy's speech enabled Iselin, under cover as a State Department official, to make his first recruits. He made regular visits to the training sites of the major liberation groups, the ALN and FLN: 'We gave hospital supplies, though mainly cigarettes, which I got from Port Lyautey and used to bring back in the back of my car. Also, we had lighters made up with an Algerian flag and "FREE ALGERIA" on them'. The CIA, Iselin told Meaney, coordinated closely with national liberation movements across North Africa, where it worked through the American Federation of Labor to infiltrate trade unions in Morocco, Tunisia and Algeria.[47]

Western trade unionists came to Africa 'in droves' from the mid- to late 1950s, writes the historian John C Stoner. Those from the AFL-CIO, he argues, 'sought to capitalize on the mythos of American anticolonialism to gain a foothold in Africa at the expense of European unions . . . which had been present (and in some cases complicit with the colonial apparatus) during the colonial period'.[48] Brown and Lovestone were sceptical of the Afro-Asian endorsement of nonalignment. Like many Americans, argues the Russian scholar Sergey Mazov, they perceived nonalignment as either 'against us' or 'for us'.[49]

In February 1967, the columnist Drew Pearson reported in the *New York Post* that Jay Lovestone received orders from CIA Director of International Organizations Cord Meyer, and that Irving Brown 'spends CIA money in Africa'.[50]

Brown was shuttled into and out of Africa. But 'the real job', according to a biographer of Lovestone, 'fell to a black woman from the ranks of the ILGWU [International Ladies' Garment Workers Union] who became Lovestone's Africa agent'.[51] This was Maida Springer, an earnest, thoughtful American with severe spectacles, who had studied at Ruskin College in Oxford and cared passionately about the rights of workers. As a Black woman in the white and male-dominated world of organised labour, she was keenly aware of the obstacles facing Black women at work. Following a meeting with George Padmore in 1945, she turned to international labour activism. She worked in a number of African countries, including Kenya, Nigeria, Tanzania, Uganda and Ghana, where she was widely known as 'Mama Maida'.[52]

Along with Brown, Maida Springer represented the fifteen million members of the AFL-CIO at the All African People's Conference in Accra. 'For once in my life', she observed with joy, 'I was somewhere I had the right paint job. I empathized with the people in Africa. I was not objective. I couldn't be objective!'[53]

It was her judgement that Irving Brown did a sterling job as part-time interpreter. The delegates at the conference sanctioned his activity she said, notwithstanding his known affiliation with the ICFTU, which was generally unpopular in Africa. She thought his 'general friendliness and usefulness with the delegations was very effective'.[54]

Maida Springer had become a housemother to Africans visiting New York in the 1950s. 'She had an old house in Brooklyn, a mother who liked to cook, a beat-up Ford to drive them around in, and two manual typewriters', according to her biographer. When the young Kenyan Tom Mboya arrived in New York in 1956, he stayed with her. She introduced him to Lovestone, which gave Mboya an opportunity—over dinner at a Chinese restaurant on Third Avenue—to explain that he wanted a trade union centre in Nairobi and scholarships for Kenyan labour leaders. Mboya got both.[55]

Springer attended the independence celebrations in Ghana on 6 March 1957 and was profoundly moved; she recalled later that she 'wept like a baby on that evening'.[56] When she returned the following year to Accra, she threw herself, as a volunteer, into the work of helping to organise the All African People's Conference.

But she came under critical scrutiny in the second half of the 1970s, when it was alleged that she was in the pay of the CIA and, like Irving Brown, had participated in espionage and covert activities to weaken and divide African labour movements. She was stung by the accusation. 'I can say without equivocation', she responded, 'that I have never been asked to do anything by the AFL-CIO that was in conflict with the early stated aims of the African Trade Union Movement'.[57]

It was also believed that Mboya had been receiving regular funds from the CIA; he was seen by the US as a leader who espoused an acceptable type of socialism in Africa.[58] American approval of Mboya was set out in a briefing to the National Security Council, which advised the president on national security and foreign policy; it was dated 17 December 1958, just days after the end of the AAPC. Mboya was described as a 'dynamic, young (29), spellbinding but essentially moderate labor leader'. It noted with satisfaction that he had chaired the Accra conference, 'and thereby added appreciably to his stature'.[59]

Mboya was appointed the head of the Kenya Federation of Labour, which was suspected to be CIA backed.[60] It was alleged that Maida Springer was Mboya's contact officer. She denied this in the course of interviews for a book published in 2004 by Yevette Richards. 'As far as CIA activities with Tom, about Tom, or even general conversations', Springer told Richards, 'I never, never had any'.[61]

In the late 1950s, the ICFTU decided to establish a regional office for Africa in Accra. It planned to use the Ghana Trades Union Congress, which was headed by the Ghanaian John Tettegah, as a continental base for pursuing its activities in Africa, and to put pressure on African unions to adopt hard anticommunist positions. But this strategy was unwelcome and unsuccessful. Instead, delegates at the All African People's Conference called for the creation of an All African Trade Union Federation (AATUF) as a non-aligned alternative to the ICFTU and to the communist-backed World Federation of Trade Unions. The AATUF, which did not come into existence for almost three years, espoused the neutralist Pan-Africanism advocated by Nkrumah.[62]

Jay Lovestone took a hard line on Ghana. A few months after independence, he wrote to Maida Springer: 'I am a bit disturbed as to the way Ghana is going . . . [and] by the game which is being played by Nkrumah and others, a game which is often played by newly-established independent governments. I refer to the game of flirting with Moscow, of signing trade treaties with them, of establishing diplomatic relations. All of this leads to neutralism a la Nehru and confusion worse confounded'.[63]

Irving Brown, too, disliked Nkrumah. The Ghanaian leader, he said, 'revelled in playing the militant leftist'.[64] But Springer remained supportive of Nkrumah and his Pan-Africanist vision. 'Oh, my God!' she exclaimed years later, when she remembered Accra in December 1958. 'Ooh! I still get goosebumps when I think of the All-African People's Conference and reflect now on the significance of it'. She added: 'This was as incredible as the Berlin Wall coming down or even more so, because people from all over the continent were meeting together and sharing problems, aspirations, and talking about an African community of support for one another'. The fact that it was meeting in an African country and organised by an African government, she said, was pathbreaking: 'This had never happened on this continent before. Couldn't have happened without an independent Ghana'.[65]

7

Atomium

I N THE SAME YEAR THAT the All African People's Conference in Accra celebrated the prospect of Africa's liberation from European colonisation, a contrasting event took place in Europe: an international exhibition that put a bright spotlight on the Belgian colonisation of the Congo. This event was Expo 58—the Exposition Universelle et Internationale de Bruxelles, also known as the Brussels World's Fair, which was held between April and October 1958. Rooted in the tradition of the Great Exhibition that was held in the Crystal Palace in London in 1851, it was the first international exhibition since the Second World War.

Expo 58 was vast: it covered nearly five hundred acres on the Heysel Plateau, just north of the city of Brussels. Forty-four nations participated, and about eighteen million people came through its gates.[1] King Baudouin of Belgium opened the exhibition, drawing attention to its slogan: 'A world for a better life for mankind'.[2] Its major theme was the application of technology and science to make the world more humane.[3]

The pavilions of the US and the Soviet Union were placed next to each other, which had the effect of drawing attention to the increasingly bitter Cold War. The Soviet pavilion put the achievement of Sputnik—the first satellite in space—at its centre and celebrated communist society. At the US pavilion, which showcased the American way of life and consumer society, visitors could watch colour television, eat ice cream and drink Coca-Cola.[4] 'We don't intend to use the hard sell', said the US commissioner general. 'We don't think we have to—not in selling America'.[5]

Seven of the Belgian pavilions were dedicated to the country's colonial possessions: the Belgian Congo and Ruanda-Urundi (now Rwanda and Burundi). They presented exhibitions on a range of activities, including the colonial administration, agriculture, Catholic missions, energy and transport, banks, insurance companies and commerce. Congolese workers were brought to Brussels to display their methods of work: tobacco industry employees made cigarettes all day long, while potters, winnowers and sculptors demonstrated their skills. Soldiers and so-called évolués were also put on show.[6]

A theatre in the Congo section presented *Congorama*: a thirty-minute show with visual effects to 'plunge' the viewer into 'the disturbing ambience of primitive life'.[7] Using film, sound recordings and animated maps, it aimed to present 'the different states of the Congo's progress from the night of prehistory to the light of civilisation'.[8] Its message was clear: the 'light of civilisation' had been provided by Belgium.

There was also a live version of *Congorama*. Nearly 600 Congolese people—183 families, including 273 men, 128 women and 197 children—had been brought to Belgium to be put on daily display in seven acres of tropical gardens. Every day they were bussed in from their lodgings and exhibited in a so-called *village indigène*—'native village'—of straw huts, behind a bamboo perimeter fence.[9] They were expected to carry out traditional village activities, including craft work. This was effectively a zoo, but of human beings.

Six decades before Expo 58, in 1897, King Leopold II of Belgium had organised a display of people from the Congo in the village of Tervuren, just outside Brussels, in conjunction with the Brussels International Exposition of that year. Three hundred Congolese people were exhibited in a village behind fences, with notices instructing visitors not to feed them. Seven died.[10]

Despite the evils perpetrated by Leopold II, the former king was celebrated at Expo 58. A bust representing him was placed at the entrance to the main Congo pavilion. Underneath it were written the words he had used to describe his purpose in Africa: 'I undertook the work of the Congo in the interest of civilisation'.[11] When King Baudouin—the great-grand-nephew of Leopold II—visited the 'native village' at Expo 58, he greeted the Congolese from a distance with a reserved wave of his hand; he did not talk to them.[12]

Every day, foreigners and Belgians came to watch the activities of the Congolese. Children tried to give them bananas, and many passersby threw insults and money at them.[13] But some of the visitors criticised the display. The Congolese 'were parked there like livestock', objected one, 'and exhibited as curious beasts'.[14] A newspaper reported an encounter wherein a white Belgian woman threw half a candy bar to a boy of about two or three years of age, which landed between his knees. His response was swift: 'Right away, without the least hesitation, the boy throws the titbit back over the fence without even looking up'.[15]

Within three months, the Congolese in the 'native village' had had enough and went home. The huts were left empty.[16]

But numbers of other Congolese people remained in Brussels for the duration of Expo 58. These were nuns, journalists, dancers, singers, soldiers. A choir known as Les Troubadours were celebrated for their performance of the *Missa Luba*, a Latin mass sung according to Congolese harmonies and traditions.

For several years, small groups of évolués had been allowed to take educational trips to Belgium, as Lumumba had done. But now, hundreds of Congolese, including a large group of soldiers, were invited for stays of a few months to visit the Expo. 'My father was allowed to go to Belgium in 1958', recalled Jamais Kolonga. 'He was very impressed by what he saw. Europeans who washed dishes and swept the streets, he didn't know that existed. There were even white beggars! That was a real eye-opener for him'. The Congolese visitors saw that they were welcome in the restaurants, cafés and movie theatres of Brussels.[17] That, too, was very different from the daily segregation they experienced in the colony.

The Congolese visitors to Expo 58 not only discovered a different Belgium, but they also discovered each other. Until now, restrictions on travel and the long distances in the Congo had meant there was little contact between residents of the various regions. But during those months in Belgium in 1958, people from different parts of the vast territory talked with each other about the situation at home and dreamed of a different future. A number of évolués were approached by Belgian politicians and trade union leaders, from different sides of the political spectrum.

The star soccer player of the Daring Football Club in Leopold-ville, Longin Ngwadi, who was nicknamed 'The Rubber Band', came to Brussels as a servant to the current governor general, Léo Pétillon, but was not able to go to the Expo site. 'We went by plane', he recalled in an interview. 'I went along as Pétillon's houseboy. I stayed in Namur and had to cook and do the laundry. Pétillon went to the world's fair to look at all the merchandise. Copper, diamonds, everything from Congo, everything from every country'. But while Pétillon was dining in Brussels with the Duke of Edinburgh and the Dutch minister of foreign affairs, Ngwadi remained behind, in the kitchen in Namur.[18]

The Daring Club was the top soccer team in the Congo. It had made the Angolan Holden Roberto—like Ngwadi, a gifted player—a national icon when he moved to Leopoldville in 1949. Another well-known player in the Daring Club was Cyrille Adoula, who was later to become prime minister of the Congo.

One of the Congolese journalists who went to Expo 58 in Brussels was the twenty-eight-year-old Joseph-Désiré Mobutu—highly intelligent, eager, ambitious and charming. He had been given the name of his great-uncle, Mobutu Sese Seko Nkuku Wa Za Banga—'all-conquering warrior, who goes from triumph to triumph'. His father, who was a catechist and a cook for the Capuchin mission-aries, had died when he was eight. This caused problems during Mobutu's childhood, as his widowed mother struggled to support her children.[19]

In some ways, Mobutu was like Patrice Lumumba: at school, he had stood up to teachers when he felt they were unjust; he was an avid reader and student; he disliked Catholic missionaries; and he was very thin and near-sighted.[20] After one year of secondary education he joined the Force Publique, the colonial troops of the Belgian Congo, as a secretary-typist; in 1954 he was promoted to the rank of sergeant. He then—again, like Lumumba—began writing articles for publication.

In 1956 Mobutu left the army to become a full-time journalist and went to Leopoldville, where he wrote for *Actualités Africaines* and the daily newspaper, *L'Avenir*. During this period, notes Georges Nzongola-Ntalaja, Mobutu was hired as an informer for the Belgian intelligence service.[21] After two years of this work, Mobutu was invited to Expo to represent the two journals at the Congrès de la Presse Coloniale, an international congress of the colonial press. It had also been arranged for him to be trained in intelligence in Brussels, under the cover of training in social work.

On the plane to Brussels, Mobutu sat next to a Belgian journalist, who later recalled that Mobutu seemed a bit anxious and plied him with questions about Belgium. At the congress, the journalist introduced Mobutu to people: 'His curiosity was insatiable: he wanted to visit everything, see everything, and understand everything'. Mobutu picked things up fast, and after a few days he got on fine.[22] Clever and amusing, he easily charmed journalists who sought him out to ask questions about the Congo.[23]

With the rising tide of African nationalism having hit the Congo, wrote Nzongola-Ntalaja, 'Belgian and US policymakers were anxious to know who was who among the emergent politicians'.[24] The visitors to Brussels were scrutinised carefully. Mobutu quickly caught the eye of an American working at the US embassy in Brussels: Lawrence Raymond Devlin, generally known as 'Larry'. A veteran of World War II and a Harvard graduate who by then was in his mid- to late thirties, Devlin had been attached to the US embassy since March 1957 as an attaché and political officer. But his position at the embassy was a cover; in fact he was working for the CIA.

Devlin retained Mobutu's services as an informer. Mobutu was now working for both the Belgians and the Americans.

* * *

THE CONGO AND RUANDA-URUNDI pavilions and the Congolese village were located in the shadows—almost at the foot—of the centrepiece of Expo 58: the Atomium. The futuristic building, Brussels's answer to Paris's Eiffel Tower of 1889, is a 355-foot-tall structure, resembling the nine atoms of a crystal of iron enlarged 160 billion times.[25] The Atomium showcased the Belgian nuclear industry, of which the nation was extremely proud. The true origin of, and reason for, this industry was the Shinkolobwe uranium mine.[26]

Not far from the Atomium was an exhibit organised by Union Minière du Haut Katanga, the multinational company that owned Shinkolobwe, to demonstrate how the uranium was mined. In addition, Belgonucleaire, a research bureau associated with Union Minière, presented its programme for the design and construction of reactors.[27] There had been a plan to build a nuclear power station at Expo 58 to supply the site with electricity, but this was cancelled due to safety concerns.

In the view of Jonathan Helmreich, an authority on the role of Congolese uranium in relations between the US and Belgium, the symbol chosen by the Belgians for the World's Fair in Brussels— 'the spectacular "Atomium" rising in silver geometric form over the gathering of exhibits from all sectors of the globe'—was fully justified.[28]

* * *

THE ATOMIC ERA CREATED new and terrifying threats to the globe, unheard of before World War II. In 1945, the Nobel-laureate physicist James Franck headed a committee of scientists at the University of Chicago that envisaged the possibility of the complete destruction of human civilisation by atomic weapons. To prevent such a catastrophe, the committee proposed a prohibition on the mining of uranium. The ban would also forego the advantages of nuclear energy, but the potential loss was seen by many as a price worth paying.[29]

Harry S Truman, America's president at the time of the bombing of Hiroshima and Nagasaki, had maintained that only the US could be trusted to develop atomic power. Even a peaceful program, it was argued, might generate fissionable materials with the potential to build bombs.

But Eisenhower, who replaced Truman in 1953, took a different approach: he attempted to dispel alarm and fear with the idea of the atom as potentially benign. In December 1953 he gave a speech to the UN General Assembly which set out a programme of 'Atoms for Peace': the promotion of peaceful uses of atomic energy by all the nations of the world. He argued that there was a 'special purpose' to promote atomic energy 'in the power-starved areas of the world'.[30]

Eisenhower also called for the creation of an International Atomic Energy Agency (IAEA) to accept fissile materials from the atomic powers, for the benefit of all nations. However, the United States possessed stockpiles of fissile materials that were much larger than those of the Soviets. It would be to the advantage of the US, therefore, if the Soviets were to lose some of their materials by donating them to the IAEA.

In 1955, under the auspices of the United Nations, Geneva hosted a major international conference called Atoms for Peace. The most popular exhibit was a working reactor installed by the US, with a blue radiation glow. Eisenhower came to see it, as did many thousands of visitors, some of whom enjoyed going right up to it and touching its parts.

The historian of science John Krige has argued that this presentation of the US reactor in Geneva was a masterpiece of marketing: 'It was intended to demystify nuclear power and to show that anyone and any nation could exploit it safely and to social advantage'.[31] Atoms for Peace exhibits were taken to many parts of the world, including Ghana.

In 1957, the IAEA was set within the family of the UN, to promote the peaceful use of nuclear energy and to inspect nuclear facilities. Its responsibilities included the monitoring of fuel in order to reveal any diversion to military purposes.

Many in the nonaligned world were persuaded by Eisenhower's speech about the value of an atomic reactor; they applied it to their own situation, with the belief that modern technology should be made available to all parts of the world. Prime Minister Nehru of India was the first to take this forward; he set up India's Atomic Energy Establishment in 1954. In the following year India accepted an offer of a reactor from Canada.

Kwame Nkrumah shared Nehru's enthusiasm for the potential of atomic power. In any case, atomic technology had already been in use in Ghana since 1952, when it was the British colony of the Gold Coast. Radiostrontium—a radioactive isotope of strontium—was used in experiments on monkeys.[32]

In 1956, the year before Ghana's independence, Nkrumah declared that Ghana should have its own atomic reactor. The British governor of the Gold Coast reported on Nkrumah's plan to the colonial secretary in London—that Nkrumah was 'examining the possibility of erecting an experimental nuclear reactor'. However, the governor anticipated a difficulty with obtaining uranium: 'It appears that one of the most important problems is the supply of fissile material, which it is understood is scarce. In the event of this Government's deciding to go on with the reactor, it will wish to seek your good offices in securing the necessary fissile material'.[33] The governor appears to have been unaware that the world's richest uranium ore was mined on the African continent—in the Belgian Congo.

Nkrumah was keen that African nations should benefit from atomic energy, but he was also concerned that the people of Africa should not be exposed to the dangers of atomic weapons testing. Other African leaders felt the same. The Conference of Independent African States in April 1958 resolved that nuclear testing should be suspended and that means should be taken to reduce the arms race. It also called for African representation in international arms-control agencies. At the All African People's Conference, in December, a resolution was passed to make the same demands. In that same year, the physics department of the University College of Ghana, on behalf of the Ministry of Defence, started a radioactive fallout monitoring service.[34]

* * *

THROUGHOUT THE 1950S, AMERICA was anxious to maintain Belgian cooperation, to ensure and protect its import of uranium from the Congo. To assist with this goal, it had signed an agreement to help fund and support Belgium's nuclear energy programme. This led to the delivery and installation of two reactors: one in Belgium, the other in the Belgian Congo. The reactor for the Congo delighted the Roman Catholic rector and founder of Lovanium

University (now the University of Kinshasa) in Leopoldville: Monseigneur Luc Gillon, a nuclear physicist with a doctorate from the University of Louvain, in Belgium, who had studied at Princeton under J Robert Oppenheimer. Since 1956, he had argued that the Belgian Congo, as the territory that had supplied the raw material for the Manhattan Project, should get the benefits of an atomic reactor.

On 3 December 1958, the Belgian ambassador to the US signed a contract relating to the reactor destined for the Congo with two very senior representatives of the American government: William A M Burden, who was shortly to take up the position of American ambassador to Belgium, and John A McCone, chairman of the US Atomic Energy Commission (who became the director of the CIA from 1961 to 1965). The contract agreed on the sale by the US to Belgium of the enriched uranium to be used in the fifty-kilowatt Training, Research, Isotopes, General Atomics (TRIGA) Mark I reactor, which had been built by the General Dynamics Corporation in California.[35]

The reactor arrived in the Congo in January 1959 and became fully operational in June.[36] It was known as the TRICO, a portmanteau of TRIGA and Congo. Its purpose was training, research and the production of isotopes for agricultural and medical purposes.

This was Africa's first nuclear reactor.

* * *

AMONG THE NUMEROUS AMERICANS visiting Brussels for Expo 58 was a brilliant financier with business interests in Africa.[37] This was Maurice Tempelsman, who became known to the American public several decades later as the partner of Jackie Kennedy Onassis. In 1984 Tempelsman moved into her Fifth Avenue apartment and stayed with her until her death ten years later. One observer described him then as 'short, portly, older looking than his actual years', adding that he smoked Dunhill cigars and was fluent in a number of foreign languages.[38]

Tempelsman was born in Belgium, but his Orthodox Jewish family fled in 1940 to escape the Nazi invasion. After two years in Jamaica, they moved to New York, where Tempelsman worked for his father, a broker of raw diamonds, in the family firm, Leon Tempelsman and Son. In 1950, when Maurice Tempelsman was only twenty-one, he persuaded the US government to buy industrial diamonds for its stockpile of strategic minerals. As the middleman in the process, he made millions of dollars.[39]

In the 1950s, Tempelsman established a close working relationship with Adlai E Stevenson, a prominent lawyer who was the US Democratic presidential candidate in 1952 and 1956. Stevenson included American Metal Climax among his company's clients and was an old friend of Harold Hochschild, the chairman of its board of trustees. American Metal Climax, which had a vast network of mines in Africa, assisted with the financing of the African-American Institute when it was founded by the CIA in 1953. Among the businessmen recruited to the board of the AAI were Hochschild, William Burden and Tempelsman. Another client of Stevenson was Reynolds Metals, on whose behalf Stevenson acted in relation to the aluminium smelter in Ghana that would be fuelled by the massive Volta Dam hydroelectric project at Akosombo.

In 1955 Stevenson went to Ghana, where he had an appointment with Nkrumah. 'Whatever happens to Ghana', said Stevenson afterwards, 'must have a profound effect, for better or for worse, on the rest of Africa and, therefore, the whole world'. He took a keen interest in anticolonial developments, but had a painfully condescending view of people living on the continent of Africa. According to a letter that found its way to the UK Foreign Office, he regarded people in Africa as 'almost indistinguishable from the coloured folk of Alabama, with their gentleness, good humour, sudden guffaws of laughter at odd trivialities, their ignorance and their lack of ambition'.[40]

Stevenson's visit to Ghana in 1955 was part of a longer tour of other territories in sub-Saharan Africa, including the Belgian Congo. His travels in the Congo were arranged by the Belgian government; afterwards, he paid tribute to Belgian colonial rule. 'Their efforts to meet and to mold the growing race consciousness', he wrote to a friend, 'is impressive indeed'.[41]

Two years later, Stevenson wrote to Nkrumah to say he would soon be in Africa again, to 'transact some legal business for some

American clients in the Union of South Africa'. And again, his trip would include Ghana. One of his clients, he wrote, was applying for a license to purchase industrial diamonds in the government market in Accra. 'This company', he told Nkrumah, 'is one of the largest factors in the industrial diamond business in America and, as a large and growing consumer of industrial diamonds, it could be a useful and stabilising influence in this industry in Ghana'.[42]

The client was Maurice Tempelsman. This fact emerges from a memorandum dated 5 June 1959 in an FBI file on Stevenson: 'Adlai Stevenson is reported to have persuaded Prime Minister Nkrumah, of Ghana, personally to intervene to secure a license for the Templesman [sic] Company' to buy diamonds in Ghana.[43] This FBI file on Stevenson is one of the 165 'Official and Confidential' files kept by J Edgar Hoover in his office suite, to which only two people had access—Hoover himself and his secretary.[44]

Stevenson's 1957 tour of Africa, as in 1955, included a visit to the Belgian Congo, where he discussed some of the activities of Leon Tempelsman and Son with high-ranking colonial officials.[45] Tempelsman's business was becoming a reliable source of funding for Stevenson's law firm. Records show that in 1958, Tempelsman paid the firm an annual retainer of $50,000.[46]

Fortune, the multinational business magazine headquartered in New York, noted Tempelsman's initiative and success in Africa. 'In a bold move for such a young man', it enthused in 1982, 'Tempelsman . . . began showing up—with Stevenson in tow—in emerging African nations. Stevenson at that time was enormously popular in Africa. That, plus the timing—so many nations were on the brink of independence—gave Tempelsman unmatched entree'.[47] At the same time, he was developing close associations with other prominent businessmen in the mining industry, such as the South African Harry Oppenheimer, the chairman of Anglo-American Corporation and De Beers Consolidated Mines.

In spite of Tempelsman's high-level contacts and increasing wealth, he managed to keep himself and his business arrangements out of the public eye, remaining 'a shadowy, mysterious figure'.[48] He carefully maintained this low profile, even when he became known in prominent social circles from the early 1980s as the partner of John F Kennedy's widow.

* * *

TEMPELSMAN WAS DISCREETLY ASSOCIATED with an American, George Wittman, who was the same age as himself—thirty in 1959—and who also had dealings in Africa. Wittman was the very clever and well-read president of G H Wittman Inc, a mining and trading family business with offices on Broadway, in New York City, that had been established in 1885. After his father died in 1958, Wittman shifted the company's focus to political and economic consulting, with an emphasis on Africa and the Middle East.

The company's activities were high powered. They were also a cover: Wittman was a CIA agent. This information emerged in an obituary written by Gina Faddis for the *Washington Times* after Wittman's death, at age ninety-one, in November 2020; Faddis was herself a retired CIA operations officer. She wrote that Wittman had been recruited into the recently formed CIA in 1951 and was a case officer in Frankfurt, Germany. 'As his career developed', reports Faddis, 'he undertook extensive sensitive assignments across the globe. He worked in this capacity until 1968'.[49] Faddis's obituary of Wittman was reproduced on the website of the Association of Former Intelligence Officers (AFIO).[50]

In 1959, Wittman's company produced a substantial study—nearly five hundred pages—of Ghana, which considered the nation's development in the light of economic, political, sociological and legal factors.[51] Wittman led the research team in Ghana, which was given ready access to officials and members of the banking and business community.[52] It was an ideal opportunity to network and make useful contacts. Over the first half of the 1960s, G H Wittman Inc operated in the Central African Republic, Congo Leopoldville, Congo Brazzaville, Gabon, Ghana, Guinea, Ivory Coast, Kenya, Liberia, Sierra Leone, Sudan, Uganda, Tanganyika (and then Tanzania) and the United Arab Republic.[53]

In 1960, Wittman went to the Congo and Ghana to work for Maurice Tempelsman as a representative for Leon Tempelsman and Son. This was both an effective CIA cover and a productive professional relationship. In Wittman's obituary in the *Washington Post*, however, Tempelsman is never mentioned.

David N Gibbs, the author of *The Political Economy of Third World Intervention*, has sought to put flesh on the skeleton of information about Tempelsman, but with scant success. 'A full discussion of Mr Tempelsman's role would be difficult', notes Gibbs, 'since little is known about him. He is not listed in *Who's Who in America*'.

But, adds Gibbs, 'He is known to have very close ties to the Central Intelligence Agency'.[54] The same point has been made by Paul Baddo, a Ghanaian diplomat and consultant: that Tempelsman had 'strong links with the CIA'.[55] This claim is highly credible following the revelation that George Wittman, Tempelsman's representative in the Congo and Ghana in the early 1960s, was a CIA agent between 1951 and 1968.[56]

In 1975, seven years after leaving the CIA, Wittman published *A Matter of Intelligence*, a novel of espionage. It is threaded with details relating to ballistic missiles, the CIA and the Pentagon. 'The defense business', noted Wittman, is 'the boom boom business, the national bull shit business'.[57]

PART III

AFRICAN JAZZ

8

The Rise of Lumumba

F OR PATRICE LUMUMBA, THE ALL African People's Conference
in Accra had been a political and personal epiphany. He returned to the Congo transformed by his exposure to the vision of
the Pan-Africanist leaders, especially that of Prime Minister Nkrumah. On 28 December 1958, about two weeks after his return, he
and his fellow leaders of the Mouvement National Congolais organised their first mass rally. It was held in Kalamu, in the cité of
Leopoldville. A crowd of around ten thousand men and women
attended, eager to hear about the MNC's plans.[1]

Lumumba spoke with passion and conviction. He announced
that the MNC had a new programme, based on the Accra Resolutions. 'We wish to carry out this programme', he said, 'with the
active collaboration of each and every Congolese: man, woman,
and child'. The Accra conference, he added, had 'marked a decisive step toward the self-realization of the African personality, and
toward the total unity of all the peoples of the African continent'.
He called for the immediate independence of the Belgian Congo,
echoing the victorious slogan of the CPP, Nkrumah's political
party: 'Self-Government Now!'[2] Lumumba's audience were excited
to hear his words of hope for real change. In chorus, they shouted
out their demand for '*Indépendance Immédiate!*'[3]

The All African People's Conference had lasted less than a
week, but it had made Lumumba into a prominent politician in the
Congo and an acknowledged leader on the African stage. It had
also made him visible to the colonial rulers of the Congo and to
foreign powers beyond the shores of Africa.

Lumumba was only thirty-three years of age. His life would never be the same again.

* * *

ON 4 JANUARY 1959, a week after the MNC rally in Leopoldville, a violent and bloody riot exploded on the streets of the Congo's capital city. It was a sunny day and, as usual on a Sunday, the streets and bars of the cité were thronged with people. The day had been chosen by Joseph Kasavubu for the Abako political party to hold its own public rally; he was concerned that Abako was losing the leadership of the independence campaign to Lumumba and the MNC.[4] The call went out to Abako supporters to assemble at the same site in Kalamu that had been used by the MNC.

But when the crowds arrived, they were informed that the rally had been prohibited by the colonial administration. They responded with outrage and fury, which spread like wildfire through the neighbourhoods. Soon, more than sixty thousand people were marching through the streets of Leopoldville.[5] The Force Publique, the colonial army, opened fire on the demonstrators to break up the protest. A fierce and bloody confrontation ensued, lasting for four days. At least five hundred people were killed; many families buried their dead in the middle of the night.[6]

The date of 4 January 1959 quickly became significant in the calendar of the Congo and is remembered annually as a tragic event in the country's painful history. It has a similar meaning to the historic date of 28 February 1948 in Ghana, when British police killed three unarmed African ex-servicemen.

The CIA was receiving reports on the riots in Leopoldville, and on 7 January 1959 the agency prepared a briefing for the National Security Council titled 'Belgian Congo'. The briefing recorded that the police force—which, it noted, was 'colored, with white officers'—intervened with gunfire, resulting in 'mob action'. The report observed that the All African People's Conference in Accra had been a catalyst to Congolese nationalism. The only Congolese leader it identified as being involved in the riots was Arthur Pinzi, the mayor of a Leopoldville suburb, 'who had just returned from [the] Accra conference'.[7]

The detailed nature of the report suggests that the CIA had a source on the ground. This may have been John Marcum, the American political scientist who had attended the AAPC. Marcum's archive contains a photograph of Kasavubu at the Abako rally; the note on the back gives the date of 4 January 1959 and explains that it was taken 'just before the Belgian Congo riots'.[8] Marcum, who was on a research trip in West Africa that was funded by a grant from the Ford Foundation, had travelled from the Ivory Coast to Accra in early December 1958 to attend the AAPC. This photograph indicates that after the conference, he went to the Congo.

The rioting in Leopoldville spread rapidly to other parts of the Congo. Some areas quickly became ungovernable; anger was at boiling point and many people refused to pay taxes. Like the protesters in Leopoldville, many people called for immediate independence.[9]

* * *

IN RESPONSE TO THE riots of January 1959, the colonial government hit back with a brutal crackdown. Many of the leaders of Abako, including Kasavubu and Daniel Kanza, were imprisoned without trial.

The Belgians living in the Congo were shocked by the violence of the unrest and by the call for immediate independence. Their occupation of the Congo had seemed to them secure—that it would last for many more years. As recently as 1955, Governor General Pétillon had said that the Belgian Congo could go on as it was for twenty-five years and there was 'really not much point in looking beyond that'.[10]

Now, in the tense shadow of the riots, the settlers' confidence in their future was suddenly shattered—and they were afraid. They were advised by the administration to avoid the cité and lonely stretches of road by night.[11]

From Brussels, the Belgian government watched the unfolding crisis with acute misgivings. They were uncertain how to react. Any hope of controlling the protests and rallies required sending additional troops from Belgium to Africa, which they were eager to avoid. The experience of France in Algeria and Indo-China offered frightening examples of what could go wrong when a colonising nation intervened militarily in a desperate measure to hold on to power. The Belgian government knew that any such intervention in the Congo—with the potential loss of Belgian lives—would be strongly opposed at home.

Moreover, criticism of Belgian rule of the Congo was being articulated not only in the Congo by Congolese, but in Belgium by Belgians. In 1953, *Le Drapeau Rouge*, a communist daily newspaper, had called for the independence of the Congo and equated Belgian rule in Africa with the Nazi occupation of Belgium.[12]

The government decided against a military solution. Instead, it chose to respond to the spirit of the demands being made by the Congolese. Within eight days of the start of the rioting, on 13 January 1959, the government promised an increase in local and district self-government. King Baudouin went even further, promising eventual independence.[13] 'Our resolve today', he declared in a radio broadcast, 'is to lead the Congolese peoples to independence in prosperity and peace without delay, but also without irresponsible rashness'.[14]

Lumumba seized the moment. He gave up his job at the brewery and threw himself into political work. For financial backing, the MNC turned to the AAPC secretariat in Accra and the Afro-Asian Solidarity Movement based in Guinea.[15]

* * *

INSPIRED BY HIS EXPERIENCE in Accra of meeting people from all over Africa, Lumumba was eager to visit other territories on the continent. In March 1959, he flew to Nigeria to participate in a conference on 'Representative Government and National Progress' at the University College, Ibadan in Nigeria.[16] The invitation was arranged by his good friend Luis López Álvarez, a Spanish poet and journalist who had moved from Paris to Brazzaville in 1957, to work for Radio Brazzaville. At that time, Brazzaville was the capital of the federated territories of French Equatorial Africa. A year after the arrival of López Álvarez, those territories voted in the referendum organised by the French government to become autonomous within the French Community; the federation was dissolved.

Lumumba had first visited López Álvarez's home in November 1958, on one of his trips across the Congo River to Brazzaville. Both men had a deeply poetic nature and they shared similar political convictions. In January 1959, when the riots in the Belgian Congo forced hundreds of Congolese to flee from the Force Publique and take refuge in French Brazzaville, López Álvarez created a committee of Congolese solidarity to assist the refugees.

López Álvarez was nearly thirty years old. He had obtained a degree in political science from the Paris Institute of Political Studies (Sciences Po) in 1957, and he ran in the literary and intellectual circles of the French capital.[17] He participated enthusiastically in the activities of the Paris-based Congress for Cultural Freedom—having no idea, like so many of those who were involved with the work of the CCF, that it was a CIA front. He sat on its executive committee and also contributed articles to *Cuadernos*, the Spanish-language journal of the CCF. It was the CCF that sponsored the conference in Ibadan, which it organised in conjunction with the University College, Ibadan's Department of Extra-Mural Studies.

As well as securing an invitation for Lumumba to attend the Ibadan Seminar, as the conference became known, López Álvarez arranged an invitation for the Congolese trade unionist and politician Cyrille Adoula, who was now a member of the MNC; this was done at Lumumba's request. A tidy, quiet man and a devout Catholic, Adoula had early on attracted the interest of American union leaders. He had been educated at a Catholic mission school in Leopoldville and worked as a bank clerk before taking a job with the labour movement in 1956, which led him into politics.

In order to reach Ibadan, Lumumba and Adoula went to Brazzaville to take the plane to Kano in Nigeria. López Álvarez went to meet them at Brazzaville Beach, the riverbank where boats dock after crossing the Congo River from Leopoldville. He found them with Joseph-Désiré Mobutu, who would shortly be leaving Africa for Brussels to start an internship with Inforcongo, the Belgian government's public relations office dealing with the Congo.[18]

Lumumba was highly impressed by Mobutu, five years his junior, and a close bond was developing between them. On Lumumba's side, it was genuine and trusting: for Lumumba, Mobutu was like a younger brother who enthusiastically supported the vision of the MNC.[19] On Mobutu's side, the friendship was cynical.

Once in Brussels, Mobutu was appointed as the MNC's representative in Belgium. This put him in an ideal position to obtain useful information about emergent Congolese politicians for his Belgian and American handlers.

Lumumba, Adoula and Mobutu would all go on to become leaders of their country. They now met as friends, but it would not be many months before trust between them broke down in irrevocable and tragic ways.

* * *

THERE WERE SOME FORTY participants at the Ibadan Seminar, as well as observers, from eighteen countries altogether. Most were from African countries, but the US, Israel, India, Britain, France and West Germany were also represented. The seminar was described by its organisers as 'the first of its kind in West Africa', offering the 'first opportunity for a direct confrontation between French-speaking and English-speaking intellectuals'.[20]

Two participants involved in the organisation of the seminar were tutors in the Department of Extra-Mural Studies at University College, Ibadan (a constituent college of the University of London). One of them was the South African writer Ezekiel Mphahlele, who was forced to live in exile from his own country, and whom Lumumba had met in Accra just three months before at the All African People's Conference.

The other tutor was Ulli Beier, a German who was the editor of *Black Orpheus*, a journal which he and the German writer Janheinz Jahn had established in Ibadan in 1957 and in which the CCF took a keen interest; from 1961 it provided the journal with financial support.[21] Named after Sartre's essay on Négritude, *Black Orpheus* made the works of Aimé Cesaire and Léopold Senghor available in English, as well as a range of African, Haitian and Cuban writings.

The Ibadan Seminar was imprinted with the invisible mark of the CIA in myriad ways. Edward Shils, a sociologist at the University of Chicago who would become the editor of the CCF-sponsored

Minerva in 1961, contributed a paper. The journalists who attended included Russell Warren Howe, a British reporter who worked as a stringer for *Newsweek* and had ties to the CIA.

A photograph of Lumumba, Adoula and López Álvarez, standing together, was taken by Mercer Cook, one of the founding members of the CIA-funded American Society of African Culture (AMSAC), who would soon become the director of the Africa programme of the Congress for Cultural Freedom.[22]

Lumumba gave his contribution to the Ibadan Seminar on the final day: 'African Unity and National Independence'. He argued that Africans needed to 'free our peoples psychologically'; a certain conformism, he warned, was noticeable on the part of many intellectuals. 'We need genuine literature and a free press that brings the opinion of the people to light', he insisted, 'rather than more propaganda leaflets and a muzzled press'. Then he expressed his earnest hope that the sponsors of the conference would assist this process: 'I hope that the Congress for Freedom and Culture will aid us along these lines'.[23] Like López Álvarez, Lumumba had no way of knowing that the Congress for Cultural Freedom was a CIA front.

Some of the papers given at the Ibadan Seminar were published in a thick book by Ibadan University Press in 1963; the title page explains that it was 'published for the Congress for Cultural Freedom'. Lumumba's paper was not included.[24]

* * *

IN JANUARY 1959, SEVERAL months before the Ibadan Seminar in Nigeria, López Álvarez flew to Paris to attend the annual meeting of the executive committee of the Congress for Cultural Freedom in Paris. He used this opportunity to appeal to the congress for help with a cherished dream: to set up an institute of Congolese studies in Brazzaville, to serve young men and women on both sides of the Congo River. It was a dream he shared with Lumumba, and it had been the subject of many animated discussions between the two men.

The CCF was delighted with the proposal. With CIA intelligence goals in mind, the organisation was keen to establish an influence in the French Congo. Moreover, the proposed cultural

centre was an ideal means to reach earnest and thoughtful young
adults in the Belgian Congo, since it took less than an hour to cross
the Congo River from Brazzaville to Leopoldville.

Within weeks, the CCF provided some initial funding for the
project, and the new institute was born—L'Institut d'Études Congolaises. A monthly allocation was put in place, which was charged
to the CIA pass-through, the Farfield Foundation, and to the Ford
Foundation. Supplementary grants were made for the salaries of
several employees and for the purchase of furniture, a mimeograph,
a tape recorder, a film projector and motor transport. An additional
grant was provided by the Charles E Merrill Trust, which was
another pass-through set up by the CIA.[25]

The institute served as a centre for local writers and artists, enabling them to meet at any time of the day and evening in the comfortable study hall and library. A plan was put in place to publish
and exhibit their work. The centre had a station wagon to take the
students to their homes, since many of them would otherwise need
to walk very long journeys. Courses were offered on the history and
culture of the region, for which teachers were soon brought from
other parts of Africa and the world. Scholarships were offered.

The library was soon filled with books ordered in collaboration
with the African Program of the Congress for Cultural Freedom.
Records of African poetry and music were provided, as well as American jazz; documentary films were shown.[26] The centre was an ideal
way to showcase American culture to young adults and to introduce
them to American values. At the same time, it provided opportunities for the agency to make contact and foster relationships with
promising individuals, some of whom would go on to be politicians.

According to the official statutes of the institute, its members
'condemned totalitarianism and attacks on freedom, from wherever
they came'; it is unclear whether or not the institute's members
were asked to declare or sign such a condemnation.[27]

An inaugural ceremony was held on 1 December 1959, to which
the Senegalese poet Léopold Senghor was invited. He gave a
speech in which he extolled the efforts and achievements of the
institute.

* * *

As THE MONTHS OF 1959 wore on, it became clear to Lumumba and other Congolese nationalists that the Belgian government was in no rush to fulfil the promise it had made in January of an increase in local and district self-government. This was largely due to the political situation in Belgium: the prime minister led a weak coalition of Christian Socialist and Liberal parties, which were in disagreement over the pace of decolonisation. The minister of the Congo, who was a Liberal, took steps to advance measures of self-rule in the colony, but when these were impeded by other ministers and the king, he had no choice but to resign in September 1959. The new minister halted much of his predecessor's legislation.[28]

Frustrated, the Congolese resistance movement turned to Ghana for help. In late September 1959, a group associated with Kasavubu and the Abako party went to Accra to mobilise public support for their cause. They presented a petition to the Foreign Ministry of Ghana, giving details of the brutalities perpetrated by Belgians and calling on Nkrumah to use his 'good offices' to share this information with the other independent African states, the Afro-Asian movement and other world organisations sympathetic to their cause. It also called upon the United Nations to set up an international commission to investigate the events in Leopoldville of 4 January 1959.[29]

Ghana responded sympathetically and provided assistance. But overall, the Abako was no longer the primary focus of Ghana's support for the Congolese, as it had been before the All African People's Conference. Since then, Ghana's support had shifted to the MNC, led by Patrice Lumumba. George Padmore established links in Paris, Brussels and Congo-Brazzaville, through which funds and political advice were secretly transmitted to Lumumba's MNC, as and when necessary.[30]

But the Mouvement National Congolais suffered from internal conflicts. By October 1959, the party had split into two: the MNC-L, under the leadership of Lumumba; and the MNC-K, led by the Kasai provincial leader Albert Kalonji, a shallow, flamboyant and unscrupulous man. Also joining the MNC-K were Adoula and

the ambitious, but weak and ineffective, Joseph Ileo.[31] The friendship between Lumumba and Adoula, which had been much in
evidence at the Ibadan Seminar earlier that year, was now contaminated by political infighting.

'During the turbulent year of 1959', Nkrumah later recorded,
'Patrice Lumumba . . . maintained close and continuous contact
with me'. The young Congolese leader was deeply grateful that
Nkrumah was willing to serve as his mentor. On 9 October 1959,
he wrote to the Ghanaian Foreign Ministry. 'May I please ask the
Prime Minister to give me the necessary guide in respect of the
plan to follow in our struggle?' he asked. 'His experience means a
lot to us'. He also asked for copies of Nkrumah's political speeches
for publication in the Congo.[32]

Lumumba spoke openly and often in public, repeating the call
for immediate independence. In Stanleyville, the capital of Orientale Province, his rallies were triumphant—'one could feel that
Lumumba had merged with his people', noted an Italian journalist. The journalist remembered seeing Lumumba's old father at one
of the rallies: 'His face bore the marks of poverty and he had the
coarse hands of a man who had hunted for food with bow and ar-
row. Now these hands embraced the son, who was carried aloft by
young people chanting: "*Uhuru*—Freedom!" '[33]

On 23-28 October 1959, the First National Congress of the
MNC-L was held in Stanleyville. On the final day of the Congress,
Lumumba gave a speech to an audience of over a thousand people
in which he drew attention to the military bases established by the
Belgians at Kamina and at Kitona. 'Why all these bases?' he asked.
He then suggested the answer: 'To intimidate you, to oppress you.
What purpose do all these military bases serve in Africa? Blacks are
peaceful men, blacks are peace-loving men. . . . All these bases, all
these arms that are here, that are aimed our way?'[34]

The Kamina military base in western Katanga—some 200 miles
from Shinkolobwe and 260 miles northwest of Elisabethville—had
been built in 1952 by Belgium, supported by NATO funding.[35] It
was gigantic, encompassing an area equivalent to that of a Belgian
province.[36] It comprised twin bases, air and military, seven miles

apart and with matching headquarters.[37] The air wing had transport aircraft capable of lifting troops and jeeps, fighter support and
a school for advanced pilots. The number of military personnel at
Kamina was estimated in 1958 to be ten thousand.[38] Amenities included garden cities for the European personnel, housing suburbs
for the Congolese workers, officers' and noncommissioned officers'
messes, with swimming pools and cultural amenities, and a well-
equipped hospital.[39]

It was Shinkolobwe, observed an American journalist, that was
'Kamina's original raison d'etre'.[40]

According to an article in the *New York Herald Tribune* in 1955,
the Kamina base had two 'global missions'. One of these was 'to
protect Belgium's rich uranium mines at Shinkolobwe' and its rich
copper deposits in the same general area. The other was 'to form a
nucleus for the protection of the entire southern half of Africa, and
probably extend that protection even further, should another world
war occur'.[41] The base was 'designed to survive a nuclear attack'.[42]

In addition to Kamina in Katanga and the military base at Kitona near Leopoldville, there was a naval installation at Banana on
the coast, to control the mouth of the Congo River. 'No one needs
to tell a military geographer', observed the *New York Herald Tribune*, 'how this will contribute to the control of all Africa, except
the Nile basin and the northern frontier'.[43]

* * *

By October 1959, the Belgian administration had had enough of
Lumumba. They had already been alarmed by his rhetoric and his
meteoric rise in popularity. Now they attributed the growing anger
in Stanleyville not to the despair and frustration of the Congolese
but to Lumumba personally. On 30 October, at the end of a congress of five nationalist parties (including the MNC-L, which had
just held its First National Congress), soldiers of the Force Publique pushed in to arrest Lumumba. The crowd reacted to stop
them with such energy that the police had to give up. Thirty people
were killed and more than a hundred were wounded.[44]

Lumumba was accused of inciting a disturbance, and a warrant for his arrest was issued. He was arrested on 1 November and

incarcerated in Stanleyville prison. His friend in Brazzaville, Luis López Álvarez, arranged for a lawyer in Paris to come to Stanleyville to defend him.[45]

The rioting in Stanleyville continued and eventually spread to Leopoldville in November and December 1959.[46]

In December, a letter from López Álvarez reached Lumumba in prison. In his reply, Lumumba expressed his fond affection for his friend and his pleasure at seeing the statutes of the Institut d'Études Congolaises, which had been delivered to him. 'I express my most fervent hope for the best success of this magnificent project', he told López Álvarez. 'My commitment continues to be whole, complete and total'. Unwittingly, Lumumba was declaring his enthusiastic support for a project financed by the CIA.

Lumumba continued his letter with a clear statement of commitment to the goal of independence through nonviolent and peaceful means. 'Dearest Luis', he ended, 'my thoughts are flying to you through the walls of my cell and, with the same love that has always united us, I embrace you fraternally'.[47]

9

'Table Ronde'

B Y THE TIME THE RAINY season took hold in October 1959, there was a sense that the thick rainfall lashing down on the Belgian Congo reflected a political thunderstorm. The Congolese were becoming increasingly uncooperative with the Belgian administration, and the government in Brussels feared it was losing control. The crisis was further inflamed when the Belgian Socialist Party, the third-largest political party in Belgium, withdrew its support for the new Belgian minister of the Congo.[1]

The government resolved to fulfil its earlier promises to cooperate with Congolese demands. At the start of November 1959, the minister of the Congo announced plans for a round-table conference in Brussels starting on 20 January 1960, to find a way forward from colonial rule to independence.

The Round Table—as it quickly became known—would bring together representatives of the various Congolese political parties for discussions with members of the Belgian Parliament and government. It would take the form of two parts: the first part, from 20 January to 20 February, would focus on political questions; the second part, from 26 April to 16 May, would look at economic issues. The venue would be the Palais des Congrès—the elegant convention centre that had been built for the 1958 World's Fair.

King Baudouin believed he had an important role to play in calming the tensions in the Congo. He went on a lightning visit to the colony in the middle of December 1959, expecting to renew the tributes he had enjoyed on his trip in 1955, when he had been widely cheered by Blacks and whites. William Burden, the American ambassador in Brussels, commented on the ongoing relationship between the king and the Congo. The royal family, he said, had originally regarded the Congo—then the Congo Free State—as their personal property. It was then handed over by King Leopold II to the Belgian government, but the influence of the royals in the Congo remained strong. 'A great deal of the reporting by the Governor Generals of the Congo and by the military of the Congo', he noted, 'went directly to the Royal Family and never went to the government at all, or at least did so in very garbled form'.[2]

King Baudouin was disappointed by the reception he received from his Congolese subjects in December 1959. Instead of the deference and respect he expected, he was met with anger and a determined call for freedom from the Belgian occupation. In Stanleyville, he was surrounded by crowds shouting, 'Free Lumumba!'[3]

* * *

THE FIRST CONGOLESE DELEGATES to the Round Table arrived in Brussels on 9 January 1960. There were eighty-one official delegates, and since most parties sent teams of advisers as well, soon there were over two hundred Congolese in the Belgian capital. 'For the Belgians', commented one historian years later, 'it was as if a contingent of Martians had landed its flying saucers at the *Palais des Congrès*'.[4] Although a number of Congolese people had visited Expo 58, they had been barely noticed by the Belgians, apart from the families caged in the human zoo. Now the people of Brussels were surprised to see people with black skin in their hotels, cafés and bars.

But one member of MNC-L was already in the Belgian capital: Joseph-Désiré Mobutu, who had arrived the previous year to work for Inforcongo and was working secretly for both the Belgian and American intelligence services as an informer.[5]

Also in the city at this time was Cyrille Adoula, the Congolese trade unionist who had gone to the Ibadan Seminar with Lumumba in March 1959; he had been a leader in the breakup of the MNC and was now a supporter of MNC-K. He had come to Belgium in December 1959 for the Sixth World Congress of the anticommunist International Confederation of Free Trade Unions, which had its headquarters in Brussels. The World Congress had been held at the Palais des Congrès, where the Round Table would be meeting. It was an important meeting, after which the AFL-CIO and the ICFTU were virtually indistinguishable.

Newsreels were filmed of the congress and its delegates—all men, mostly white, smoking cigarettes; George Meany, the president of the AFL-CIO, can be seen with a cigar.[6] But there were a few men with black skin, including Adoula and Tom Mboya, the Kenya trade union leader who had chaired the All African People's Conference in Accra.

Mboya was representing the Kenya Federation of Labour. By now, he had established a firm association with the noncommunist unions of the West. When a meeting was called in Accra in November 1959 for the convening of an All African Trade Union Federation (AATUF) congress, as a nonaligned alternative to the ICFTU and to the World Federation of Trade Unions, Mboya chose instead to attend a concurrent meeting of the ICFTU in Lagos.[7]

The Kenya labour movement was receiving contributions from the AFL-CIO, the ICFTU and some of the international trade secretariats affiliated with the ICFTU, among other sources. David Goldsworthy, a biographer of Mboya, refers to the Kenya Federation of Labour's 'insatiable demand for money from ICFTU which, once despatched, seemed simply to evaporate'. Since the CIA's role in helping to finance foreign aid programmes of the AFL-CIO and, by extension, the ICFTU, was common knowledge, Mboya's critics argued that he had become a tool of American policy. According to Goldsworthy, however, Mboya simply 'wanted the money for domestic political purposes and had no qualms about its sources'.[8]

Cyrille Adoula was following a path similar to that of Mboya. Strongly anticommunist, he was secretary general of the Federation Générale du Travail du Kongo, which belonged to the ICFTU, and he was elected a substitute member of the ICFTU executive board at the Sixth World Congress in 1959. Nearly ten years older than Mboya, he was thirty-eight by the time of the Sixth Congress, and married with three children.

Lumumba understood the importance of trade unions in the political work of a freedom movement. He founded the Syndicat

National des Travailleurs Congolais (SNTC) as the labour arm of
the MNC, which was intended to replace those unions that were
foreign imports or closely associated with foreign unions. The brother-
in-law of Adoula, Alphonse Roger Kithima, was made general secretary. Soon, however, Kithima moved close to the ICFTU and
broke his allegiance to Lumumba.[9]

* * *

IN THE LEAD-UP TO the Round Table, the Belgian government was
busy encouraging and fostering the creation of many small Congolese political parties that would cooperate with the colonisers. There
were also parties with particular interests, such as the Confédéra-
tion des Associations Tribales du Katanga (CONAKAT) in Katanga, led by Moise Tshombe, which was financed by Union Minière
and which advocated the secession of Katanga from the Congo.

But despite the substantial differences in approach, the leaders
of all the Congolese political groups in Brussels formed a united
front in their dealings with Belgium. Their chief concern in the
first weeks of January 1960 was the absence of Lumumba, who was
in prison in Stanleyville. They regarded Lumumba as the most important voice in the nationalist struggle, and on 19 January they
insisted that he be set free and brought to Brussels; Kasavubu was
one of the principal spokesmen.[10] This demand had become urgent,
since the talks were scheduled to start the following day.

But Lumumba was still in prison on the first day of the Round
Table in Brussels. The next day, he appeared before the Stanleyville
Tribunal and was sentenced to six months imprisonment, with immediate effect. Then, on the following day, the colonial administration ruled that Lumumba should be transferred to the maximum
security prison in Jadotville (now Likasi) in Katanga. Lumumba
sent a telegram to his lawyer:

WAS TRANSFERED JADOTVILLE UNDER HIDEOUS CIRCUM-
STANCES THROWN ON PLANE BAREFOOT SHIRTLESS HAND-
CUFFED AND PHYSICALLY ASSAULTED TILL ARRIVED ON BOARD
STOP TORTURE CONTINUES ALL MY POSSESSIONS REMAIN PRISON
STAN[LEYVILLE] AND NO CHANGE SHIRT.

He added that he was 'keeping calm and collected'.[11]

The Congolese politicians at the Round Table in Brussels continued to exert heavy pressure on the Belgian government to release Lumumba from jail and bring him to Belgium. His release, they said, was nothing less than a condition of their active participation in the talks.

The government had no choice but to give in. On the same day that Lumumba was sent to Jadotville, Brussels sent an order to Leopoldville that Lumumba be released from captivity and flown to Belgium. Governor General Hendrik Cornelis vigorously opposed the decision, but he was overruled.

Lumumba was photographed at the start of his long journey: he looked exhausted, with bare feet and in dirty prison clothes.[12] In a speech the following month, he recalled this painful episode and the support of the Congolese people: 'I didn't have anything, no suit, no shoes, absolutely nothing. The authorities had to find me a suit and other things so I could get dressed. The Africans took up a collection and bought me the rest of the clothes I needed. I was escorted from Jadotville by the district commissioner and military jeeps'.

When he arrived at Elisabethville airport, he was astonished—and profoundly moved—to see the huge crowds of people waiting for him: 'There were at least ten thousand Congolese there; they were delighted, and kept shouting, right there in front of the provincial commissioner: "Down with colonialism, down with the colonialists, long live immediate independence!"'[13]

He was then put on a flight to Brussels.

* * *

LUMUMBA ARRIVED IN BRUSSELS on 25 January. He was wearing bandages on both wrists, to protect the injuries inflicted by his handcuffs and mistreatment. He was greeted at the airport as a hero. The Round Table members of the MNC were allowed to welcome him, and they rushed up the steps of the plane as he emerged, to hug him tightly. The joy on Lumumba's face was captured by the photographers and cameramen who had come to film his arrival.[14]

Joseph-Désiré Mobutu, since he was not a member of the Round Table, was prevented from joining them by a policeman.

Upset, he turned to his companion—Luis López Álvarez, who had arrived in Brussels the day before and who had been driven to the airport by Mobutu. López Álvarez took Mobutu with him to the airport terrace, to watch the arrival of Lumumba's plane. As Lumumba appeared at the top of the steps, Mobutu called out, 'Vive Lumumba! Vive le M.N.C.!'[15]

One of the people waiting patiently for Lumumba was an old Belgian woman, carrying a bunch of flowers. When she saw him, she rushed up to him and thrust the flowers into his arms, kissing him. 'I am only one poor woman', she said, 'but there are millions of others like myself. In their name I want to salute a fighter for freedom'.[16]

López Álvarez noted a bank of police officers in the arrival hall, where he and Mobutu were waiting for Lumumba. As he embraced Lumumba, he whispered into his ear instructions about where to exit the airport in order to avoid the police.

With Mobutu, López Álvarez took Lumumba to his room at the Hotel Cosmopolitan, where the MNC-L delegation and López Álvarez were staying. There, Lumumba was examined by a doctor. Not only did he have heavy bruising on his wrists, but his back was ploughed with long scars caused by recent beatings—slightly diagonal, about twenty centimetres in length, overlapping each other. They were covered in places by fresh scabs. The doctor was also concerned about his low blood pressure. López Álvarez asked Lumumba to tell him when he had been beaten, but his friend replied several times: 'No, don't worry about it, it's of no importance'. López Álvarez looked after him as carefully as he could and managed to prevent him from being disturbed for as long as possible, to give him some rest.[17]

At the end of the afternoon, they went downstairs to join other members of MNC-L for a session of photographs. There they found that Mobutu had hung up some sheets on the wall, on which he had written in large letters, 'Vive Lumumba! Vive le M.N.C.! Vive le Congo Uni!' These were Mobutu's own sheets, which he had prepared during the night. His apparent support for MNC-L was carefully displayed for all to see.[18]

* * *

MANY FOREIGN CORRESPONDENTS WERE in Brussels to report on the Round Table. One of them was López Álvarez, who was taken by Mobutu to the office where he needed to obtain formal accreditation as a journalist.

Another journalist was Colin Legum, a South African, who went to the Hotel Cosmopolitan to interview Lumumba. Legum noted his modest accommodation. It was 'a small, plain room', he observed, 'with two plain narrow beds, both too short for the length of their occupant. . . .The telephone never stopped ringing; young men padded in and out of the room constantly; some of them went barefooted and wore their early morning pajamas'. He was impressed by Lumumba's powers of concentration: although he spoke for hours and was frequently interrupted, he never lost the thread of what he was saying.

Lumumba spoke to Legum of his great admiration for Nkrumah and Ghana. He also made it clear that he welcomed cooperation with the Belgians.

Next, Legum went to see Kasavubu. 'The second Congo Headquarters', he recorded, was 'at the ritzy Plaza hotel where the Abako delegation stayed. Unlike Lumumba's room, Kasavubu's was large and elegantly decorated in Regency red-and-white striped wallpaper, with satin curtains and coverings'. In contrast with Lumumba, noted Legum, Kasavubu's attitude towards Belgium was negative and unconstructive.

The lobby of the Plaza Hotel was full of delegates and 'of strangers firmly stuck behind their papers'. Some of them, believed Legum, 'were plain-clothes policemen keeping an eye on what was going on; others were "contact men" trying to nobble the delegates with promises of foreign aid and propositions for commercial transactions'.

Cyrille Adoula was also staying at the expensive Plaza. López Álvarez had spent some time talking to him, sharing his concern about the breakup of the MNC into two sections; he reminded Adoula of the time the three men had spent together in Ibadan the previous year. Adoula reassured him. Lumumba, he said, was still the object of his affection and, in his view, far outclassed the other Congolese leaders. López Álvarez said that he wanted to organise a reconciliation between the two men. But it turned out to be unnecessary, for as soon as Adoula and Lumumba saw each other in the corridors of the Palais des Congrès, they exclaimed with pleasure and embraced.

The Congolese visitors to Brussels met together in different parts of the city. The younger delegates took over a café in downtown Brussels, which became a place for all the Congolese visitors—from every political party—to meet at night. 'Many of the leaders', observed Legum, 'were now meeting each other for the first time, and making friends—or enemies'.[19]

Thomas Kanza, who was working in Brussels for the European Common Market, acted as a liaison between the various conference participants. As the first Congolese person to graduate from the prestigious Louvain University and to have studied at Harvard, he commanded respect on all sides. He was the editor of *Congo*, the first weekly journal produced by and for Congolese.[20]

Kanza decided to invite some musicians from the Congo to Brussels, wrote Gary Stewart in *Rumba on the River*. He arranged for the celebrated musician Joseph Kabasele Tshamala, known to everyone as Le Grand Kallé, to come to Brussels with his band, African Jazz. Their arrival brought the delegates a 'little taste of home'.[21]

Some members of the Congo's other great band—OK Jazz (later known as TPOK Jazz)—also joined the group (but not its famous leader, Franco Luambo Makiadi, who at the time was unable to travel to Belgium).[22]

Kabasele composed several songs especially for the conference, such as 'Table Ronde', which was written in the Congolese rumba style. Vicky Longomba, a vocalist with OK Jazz, wrote a song called 'Vive Lumumba Patrice'.

The musicians played together all over Brussels. Some evenings, they could be found in the smart Plaza Hotel, where Kasavubu and Adoula were staying; on other evenings, they performed in bars popular with the Congolese. According to a singer from Guadaloupe who was covering the Round Table for the French public radio service, the RTF, the songs 'sent a musical shock wave. It was pretty extraordinary, this spontaneous, natural music'.[23]

'The foreign press interviewed me', said Kabasele. 'All could well believe that we were from Congo', he added dryly, 'but not that we were capable of making such beautiful, such impressive music'.[24] One of the musicians remembered that 'people came, women especially, to see if [my color] came off. . . . They picked up the instruments to see if they were real. People thought we had put a tape on'. Another said, 'It was the first time they had seen an African guitarist, more specifically Congolese'.[25]

* * *

ONCE LUMUMBA ARRIVED EVENTS moved fast, and he dominated the proceedings of the Round Table.[26] The delegates from the Congo continued to present a united front, and the Belgian opposition parties sided with them openly, which gave them a valuable advantage. They demanded unconditional independence within six months and insisted that all decisions must be binding—not simply consultative, which is what the Belgians were pushing for.

Within days of Lumumba's arrival on 27 January 1960, an agreement was reached that the Congo would become independent on 30 June that year—in five months. It would be a unified state, with considerable devolution to the six provinces. The legislature would be composed of a Chamber of Representatives and a Senate. The elections would be held in May 1960.

When the June date was fixed, the delegates were overjoyed. Many of them went to the Plaza Hotel to dance the night away to the music of Joseph Kabasele and African Jazz. Kabasele introduced a new song, which he had written that day, especially for the occasion, 'Indépendance Cha-Cha'. The song, written in Lingala, paid tribute to the Congolese for their achievement of freedom and called on all the leaders to work together. Its 'simple but eloquent words', commented Stewart, 'saluted Congolese leaders and their parties by name set to music of almost uncontrolled exuberance'.[27]

Indépendance cha cha to zui e

O Kimpuanza cha cha tubakidi

O Table ronde cha cha ba gagner O

O dipanda cha cha to zui e

Here we are, independent at last!
Long live Liberty, cha-cha
Victory at the political roundtable!
Long live Independence,
We have won.[28]

The song travelled swiftly around Africa as an anthem of freedom. Almost immediately in Northern Rhodesia, the British colony that shared a border with the Congo, the resistance campaign against British rule became known as the 'Cha Cha Cha'.

Luis López Álvarez sent a telegram reporting on the outcome of the Round Table to the second All African People's Conference, which had opened in Tunis on 25 January 1960. Some 180 delegates had arrived, from about thirty African countries.[29] When the news from Brussels was announced, there was exhilaration and joy. 'Everybody in the hall was silent for a moment; then the applause broke loose', wrote Colin Legum. 'It was a memorable moment in the history of Pan-Africanism'.

He added, 'Only a short year earlier, Patrice Lumumba had appeared on its platform at the first conference in Accra; then he was an unknown leader from a country without a nationalist movement. Who could have predicted the swift transformation of his, and of the Congo's fortunes?'[30]

* * *

THE FIRST SET OF discussions at the Round Table, which focused on political issues, lasted for almost a month and was reasonably productive as a way forward for the Congolese delegates. Governor General Cornelis created a college of six commissioners, including Kasavubu and Lumumba, who were put in nominal control of the Congo's major departments of administration. Once back in the Congo, Lumumba quickly went to work, devoting himself to the role at all hours.[31]

The second part of the Round Table, which dealt with economic matters, lasted from 26 April to 16 May. This was successful from the point of view of the Belgians—but not of the Congolese. Lumumba sent Mario Cardoso, a teaching assistant in psychology and education at Lovanium University, as the representative of the MNC-L. Other major parties also relied on university students and recent graduates. This put them at a disadvantage; as Georges Nzongola-Ntalaja notes, they had to negotiate with prominent Belgian experts, some of whom were their professors.

Nzongola-Ntalaja's analysis of the process is devastating: 'Negotiating with such young, inexperienced, and politically insignificant delegates who needed Belgian expertise to make sense of the complex issues at stake, the Belgians laid the groundwork for the third rape of the Congo, economically speaking, the first and second having taken place under King Leopold II and the colonial state, respectively'.

The Belgian authorities, he adds, 'cynically used the resolutions of the conference to privatize the enormous state portfolios in major colonial trusts such as the Comité Spécial du Katanga (CSK) and the Comité National du Kivu (CNKi) and transferring these assets to Belgium'. They also allowed many private companies operating in the Congo to transfer their headquarters to Belgium, 'thus denying the new state a large amount of tax income, while leaving to it virtually all of the public debt'.[32]

Thomas Kanza took an equally bleak view of these developments. Nearly every problem was touched on, he commented bitterly some years later, 'except those of really vital importance to any state's survival—the economic, financial, military and diplomatic ones'. In this, he argued, 'the Belgians systematically betrayed the good faith of the Congolese'.[33]

During this period, the Loi Fondamentale—a temporary constitution for the new nation of the Congo—was drafted; it was enacted by the Belgian government on 19 May. The law adopted structures which virtually reproduced the constitutional monarchy of Belgium and was riddled with problems for the Congo.[34] It has been described as 'patently incompatible' with the context of Congolese politics and 'one of the most complicated and cumbersome instruments the Congolese could possibly have anticipated'.[35] It still needed to be passed by the new Congolese Parliament, following independence.

The Belgians made all these concessions, maintains Nzongola-Ntalaja, 'because they were confident that their continued presence in the Congo would protect and advance their interests. As they saw it, they would remain associated with state power through the army . . . and through the government, the judiciary, the civil service and state enterprises'.

At the same time, Belgian companies expected to continue their exploitation of Congolese resources, and the Catholic missionaries expected to remain involved in the religious, educational and health ministries.[36]

The Congolese people joyfully embraced the promise of freedom, just a few months away. But their long history of occupation and deprivation had provided little in the way of preparation for self-government. The colony had fewer than thirty African university graduates, and out of some five thousand management-level positions in the civil service, only three were held by Congolese.[37]

Inevitably, many of the Congolese politicians taking up key roles didn't trust the Belgians. 'A lot of them', recalled Andrew Steigman, a young foreign service officer attached to the US embassy in Leopoldville from March 1960, 'very much wanted to talk to the Americans'. They felt inexperienced and wanted guidance: 'They really didn't know what they were dealing with or how they were going to cope, and they were coming around looking for advice and counsel'.

At the time, in the months leading up to independence, the American official presence was a consulate general with a small staff, including a CIA officer. Both the political officer, said Steigman, 'and the CIA guy, we had them make contacts. They were the two people, really, working in the political field and were starting to meet people and talk to them and get a feel for them'.[38] These relationships quickly put down roots, which were energetically nourished with financial rewards by the CIA.

10

Ambassador Burden

THROUGHOUT THE ROUND TABLE, A phalanx of journalists from all over the world sat at the back of the room, writing reports to send home. The American magazine *Time* described the conference as a 'mad melange of inflammatory speeches, door-slamming walkouts, rival press conferences and angry communiqués'.[1] It was headline news. But behind the headlines was another story, which was kept very quiet: negotiations about the future of the Congo between Belgium and the USA. At their centre was a 'pouchy, owlish' six-foot-one-inch American, William 'Bill' Armistead Moale Burden Jr, who had flown to Brussels in early September 1959 as the new US ambassador to Belgium and the Belgian Congo.[2]

Burden, heir to the Vanderbilt fortune, was a wealthy New Yorker and patron of the arts. He had made substantial contributions to the Republican Party in the 1956 presidential campaign, hoping to be rewarded with the role of American ambassador in France.[3] Instead, he was offered Belgium, which he declined—he hankered for the sophistication of diplomatic life in Paris. But when it became clear that France was not in the cards, he was ready to compromise, and when he was offered Belgium a second time, he accepted. He was aware, too, that Belgium and its African colony were going through a period of change of great importance to the US. And Belgium— unlike France—had a monarchy, which had a special appeal for Burden, who relished opulence. He knew that the American ambassador would be expected to participate in many lavish royal events.

Burden and his wife, Peggy, resolved to make a success of the appointment. They took his Cadillac to Brussels, along with some favourite paintings, the best butler he had ever had and an excellent French chef. Keen to establish his skill as a wine connoisseur, he also obtained a 'superb cellar of Bordeaux wines, including fifty cases of irreplaceable Chateau [Cheval] Blanc, 1947', which were conveyed to the embassy from Bonn in two truckloads. Wine from New York was added to the cellar. This collection of vintage wines, he wrote with considerable satisfaction some years later, 'made my reputation'.[4]

Burden wrote a thick memoir in his later years—*Peggy and I: A Life Too Busy for a Dull Moment*. In it, he recorded a life of luxury, expensive meals and the purchase of art and influence. His granddaughter, Wendy Burden, also wrote a memoir, *Dead End Gene Pool*, which was a caustic account of growing up with William and Peggy Burden in their Fifth Avenue apartment, cared for by a chain-smoking nanny. Her father, their eldest son, killed himself when she was six, after her grandparents went to Brussels. In her memoir, Wendy Burden portrays her grandfather as 'a casual anti-Semite and a serious alcoholic'.[5] William and Peggy Burden were rarely seen without an alcoholic drink and spent several weeks in a clinic every year to dry out. Once, while visiting Paris, when he had just seen the latest model Mercedes-Benz, William called his private secretary in New York to instruct her to order five of them—one to be delivered in a few hours to him in Paris.[6]

Dead End Gene Pool gives the impression that Burden was superficial and dull witted. But in fact, he appears to have been astutely intelligent, as well as ruthless. His professional background was as an aviation analyst, and during World War II he was US assistant secretary of commerce for air. In a debate in the British House of Commons towards the end of the war, he was described as 'one of the greatest experts on this subject in the world'.[7]

He was intensely interested in national defence and took the credit for convincing President Truman to go ahead with America's development of the hugely destructive hydrogen bomb, over Robert Oppenheimer's vigorous objections. The pride he felt in his involvement is manifest in *Peggy and I*, where the only illustration in colour is that of the 'Fireball of the world's first thermonuclear explosion, Eniwetok Proving Grounds, November 1, 1952'.[8]

Nicholson Baker, who has written with perspicacity on the horror of war, has described Burden as a 'mass-destructionist'. He notes that Burden was the least well known of the US Air Force's three most influential proponents of infectious warfare—'united in a belief that weaponised disease was the way to win the war with the Communists'. Burden took tours of the US Army's Special Operations Division, based at Fort Detrick, fifty miles from Washington in the Maryland town of Frederick, which—shrouded in secrecy—was the centre of the US biological weapons programme. Burden, opposed to any sort of retaliation-only restriction on the use of biological weapons, asked in November 1951, 'What is being done about the policy of using BW [biological weapons] for other than retaliatory purposes?'[9]

In 1957 he was appointed a public trustee of the Pentagon's Institute for Defense Analyses, a weapons-research think tank, which he later described as 'one of the top priorities of my life'; he was elected chairman of the institute in May 1959.[10]

* * *

BURDEN'S BUSINESS INTERESTS WERE wide ranging. He founded the Wall Street investment company that bears his name and, at various times, was a director of Lockheed Aircraft Corporation, the CBS television network, Hanover Bank and Allied Chemical, as well as other major companies. He was also a director of American Metal Climax, a mining company with extensive holdings in central Africa; it was a large shareholder in Rhodesian Selection Trust, which was closely linked to the Belgian Congo and obtained much of its energy from the Congo's hydroelectric sources.[11]

Burden saw himself as a central figure in the mining world of Katanga and Belgium. 'Having been in the mining business as a director of American Metals Climax', he stated some years after leaving Brussels, 'I knew a great many people in the mining business, and a great many people in the Union Minière, who had direct knowledge of Congo affairs and who were much more realistic about what was likely to happen than the people in the Belgian government'.

An especially useful contact, said Burden in an interview in 1971, was 'Mr. Sengier, who was the famous Union Minière man who brought the raw material necessary to produce uranium to the United States in the early stages of the war, on his own initiative and at his own risk'.[12]

Burden was one of a number of powerful, rich men associated with the Eisenhower administration who had financial interests in companies with a stake in Belgium and the Belgian Congo. Another was Christian A Herter, the secretary of state, who had family ties to Mobil Oil, with direct investments in the Congo. C Douglas Dillon, the undersecretary of state, had family ties to Dillon, Read and Company, which had managed the Belgian Congo's bond issues. Thomas Gates, the secretary of defense, had ties to Drexel and Co and to Morgan Guaranty Trust, which had managed two $20 million loans to the Belgian Congo.

Robert 'Bob' Murphy was a director of Morgan Guaranty Trust.[13] Murphy, who retired from the State Department in 1959, was one of Burden's predecessors in the role of US ambassador to Belgium, from 1949 to 1952. During that period, the US was at war in Korea and concerned about protecting its exclusive supply of Congolese uranium ore. In November 1950 Murphy visited the Congo in order to evaluate the security of the Shinkolobwe area against outside attacks.[14] Murphy saved the US a huge amount of money in 1951 over the purchase of Congolese ore. 'For years', he wrote later in his memoir, 'we had been able to import substantial amounts of uranium ore from Katanga at prices below what was paid elsewhere, but now Union Minière justifiably felt it was entitled to a price increase. This amounted to a number of million dollars annually'. Murphy was summoned to Washington for negotiations with Belgium; he suggested offering half the amount, which was accepted.[15]

* * *

THERE WERE TANGIBLE LINKS between William Burden and the CIA. He was a director of the Farfield Foundation, the CIA front that financed such cultural organisations as the Congress for Cultural Freedom and its various projects and publications. Burden's name is listed on the foundation's letterhead.[16]

Burden was closely associated with the Museum of Modern Art (MoMA) in New York, to which he donated valuable gifts of sculptures and paintings. Here, too, was a link with the CIA, which gave generous funding to MoMA. Burden was a trustee from 1943 and was elected as president in 1953; he was elected annually until 1959, when he resigned to go to Belgium (reprising this role after his return to New York).[17] The museum's board 'was a who's who of CIA connections', according to one commentator. 'Nearly everyone involved at the museum', he adds, 'had government connections, whether in the State Department, Foreign Service, or CIA'.[18]

According to David Anfam, an authority on modern American art, the CIA was eager to support MoMA in order to promote abstract expressionism—which was developed after the Second World War by artists such as Jackson Pollock—as a foil to the Soviet realist style. It is 'a well-documented fact', observed Anfam in 2016, that the CIA co-opted abstract expressionism in their propaganda war against Russia. He believes that understanding the appeal of abstract expressionism to the CIA is easy: the artworks produced under the movement showed that 'America was the land of the free, whereas Russia was locked up, culturally speaking'.[19] The success of abstract expressionism also enabled New York to challenge Paris's role as the centre of Western art.

Burden referred to Allen Dulles, the director of the CIA under Eisenhower, as 'a lifelong friend'.[20] Dulles, like Burden, had close ties with American Metal Climax. The chairman of the board of trustees of American Metal Climax was Harold Hochschild, who collaborated with the CIA in various ways, especially in Africa, and was well known to Dulles.[21] Hochschild had been one of the founders of American Metal Climax, which had started life as American Metal Company and was later known as AMAX. American Metal Climax was part of a huge network; it had mines and smelters in Africa and Mexico and the US, company headquarters in New York, offices in other parts of the world and ships that freighted the ore. Much of the network belonged to subsidiaries or affiliates or joint ventures with other corporations.[22]

All these connections came together with the foundation of the African-American Institute in 1953, which was put on a solid financial footing by the CIA, with assistance from American Metal Climax.

Dulles recruited prominent businessmen to the AAI board, in order 'to take on this responsibility as a public service in the national interest'. Trustees included William Burden; Harold Hochschild; Dana Creel, later the head of the Rockefeller Brothers Fund; and Alan Pifer, later the head of the Carnegie Corporation.[23]

The son of Harold Hochschild was Adam Hochschild, who published *King Leopold's Ghost* in 1998. In 1986 he published *Half the Way Home: A Memoir of Father and Son*, about his childhood, which refers to the AAI—'a new organisation Father had helped start: the African-American Institute'. In the book, Hochschild explains that his father had been chairman of its board for a decade. He then describes his father's reaction when the media revealed in the 1960s that the AAI was a CIA front. 'The next time I saw him', he writes, 'he seemed uncomfortable. He defended the link, saying that in its early years there was nowhere else the Institute could have gotten enough money for its work. But he was clearly embarrassed that the whole thing had had to be kept secret'.[24]

Other members of the AAI board included African American intellectuals and writers, such as Horace Mann Bond of the CIA-funded AMSAC; Edwin S. Munger of the American Universities Field Staff; and Bob Keith, the chief editor of the AAI's journal, *Africa Special Report*. All three men had attended the All African People's Conference in Accra in 1958.

Newly appointed as the US ambassador to Belgium in 1959, Burden was briefed on relevant CIA activities in late September 1959.[25] Two months later, he was concerned about the prospect of unrest in the Congo. He wrote to Dulles to ask if the CIA had done any work on the degree to which 'new weapons, such as some of the newer gases' might be used to deal with the type of rioting occurring in the various countries of Africa, with particular reference to the Congo. The agency's Africa Division provided some notes on this topic for a planned conversation between Dulles and Burden.[26]

* * *

IN MARCH 1960, AMBASSADOR Burden went on a three week fact-finding tour of the Congo with his wife and a group of Americans attached to the Brussels embassy. Owen Roberts, who was a consular officer in Leopoldville in 1958–1960, recalled the tour some years later. 'It was a revelation', he marvelled. 'They had tape recorders and secretaries, extensive appointments made from Brussels and they proceeded to analyze the whole situation in a few days. They were a big operation'.[27]

Burden lists the members of the group in *Peggy and I*. But he omits one important member of the group: Larry Devlin.[28] Devlin's chief responsibility at this time was to prepare for his forthcoming post as the CIA's chief of station in the Congo; he expected to move there at the time of independence. He had been appointed in late August 1959, following a briefing on the Congo in 1958 by Allen Dulles, who was on a visit to Brussels.[29] 'I was assigned to serve as his driver, bodyguard, and general man Friday', recalled Devlin years later, 'for in those times directors travelled without an entourage'. They also lunched together. Dulles told Devlin that the United States could not afford to lose the Belgian Congo to the Soviet Union: 'He impressed on me that I would be playing a key role in his plans'.[30]

Devlin agreed with Dulles's analysis. Soviet control of the Congo, he wrote in his memoir, *Chief of Station, Congo*, 'would give the Soviet Union a near monopoly on the production of cobalt, a critical mineral used in missiles and many other weapons systems, since the Congo and the USSR were the world's main suppliers of the mineral'. Such a scenario, he argued, would put America's own weapons programme at a severe disadvantage.[31]

Cobalt, which was mined in the Congo, was indeed a strategic mineral of great value to the US. However, it was nowhere near as 'critical' as the uranium from the Shinkolobwe mine. It is possible that Devlin was using the word 'cobalt' as a cover for uranium, as it had been used in World War II; Congolese uranium ore had been packed in barrels marked 'Special Cobalt' for the journey from Shinkolobwe to the US.[32]

* * *

AMBASSADOR BURDEN, MRS BURDEN, Larry Devlin and other members of the tour to the Congo flew from Leopoldville to Luluabourg (now Kananga), the capital of Kasai province, with Albert

Kalonji, the leader of the Luba people, known as Baluba. Kalonji, who was the leader of the MNC faction that had pulled away from the Lumumba-supporting branch of the party, was becoming increasingly hostile towards Lumumba.[33]

Moving on to Katanga, Burden's group visited some of the large mines and refineries of Union Minière. Katanga, noted Burden, contained 'very large copper mines, very rich uranium deposits and important diamond mines'. The 'general attitude' of Union Minière, he added, was that despite independence, 'over the long run things will work out all right and that they will continue to show confidence in the new country by continuing to make investments and modernizing their properties'.[34] In Elisabethville, the capital of Katanga, Ambassador Burden stayed at the Union Minière guest house.[35]

Burden returned to Brussels at the start of April 1960 and made a number of recommendations to Washington. One of these was to send a 'top notch Ambassador' to Leopoldville since, after 30 June, it would be necessary to replace the consulate general in the Congo with a fully fledged embassy. Burden's focus on planning greatly impressed Devlin, who thought he was 'one of the few people who showed any interest in the fact that the Congo was becoming independent'.[36]

* * *

DURING THE PERIOD OF the Round Table in Brussels, Burden obtained permission from the Belgian government to meet some of the Congolese delegates.[37] One of these was Lumumba, whom he invited to the American embassy. Judging by Burden's report to Washington on the meeting, he disliked Lumumba at first sight and felt a personal animosity towards the younger man. The Congolese leader arrived half an hour late, said Burden. Then he 'kept a taxi waiting in front of the Embassy for the forty minutes or so which was covered by our conversation'. This was worth noting, he observed, 'from the financial point of view'.

Lumumba was 'a highly articulate, sophisticated, subtle and unprincipled intelligence', judged Burden. 'He gives the impression of a man who would probably go far', he added, 'in spite of the fact that almost nobody trusts him'. In his opinion, Lumumba was dangerously left wing. Yet Lumumba had expressed a favourable opinion of the US. This, believed Burden, 'was due in no small measure to the feeling that the American Negroes come in important numbers originally from the Congo and are hence the "brothers" of the Congolese'.[38]

Burden and Lumumba did not have a shared language in which to communicate. Burden claimed fluency in French, the official language of Belgium along with Flemish, and the official language of the Belgian Congo. But as his memoir makes clear, he struggled with French and had to take intensive lessons in order to cope with the most basic demands of diplomatic life in Brussels.[39]

But the real obstacle to any understanding between the two men was the difference in their experience, backgrounds and attitudes. The American was rich and privileged, with enhanced status in his own country because of the colour of his skin; his book reflects a deeply held racism. The Congolese came from a poor family and was treated as a second-class citizen within his own country, also because of the colour of his skin. He was suspicious of white Belgians as a result of his experience.

But he was not suspicious enough of white Americans. Frank Carlucci III, who was attached to the US embassy in Leopoldville shortly after independence, described an episode that revealed the trust Lumumba initially felt in Americans, as opposed to Europeans. Lumumba had misunderstood Carlucci about an issue and screamed at him, 'You Europeans are all hypocrites. You promised me'. Shortly afterwards, Carlucci asked Lumumba why he had screamed at him. Lumumba replied, 'I didn't realize you were an American. I thought you were European'.[40]

Larry Devlin suggests in his memoir that he himself was less concerned about the colour of an individual's skin than with the individual's potential to advance his professional objectives. And, unlike Burden, Devlin spoke French fluently: his wife, Colette, was a Frenchwoman he had met in Algiers during World War II, when they were both engaged in intelligence work. Devlin was therefore able to converse with Congolese people who spoke French, but he did not learn any of the Congo's 242 languages, including Lingala, Kiswahili, Kikongo and Tshiluba.

One of the contacts Devlin established in Brussels during the Round Table was with Victor Nendaka, an ambitious politician who paid a visit to the American embassy on his own accord, without an invitation. Nendaka had previously been the vice president of MNC-L, but by the time of the Round Table he had left Lumumba's group for MNC-K. According to Devlin, Nendaka went to the embassy and 'warned a political officer that Lumumba was already working closely with the Soviets. The officer, aware of my future assignment in the Congo, introduced me to Nendaka'.

Devlin was grateful for this introduction. Although Nendaka had no experience in intelligence, Devlin wrote years later, 'he proved to be a quick learner'. He was self-taught and had 'a brilliant mind'; Nendaka's wife told Devlin that when they were first married, he preferred to stay home and read books, rather than going out to dance and drink beer. Now, as the Congo prepared for independence, Nendaka was an ideal contact for Devlin: 'he 'recognised that American support was essential to the success of the new government and started to cultivate the most important officials in our embassy as I began to focus on him. The result was that we eventually became close friends'.[41] This friendship was to have huge ramifications for the Congo after independence.

* * *

AMBASSADOR BURDEN GAVE A reception in Brussels in January 1960 for the Congolese men attending the Round Table.[42] One of the guests was Joseph-Désiré Mobutu. 'I met him', said Devlin many years later, 'as I met a number of the leaders after the end of the round table conference, [when] Ambassador Burden gave a reception'.[43] At the reception, he added, 'We each took the names of x number, I don't remember [how many], of Congolese, and tried to get an idea of who they were, if they were intelligent, competent, because what we had up until that time, [were] assessments provided by the Belgians'.

From this, indicated Devlin, emerged the connection with Mobutu: 'the reaction was that, here is a man who is a strong nationalist, intelligent, and who seems to have leadership qualities along with others. For several of the others, the reaction was rather negative'.[44]

This was not truthful, since Mobutu was already serving Devlin as an informer.

There was widespread suspicion of Mobutu in Congolese circles during the Round Table. It was widely believed that he had been an informer in the pay of Belgium from the late 1950s. Jef Van Bilsen, who was at the Round Table as an advisor to Abako, personally warned Lumumba that Mobutu was working as an informer. He pointed out that this made MNC-L vulnerable, given Mobutu's prominent role in the party. Lumumba responded that he was already aware of this and that it was an innocent way for Mobutu to bring in some extra income. Lumumba knew personally the difficulties of financial hardship, but he had also developed a dangerously soft spot for Mobutu.

The network of part-time informers to the Belgian Security Service was extensive; on 11 April 1961 *Kongo dia Ngunga*, the principal organ of Abako, devoted several pages to a list of informers discovered in Belgian colonial records.[45]

Mobutu's relationship with Devlin was explored at an important conference on events in the Congo in 1960–1961, which was held in 2004 at the Woodrow Wilson International Center for Scholars in Washington, DC.[46] Attendees included Larry Devlin; Thomas Kanza, who represented Lumumba's government at the UN and was later a minister in the government of President Laurent-Désiré Kabila; Cléophas Kamitatu, the provincial president of the Parti Solidaire Africain; the political scientist Georges Nzongola-Ntalaja, who describes himself as 'a scholar of the Congo as well as a native of the Congo';[47] Stephen R Weissman, former staff director of the US House of Representatives Subcommittee on Africa, who is an expert on US foreign policy in the Congo; and the American political scientist Herbert F Weiss, who conducted research on the Congo for the Massachusetts Institute of Technology (MIT) between September 1959 and mid-1962.[48]

Nzongola-Ntalaja asked probing questions about the CIA's use of Mobutu as an agent. But this was firmly resisted by Devlin.

There was a clear distinction, he said, between an agent and a coop-erator. 'He was never an agent by my assessment', explained Devlin; rather, 'he was a cooperator, because we both seemed to be going in the same direction and therefore there was a certain collaboration'.

Devlin was adamant that Mobutu was never 'recruited'. When asked if Mobutu was given a stipend, he evaded the question. 'You don't have to be an agent to receive a stipend', he argued defen-sively. 'An agent is a person to whom we'd say: "we expect you to do this and do that". Mobutu was never a person to whom we could say "do this and this and this"'.[49]

But what Devlin *did* acknowledge was that the CIA had as-sessed the Congolese politicians long before independence. There were still several months to go before the Congo's first democratic election in its history. But the CIA had already identified Mobutu as a future leader who was susceptible to American influence—someone to cultivate and to promote.

PART IV

AMERICA AND AFRICA

11

The Africa Division of the CIA

IN THE MIDDLE OF NOVEMBER 1959, just a few months after Larry Devlin's appointment as CIA chief of station in the Congo, a dedicated Africa Division was created in the CIA's Directorate of Plans.[1] Previously, the African continent had been covered by the Near East and Africa Division. Henceforth, the number of CIA stations in Africa increased rapidly, by over 50 per cent between 1959 and 1963.[2]

The first chief of the Africa Division was Bronson Tweedy. Known as 'Brons' by friends and colleagues, Tweedy was a Princeton-educated, old-school 'career spook', with a background in naval intelligence during World War II.[3] After the war he returned to his prewar career in advertising and was then recruited by the CIA. Well-built and greying around the temples, he was described by an investigative journalist as cosmopolitan in manner, with a 'mellow film star voice'.[4] Before being appointed as head of the Africa Division, he had served as chief of station in Vienna and then London.

In his new position, Tweedy reported to Richard ('Dick') M Bissell Jr, deputy director for plans (DDP) from the start of 1959; Tweedy's deputy was Glenn Fields. Dick Bissell reported to Allen Dulles, the director of the agency as a whole. Bissell's deputy was Richard Helms, who went on to become director of the CIA in 1966–1973 and was convicted in 1977 of misleading Congress in relation to covert operations in Chile.

The Directorate of Plans was responsible for CIA clandestine operations, which included the removal from power of foreign leaders who were seen as a threat to US interests—such as Jacobo

Arbenz, the president of Guatemala, whose 1952 land reform programme had enraged wealthy planters and the United Fruit Company, a huge American corporation. Arbenz was overthrown in 1954
in a CIA operation code-named PBSUCCESS.[5]

The CIA was housed at this time in about forty offices that
were scattered around Washington, DC, many of them in the area
known as Foggy Bottom.[6] A huge new headquarters was being
constructed in Langley, Virginia, but it was not ready for service
until September 1961.

John Stockwell recalled his experience of working for the CIA
in his memoir, *In Search of Enemies*. The Africa Division, he recalled,
was rooted not only in the concrete offices of Washington, but in a
network of relationships across the world. The clandestine services,
he wrote, 'is a small clubbish unit of 4,500 people compartmented
into geographic divisions. Africa Division itself had less than 400
staffers and after ten years I knew nearly all of them. Our assignments and operational travels overlapped and crisscrossed like the
trails of migrating wildebeest on an East African plain'. He added,
'A night on the town in Paris, a three-day course in lock-picking at
headquarters, lunch in a Nairobi restaurant, all years apart, can be
enough for a kind of understanding rare in other lines of work'.[7]

* * *

THE AFRICA DIVISION WAS created against a background of concern at the highest levels in Washington about the way forward for
Africa. Bleak opinions were expressed about the future of the continent, with the exception of South Africa. At a meeting on 14 January 1960 of the National Security Council, President Eisenhower
reviewed the matter of US policy towards Africa. There was a perceived need, he observed, for 'access to such military rights and facilities and strategic resources as may be required in our national
security interests'.

Allen Dulles explained to the council the position of the CIA.
The chances in Africa of 'orderly economic development and political progress towards self-determination', he asserted dismissively,
were 'just about nil'. The president agreed. So did Vice President
Nixon. He reported that Ghana, according to the British, 'had only a

50 per cent chance for an orderly development'. Nixon then offered his personal opinion of people living on the African continent. 'Some of the peoples of Africa', he maintained, 'have been out of the trees for only about fifty years'.

Later in the meeting, Maurice Stans, a senior member of the Eisenhower administration who had recently visited the Belgian Congo, suggested that Nixon was being too generous in his opinion of Africans. He himself, he said, had 'formed the impression that many Africans still belonged in the trees'. No one at the meeting— including Eisenhower and Dulles—challenged these deeply offensive characterisations by Nixon and Stans.

Nixon shared his conviction that America should associate with 'the strong men' in Africa. 'We must recognize, although we cannot say it publicly', he argued to the council, 'that we need the strong men of Africa on our side'. Nixon pushed his argument further. He believed that it would be impossible to stop the process of independence in Africa. It was therefore necessary, he said, not simply to support 'strong men' but actively, in some cases, to develop 'military strong men as an offset to Communist development of the labor unions'. Such a policy ran counter to America's publicly stated commitment to democracy for all nations. But Eisenhower agreed.[8]

* * *

AT THE START OF April 1960, Tweedy produced a memorandum for CIA use on American policy in the Belgian Congo. Its particular concern was the handling of Lumumba, who had been working since 14 March as one of the six commissionaires responsible for the administration of the Belgian colony in the lead-up to independence. 'Our feeling', said Tweedy, 'is that there is so much at stake in preventing the placing of Lumumba in a prominent role . . .that although we admittedly do not have great resources we should make every effort possible'. A handwritten note by Tweedy at the bottom of the memorandum called for swift action: 'P.S. Irrespective of any Belgian financial support, it is most important that some CS [Clandestine Services] money and influence get in there quick!'[9]

But despite his wish to diminish Lumumba's role, Tweedy judged that it would be unwise to alienate him and his supporters.

A couple of weeks later, Tweedy wrote to Joseph Satterthwaite, the assistant secretary for African affairs, with a careful warning: 'Although we consider him unscrupulous and willing to accept aid from anyone if it would help him, we suggest the possibility of limited funding to Lumumba along with other selected leaders. This would provide relatively more help to other leaders but would also keep the door open for future Lumumba contacts and perhaps avoid alienating him if he learns of our support to other leaders'.

Tweedy added, 'We are opposed to any "stop Lumumba" campaign. He is one of the few, if not [the] only, Congolese leaders with a Congo-wide appeal and standing. We feel it is almost certain that he will play an important political role in the Congo for at least the next two years. Thus, an anti Lumumba campaign could backfire'.[10]

The cautious approach to Lumumba was by no means shared by senior officials in the Belgian government. On 1 March 1960, a plan to 'eliminate' him was drawn up by Count Harold d'Aspremont Lynden, the assistant private secretary to the prime minister, and Professor Arthur Doucy of the Université Libre de Bruxelles. The count was a nephew of the grand marshal of the royal court, who was closely associated with the royal family and also had connections with the huge enterprises of Société Générale and Union Minière. The plan he developed with Doucy included the organisation of political forces opposed to Lumumba: 'Political Action: Man to eliminate is Lumumba . . . regroup moderate forces by province . . . : Katanga: Conakat . . . Kasai: Kalonji. . . . It would be necessary to make available to these parties technicians, propaganda and funds'.[11] The total cost, he suggested, could be a maximum of 50 million Belgian francs.[12]

This antagonistic and aggressive attitude to Lumumba was shared by Ambassador Burden. 'Lumumba, you remember', he observed some years later, 'was the Communist-inspired leader, which many well-meaning people in the United States thought represented the true spirit of the Congolese, carefully neglecting the fact that he was actually working if not directly for the Russians, very closely with them'.

Then Burden expressed his hostility to the Congolese leader in even stronger terms. 'Lumumba was such a damn nuisance', he declared, 'it was perfectly obvious that the way to get rid of him was through political assassination'.

Political assassination, added Burden, 'is something which the United States has not been willing to engage in, much to our damage, as we see in the present situation in Vietnam'. At the time Burden made this point, the US was embroiled in the Vietnam War. 'The death of one or two people in North Vietnam', argued Burden, 'might shorten the war by a year or more, and is certainly thoroughly justified, in my opinion, by history and everything else'. Political assassination for Burden was nothing less than murder.

The Belgians, remembered Burden, 'were sort of toying with the idea of seeing to it that Lumumba was assassinated'. This was a view, he said, which he told them he shared. 'I went beyond my instructions', he stated frankly, 'and said, well, I didn't think it would be a bad idea either, but I naturally never reported this to Washington'.[13]

* * *

AMBASSADOR BURDEN HOSTED HIS first formal dinner in the American embassy in Brussels in October 1959. The guest of honour was John McCone, chairman of the US Atomic Energy Commission. McCone, a multimillionaire industrialist from California, had been undersecretary of the Air Force in 1950; he had returned to private industry before moving to the top role at the Atomic Energy Commission in 1958.

Strong-willed and stern, McCone had aroused considerable hostility in his rise to the top. He had outraged scientists at the California Institute of Technology—Caltech—in 1956, when he accused them of attempting to 'create fear in the minds of the uninformed that radioactive fallout from H-bomb tests endangers life'.[14] Like Burden, he energetically supported the testing of the hydrogen bomb. In *The Invisible Government*, David Wise and Thomas B Ross report that during his government service, McCone gained a reputation as an 'uncompromising supporter of John Foster Dulles' doctrine of massive retaliation, the Air Force's atomic warfare theories, and the hard-line strategy against the Soviet Union'.[15]

McCone's reason for going to Brussels in October 1959 was to meet with the president of the European Atomic Energy Community, known as EURATOM. He was on the way back to the US following a ten-day visit to the Soviet Union for discussions with his Russian counterpart and for an inspection of Soviet atomic facilities. An important motive for the trip, he said before leaving the US, was to obtain information—'but he didn't know just how much'—'with respect to data on Soviet uranium ore reserves, a matter that has been carefully guarded in the past'.[16]

Zhores A Medvedev, a dissident scientist in Moscow—who defected to the West in 1973—stated in 2000 that from 1950, uranium mining had been 'one of the most closely guarded state secrets' of the Soviet Union.[17]

The year prior to McCone's visit, the CIA and the intelligence organisations of the Department of State, the army, the navy, the air force, the Joint Staff and the Atomic Energy Commission produced a top-secret report titled 'The Soviet Atomic Energy Program'. The report set out estimates both of uranium ore production by the Soviet bloc up to 1957, and of projected production. The estimated future production of recoverable uranium ore in the USSR, as illustrated by a table in the report, would be 4,500 metric tons in 1958, 4,900 in 1959, 5,500 in 1960, and 6,000 in 1961. Considering the Soviet bloc inclusively, the table set out an estimated production of 12,000 metric tons in 1958, 13,400 in 1959, 14,400 in 1960, and 15,300 in 1961.[18] The report stressed that these figures were necessarily estimates, but its authors had used all the sources that were available.

McCone's visit to Brussels took place against a background of intense negotiations over Congolese uranium. These were triggered by efforts by Edgar Sengier, the managing director of Union Minière, to market to the US the uranium stocks that the company would have above ground at the Shinkolobwe mine when the existing contract expired. In April 1959, Sengier offered to sell one thousand tons at the 'very low' price of seven dollars per pound.[19]

* * *

IN OCTOBER 1959, AFTER a series of meetings in Brussels and dinner with Sengier, Ambassador Burden strongly recommended the purchase of 1,500 tons of uranium ore from Union Minière for $26 million over a period of years.[20] This was a substantial amount: almost half the amount of approximately 3,310 tons that had been delivered from the Congo to the US in the course of World War II for the Manhattan Project.[21]

As a vigorous advocate of all weapons necessary to secure national defence, Burden was conscious of the key role he had played in the decision of the American government to proceed with development of the hydrogen bomb. He was not prepared to risk allowing the Soviet Union to obtain the Congo's uniquely rich uranium. Eisenhower was also in favour of purchasing the ore. For him, too, it was a critical military and strategic decision.

Secretary of State Christian Herter, however, advised caution. He warned that such a move would trigger problems with Canada. This was because the US had signed extensive options to purchase Canadian uranium but had failed thus far to exercise them. Were the US to purchase more uranium from Belgium, Herter pointed out, Canada might insist on a revision of the options.[22]

When Burden met McCone in Brussels, he pushed the case for the purchase of the Congolese uranium. No doubt he was aware through his Union Minière contacts that the Shinkolobwe mine in Katanga was still, in 1959, producing valuable ore.[23] By 1959, new technologies had enabled lower-quality uranium to be enriched to a fissionable quality, thus diminishing the dependence on the Shinkolobwe material. But there was always the risk that the rich Congolese ore would be of value to the Soviet Union.

By the time McCone left Belgium for the US, Ambassador Burden thought he had convinced him that the US should buy 1,500 tons of uranium from Sengier. McCone was keen for America to purchase the ore. But he shared Herter's concerns about the potential risk of alienating Canada. He could not devise a way of buying ore from the Belgians while at the same time making a public announcement that the Atomic Energy Commission would not be purchasing any more Canadian ore.[24] Shortly after McCone's meeting with Burden in Brussels, it was announced that uranium procurement from Canada would not be increased and that the

US Atomic Energy Commission 'already is buying more uranium oxide (U308) than it really needs'.[25] It was also decided in late 1959 not to buy the ore offered to the US by Union Minière. But leaving the rich uranium in Katanga vulnerable to purchase or seizure by the Soviet Union remained a source of huge concern to some very powerful figures in America.

12

Voice of Africa

AFTER INDEPENDENCE, NKRUMAH HAD ASKED his trusted friend George Padmore to move from Britain to Ghana to take on the role of 'advisor to the prime minister on African Affairs'. It would be a crucial post in the implementation of their shared vision for Africa. Padmore would report directly to the prime minister, not to the Foreign Ministry, which would give him considerable freedom. Padmore accepted the post with pleasure and started work in December 1957. His wife, Dorothy Pizer, joined him in Accra, and they settled into a sunny home with a beautiful garden of flamboyant trees and bougainvillea.[1]

But Padmore had no plans to relax. He was working 'at top speed', he wrote in a letter to W E B Du Bois in February 1958, as he threw himself into the planning of the first Conference of Independent African States in Accra in April 1958. For this, he went on a tour of 'all the capitals' of the independent states.[2]

His chief aim was to give liberation movements all over the continent the help and support they needed, on a range of fronts. His office established and coordinated the African Affairs Centre, a large complex of buildings near the Accra airport, to house refugees and students from the colonies of Africa. Alfred Hutchinson, the refugee from South Africa who unexpectedly turned up at the AAPC, was immediately taken under Padmore's wing and given shelter and support. Félix-Roland Moumié, the anticolonialist leader from Cameroon who attended the AAPC, proceeded to use Accra as a base from which to organise the guerrilla movement in his home country against French occupation.[3]

Education was a central focus of support for freedom fighters. 'My feeling', noted T Ras Makonnen, who ran the African Affairs Centre, 'was that we had to provide a training as well as a refuge. We would be fools to let the communists train such people'.[4] Robert Mugabe, who would be the first democratically elected premier of Zimbabwe in 1980, went to Ghana in 1958, where he studied and taught; there he met his future wife, the Ghanaian Sally Hayfron. Hastings Banda, who became the founding prime minister of independent Malawi in 1964, benefited from Ghana's support as well. He practised medicine in Kumasi in Ghana, until Nkrumah persuaded him in 1958 to return to Nyasaland to take part in its campaign for independence.[5]

One student from Nyasaland—Bright Nyondo—recalled in 1961 that it was because of Padmore's ability to connect the changes in Ghana with Nyasaland's own struggle that he went to Accra to study. 'I was much impressed', he said, 'by his simplicity, by his sincerity, by his sympathy with my efforts to educate myself and, above all, by his great interest in my country Nyasaland'. Nyondo completed his primary- and secondary-school education in Ghana.[6]

Padmore 'took care of Africa', observes Cameron Duodu, 'enabling Nkrumah to devote himself to the affairs of Ghana'.[7] Their dream of Pan-Africanism was achieving real success in some parts of the continent. On 1 May 1959, Nkrumah and President Sékou Touré of Guinea announced that their two countries had forged a union, with common citizenship and a shared national flag and anthem. The two leaders also extended an invitation to other African states to join them. President William Tubman of Liberia invited Touré and Nkrumah to a conference in mid-July at Sanniquellie, a small Liberian village. After intense negotiations over four days, they issued the Sanniquellie Declaration, which formulated six principles for the achievement of a community of independent African states.[8]

The CIA, monitoring developments in Ghana, took note of Padmore's central role. In June 1959, a report was sent to CIA headquarters after the inauguration by the Convention People's Party of a school for party members, to train them in political work. It noted that Padmore gave the first lecture, which concluded with the prediction that 'within the next fifty years the whole world will be toeing the socialist line'. The new school, noted the report, was located at the African Affairs Centre near the airport and took place every weekend.[9]

* * *

IN EARLY 1959, PADMORE predicted confidently that there would 'be a United States of Africa, in our own lifetime, in all Africa'.[10] But his own lifetime was about to be suddenly cut short. He was feeling increasingly unwell and went to London for medical treatment, where he was diagnosed with a liver ailment. On 23 September 1959, he died at age fifty-six.

Nkrumah was overwhelmed with grief. 'One day', he said sorrowfully in a tribute over Ghana's radio, 'the whole of Africa will surely be free and united and when the final tale is told, the significance of George Padmore's work will be revealed'.[11]

Pizer carried her husband's ashes from London to Accra, where she was met at the airport by a sombre group. Arrangements were made for the laying of his ashes to rest within a wall at Christiansborg Castle. Patrice Lumumba was one of the special guests invited to the memorial, along with Nnamdi Azikiwe of Nigeria.[12] But it was impossible for Lumumba to attend. Based in Stanleyville, where he was immersed in political work and speaking at public rallies, he was under heavy surveillance by the colonial administration.

St Clair Drake, an African American sociologist working at the University of Ghana, was invited to the ceremony. It was a powerful symbol of return, he wrote later, for those who had been cruelly taken away from Africa's shores.[13] It took place on a parapet in the castle 'with the slave pens down below us where they used to hold the slaves before they sent them on across the Gulf of Guinea'.

Nkrumah 'looked out where the surf was beating in against the walls of the slave castle', recorded Drake. Then the prime minister drew a link between the history of Padmore's family—his grandfather had been a slave in Trinidad—and the centuries of evil witnessed by the castle. Nkrumah spoke with great emotion: 'Who knows, but from this very spot, [Padmore's] ancestors were carried out across the ocean there, while the kinsmen stood weeping here as silent sentinel. We've brought his ashes home to rest'. Then Nkrumah 'slammed them up in the wall', wrote Drake, 'got his handkerchief and started crying'.[14]

The place in the wall containing Padmore's ashes was marked with a small sign: 'George Padmore, born in Trinidad, died in London, he loved Africa more than life, *requiescat in pace*'.

In Ghana and around the world, many people were celebrating the achievements of Padmore's life. But the CIA was deliberately smearing his reputation. In December 1959 the CIA-backed journal *Encounter* published a critical article on Padmore by Russell Warren Howe, the journalist with ties to the CIA who had attended the Ibadan Seminar in March. The article referred to a 'revolt of other African leaders' against Padmore at the All African People's Conference and portrayed him as contemptuous of Africans. The claims of this article have been interrogated by Carol Polsgrove, an expert on Padmore. 'Howe's CIA association and the identifiable errors of fact and interpretation in his article', she observes, 'undermine its credibility'.[15]

Criticism of Padmore had appeared in *Encounter* long before his death. A scathing review of his 1956 book *Pan-Africanism or Communism?* described it as 'infuriating'; it classified Padmore among those 'who have revolted against Communist conduct and cynicism, but can never free themselves from Communist ideology'. The review was written by Rita Hinden, who was carefully selected for the task. Michael Josselson, the CIA agent who had set up the Congress for Cultural Freedom, had told Irving Kristol, the coeditor of *Encounter*, that he should run a review 'by one of "our" people'; elsewhere, Josselson described Hinden as 'one of us'.[16]

Pizer remained in Accra until her death in 1964, when she suffered a heart attack. Like her husband, she died young, at fifty-eight.

* * *

PADMORE'S DEATH LEFT A gaping hole in the Pan-Africanist activities of Nkrumah's government. To fill it, substantial changes were made in the organisation of his office. They were intended, explained Nkrumah, 'to put the work begun by the late Mr. George Padmore on a permanent basis'.[17]

The long-winded name of the Office of the Adviser on African Affairs became the more succinct Bureau of African Affairs, known as the BAA. Aloysius K Barden, an ex-serviceman from World War II who had been Padmore's assistant, was made secretary of the bureau. Soon he became director.

Ambitious plans were made—and swiftly implemented—for the expansion of the structure created by Padmore to include an information office, a research department, a protocol division, a printing press and publications section, a library, a linguistic secretariat and a conference section.[18]

A new advisory body, named the African Affairs Committee, was established by Nkrumah as a way of fusing the bureau, the African Affairs Centre and the All African People's Conference secretariat. Weekly meetings were held, gathering together some of the most important figures of Ghanaian politics; Nkrumah, who was chair of the committee, attended every meeting. At the first meeting, on 19 October 1959, Kojo Botsio and Nathaniel Welbeck, who were close to Nkrumah and had been members of his government since independence in 1957, attended as representatives of the Convention People's Party.

At a meeting on 19 November 1959, the African Affairs Committee resolved to create an intelligence service expressly to deal with African affairs. The idea of such an intelligence service had been supported by Padmore before his death. It would supplement, and be separate from, the Foreign Research Service Bureau (FRSB), Ghana's intelligence service, which was attached to the Foreign Ministry. It was agreed that the bureau would appoint several agents as political attachés to each Ghanaian diplomatic mission in Africa; they would use their official cover to collect information and to provide support to liberation movements. The agents would be permitted to use the wireless transmitter in the mission, employing a separate code for communication with headquarters. The bureau would use the diplomatic bag for the transmission of messages and supplies, but under a separate seal.[19]

Barden undertook perilous journeys throughout Africa, under various guises, in order to communicate with the bureau's network of agents; he conveyed Nkrumah's directives, along with medical supplies and anticolonial literature to be given out to freedom fighters.[20]

The political activist Kofi Batsa, who was not yet thirty years of age, was the principal research officer at the bureau. He travelled widely and used his role as a journalist as cover to make contacts with freedom fighters: 'I travelled continuously. I travelled throughout West Africa. I went to Kenya, Tanganyika, Zanzibar, to the Congo and Angola, to all those countries where there was a liberation movement slowly developing and where the prospects of Independence were on the horizon. . . . I made, for example, twenty eight trips in 1960, the first year of this activity. . . . I worked closely with a whole generation of leaders'.[21]

Requests for help from outside Ghana were met with expressions of solidarity and, whenever possible, practical assistance. 'We in Ghana', replied Barden in July 1960 to a Mozambican freedom fighter in exile in Swaziland, 'sympathise with you in your struggle and your sufferings and are willing to give every possible assistance in our power'.[22]

Nathaniel Welbeck established a close collaboration between the bureau and the Convention People's Party. Tall, athletic and a keen stamp collector, Welbeck was a much-liked and flamboyant minister of state. In May 1960 he became chairman of the bureau. A letter from Welbeck to Nkrumah, headed 'Operation Independence, Transfer of Financial Aid to Freedom Fighters', reveals the confident vision of the bureau. The Ghana government, it said, 'had made its intention clear to give financial assistance to all Freedom Fighters in their attempt to free themselves from imperialist yoke. . . . Fortunately, we are in a better position than most, if not more than all the independent African States, who have also pledged themselves to that end. We are in a better position because we have the effective machinery to deal with the problem; our financial position is rosier'. The letter added, 'We have well laid flexible plans to suit in each turn, the ever changing manoeuvres of the imperialist tactics'.[23]

The bureau provided scholarships to fourteen Mozambicans to study party organisation in Ghana. It organised their travel carefully; special permits were arranged for their journey to Accra via Tanganyika, and their expenses were covered by the bureau. Their travel also depended on the help and protection of liberation movements en route.[24]

Simon Zukas, a Zambian freedom fighter, recalled many years later the valuable support provided by Ghana. In 1960, while Zukas was living in exile in the UK, Reuben Kamanga, one of the cofounders of the Anti Federation Action Committee, went to London from Cairo and obtained a donation of some £30,000 from the Ghanaian high commissioner.[25] 'He entrusted it to me for disbursement on instructions from himself or from Kenneth Kaunda', Zukas wrote. 'I kept the money on deposit at my bank and disbursed or remitted from it when instructed. I accounted fully to Reuben Kamanga when we met again in 1964'.[26]

By early 1960, freedom fighters were flocking to Ghana from South Africa, the Rhodesias, Tanganyika, Algeria, Cameroon, Angola and other European-ruled colonies. The Bureau of African Affairs provided them with visas, clothing, a small stipend, basic toiletries and literacy classes.

'Ghana was the base of anti-imperialist movements', stated Ndeh Ntumazah, the leader of One Kamerun, a branch in British Cameroon of the Union of the People of Cameroon, led by Félix-Roland Moumié. 'It was our haven, our springboard. It was from Ghana that members of the UPC took off for further studies or military training in China and Vietnam. We were very welcome and our travels financed. Nkrumah was always in the forefront of anti-colonialist movements'.[27]

Under Nkrumah's guidance, the bureau developed centres of education for the freedom fighters and exiles. In November 1960, the Kwame Nkrumah Youth Training School was opened for young people from Nyasaland and for 108 Gambians, of whom 50 returned to their country after completing a course in youth leadership.

In 1959, Nkrumah initiated plans for a college at Winneba, a port in the south of Ghana, to offer training in ideology, economics and administration to students from Ghana and elsewhere in Africa. At the dedication ceremony in 1960, Nkrumah said, 'I see before my mind's eye a great monolithic party growing up, united and strong, spreading its protective wings over the whole of Africa—from Algiers in the North to Capetown in the South, from Cape Guardafui in the East to Dakar in the West'.[28]

The transformation of the Winneba site into an academy for the training and education of future leaders of Africa was a profoundly meaningful act. Winneba had been built as a slaving port—Fort Winneba—in the late seventeenth century by the Royal African Company, an English trading company under royal patronage. Between 1662 and 1731, the RAC transported approximately 212,000 slaves, of whom 44,000 died en route. Many were branded with the letters 'DY' for the company's governor, the Duke of York; others were branded with the company's initials, RAC, on their chests. The company's profits substantially increased the wealth and financial power of those who controlled the city of London.[29]

* * *

THE BUREAU OF AFRICAN Affairs maintained one of the largest presses in Africa, publishing newspapers and magazines to spread Nkrumah's Pan-Africanist views across the continent. Best known was *Voice of Africa*, which was published every Friday, *The Spark* (and its French version, *L'Étincelle*), *The African Chronicler, Freedom Fighter* and *The Information Bulletin on African Affairs*.[30] Batsa was editor of both *Voice of Africa* and *The Spark*.

The message of *Voice of Africa* was clear: 'In Unity Lies our Salvation'. It encouraged its readers to learn from mistakes and to build a future of freedom:

> Ours is the Voice of Africa: the voice of the African peoples—terrorised, enslaved, deceived and exploited. Ours is the voice of peace and freedom.
>
> We bring the dawn of a new era in the world—the dawn of the new Africa.
>
> Long Live Freedom Fighters of Africa.
>
> Long Live the African Revolution.
>
> Long Live a Union Government of Africa.

The journal published a wide range of articles, such as 'Imperialist Weakening' and 'Dangers of NATO War Bases in Africa'.

'Above all, read; read', it instructed earnestly. 'Read everything; something of everything. . . . It will enable you to develop a critical acumen . . . to sharpen your sword for the rapidly approaching final show-down with the foreign oppression'. This focus on reading very much represented the convictions of Nkrumah, himself a voracious reader. Genoveva Marais recorded Nkrumah's efforts to encourage reading among his close associates:

> 'You don't read enough', he would declare, to me or to his other close associates. He would turn to the shelves behind him. These were full of books and he would carefully study the titles. Then he would take one from a shelf. The person before him might be a Minister or a civil servant (or it might be me!).
>
> 'Let me have a summary of this book', he would say. 'I have to prepare a paper on the subject'.
>
> This might or might not have been true; but it forced the recipient not only to read but to thoroughly study and absorb the subject.[31]

Nkrumah was certainly bookish, but he was by no means an intellectual snob. He and the staff of the BAA were eager to communicate with as many people as possible throughout Africa, but they were aware that most of them had never been given the opportunity to learn to read. It was therefore decided to include cartoons in the publications, which visualised the important message of unity.

Batsa was proud of the bureau's achievement in delivering *Voice of Africa* and *The Spark* all over the continent.[32] 'We were banned in many countries still under colonial rule', he wrote, 'but we managed to reach most countries by one means or another. . . . No frontier was safe!'[33] The British-ruled Federation of Rhodesia and Nyasaland banned *Voice of Africa* in July 1960, alleging it was seditious.[34] Alphonse Ebassa, a freedom fighter in Sierra Leone, requested more copies; propaganda, he told the bureau, was proving to be more powerful than guns.[35]

Voice of Africa carried information about another means of information and propaganda: the transmission times and wavelengths of Radio Ghana. Each transmission would start with the sound of drums and station identification: 'This is the Voice of Africa coming to you from Radio Ghana, Accra'.[36] For three hours a day, explained Nkrumah in a speech to mark the opening of the Ghana External Broadcasting Service, programmes were broadcast from Accra in Arabic, English, French, Hausa, Portuguese and Kiswahili. Twenty-one news bulletins were broadcast daily, as well as news talks and newsreels, to Africa and throughout the world.

'The voice of this service will not necessarily be the Voice of Ghana', declared Nkrumah firmly. 'Indeed, it will be the voice of Africa'.[37] The purpose of the service was to provide accurate accounts of events that were not available from foreign-controlled and foreign-dominated radio stations. In Ghana, these foreign radio stations included Voice of America, which was broadcast from Liberia, and the BBC.[38]

Voice of America was overseen by the US Information Agency, known as USIA, which coordinated at that time with the CIA. According to Christopher Simpson, in *Science of Coercion*, 'USIA and CIA work was first coordinated through "country plans" monitored by area specialists at President Truman's secretive Psychological Strategy Board (established in 1951) and, later, at the National Security Council under President Eisenhower'.[39]

The news items produced in the Radio Ghana newsroom were given to the various language sections to translate and broadcast. The actual delivery was entrusted to broadcasters recruited from the language areas. Cameron Duodu, who was chief writer in the newsroom at one stage of his career, recalls that these broadcasters would have been recommended—or at least approved—by political parties whose Pan-African sympathies were known to the Bureau of African Affairs.

Duodu's contributions were initially read in English by Sam Morris, a West Indian broadcaster who worked at Nkrumah's publicity secretariat, with a translation in French by the prime minister's French interpreter. Later, Duodu read his own commentaries.

'I enjoyed doing my stint as a pioneer African affairs commentator', he reflected many years later, 'because I chose the subjects myself and no-one told me how to treat them'. He appreciated this opportunity to keep in touch with developments throughout Africa and to tell people about them. 'I considered it a duty', he explains, 'to pass on my knowledge'.[40]

* * *

THE ACTIVITIES OF GHANA's Bureau of African Affairs were carefully monitored in Washington. The bureau was heavily criticised in a report titled *Ghanaian Subversion in Africa*, which was prepared by the State Department with assistance from a 'knowledgeable CIA representative'.

If Nkrumah had been shown the report, he would have been delighted by its claims. 'Ghana's influence, or interference', it judged, 'is felt in all sections of the continent'. The core of the widespread subversion activities, it stated, was Ghana's Bureau of African Affairs: 'Under the direct supervision of Nkrumah it masterminds the activities of more than 100 agents throughout Africa'. Other subversion activities included the African Affairs Center, housing political exiles. 'Word-of-mouth underground is another technique used to advantage', observed the report with disapproval. 'Perhaps the most important single tool in the subversion movement', it added, were the institutions providing education.[41]

13

American CIA Agent and Kenyan CIA Asset

A S 30 JUNE 1960—THE DATE set for the Congo's independence from Belgium—grew ever closer, the Directorate of Plans at the CIA was carefully penetrating the region. One of the agents it used in its Congo operations was Howard Imbrey, a fortyish American from New York City who was a veteran of the wartime intelligence agency, the OSS.[1] He joined the agency in 1948 and five years later became the Communist Party officer for what was then the Near Eastern/African Division; the position required him to develop agents locally to report on the spread of communism within their borders.

For his Congo-related work, Imbrey operated under nonofficial cover (NOC). This was a new development for Imbrey; on his earlier assignments in India, Sri Lanka and Ethiopia, he had been attached to the US embassy. Speaking about these posts, he noted sardonically that his diplomatic cover did little to conceal his CIA role, since the State Department officials 'did not want us confused with the Foreign Service'. Instead of designating them with the rank of the standard FSO (Foreign Service Officer), he recalled, 'we were always registered as FSR [Foreign Service Reserve Officer], where everybody looked down the list and spotted us right away'.[2]

The CIA had 'a very big operation' in Addis Ababa, the Ethiopian capital, where Imbrey worked from 1956 to 1958. 'As a matter of fact', he recalled years later, 'we had bugs on the Soviets, Czechs, Egyptians and I think a Bulgarian came in'. At the US embassy, he added, 'there was a wing which was known by the locals as the CIA wing. In the basement we had many tape recorders and a number of people spent the entire day translating from the various take on these things. We had a house rather far out in which the tape recorders were running night and day causing a great deal of problems for us because we have to explain the high bill for electricity, which we did by getting somebody in the telephone company to ignore it'.[3]

But serious problems were caused by the heat generated by the running of the equipment, so they repeatedly had to buy fans, which often didn't work. In addition, said Imbrey:

We had a central place where the telephone lines were connected to our apparatus. This was about four feet underground and we built in the house of a former agent, we built a garage around it to make it appear as if it were a garage and then we buried this stuff.

Well, about every four or five months they would decide to extend the telephone lines which would mean we'd have to go there, unbury the lines, put them near the surface so that they would find them, but they wouldn't find our bugs and to do that you have to get through Ethiopian mud which sticks like a [word indistinct]. It was a six hour job getting this stuff to the surface and then getting it back in until we all hated it.

'It was a successful operation', Imbrey reflected with his usual dry humour, 'except that the people never said anything much over the phone'.[4]

As an NOC in the Congo, Imbrey was in far more danger than he had been in his previous postings: he was required to deny any connection with the US government. Should he be exposed as a CIA agent, he would be unable to expect diplomatic immunity or any kind of protection. In this way, the government had recourse to plausible deniability.

Larry Devlin was operating under official cover in the Congo, but he had operated as an NOC earlier in his CIA career. For his first post, he worked under the cover of writer for Fodor travel

guides in Europe—a front for agents abroad that was widely employed by the CIA in this period (and which was exposed in the
1970s, during the Watergate scandal).[5]

Imbrey maintained absolute secrecy for most of his life about
his CIA career. When the Church Committee investigated the role
of the agency in the Congo in the mid-1970s, interviewing a range
of CIA personnel, Imbrey was completely invisible. But in 2001—
at age eighty—Imbrey suddenly abandoned his commitment to
secrecy. In February of that year, he gave a candid interview in his
home to a high school senior. Then, four months later, he gave a
long interview to the oral historian Charles Stuart Kennedy under
the auspices of the Foreign Affairs Oral History Project, which is
organised by the Association for Diplomatic Studies and Training (ADST). The project's interviews provide a valuable source of
information about former participants in US foreign affairs since
World War II. Imbrey died the year after his interview with Kennedy; his obituary in the *Washington Post* acknowledged his role at
the CIA.

When Devlin published his memoir, *Chief of Station, Congo*, in
2007, he made no mention of Howard Imbrey. However, he included Imbrey's wife in his short list of acknowledgements: 'Ina
Imbrey for locating phone numbers and arranging contacts'.[6]

It is unclear why Imbrey chose to reveal his CIA career in his
eighth decade, but he appears to have had a strong and independent mind. A colleague in the diplomatic service described him as
'amusing, mischievous, a bit vicious in fact, not high-minded'. He
was extremely clever and gifted at languages: fluent in French, Ital-
ian, Urdu and Hindi, and with a working knowledge of Singhalese,
Sanskrit, Portuguese, Latin and Greek.[7]

* * *

IN THE INTERVIEWS HE gave in 2001, Imbrey explained the context
in which he had started work in the Congo: 'Africa was emerging.
As of '58 . . . we saw this all coming, there was independence for all
of the African regions and we knew we had to get in there before
the Soviets'. This was the reason for his shift to unofficial cover: 'So,
they told us to go outside the agency, develop a business, and work

at the United Nations in getting sources there and see what we could do'.

Imbrey set up a public relations office in New York, with the name Overseas Regional Surveys Associates (ORSA)—one of those titles that 'are as meaningless as possible' in the pursuit of the spy game, as put by a cultural historian writing about the CIA in the Cold War.[8] Imbrey's junior partner in the project was Thomas L Goodman, formerly an explorer in Southeast Asia for a US museum.

The headquarters of ORSA was located at 333 East 46th Street, a newly built twenty-storey high-rise. It was ideally placed for the purpose of their covert work: the building was only a couple of blocks from the United Nations, which facilitated easy access to delegates and events. There were opportunities for casual meetings with UN delegates and staff, since the building provided office accommodation for some employees of permanent missions to the UN.[9] It also housed the offices of some Africa-related organisations, such as the African Research Foundation, which received CIA funding and had activities in Nairobi.[10] The ORSA office building was situated next door to the African-American Institute, another CIA front, which similarly benefited from proximity to the UN.

To establish their cover of working in Africa for ORSA, Imbrey and Goodman initiated overt projects that were clearly associated with the firm. These were featured in *Fortune* magazine, which published an article on their efforts to support small enterprises in various African territories, matching the investments of locals with an idea for a business. In Ibadan, they facilitated the manufacturing business of rear-end carriers for bicycles, and in the Congo, they worked with a Congolese man to develop a plan for processing pharmaceuticals in Leopoldville. Other projects included the making of wax candles. The placement of the story in *Fortune* may have been arranged by the CIA; it was then republished in *Negro Digest*.[11]

Imbrey served as a contact in the US for CIA assets—that is, sources of intelligence who provided information but were not agency personnel—who had come from Africa. One such asset was Washington Aggrey Jalang'o Okumu, a Kenyan who was brought to the US in 1958 to study at Iowa Wesleyan University on the recommendation of Tom Mboya. He was then in his early twenties, fifteen years younger than Imbrey. He was opposed to European colonisation in Africa and was profoundly influenced by the ideals of Pan-Africanism and the vision of Nkrumah.[12] In nearly thirteen hours of interviews in 2016 with the American historian Nancy J Jacobs, Okumu gave an account of his life and his involvement with the CIA. With Okumu's permission, Jacobs published a detailed account and analysis of the interviews.

Okumu told Jacobs that he was the CIA's 'blue-eyed boy'.[13] His connection with the agency, he explained, had been initiated by Imbrey and Goodman. 'They telephoned me and said they were looking for Kenyan or African students who are politically conscious. And know about Africa and African leaders. And possibly had relationships with them'. When pressed by Jacobs, he could not say much more about them. 'What! They didn't call and say, "Here we are . . . CIA". . . . They may call, and even at that time you don't know who they are. I don't think Howard [Imbrey] or Tom [Goodman] even now if they call me would think that I know who they are. They still would want to believe that I didn't know who they are. After forty years. . . . Do you think they would tell you?'[14]

The racism Okumu encountered in the US horrified him. 'In Iowa', he told Jacobs, 'I knew I could not go to bed because I was afraid I would be lynched. I knew I was going to die!'

He eventually fled Iowa to attend Harvard University, where he enrolled in the 1959 International Student Relations Seminar (ISRS), a summer programme.[15] According to Karen M Paget in *Patriotic Betrayal*, the ISRS was established as a recruiting vehicle by the CIA in 1953; it was first directed by CIA employee Ted Harris, who had been the National Student Association's president in the late 1940s and went on to become AMSAC's associate director.[16]

Harvard University, which has been described as having a 'cozy relationship with the CIA' over the years,[17] was where Larry Devlin, a student in international relations, was recruited to the agency. He didn't finish his degree but went directly into the Office of Policy Coordination (OPC), the covert operation wing of the CIA at that time.[18]

The ISRS, which Okumu attended in 1959, gave the CIA time to conduct background security checks, explains Paget.[19] Okumu evidently met their criteria, regardless of his weak grades from Iowa; it was the sponsorship of the CIA, he told Jacobs, which then got him into undergraduate studies at Harvard. He received some funding from the CIA front the African-American Institute.[20]

Okumu explained to Jacobs the nature of his ambitions and great hopes at that time: 'I had a burning desire to get education and come back as a leader of my country'. But this was not to be. When he returned to Kenya, he worked for a railway parastatal and then for the government, but was imprisoned in 1968 for alleged corruption. 'My life was mixed up', he said, 'in the relationship between Tom Mboya and Oginga Odinga and that mix-up ruined my life forever. I was never able later to pursue a career and stick to it without being hit up by the powerful friends or enemies of either side'.

The Kenyan government may have had another reason to turn sour on Okumu, suggests Jacobs: that he had continued his connection with the CIA while working for the railway parastatal.

After his release from prison, Okumu worked as a commercial attaché in the US embassy in Nairobi for half a year. He left Kenya in 1971 to work for the UN Industrial Development Organisation in Vienna, where he stayed for fifteen years. While he worked for UNIDO, he became involved in secret negotiations between B J Vorster, the prime minister of apartheid South Africa, and Julius Nyerere, the president of Tanzania, in the mid 1970s. This involved secret visits to Pretoria, arranged by the South African Bureau of State Security (BOSS), an organisation that sought to crush resistance to white minority rule with brutality and murder. It is unclear how Okumu became entangled in these developments and to what extent the CIA may have played a role. Jacobs illustrates her article with a photograph from August 1976, showing Okumu with

Vorster, with another South African government official and with Hendrik van den Bergh, the head of BOSS. Another photograph shows Okumu in 1977 sitting in the company of Ian Smith, the prime minister of the illegal and deeply racist government of Rhodesia, now Zimbabwe.

Okumu moved into the public arena—and the news—in 1994, as the mediator who brought the Inkatha Freedom Party of Mangosuthu Buthelezi, the Zulu leader, into South Africa's first democratic election. The CIA may have been operating in the shadows of these negotiations: in June 1991, Buthelezi had announced to journalists that he had met with 'the head of the Central Intelligence Agency' in Washington.[21]

Okumu received widespread acclaim for his role as mediator. Some doubts have been cast on his importance, on the grounds that the forces leading Buthelezi into the election were much bigger; it has been suggested that Okumu's intervention was limited to that of a face-saving device for the IFP leader.[22] If so, it would nonetheless have made a valuable contribution to the outcome.

In the judgement of Jacobs, Okumu was an unreliable witness; she describes him as 'an opportunistic and shadowy go-between for hire by white American, South African, and British conservative Christians'.[23] However, much of the information he gave about his dealings with the CIA appears to be accurate; it is backed up by his references to Howard Imbrey and Thomas Goodman.

* * *

HAVING SET UP ORSA, Howard Imbrey spent most of his time at the UN, 'visiting Africans and encouraging them'. But soon, 'the whole thing changed because they sent me out' to Leopoldville—'I guess it was in April and May of 1960'—to help with the CIA station. This work involved 'developing sources for the oncoming independence of the Congo and I did all sorts of jobs along with the chief of station and a couple of other guys'. He left the Congo 'shortly after independence' on 30 June.

The objectives of the agency in preindependent Congo were set out clearly in a CIA paper titled 'CIA Position in Belgian Congo Re Political Action Operations'. The paper was not dated, but its provenance reveals it was produced in 1960 (evidently in the period leading up to the end of June). Using the cryptonym KUBARK to refer to the agency, it noted, 'The role of KUBARK in the Belgian Congo during the period prior to 30 June 1960 should be to ensure that U.S. aims for the area, both the Congo and the other parts of the continent whose relationship with the Congo will affect our aims, can be implemented'. These aims were made explicit: the election of a government oriented to the West and friendly to the US, and the identification, isolation and exclusion of groups that were supported by, or oriented towards, the Soviet bloc.[24]

In order to assist the election of a government oriented to the West, Imbrey was 'passing money most of the time' to people in the Congo. 'Yes', he told Charles Stuart Kennedy. 'I was in hotels and dealing with the people the best we could and passing out money'. One of 'my people', he added, was 'Al Canharogey, who was to play a larger part with the Baluba element'. Here, the transcriber of the interview appears to have misunderstood Imbrey's pronunciation of the name of Albert Kalonji, who was the leader of MNC-K. Heavily influenced by the CIA, Kalonji became an increasingly bitter enemy of Lumumba.

Imbrey was also passing out money and talking with 'Cyrille Adoula who became the prime minister'. Other recipients were Victor Nendaka, Joseph Ileo and Justin Bomboko.

It is unclear to what extent Imbrey was in contact with Joseph-Désiré Mobutu. When asked, 'How about Mobutu? Was he a figure while you were there?' Imbrey replied, 'No. That was about '62 or '63'. Given that Mobutu was one of the politicians benefiting from CIA support throughout this period, it is possible that Imbrey did not want to admit that he had cultivated him. It is evident from his interview with Kennedy that he had a very low opinion of Mobutu, making a reference to 'Mobutu, Mugabe, all the thieves'. He also had a low opinion of Kasavubu: 'never a terribly important character, just wishy, washy'.

It is also unclear whether or not Imbrey passed funds to Lumumba. Right up to the last fortnight before independence, John D Tomlinson, the US consul general in Leopoldville, took the view that Lumumba should be cultivated. In a telegram to the State Department, Tomlinson argued that there would be 'widespread chaos if [a] government of national unity, including Lumumba, cannot be formed'.

Lumumba, he said, should be included in American plans for the new Congolese government: 'Untrustworthy and unreliable as Lumumba is, and despite the fear of him by other leaders, we see no better alternative on the horizon than a government built around him, preferably a government embracing the other major parties, with an appropriate cut in the pie'. He argued, 'If the wherewithal is immediately provided in the form of substantial financial aid by the Belgians and ourselves together with our ICA program'—the International Cooperation Administration (the predecessor until 1961 of the Agency for International Development)—'there is as good a chance as any [of] keeping such a government reasonably oriented toward the West'.[25]

Imbrey described the process of handing out funds to promising individuals: 'So, we're dealing with all of these people and passing out a lot of pittances. It wasn't a lot of money. We were passing out money to enable them to form their political cadres and get around the country and talk'. The process required a great deal of travel. But this was not difficult, said Imbrey, 'because the Belgians had made an infrastructure that was unbelievable between the river traffic and the road traffic of at least 50,000 miles of paved roads'.

Another advantage appreciated by Imbrey was his close friendship with Clare Hayes Timberlake, the American diplomat who arrived after the Congo's independence to take over from Tomlinson. His role was that of US ambassador; the embassy had replaced the consulate general after independence, as the Congo was now self-governing.

Timberlake was appointed on 5 July and presented his credentials on 25 July. His deputy chief of mission was Robinson 'Rob' McIlvaine, who had arrived in Leopoldville on 25 June, just days before independence.[26] 'We got tons of people at that point', said Andrew Steigman, a member of the diplomatic staff. 'We got two political officers. We got Army, Navy and Air Force attachés. We got additional CIA personnel. We got additional administrative help. The staff suddenly tripled'.[27]

Like Imbrey, Timberlake was a gifted linguist: he could speak Arabic, French, German, Italian, Portuguese and Spanish. He had joined the Foreign Service in 1930, and his service included a stint in Spain during the Civil War, when he was stationed at the US Consulate in the Nationalist port of Vigo. Immediately after the end of World War II, he served as assistant chief—and then chief—of the Division of African Affairs in the State Department. In 1948 Timberlake was sent as US consul to Bombay, where he met Imbrey; Timberlake was the best man at Imbrey's wedding, who later described them as 'old, old friends'.[28]

* * *

IN HIS INTERVIEW WITH the high school senior, Imbrey explained carefully the vital significance of the Congo to the US: 'We didn't want the Russians to get all of the Uranium. They had Uranium of their own, but we certainly didn't want them to control any of the ores that were coming out of Congo. We did our best to prevent them. . . . During the Cold War we tried to prevent the Soviets from getting into a position of power anywhere on the earth'.

The uranium, he added, made the Congo important in a way that was simply not applicable to other African countries: 'the other African countries didn't have anything. They're bankrupt, most of them are bankrupt. Let's see, Ivory Coast had a logging industry, Nigeria had no oil at that time, and there was no question of Nigeria as having any importance at all'.

'Our primary task', he said, 'was to keep out the Soviets'.

Imbrey insisted that the CIA did not act independently of the government, but in partnership with it. The State Department, he said, was responsible for policy: 'When that policy calls for some sort of an operation such as the undermining of an individual, the undermining of a government, or any kind of an action of that sort, the State Department makes that decision that this has to be done. It turns to CIA and says, how are you going to do it for us?' In response, the CIA presented a number of programmes to tackle the State Department's problem. 'Then, the many organs of government meet at the National Security Council, and decide that this CIA programme is appropriate in accordance with the State Department's needs'. He continued, 'At that point, the President issues a finding saying that this is in the interest of the United States; and at that point, only, does the money come for CIA to operate. So CIA does not have any independent mode. The money controls them'.[29]

* * *

ANOTHER CIA FRONT IN which Imbrey was involved was Worldwide Information Services, a commercial news network set up in 1958 that relied on newspaper stringers; it also provided services in commercial intelligence and market research. Its headquarters were at 660 First Avenue, in New York; in addition, there was a European base at 17 rue Vernet in Paris and a Japanese base in Tokyo. Like Overseas Regional Surveys Associates, it provided an ideal cover for CIA agents. In 1963, Imbrey became bureau chief of Worldwide Information Services in Paris.[30]

Worldwide Information Services provided an excellent means of making contact with important individuals from Africa. 'I was handling all the many, many African agents', recalled Imbrey. 'Now, try to meet an African on the streets; everybody in Africa, white and black, played their own role. But, if a black happens to be passing through Paris one can get at him in a cafe, a movie, wherever you like and nobody thinks anything of it'. Imbrey was handling about ten to fourteen agents regularly from various parts of Africa. If anybody had a problem seeing an agent, they sent them to Paris and Imbrey would debrief them: 'That was my role'. After Paris, he moved to Belgium and then to Rome.[31]

Both Imbrey and Washington Okumu gave interviews close to the ends of their lives, revealing the sharp differences in their experiences of working for the CIA. Imbrey was a career CIA professional, with a salary, health care and a pension. He appears to have enjoyed his work; he was confident and proud of what he had achieved. Okumu's work for the CIA made him feel intensely vulnerable. It was less predictable than Imbrey's, much less under his own control and far more dangerous. In his interviews with Jacobs, he referred repeatedly to a fear of assassination.[32]

Okumu never lost his Pan-African ideals, which underpin his first book, *Lumumba's Congo: Roots of Conflict* (1962). The foreword was written by the Harvard professor of Politics and International Relations Rupert Emerson, who described Okumu as an 'angry young African', too nationalist to be capable of an impartial critique of Lumumba or of decolonisation.[33]

Okumu was at pains to emphasise that Lumumba was the Congo's 'first democratically elected prime minister'.[34] Imbrey, however, despised Lumumba. He believed that Lumumba had 'ties' with communists, although he was not a communist in terms of his ideology. 'Communism', said Imbrey, 'doesn't mean terribly much in most of Africa. The political development of most of the people didn't. . . . There were already Communists [laughs] at the village level. That's how they lived'.[35]

In 2002, Okumu published *The African Renaissance*, a thick and detailed book that sets out an optimistic vision of Africa's future and advocates the development of science and technology; it refers to his association with the African Renaissance Institute, based in Botswana. The book describes Africa as the cradle of mankind, 'yet the poorest continent', which suffered the horror of the Atlantic slave trade. It sets out in detail the vision and achievement of the All African People's Conference in Accra in 1958 and of Nkrumah: 'Like Nelson Mandela, he is perhaps one of Africa's most important leaders. . . . Nkrumah had a keen perception of the common destiny of the peoples of the Third World. Though he was a Pan-Africanist his vision was internationalist. In many respects it was his understanding of the international character of the class struggle that turned him into such a forceful advocate of Pan-Africanism'. Nkrumah's 'message of liberation, though drawn from the experience of Africa', insists Okumu, 'is profoundly universal; hence, his inspiration of a Black Renaissance in terms of African nationalism'.[36]

Such a position was in sharp contrast with that of Okumu's handler, Howard Imbrey. For Imbrey, Pan-Africanism and non-alignment were more or less the same thing as communism. Speaking about the United Nations and V K Krishna Menon, who was

India's ambassador to the UN in 1952–1962 and close to Nehru, Imbrey declared, 'We really hated them'. Then he added sourly that Menon 'was under the anti-colonist credentials. So, I'm sure he and Kwame Nkrumah got on very well'.[37]

Okumu died in many ways a disappointed man. 'Not only do I cherish peace', he said, 'I toyed with the idea of building a Peace Institute. It was not to be, but I did not let go of the dream'.[38] When he became involved with the CIA in his early twenties, he believed doing so would enable him to follow his dream. But the CIA had different ideas. His involvement came at a huge cost for Okumu, who was at the mercy of the agency's demands. When asked by Jacobs how long his service to the agency had lasted, he initially said from 1960 to 1988. But then he added: 'It goes on. They can always come back. Maybe through the back door for rent without you knowing. They don't tell you I am sending so and so. An American friend may call you and say they want to talk to you'.

The CIA was always nearby. 'When you are CIA', Okumu told Jacobs, 'you are CIA, you don't stop. That is the time when you are most useful to them, so they will be at your tail every five minutes. You can assume they were under my bed. The Americans were everywhere'.[39]

PART V

'INDÉPENDANCE CHA CHA'

14

'The Courageous Have Won'

A T AROUND THE SAME TIME that Howard Imbrey arrived in the Belgian Congo, Joseph Kabasele and African Jazz arrived home from Europe. With them came a Belgian jazz drummer, Charles Hénault, who had been recruited to the group. He was astonished by the tremendous enthusiasm of the band's homecoming welcome. They crossed the river from Brazzaville, where their flight from Paris had landed, to Leopoldville. Then, to Hénault's astonishment, he saw that 'cars were waiting for us. And we rode around all of [Leopoldville], oh la la! The modern city and the old city. People were screaming, they threw flowers at us. It was crazy. It was crazy. It was almost like a president's motorcade. It was incredible. And the horns, and the noise. The noise as though there were some big wedding going on'.[1]

Kabasele's song 'Indépendance Cha Cha', which he had composed in Brussels to celebrate the agreement struck at the Round Table, 'seemed to flow in overlapping waves from every record player and sound system in the cité'.[2]

Kabasele, who supported Lumumba, took him around town in his big white convertible. But, like other Congolese musicians, he chose not to take sides in the lyrics of his songs. Instead, they celebrated the imminence of independence and urged unity.[3]

In the weeks leading up to the elections, the various political parties presented to the public their candidates for the new Chamber of Deputies. MNC-L was one of the few parties not to identify with any one ethnic group but to campaign on a platform of national unity; the Parti Solidaire Africain (PSA), led by Antoine

Gizenga, took the same approach. But most of the political parties were rooted in local interests, such as Kasavubu's Abako.

Nkrumah urged Lumumba to prioritise the need for unity. He believed that women could play an important role in this process by bringing people together. He therefore asked Madame Andrée Blouin, a political activist and feminist from Congo Brazzaville, to go to the Belgian Congo, to 'make a call to Africa's women—to help bring the men together, setting aside the old quarrels between peoples'.[4]

Blouin, the daughter of a very young Banziri woman and a French businessman, had been placed as a child in the 1920s in a Roman Catholic orphanage in Brazzaville. She had been mistreated by the nuns, who viewed her interracial origin as a sin. As an adult, she found it a struggle to define herself. 'I am not white, I am not black', she said finally, 'I am African'.[5]

After the independence of Guinea in 1958, she went to live there, trying to support the new nation as it dealt with the hardships created by France's angry departure. There she met Kwame Nkrumah through Sékou Touré, Guinea's president. Blouin and Nkrumah swiftly developed a deep admiration for each other. Through her friendships with Nkrumah and Touré, Blouin was introduced in Conakry to Antoine Gizenga, who had just returned to Africa from a visit to Moscow, Berlin, Bonn and Paris.[6]

Gizenga had been ordained as a Catholic priest in 1947 and had run a parish in his home region of Kwilu, but then left the priesthood. A man of few words, he had none of Lumumba's charisma and popular appeal, but was respected by many Congolese for his keen sense of justice and his honesty. He habitually wore dark glasses, which gave him a sinister appearance to those who had reason to dislike him—including Howard Imbrey. 'Gizenga', said Imbrey dismissively, 'was early on, a . . . what would you call it, a puppet of the Soviets. They found him, they found that he had a following. He had a following in the north-east of Congo among his own tribespeople. I forget what tribe they were. But at any rate, he was able to raise an army of his own. He was immediately somebody we didn't like'.[7]

As someone who was quiet and formal in his manner, as well as firm and reliable—'a man of iron'—Gizenga made a favourable impression on Andrée Blouin. And she, in turn, made a favourable impression on him. In his 2011 memoir, *Ma Vie et Mes Luttes*— 'My Life and My Struggles'—Gizenga recalled being struck that this 'mother of three children, the eldest of whom was already 20 and the youngest 4, still had an ardent desire to serve the African cause alongside progressive leaders'.[8] By then nearly forty, Blouin was older than both Gizenga and Lumumba, who were in their mid-thirties.

Like Nkrumah, Gizenga was keen for Madame Blouin to go to the Congo, and while he was still in Conakry he arranged to meet her. He wanted to obtain her husband's permission: 'Everything depends on your husband, who must give his consent to your departure'. But she brushed this aside. 'Everything', she replied in exhilaration at the prospect of joining the struggle in the Congo, 'depends on me, who wishes to go and serve the country of my ancestors. My husband *must* agree'. She arrived in Leopoldville in April.[9]

Blouin travelled widely through the Congo with Gizenga and other members of the PSA.[10] By the end of May 1960, she had enrolled forty-five thousand female members in the Feminine Movement for African Solidarity in the Kwango-Kwilu area. In her memoir, *My Country, Africa*, she described the resentment she suffered from the colonial administration, who 'did all they could to harass our caravan. They banned our meetings. They cut off our ferry boats. Sometimes we had to wait two days in the heart of the bush, without food'.[11]

One Congolese woman described her astonishment at watching Blouin address a meeting. She saw people dancing, while Blouin stood, haranguing the crowd—'Nobody has ever seen a woman like her, giving out orders to thousands of men'.[12] She thought Blouin was a white woman, but dressed in village clothes and speaking Kikongo—a language Blouin had learned while growing up in the orphanage in Brazzaville.

Herbert Weiss, who participated in the Wilson Center conference on the Congo in 2004, arrived in the Congo in December 1959 as a young MIT field researcher in order to study the independence struggle. In the course of his research, he travelled through the territory of the Parti Solidaire Africain at the end of April, observing how the party mobilised grassroots support and handled its election campaign.[13] He found Blouin fascinating. 'Who is this woman?' he remembered thinking. 'She's wearing very fine perfumes. She has an air of Paris about her'.[14] They became lifelong friends.[15]

After Lumumba returned to the Congo from Brussels in early 1960 to serve as one of the six commissionaires in the lead-up to independence, Gizenga took Blouin to meet him. According to her memoir, Blouin noticed that he constantly moved his 'fine, long, nervous hands' and was at pains to make her feel welcome and comfortable: 'Patrice was his characteristically natural self at our meeting with him. It was he who came to the door of his residence to receive us. Laughing, his white teeth shining, he shook our hands warmly. He wore black trousers and a white shirt. With a feline step he led us into his receiving room'. Blouin 'felt a great deal of joy in his easy manner'.[16]

The US Consulate General in Leopoldville were deeply suspicious of Blouin—and mistakenly assumed she was from Guinea. A telegram to Washington noted, 'Czech consul Virius and Guinean Councillor to PSA, Mme Blouin, and other Communist or leftist influences are at work, though immediate aims not clear'.[17]

The Leopoldville secret police were also suspicious. One evening, in the company of Blouin and Gizenga, Lumumba produced a report from the police that referred to Blouin as 'a *métisse* woman from Guinea who was raised in Brazzaville. She is a courtesan. After having been the mistress of Sékou Touré she became in turn that of N'Krumah, Tubman, Modibo Keita [the president of Mali] and other well-known African leaders. Today Gizenga is the favoured one. This woman must not remain in the Congo'.

'Congratulations!' remarked Lumumba to Blouin as he read the report aloud. 'You're a success. The Belgian Secret Service is very concerned about you'. Then he read out more of the report: 'Madame Blouin has a gift for speaking. Already she is in demand in several provinces to organise new groups of her feminine movement. She is all the more dangerous because she scorns money and sex. She is sincere and tireless. A fanatic'.

The logic of this analysis, commented Gizenga dryly, was 'astonishing'.[18] To the Belgian secret police she was both a whore and a saint; they had no idea how to thwart her.

* * *

BELGIUM WANTED THE GOVERNMENT of the Congo after independence to be responsive to Belgian interests. It threw a lot of money at the Parti National du Progrès (PNP), which was a coalition of more than twenty local parties from around the country. In Katanga, commercial and mining interests—especially Union Minière—heavily subsidised and dominated CONAKAT, which had been created in November 1958 and was led by Moise Tshombe. Its key policy was the secession of the province from the rest of the Congo, which would enable foreign businesses to maintain their investments. Those businesses had much to lose: between 1950 and 1959, Union Minière's net profits were 31 billion Belgian francs, a sum that is equivalent to over US\$5.5 billion in late 2020.[19]

A British diplomat was told by a well-informed Belgian that Union Minière had 'taken up the position that under no circumstances could they envisage the Katanga being governed by a central native body. (They might accept a provincial puppet government.)'[20] There was evidence that the Belgian government shared this position. In February 1960 a British official in Elisabethville reported to the consul general in Leopoldville that 'the secession of the Katanga will . . . be inevitable and easy. Indeed, some go as far as to say that this is just the result the Belgian Government hope from a deliberate, and Machiavellian, policy'.[21]

* * *

THE ELECTION TOOK PLACE between 11 and 22 May. For the first time in the history of the colony, all adult male citizens twenty-one and over were enrolled to vote, regardless of their colour. Women were not given the vote. In Belgium, women had voted for the first time in parliamentary elections in 1949; it was one of the last western European countries to give women the right to vote. But in 1960, this right was kept from Congolese women.

There was a massive turnout: nearly 82 percent. MNC-Lumumba emerged as the strongest party, gaining 33 of the 137 seats in the Chamber of Deputies (25 per cent). The coalition party favoured by Belgium, the PNP, followed with 22. Next came the Parti Solidaire Africain, led by Gizenga, which won 13. Abako, led by Kasavubu, won 12. The Centre de Regroupement Africain (CEREA) gained 10 seats, and MNC-Kalonji gained 8 seats, as did CONAKAT, the Katanga party of Moise Tshombe and Union Minière. Six seats were won by the Association Générale des Baluba du Katanga (BALUBAKAT). The remaining seats were won by other parties.[22]

Since no single party had sufficient seats to govern on its own, it was necessary to form a government of unity. The Belgian minister of African affairs, W J Ganshof van der Meersch, who was in the Congo to supervise negotiations, promptly nominated Kasavubu to form a government; his nomination had the official support of King Baudouin.[23]

Lumumba angrily pointed out that this was wholly improper. At a press conference in mid-June, he exclaimed, 'In accordance with democratic principles, it is the MNC—the party which won more votes than any other in the elections—that should form the government. The king of the Belgians should call upon the MNC to form the government. . . . The MNC should have the right to call on minority parties to consolidate its majority'.

'But what', he asked in frustration, 'is happening today?' He was suspicious, he said, that the 'Belgian Government and the royal palace are absolutely determined to keep the MNC out of power. They are now urging minority groups to form a coalition on artificial bases, so as to appoint a puppet government, which I swear the people will reject tomorrow if these manoeuvres behind the scenes succeed'.[24]

But in any case, Kasavubu was unable to form a government: he was defeated on straight votes three times running in the Chamber of Deputies.[25]

Lumumba's MNC-L successfully entered into a coalition with the PSA, CEREA and other parties to obtain a working majority.

Baudouin had therefore no choice but to recognise Lumumba as prime minister.

In the lead-up to the elections, Joseph-Désiré Mobutu had remained in Brussels as head of the MNC-L office, at Lumumba's request. Now he was back in the Congo, and Lumumba gave him the office of secretary of state to the presidency, a key position.[26] Antoine Gizenga was appointed deputy prime minister. Justin Bomboko was appointed minister of foreign affairs. Anicet Kashamura, the cofounder of CEREA, was appointed minister of information and cultural affairs, and Thomas Kanza was made UN ambassador, with ministerial status. Andrée Blouin was appointed to chief of protocol in the cabinet. She remained a member of Lumumba's inner circle, as she had been before the election, working closely with him. Some members of the press dubbed them 'team Lumum-Blouin'.[27]

From Accra, Nkrumah was monitoring developments and sending advice through his personal envoy in the Congo, Andrew Yaw K Djin, a businessman well known for his discretion.[28] Nkrumah urged Lumumba to facilitate the election of Kasavubu as head of state, on the grounds that the Bakongo people were too important to be thrust aside. Lumumba followed his advice.

Joseph Ileo was appointed president of the Senate. He was one of the politicians being passed money by Imbrey. 'A chap we followed', recalled Imbrey with contempt in one of the two interviews he gave in 2001, 'was named Josef Laho [as heard by the transcriber] who I think was demented'.[29]

Senior figures in Washington were also watching closely. Although concerned about the election of Lumumba, they regarded the presidency of Ileo as a good outcome. At a meeting of the National Security Council, Charles P Cabell, an air force general who was deputy director of the CIA, 'mentioned briefly the fact of the election of Joseph Ileo to the Presidency of the Congo Senate'. He expressed satisfaction at the influence of the CIA through the disbursement of funds to individuals such as Ileo. He reminded those at the meeting that Ileo was already under some degree of influence by the US. 'We may', he said, 'have secured some influence with this potentially useful individual'.[30]

* * *

On 29 June 1960, King Baudouin arrived in the Congo for the ceremony of independence the following day. As he was driven from the airport, his entourage slowed down to allow him to stand up and salute the flag of an honour guard of the Force Publique by the side of the road. Suddenly, a smartly dressed man named Ambroise Boimbo, a former soldier proudly wearing his medals, ran out of the crowd lining the route and snatched Baudouin's sword out of its scabbard.[31] This was not intended as an act of personal aggression against Baudouin, but as a powerful symbol of the transfer of power. The German photojournalist Robert Lebeck, who was there at that moment, took a series of photographs to record the episode. Boimbo was wrestled to the ground by Belgian and Congolese gendarmes and thrown into a police jeep. He was apparently released the next day.[32]

The morning of 30 June 1960 in Leopoldville was cool and clear. Guns fired a salute to proclaim freedom for the country's fourteen million people.[33] The ceremony of independence took place in the House of Parliament—the Palais de la Nation—which faced the Congo River with a view of Brazzaville on the opposite bank. In front of the building was a monument to Leopold II, which the Congolese attending the ceremony were obliged to pass on their way inside. Once inside, they had to pass a bronze bust of Leopold II.[34] All were painful reminders of the Congo's history.

Eve Blouin, Andrée Blouin's daughter, who was then a child, remembers the day vividly: 'I climbed up the tamarind tree shading our courtyard to witness the madness in the streets. Crowds of Belgians and Congolese had gathered to see the youthful King Baudouin the First who had come to the Congo for the occasion. . . . From the highest branches, we could see the convoy of official black convertible cars following King Baudouin to the Sainte-Anne cathedral for the *Te Deum* celebration before heading to the Palais de la Nation, where the official and solemn ceremony of Independence would take place'. She further recalls, 'The speakers in the streets of Leopoldville blasted the popular song "Indépendance Tcha Tcha" by Grand Kallé and his African Jazz band'.[35]

Guests at the Palais de la Nation included Ralph Bunche, who attended as the representative of the United Nations, just as he had done at the independence of Ghana in Accra in 1957. There were delegations from the USSR and from the US; the American group was led by Bob Murphy, the foreign service officer who had been US ambassador to Belgium in 1949–1952.

King Baudouin was wearing his sword, which had been retrieved from Ambroise Boimbo. As he stood up to give a speech, a warm atmosphere of goodwill suffused the room. But it was instantly shattered by the king's tasteless remarks. 'The independence of the Congo', he declared, 'is formed by the outcome of the work conceived by King Leopold II's genius, undertaken by him with tenacious and continuous courage with Belgium's perseverance'. For eighty years, he said, Belgium had sent to the Congo 'the best of its sons'. These 'pioneers', he added, had built communications, founded a medical service, modernised agriculture and built cities and industries and schools—'raising the well-being of your populations and equipping the country with technicians indispensable to its development'.[36]

This was an extraordinary claim. 'Today', observed the correspondent for the *New York Times*, who was present at the event, 'barely half of the Congolese can read and write, and only sixteen Congolese are university or college graduates. There are no Congolese doctors, lawyers or engineers, and no African officers in the 25,000-man Congolese Army'.[37]

Baudouin concluded his speech in a deeply paternalistic tone. 'It is now up to you, gentlemen', he said to the Congolese in front of him, 'to show that you are worthy of our confidence'. Outside the Palais de la Nation, where thousands of people were following the speeches through loudspeakers, there was fury and hurt.

The previous evening, Prime Minister Lumumba had accepted the maroon sash of the Order of the Crown, Belgium's highest decoration, which he was now wearing. But as he listened to Baudouin's speech, he became increasingly distressed and, as a photograph of the event shows, he furiously wrote down some notes.[38]

Baudouin's speech was followed by a diplomatic response from President Kasavubu. Then Lumumba—although he had not been included in the list of speakers—approached the microphone.

The day of 30 June 1960, asserted Lumumba, would be known for the 'glorious history of our struggle for liberty'. No Congolese, he insisted, would ever forget the struggle in which 'we have not spared our strength, our privations, our sufferings or our blood'. It was a struggle, he went on, that was indispensable for putting an end to the 'humiliating slavery which had been imposed on us by force'. He added that colonialism had left wounds too keen and too painful to be wiped from memory. Lumumba reminded members of the new Parliament of 'the ironies, the insults, the blows that we had to submit to morning, noon and night because we were Negroes'. Lumumba drew attention to the UN Charter. He declared that the Congo must be made the 'rallying point of all Africa' and that the nation must put an end to the oppression of free thought and give to all citizens the fundamental liberties guaranteed in the United Nations Universal Declaration of Human Rights.[39]

At a number of different moments throughout the speech, the Congolese in the hall broke into applause. The Soviet diplomats, noted the *New York Times* correspondent, 'seemed to be enjoying the occasion'.[40]

Baudouin, however, was deeply upset; it looked as if he was going to walk out of the hall, but he was persuaded to stay. Bob Murphy noted that 'the veins in his forehead stood out as indication of the violence of his feelings'. Murphy condemned Lumumba for delivering 'an inflammatory and bitter recital of all the wrongs, real and imaginary, committed in the past by Europeans in the Congo'.[41]

A few years later, Malcolm X, at the founding rally of the Organization of Afro-American Unity in Manhattan in June 1964, told his listeners about Lumumba's Independence Day speech. 'You should take that speech and tack it up over your door. This is what Lumumba said: You aren't giving us anything. Why, can you take back these scars that you put on our bodies? Can you give us back the limbs that you cut off while you were here?'[42]

In a radio broadcast in New York five months later, Malcolm X compared the Congo with America:

> The basic cause of most of the trouble in the Congo right now is the intervention of outsiders—the fighting that is going on over the mineral wealth of the Congo and over the strategic position that the Congo represents on the African continent. And in order to justify it, they are doing it at the expense of the Congolese, by trying to make it appear that the people are savages. And I think, as one of the gentlemen mentioned earlier, if there are savages in the Congo then there are worse savages in Mississippi, Alabama, and New York City, and probably some in Washington, D.C., too.[43]

Lumumba, Malcolm X believed, was the 'greatest black man who ever walked the African continent'.[44]

* * *

THE EXUBERANCE OF INDEPENDENCE in Ghana on 6 March 1957, three years before the independence of the Congo, had been un-qualified: there was an overwhelming sense of happiness and hope for the future. Many in the crowds at the celebrations—including Ghana's guests, such as Reverend Martin Luther King Jr—wept with joy.

The transfer of power from Belgium to the Congo on 30 June 1960 was similarly unforgettable. The dominant word, as recorded by the Congolese historian Ndaywel è Nziem, was 'indépendance': 'uhuru' in Kiswahili, 'kimpwanza' in Kikongo, and 'dipanda' in Lingala. Women wore pagnes bearing the word 'indépendance', while the markets and public places reverberated with 'this magical word'.[45] All night long, people danced to the songs of freedom. Kabasele and African Jazz had written a new song, 'Bilombe ba Gagne', meaning 'The Courageous Have Won':

Such was the state of things yesterday
The black man knew poverty
Forced labour, the whip

Whatever he said, his words met with a poor reception:
'Monkey, shut up!'[46]

The lyrics echoed the speech given by Lumumba at the Palais de la Nation.

* * *

BUT THERE WAS AN edge of tension in the atmosphere. Baudouin's speech had introduced a sour note, and the tragic history of the former colony seemed to press down on the hopes of so many for the future.

The American consul in Brazzaville, Alan W Lukens, was a member of the US delegation to Congo's independence celebrations. 'I'll never forget that day', he said in a spirit of sympathy for the new nation. 'We were all sitting in the stands watching the parade, consisting of goose-stepping African soldiers led by Belgian—mostly Flemish—non-coms [noncommissioned officers], who were screaming at them as they went by in the parade. I said to my wife at that point, "This is not going to last. They won't accept this".'[47]

In the evening, Lumumba's friend Luis López Álvarez went on a long walk in Brazzaville near the rapids of the Congo River. In the distance he could see the blue and green lights of Leopoldville, reflected on the river. His heart was full of joy at 'the independence of our Congo', he wrote later. But he was seized 'with a thousand fears' about the immediate future of his friend Patrice, 'knowing him alone and distraught' among people who had come from all over the world. 'Staying on the north bank of the river', he wrote with emotion, 'I witnessed the independence of our country, seriously thinking of the battle the next days would bring'.[48]

15

Year of Africa

G HANA WAS ONE OF THE first nations to open an embassy in in-dependent Congo. Andrew Djin, Nkrumah's personal envoy in Leopoldville, was appointed Ghana's official ambassador. The embassy was centrally located in the city, on the steep bank of the Congo River.[1]

Djin worked with Ghana's government to send to the Congo some of the professionals it so badly needed: doctors, nurses, po-licemen, engineers, electricians, civil servants and other trained per-sonnel. Some of them flew to the Congo in Egyptian planes, while others went by Ghana Airways, flown by Ghanaians. The Congo-lese who saw these planes arriving could hardly believe their eyes: with fewer than twenty university graduates in their own country, they were stunned to see pilots with Black skin.[2]

On the day of the Congo's independence, Ghana's *Daily Graphic* published a full-page article about its new prime minister: 'Lu-mumba Rose to Power from a Prison Cell'. It was written by a Swiss journalist, François Bondy, who was the editor of the French magazine *Preuves*, which—like the UK-based *Encounter*, the Ital-ian *Tempo Presente* and the Latin American *Cuadernos*—was af-filiated with the Paris-based Congress for Cultural Freedom and funded covertly by the CIA.

Bondy had joined the CCF in 1950, becoming the director of its publications. The following year, he established *Preuves*, which he edited until 1969; it swiftly became one of the most important literary reviews in Europe. As a magazine aiming at an Atlanti-cist, antineutralist and pro-American consensus, observes Frances

Stonor Saunders in *Who Paid the Piper?*, '*Preuves* was unmistakably the house organ of the Congress'.[3] It was based and published in Paris, the home of the CCF headquarters, and thus had a closer relationship with the CCF than the congress's other journals.[4]

The London *Times* later described *Preuves* as 'one of the decisive weapons of the West in the cultural cold war with the communist East'; Bondy, it claimed, helped to win the Cold War intellectually long before it was won over politically.

As well as editing *Preuves*, Bondy wrote on occasion for the Forum Service, a syndication organisation that mailed articles to editors in Africa, Asia and Latin America, offering free reproduction rights.[5] It was a CIA front, later known as Forum World Features, which the *New York Times* in 1977 described as 'perhaps the most widely circulated of the C.I.A.-owned news services'.[6] According to the journalist Russell Warren Howe, who had links with the CIA, it was set up to provide what was regarded as 'balanced, informed reporting' for the press of developing countries.[7] It was possibly through the Forum Service that Bondy's article on Lumumba reached the *Daily Graphic*.

Bondy reported that upon his arrival in the Congo, he had first seen Lumumba's face on the shirt of his taxi driver, where it was printed—on the front and back—with the inscription 'Indépendance—30 Juin'. Finding Lumumba in person was more challenging, however. He finally caught up with him in Stanleyville, where he hung around Lumumba's home and office, hoping for an interview. All of a sudden, the prime minister suggested going for a drive and a chat. 'We got into his open American cab', reported Bondy, 'and the chauffeur drove off. From all the streets there echoed the cry "Uhuru"'.

Whenever Lumumba travelled somewhere, observed Bondy, 'his journey lasts many hours since in every village the inhabitants throw trees in the road, block the route and refuse to let him go until he has made a speech'. In Bondy's account, the All African People's Conference in Accra in 1958 is given significance as an event that 'played a decisive role in the history of the Congo'.

Bondy's article reveals an open mind in relation to Lumumba, whom he portrays sympathetically as someone with 'unshakeable calm'.[8] He shows, too, that Lumumba was hugely popular in the Congo—a perception shared by Bronson Tweedy, who was concerned to prevent any 'stop Lumumba' campaign on the grounds that Lumumba was 'one of the few, if not [the] only, Congolese leaders with a Congo-wide appeal and standing'.[9] Neither Bondy nor Tweedy at this stage were showing any of the antipathy for Lumumba that was felt so strongly by Bill Burden and Larry Devlin.

But Bondy's article demonstrates far more interest in white people—whom he referred to as 'Europeans'—than with the majority population of the Congo. Bondy concluded his article with a tribute to Belgian colonisation as a form of rule which, 'for all its sins and shortcomings, may justly be described as the great even noble legacy of the Belgian administration'.

On his way to the Belgian Congo, Bondy travelled via Brazzaville, which he described as 'the sleepy and dilapidated capital of the French Congo'. While there, he heard Lumumba's name constantly.[10]

Possibly he met with Lumumba's friend Luis López Álvarez, who was also a member of the Congress for Cultural Freedom; both men had published articles in *Cuadernos*. But whereas López Álvarez was almost certainly ignorant of the CIA's role in the congress, it seems likely that Bondy knew of it. Stonor Saunders includes him in the list of those who were aware that Mike Josselson, who had set up the congress and managed it in Paris—and with whom Bondy worked closely—was a CIA agent. 'Not all of them were "witting" in the sense that they were active participants in the deception', comments Stonor Saunders. 'But they all *knew*, and had known for some time. And if they didn't, they were, said their critics, cultivatedly, and culpably, ignorant'.[11]

Chantal Hunt, the wife of Josselson's assistant, John Hunt, told Stonor Saunders in 1997 that she was surprised that anyone involved with the CCF in Paris would deny knowledge of the agency's role. She herself had worked for the French Ministry of Culture and, briefly, for the CCF. 'Everyone in France, in my circle at least', she told Stonor Saunders, 'knew the truth about who was behind the Congress. They all talked about it. They would say,

"Why do you want to go and work there? It's CIA". Everyone knew except, apparently, those who worked for it. Isn't that odd? I always thought so'.[12]

* * *

AT THE TIME OF the All African People's Conference in 1958, there were only nine independent countries across Africa. But in 1960 alone, seventeen African nations became independent, and by the end of the year Africa represented one-quarter of the UN's member states. 'Bunche Says '60 Is Year of Africa', reported the *New York Times* on 17 February—a slogan that was picked up widely and with enthusiasm.[13] There was a growing sense of hope and optimism across the continent.

But the injustices continued. On 21 March of that year, in the town of Sharpeville, South Africa, the police opened fire on a peaceful protest against the racist pass laws, which required Black South Africans to carry pass books at all times. Sixty-nine unarmed people were massacred and many were badly injured.

This was a defining moment in South Africa's freedom struggle. In solidarity with the victims, Chief Albert Luthuli (the president general of the African National Congress), Nelson Mandela and other ANC members all burned their own passes. Just over a month later, the UN General Assembly discussed apartheid for the first time, declaring that it was in violation of the UN Charter.

* * *

ON 1 JULY 1960—THE day after the independence of the Congo—the Republic of Ghana was proclaimed. On 27 April, a general election had been held, alongside a referendum on the creation of an executive presidency. The referendum in favour of the presidency passed, and Nkrumah, who won the election, became Ghana's first president. The role of governor general, which had been held by Lord Listowel since independence, was obsolete now that Ghana was a republic. A photograph of Listowel walking to his plane to leave Ghana shows Nkrumah cheerfully waving goodbye to the representative of Elizabeth II.

Now fifty years old, Nkrumah was confidently holding the reins of his government. His office and residence had moved from

Christiansborg Castle to Flagstaff House, in the middle of Accra, which had been the army's headquarters during colonial days. Work at Flagstaff House, noted Tawia Adamafio, minister for presidential affairs, 'was mountainous and urgent every minute'.[14]

Under Nkrumah, Ghana was building a new postcolonial infrastructure to benefit the majority of citizens. Since 1954, Nkrumah had been eager to see the introduction of compulsory and free primary education, and his government was working to accomplish this by 1961, which it did. The school population in Ghana quickly shot up; whereas in 1960 the number of students enrolled in first grade was just over 123,000, the number enrolled in September 1961 was almost 100,000 more. 'Schools sprang up like mushrooms all over the country', wrote Adamafio, and 'a great spirit of educational endeavour seized the people and propelled them on to enthusiastic voluntary effort in the provision of school accommodation'. Most villages boasted at least one primary school.[15]

Teacher-training enrolment increased from 1,916 in 1951 to 4,552 in 1961—an increase of 137.5 per cent. University students in that period increased from 208 to 1,204. The number of hospital beds went up from 2,368 to 6,155. Gravel roads increased by nearly 60 per cent. Telephones increased by over 345 per cent.[16]

Under colonial rule, Ghana's economy had been made dependent on one cash crop: cocoa. This was a huge threat to the economic future of the newly independent country, since the demand for cocoa was dependent on the consumption levels of a handful of Western nations. Moreover, notes Kofi Buenor Hadjor, a press aide to Nkrumah and later the editor of *New Africa*, 'the African producer of cocoa was left with very little after the European marketing firms and the colonial tax-men were through with him'.[17]

Despite this obstacle, according to Hadjor, the results of Nkrumah's strategy were impressive: 'The state invested in oil and sugar refineries, meat-canning, soap- and paint-making factories, and a vehicle-assembly plant. Investments were also directed towards agro-related industries so as to provide the foundation for meat-canning and sugar production. Other initiatives in this sector were designed to lower Ghana's dependence on food imports such as meat, rice and sugar'. As a result of these policies, 'Ghana's real gross national product increased by 24.5 per cent between 1960 and 1965'. The new enterprises established during this period, Hadjor adds, 'provided the country with a new structural foundation for economic growth. And this occurred despite the dramatic decline in the price of cocoa during the years 1960 to 1965'.[18]

Not all Nkrumah's policies were popular with everybody. Some Ghanaians had reservations about his massive project to build the Volta River dam at Akosombo in order to produce hydroelectric power for processing Ghana's bauxite into aluminium. 'New nations', declared Nkrumah, 'which are determined by every possible means to catch up in industrial strength', must aim for 'large-scale industrial advance. Electricity is the basis for industrialisation'.[19] But Dr Joseph Boakye Danquah, leader of the opposition, described the hydroelectric project as a 'communist inspired prestige undertaking'.[20] He 'tried his utmost to ditch the project'.[21]

Nkrumah persevered. He sought and eventually obtained American funding and technological expertise. Work on the dam started in 1961, and it was inaugurated in January 1966, creating the Volta Lake, which is the third-largest artificial lake in the world by volume. The resettlement of eighty thousand people into fifty-two new villages was partnered with the introduction of better living conditions and farming methods, but many people were traumatised when their homes and farms were flooded.[22] There was concern, too, about the environmental impact.

The hydroelectric power plant fuelled the aluminium smelter and also provided electricity to urban centres. In 2020 the Akosombo Dam provided 85 per cent of Ghana's electricity and also supplied Togo and Benin with power.[23]

One of Nkrumah's actions that worried even some of his most loyal supporters was the Preventive Detention Act of 1958, which gave the government power to detain offenders without trial for five years. Joseph Godson Amamoo, who served as a diplomat for Nkrumah's government in London, Hungary and Vienna, pays tributes to the government's huge and transformative achievements in *The Ghanaian Revolution*.[24] But he is also conscious that mistakes were made, including the Preventive Detention Act. In *Ghana:* 50 *Years of Independence*, Amamoo describes the act as 'notorious', because it meant that the vaguest suspicion of political disaffection could lead to swift arrest and detention and to 'outrageous violations of human rights'.[25]

Geoffrey Bing, a British left-wing lawyer who was Nkrumah's attorney general and trusted advisor (much loathed by the British government), was deeply troubled by the act. As a former British member of Parliament he had opposed the Special Powers Act in Northern Ireland, under which political offenders could be imprisoned without trial. 'As a stubborn opponent of preventive detention anywhere in the United Kingdom', he observed in his memoir, 'I would, for this reason alone, have found it hard to accept it in Ghana'. His view was modified shortly after the bill was passed: 'A dangerous tribal conspiracy was discovered. It was clear that it could only be dealt with effectively by the use of special powers'. But his scruples never entirely left him.[26]

Nkrumah was not without powerful political enemies. His most notable opponent was Dr J B Danquah, who had stood unsuccessfully as a presidential candidate against him in April 1960. Danquah had taken a vigorous role in the struggle for independence from Britain and was widely respected as one of Ghana's founding fathers. A lawyer of distinction, Danquah was the section chairman of the Europe-based International Commission of Jurists, which was revealed in 1967 to have received CIA funding through the American Fund for Free Jurists.[27] (Following this revelation, the ICJ successfully pulled away and established itself as an independent organisation.) Slightly more than three thousand subscribers received ICJ publications in Africa in the early 1960s.[28]

Danquah developed a close association with Pauli Murray, a thin, intense African American lawyer, who arrived in Accra in February 1960 to serve as a faculty member in the newly established Ghana School of Law. She had been urged to take up the position by the trade unionist Maida Springer, who lived near her in Brooklyn and was a close friend. Through Springer, Murray had met the Kenyan leader Tom Mboya; in 1956, she picked him up from the airport to take him to Springer's home. She also met with Nyerere and other African nationalist leaders.[29]

Murray was a formidable intellectual who was also a poet and later became a priest in the Episcopal church. But, as an interracial woman and active resister of Jim Crow, she faced many obstacles in her daily and her professional life. She had a keen personal sense of the sufferings wrought through racial oppression: her grandmother had been born into slavery, and she herself had been brought up by her maternal grandparents in the bitter conditions of segregation.

Another difficulty for Murray was that she was sexually attracted to women at a time when homosexuality was against the law in the US and generated prejudice and hatred. Recent interpretations of her archives reveal that she battled with gender dysphoria; had the term existed in the 1930s and 1940s, argues the Black feminist scholar Brittney Cooper, Murray might have identified as a trans man.[30] Biographies published in 2016 and 2017 reveal that well into middle age, Murray tried to obtain hormone replacement therapy as a means of transitioning gender, but without success; the treatment scarcely existed before the mid-1960s, and even then it was seldom available to women who identified as men.[31]

Yet another factor that made Murray feel vulnerable was her political past: she had worked for a number of the organisations singled out as communist by the House Un-American Activities Committee. Because of this, when applying for a position at Cornell University she decided to submit a six-page memorandum detailing 'pertinent data on my background and organizational affiliations which may be useful to you in the event the State Department requires a loyalty investigation of all prospective personnel'.[32] She stated that in each case she had taken an anticommunist position.

Murray wrote a family memoir in 1956 titled *Proud Shoes*. Its tone, argues Sarah Azaransky in a study of Murray's life and work, is defiant of the insinuation that she had communist connections 'or that she was disloyal to the American government and to the ideals of American democracy'. Yet, adds Azaransky, 'Murray's project can also be read as deeply apologetic. . . . Instead of calling into question the state's use of suspicion to discredit people involved in freedom struggles . . . Murray went to great lengths to show that she did not deserve suspicion'.[33]

In Ghana, Murray was miserable. She had never left the US before, and she was far away from the person whom she was closest to: Irene Barlow, known as Renee, who was three years younger than Murray. 'Tall, sophisticated and white', observes Rosalind Rosenberg in a biography of Murray, 'Barlow appeared to have little in common with Murray'. In comparison with Barlow, Murray said she felt she was 'a vagabond, a Pixie!' But they had both suffered a 'hardscrabble life' and shared the Episcopalian faith. They did not live together in the same household, but theirs was a profound union that gave Murray the 'guiding hand' and 'spiritual embrace' she had longed for.[34] She wrote long and thoughtful letters to Renee from Ghana.[35]

Many aspects of life in Ghana were unbearable to Murray. Her house was still being built, and she had to live in a place with 'intolerable heat, noxious smells, and ubiquitous insects'.[36] She liaised with the US embassy, under Ambassador Wilson C Flake, and socialised with Earl Link, an African American on the staff who was known in Ghana for his 'superb and booming bass singing voice'.[37] But she did not fit easily into the large community of African Americans who had moved to Accra in support of Dr Nkrumah and independent Ghana.

In 1960, Maida Springer was travelling through Africa in the course of her work for the AFL-CIO and stopped in Accra to see Murray. She was alarmed by what she found: Murray told her that she was living in a police state and wanted to leave. Springer defended Nkrumah, arguing that allowances should be made at this moment of decolonisation, but Murray disagreed. Springer later told her biographer, 'My passionate feeling about Africa she certainly did not share. She was too cool-headed and intellectually searching and was unwilling to make any compromises for undemocratic practices in Africa'.[38]

Murray believed that Nkrumah was becoming a dictator and feared she was at risk of arrest, because she was spending time with members of the political opposition, including J B Danquah. She ensured that Earl Link, her closest contact at the US embassy, knew where she was whenever she left the capital city, in case she needed to be rescued.[39] As a precaution, she sent all her lecture notes to the CIA, through Link, as evidence against any charge that she was seeking to proselytise her students. It appears that Link was not simply a contact with the CIA but also a CIA agent under cover of his work at the embassy.

Murray spoke freely about her unhappiness to Lloyd Garrison Jr, a *New York Times* correspondent covering West Africa, who was the son of her mentor in the legal profession. The man she was in contact with at the US embassy, she told him, was a CIA agent. 'If she confided to Garrison that she was in contact with an African American CIA agent (as Garrison reported to State Department officials)', observes Kevin K Gaines in *American Africans in Ghana*, 'she could have been something more than an unwitting asset. At the very least, Murray championed American influence in Ghana with a steadfastness that made her serviceable to those engaged in gathering intelligence'.[40] This steadfastness led her in June 1960 to join the CIA-backed American Society of African Culture (AMSAC).

Murray and Nkrumah were both extraordinary, courageous individuals with brilliant intellects and deep social concern. And in Accra, not far from each other's homes, they both listened frequently to much-loved Western classical music. Beethoven's *Pathétique* and various sonatas by Brahms afforded Murray particular pleasure, as she wrote in her letters to Renee.[41] Nkrumah, for his part, listened to Haydn's *Creation* or Handel's *Messiah* for hours on end. He frequently asked Genoveva Marais to listen with him, often over the telephone, with the music turned up as loudly as it would go.[42]

Murray's dislike for Nkrumah did not diminish, even once she had left Ghana. 'His attempts to gain hegemony or leadership over various countries failed. In my opinion, he was a real tragedy', she stated in an interview in 1976 for the Southern Oral History Program Collection. 'Perhaps it was unfortunate', she added, 'that he spent so many years in the United States and got this sense of what it must be to have a big country, a subcontinent united and

the power of a subcontinent. I've often felt that his sojourn in the
United States made a tremendous impact and contributed to this
obsession of a United States of Africa'.

Lumumba, said Murray, was Nkrumah's protégé. This was an accurate claim in the sense that Nkrumah acted as the younger man's
mentor, but it was intended by Murray to suggest an excessive and
unthinking allegiance on Lumumba's part. She also referred to a
rumour that 'he, Nkrumah, almost bled the country of money to
help Lumumba bring about a domination of the then Congo'.[43]

Murray visited the Congo in mid-June 1960, shortly before
independence. The reason for her visit was 'to secure information
for the Ghanaian government on how safely to rescue a group of
South Africans at risk of arrest for their role in protesting apartheid', writes Rosenberg, using Murray's diary as a source. The visit
was 'dangerous and difficult', adds Rosenberg.[44] Further details on
this visit have not been found.

* * *

WASHINGTON, DC, WAS REASONABLY well disposed towards Nkrumah in 1958, argues the historian Ebere Nwaubani. It had been ir-
ritated by his move 'towards an activist, African-centered foreign
policy and more so by its accompanying rhetoric', but the relationship between the two nations was sufficiently resilient to withstand
this development. 'Our trade relations with Ghana, including access to raw materials produced in Ghana, are good', Ambassador
Flake reported to Washington in October 1959. 'Our political relations with Ghana are friendly and fruitful'.[45]

But the more Accra asserted itself throughout Africa, Nwaubani notes, the more the US worried about the general direction
of Ghana's foreign policy. By 1960, it was increasingly alarmed by
Lumumba's close relationship with the Ghanaian leader. In February 1960, Washington resolved to 'discourage, whenever possible,
Ghana's current tendency to support extremist elements in neigh-
boring African countries'.[46] The US planned a redefinition of its
relationship with Ghana.[47]

One of America's concerns about Nkrumah was his continuing and active interest in atomic matters, including his profound

opposition to atomic weapons testing in Africa. He was clear-sighted about the risks of atomic weapons for Africa, which he regarded as atomic imperialism. When France started in 1960 to test its atomic bombs in the Sahara Desert, Nkrumah actively supported global campaigns against it—on the grounds that it contaminated the people of Africa, who had not even been consulted.

In April 1960, a Positive Action Conference for Peace and Security in Africa was held in Accra, where 250 delegates represented twenty-five African countries; observers from non-African countries also took part. Speaking at the conference, Nkrumah lamented, 'Winds carried the poisonous debris from the explosion to various parts of Africa, including Ghana. . . . From the point of view of genetics these atomic tests are extremely bad and can have the most disastrous effects. The French test last February resulted in a very substantial increase in radio-activity'. This was proved, he said, by the work of the British and Canadian scientists who were manning monitoring stations in Ghana.[48]

* * *

THOUGH FIRMLY OPPOSED TO atomic weapons, Nkrumah was enthusiastic about the possibility of atomic power to produce energy. The Ghanaian president believed that atomic power should be available to all countries, including those emerging from colonisation. Since 1952, scientists in Ghana had been working with isotopes, including experiments with radiostrontium on monkeys. Ghana joined the IAEA on 28 September 1960, three years after the foundation of the agency in July 1957.[49]

That same year, Nkrumah announced a decision to establish the Ghana Atomic Energy Commission and to build an atomic reactor. It would be located on the outskirts of Accra in an area called Kwabenya, which was swiftly dubbed 'Atomic Junction'. At first Nkrumah asked Canada—which had assisted India—for help with obtaining a reactor, but, under pressure from the US, Canada declined the request. Nkrumah then turned to the Soviet Union, which promised to provide Ghana with a two-megawatt research reactor for training a cadre of Ghanaian nuclear specialists. It also promised to provide experts, including physicists, geologists and engineers. In February 1961, an agreement was signed between the two nations.[50]

A few years later, Nkrumah explained his thinking behind Ghana's plans for a reactor. 'We were fully aware', he said, 'that our motives might be misconstrued, for the setting up of an Atomic Reactor is the first practical step to building an Atomic bomb'. But Ghana's sole motive, he explained, was simply to enable the young nation 'to take every advantage of the decisive methods of research and development, which mark our modern world'. It was essential to do this, he added, 'if we are to impart to our development the acceleration, which is required to break even with more advanced economies. We have therefore been compelled to enter the field of Atomic energy, because this already promises to yield the greatest economic source of power since the beginning of man'.[51]

With these words, Nkrumah echoed the spirit of Eisenhower's Atoms for Peace speech—but this stance was evidently not regarded by Washington as appropriate for Ghana. By contrast, the US had agreed to deliver the TRICO atomic reactor to the Congo in 1958, when it had no reason to expect the Congo to achieve majority rule in the near future. And again by contrast, it was in discussions with apartheid South Africa to supply enriched uranium for an atomic reactor, known as SAFARI, construction on which began in 1961 and continued until 1965, when it achieved criticality. It appears that from the point of view of the US government, a necessary qualification in Africa for access to a reactor was colonial occupation or white minority rule.

16

Things Fall Apart

D ESPITE THE MOMENTS OF TENSION on the day of independence, the Congo was joyful and calm. For the first time
in their history, the Congolese had a government that had been
elected by them on a democratic basis.

Lumumba and his family had been living in a home on Boulevard Albert 1er. This street (known today as Boulevard 30 Juin, to
mark the day of freedom) lay in the central part of Leopoldville,
which during the colonial era had been exclusively for people with
white skin. In February 1960, Lumumba had been able to purchase
this house by virtue of his nomination to the college of six commissioners.[1] Now the family were preparing to move into the official
residence of the prime minister on Avenue Tilkens (now Avenue
du Fleuve Congo), which runs along the river upstream from the
Palais de la Nation. It had previously been the official residence of
Governor General Cornelis, who moved out in the first week of
July.

Joseph Kasavubu moved into the president's official residence
on Mont Stanley (now Mont Ngaliema), the former residence of
the governor of Leopoldville Province, which overlooked the Kin-
suka rapids of the Congo River.

But suddenly, less than a week after Independence Day, the period of building and of change was shattered. On 5 July, a mutiny
broke out among the ranks of the national security force, the Force
Publique. This army of twenty-five thousand strong had expected
their lives to improve substantially at independence, but nothing had changed: all the officers were Belgian, and not one army

sergeant had even been made a 2nd lieutenant.[2] Conditions of service and of pay had remained the same.

As Nzongola-Ntalaja explains, the explosion of anger among the soldiers of the Force Publique had started with General Émile Janssens, commander of the colonial army, who had been kept at his post by the new government of independent Congo. 'Given the chance of discontent for lack of promotions among non-commissioned officers and the rank and file . . . the general convened a meeting of the troops at the main army camp in Kinshasa on 4 July'. Nzongola-Ntalaja describes what happened next: 'On the big blackboard in front of the excited troops, he wrote the following words: "before independence = after independence". For the men in uniform, he told them, there would be no changes as a result of independence; discipline would be maintained as usual, and white officers would remain in command'.[3]

Many Belgian citizens panicked, fearful for their safety. Six thousand of them fled for Brazzaville on the night of 7 July and the next day. 'I went around my neighbourhood', said Frank Carlucci, second secretary at the US embassy, 'and remember a houseboy coming out and telling me his employer had said, "Take everything; it's all yours". Another said, "They left the phonograph playing. Should I turn it off?" People fled literally in their nightgowns. The neighbourhoods were deserted for quite some time'.[4] Within forty-eight hours, Leopoldville had barely any magistrates, doctors, technicians or administrators.[5]

On 10 July, the Belgian government sent Belgian paratroops and other crack units to the Congo, claiming their purpose was to protect Belgian citizens. Before long, ten thousand Belgian troops had entered the country.[6]

The military intervention contravened international law. In 1957, the UN General Assembly had adopted a resolution instructing member states 'to develop amicable and tolerant relationships, based on e.g. non-intervention in the internal affairs of the States'.[7] It built on a 1949 resolution asking member states 'to refrain . . . from any direct or indirect action intended to jeopardise the freedom, the independence or the integrity of any State, to incite any State to internal struggle'.[8] The Loi Fondamentale agreed upon between Belgium and the Congo on 19 May during the Round Table had set out a Treaty for Friendship, Assistance and Collaboration—but in no way did this qualify Belgium to intervene militarily.

The new Congo government was deeply suspicious of Belgium's motives. Such a swift return of Belgian troops—within ten days—was a disturbing indication that they had plans to recolonise the territory. Then, on 11 July, Moise Tshombe's CONAKAT Party announced the secession of Katanga. This move was actively supported by the Belgian government and also by Union Minière, which now paid all its taxes to the Tshombe government—not to the central government.

Prime Minister Lumumba's first inclination was to appeal to the US for support, even though the US was a NATO ally of Belgium.[9] This is a sign of the confidence and faith Lumumba had at this time in America's support for the decolonising nations of Africa and for democracy. He approached US ambassador Timberlake, asking for military assistance from the American government to force the Belgian troops out; the Congolese government confirmed in writing its request for a contingent of three thousand men to be sent without delay to Leopoldville.[10]

But to Lumumba's surprise and disappointment, American military help was not forthcoming. The US advised the Congolese government to turn to the United Nations as the most appropriate recourse for help.

In fact, the US was already responding to the new developments in the Congo with military manoeuvres—but not the kind that Lumumba was asking for. On 9 July, the US had sent the USS Wasp, a US Navy aircraft carrier, to the South Atlantic, off the Congo's coast, with six military helicopters.[11] Charlie La Marr, then a gunnery sergeant in the US Marine Corps, was on this operation. 'The Wasp took off their fighters', he said later, 'and put us aboard. We went to the Congo'.

The task force returned to the US on 1 August. The operation was described officially as an effort to calm things down in the Congo and to assist a potential mass evacuation of Americans. But La

Marr—in a 2002 online conversation with some other veterans—explained that it was nothing of the sort. In fact, it was a reconnaissance operation. 'We were there', he said, 'to photograph and map portions of the west coast of Africa for future Marine amphibious landings. The Congo war brought it on'.[12]

Ed Shea, a marine involved in an exercise in 1961 in the Gulf of Guinea, described the deployments to the Congo in 1960 as 'efforts made by US Navy UDT [underwater demolition team] and 2nd Marine Division Recon personnel to examine underwater and shoreline alike for obstacles and conditions of recognized importance to forces contemplating the landing of Battalion and larger sized Landing Teams of the time'. He adds, 'No deployments or reconnaissance of a similar nature were known to have occurred previously in the same region'.[13]

Prime Minister Lumumba and his government had no idea about the American naval operation. He consulted Ralph Bunche, who was in Leopoldville as the representative of UN Secretary General Dag Hammarskjöld, to ask for United Nations help to protect the Congo and its independence. Then Lumumba and Kasavubu sent a cable to New York, requesting UN military assistance to remove the Belgians and to end the secession of Katanga.

Hammarskjöld, who had been keenly aware of Belgium's failure to prepare its colony for self-government, had already prepared the groundwork to send technical and other assistance to the Congo. Now, in this newly critical situation, he asked the Security Council to meet immediately to review the situation. On 14 July, it passed a resolution calling on Belgium to withdraw all its troops from the Congo and for the UN to provide military and other assistance to the new republic. The operation would be known as the Organisation des Nations Unies au Congo, or ONUC.

The first three thousand UN soldiers, all from African nations, arrived within three days, followed by ten thousand more in the next two weeks. One UN unit was sent to Camp Hardy at Thysville, near Leopoldville. All along the route, civilians cheered them, and the soldiers at Camp Hardy greeted them with smiles. The Casques Bleus—as the UN soldiers were called because of their blue helmets—were pleased and relieved; they had been led to expect a frosty welcome.[14]

In addition, a large civilian UN task force was sent to help fill the void in public administration—at airfields, in hospitals, in communications, at the central bank, in the police and for other essential services.[15] The void was growing larger as more and more Belgians left the newly independent country. In the eighteen-hundred-bed Leopoldville general hospital, only three doctors stayed on—an American surgeon, a Belgian specialist in internal medicine and an Egyptian gynaecologist. Many industries and businesses were run by skeleton staffs, and courts were closed.[16]

The situation was deteriorating rapidly. It was further aggravated when Kasavubu and Lumumba were denied landing rights on a flight to Elisabethville, which was under the control of Belgian troops. They then broke off the Congo's relations with Belgium.

Lumumba and Kasavubu sought to reassure the soldiers of the Force Publique, promising better conditions of service and promotions, and that racial discrimination would be made illegal. As a marker of change, the name Force Publique was changed to Armée Nationale Congolaise. As well, the senior Belgians who had run the force were dismissed and replaced. Victor Lundula, who had served as an elected mayor of a commune in the city of Jadotville from 1957 to 1960 (following the very first municipal elections held in the Belgian Congo in 1957 in three cities only, namely Leopoldville, Elisabethville and Jadotville), was appointed commander in chief of the army, with the rank of general. Joseph-Désiré Mobutu was made his chief of staff, with the rank of lieutenant colonel.

Both appointments, Nzongola-Ntalaja observed, were 'ill-advised'. Lundula did not have the qualifications to manage a modern army. As for Mobutu, 'Lumumba made a serious blunder based on his political naivety and his overconfidence with regard to commanding the loyalty of the people in his entourage'. He ignored the well-founded rumours about Mobutu's ties to the Belgian and American intelligence services. 'In appointing Mobutu to this sensitive position', Nzongola-Ntalaja wrote, Lumumba 'had unwittingly chosen his own Judas'.[17]

Antoine Gizenga, Lumumba's loyal deputy prime minister, saw that Mobutu had wormed his way into the appointment and that, once he had it, he made little effort to go and see the soldiers and tackle their concerns.[18] He sought to intervene. While Mobutu was out of the capital on an unofficial trip, Gizenga gave his post to Maurice Mpolo, the minister of youth and sports.

When Mobutu returned to Leopoldville, he was furious at the change and went to Lumumba to demand the role back. But, complained Gizenga, Lumumba was 'too sentimental' and didn't perceive the danger that roamed around him. Lumumba had a weakness for Mobutu, Gizenga noted with frustration; he regarded him as 'his son, a sweet lamb' and was affected by his tears. Instead of supporting Gizenga's intervention, Lumumba instructed Mpolo to leave the army and return to his ministry. Mpolo did. Mobutu then ordered his arrest, but his soldiers failed to carry out the order.

Charmed by Mobutu, Lumumba was giving him, rather than Gizenga, the benefit of the doubt. He was concerned by Gizenga's harsh judgment of his new chief of staff and asked him to be more understanding.[19]

* * *

NKRUMAH WAS DETERMINED TO do everything possible to support the liberty of the Congo. On 15 July, almost 1,200 Ghanaian soldiers were flown to Leopoldville; 192 more were waiting in Accra for transport, with 156 trucks and 160 tons of stores.[20] By 25 July, Ghanaian troops, numbering 2,340, were the largest single national contingent in the UN force, which by then totalled 8,396; there were also about 37 Ghanaian police officers in the Congo. Senior Ghanaian ministers and officials visited the Congo frequently.[21]

But tensions were emerging that had not been anticipated by Nkrumah. The cause was the commander in chief of the Ghanaian contingent: Major General Henry Templer Alexander, who had been seconded from the British Army to serve as Ghana's chief of defence. According to the magazine *Topic*, he was a 'handsome, whipcord soldier, slight but with huge black eyebrows and clipped, greying moustache'.[22]

Alexander was 'an experienced senior military officer', noted Indar Jit Rikhye, a major general in the Indian army who was serving as Hammarskjöld's military advisor in the Congo.[23] Still, Rikhye believed that Alexander had little understanding of the politics of peacekeeping, and he looked at the Congo crisis through the prism of imperial policing. What he did not seem to understand was that the UN was not an imperial power and was not entitled to enforce its will on the Congolese.[24] And since Alexander did not speak French, Lingala, Kiswahili or Kikongo, he had to rely on English speakers to obtain any sense of what was going on.[25] Alexander avoided the British embassy, apparently on the grounds that it was too closely linked with colonialism. Instead, he chose to seek logistic support from the American embassy.[26]

In *African Tightrope*, a memoir Alexander later wrote about his two years as Nkrumah's chief of staff, he drew attention to his close contact with the US embassy, including with the thin-as-a-reed Clare Timberlake, the new American ambassador. On his arrival in the Congo, recorded Alexander, 'I was seen immediately by Mr. Timberlake—a man to whom I took an immediate liking'.[27] And the liking was mutual: on 15 July, Timberlake reported to Washington that Alexander was 'level-headed and broad gauged'.[28] Alexander was also in close contact with the US ambassador in Ghana.

Most of the officers of the Ghanaian troops were white. Even though it had been three years since Ghana's independence, Alexander had failed to reconstitute the Ghanaian units that went to the Congo so that they would be officered by Ghanaians.[29] Alexander displayed a deeply held racism; in his memoir he observed that 'Life to the African is of much less value than to the European'.[30] After arriving in July to take up the post of CIA chief of station, Larry Devlin witnessed an occasion in which Alexander stated that the Congolese leadership 'had not yet come down from the trees'. Luckily, noted Devlin, neither Bomboko nor Kanza, who were present, 'appeared to have heard this offensive remark'.[31]

An immediate problem caused by Alexander was his decision on 15 July to disarm the ANC troops. This action—and Alexander's 'forceful personality'—was widely admired by the Western press.[32] From Accra, the British high commissioner reported to London on Alexander's heroic exploits. It was only because of Alexander, he said, that 'mass murder and looting' had been prevented in Leopoldville, and that Alexander, 'single-handed', had prevented a huge mob from lynching someone. It was particularly impressive, he said, because 'Bunche was not backing him'. Bunche, he added, 'though he may be a first-class mediator, is evidently quite useless as a man of action in a situation like this. He spent all his time wandering between his hotel room and the American Embassy for comfort and Coca-Cola', while Alexander moved from one trouble spot to another.[33]

But Lumumba and his government were appalled by the disarming of the ANC. So, too, were Hammarskjöld and Bunche—all the more so since Alexander was not a member of the UN command. To sideline Alexander, Hammarskjöld quickly named Bunche as the acting force commander (on Bunche's own recommendation), in addition to his position as special representative.[34] Bunche continued in this role until the arrival of Major General Carl von Horn to act as the supreme commander of the UN force in the Congo.

Bunche insisted that the weapons of ANC soldiers be handed back to them. When Bunche returned to New York, 'obviously very tired', he had 'a good deal to say' about Alexander. 'This rather swashbuckling soldier', he said with evident irritation, 'thought that he had answers to the problems of the Congolese army and the maintenance of order and he had taken a strong but mistaken position on the question of disarming the Congolese troops'. Speaking to Rajeshwar Dayal, the Indian diplomat who was preparing to go to the Congo to take over Bunche's role of Hammarskjöld's special representative, Bunche warned him that Alexander was a troublemaker.[35]

Alexander did not seem to understand, Bunche complained, that the United Nations force was a 'peace force, not a fighting force', and that it could use arms only in self-defence. It was absolutely necessary that UN troops should avoid getting into the 'extreme position of having to shoot Congolese'.[36]

But Alexander was ambitious. On several occasions, he put himself forward as the ideal man to take responsibility for the UN's operational activities in the Congo. He was eager to be at the heart of the action and seemed not to be aware of his unsuitability for the post. Moreover, he did not realise that, as von Horn put it, the 'concept of this military scion of a colonial power being given *carte blanche* in the Congo was totally unthinkable'.[37]

Andrew Djin, Ghana's ambassador to the Congo, was increasingly suspicious of Alexander; he sent urgent messages to Nkrumah warning him about Alexander's 'intrigue and subversive action'.[38] The dislike was mutual. Alexander depicted Djin in his memoir as 'a black racist, anti-white and virulently anti-Belgian'.[39]

* * *

AN ABSOLUTE PRIORITY FOR Lumumba and Kasavubu was to force the Belgian troops out of the Congo. On 17 July, they gave an ultimatum to Bunche: they would call for Soviet military intervention if the UN had not pushed the Belgian troops out of the Congo within two days. The ultimatum was set out in a letter, which Lumumba gave to Alexander in Stanleyville.

Alexander then flew to Leopoldville with Carlucci and radioed Ambassador Timberlake, asking him to meet him on arrival at Ndjili airport, together with Bunche and the commander of the Belgian metropolitan troops. At the airport, Alexander handed the letter to Bunche, observing that the request it contained was impossible. The meeting at the airport was described in detail by Timberlake to the State Department on 18 July, in a cable that was copied to the small group of men involved in the developing crisis:

> Alexander feels Kasavubu not happy with direction being taken by Lumumba but seems to be weak and under latter's thumb. Alexander feels Lumumba is irrational and so does Bunche. I think at very least we are dealing with man who is temporarily irrational.
>
> I talked at length with Bomboko and Kanza who said they would call Cabinet meeting to be held on arrival Kasavubu and

Lumumba and would meanwhile line up Cabinet members they know or might persuade to go against any such ultimatum. Bomboko considers it illegal since it has neither Cabinet nor Parliamentary approval.[40]

The cable reflects the confidence that Timberlake felt in Alexander. It was sent with a high precedence: NIACT, or 'night action', which meant that it had to be delivered immediately to the addressee, even in the middle of the night.

The demand by Lumumba and Kasavubu did push some Belgian troops back to their bases at Kamina and Kitona.[41] But it was otherwise futile: Bunche did not accept the ultimatum, arguing that it was unrealistic.

Some of Lumumba's supporters were concerned about his strategies to remove the Belgians. 'He's trying to please everyone', complained his deputy, Antoine Gizenga, to Andrée Blouin. 'With his methods, we are heading for disaster'. Gizenga was grateful for Nkrumah's influence on his leader. Blouin, in turn, was grateful for Gizenga. 'This man of iron was a loyal friend', she observed. 'He also saw the situation as it was. His silence was his strong card. He listened and he watched. But he was tenacious; he never forgot his ultimate purpose'.[42]

Threats to the new government were increasing rapidly, on all fronts. 'Traitors were organizing everywhere', Blouin noted in her memoir, *My Country, Africa*. 'In the vice prime minister's office, dossiers disappeared from Gizenga's desk as well as from mine. I realised my desk was being systematically searched, every day. When I locked the drawers with a key, they were callously forced'.[43]

William Burden, the US ambassador in Brussels, had received the NIACT telegram sent by Timberlake. The next day, he made his first official recommendation—and possibly the first official recommendation to this effect made by any American diplomat, politician, military man or CIA agent—that the US overthrow Lumumba's government.[44] He sent the following cable to the State Department:

Lumumba has now maneuvered himself into position of opposition to the West, resistance to United Nations and increasing dependence on Soviet Union and on Congolese supporters
(Kashamura, Gizenga) who are pursuing Soviet's ends. Only
prudent therefore, to plan on basis that Lumumba government
threatens our vital interests in Congo and Africa generally.

A principal objective of our political and diplomatic action must
therefore be to destroy Lumumba government as now constituted,
but at same time we must find or develop another horse to back
which would be acceptable in rest of Africa and defensible against
Soviet political attack.[45]

He suggested that US policy might include encouraging 'the Congolese parliament to repudiate Lumumba'. He added that CIA
representatives in Brussels would make a number of suggestions
through their own channels to Leopoldville and Washington.[46]

Just two days later, a meeting of the US National Security Council discussed the Congo. In it, Dulles argued that 'in Lumumba we
were faced with a person who was a Castro or worse'. It was safe,
added Dulles, 'to go on the assumption that Lumumba has been
bought by the Communists; this also, however, fits with his own
orientation'.[47]

Burden's memoir presents this development as one that was
driven by Dulles. But it is clear that he himself had an instrumental
role. After the meeting of the NSC, Dulles 'flew to Brussels for a
quick survey' and briefed Burden on the council's recent decisions.[48]

The CIA's attitudes toward Lumumba had hardened into enmity.

17

Eisenhower Snubs Lumumba

F OR LUMUMBA, IT WAS AN urgent priority to consult with Secretary General Hammarskjöld and his senior advisors at the United Nations in New York. On 22 July 1960, he left the Congo en route to the US, with fourteen ministers and political leaders. They flew on a Ghanaian plane to Accra, which was their first stop. Ghana had become a nation of huge significance to Lumumba ever since the 1958 All African People's Conference, which had transformed his political life so completely. A huge welcome awaited him; so many thousands of people were waiting on the airfield that the pilot had concerns about how to land safely.

The Congolese prime minister spent two hours in discussions with President Nkrumah, who greeted him with real affection and pleasure. In many ways Nkrumah had become a father figure to the younger man. It was a close personal relationship as well as a profound political alliance. Now, Nkrumah gave Lumumba advice on his forthcoming visit to the UN.

When Lumumba arrived at New York's International Airport on 25 July, he was met with a nineteen-gun salute, as a foreign head of government. He was then escorted at once to the UN, where he was received by Hammarskjöld with warm words of welcome.[1]

The Congolese delegation stayed at the Barclay Hotel in midtown Manhattan, where Thomas Kanza, the Congo's ambassador to the UN, was already staying. The Kenyan trade unionist Tom Mboya had arrived at the same hotel the day before Lumumba.[2] The two men had established a friendship at the All African People's Conference, and now, meeting in New York, they were able to discuss their memories of the conference in Kiswahili, a language they shared. But they had moved sharply apart politically. Mboya was increasingly pro-Western and operated in the shadows of the CIA, while Lumumba remained firmly committed to Pan-Africanism and nonalignment.

Mboya had gone to New York to attend a one-day conference called the Quest for Higher Education in East and Central Africa, convened by the Phelps-Stokes Fund, an American nonprofit foundation.[3] He was hoping the conference would support efforts to airlift several hundred East and Central African students to the US, for whom college places and financial aid were available. Among those present at the conference were representatives of the CIA-backed African-American Institute and the American Society of African Culture (AMSAC).[4]

The Airlift Africa Project, as it was called, had already brought a number of African students to study in the US, including Washington Okumu from Kenya. In 1962, it would bring Barack Obama Sr, the father of former president Barack Obama. The project was underwritten by the Kennedy Foundation and the African-American Students Foundation, of which Mrs Ralph Bunche was a director. She, the actor Sidney Poitier and the baseball player Jackie Robinson, who was the first African American to play in Major League Baseball, all gave time and funds to the foundation, in their wish to support the education of young people in Africa.

But Airlift Africa was more than simply a project to educate young people; it was linked to the CIA as a 'sheep dipping' project, intended to groom future pro-American leaders of newly independent English-speaking states in Africa. Okumu, as someone who wanted very much to become a leader of his country, was the kind of candidate who fitted the bill perfectly.

There was growing suspicion by now in Kenya, the US and elsewhere that Mboya was working for the CIA, which triggered concern about the Airlift Africa Project. Opposition to the project was also increasing in the British colonial government of Kenya, on the grounds that it was an amateur endeavour that was diverting students from education in Kenya and Britain.[5]

* * *

ALONG WITH OTHER UN ambassadors from Africa, Thomas Kanza
and Alexander Quaison-Sackey (Ghana's UN ambassador, who in
1964 became the first Black African to serve as president of the UN
General Assembly) took Lumumba under their wing during his
trip to New York. Lumumba met with Hammarskjöld and his closest advisers on three consecutive days—24, 25 and 26 July 1960.[6] On
one of them, Hammarskjöld hosted a lunch for Lumumba and
members of the Security Council.

Lumumba put pressure on the UN secretariat and the Security Council to push the Belgian troops out of the Congo and also
to dispatch UN troops to Katanga. He believed that the democratically elected government of the Congo, which he led as prime
minister, was faced with a severe and urgent threat. He was keenly
disappointed when he was told that the UN had to rely on negotiation to get into Katanga, not on force.[7]

The issue of Katanga's secession was a complex one for the UN.
Thomas Kanza was grimly aware that the British government gave
theoretic and verbal support to the UN action and its refusal to accept the secession, but at the same time the nation 'did nothing to
stop bankers and businessmen, who wanted to collaborate with the
Belgians, from safeguarding their interests through the survival of
their political pawns in Katanga'.[8] Much the same was true for the
US. 'It is clear', observed David Gibbs in *The Political Economy of
Third World Intervention*, 'that the Eisenhower administration was
nearly unanimous in its support of Katanga'.[9]

* * *

ON 25 JULY, THE National Security Council met in President Eisenhower's summer residence in Newport to discuss the Congo.
John McCone, chairman of the US Atomic Energy Commission,
told Eisenhower and his senior advisors that the Congo was no
longer considered an important source of uranium for the US.

At the same meeting, Allen Dulles expressed serious worry
about the activities in the Congo of Louis Edgar Detwiler,[10] an
American businessman who had attempted to establish profitable
business arrangements to exploit Africa's valuable resources. In

1952, Detwiler and Dr Horace Mann Bond, the president of Lincoln University, had tried—but failed—to interest Nkrumah in a huge project, hinting at US financial backing.[11]

Detwiler had signed a fifty-year contract with Lumumba to develop the Congo's mineral, oil, gas and hydroelectric power resources. However, Lumumba retained the option of annulling the contract, and in any case it still had to be approved by Parliament. Lumumba's agreement with Detwiler had been made openly. When Lumumba had flown to Accra on the first leg of his journey to New York, Detwiler accompanied him. Ghana's *Daily Graphic* reported on 23 July that Lumumba had arrived with 'Mr Edgar Detwiler, an American businessman with whom he had signed a financial and technical agreement yesterday for developing the Congo'.[12]

At midnight on 26 July, the day after the meeting of the NSC, Henry Cabot Lodge, the US ambassador to the United Nations, reported that he had called on Lumumba at his hotel to warn him against Detwiler. Lumumba explained that he had believed that Detwiler enjoyed State Department support. Lodge then told him that 'there were all kinds of Americans, good and bad'. He urged Lumumba to talk with Ambassador Timberlake whenever he needed information about individual Americans.[13]

The contract with Detwiler did not go ahead. But because of the Detwiler episode, Herbert Weiss observed, America's opinion of Lumumba fell even lower; it was thought 'this guy is a total nut, he sells his country's resources to a crook'.[14]

* * *

LUMUMBA DECIDED TO USE his visit to the US to go to Washington, DC. It was agreed with American officials that he would go to the capital on 27 July, when he would meet with President Eisenhower and Secretary of State Christian Herter. But as it turned out, he met only with Herter and Undersecretary of State Douglas Dillon.

Their response to Lumumba was intensely hostile. According to Dillon, Lumumba seemed to have an irrational, almost 'psychotic' personality. 'When he was in the State Department meeting either with me or with the Secretary in my presence', said Dillon, 'he would never look you in the eye. He looked up at the sky. And a tremendous flow of words came out. He spoke in French, and he spoke it very fluently. And his words didn't ever have any relation to the particular things that we wanted to discuss [redacted]. You had a feeling that he was a person that was gripped by this fervor that I can only characterize as messianic [redacted]. He was just not a rational being'.

The United States government was no longer willing to work with Lumumba: 'The impression that was left was [redacted] very bad, that this was an individual whom it was impossible to deal with. And the feelings of the Government as a result of this sharpened very considerably at that time [redacted]'. Dillon added, 'We [had] hoped to see him and see what we could do to come to a better understanding with him'.[15] But Dillon was in full agreement with Dulles, who just a week earlier had compared Lumumba unfavourably to Castro.[16]

Lumumba's own priority at the meeting with Herter and Dillon was altogether different from theirs: Lumumba wanted the US to help remove Belgian forces out of the Congo. The Congo, he insisted, 'does not wish to be exploited and that if any conditions are attached to assistance it will not be accepted. He said that the United States needs Congolese resources such as uranium, and the Congo needs American products. He said he hoped the United States would use its influence with the Belgian Government [so] that the latter might understand that its actions are contrary to its own best interests and contrary to the interests of the West in general.'[17]

* * *

PRIME MINISTER LUMUMBA DID not meet with President Eisenhower. Kanza was informed that Eisenhower would be out of town at the time of Lumumba's visit to Washington.[18] Kanza believed there were two reasons for this diplomatic refusal. The first was that, while in New York, Lumumba had had two unofficial meetings with the Soviet deputy foreign minister Vasily V Kuznetsov. The meeting was not in the least sensational, but Radio Moscow made a point of claiming that Lumumba had agreed during the meeting to visit Moscow.

At the 2004 Wilson Center conference on the history of the Congo in 1960–1961, Kanza put forward another reason for Eisenhower's refusal to meet Lumumba. This reason, he said, emerged out of a meeting in July 1960 between Lumumba and a group of American businessmen in New York, which Kanza (who was there) described in some detail in his 1972 book, *Conflict in the Congo: The Rise and Fall of Lumumba*.

Lumumba was asked, 'What will you do [after independence] with old agreements signed by the Belgians?' 'The exploitation of the mineral riches of the Congo', answered Lumumba, 'should be primarily for the profit of our own people and other Africans'. Then one of those present, who was the head of a New York bank, asked him, 'Do you know, for instance, that Congolese uranium is sold in the United States as Belgian uranium, according to a legal and formal agreement between ourselves and Belgium?'

Kanza guessed what Lumumba would say and swiftly intervened in Lingala, warning him not to reply. But Lumumba's reaction to Kanza's advice was 'Why ever not?' He replied to the American banker, 'As I have said, Belgium won't have a monopoly in the Congo now. From now on we are an independent and sovereign state. Belgium doesn't produce any uranium; it would be to the advantage of both our countries if the Congo and the US worked out their own agreements in future'.

The Americans present, noted Kanza, all of whom represented powerful financial interests, 'looked at one another and exchanged meaningful smiles'.[19]

Later that evening, Kanza received a phone call from an adviser to Eisenhower. 'Look Mr. Kanza', he said. 'I'm sorry, tell your Prime Minister that the President prefers to go and play golf than to meet Lumumba'.[20]

* * *

ON 2 AUGUST 1960, Lumumba left the US to return home. It had been his first visit to the US—a nation he had admired and spoken about with such great enthusiasm, because of its triumph over colonisation and its achievement of self-determination. He had hoped that Americans would be natural allies with the Congolese in their own struggle for freedom. But he came away deeply disillusioned: the visit had confirmed the US government's refusal to help end the Belgian military presence in the Congo.

Far from feeling any sense of support, he was being increasingly criticised by the American media, which now pointed a finger at his use of a Soviet Ilyushin aircraft to fly to the US. This meant, they said, that he was a communist.

In fact, the Congolese prime minister had made a request to the US State Department for the loan of an official airplane; the request had been approved by Ambassador Timberlake and also Ralph Bunche, on behalf of the UN. But in the end it was refused. The Undersecretary of State for Political Affairs, Livingston T Merchant, reported to Secretary of State Herter in a telephone conversation on 21 July that as far he was concerned, there was 'nothing in it for us and it would be more to our advantage if he came by Soviet plane'. The memorandum of the conversation does not explain the nature of this advantage, but it was presumably the impression it would generate that Lumumba was pro-Soviet.

The conversation had been triggered by an earlier phone call between Ambassador Burden in Brussels and Ambassador Timberlake in Leopoldville. Merchant told Herter that he would phone Burden to report on what had been decided.[21]

With no other choice available, Lumumba had accepted the gift of a plane from the Soviet Union.[22] For this, Tom Brady of the *New York Times* took him to task. 'What was I to do?' Lumumba responded indignantly. 'Now it is said that I am a Communist. But judge for yourself what was more important: to be regarded a Communist or to turn down an opportunity to go to the UN to defend our interests there? Judge for yourself'.[23]

For many people, in fact, air travel in the Congo at this time was not a straightforward choice of Soviet versus American. General Alexander himself had flown in a Soviet IL-18 from Ghana to the Congo—and greatly enjoyed the experience. 'The Russian crew', he wrote warmly in his memoir, 'were the height of affability'. When they crossed the equator, 'the pilot put on a beard and I was regaled with Russian champagne and caviar'. When he landed at Leopoldville, Alexander recalled with jovial pleasure, 'I was in a frame of mind to handle any awkward situation!'[24]

* * *

ON HIS WAY BACK to the Congo from America, Lumumba paid a short visit to several African leaders: President Habib Bourguiba of Tunisia, King Mohammed V of Morocco, President William Tubman of Liberia, President Sékou Touré of Guinea, President Sylvanus Olympia of the tiny Republic of Togo—and Nkrumah for a second time within a fortnight.

At every stop, he was cheered by huge and enthusiastic crowds. All the leaders he met expressed their sympathy toward the Congo's difficulties, which were increasing rapidly. On 8 August, Albert Kalonji—following the path of Moise Tshombe in Katanga—announced the autonomy of South Kasai, Lumumba's home province. It was a region rich in diamonds, with heavy involvement by Western business interests, notably the Belgian company Forminiere and the American firm Leon Tempelsman and Son; both companies were suspected of aiding and abetting the secession.

Almost immediately, Kasai's diamonds were sent across the Congo River to Congo Brazzaville, which promptly became the world's largest exporter of diamonds—even though it had no diamond mine of its own.[25] At the time, Congo Brazzaville was preparing for its own independence, set for 15 August 1960. Its political leadership worked closely with Western powers, especially France, and with foreign businesses. The first president was Abbé Fulbert Youlou, who was described dismissively by the US consul, Alan W Lukens, as 'a five-foot excommunicated priest, who walked around in Dior caftans, and was sort of ridiculed as a French puppet'.[26]

Some of the African leaders visited by Lumumba pledged military support, should it become necessary, in order to remove Belgian troops and to end the secession of Katanga and Kasai.[27] 'Hundreds, thousands of Guineans', reported Lumumba in a speech on his return to Leopoldville, 'have volunteered to come serve the Congo'.[28]

The most important stop on Lumumba's tour was Ghana. Nkrumah marked Lumumba's visit with a speech to the Ghana National Assembly on 8 August. 'This is a turning point', began Ghana's president, 'in the history of Africa'. Then he emphasised the importance of supporting the Congo: 'If we allow the independence of the Congo to be compromised in any way by the imperialist and capitalist forces, we shall expose the sovereignty and independence of all Africa to grave risk'.

The struggle of the Congo, he insisted, 'is therefore our struggle. It is incumbent on us to take our stand by our brothers in the Congo in the full knowledge that only Africa can fight for its destiny'.[29]

For two days, Nkrumah and Lumumba talked together intently. They agreed to call a summit conference of independent African leaders from 25 to 30 August in Leopoldville, to consider the situation in the Congo.

But the most important result of their discussions was a secret one: the signing of an accord for the Union of Ghana and the Congo.[30] It was a short document, but it presented a powerful vision of a possible future Union of African States, which any state or territory in Africa could join. The union would have a republican constitution with a federal framework: a federal parliament and a federal head of state. This government would be responsible for foreign affairs, defence, a common currency and economic planning and development; there would be no customs barriers between any parts of the federation.

The capital of the union would be Leopoldville—which, argues one of Nkrumah's biographers, is 'a striking indication of Nkrumah's lack of personal ambition'.[31] Above all, it was an acknowledgement of the central importance of the Congo in Africa.

PART VI

YQPROP

18

Bribery, Bugging and Green Berets

'THE INITIATIVE IN THE CONGO lay in Accra', observed the South African journalist Colin Legum in his 1961 study, *Congo Disaster*. From there, 'President Nkrumah kept in daily contact with Léopoldville and the UN Headquarters, and carried on rapid consultations with other African states through his Ambassadors in their capitals, as well as through their Ambassadors in Accra'.[1]

There were posters on the streets of Accra calling for the support of the Ghanaian troops, and campaigns for cigarettes and other comforts for the soldiers away from home.[2] Radio Ghana transmitted a special programme from Accra to be rebroadcast by willing Congolese radio stations and by a special broadcasting unit set up by the Ghana Army, which carried messages to individual Ghanaian soldiers from their families and friends.

The programme's signature tune was played by E T Mensah and his Tempos, a hugely popular Highlife band. It was quickly remembered because of its catchy words:

Congo! .... Congo!
River Congo!
Me no sabe swim
Water dey take me go!
Congoooo!
Congooooo!

Me no sabe swim,
Water dey take me go!

'Grown men wept when it came on the air', said Cameron Duodu, who was working for Radio Ghana, 'for the Congo was a chaotic and dangerous place and almost everyone feared for those who went there and lived in fear that they might never return home alive'.[3]

On 1 August, Ghana's *Daily Graphic* published a photograph of three Ghana police officers managing the air-radio station in Leopoldville. It also quoted from a welcome by the Congolese minister of health to a Ghanaian medical team bringing doctors, four nursing sisters, a radiographer and a laboratory technician. 'Regard Congo as your own country and save the lives of its people', said the minister gratefully. 'We have confidence in you more than anybody else'. He went on: 'Work as you work at home in Ghana. This is your own home. We won't forget this'.[4]

Nkrumah created a new Ghana Office in the Congo to serve as an administrative liaison between himself and Lumumba. To lead it, Michael Dei-Anang—a first-class civil servant—was released from his routine work as principal secretary of the Foreign Ministry.[5]

In addition, a dedicated coordinating committee was established in Accra to assist the Congo, under the chairmanship of Kwaku Boateng, the minister of information.[6] Members of the committee included Colonel Eric Otu, the senior Ghanaian officer in the army; Geoffrey Bing, the attorney general; General Alexander; and a military officer with logistics expertise. Richard Quarshie was appointed secretary to the committee. On 12 July, the committee sent a mission to Leopoldville.[7]

Another member of the committee was Aloysius K Barden, the director of the Bureau of African Affairs, who was increasingly involved in the Congo. At the end of July, he moved to Leopoldville to coordinate the work of the BAA agents working there. 'I left for Congo to assist our brothers in consolidating their newly hard-won independence', he wrote to a friend in Uganda on 30 July, 'and also to achieve their territorial integrity and sovereignty which are being threatened by mass invasion of Belgium imperialists'.[8] Barden returned briefly to Accra to submit a report to Nkrumah; he then returned immediately to his work in the Congo.[9]

* * *

BOTH GHANA AND THE US were embroiled in the developing crisis of the Congo. But 'almost from the beginning', argues historian Nwaubani Ebere, 'the two had fundamental differences on the issue'.[10] The most fundamental difference was that of purpose. Ghana was seeking to protect the legitimate government of the Congo and was making considerable sacrifices in order to achieve that goal. The US, by contrast, was seeking to undermine Lumumba and his government and to advance the perceived interests of the US. In this process, the CIA took a key role.

Larry Devlin arrived in Leopoldville as the CIA chief of station of the Congo 'in early July (probably the 10th or 11th) 1960', about ten days after independence and five days after the mutiny of the army.[11] His cover was that of political officer in the embassy, and his office was next door to that of Ambassador Timberlake, with whom he forged a friendship. Sometimes, commented Devlin, there was friction between foreign service officers and CIA personnel in an embassy, but not under Ambassador Timberlake, who 'set the tone from the outset, making it clear that he would not tolerate any kind of turf wars or infighting'.[12] Devlin already had a close relationship with Bill Burden, who was close to Timberlake; these links quickly translated into a triangle of men who were of one mind.[13]

'Shortly after my arrival', wrote Devlin in *Chief of Station, Congo*, 'I drove in a borrowed car to a house in Binza—a suburb of Leopoldville on a hill overlooking the city—where I met an agent who had been on the books for some time. He was one of the few agents I inherited and I had to start building up a network from scratch'.[14] This gives the impression that the CIA presence in the Congo was patchy at best. Such a picture was frequently promoted by officials. 'The CIA had had one agent in the Congo' observed Owen W Roberts, who was the consular and commercial officer in the embassy in Leopoldville.[15]

But judging even by Devlin's sparse account, this was misleading. He had a deputy, Eugene Leroy Jeffers Jr, who served under cover of political officer at the embassy. He also had a 'deep cover agent' who worked in secret at the office of Pierre Mulele.[16] Since Mulele was the minister of education in Lumumba's cabinet and a central figure among Lumumbists, his appointment afforded a valuable source of information for Devlin. Two additional assets were referred to by Devlin as 'Dad' and 'Bobby'.

One of Devlin's agents was 'Jacques', a Belgian who owned a plantation. 'Jef, my new deputy', Devlin recorded, 'was his case officer and soon had him [Jacques] suggesting anti-Lumumba story lines to his friend the newspaper editor, and getting steady feedback from all his sources'. In addition, wrote Devlin, 'We were already monitoring parliament and encouraging and guiding the actions of various parliamentary opposition groups that we had penetrated. We were seeking political leaders who might marshal their supporters against Lumumba when a vote of confidence was called'.[17]

Jacques used his contacts with the youth, with labour leaders and with Abako to foment demonstrations against Lumumba in the weeks that followed independence.[18] This may explain a crowd encountered by Lumumba in front of the prime minister's residence when he returned from the US in late June 1960: a gathering of adolescent girls wearing white shirts, orange skirts and blue caps, the uniform of the youth of Abako, who cried out, 'Down with Lumumba! Down with the traitor government!'[19]

Devlin was highly appreciative of a temporary duty officer who worked under official cover in the embassy. This asset, referred to by Devlin as 'Mike', was experienced and extremely competent, as well as fluent in French. 'He had been sent to the Congo by his home station', Devlin wrote (though without identifying which home country this was), 'with instructions to develop contacts among that nation's troops assigned to the United Nations military force. Though I appreciated the other station's needs, I quickly drafted Mike to serve as a station case officer because we needed all the help we could get against our local and Soviet targets'. Mike remained in the Congo for several months.[20]

A woman working with the CIA was attached to the US embassy, but Devlin made no mention of her. Apart from this woman and Alison Palmer, the vice consul, the embassy staff were 'essentially an all-male group'.[21]

A number of Americans were living in the Congo at this time, and the US embassy tried to recruit some of them as sources of information. One of these was Herbert Weiss, who refused. 'My relationship with the US Embassy in Leopoldville was strained', he recalled many years later, 'and one reason was that they assumed I would be a reasonable source of information on the grounds that I had worked at the State Department less than a year earlier'. This, thought Weiss, 'was understandable'. But he was not in a position to assist. 'I could not be helpful with raw information, because I was in the Congo under academic auspices for the Centre of International Studies at M.I.T. I had presented myself to the Congolese leaders and party representatives as an independent scholar. I felt that sharing such information with any government or intelligence agency was inconsistent with this, especially where I was given free access to their supporters'. He added, 'And no one at the US embassy ever asked for my opinion as to what I thought US policy should be. On this, I think I would have given them a full answer had they ever asked. I would have said that in my opinion, Lumumba is entirely open to negotiations, especially with the United States, and I would urge you to enter into negotiations with him'.[22]

* * *

ONE OF DEVLIN'S REGULAR visitors was Albert Kalonji, who announced the secession of South Kasai in August 1960. Kalonji 'was seeking American support to overthrow Lumumba', recalled Devlin in his memoir, 'and he wasn't the only one, for several other politicians visited me with the same idea in mind'.[23] Given that Devlin and other CIA officials were actively inspiring Kalonji and other politicians to oppose Lumumba, this statement was disingenuous at best.

Howard Imbrey passed out money to selected politicians while he was in the Congo. This was a task in which Devlin, too, took a role after his arrival. By now, payments were being made to the five members who formed the nucleus of the Binza group, so-called because its members lived in the elite Leopoldville suburb of Binza, where only white people had lived before independence. This powerful clique comprised Mobutu, army chief of staff; Victor Nendaka; Justin Bomboko, foreign minister; Albert Ndele, finance aide; and Damien Kandolo.[24] Also on the list of recipients were Kasavubu, the Senate president Joseph Ileo and Cyrille Adoula.[25]

Further information about the bribing of Congolese politicians emerged in 1975 in the course of the wide-ranging and revelatory investigations of the Church Committee, a US Senate committee chaired by Democratic senator Frank Church to investigate the intelligence activities of the US government. An important dimension of its investigation was the events taking place in the Congo in 1960–1961.

In the course of the Church Committee investigation, Douglas Dillon was asked, 'Were you aware that the US was supplying financial support or other kinds of support to "moderate" politicians within the Congo who would be opponents of Lumumba?' He replied, 'Not in detail, but certainly the general fact that we would be doing that, yes'.[26]

Soldiers were also bribed by the CIA. UN liaison officers attached to Mobutu noted 'the constant comings and goings of some Western military attaches who visited Mobutu with bulging briefcases containing thick brown paper packets which they obligingly deposited on the table'. The UN officers did not know what they contained, but 'could not help making guesses'. A senior UN official believed that with this money, Mobutu's men became 'by far the most affluent soldiers in Africa'.[27]

The historian David Gibbs has commented that these highly paid soldiers may not have numbered more than a few hundred. But, he adds, they constituted virtually the only functioning units in the Armée Nationale Congolaise. 'With such a political base', he points out, 'Mobutu was able to play a decisive role. The CIA used Mobutu and his soldiers as a free-lance strike force'.[28]

It has been alleged that Frank Carlucci, a political officer at the US embassy, was working for the agency. He vigorously denied these allegations.[29] Between 1957 and 1959, Carlucci had been on the staff of the US embassy in Johannesburg as a commercial officer; whether or not he was CIA, he worked hard to collect intelligence on the Pan Africanist Congress. In an interview in 1997, he recalled, 'I got acquainted with the movement, which, interestingly, nobody in Pretoria had been able to do. Our embassy was constrained from attending the meetings. The meetings were in Johannesburg. So I established a relationship, a personal relationship, with some of the political officers in Pretoria and reported to them'.[30]

The Pan Africanist Congress in South Africa, abbreviated as the PAC, had been founded in 1959 by Mangaliso Robert Sobukwe, a university lecturer, as a breakaway movement from the African National Congress (ANC), identifying itself as Black nationalist and anticommunist. The PAC's anticommunism attracted the attention of Washington. According to Denis Herbstein in *White Lies*, the ANC later suggested that its new rival was a CIA creation, the conception taking place in the Johannesburg offices of the United States Information Service, where Potlake Leballo, the national secretary of the PAC, had been employed. This allegation has been challenged as factually inaccurate. But in any case, as Herbstein notes, the split was not displeasing to Pretoria: 'The new congress might weaken the ANC, whose non-racial demands could not possibly be appeased, but the message of "Africa for the Africans" might, with skill, be blended into the realm of "separate development"'.[31]

At the end of his posting in South Africa, Carlucci went back to the US for French-language training before being sent to the Congo in 1960, fifteen days before independence. When he first arrived, he did not have much contact with the CIA. Nonetheless, he considered it a priority to collect intelligence:

I persuaded the DCM [deputy chief of mission], Rob McIlvaine, a marvelous man, to allow me to rent a Volkswagen so I had my own car and didn't go around in an embassy chauffeured car. I then got myself some press credentials because the press moved around more freely than anybody else could. Lumumba tended to hold a press conference a day and I figured it was important to get into those. Then I got myself a pass to the Parliament which was in formation. And basically spent all day outside the embassy. Just floating in from time to time.

Carlucci described Lumumba as 'an absolute spellbinder, a very charismatic man'.[32]

There is a brief mention in Devlin's memoir of the bugging of the telephones of an office belonging to 'the Czechs'—presumably Czechoslovakia's embassy. This required a house nearby to use as a listening post, which was organised by 'Jeff' and an American technician sent out to the Congo to assist them. Few details are given by Devlin, apart from an episode in which the technician, groping for wires in the darkness, wrapped his hand around a snake.[33]

Devlin's memoir is threaded with moments of danger when he remained cool and collected, taking 'a deep drag' on a cigarette. But the book is incomplete and unreliable: it is a collection of anecdotes, often implausible, tied loosely together. At times it appears to be deliberately misleading. In any case, many aspects of his life appear to have been routine. His wife, Colette, and daughter, Maureen, joined him in Leopoldville, where Colette enjoyed teaching her cook to prepare favourite dishes and Maureen went to a riding club. They lived in a house less than a hundred yards from the Ghana embassy and near the residence of the Timberlakes.

Alison Palmer, the US vice consul, was candid about the advantages of being a well-funded American in Leopoldville: 'We had a two-hour lunch hour and I would go to the swimming pool with some friends and we would play a couple of sets of tennis and then cool off in the pool and then have lunch and get back to work again. (laughs) And I belonged to the riding club there and did a lot of riding'.[34]

The pleasures of Devlin's family life did not prevent him from admiring Madame Blouin, Lumumba's chief of protocol. To his eyes, she was 'a striking, light-skinned beauty'. He regretted that she was 'anti-white and reportedly had considerable influence with Lumumba', but all the same he found her 'tantalizing'.[35]

Less tantalising was Daphne Park, Devlin's MI6 counterpart in the Congo, who had arrived in 1959 under cover of first consul at the British embassy and cut a short, stout and frumpy figure. 'For years and years', Park told a *Guardian* journalist in 1979, 'I have looked like a missionary, which was a great advantage in my career'.[36] According to one British correspondent in Leopoldville in 1960, Park was 'to be seen everywhere, a large bespectacled lady, usually with cigarette ash on her ample bosom'.[37] Another British correspondent in the Congo described her as a 'very unusual political secretary, a large, jolly and immensely well-informed girl. . . . She drives a small car, always full of people, and successfully invites the most astonishing collection of rival African leaders to her house outside Leo'.[38]

Park and Devlin became good friends, sharing similar attitudes towards events in the Congo. 'While Daphne and I worked separately and did not have any joint operations', Devlin recalled in his memoir, 'we knew each other well and had come to similar conclusions'. She was, he thought, 'one of the best intelligence officers I have ever encountered'.[39] She abhorred communism and the Soviet Union and felt a strong hostility towards the UN, strongly disapproving of Hammarskjöld. 'The United Nations force had very curious ground rules concerning non-intervention', she observed in 1989 in an interview with the *New Yorker*, 'which caused me to become disillusioned with the United Nations forever'.[40]

'I was interesting to many of the African nationalists', said Park, 'because I travelled up and down the coast a lot—to Ghana, Nigeria, and French West Africa. When I first arrived, I used to go to fetch the Embassy mail from Accra. Most people liked to do it once or twice but then got bored, whereas I didn't mind. One had to cross the river to Brazzaville, then fly to Douala, often getting stuck in Gabon en route. One would get as far as Lagos, then get stuck again before reaching Accra. It could take three days'. She added, 'I was meeting and talking with people all the way, so I knew what was in the air'.[41]

She regarded her job in MI6 as not simply intelligence gathering, but also intervention. 'Once you get really good inside intelligence about any group', she explained in a television documentary in 1992, 'you are able to learn where the levers are, and what one man fears of another. . . .You set people discreetly against one another. . . . They destroy each other, we don't destroy them'.[42]

* * *

THE CIA NOT ONLY had a station in Leopoldville, which managed all the agency's operations in the Congo under the direction of the chief of station, but also had a base in Elisabethville. This base—in accordance with the standard model for CIA operations in individual countries—was subordinate to the station but also communicated directly with headquarters in Washington. The same model applied to a CIA base in Bukavu, the capital of Kivu (which was headed by William H Dunbar in 1963).[43] When Devlin first arrived in the Congo, the chief of base in Elisabethville was John Anderton, who shared the post with a communicator. Though a dedicated officer, Anderton was bitter. He had already served as chief of station in Saigon, so he was far too senior to head the Katangan base. He left the Congo as soon as he could be relieved, after about a month.

The relief arrived in July 1960, in the form of David D Doyle, who was a good friend of Bronson Tweedy; their fathers had been classmates at Princeton. Doyle later gave an account of his time in the Congo in his memoir, *True Men and Traitors*. Unlike Anderton, he welcomed the post—'every day was a new challenge, a new adventure'.[44]

Doyle spent his first three weeks in the Congo in Leopoldville, assisting Devlin; he handled a few agents and a prospective agent. He lived with two other clandestine services officers, 'Mike' and 'Gene', in a small furnished house. 'They were out there day and night', he recalled, 'recruiting agents and running them under conditions of dangerous public disorder'.[45]

In early September, he flew to Elisabethville, staying there until April the following year. It was a complicated post, since the breakaway province of Katanga was not recognised by the US; this meant that it was difficult for Devlin, as an accredited diplomat to the Congo, to go there.[46] Doyle himself was under the cover of the Department of Defense, yet serving in a US foreign service post that had no military presence. He and the US consul, Bill Canup, kept quiet about his 'irregular status'.[47]

Also at the Elisabethville base were two communicators, 'Frenchy', the radio operator with whom Doyle shared a 'ramshackle bungalow', and a second man. A third member of the team, for a short time, was a 'girl' from headquarters.[48]

Doyle despised Lumumba. He regarded him as 'simply an unstable former postal clerk with great political charisma, who was leaning towards the Communist bloc'. Lumumba, he noted with concern, had 'brought in a dozen or so IL-14 aircraft with full duplicate Soviet crews to transport his troops against the Katanga and Kasai secessions . . . [and] a second Soviet airlift of Congolese troops to the Katanga appeared likely'.[49]

For Doyle, Major Guy Weber of the Belgian army was 'one of the heroes', because he 'stood firm and kept his troops in order'. Weber later became the military advisor to Moise Tshombe, the self-styled president of Katanga. Doyle was less enthusiastic about the 'mixed bag of foreign mercenaries' who were brought into Katanga once Belgium started finally to pull out their officers and noncommissioned officers.[50]

Doyle started CIA operations in Katanga 'virtually from scratch', according to his memoir. 'My orders in Elisabethville', he explained, 'were simply to recruit a stable of agents who could keep us informed—among both the Katangan government and its white supporters, and the main tribal opposition, the Balubas'. He swiftly brought new people into his outfit. 'I set out to conduct the standard recruitment cycle: to spot people who looked like good agent prospects, to contact and assess them, and to develop and recruit those who would make good agents. The task was not easy. The US consulate had been there for forty years, but mainly because of the US private sector's mining interests in the region'.[51]

Although Doyle claimed to have started CIA operations in Katanga 'virtually from scratch', this was not the case. American intelligence had been operating there since World War II; in 1944, the OSS station in Leopoldville had made a strong case to headquarters in Washington that a second US consulate be opened in Elisabethville, to facilitate effective intelligence work in the area. The

State Department had been arguing energetically for the setting up of a consulate in Katanga for some time.[52] The reason for this need was the Shinkolobwe mine. The mine is not mentioned in *True Men and Traitors*, but its omission is meaningless since everything about Shinkolobwe was regarded as top secret. In any case, Doyle's memoir is unreliable, much like Devlin's.

* * *

IN SEPTEMBER 1960, ANOTHER CIA official arrived in the Congo: George Wittman, who presented himself as an American business-man. He established himself in the Memling, the luxury hotel in the centre of Leopoldville.[53] Good-looking and well-dressed, Wit-tman mixed easily among the other foreign white businessmen staying at the Memling.

Wittman was in and out of the Congo over the following year and also visited Ghana. He wrote eloquent and lively accounts of his meetings and travels, which he sent to Maurice Tempelsman.[54] Since Wittman was a professional agent working for the CIA and, in any case, Tempelsman was seemingly linked in some way to the CIA, it is reasonable to assume that these reports—or versions of them—reached CIA headquarters.[55]

They reveal that Wittman stayed carefully in the shadows; his guide 'for everything at this stage', he wrote, was 'velvet paws'.[56] Nonetheless, he attracted attention in October 1960 when—according to his account to Tempelsman—he rescued Albert Ndele, the Congolese finance minister, from a bloody attack by about fif-teen Lumumbists and carried him to safety. The episode was writ-ten up as a heroic adventure in a number of American newspapers and also in the alumni magazine of Wittman's college.[57]

Tempelsman used his connection with Adlai Stevenson to infiltrate Wittman into the networks of the UN in the Congo. In September 1960, David Gibbs records in *The Political Economy of Third World Intervention*, Stevenson introduced Wittman to Sture Linnér, ONUC's Swedish chief of civilian operations, with the following letter:

Mr. Wittman is going to the Congo as a representative of Mr. Tempelsman's firm . . . [and] would be very glad to place at the

disposal of the United Nations authorities and the Congo government whatever technical assistance in the field of mineral development they may desire. . . .

I understand what pressures you must be under, and the only
purpose of this letter is to assure you that Mr. Wittman would be
glad to be of whatever help he can should his services be required.

Linnér replied to say that he would be 'happy to cooperate with
Mr. Wittman in any way that would seem useful to all parties
concerned'.

Stevenson also met with Secretary General Hammarskjöld
'about the Congo on behalf of his client, Maurice Tempelsman'.
Tempelsman reportedly worked 'hand in glove with the CIA Station' in Leopoldville, Gibbs writes, and developed close ties to the
station chief, Larry Devlin.[58]

As soon as he arrived in the Congo, Wittman sought to make
useful contacts and went to dinner gatherings. He was pleased
when Ambassador Timberlake asked him 'to stay after cocktails
to have a light dinner with him'.[59]

The first secretary, it turned out, was an old acquaintance. To
this friend Wittman explained 'the main purpose for my visit': to
assess the best approach in relation to a barter programme with the
Congolese government.[60]

'There is no sign at this early stage of other diamond activity',
reported Wittman to Tempelsman.[61] As before, it is likely that
Wittman used the word 'diamond' as a camouflage for uranium and
possibly other strategic minerals. This was the cover that had been
used by the OSS during World War II to refer to uranium from
the Shinkolobwe mine: 'Own job, *under cover of trying to look for
ind[ustrial] diamonds*, getting illegally to Germany', said one OSS
agent in this top-secret mission in the Congo, 'was to find uranium
sources'.[62]

David Gibbs examines Tempelsman's barter scheme. It was 'of
dubious value' to the US government, observes Gibbs, since America's strategic stockpile was amply supplied with industrial diamonds. 'We have a very large surplus of industrial diamonds in the

stockpile already', noted the State Department. 'The diamonds we would obtain from the barter deal would be of no use to us at all'.[63]

If Wittman *was* referring to uranium, he needed to disguise it. He had arranged with the embassy to send his secret reports to the US via the official pouch, but this was not completely secure.[64] He soon established a channel for secret information through a Brazzaville contact, while arranging for cables without sensitivity to be sent directly to the Memling hotel.[65]

* * *

OFFICIALLY, THERE WERE NO American troops in the Congo. But working closely with Ambassador Timberlake was a team of US Green Berets—a Tenth Special Forces Group, led by Sully deFontaine, an American born in Belgium to French parents, who had served in the OSS during World War II.[66]

A request for this team, conceived as a rapid response unit, had been submitted to the US government by Ambassador Timberlake, in order to 'evacuate Americans and Europeans from remote jungle outposts', according to Jack Lawson, who wrote an account of the mission in *The Slaver's Wheel* (2009).[67]

Lawson states that his book is based on the memoirs of Sully deFontaine. He does not provide documentary sources, apart from an appendix, which contains an image of a list of 'American Embassy Personnel and Americans living in Leopoldville and the Congo as of August 1960'. The list includes 'Fontaine, Lt. Sully', and it identifies him as 'USAF'. This fits with the claim by Lawson that when deFontaine was around the embassy, he used the cover of air force first lieutenant to obscure the reason for his access to Timberlake.[68] In addition, corroborating accounts of the evacuation mission exist elsewhere, including a report in the official history of the US Army.[69] Still, the lack of documentary sources makes it impossible to verify the details of the mission—and of subsequent events—presented by Lawson.

There were eight men in deFontaine's rapid response unit, according to Lawson, including Captain Albert Valentine Clement, a pilot whose nicknames included 'Jake' and 'Snake', and Sergeant Stefan Mazak. Sergeant Edward Cournoyer, a French-speaking air force radio communications specialist, was another member of the team; because of his fluency in French, he was called 'Frenchy' by the team. Sully deFontaine was apparently shocked when he saw how much electronics equipment the air force had stowed for Cournoyer on the cargo plane that took the unit to the Congo. 'Frenchy had about every conceivable piece of shortwave radio equipment that existed. It was all in huge containers and each container was tied down to the floor'.[70]

It may have been a coincidence that the communicator working for deFontaine had the same nickname—Frenchy—as the communicator working for Doyle. But it is also possible they were the same man. If that is so, it may indicate that deFontaine's operation was used to deliver powerful radio equipment to the CIA base in Elisabethville.

Only deFontaine, Clements, Mazak and Cournoyer went out to the Congo on 13 July; the others remained on standby in Germany, in case of an emergency. Their cover was that of being French Canadian Red Cross medical personnel; they were instructed not to indicate in any way that they were American military. The code name of the classified operation, according to Lawson, was 'Robert Seven'. Only a few people at the embassy were aware of it, and 'a purposeful disconnection' was maintained between CIA operations and the Special Forces team. The operations centre was based at an airfield in Brazzaville, on the other side of the Congo River, which was considered safer.[71] To this headquarters flew the remainder of the unit: eighteen pilots from the US Army and Air Force. Helicopters and single-engine planes were flown in.

Cournoyer, the radio specialist, was in communication with the navy task force that was cruising about two hundred miles off the Congo's coast. The USS Wasp was acting as a communications relay station to the USAREUR—the US European Command—because of the power of its communications equipment. According to Lawson, it had been decided that in case of an emergency, such as the American embassy being stormed by rebels, the naval task force would send in the marines.[72]

On 20 July, deFontaine met Patrice Lumumba and Antoine Gizenga, following an incident in which deFontaine and Mazak—under their cover as French Canadian medics—assisted an injured soldier. In Lawson's telling, this soldier was a 'rebel'; the Green Berets gave him morphine. Afterwards, Lumumba went towards them, to thank them for assisting the soldier, and introduced them to Gizenga.

DeFontaine reported that Operation Robert Seven rescued 239 people. By the end of July, all the members of his unit had left the Congo. He alone remained, according to Lawson's account, 'to assist the United Nations troops that were arriving and to gather as much information as he could on the intentions of the Lumumba government for Ambassador Timberlake'.[73] Lawson writes that deFontaine was no longer pretending to be a French Canadian Red Cross medic. He was now operating under a new alias—that of Robert DuJardin, a Frenchman.

In mid-July, deFontaine (as DuJardin) met Ralph Bunche by chance in a hotel elevator, and Bunche asked him to act as interpreter for him at a lunch with some French-speaking teachers. The lunch did not materialise. But deFontaine returned to the hotel on 25 July to see Bunche, with a request from Timberlake: that DuJardin be issued credentials identifying him as working for the UN. Bunche agreed. He had been given to understand that the man calling himself DuJardin was an air force lieutenant assigned to the US embassy. He had no idea that DuJardin was a Green Beret.

DeFontaine said he was given the role of French major/commandant with the UN peacekeeping forces and issued an 'ONU' armband.[74] No record of such a soldier in ONUC has been found in relevant UN files. Given the chaos and confusion in the Congo at the time, however, the lack of extant documentation does not necessarily disqualify his story.

He was one of a number of soldiers employed unofficially by the US in the Congo. The US also used some of the white mercenaries of different nationalities (notably British, French, Belgian, South African and Rhodesian) who were employed by Moise Tshombe in Katanga. According to the summary of an interview with Larry Devlin for the Church Committee in 1975, Devlin said that he had

had 'important contact' with Mike Hoare and his men. 'Mad Mike' Hoare was a notorious white mercenary who reportedly told journalists in 1964 that 'killing African nationalists is as if one is killing an animal'.[75]

Devlin claimed that his station 'gave no direct or indirect support' to the white mercenaries, but this is not necessarily true; nor does it exclude the possibility that mercenaries supported him and his operations.[76] Several of them, including Hoare, later claimed to have worked with the CIA in the Congo.[77] It is not possible to verify these stories, but there appears to be a pattern, suggesting some degree of accuracy.

* * *

CHIEF OF STATION DEVLIN flew to Paris in late July 1960 for a meeting about the Congo crisis with three US ambassadors: Burden, Timberlake and Amory Houghton, the ambassador to France. It emerged from their discussions that *Time* magazine was planning to do a cover story on Lumumba. Timberlake was appalled. 'Celebrity coverage at home', he complained, 'will make him even more difficult to deal with. He's a first-class headache as it is'. Burden advised him to get the story killed or modified—but Timberlake responded that he had tried to lean on the *Time* man in Leopoldville, without success. The story had already been sent to New York.

Burden's response was swift. He was a friend of Henry Luce, the owner of *Time* (as well as of *Life*, *Fortune* and *Sports Illustrated*), and his wife, the celebrated author and diplomat Clare Booth Luce. Burden acted to exploit this connection. Devlin witnessed his accomplished handling of the situation, which he recorded in his memoir:

'You can't expect much from a journalist at that level', Burden said pulling out his address book and flipping through the pages. He picked up the phone and put a call through to the personal assistant of Henry Luce, *Time*'s owner.

Luce soon returned the call. After a brief, friendly exchange that made clear his personal relationship with Luce, Burden bluntly told him that he would have to change the Lumumba cover story. Luce apparently said that the magazine was about to go to press. 'Oh, come on, Henry', Burden said, 'you must have other cover stories in the can'. They chatted for a few more minutes before Burden hung up.

A few days later, Devlin flew to the US for briefings with Allen Dulles and picked up a copy of *Time*. It had a different cover story: Lumumba had been relegated to the inside pages.[78]

19

The Road to Calvary

O NCE DEVLIN HAD RETURNED TO the Congo from Washington in late July, the CIA plot targeting Lumumba rapidly
took shape. On 17 August, Devlin sent a cable to CIA headquarters,
warning of a communist plan—for which there was no evidence—
to take over the Congo. 'Lumumba, Kashamura, Ghanaian Ambassador Djin and Madame Blouin', asserted Devlin, 'are all anti-white
and latter Communist. So are Momo Toure, Yansan Sekou, and
Louis Behanzin, Guinean advisers'. He added that Serge Michel—
who was attached to the Algerian provisional government and was
currently serving Lumumba as his press attaché—was 'even more
in the Commie camp and anti-western'. The situation, he warned,
'is rapidly getting worse and the Commie design now seems suddenly clear. It is already late'.[1]

Bronson Tweedy responded to the cable the same day. He was
seeking State Department approval, he assured Devlin, to remove
Lumumba from power.

Ambassador Timberlake, too, sent a cable on 17 August to the
State Department. He warned that Ghana was 'giving aid and comfort to Lumumba and the Communists', and that Ghana, along
with Guinea, 'would oppose any change in the Government of the
Congo and any action of the UN which would reduce Lumumba's
power or change his political course'.[2]

The next day, at nine am, in the summer residence of President
Eisenhower, a meeting of the National Security Council was held to
discuss the Congo. Undersecretary of State Dillon presented background information to the council and asserted that Lumumba was

serving the Soviets. Allen Dulles agreed, adding that Lumumba was 'in Soviet pay'. Timberlake, added Dulles, was concerned that the ANC was armed and that Lumumba 'could use it to terrorize the whites. He might force all the whites out except for the Soviet technicians'. The discussion was written up in a memorandum by Robert H Johnson:

> Dulles argued that it was 'important to preserve Katanga as a sep-arate viable asset'.
>
> Eisenhower was in agreement: he suggested it might be a good idea if the UN were to recognize Katanga, even though that view contradicted America's official position.
>
> The clear consensus around the table was that Lumumba was a threat to American interests and had to be removed. Maurice Stans hoped this could be achieved without violence. 'We might base ourselves on Tshombe and Kasavubu', he suggested, 'and throw out Lumumba by peaceful means'.[3]

Meanwhile, on the same day as the meeting of the NSC, Devlin sent a dramatic cable from Leopoldville: 'Embassy and Station believe Congo experiencing classic Communist effort take over government. Many forces at work here: Soviets, Czechs, Guineans, Ghanaians, Communist Party, etc. Although difficult determine major influencing factors to predict outcome struggle for power, decisive period not far off'. There was no basis for such an alarming report. But it justified Devlin's proposal for an operation 'to assist a Congolese effort to organize opposition to Prime Minister Patrice Lumumba with the aim of replacing him with a more moderate and pro-Western government'. He sent a follow-up cable, report-ing that Timberlake approved of the plan.[4]

Two days later, on 19 August, the CIA authorised the station in Leopoldville to proceed.

* * *

THIS WAS THE FIRST big undertaking of the CIA's Africa Division, and it was given every priority. It was at the top of the agenda at a meeting on 25 August 1960 of the National Security Council subcommittee responsible for the planning of covert operations. Known as the 'Special Group', members included Allen Dulles; Livingston Merchant, from the State Department; John N Irwin II, the assistant secretary of defense for International Security Affairs; and Gordon Gray, the White House security advisor. The Special Group agreed to keep all options open for the possible removal of Lumumba.[5]

The meaning of this agreement was clarified by the release in April 2018 of the transcript of Dillon's 1975 testimony to the Church Committee, under questioning by counsel Frederick D Baron. Their exchange reveals details about the meeting of the Special Group on 25 August 1960:

> *Mr. Baron.* From your knowledge of Special Group meetings and minutes, it is your reading of this sentence that 'it was finally agreed that planning for the Congo would not necessarily rule out consideration of any particular kind of activity which might contribute to getting rid of Lumumba'—you would read that sentence to indicate that an assassination was within the bounds of the kind of activity that might be used to get rid of Lumumba?
>
> *Mr. Dillon.* Yes, I would.
>
> *Mr. Baron.* And you were commenting before that Mr. Dulles might be expected by, say, some members of the Special Group, to return to the Special Group if an assassination were being mounted?
>
> *Mr. Dillon.* Not only that, but anything being mounted, I mean whatever action to get rid of Lumumba . . .—and Gordon Gray. I think they would have kept him notified, because he was sort of central in this thing, they wouldn't do anything without his at least knowing about it.

This reference to Gray, the White House security advisor, was picked up by Counsel Baron, who asked Dillon about the role of Eisenhower in the acceptance of assassination as a means to get rid of Lumumba:

> *Mr. Baron.* . . . Mr. Gray commented . . . that his associate had
> expressed extremely strong feelings on the necessity for very
> straightforward action in this situation, and wondered whether
> the plans as outlined were sufficient to accomplish this. . . . Let
> me represent to you that we have testimony from Thomas Par-
> rott [the secretary of the Special Group on CIA activity in rela-
> tion to the Congo], who took the minutes for this meeting and
> other Special Group meetings, that when he used the phrase
> 'Mr. Gray's associate or Mr. Gray's friend', he was referring eu-
> phemistically to the President.
>
> *Mr. Dillon.* That is what I would more or less have assumed. But as
> long as you have that testimony, my assumption is probably correct.[6]

Robert H Johnson also gave testimony in 1975 to the Church
Committee, which substantiates the statements by Dillon. Johnson testified that when he was taking notes of an NSC meeting
in the summer of 1960, evidently the meeting on 18 August, President Eisenhower 'said something—I can no longer remember his
words—that came across to me as an order for the assassination of
Lumumba'. Eisenhower turned to Dulles and said something to
the effect that Lumumba should be eliminated, in the full hearing
of all those in attendance.

According to Johnson, there was a stunned silence for about
fifteen seconds, and then the meeting continued. There was no discussion, he explained; the meeting 'simply moved on'. But he could
remember his 'sense of that moment quite clearly because the President's statement came as a great shock to me'. He said he had
heard of nothing like that since.

John Irwin, the assistant secretary of defense who was at the
meeting, said later to the Church Committee that he could not
recall any plan for assassination. But, he added, 'It is my general
opinion that it would be improper for the Director of Central Intelligence to undertake an assassination operation without an express directive from the President'.[7]

The president needed enough information to stop an action,
argues Peter Grose in his biography of Allen Dulles, but not so

much that 'plausible deniability' is lost—that is, the ability to deny knowledge of a secret undertaking if it were to become public. 'Defenders of presidential virtue only insult Eisenhower's intelligence', Grose observes, 'in suggesting that he did not understand the intimations he was receiving from his aides and the signals he was sending when he let the opportunities pass without a negative response. At any point between July and October of 1960 Eisenhower could have told Allen or Bissell that their efforts to immobilize Lumumba should stop short of actual assassination'.

'This', adds Grose, 'he did not do'.[8]

* * *

On 27 August, two days after the meeting of the Special Group, Dulles sent an urgent cable to Devlin. 'Lumumba's removal', it read, 'must be an urgent and prime object and . . . should be a high priority of our covert actions'. Dulles cited 'high quarters here' as the source of this 'clearcut conclusion'.[9] Since the CIA director's only superior is the president, this was a clear reference to Eisenhower.[10]

Devlin was given an additional $100,000 to accomplish his goal by whatever means possible.[11] 'To the best of my knowledge', he wrote in his memoir, 'no other station chief had ever been given such latitude. . . . If further evidence was required that Washington supported our own conclusion about replacing Lumumba, that was it'.[12]

Meanwhile, Dulles had been keeping in close touch with his friend Bill Burden. He flew to Brussels for 'a quick survey' with him. 'He briefed me on the recent decisions of the National Security Council', Burden records in his memoir. 'The leader we could depend on in a showdown with Lumumba', Dulles told Burden, 'was young Colonel Joseph Mobutu, second in command of the Congolese army'.[13]

* * *

Lumumba had despaired at the UN's inability to remove Belgian troops and to bring Katanga back into the Congo. On 21 August, he followed up on the earlier threat he had made—and appealed to the Soviet Union for help. This appeal was made a full three days after Devlin's warning to Washington that 'Commie design now seems suddenly clear. It is already late'. This suggests that Devlin was motivated less by evidence than by a wish to justify his actions.[14]

Eisenhower later stated, in the second volume of his autobiography, that a Soviet ship with trucks and technicians arrived in the Congo in late August; it was estimated, he added, that two hundred Soviet technicians, in addition to some air crews, were in the Congo without UN authority. He described this as a 'Soviet invasion'.[15]

But David Gibbs argues in *The Political Economy of Third World Intervention* that the role of the Soviet Union in the Congo was minimal. 'There is no evidence', he writes, 'that the Soviets actually sought to take control of the Congo'. Even if the Soviets did intend to seize power, he adds, 'it is very doubtful that they could have done so'. He illustrates the point with figures for both sides: 'At its height the Communist intervention in the Congo comprised no more than 380 Soviets and Czechoslovaks—against 14,000 UN troops and many thousands of Belgian military officers, mercenaries and technical aides'.

Gibbs acknowledges that Lumumba's party, the MNC-L, received funds from the Belgian Communist Party, but points out that it was also funded by the right-wing Liberal Party of Belgium and by colonial business interests. Indeed, it may have been funded by the CIA, which had advocated the funding of Lumumba in April 1960, less than four months earlier.

There is little evidence, adds Gibbs, to suggest that Lumumba personally was a communist—a point recognised and accepted by American officials.[16] Frank Carlucci made a broader point about the role of the Soviet Union in the Congo in an interview with Charles Stuart Kennedy in 1997:

> *Q*: At that time, did we see the . . . Were the Soviets or the Soviet embassy, was it a real competition? I mean did you find yourself jostling the Soviet political officers or not?
>
> *CARLUCCI*: No. I can't recall the Soviet embassy being that active.[17]

In any case, it was not Lumumba that was the problem, Bronson Tweedy believed. 'The concern with Lumumba', he explained in his testimony to the Church Committee in 1975, 'was not really the concern with Lumumba as a person. It was concern at this very pregnant point in the new African development [with] the effect on the balance of the Continent of a disintegration of the Congo'. The real trigger for such intense American interest, he added, were the resources of the Congo: 'The Congo, after all, was the largest geographical expression. Contained in it were *enormously important mineral resources* [redacted]. . . . This was why Washington [redacted] was so concerned about Lumumba, not because there was something unique about Lumumba, but it was the Congo [redacted]'.[18]

The standard explanation for American behaviour in the Congo is that it aimed to 'hold the line against Soviet incursion', observes Ebere Nwaubani. But there is 'more plausibility', he adds, 'in arguing that there was a fusion of strategic interests (especially anti-Sovietism, access to Congo's uranium deposits, the geographical size of the country and its location at the heart of Africa), as well as what Stephen Weissman has identified as a deeply ingrained "NATO reflex in [United States] African policy"'.[19]

* * *

ON 25 AUGUST, THE day when the Special Group resolved not to 'rule out' consideration of 'any particular kind of activity which might contribute to getting rid of Lumumba', the Congolese prime minister attended the first day of the conference in Leopoldville of independent African states. He and Nkrumah had made plans for this meeting when they met in Accra earlier in the month: to chart a clear path on African economic and political cooperation.[20]

Yuri Zhukov, a Soviet advisor who had just arrived in the Congo, saw the flags of many African countries waving over the entrance of the Parliament building as he drove past—the flags of the Congo, Ghana, Guinea, the Cameroons, Togo, Ethiopia, Liberia, the Sudan, Morocco and the United Arab Republic, the union of Egypt and Syria.[21] Delegates included Frantz Fanon and his friend Félix-Roland Moumié, the Cameroonian freedom fighter who had moved to the Congo in 1960 to lend his support to Lumumba. Fanon and Moumié had established a fond friendship with each other and with Lumumba in Accra in 1958.

Lumumba gave the opening speech at the conference, in which he referred explicitly to the threat of the West's greed for the Congo's resources. 'Our Katanga because of its uranium, copper and gold', warned Lumumba, 'and our Bakwanga in Kasai because of its diamonds have become hotbeds of imperialist intrigues. The object of these intrigues is to recapture economic control of our country'. Lumumba went on to insist that 'our future, our destiny, a free Africa, is our affair. . . . We all know and the whole world knows it, that Algeria is not French, that Angola is not Portuguese, that Kenya is not English, that Ruanda-Urundi is not Belgian. . . . We know the objects of the West. Yesterday they split us on the level of a tribe, clan and village. Today, with Africa liberating herself, they seek to divide us on the level of states'.

'In Africa', he argued, 'they want to create antagonistic blocs, satellites, and, having begun from that stage of the cold war, deepen the division in order to perpetuate their rule'.[22]

Little did Lumumba realise that even as he was speaking, an American plot was afoot at the conference, disrupting its progress. 'One of our early operations', Devlin reported in his memoir, 'was an anti-Lumumba demonstration when the latter spoke at a meeting of African foreign ministers held in Leopoldville on August 25'. On Lumumba's arrival, protestors shouted, 'À bas Lumumba!'—Down with Lumumba! When he started to speak to the delegates, he was drowned out by the mob, who chanted anti-Lumumba slogans.

Devlin regarded the success of the operation with satisfaction: 'This undermined Lumumba's image of a man loved by his people and in full control of the nation. He had counted on the conference to strengthen his position within the pan-African movement, but instead the delegates were caught up in the reality of the Congo situation'.[23]

The CIA-inspired protest was filmed by a Pathé cameraman and was screened in a newsreel that was shown around the world.[24] It gave an entirely false impression of people's attitudes in the Congo.

On the first evening of the conference, Prime Minister Lumumba gave a dinner for the delegates, the diplomatic corps and foreign visitors to Leopoldville. 'A military band played in a shady flood-lit garden on the bank of the mighty African river', observed Zhukov with pleasure. Along with other guests, he was met formally by Lumumba on his arrival. 'His energetic, animated face', noted Zhukov, 'instantly impresses itself on one's memory—the piercing, glowing brown eyes that reflect profound assurance and spiritual dignity seem to look into your very soul'.[25]

One of the delegates to the conference was Washington Okumu, the Kenyan CIA asset handled by Howard Imbrey; he stayed at the Regina Hotel in the centre of Leopoldville, not far from the railway station.[26] Before independence, Congolese people had been barred from entering the hotel, unless they were servants. Now, some Congolese politicians were living there. Also staying at the hotel was 'Dad'—one of Devlin's long-standing agents, whose cover in the Congo was as a businessman. Devlin described the Regina as 'one of the oldest and most rundown hotels in town with little to recommend it, but at least it had a bar, live music, and dancing'.[27] It was a far cry from the luxurious Memling, where George Wittman stayed in Leopoldville.

Andrée Blouin was even less impressed than Devlin with the Regina Hotel, observing that it was the 'center of activity for the Belgians and those through whom they planned to work'. Here, she added, 'the aspiring politicians of the so-called "moderate" parties met. Congolese who only a little earlier had been stiffly excluded from the establishment took intense delight in using its rooms and bars noisily. Exuberant in their new privileges, they conspired there with their former tormentors with the greatest satisfaction. . . . There they were, every day, drinking, shouting, gesticulating, plotting against their country and those who were trying to save it'. Lumumba, she said, referred with contempt to 'the Belgians' puppets who are proliferating their plots at the Hotel Regina'.[28]

Okumu's travel and hotel bills were funded by different organisations, including the CIA. His reason for being in the Congo in August 1960 is unclear, but it is likely that the CIA wanted a pair of discreet eyes at the conference of independent African states. CIA officials operating in the Congo had white skin and would have stood out; the problem was solved by Okumu.

Okumu may have had his own reasons for visiting the Congo—perhaps to conduct research for the book he published two years later about Lumumba. In his interviews with Nancy Jacobs, he expressed his appreciation for the comfort provided by the CIA on his travels. 'Wherever I was, the CIA would put somebody there to pay your hotel bills, and so on. And I said they made your life comfortable. All I needed to do was work and I loved to work. I loved [writing] the book'. This was Okumu's first return to Africa, on a tour that included Mali, Liberia and Ghana, where he said he met President Nkrumah.[29]

* * *

LUMUMBA HAD EXPRESSED PROFOUND confidence in the future of the Congo and of Africa in his opening speech to the conference. But this confidence was dealt a heavy blow on 5 September. Unexpectedly, President Kasavubu suddenly dismissed him as prime minister and entrusted Joseph Ileo, the president of the Senate, with the formation of a new government. Kasavubu made the announcement on the radio at 8.15 pm.

'The door opened on a gulf', recalled Blouin, 'and the Congo plunged into the abyss. Alone, at night, like a mad woman I raced to the home of the prime minister'. A dense crowd had gathered outside the prime minister's residence, including 'ministers, members of the NCM [Mouvement National Congolais], journalists, and the mere curious'. Guards prevented Blouin from entering: 'My heart aching, I sat in my car in front of the residence for a long time, waiting for the results. The very thing I had dreaded had come to pass. It broke like a thunderclap over the young republic, blasting its new life'.[30]

Less than six weeks had passed since the Congo had achieved its independence and since Patrice Lumumba had been sworn in as its first democratically elected prime minister.

Devlin argued in his memoir that under the Loi Fondamentale, drawn up earlier that year in Brussels, 'the president had the legal authority to dismiss the prime minister and replace him with another person but the replacement needed to obtain a vote of confidence from parliament'.[31] In fact, however, the president did not have this legal authority, since the law had not yet been ratified by the Congolese Parliament.

At 9.05 pm, less than forty-five minutes after Kasavubu's announcement, Lumumba arrived at Radio Leopoldville to challenge his dismissal on national radio. 'No one, not even the president of the republic', he declared, 'has the right to dismiss a government elected by the people; only the people can do so'. He added that Kasavubu's appointment as head of state should be revoked.

A number of people in the studio applauded his speech, shouting out, 'Long live Lumumba!', 'Long live the Prime Minister', 'Long live the republic!' He spoke on the radio twice more that evening.[32]

Cameron Duodu was following events in the Congo carefully for Radio Ghana and trying to understand what was going on. 'As far as Radio Ghana was concerned', he recalled later, 'the assiduous work done by our monitoring service—French speakers recording the speech, transcribing it in French and then translating it into English, all at full speed—enabled us to capture Lumumba's speech direct from the Parliamentary chamber in Leopoldville. We broadcast it all to Ghana and the outside world, in both English and French'. He took 'special pride', he said, that as the editor on duty, 'I was able to allow our people to partake of a very important moment in African history at the time it was happening'.[33]

On 7 September, the Chamber of Deputies met to discuss Kasavubu's action, sitting in session until three am. The deputies agreed—by sixty votes to nineteen—to annul the decisions whereby the prime minister and the head of state had dismissed each other.[34] The next day, the Senate met and confirmed the decision of the chamber, by a vote of forty-one for Lumumba, two against and six abstaining, including Ileo and Adoula; twenty-nine members were absent.[35]

It was a triumph for Lumumba. But at this moment of strength, Gizenga noted with intense frustration and regret, he made a dangerous and irrevocable mistake: he failed to act against those who had plotted against him.[36]

* * *

GIZENGA'S ANXIETIES WERE QUICKLY justified. On 11 September, Lumumba's series of victories against his enemies suddenly hit a brick wall: at four pm he was prevented from speaking on Radio Leopoldville. Aware of the power of the prime minister's oratory and his massive popularity, his enemies silenced this means of communication with Congolese citizens. Kasavubu, though, was allowed to continue speaking on Radio Brazzaville, with the encouragement of his political ally, the Abbé Fulbert Youlou.

To Lumumba's horror, he saw that the men preventing him from making a broadcast were Ghanaian UN soldiers. To him, this was a double betrayal: first, they were UN troops; and second, they came from the very nation that had been urging him to take the path that had led to this moment.

The leader of the men was Colonel Joseph A Ankrah, the brigade commander of the force based at Luluabourg in Kasai. Anicet Kashamura witnessed the bitter dialogue between the two men, in which Ankrah accused Lumumba of being a communist. Lumumba, in disgust, described Ankrah as a traitor to the UN and to Ghana's president.[37]

Lumumba immediately sent a hurt and angry message to Nkrumah. 'I hasten', he wrote, 'to express to you my indignation regarding the aggressive and hostile attitude of Ghanaian soldiers towards me and my Government'. The Ghanaian troops, he reported, seized the arms of his guards and 'even wanted to shoot me and my soldiers'. He referred as well to a hostile declaration by General Alexander in London against the Armée Nationale Congolaise.

In the circumstances, he declared, 'I feel obliged to renounce the help of your troops in view of the fact that they are in a state of war against our Republic. Instead of helping us in our difficulties, your soldiers are openly siding with the enemy to fight us'.[38]

The truth behind the episode was revealed to Nkrumah on 12 September in a message from Djin, his ambassador in the Congo. It was Colonel Ankrah, said Djin, who was chiefly implicated in the refusal to let Lumumba speak over the radio. Ankrah, he added, was very close to General Alexander. 'If you would allow me', wrote Djin to Nkrumah, 'I would say that this is the culminating point of Gen. Alexander's intrigue and subversive action which I have time and again pointed out and which was also confirmed by all the delegations which had paid a visit to the Congo'. He urged the immediate dismissal of Alexander from his post and of all the white soldiers in the Ghana contingent of ONUC.[39]

Nkrumah was horrified. He at once replied to Lumumba's note, explaining that he found himself in an 'embarrassing and invidious position' with respect to the way the Ghanaian troops were being used in the Congo. He added that he had been 'fighting like mad day and night on your behalf'. He sent to Lumumba a copy of a letter he had just sent to Secretary General Hammarskjöld, in which he warned that if Lumumba were not allowed to use his own radio station at Leopoldville to inform the Congolese people of the critical situation, then Ghana would withdraw her troops from the UN Command—and place them entirely at the disposal of the legitimate government headed by Lumumba.

On the same day, 12 September, Nkrumah sent a further—and lengthy—note to Lumumba. 'You cannot afford, my brother', he urged, 'to be harsh and uncompromising. Do not force Kasavubu out now. It will bring you too much trouble in Léopoldville when you want calm there now'. He gave detailed advice on cabinet reorganisation, recommending that Lumumba should work through a small inner cabinet for quick decisions, and appoint a separate technical cabinet to ensure effective cooperation with the UN and with foreign states. In any crisis, he assured Lumumba, he himself would mobilise the Afro-Asian bloc, as he was now doing.

'Brother', he insisted, 'we have been in the game for some time now and we know how to handle the imperialists and the colonialists. The only colonialist or imperialist I trust is a dead one'. Nkrumah urged Lumumba to avoid any future misjudgements. He concluded his message with a powerful exhortation: 'Patrice, I have surveyed the position in the Congo very, very carefully. If you fail you have only yourself to blame and it will be due to your unwillingness to face the facts of life or as the Germans call it, "real politik". Your failure will be a great blow to the African liberation movement, and you cannot afford to fail'.[40]

* * *

LUMUMBA WAS ARRESTED ON 12 September. A warrant for his arrest had been issued by the order of Chief of Staff Joseph-Désiré Mobutu, on the grounds that Lumumba had rejected as illegal the attempt to dismiss him as prime minister. Lumumba was released later that day, largely due to the energetic interventions of Djin. As before, Djin held Alexander responsible. He reported to Nkrumah that the prestige of Ghana 'had been run down to its lowest ebb by General Alexander's intrigues'. Unaware of Djin's efforts, Lumumba wrote again to Nkrumah, objecting to the 'hostile attitude of the Ghana troops'.

But then, when Lumumba was told of Djin's attempts to release him, his attitude to Ghana changed instantly. 'I gathered from the remarkable change in Lumumba's attitude towards me and from the friendly smile on the faces of his Cabinet Ministers', wrote Djin to Nkrumah on 15 September, 'that the part I played for his release had gone home to Lumumba and his Cabinet Ministers who on the previous day had insulted me as treacherous'.[41]

The bitter tussle in Leopoldville continued. On 13 September, the Chamber of Deputies and the Senate voted at a joint meeting to back Lumumba, as the legitimate prime minister of the Congo, by eighty-eight votes to five, with three abstentions. The next day, President Kasavubu prorogued Parliament, but the president of the Chamber of Deputies and the vice president of the Senate refused to recognise the instruction.

* * *

THE PARLIAMENTARY VOTE AND the failure of Kasavubu to prorogue Parliament had frustrated the plan to remove Lumumba from power. Now Mobutu and his supporters turned to a more extreme, military measure. Mobutu went on Radio Brazzaville on 14 September to announce that the army had seized power, suspending civilian rule of the Congo until 31 December.

Devlin later claimed that the CIA was responsible for this ruthless development. According to a summary by the Church Committee of an interview with Devlin on 22 August 1975, Devlin contended 'that the *coup* of Mobutu seized control [and] was arranged and supported, and indeed, managed, by the Central Intelligence Agency'.[42]

Mobutu established a College of Commissioners to serve as a government. This council comprised Congolese university graduates and last-year students from both Lovanium and foreign universities. Justin Bomboko was appointed its president, Albert Ndele became vice president and Victor Nendaka was made chief of the security police—the dreaded Sûreté Nationale.[43] All three men were being funded by the CIA. So too was Kasavubu, who was kept on as president; he signed the decree that 'legalized' Mobutu's dictatorship.

Mobutu closed the Soviet and Czech embassies and ordered all Soviet and Czech diplomats and technicians to leave the Congo within forty-eight hours. 'It was an exciting moment', recalled Devlin in his memoir. 'Our efforts to remove Lumumba and prevent the Soviet Union from gaining control of the Congo were at last bearing fruit'.[44]

The following day, Lumumba took refuge in the Ghana officers' mess. He asked the UN for protection, and Rajeshwar Dayal, the Indian diplomat who had arrived in the Congo on 5 September 1960 to take over from Ralph Bunche as Hammarskjöld's special representative, responded immediately. He arranged for Ghanaian troops to escort Lumumba out of the camp at nightfall and take him safely home.

When Mobutu announced the coup on the radio, Devlin and Andrée Blouin were at the home of Alison 'Tally' Palmer, the American vice consul, in her apartment building overlooking the Congo River.[45] 'Shortly after her arrival', recorded Devlin, 'Andrée Blouin, the prime minister's glamorous and beautiful chief of protocol, received a phone call and departed in a great rush'.[46]

Blouin was devastated. 'The days that followed Mobutu's seizing of power', she said later, 'were like a modern apocalypse. The Congo was on the edge of madness. Kasavubu had at least pretended to conform to the constitutional laws drawn up by Belgian lawyers. Mobutu made no such pretences. Democracy was completely overthrown and replaced by a military dictatorship'. Parliament was closed by Mobutu's orders and rigorously guarded by soldiers.[47]

For Lumumba, Mobutu's coup was the start of his road to calvary, said Blouin. From then on, 'the conspiracies against him were carried on openly. Each day, Kasavubu crossed the river to Brazzaville to consult with Youlou and the Belgian embassy there on decisions for the young republic'. For a few hours every day, Radio-Congo broadcast from Brazzaville 'the most vile calumnies against us'.[48]

At a press conference on the morning of the coup, Bomboko had announced the expulsion of the Ghanaian, Guinean and Egyptian UN contingents in the UN Command. Among a number of individuals issued with an expulsion order was Andrée Blouin; when her mother, Josephine, heard the news over the radio, she suffered a heart attack. Blouin begged Mobutu over the phone for more time. She was granted just forty-eight hours.[49]

Félix-Roland Moumié was deported to Ghana. On arrival, he met with Fanon, who was in Accra at the time, and together they went to see Nkrumah; the president had asked Moumié to write a report on what he had witnessed in the Congo. On 1 October, Fanon and Moumié left Ghana for Rome. From there, Fanon went to Cairo and Moumié went to Geneva.[50] Within weeks of his arrival, Moumié was poisoned by an agent of the SDECE, the French foreign intelligence service, who put thallium in his drink during dinner at a restaurant. The thirty-four-year-old suffered agony in the hospital for two weeks, eventually dying on 3 November 1960.[51]

* * *

IN BRUSSELS, AMBASSADOR BURDEN welcomed Mobutu's seizure of power. 'Peace came slowly as Lumumba's power dwindled', he wrote in his memoir with satisfaction. 'Finally a coup by Kasavubu and Colonel Mobutu brought about a consolidation'.[52]

But some Americans in the Congo had doubts about Mobutu. 'I think Larry Devlin and I went to see [Mobutu] shortly after he took over', commented Frank Carlucci many years later, after Mobutu had been president of the Congo for several decades. 'I walked out of there saying, "Larry, this guy can't last 10 days!"' Carlucci added a self-mocking aside: 'Shows you how good a political leader analyst I was'.[53]

On 17 September Lumumba wrote to Nkrumah to inform him of his plans to move the seat of Parliament and the government to Stanleyville. Gizenga was already there, with some other ministers of the legitimate government. Lumumba concluded his message with an expression of renewed trust and loyalty. 'You can rely on me', he told Nkrumah, 'and I can on you. Today we are one, and our countries are one'.[54]

20

The Poison Plot

Politically, Lumumba 'was dead', feared his friend and chief of protocol Andrée Blouin. 'Invisible hands were strangling him, and those invisible hands came from far away. Very far away'.[1] Blouin was right, but only up to a point. She was unaware that those invisible hands did not simply want Lumumba's political death—they were also planning his physical death.

Five days after Mobutu seized power, Dick Bissell and Bronson Tweedy sent Devlin a cable from headquarters, stressing that he should not discuss its contents with anybody. It instructed Devlin that he would soon be visited by a messenger from CIA headquarters, who would announce himself as 'Sid from Paris'.[2] Devlin was instructed to see him urgently.

The cable bore the codeword 'YQPROP': a combination of 'PROP', which was normally used to denote sensitive personnel matters,[3] and 'YQ', which denoted the operation to assassinate Lumumba. It indicated extraordinary sensitivity, restricting circulation at CIA headquarters to Allen Dulles, Dick Bissell, Bronson Tweedy and Tweedy's deputy, Glenn Fields. In Tweedy's testimony to the Church Committee, he confirmed the designation of 'YQPROP'. He added helpfully, 'We could have attempted to assassinate 500,000 people and there would always have been an additional channel set up'.[4]

Devlin was told that Sid from Paris would phone him and set up a time for a meeting. But the meeting would take place one hour earlier than the time mentioned, and 'Sid' would be in the main entrance of the New Stanley Hotel, carrying an unrolled copy of *Paris Match* in his left hand.[5]

On 21 September 1960, a meeting of the National Security Council occurred during which Allen Dulles—in the presence of President Eisenhower—observed that 'Mobutu appeared to be the effective power in the Congo for the moment but Lumumba was not yet disposed of and remained a grave danger as long as he was not disposed of'.[6]

In the late afternoon of 26 September, Devlin left work and made his way to his car. A man seated at a café across the street got up and strolled over, introducing himself as 'Sid from Paris'. In fact, he was Dr Sidney Gottlieb, a biochemist in the CIA's Deputy Directorate of Plans.

Gottlieb oversaw a vast range of secret drug and mind-control experiments for the CIA in the 1950s and 1960s. As shown by Stephen Kinzer in *Poisoner in Chief*, a chilling study of Gottlieb and his exploits, the experiments were conducted on an epic scale. He was known to some, writes the security analyst Gordon Corera, 'as the "dark sorcerer" for his conjuring in the most sinister recesses of the CIA. . . . With his club foot, he was perhaps too easy to caricature as a cross between a Bond villain and Dr Strangelove, a scientist who always wanted to push further without worrying about the morality of where it all led'.[7]

Dr Gottlieb had joined the agency in 1951 as chief of the Chemical Division of the Technical Services Division (TSD), which utilised the US Army's Special Operations Division at Fort Detrick to secretly produce toxins for the agency and develop delivery systems. This was the centre in which Ambassador Burden, an advocate of biological weapons, took a keen interest.

Gottlieb was part of an informal group of CIA chemists known as the 'Health Alteration Committee', who came together in early 1960 as a response to Eisenhower's 'renewed conviction', according to Kinzer, 'that the best way to deal with some unfriendly foreign leaders was to kill them'.[8]

He was the head of MKUltra, a mind-control project researching methods of altering human behaviour, which began in 1953 and conducted experiments on three continents. The project has been largely associated with research on LSD. But the use of hallucinogens, states Jeffrey Richelson in *The Wizards of Langley*, was only one element of MKUltra. 'Subprojects included electrical brain stimulation and the implanting of electrodes in the brains of several species of animals', he reports, 'to enable experimenters to direct the animals by remote control, in the hope they could be further wired and used for eavesdropping'.[9]

In January 1973, most records relating to MKUltra were destroyed by TSD on the verbal orders of Dr Gottlieb.[10] Some records, however, escaped destruction and later surfaced; they were the subject of scrutiny by the Church Committee in 1975 and then by a Senate Select Committee investigating 'Project MKUltra' in 1977.

In 1975, the deputy director of the CIA revealed that over thirty universities and institutions were involved in an 'extensive testing and experimentation' programme that included covert drug tests on unwitting citizens 'at all social levels, high and low, native Americans and foreign'.[11] There were 149 MKUltra subprojects, which appeared to have some connection with research into behavioural modification, drug acquisition and testing or administering drugs surreptitiously. There were 33 additional subprojects 'concerning certain intelligence activities previously funded under MKULTRA which had nothing to do either with behavioural modification, drugs, and toxins or with any other related matters'.[12]

MKUltra's human subjects were 'almost all of them unwitting', observed Rupert Cornwell in an obituary for Gottlieb in 1999; they 'were society's outcasts: prostitutes and their clients, mental patients, convicted criminals—people, in the words of one of Gottlieb's colleagues, "who could not fight back"'. The most bizarre brainwave of Gottlieb (himself a frequent user of LSD), adds Cornwell, was to set up a string of CIA-controlled brothels in San Francisco which operated for eight years: 'Prostitutes would slip drugs to their customers, and the results would be observed by agency officials through two-way mirrors'.[13]

Gottlieb is frequently mentioned and quoted in the Church Committee's 1975 report.[14] But there is a massive gap in information, because Gottlieb's testimonies are missing.[15] These testimonies are among a number of transcripts that the Assassination Records Review Board found to be missing from Senate files once it undertook a search after the passing of the 1992 JFK Assassination Records Collection Act. In the case of these files, as Rex Bradford, the president of the Mary Ferrell Foundation, has observed, 'there is simply no known extant transcript to be declassified'.[16]

It is possible that Gottlieb may have developed plans not only to assassinate Lumumba, but also to assassinate or incapacitate other individuals in or from Africa. In testimony to the Church Committee that was quoted in its report, Gottlieb referred to an inquiry from Bissell 'generally about technical means of assassination or incapacitation that could be developed or procured by the CIA'. Gottlieb replied that the CIA 'had access to lethal or potentially lethal biological materials that could be used in this manner'. Following this exchange, Gottlieb discussed assassination capabilities with Bissell in the context of 'one or two meetings about Africa'.[17]

An additional and deeply worrying concern is that no documents are available regarding the use overseas of MKUltra materials—a procedure that was designated MKDelta. All documents relating to MKDelta were destroyed. The use of these substances abroad began in the early 1950s.[18] There is a reference to MKDelta in a set of CIA internal notes—titled 'DAIRY [sic] NOTES'—produced on 27 September 1963.[19] The notes, which connect MKDelta to TSD, are heavily redacted.[20]

The 1977 Senate inquiry report into Project MKUltra referred briefly to MKDelta: 'A special procedure designated MKDELTA, was established to govern the use of MKULTRA materials abroad. Such materials were used on a number of occasions. Because MKULTRA records were destroyed, it is impossible to reconstruct the operational use of MKULTRA materials by the CIA overseas; it has been determined that the use of these materials abroad began in 1953, and possibly as early as 1950. Drugs were used primarily as an aid to interrogations'.

But, adds the report, 'MKULTRA/MKDELTA materials were also used for harassment, discrediting, or disabling purposes'. By

1963 the number of operations and subjects had increased substantially.[21] MKUltra was terminated in the late 1960s.[22]

There are nine uses of the word 'overseas' in the Senate inquiry report, mostly referring to experiments conducted on individuals. But in no case is the overseas nation specified.

Urgent questions emerge from any study of MKUltra and MK-Delta: What procedures were used overseas? Were they used in African nations?

If the CIA were ready and willing to kill the elected premier of the Congo, there is no reason to assume they would shrink from using procedures against Congolese people that involved the alteration of human behaviour. Burt V Wides, the chief of the investigations into the CIA for the Church Committee, was deeply concerned that he had seen 'sworn statements that the use of biological warfare was contemplated in the Congo'.[23] He tried to find out more about these statements, but without success. It is conceivable that plans for biological warfare were connected to MKUltra/MKDelta.

* * *

THE CIA'S INVOLVEMENT IN planning assassinations goes back at least to 1954, when it prepared a nineteen-page manual for killings. 'The essential point of assassination', it states rather obviously, 'is the death of the subject'. And although it 'is possible to kill a man with the bare hands . . . the simplest local tools are often much [sic] the most efficient means of assassination. A hammer, ax, wrench, screwdriver, fire poker, kitchen knife, lamp stand or anything hard, heavy and handy will suffice'. The 'most efficient accident, in simple assassination', recommends the manual, 'is a fall of 75 feet or more onto a hard surface'.[24] Such methods were challenging to apply in relation to foreign leaders. But there was a solution, argued Gottlieb: poison. It could be invisible, untraceable and, if handled well, not liable to generate suspicions of foul play.[25]

Fidel Castro was the target of various toxins prepared by Gottlieb, who devised their application in methods including lethal pills and poisonous cigars. One plot involved a diving suit, which seemed a promising way of poisoning the Cuban leader because he was a keen scuba diver. According to a CIA officer some years later, the

Technical Services Division 'bought a diving suit, dusted it inside with a fungus which would produce Madura foot, a chronic skin disease, and contaminated the breathing apparatus with a tubercle bacillus'. The plan was to ask the lawyer who would be meeting Castro to discuss the issue of the Cuban American prisoners captured during the Bay of Pigs invasion to present Castro with the suit. But the plot had to be abandoned when the lawyer decided to give Castro a different diving suit.[26]

Sid Gottlieb's activities were investigated by the Church Committee in connection with its careful examination in 1975 of the CIA's plots to assassinate foreign leaders, which led to its report, *Alleged Assassination Plots Involving Foreign Leaders*. Gottlieb testified that Richard Helms, the agency's deputy director of plans, ordered him to destroy records of all the tests on toxins considered for the murder of Lumumba.[27]

Gottlieb finally selected botulinum, because it would produce a death like the one caused by diseases common in the Congo. He produced a dedicated poison kit, including protective gloves and a mask. It was agreed that Gottlieb himself would take the kit to Leopoldville, to hand over to Devlin. Once in Leopoldville, Gottlieb gave Devlin the kit. It contained a hypodermic needle, which, he told Devlin, should be used to inject the toxic substance into anything that Lumumba would put into his mouth. This could be food or a toothbrush. After Lumumba had been killed by the poison, explained Gottlieb, his autopsy would show 'normal traces found in people who die of certain diseases'.[28]

In the course of the Church Committee hearings, Devlin said he had asked Gottlieb if the president had authorised the operation. Gottlieb had confirmed this:

Q: Your understanding then was that these instructions were instructions coming to you from the office of the President?

Hedgman [the Church Committee pseudonym for Devlin]: That's correct.

Q: Or that he had instructed the Agency, and they were passed on to you?

Hedgman: That's right.

Q: You are not the least unclear whether [redacted] the President's name had been invoked in some fashion?

Hedgman: At the time, I certainly felt that I was under instructions from the President, yes.[29]

These revelations shocked John Stockwell; it was directly because of them that he left the CIA and then acted as an energetic whistleblower. The agency's programmes, he wrote, 'appalled me: kinky, slightly depraved, drug/sex experiments involving unwitting Americans, who were secretly filmed by the CIA for later viewing by pseudoscientists of the CIA's Technical Services Division'.

For years, added Stockwell, 'I had defended the CIA to my parents and to our friends. "Take it from me, a CIA insider", I had always sworn, "the CIA simply does not assassinate or use drugs"'.[30] Then he learned about the information emerging from the Church Committee investigations: 'The former deputy director of plans (operations), Richard Bissell, testified that feasibility studies of how to assassinate Patrice Lumumba had been made. . . . Sid Gottlieb, the CIA chief of the Office of Technical Services had hand-carried poison to Kinshasa for the Lumumba operation'.[31]

The Church Committee exposed this extraordinary information about Gottlieb's plan to poison Lumumba. But it failed to ask what *else* Gottlieb might have been doing in the Congo. In late August 1960—fully a month before Gottlieb delivered the poison to Devlin—the political scientist René Lemarchand came across the chemist in Bukavu, the capital of Kivu province. According to Lemarchand, Gottlieb introduced himself 'as a Canadian businessman, who knew Lumumba, and was eager to displace Belgian interests in the Kivu'.[32] Lemarchand was never able to discover the real nature of his activities in Bukavu.

* * *

IN THE WEEK THAT Gottlieb arrived in the Congo, George Wittman reported to Tempelsman that he was busy developing 'direct lines' to leading politicians such as Kasavubu, Ileo, Lumumba, Kalonji, Tshombe and Mario Cardoso. 'They are now all aware of my existence', he reported, 'and in different manners have made it clear that whenever I want to make the final official approach they are delighted to receive me'.[33] Here, Wittman was presumably referring to the barter deal. The commissioners, he judged, 'are now in effect the government from an administrative standpoint. They are the ones through which business must flow. They are in lieu of the usual political organisation and the usual civil service'.[34]

Wittman had by then established a rapport with Mobutu. He accompanied Mobutu on a raid with his soldiers, where he witnessed them beating people with rifle butts: 'There is a delight in their work that makes up for the lack of finesse'.[35]

'Diamond smuggling is apparently at a high rate these days', reported Wittman; as in his earlier reports, he was possibly using 'diamonds' as a cover word for uranium. 'Leopoldville is full of seedy characters trying to arrange deals'.[36] From a secret source using intercepted cable traffic, Wittman learned of a Swiss operation to procure up to $40 million worth of illegal diamonds in the Congo. 'Whether such an amount is available is questionable', observed Wittman. He was considering using his source for side assignments.[37]

The CIA was operating under the radar in the Congo, but its personnel were on occasion noticed by American visitors. One of these was Ulric Haynes Jr, a young African American attorney who accompanied Democratic diplomat W Averell Harriman—who had been US ambassador to the Soviet Union during World War II—to the Congo in September 1960, on a fact-finding mission for Senator John F Kennedy. Haynes thought that his driver was probably a CIA asset. 'I was driven around—I can't remember how this happened', he said later, 'by a Congolese who was a junior executive in an American oil company in the Congo. In retrospect, I believe that he was one of the CIA contacts in the Congo'.[38]

Links to American oil companies were good covers. Sully de-Fontaine allegedly stayed for a time in Leopoldville in a villa owned by Ed Maley, a Mobil Oil executive, whom deFontaine had met at the embassy. 'Curiously', notes Jack Lawson in *The Slaver's Wheel*, 'Sully saw him there every time he reported to the ambassador and

he soon suspected that Maley was an operative for the Central Intelligence Agency. For someone in the oil business, the man seemed
to know more than anyone in the embassy about what was happening in the Congo'.[39]

Lawson's account of deFontaine's time in the Congo offers details that seem authentic, such as his visits to the restaurant Titin,
next door to the Regina Hotel. But his claims do not fit with one
crucial development in the CIA's plot to kill Lumumba. DeFontaine would later claim that he became a bodyguard for Lumumba,
using the pseudonym of Robert Solvay; he said he was perceived
as trustworthy by Lumumba and his advisors because of family
links to the Communist Party in Belgium. According to Lawson,
deFontaine 'once accompanied Lumumba to Rabat, Morocco as
his bodyguard. That's when the infamous "Toothpaste Assassination Plot" to kill Lumumba with poisonous toothpaste was to have
occurred'.[40]

But this is simply not possible, since Gottlieb delivered the poison to Devlin in late September. By then, deFontaine was long gone.
Lawson's account records that on 21 August 1960, Timberlake told
deFontaine that he was booked on a flight to leave the Congo the
following day.[41] Possibly deFontaine stayed secretly in the Congo.
But the discrepancy—without an explicit explanation—is too great
to ignore and weakens the credibility of deFontaine's memoirs.

* * *

LUMUMBA HAD WITHDRAWN DURING this period to his private
home on Boulevard Albert 1er, where he was protected by a UN
guard.[42] On 20 September, Chief of Staff Mobutu issued an order
for Lumumba's arrest. Antoine Gizenga, the deputy prime minister, had already been arrested and placed in an underground prison
outside Leopoldville. The UN firmly refused to countenance the
arrest of Lumumba; Hammarskjöld insisted that Lumumba must
be part of any political settlement.

The next day, Mobutu sent a party of soldiers to Lumumba's house to arrest him, but they were turned away by the UN
guard.[43] The US then asked the UN to allow Mobutu's forces to
arrest Lumumba, but Hammarskjöld reiterated his earlier refusal.[44]

Lumumba returned to his official residence on the palm-lined Avenue Tilkens.

Hammarskjöld's position was adamantly maintained by Rajeshwar Dayal, who had arrived in the first week of September. Dayal, who was close to his prime minister, Jawaharlal Nehru, shared Nehru's commitment to the legitimate government of Prime Minister Lumumba. From the moment of his arrival in the Congo, Dayal was uncompromising in his support for Lumumba and his ministers. This was not out of personal loyalty, but because he considered it an absolute requirement of justice and of the UN Charter. In his early fifties, the patrician Dayal was highly regarded in India and at the UN as a 'diplomat of unusual perspicacity' and 'a man of supreme patience'.[45]

Under the protection of the UN, Lumumba's residence was guarded day and night by two platoons of Ghana rifles.[46] Lumumba went into and out of the residence freely. 'He was in the habit of going out in his motorcar for fresh air, for shopping or to visit friends', noted General Rikhye. 'He was a frequent visitor of the various restaurants where his party supporters were; he would join them very often, make speeches and then he would return to his residence'.[47]

* * *

DAYAL SUSPECTED THAT MOBUTU was not the unqualified strong leader that was energetically portrayed by the Western media. Wittman thought the same—that Mobutu 'is a bit over his head having assumed leadership of his gorillas whom he has to let eat every now and then to keep them happy'.[48]

On 22 September, Mobutu turned up at UN headquarters 'overworked and bewildered' and presented to Dayal a proposal for reconciliation with Lumumba. 'Mobutu was exhausted and unshaven', recorded Dayal. 'His plan was to get Kasavubu and Lumumba together under UN auspices. The next step would be to have a Round Table Conference'.

Dayal was keen to see a reconciliation between the Congo's leading politicians. He responded with alacrity, asking Mobutu if the different parties were in support of the plan. Mobutu then telephoned Kasavubu, who was evasive but made an appointment for the following morning. Mobutu could not telephone Lumumba, as Lumumba's telephone line had been cut, but Mobutu sent him a letter. Lumumba replied, inviting Mobutu to visit him for talks the next day and asking for the release of Gizenga, Mpolo and two secretaries of state who had been arrested, as a gesture of sincerity. Mobutu was in a dilemma, Dayal thought, but 'he decided to release all four to demonstrate his "generosity and fear of God"'.[49]

At first, Mobutu 'was as good as his word', to Dayal's relief. But it did not last. Mobutu, 'who had been frightened by his own soldiers into playing a mediatory role—although a very short-lived one', quickly recovered his bullish confidence. He called off the reconciliation plan.[50]

Rajeshwar Dayal had become an intense irritation to George Wittman. 'The UN command here (in the form of Dayal personally)', complained Wittman crossly to Tempelsman, 'has for some fantastic reason chosen to lean now toward some form of support of Lumumba'. The 'entire attitude of Dayal', he added in exasperation, 'is best understood in recounting the following conversation between William Anderson of UPI [United Press International] and Dayal . . . at a special press party':

Anderson: Mr Dayal, if Colonel Mobutu goes to New York, through what mechanism will the U.N. continue to deal?
Dayal: Through the only legally elected body.
Anderson: Will that mean the Commissaire [illegible word]?
Dayal: No . . . the Commissaire is solely a creation of Mobutu's. The parliament is the only duly elected body as is the government formed under it.
Anderson: You mean to say that you would then deal with Lumumba's Government and him?
Dayal: We certainly would. . . . After all he is still the only duly elected leader here and we must proceed on the basis of democratic principle.[51]

Dayal's position was in sharp contrast with that of General Alexander. They were both serving the UN in the Congo, but whereas

Dayal supported the legitimate government led by Lumumba, Alexander was effectively allied to the American presence in Leopoldville, which was working to remove Lumumba.

* * *

THE AMERICAN PRESENCE, LED by Devlin, was considering the possibility of involving Holden Roberto in the YQPROP operation to eliminate Lumumba. Roberto was the leader of União das Populações do Norte de Angola (UPA), a political party created in exile in 1954 in the Congo to resist Portuguese rule in Angola. Roberto had been receiving funds from the CIA since 1955. After the independence of the Congo, Roberto had returned to Leopoldville, where he had spent his childhood. Ever since the All African People's Conference in Accra in December 1958, he had been a friend of Lumumba, who now permitted him to transmit political broadcasts into Angola on behalf of the UPA. Roberto used a variety of pseudonyms at different times, and in the Congo, after independence, he adopted the nom de guerre José Gilmore.[52] He was ignorant, however, of the cryptonym used by the CIA to refer to him in cable traffic between the CIA station in Leopoldville and headquarters in Washington: KALISLE/1. The digraph 'KA' designated Angola.

Devlin cabled Tweedy that a 'new possibility' existed in light of forthcoming talks between himself and Roberto, scheduled for 29 September. In particular, he thought that Roberto might serve as the third-country national that was needed in the plot to eliminate Lumumba, as Devlin and Washington had agreed upon. A third-country agent—someone who was neither American nor Congolese—was desirable because he would provide deep cover and avoid association with the US should his actions be exposed. But it was unclear to Devlin whether Roberto qualified as a third-country national: he was Angolan, not Congolese, but on the other hand he was living in the Congo.

Roberto was afraid, thought Devlin, that if Lumumba returned to power as prime minister, he would support the Movimento Popular de Libertação de Angola (MPLA), rather than the UPA. The MPLA, the other principal party dedicated to the liberation of

Angola, had been set up in 1956 and was based in Conakry, Guinea's capital, where it was given support by Sékou Touré.

Roberto insisted on immediate action. Devlin therefore proposed to Tweedy that he 'explore KALISLE 1 thinking soonest to see how far he willing go and determine his assets'. Tweedy authorised the exploratory talks, so that Devlin could assess Roberto's 'attitude toward possible active agent or cut-out role'. But the discussion was eventually dropped: KALISLE/1 did not fit the bill required for the deadly YQPROP mission.[53]

* * *

MOBUTU HAD FAILED TO get Lumumba arrested, largely because of the unwavering position taken by Dayal. Devlin's next step was to arrange for the release to the public of letters exchanged between Lumumba and Nkrumah between August and September, which had been stolen. It was given out that they had been found in Lumumba's briefcase during his arrest on 14 September 1960. Also released were two letters alleged to have been sent by Lumumba and Gizenga to the Soviets and the Chinese. All the letters were published in the Congolese press and caused a sensation. Many people believed that the letters were genuine.

Dayal, however, was suspicious that while some of the letters might be authentic, two—which were extremely damaging to Lumumba—were forgeries. One of the two, ostensibly written by Lumumba, contained a plan to replace the UN with a Soviet operation and to initiate a wave of executions and arrests. Dayal showed the letter to some experts, who were 'categorical that it was a crude forgery'. It was clear, judged Dayal, 'that some foreign hand was behind the conspiracy, for the Congolese did not have the means—or the experience—to produce such a document'.[54] Dayal did not identify the nationality of the 'foreign hand'; he may not have known, and even if he had known he would have been prevented by his position from making any kind of formal accusation.

The foreign hand may have been George Wittman. 'I have the photocopies of Kwame Nkrumah's letters to Lumumba as well as Lumumba's letters to the Soviets and Chinese', he reported to Tempelsman on 30 September 1960.[55] Wittman did not explain where he had obtained the photocopies or what he had done with them, but the fact that he had them at all suggests an involvement.

Supporters of Mobutu as well as some foreign correspondents described the letters as evidence of Nkrumah interfering in the Congo and wanting to take over the country. It was said, too, that they revealed Nkrumah's hatred of the West, notably Nkrumah's comment that 'The only colonialist or imperialist that I trust is a dead one'.

Mobutu exploited the letters to demand the immediate withdrawal of the Ghana Brigade from the Congo.[56] He also insisted on the closure of the Ghana embassy, describing it as a centre of communist subversion.

It was true that Nkrumah had written to Lumumba in tones that were more militant than his usual public stance. Possibly he felt that such candour would help to bring Lumumba to his way of thinking; in any case, the letters were not intended for the eyes of anyone but Lumumba.

Moreover, Nkrumah urged caution throughout the letters, as was clear from any reading of them. He advised Lumumba to seek a reconciliation with Kasavubu and to build a broad coalition government, in order to stabilise the Congo; it was essential, he had written, to work with and within the UN framework. He advocated tactical action and advised Lumumba to stay 'as cool as a cucumber'. The letters were praised by some commentators, including the South African journalist and commentator Colin Legum, who said they contained 'sound advice'.[57]

For Nkrumah, the release of the letters was a disturbing development. It was also bad timing to find himself under such a cloud, for he was about to go to New York for the Fifteenth Session of the UN General Assembly.

The front page of Ghana's *Daily Graphic* on the day of Ghana's independence from Britain, 6 March 1957. Prime Minister Kwame Nkrumah, with his arm raised, proclaims the midnight transfer of power. CREDIT: Daily Graphic, *front page, 6 March 1957*

The Gold Coast cabinet at the time of the election on 17 July 1956, which led to the independence of Ghana the following year. Nkrumah is seated centre, with K A Gbedemah to his left and Kojo Botsio to his right. Nathaniel Welbeck is standing 2nd from left. CREDIT: *Moorland-Spingarn Research Center, Howard University, Manuscript Division, Dabu Gizenga Collection on Kwame Nkrumah, Series F, Box 128-26, Folder 606*

Ghana's Finance Minister Komla A Gbedemah (far R), US Vice President Richard M Nixon and Pat Nixon (second and third from R) at Ghana's independence celebrations, March 1957. Later that year, Gbedemah was refused a seat in a US restaurant because he was Black. By way of apology, President Eisenhower invited him to breakfast at the White House with himself and Nixon. CREDIT: *National Archives, photo no. 306-RNT-12-16*

President Eisenhower and Prime Minister Nkrumah meet in Washington, July 1958. Subsequently, Eisenhower became exasperated with Nkrumah, accusing him of being pro-Soviet. Eisenhower authorised the CIA to assassinate Lumumba. CREDIT: *Everett Collection Historical / Alamy Stock Photo*

William A M Burden, the outgoing President of the Museum of Modern Art (MoMA) in New York in 1959, with Mrs John D Rockefeller 3rd, incoming President. Burden left MoMA temporarily when he was appointed US Ambassador to Belgium. MoMA received funds from the CIA, with which Burden was closely associated. CREDIT: *AP92. Digital image © 2021. The Museum of Modern Art, New York/ Scala, Florence*

Atomium, the centrepiece of Expo 58 in Brussels. Belgium's nuclear prestige was rooted in the exploitation of the Shinkolobwe mine in the Belgian Congo. Shinkolobwe supplied the uranium used to build the atomic bombs dropped on Japan in 1945. CREDIT: © *Dolf Kruger / Nederlands Fotomuseum*

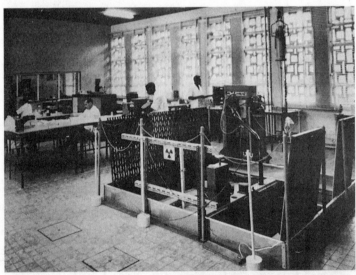

The Triga atomic reactor in the TRICO Centre at Lovanium University in Leopoldville, June 1959. In August 1960, CIA Chief of Station Larry Devlin was instructed by the CIA to remove the rods from the reactor, but judged the order too dangerous to follow. CREDIT: *Photo by R. Minnaert from Luc Gillon,* Servir: en Actes et en Vérité *(Paris–Gembloux: Duculot, 1988)*

'Hands Off Africa! Africa Must Be Free!' Kwame Nkrumah opens the All African People's Conference in Accra on 8 December 1958, attended by delegates from all over the continent and observers from the US and elsewhere. CREDIT: *African Activist Archive Project, African Studies Center, Michigan State University*

Frantz Fanon addressing the All African People's Conference in Accra. Describing atrocities by the French colonial authorities in Algeria, he argued that violence is necessary sometimes to obtain freedom. Fanon took the conference by storm. CREDIT: *Archives Frantz Fanon / IMEC*

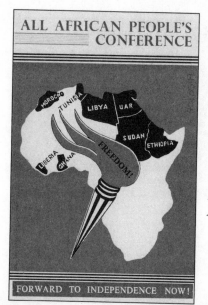

The cover of the 'All African People's Conference' leaflet, 1958, showing the nations of Africa that were free from colonialism. The leaflet begins: 'Attention, all Africans! Have you heard the clarion call to action?—HANDS OFF AFRICA!' CREDIT: *W E B Du Bois Papers (MS 312), Department of Special Collections and University Archives, W E B Du Bois Library, University of Massachusetts Amherst*

The five founders of the Non-Aligned Movement on 29 September 1960 in New York, where they are attending the UN General Assembly. In the forefront, L-R: India's Prime Minister Jawaharlal Nehru; Nkrumah; Egypt's President Gamal Abdel Nasser; Indonesia's President Sukarno; and Yugoslavia's President Josip Broz Tito. CREDIT: *Harvey Lippman / AP / Shutterstock*

The Pan Africanist George Padmore (L) from Trinidad, who moved to Ghana after independence as Nkrumah's Advisor on African Affairs, to support liberation movements across Africa. He is in his garden in Accra with his wife Dorothy Pizer, not long before his death in September 1959, aged 56. CREDIT: *Courtesy of Beatrice Anne Pizer*

The cover of the Pan-African magazine *Voice of Africa*, February 1961, which was distributed across Africa by Ghana's Bureau of African Affairs. The magazine urged: 'Towards African Independence and Unity: Tomorrow the United States of Africa!' CREDIT: *Cover of* Voice of Africa, *Vol. 1, no. 2, February 1961*

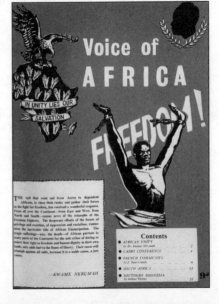

Patrice Lumumba in Brussels for the Round Table, organised by Belgium in 1960 to discuss the future of the Congo. Recently released from prison, where he was brutally treated, Lumumba's wrists are bandaged. He is in front of a banner bearing words painted by Joseph-Désiré Mobutu: '*Vive Lumumba! Vive le MNC! Vive le Congo Uni!*' CREDIT: *The photograph was taken on 26 January 1960 by Harry Pot. Fotocollectie ANeFo, The National Archives of The Netherlands, Bestanddeelnummer: 910-9733*

The famous Congolese musician Le Grand Kallé—Joseph Kabasele Tshamala—and his band African Jazz, playing at the Plaza Hotel in Brussels during the Round Table. While in Brussels, Kabasele (facing the microphone) wrote '*Table Ronde*' and '*Indépendance Cha Cha*', the song which became an anthem of freedom across Africa. CREDIT: *HP.2005.60.7, collection RMCA Tervuren; photo R. Stalin (Inforcongo), 1960, RMCA Tervuren* ©

Andrée Blouin, a political activist from Congo Brazzaville, campaigning in the Belgian Congo in the months leading up to independence. She joined Lumumba's inner circle and some of the press dubbed them 'team Lumum-Blouin'. CREDIT: *Herbert F. Weiss Collection, EEPA 2020-005, Eliot Elisofon Photographic Archives, National Museum of African Art, Smithsonian Institution*

A woman in Leopoldville in June 1960 looks forward to the day of freedom from Belgium at the end of the month. Her dress bears the words *CONGO INDEPEN- DANCE 1960* and images of children facing a sun-filled horizon of freedom. CREDIT: *Belga Photo Archives / PA Images*

High emotion and hope at the Congo's independence celebrations in the King Baudouin Stadium in Leopold- ville, 1 July 1960. CREDIT: *Belga Photo Archives / PA Images*

The first Congolese govern- ment was approved by Parliament on the night of 23-24 June 1960. After the vote, Ministers Anicet Kashamura (L) and Tamusu Fumu (R) reached for the beard of Prime Minister Lumumba (centre) in a gesture of enthusiasm. Members of several parties had decided to grow a beard until Congo's independence. CREDIT: *R Stalin / Congo- presse (Liberas Ghent, Archives of Henri and Hélène Guillaume)*

Young women celebrate their freedom from colonial rule in Leopoldville on 1 July 1960. Ten weeks later, Mobutu—with the backing of the CIA—announced that the army had seized power. CREDIT: *Belga Photo Archives / PA Images*

Nkrumah welcomes Lumumba to Ghana on 8 August 1960. Ghana energetically supported the democratically elected government of the Congo. CREDIT: *Rue des Archives, 3 bis, rue Pelleport, Paris / Granger Historical Picture Archive*

Larry Devlin, CIA Chief of Station in newly independent Congo, looks out at the Congo River from Leopoldville Beach. Before his posting to the Congo in July 1960, he operated under official cover at the US Embassy in Brussels, working closely with Ambassador Burden. CREDIT: *From Larry Devlin*, Chief of Station, Congo: Fighting the Cold War in a Hot Zone *(New York: PublicAffairs, 2007)*

An anti-Lumumba demonstration outside the meeting of Independent African States in Leopoldville on 25 August 1960. The protest was orchestrated by the CIA to undermine Lumumba's reputation. This is a still from the newsreel 'Congo: Anti Lumumba Protest at Pan-African Conference'. CREDIT: *Reuters Historical Collection via British Pathé*

Rajeshwar Dayal (L) of India is briefed by UN Undersecretary Ralph Bunche at UN headquarters in New York on 2 September 1960, two days before Dayal's departure for the Congo. Dayal succeeded Bunche as Hammarskjöld's Personal Representative in the Congo and did everything in his power to support Lumumba. CREDIT: *UN Photo / Teddy Chen*

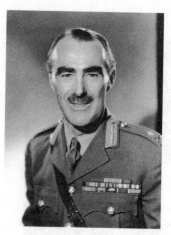

Major General Henry T Alexander, British Chief of Defence Staff of the Ghana Armed Forces, who led Ghana's UN troops in the Congo. Alexander betrayed the trust of Nkrumah. CREDIT: © *National Portrait Gallery, London*

At a press conference in Leopold-ville on 20 July 1960, Lumumba (centre) calls for international support to throw Belgian troops out of the Congo. Mobutu, who stands at Lumumba's left in an apparent show of support, is plotting with the CIA to remove him from power. CREDIT: *Bettman / Getty Images*

UN Secretary General Dag Hammarskjöld welcomes Nkrumah to the UN on 7 March 1961. Nkrumah will shortly address the General Assembly, with a firm message: 'The first task of the United Nations is to allow the Congolese people to be ruled by a government of their own choice.' CREDIT: *UN Photo / Yutaka Nagata*

Nkrumah addresses the UN General Assembly on 23 September 1960. He called for a permanent seat for an African nation on the UN Security Council. CREDIT: *UN Photo / Yutaka Nagata*

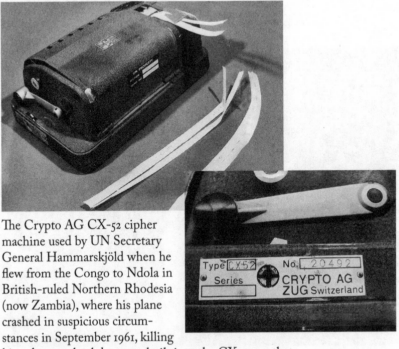

The Crypto AG CX-52 cipher machine used by UN Secretary General Hammarskjöld when he flew from the Congo to Ndola in British-ruled Northern Rhodesia (now Zambia), where his plane crashed in suspicious circumstances in September 1961, killing him. A secret backdoor was built into the CX-52, so that every message could be read by the CIA and the National Security Agency. CREDIT: *United Nations Archives,* *S-0727-0005-02*

Lumumba at Leopoldville airport on 2 December 1960, after his capture by Mobutu's troops. He was murdered the following month, together with Joseph Okito, Senate Vice-President, and Maurice Mpolo, Minister of Youth and Sport. CREDIT: *Horst Faas / AP / Shutterstock*

In shock and anger at Lumumba's killing, protesters march through London in February 1961. CREDIT: *10513830 Marx Memorial Library / Mary Evans*

Outrage erupts in Cairo at Lumumba's murder and a car is set ablaze outside the US Embassy on 15 February 1961. CREDIT: *AP Photo / Shutterstock*

Ghana's *Daily Graphic* on 14 February 1961, the day after the news of the killings of Lumumba, Mpolo and Okito. Nkrumah's Egyptian wife, Fathia, kisses the cheek of Patrice Lumumba Jr in Cairo, where Lumumba had sent his eldest sons to safety. CREDIT: Daily Graphic, *front page, 14 February 1961*

Louis Armstrong in a Ghanaian newspaper advertisement for his forthcoming concerts in Accra in October 1960. Armstrong went on an eleven-week tour of Africa as a jazz ambassador for the US, organised in collaboration with Pepsi Cola. The tour also took Armstrong to the Congo. CREDIT: Daily Graphic, *26 September 1960, p. 4*

Louis Armstrong (L), Lucille Wilson Armstrong and Nkrumah (R) in Accra in 1956. Armstrong saw a Ghanaian woman who resembled his mother and wrote to a friend: 'I came from here, way back. At least my people did. Now I know this is my country too'. CREDIT: *Louis Armstrong House Museum and Archives, New York*

Members of the US Embassy in Leopoldville at a concert by Louis Armstrong and the All Stars in Elisabethville in November 1960. Larry Devlin enthused about Armstrong's visit in his memoir. Armstrong's concerts served as a Trojan Horse for US officials to visit Katanga, which had seceded from the Congo and was not officially recognised by the US or the UN. CREDIT: *United Nations Archives, S-0805-0012-03*

Businessman Maurice Tempelsman with his partner Jacqueline Kennedy Onassis at a gala in New York, 1986. Tempelsman employed CIA official George Wittman as his company's representative in the Congo in the early 1960s. Larry Devlin worked for Tempelsman as his representative in the Congo after he retired from the CIA in 1974. CREDIT: *Photo by Sonia Moskowitz, Images Press / Getty Images*

President John F Kennedy welcomes President Nkrumah to Washington DC on 8 March 1961. The previous month, Nkrumah had protested vigorously to Kennedy about the delivery by the CIA of Fouga fighter jets to Katanga, in violation of UN Security Council resolutions and US official policy. CREDIT: *Robert Knudsen. White House Photographs. John F. Kennedy Presidential Library and Museum, Boston*

Holden Roberto (R), leader of the Angolan People's Union (UPA), interviewed on 29 June 1961 outside the movement's headquarters in Leopoldville. Roberto and his movement were bankrolled by the CIA and refused to join a united front with the MPLA, also fighting for the liberation of Angola from Portuguese rule. CREDIT: *Horst Faas / AP / Shutterstock*

Kenyan trade unionist Tom Mboya in New York on 23 February 1962. He is wearing the ring noted by Ghana's *Daily Graphic* in 1958: 'On this ring the outline of Africa is carved in black and across the face is written the word "freedom". If you ask him about it he will say that it is his engagement ring and that he is engaged to politics. At this rate, it looks as though he will marry the girl.' Mboya was in a close relationship with the CIA. CREDIT: *Associated Press / Shutterstock*

UN Secretary General Hammarskjöld (L) at a reception in Leopoldville on 15 September 1961, in conversation with Premier Cyrille Adoula (R) and Vice-Premier Antoine Gizenga (wearing glasses). A month earlier, Adoula had been inserted into power by the CIA. Two days after this reception, Hammarskjöld was killed in a plane crash in Northern Rhodesia, south of the Congolese border. CREDIT: *UN Photo / BZ*

An invitation to a festival in Lagos in December 1961 of African American musicians. It was organised by the American Society of African Culture (AMSAC), a CIA front based in New York, which opened an office in Lagos during the festival. CREDIT: *Moorland-Spingarn Research Center, Howard University, American Society of African Culture (AMSAC) Manuscript Collection, Box 41*

A. M. S. A. C.

American Society of African Culture

request the pleasure of the company of

---

at

The King George V Stadium, Lagos

December 18th and 19th at 8.30 p.m.

at

the A. M. S. A. C. "Festival of Arts."

GRATIS

African American musical stars arrive in Lagos in December 1961 to perform in a festival organised by AMSAC. Dr Horace Mann Bond, standing at L, was a founder and the President of AMSAC. The stars—including Randy Weston (centre L) and Nina Simone (centre R)—were unaware that AMSAC was a CIA front. CREDIT: *Moorland-Spingarn Research Center, Howard University, American Society of African Culture (AMSAC) Manuscript Collection, Box 41*

The Mbari Club in Ibadan, Nigeria, in 1961, one of various cultural centres in Africa set up and funded by the Congress for Cultural Freedom,
a CIA front. Wole Soyinka was outraged when he learned of the CIA's
secret patronage, denouncing it as 'the Devil himself, romping in our
post-colonial Garden of Eden and gorging on the fruits of the Tree of
Knowledge!' CREDIT: *Harry Ransom Center, The University of Texas at
Austin*

South African writer Es'kia
(formerly Ezekiel) Mphahlele, the
director from 1961 of the Africa
Program of the Congress for
Cultural Freedom. When the
Congress was exposed as a CIA
front, Mphahlele declared: 'Yes,
the CIA stinks....We were had'.
CREDIT: © *Bailey's African
History Archives, photograph by*
Drum *photographer*

Leaders of the CIA-supported coup d'état in Ghana that overthrew the civilian government of Nkrumah on 24 February 1966, at a press conference a week later, flanked by men with drawn rifles. Seated L to R: Emmanuel K Kotoka, Joseph A Ankrah, J W K Harlley and A K Deku. CREDIT: *Photographer: Priya Ramrakha. The LIFE Picture Collection / Getty*

President Mobutu Sese Seko (second from L) in a meeting with President Nixon (second from R) in the Oval Office on 10 October 1973. Backed by the US, Mobutu ruled the Congo (which he renamed Zaire in 1971) until 1997. CREDIT: *Photographer: Jack E. Kightlinger. National Archives Identifier: 194548; NLRN-WHPO-E1609-10.*

PART VII

THE GLOBAL GAME

21

Africa at the United Nations

THE FIFTEENTH SESSION OF THE UN General Assembly
opened in New York on Tuesday 20 September 1960—a crisp,
fresh day, with a touch of fall in the air. Several thousand representatives of nations from all corners of the globe had descended
on the city. It was a markedly different assembly from those of the
past: sixteen newly independent African states were to be admitted as members of the organisation.[1] And with the problem of the
Congo dominating the activities of the UN, observed Rajeshwar
Dayal, the Fifteenth Session 'virtually became an African session'.[2]

Nkrumah arrived in New York 'somewhat subdued', as his letters to Lumumba had been released only a few days earlier'. But
he was determined to make the best of this opportunity to support
Lumumba on the world stage. He was invited to a private dinner
with Secretary General Hammarskjöld to discuss matters in the
Congo. Hammarskjöld also met privately with other leaders of the
Afro-Asian bloc—Prime Minister Nehru, President Nasser, President Sékou Touré and Prince Moulay Hassan of Morocco, who
added their voices to that of Nkrumah.[3]

Castro was welcomed by the UN in its Turtle Bay precinct. But
he was not welcomed by America. Reservations had been made
for him at the plush Shelburne Hotel in Midtown, just steps from
Grand Central Station. On arrival, however, he was asked for a cash
advance of $10,000 to cover any damage his delegation might cause.
Outraged by this extraordinary demand, he refused; he was already
furious that his travel in New York had been restricted by the State
Department to the island of Manhattan.

At the suggestion of Malcolm X and other civil rights leaders, Castro and his delegation went to Harlem to stay in the Hotel Theresa, on the southwest corner of 125th Street and Seventh Avenue. When it had opened in 1913, the hotel had an all-white clientele and staff. But in 1940, it opened to all races at a time when Blacks were generally not accepted in Manhattan hotel rooms and restaurants. By 1960, it was favoured with fond affection—as a kind of Waldorf Astoria of Harlem—by New York's African American community.[4]

A host of international leaders travelled uptown over the next several weeks to meet with Castro. When Nkrumah arrived in front of the hotel, a large crowd shouted, 'Long live Nkrumah!'[5] Several thousand people gathered to welcome Nasser, some holding 'Viva Nasser!' and 'Viva Castro!' signs; others held up signs that read, 'Congo for the Congolese' and 'Allah is the Greatest'. Castro's aides flew a Cuban flag above the hotel.

The American writer Maya Angelou was living in New York at the time. As soon as she and her friends heard about Castro's relocation to the Hotel Theresa, she later recalled in *The Heart of a Woman*, 'we were on the street in the rain, finding cabs or private cars or heading for subways. We were going to welcome the Cubans to Harlem'. But so great was the neighbourhood support for Castro that they were unable to get close to the hotel, even though it was eleven o'clock on a Monday evening. Thousands of people had filled the streets and sidewalks, and the police had cordoned off the area.[6]

Khrushchev went to Harlem to visit Castro, which triggered a heavy police response around the hotel. 'White and nervous', noted Angelou, they 'guarded the intersections of 125th Street and Seventh Avenue, which even in normal times was accepted as the most popular and possibly most dangerous crossroad in black America'. Castro and Khrushchev embraced publicly on 125th Street, 'as the Cubans applauded and the Russians smiled broadly'. Black people, recorded Angelou, joined the applause.[7]

* * *

ON THURSDAY 22 SEPTEMBER, President Eisenhower addressed the representatives of UN member states in the vast hall of the

General Assembly. With his military bearing and dressed in a simple grey suit, he exerted an air of quiet authority. The first third of his speech was devoted to Africa, making special reference to the Congo. He drew a parallel between America's overthrow of British rule in the eighteenth century and the achievement of independence by the colonised territories of Africa—the same powerful analogy that had been highlighted by Nkrumah at the All African People's Conference in Accra in 1958 and had subsequently been taken up by Lumumba in his speeches.

Eisenhower proposed that member states should pledge a commitment to African people's right to make their own choices about how they wished to live. He applied the message to the Congo: 'The people of the Congo are entitled to build up their country in peace and freedom. Intervention by other nations in their internal affairs would deny them that right and create a focus of conflict in the heart of Africa'.[8] The implicit criticism was directed at the Soviet Union and also at the nonaligned nations, especially in Africa.

Eisenhower's apparent support for the autonomy of the Congo was, however, deeply hypocritical. His government was actively targeting the legitimate government of the Congo and, just a month prior, had authorised the consideration of 'any particular kind of activity which might contribute to getting rid of Lumumba'. On 19 September 1960, three days before the opening of the General Assembly, Eisenhower had expressed a wish for the death of Lumumba in a conversation with British Foreign Minister Lord Home. According to the minutes of their meeting, 'The president expressed his wish that Lumumba would fall into a river full of crocodiles'. Lord Home agreed, though in language that was less explicit.[9] The day before Eisenhower's speech to the General Assembly, Larry Devlin had received the cable telling him to expect Dr Gottlieb in Leopoldville, in connection with the plan to assassinate Lumumba.

Eisenhower concluded his speech to the General Assembly with a call for peace in the world: 'We of the United States will join with you in making a mounting effort to build the structure of true peace—a peace in which all peoples may progress constantly to higher levels of human achievement. The means are at hand. We have but to use them with a wisdom and energy worthy of our cause'.[10]

The president's words were mostly well received. Castro, however, did not applaud.

Following his speech, President Eisenhower hosted a luncheon at the Waldorf Astoria for the delegation heads of the Latin American states—but neither Cuba nor the Dominican Republic was invited. Castro, meanwhile, hosted a gathering of a dozen Black employees of the Hotel Theresa in its coffee shop.[11]

Eisenhower and Christian A Herter, his secretary of state, also met with President Nkrumah, President Tito of Yugoslavia and two others, including W M Q Halm, Ghana's ambassador to the US.[12] Nkrumah welcomed the meeting; he wanted to reach some sort of understanding with Eisenhower in relation to the leadership crisis in the Congo.

But Eisenhower did not engage with the issue, notes the historian Richard Mahoney, preferring to reminisce about his days as supreme Allied commander in World War II. The Ghanaian president pressed him further. 'Our policy', responded Eisenhower, 'is to solve problems through the UN even when we ourselves would prefer them worked out in another way'. Nkrumah left the meeting 'heartily dissatisfied with the American's assurances about working through the UN', observes Mahoney. He 'most surely suspected that Eisenhower's assurance was outright fiction'.[13]

* * *

AT 10.30 THE NEXT day, Friday 23 September, it was Nkrumah's turn to address the General Assembly. Walking slowly to the rostrum, he made a deep impression on the many world leaders around him. Nkrumah's private secretary, Erica Powell, watched with pride. 'The rich colours of gold, scarlet, emerald and white of the Kente cloth he was wearing', she thought, 'gave his whole being a radiance against the sombre background'.[14]

Like many other leaders of newly independent nations, Nkrumah was conscious of the significance of sartorial decisions. He had

designed a simple outfit for men to wear in Ghana, which he regarded as appropriate for a young, developing nation. 'This uniform
will do away with all these problems', he told Genoveva Marais,
'for I'm impatient with Western clothes'.[15] He tried hard to divest
lawyers in Ghana of their wigs and gowns, describing them as relics
of a colonial anachronism, but his urging was resisted by most of
the lawyers.[16]

When Nkrumah began to deliver his speech to the General Assembly, Powell noted, 'it was in a quiet modulated voice, almost
with reverence. But as he warmed to his subject, true orator that he
was, he gave his speech all the punch and vehemence that he had
written into it'.[17]

Disciplined as always, Nkrumah gave a speech that was carefully
timed and lasted exactly one hour. His chief focus was the Congo,
and he followed up on Eisenhower's themes—but in a markedly
different direction. He called for an end to colonial rule, for support
for the legitimate government of Lumumba and for the UN to use
only African nations and troops to create an African solution to the
problem. He recommended that African nations avoid military al-
liances with countries outside the continent and called for a revised
UN Charter, with a permanent seat for an African nation on the
Security Council.[18]

He also criticised the UN for its failure to remove Belgian troops
from the Congo and to end the secession of Katanga. 'It is no more
possible for a saint to be neutral on the issue of good and evil', he
said slowly, but firmly, 'than for the United Nations to be neutral on
the issue of legality and illegality'.[19]

He added that 'imperialist intrigue, stark and naked, was desperately at work' to prevent a reconciliation between Kasavubu and
Lumumba. 'To do anything to damage the prestige and authority
of that government', insisted Nkrumah, 'would be to undermine
the whole basis of democracy in Africa'.

He continued with passion, 'Now I, an African, stand before
this august Assembly of the United Nations and speak with a voice
of peace and freedom, proclaiming to the world the dawn of a new
era'. He further emphasised the importance of the UN:

I look upon the United Nations as the only organization that holds out any hope for the future of mankind. . . . The United Nations must therefore face up to its responsibilities, and ask those who would bury their heads like the proverbial ostrich in their imperialist sands, to pull their heads out and look at the blazing African sun now travelling across the sky of Africa's redemption. . . .

This is a new day in Africa and as I speak now, thirteen new African nations have taken their seats this year in this august Assembly as independent sovereign states. . . . There are now twenty-two of us in this Assembly and there are yet more to come.[20]

The assembly listened to Nkrumah's speech in silence, with rapt attention; when he reached the end, he received a standing ovation. Although leading a nation with only 2 per cent of Africa's population, he came across as the continent's spokesman.[21] Khrushchev, one of the first to rush up to meet him as he stepped down from the podium, congratulated him warmly.[22]

The United States, however, had a different reaction. They heard the speech as an alarming signal that Nkrumah had crossed over to the Soviet side. Within a few hours, Secretary Herter denounced Nkrumah's words to the press. 'As much as I heard of it', he said bitterly, 'it sounded to me as though he were very definitely making a bid for the leadership of what you would call a left-wing group of African states. . . . I think he has marked himself as very definitely leaning toward the Soviet bloc'.[23] Herter had not even heard all of Nkrumah's speech, as he himself acknowledged. Nonetheless, his statement had been cleared by the White House.[24]

Nkrumah was astonished by this reaction. He promptly issued a response, declaring that Herter 'was, in fact, the last person from whom I would expect such a remark'.[25] The secretary of state's accusation seemed absurd, given that Ghana was trying to protect the Congo crisis from both superpowers and from the conflict of the Cold War. Nkrumah had sought to dissuade Lumumba from asking for Soviet aid, unless under the auspices of the UN; for him, the only way forward was to Africanise the crisis. But such neutralism was anathema to the US administration, which took a wholly US-centred position: if you are not with us, you are against us.

Until September 1960, notes Ebere Nwaubani, Washington had kept its exasperation with Accra out of the public domain. But Herter's statement to the press changed this.[26]

Eisenhower wrote in his memoirs that 'Mr. Nkrumah went directly from my room to the United Nations General Assembly and within forty-five minutes cut loose with a speech following the Khrushchev line in strong criticism of Secretary General Hammarskjöld'.[27] But this was not so. In fact, Nkrumah went out of his way to canvass support for Hammarskjöld; in his speech, he had expressed his 'personal appreciation' of the way Hammarskjöld had 'handled a most difficult task' in the Congo. He had added that it would be 'entirely wrong to blame either the Security Council or any senior officials of the United Nations for what has taken place'. Certainly, he had found fault with the UN's failure to distinguish between legal and illegal authorities, but he attributed this to 'in essence the growing pains of the United Nations'.[28]

On 24 September, the day after Nkrumah's speech, Joseph Satterthwaite, the assistant secretary of state for African affairs, attempted—on Herter's instruction—to meet Nkrumah to make a formal protest about his speech. Nkrumah, by now incensed over America's behaviour, refused to see him. All Satterthwaite could manage was a telephone conversation with Alexander Quaison-Sackey, the Ghanaian ambassador to the UN. Satterthwaite told him that the US was less offended by Nkrumah's speech than by his apparent commonality with the 'Communists'.[29]

The American position may have been hardened by a report from George Wittman in Ghana, sent on the same day that Eisenhower gave his speech to the UN General Assembly. Accra, he wrote, 'is currently the chief depot of Soviet diplomatic, trade and technical personnel'. The Soviet diplomats expelled from the Congo, he added, had made their way to Ghana. Referring disdainfully to Nkrumah as 'Kwame', Wittman reported that Accra was 'a hotbed of confused information. . . . It is as if one great long political conference without a beginning or an end is in progress'.[30]

* * *

Nkrumah's speech at the General Assembly was followed by that of Nikita Khrushchev. Like the American and Ghanaian presidents, Khrushchev, too, focused on Africa and the Congo. But, unlike Nkrumah, he *did* attack the US; in doing so, he drew attention to the real reason for the Congo's appeal to the US. 'Raw materials for nuclear weapons such as uranium, cobalt and titanium', he declared, 'as well as cheap labour—that is what the monopolists are afraid of losing in the Congo'. He went on: 'We have stood, we stand, and always will stand, for the right of the peoples of Africa, just as those of other continents, to establish, whatever regime they please in their countries, on attaining their freedom from colonial oppression . . . [and] against any interference by imperialists in the domestic affairs of countries which are emancipating themselves from colonial dependence, against discreditable methods such as those used in the Congo'.[31]

Khrushchev attacked Hammarskjöld for 'doing the dirty work' of the colonialists. He proposed that the post of UN secretary general be abolished and replaced by a troika: an executive of three people that would reflect the current global distribution of power. It would include one representative each from the Western nations, the communist nations and the nonaligned nations.[32]

Hammarskjöld was sending reports from New York to Dayal in the Congo during the assembly. 'Roundup of a day in the cold war', he wrote to Dayal after the speeches by Nkrumah and Khrushchev. But at least, he added hopefully, 'all got definite proof that if the Afro-Asians stick together, or if only the Africans stick together, they represent a new big power to which certain others have to bow'.[33]

When it was Castro's turn to address the assembly, the Cuban leader spoke without a break for 269 minutes—nearly four and a half hours (still, in 2021, a UN record), which pushed a UN steering committee back a full day.[34] He achieved this marathon without referring to any notes. 'In his battle dress with his jet black hair and beard', noted Erica Powell admiringly, 'he looked more as if he were enacting a Shakespearean tragedy, raising his arms in supplication, throwing his head back in agony, pounding the lectern and thumping his chest'.[35] He accused the United States of trying to topple his new government—an accusation that was wholly justified.

* * *

HAMMARSKJÖLD RESPONDED TO KHRUSHCHEV after the weekend recess of the assembly. He spoke calmly, but firmly. His speech made clear the uncompromising commitment of the UN to the newly decolonised, less powerful nations that were represented in front of him. When he had finished his speech, members of the assembly rose to their feet and gave him a thunderous ovation that lasted several minutes. But Khrushchev responded with a 'biting and personal' attack, wrote Dayal, taunting Hammarskjöld with the praise he had received from 'imperialist countries' for acting as an agent of their interests. He called on the secretary general to resign.

Hammarskjöld replied later that day, refusing to resign. 'It is very easy to resign', he said. 'It is not so easy to stay on. It is very easy to bow to the wish of a big Power. It is another matter to resist'. His speech was punctuated with applause, clearly indicating the support of most member states, especially those from Africa and Asia. Any change in leadership would jeopardise the UN mission in the Congo.[36]

Eisenhower met on Tuesday 27 September with UK prime minister Harold Macmillan in New York City. Consistent with the theme of the General Assembly, they focused on the Congo and—as Eisenhower later recalled in his memoir—they compared notes on 'the troublesome activities' of Lumumba.[37]

On the same day, Ian Scott, the British ambassador in Leopoldville, sent a telegram to the Foreign Office in London, advocating for a more active policy to neutralise Lumumba. This led to an exchange between senior officials at the Foreign Office, which set out the same aim as that of the United States—namely, murder. 'I see only two possible solutions to the problem' of Lumumba, wrote Howard F T Smith, the assistant head of the African Department of the Foreign Office, on 28 September. 'The first', he said, 'is the simple one of ensuring Lumumba's removal from the scene by killing him. This should in fact solve the problem'. The alternative would be to find a way of diminishing his power. But, he added, his preference 'would be for Lumumba to be removed from the scene altogether'. Smith, who has been described as 'a toughie if ever there was one', became director general of MI5 in 1979–1981.[38]

A D M Ross, the assistant undersecretary in the Foreign Office, agreed with Smith. 'There is much to be said for eliminating Lumumba', he replied. But, he added regretfully, 'unless Mobutu can get him arrested and executed promptly, he is likely to survive and continue to plague us all'.[39]

Wittman sent a similar message to Tempelsman from Leopoldville on 30 September. Unless Lumumba's enemies 'kill him or effectively imprison him', he warned, 'it is hard not to see him landing on his feet in a final analysis. He is still personally the strongest leader of the bunch and they know it—often down but never out'.[40]

* * *

ON 1 OCTOBER 1960, President Eisenhower was told that the leaders of five neutral nations had jointly submitted to the UN General Assembly a resolution calling for a meeting between Eisenhower and Khrushchev, to find a way of solving the problems affecting East-West relations. One of the cosigners was Nkrumah; the others were Nehru, Tito, Nasser and Sukarno. To the American president this proposal seemed 'totally illogical; at worst it seemed an act of effrontery'. He made sure the resolution was defeated.[41]

Nkrumah was bitterly disappointed at the blunt refusal of the US to consider the point of view of other world leaders. He was appalled, too, by the angry and biased coverage of Khrushchev's speech in the US media. In his judgement, it was simply inaccurate. 'The Prime Minister was so disgusted', Erica Powell wrote, 'that he never looked at another television news programme all the time we were there'.

Nkrumah himself did not escape attack. Americans were led to believe, noted Powell, that he was a communist and 'in Mr Khrushchev's pocket'. Letters flooded in to Nkrumah from angry Americans, many of which were insulting. 'I felt angry and sad', wrote Powell, 'that so many people could be so easily misled'.[42]

22

Spying on the UN

O N 29 SEPTEMBER 1960, TWO days after President Eisenhower and British prime minister Macmillan compared notes on the 'troublesome activities' of Lumumba, the Congolese leader left his official residence and went to the cité, where he strolled around with friends and colleagues. They stopped for a while in a bar, where Lumumba danced the cha-cha-cha to enthusiastic applause. Then he took the microphone and spoke earnestly for half an hour to a large crowd gathering around him.

Later, as the evening drew in, he went to see his loyal friend Anicet Kashamura, the minister of information and cultural affairs. At Kashamura's home, Lumumba gave another speech—this time, to a group of journalists. He was suspicious, he said, of American activities in the Congo, which he believed were not in the interests of the Congo.

Only a few weeks earlier, Lumumba had expressed genuine admiration for America, especially its successful battle against British colonisation. But his enthusiasm had vanished, following the bitter disappointment of his visit to the US between 22 July and 2 August.

Turning to Kashamura and his other friends and colleagues, he said that it was up to them to carry on the fight. 'For me', he added quietly, 'it's finished. I feel that I am going to die. I will die like Gandhi. If I die tomorrow, it's because a foreigner gave arms to a Congolese'.[1]

* * *

AMERICAN INTERVENTION IN THE Congo was being planned far away from Africa—in Brussels, in Washington and in the UN complex in New York. There, behind the scenes of the General Assembly, the US was spinning a spider's web of influence on the delegates from African countries.

Owen W Roberts, a Foreign Service officer serving as an economic and commercial assistant at the US consulate in Leopoldville, had been brought home in July 1960. Regarded as an expert on Congolese affairs, he was given the role of analyst in the Bureau of Intelligence and Research (INR), the intelligence agency of the State Department. Unlike the CIA, the INR is strictly an analytical bureau, with the role of keeping diplomats and officials well informed. 'The absence of cloak-and-dagger in INR', note David Wise and Thomas B Ross in *The Invisible Government*, 'is reflected in the fact that it is the only member of USIB [the United States Intelligence Board] whose intelligence budget is part of the public record'.[2]

Years later Roberts elaborated on his role in INR, explaining, 'We were very much on the side of being strictly analysts and not getting involved in policy'. Even so, he became the main US contact in Washington with Congolese visitors—'a very active role for somebody who was, strictly speaking, an INR analyst'. He served as escort officer for Lumumba when he visited Washington and stayed in Blair House, the president's official guest house; Roberts was the single liaison officer for the eighteen ministers who accompanied Lumumba.

It occurred to Roberts 'that we needed to put together and legitimize a Congolese leadership. So I started suggesting to my INR bosses, and even at inter-office meetings, that we assemble a kind of a constitutional committee meeting in Leopoldville, which would also elect a leadership'. This was his first introduction to the fact that INR 'generally doesn't directly put up policy ideas like that'. What you do instead, he discovered, 'is go around and talk to other people about your ideas'.

Roberts explained how this worked at the United Nations, when lobbying African member states. African diplomats, he said, tended 'to follow the "Third World" approach and many voted in blocs, often without much reference to home ministries. Our tactic was to get specific instructions sent out by Foreign Ministries to their UN [General Assembly] delegations. [International Organization Affairs] would draft such demarches for our Embassies to local capitals, get clearances in the Department, coordinate with allies, and cable them out'.

He recalled, 'I tried to contact as many delegates as possible, sometimes numbering ten to even twenty per country. I would argue our case and try to confirm their positions and especially their instructions'.[3]

Roberts was one of a number of State Department officials trying to exert influence at, and through, the UN. Thompson R Buchanan, who was responsible for Communist Economic Affairs in the State Department, highlighted the importance of the UN in relation to the Congo. He and Phil Habib, a colleague, 'were proudest of our work on the Congo. There we proposed that the UN be used as a type of firewall to prevent the Russians from moving in with the help of the radical nationalist, Patrice Lumumba'. When Buchanan and Habib were asked how much this would cost, Habib estimated around $200 million.[4]

'Our responsibility', said Buchanan, 'was not day-to-day policy but action programs designed to block Soviet moves in a given country. In that sense we were very active in the Congo. We kept heckling the African bureau to set up UN and bilateral programs to provide aid in a variety of fields . . . in the security field, in the agricultural field, all the logical programs that would interest an undeveloped country that had nothing'.[5]

* * *

THE CIA, TOO, WAS ACTIVE at the UN. 'I was aware', said Roberts, 'that the CIA to some extent was also contacting people, because I knew one or two of the CIA agents. Once in a while I would see them'. He was also aware that the CIA sought to buy support for American positions: 'The CIA made some payoffs, I know, to Congolese delegations, and maybe to some others'. Occasionally, he said, 'an African would be confused as to whether I was a satchel carrier or not'—that is, whether or not he was one of the Americans carrying cash to bribe delegates.[6]

By law, the CIA is not allowed to operate within the US. This does not apply to the UN complex in New York, since the complex is extraterritorial. But any covert activity at the UN defies the General Convention on the Privileges and Immunities of the United Nations, a multilateral treaty from 1946.[7] Furthermore, any kind of intrusion by the US in particular ran counter to the agreement entered into between the United States and the United Nations in 1947, which included the following provision: 'The headquarters district shall be inviolable. Federal, state or local officers or officials of the United States, whether administrative, judicial, military or police, shall not enter the headquarters district to perform any official duties therein except with the consent of and under conditions agreed to by the Secretary-General'.[8]

* * *

THE CIA's ROLE AT THE UN was considerably larger than indicated by Owen Roberts. One of its heavily funded fronts, the African-American Institute, was only a few minutes' walk away, facilitating easy access for AAI staff to the UN buildings, where they could network easily. By the same token, it was a straightforward matter to invite delegates to the welcoming and 'plush' offices of the AAI.[9]

Next door to the AAI were the headquarters of the Overseas Regional Surveys Associates, the public relations company set up by CIA agent Howard Imbrey as a cover for his clandestine activities. 'I . . . spent most of my time at the UN visiting Africans and encouraging them', said Imbrey. He worked hard at 'getting sources there and see[ing] what we could do'.[10]

He was also in contact with sources associated with the UN in other parts of the world. As the handler of Washington Okumu, he may have facilitated Okumu's recruitment to the UN Industrial Development Organisation in Vienna in 1971.[11]

Yet another method used by the CIA to influence decisions at the UN was the covert funding of some nongovernmental organisations (NGOs) that had 'consultative status' at the UN. This status had been specified in the UN Charter when it was founded in 1945 as a way of enabling NGOs to participate in various commissions and official meetings. As the practice developed, it also gave NGOs increasing access to the delegations of member states.[12]

A key assumption about consultative status, explains Peter Willetts, professor of global politics at City, University of London, was that NGOs should be independent from governments.[13] While NGOs could receive government funds for their operational programmes, it was initially taken for granted that such funding would be specified in their annual reports.

In February 1967, as discussed in Chapter 5 of this book, the *New York Times* ran a series of articles exposing the covert funding and ties of the CIA. These articles revealed that many academic and international organisations were receiving funds from the CIA, and that some of these were anticommunist NGOs enjoying UN consultative status.[14] This disclosure was met with anger by many at the UN, sharpening a concern that the West was dominating the NGO system. The covert provision of funds to a few NGOs was considered to be outrageous, notes Willetts, and it called into question the legitimacy of all NGOs holding consultative status.

Some of the NGOs receiving funds from the CIA were involved in African countries, such as the International Commission of Jurists, the International Confederation of Free Trade Unions, the World Assembly of Youth, and Pax Romana, an international lay Catholic movement.[15] The funds were funnelled through foundations with links to the CIA and through sham conduits. The World Assembly of Youth, for example, received CIA financing through the Foundation for Youth and Student Affairs, which has been described as a 'mail drop' (and which also supplied CIA funds to the National Student Association and other student groups).[16]

Strong objections were made. Dr Waldron Ramsay, a Barbardian lawyer heading the Permanent Mission of Tanzania, led the attack, demanding a review of the criteria for admission to consultative status, a redefinition of the requirements and a review of NGO rights at the UN. After a long and intensive review process, one of the main changes adopted was to require the 'basic resources' of every NGO to be derived from its membership.[17] Attempts were also made to block NGO activity on human rights, but the negotiations led to a compromise.[18]

In the General Assembly's 1967 debate on preparations for an International Conference on Human Rights, there was widespread support for attacks on NGOs by the Afro-Asian member states. The assembly's decision to invite NGO observers to the conference was sustained—but only by one vote.[19] The reaction to the news stories about CIA funding of some NGOs, observes Willetts, was the biggest upheaval in the history of the UN's relationship with NGOs.[20]

* * *

IT WAS NOT ONLY delegates representing their countries at the UN who were the targets of American intelligence. So was the UN itself.

This was not a fresh development. In 1949, four years after the founding of the UN, Trygve Lie, a Norwegian who was the first UN secretary general, reached a clandestine agreement with the US Department of State for US agents to screen American staff in the UN complex. This period was later recalled by Shirley Hazzard, an Australian novelist who was working at the UN secretariat as a typist. In the first instance, she wrote in *Countenance of Truth*, screenings were directed at American citizens who constituted about half the UN headquarters personnel—about two thousand women and men.[21]

Hans Singer, a British development economist who joined the UN in 1947, became a target of the vicious hunt for communists led by Senator Joseph McCarthy. Singer was the secretary of the Committee of the Special UN Fund for Economic Development (SUNFED), which, he recalled years later, was loathed by McCarthy as 'part of a communist world conspiracy to take money out of the pockets of American tax payers and use it for the benefit of left-leaning characters in the Third World'. Singer was not an American citizen, which gave him protection: 'I was called before the McCarthy committee . . . [but] as a British citizen, I was under no obligation to appear'.

The UN, said Singer, 'was considered to be the centre of the communist conspiracy'. This was because 'the people there, especially from communist countries, had diplomatic immunity. The

McCarthy committee more or less considered all the citizens from these countries—Russians, Poles, Czechs, etc.—in the UN as spies'. The McCarthy period, Singer believed, 'was a dreadful period' at the UN:

> The staff became demoralized, especially the American staff members. People were watching with whom you were seen. The McCarthy committee had a room in the UN building—I think, on a lower floor; anyway the Economics Department was high up, so to us everything seemed to be on a lower floor. People were brought before this committee.
>
> Trygve Lie forced them to testify. He more or less gave them to understand, that if they refused to testify, that would amount to an admission of guilt. They would be fired, more or less. Trygve Lie was very compliant with the Americans. He was in that respect a very weak Secretary-General, very weak.[22]

The influence of the secret agreement was extended beyond Americans to UN employees of other nationalities, and it permeated UN specialised agencies abroad, such as the United Nations Educational, Scientific and Cultural Organisation (UNESCO) and the Food and Agriculture Organisation. 'That the international civil service should be denied independence at the outset', Hazzard observed, 'was a conclusive defeat for any practical realisation of the United Nations concept'.[23]

Abraham Feller, the chief legal counsel of the UN at the time and an American himself, 'knew it was completely wrong and illegal', said Singer, 'to force American staff members to testify and to put [the committee] in the UN building'.[24] Feller was deeply troubled by these practises. He died following a fall out of his twelfth-floor apartment in New York City. The death was labelled a suicide; he was forty-seven years old.[25]

Dag Hammarskjöld took over from Lie in early April 1953. According to Brian Urquhart's biography of Hammarskjöld, the scrutiny of the UN by the FBI had been strengthened just a few months before Hammarskjöld was appointed secretary general:

'On January 9 [1953], President Truman . . . introduced a procedure by which the U.S. government would provide the Secretary-
General with information on U.S. candidates for employment and
would empower the U.S. Civil Service Commission to investigate
the loyalty of Americans already employed by the UN'.[26] When
Eisenhower took over as president from Truman on 20 January, he
strengthened the FBI's means of scrutinising the UN. His administration's new representative to the UN, Henry Cabot Lodge Jr,
asked the FBI—as one of his first official acts—to investigate all
members of the US mission to the UN, as well as US members of
the secretariat itself.

The extent of the FBI's activities was revealed during an incident in the public gallery of the Security Council, when an American agent in plain clothes attempted to take a demonstrator away
from UN guards. Hammarskjöld was appalled. He also learned that
a senior official had been given a detailed questionnaire on his relations with various people and his views on communism. Hammarskjöld protested vigorously to the US mission and called for a full
investigation.[27]

In March 1953, Ralph Bunche became a victim of the witch hunt.
He was summoned by the Senate Internal Subcommittee counsel
to respond to the allegation that he was a 'concealed' communist.
Thus began 'a painful and Kafkaesque period in Bunche's life', comments his biographer, Brian Urquhart, 'which disgusted him and
which he passionately resented'. It was not until the following year
that Bunche's loyalty to America was publicly acknowledged.[28]

In November 1953, Hammarskjöld found an opportunity to
challenge and stop the American intrusions. He made use, Urquhart records, 'of the opportunity provided by a remark by FBI
Director J. Edgar Hoover that the extraterritorial status of international organizations in the US made it impossible for the FBI to
operate on their premises'. He exploited this statement to demand
the immediate removal of the FBI from UN headquarters.[29]

* * *

HAMMARSKJÖLD WAS SATISFIED BY the end of 1953, his first year at
the helm, that he had removed the FBI from the UN. But other

American intelligence agencies were operating at the international organisation: the State Department's Bureau of Intelligence and Research and the CIA, who sought to influence and bribe foreign delegations to the UN. Hammarskjöld may have heard rumours of these activities, but he is not likely to have been aware of their extent.

Nor did he have any idea of an even more intrusive form of spying on the UN, which directly targeted himself and his staff: their most secret communications were being intercepted by the National Security Agency and the CIA. It emerged decades later that the cipher machines used by the UN were not secure. A top-secret backdoor was built into each one, so that every message sent in cipher could be read in real time by American intelligence agencies.[30]

The machines were produced by Crypto AG, a company founded by Boris Hagelin in the Swiss canton of Zug. Crypto AG was secretly owned by the CIA, in a clandestine partnership with West German foreign intelligence, the BND. At least four countries—Israel, Sweden, Switzerland and the United Kingdom—were aware of the operation or were supplied with intelligence from it by the United States or West Germany.

In February 2020, the *Washington Post* and ZDF, a German public broadcaster, revealed that they had obtained a classified, comprehensive CIA history of this operation. The internal account, they said, 'identifies the CIA officers who ran the programme and the company executives entrusted to execute it. It traces the origin of the venture as well as the internal conflicts that nearly derailed it. It describes how the United States and its allies exploited other nations' gullibility for years, taking their money and stealing their secrets'.[31] The operation was known at first by the code name 'Thesaurus', later by 'Rubicon'.

Initially, the CIA and Boris Hagelin worked together on the basis of a handshake deal. Then, in 1960, they entered into a 'licensing agreement' that paid Hagelin $855,000 to renew and confirm his commitment to the deal, according to the *Washington Post*. The agency paid Hagelin '$70,000 a year in retainer and started giving his company cash infusions of $10,000 for "marketing" expenses to ensure that Crypto—and not other upstarts in the encryption business—locked down contracts with most of the world's governments'. The scheme was designed to prevent adversaries from acquiring the technology: 'within a decade, the whole Crypto operation belonged to the CIA and BND'.

With no knowledge of this deceit, more than 120 countries used Crypto AG encryption equipment from the 1950s well into the 2000s. The files seen by the *Washington Post* do not include a comprehensive list, but they identify at least 62 customers, including Ghana and a number of other African countries.[32] In every case, as the economic analyst J W Smith has observed, the widespread use of these cipher machines gave the US an insurmountable advantage—that of holding 'a mirror behind everyone else's back'.[33]

America's main adversaries, including the Soviet Union and China, were suspicious of Crypto AG's ties to the West. To avoid risk, they chose not to use the machines.

Full details of the UN's use of Crypto AG's cryptograph machines have not yet emerged, but it is known that Secretary General Hammarskjöld's office used Crypto's CX-52. This means that when he and his mission went overseas, all their top-secret, encrypted cable traffic was fully—and immediately—read by the National Security Agency and the CIA.

In September 1961, Hammarskjöld flew from the Congo to the British protectorate of Northern Rhodesia, travelling with two CX-52s. It would be the last journey he made. The plane he was on crashed near the airport of Ndola, not far from the Congo border, killing him and the other passengers and crew. In the immediate aftermath of the crash, one cipher machine was found at the crash site by Rhodesian officials. Another was allegedly looted from the site by D Moyo, L Daka and P Banda, charcoal burners working nearby who were found guilty on highly questionable evidence; they were imprisoned for eighteen months with hard labour, and Banda was beaten. The three men gave witness statements to the Rhodesian Commission of Inquiry into the crash, in which they reported hearing an explosion in the middle of the night; Daka said 'he then saw a lot of fire . . . he also saw something coming down and breaking the trees'.

At dawn, they discovered the crash, as did many others—belying the official statement that the crash site was discovered at 3.10 pm.

The testimonies of Moyo, Daka and Banda were dismissed as unreliable, and one critic of the Rhodesian inquiry wondered if they had been accused of looting in order to discredit their testimony.[34]

In its report of 1962, the Rhodesian Commission of Inquiry identified pilot error as the cause of the crash, but solely on the basis of an elimination of the other suggested causes. A UN inquiry, however, which issued its report in the same year, reached an open verdict and stated that it could not rule out sabotage or attack.[35] The British high commissioner in the Rhodesian Federation, Cuthbert Alport, was at Ndola airport on the night of the crash; he closed down the airport when the plane failed to land, on the inexplicable grounds that it must have 'gone elsewhere'. Over the next few days, he resisted the UN's request that he return the cipher machine found at the crash site. Alport's resistance has been scrutinised by Mohamed Chande Othman, the former chief justice of Tanzania, who was appointed by the UN Secretary General in 2015 to lead a fresh UN investigation (ongoing to 2022) into the cause of Hammarskjöld's death. 'Alport's behavior', states Othman, 'suggests that he had a reason to seek to refuse to return United Nations property, including Hammarskjöld's CX-52, to the United Nations, although this was eventually done'.[36]

In the course of his inquiries, Judge Othman asked the United States to comment on the allegation that transmissions from Hammarskjöld's CX-52 cipher machine were intercepted by the US. The response was unhelpful: it stated that the US 'ha[s] no comments on this item'.[37]

Othman continues to attach importance to the matter of the cipher machine. In a report submitted to the UN secretary general in 2019, he stated, 'Communications sent from the CX-52 cryptographic machine used by Hammarskjöld appear to have been intercepted by British and United States signals and intelligence agencies as a result of a secret interception and decryption setting that those agencies held that enabled them to intercept surreptitiously'.[38]

This is significant, given the many questions and suspicions that hang over the tragic deaths of Hammarskjöld and all those who were travelling with him. 'It appears plausible', observed Othman in 2017, 'that an external attack or threat may have been a cause of the crash, whether by way of a direct attack . . . or by causing a momentary distraction of the pilots'.[39]

It is reasonable to assume that if the secretary general's team used a CX-52, Crypto AG machines were also used by other UN missions in the 1960s. UN headquarters in New York and, possibly, Geneva, would have had technical departments encrypting outgoing messages and decrypting incoming ones from all over the world.

The CIA asserted in its internal account of Thesaurus that the control and use of the Crypto AG machines was 'the intelligence coup of the century'. Foreign governments, it reported with satisfaction, 'were paying good money to the U.S. and West Germany for the privilege of having their most secret communications read'.[40] They were paying, explains J W Smith, to play 'a high-stakes diplomatic poker game' in which the US had an insurmountable advantage in trade negotiations. 'They knew the most intimate secrets of nonaligned nations attempting to ally together to develop their industries and internal economies'.[41]

For the UN, it was a major handicap. It meant that the CIA was always ahead—constantly aware of its secret discussions and negotiations. The unique advantage of the CIA defeated the very basis of the UN Charter, which the US had agreed to as a member state. The charter was built on the commitment to 'the equal rights . . . of nations large and small'.[42] But the secret back door of the Crypto AG machines wrecked such equality. The US obtained classified information that enabled it to exert an influence over decisions and events—in its own favour.

23

'Lumumba Assails US on Uranium'

T HE ATOMIC REACTOR AT LOVANIUM University in Leopoldville —the TRICO—had been in operation since May 1959, and the centre was flourishing. Radioisotopes were being produced for use in various studies, and plans for future projects were being developed. Congolese students, as well as students from other African countries, were taking courses involving the reactor. At the same time, a library of relevant journals and reports was being energetically developed.[1] Representatives of the International Atomic Energy Agency secretariat, headquartered in Vienna, visited the TRICO Centre in 1960 and were favourably impressed.[2]

An IAEA report noted that a visiting professor was sent to Leopoldville in May and June 1960 in connection with a course on the application of radioisotopes in medicine.[3] This professor appears to have been Engelbert Broda, an Austrian chemist who moved to Britain in the late 1930s to escape Nazi persecution.[4]

From the end of 1941, Broda had been attached to the Cavendish Laboratory at Cambridge University, working on radiochemistry as a team member of Tube Alloys, Britain's atomic bomb project. He was trailed and watched by MI5, which suspected that he was a communist and was sharing atomic secrets with the Soviet Union.[5] In 2009, documents in Russian archives revealed that this was indeed the case and that, along with thousands of other pages of information, Broda—under the cover name of 'Eric'—had delivered to the Soviets the plans for one of the Manhattan Project's early nuclear reactors.[6] In August 1943, Broda was described by Soviet intelligence as 'at pres., the main source of info. on work being done on E'. 'E' stood for 'Enormous', the code name for the Manhattan Project.

Broda passed on these secrets out of deeply held moral and political convictions. He shared the fear of many in the 1930s that fascism would prevail, and he felt impelled to assist Russia when it joined the Allies. In his view, it was wrong and dangerous that Russia was kept in the dark about developments in the atomic field.[7]

After the war, Broda was anxious to get away from any military uses of atomic research, and there is no evidence to suggest that he continued to spy for the Soviet Union. In 1947 he returned to Austria, where he worked at the University of Vienna. He was the head of the only university section in Vienna concerned with radio-chemistry and was a familiar figure at the IAEA; he wrote standard texts on isotopes and their applications. He was involved in the Pugwash movement—the campaign by scientists for disarmament and détente—almost as soon as it was founded in 1957. His work in the Congo was consistent with this shift in interests; in the following year he did similar work in Egypt, and later in Japan.[8]

But as far as the CIA was concerned, Broda was still involved in espionage for the Soviet Union. A CIA document released in 2000 (undated but evidently produced during the period when Broda was working in Vienna) identifies him as a 'Soviet Spy'. It includes him in a list of 'Staff of the Vienna Technische Hochschule who have Communist affiliations and sympathies' and who were mentioned in the biweekly reports of the United States Air Force Academy.[9] His scientific work was monitored: other records released by the CIA in 2000–2001 include documents listing the scientific publications and work of a number of scientists in Europe during the 1950s, including those of Broda.[10]

If the CIA believed that Broda continued to spy for the Soviets after the war and was still following his activities in 1960, it would have known that he went to work at the TRICO Centre in the Congo in the two months leading up to independence.

His presence there would have strengthened the agency's sense of
America's urgent need to control the region and to prevent Soviet
penetration.

* * *

Monseigneur Luc Gillon, the nuclear physicist and rector of
Lovanium University, was immensely proud of the TRICO Centre.
It was he who had energetically led the demand that the Belgian
Congo should be given an atomic reactor, on the grounds that it
had supplied the uranium necessary for the Manhattan Project.[11]

But the US was not so happy. In December 1958, William Burden and John McCone had signed a contract agreeing to the delivery of the enriched uranium to be used in the TRICO; the US-built
reactor was then delivered to Leopoldville. But then the Congo had
been a Belgian colony; now it was under the control of the Congolese themselves. The crisis enveloping the Congo heightened Washington's concern. There was a risk that the fissionable material in the
reactor could be stolen.[12] An even more worrying risk, as perceived
by the CIA, was that the reactor could get into the wrong hands.
The idea of this atomic technology being under the control of Lumumba, demonised as a dangerous left-wing militant, was perceived
as a serious threat. And if Broda was known to be working at the
centre, the threat was magnified.

In August 1960 the CIA sent a cable to Larry Devlin in Leopoldville, instructing him to go to the TRICO and remove the rods,
which are used in a reactor to control the fission rate of uranium.
Devlin was told to advise Gillon of the instruction and then to bury
the rods somewhere they could not be found. The request, said the
cable, had come from the US Atomic Energy Commission. Devlin
was horrified; he had no intention of touching the reactor. But he
readily followed the order to speak to Gillon. 'I put my fears in
neutral', he recalled later, 'and drove to Lovanium, passing through
three road blocks on the way'.

When Devlin told Gillon of the instruction to remove the rods
from the reactor, the rector was adamantly opposed. It was a crazy
idea, Gillon told Devlin firmly; in any case, it would be impossible

to carry out the mission in secrecy. It would be far safer, he said, to leave the rods in the reactor.

Lars Öhrström, professor of inorganic chemistry at Chalmers University, confirms the good sense of Gillon's advice. If the TRICO fuel rods had been unused, notes Öhrström, they would have been safe to handle. But they had been operational since June 1959—and once the rods in a reactor have been irradiated and the nuclear reactions have started, they present a serious threat to health.[13]

Devlin reported Gillon's views to Washington. 'Happily', he wrote, he never heard another word about the matter.[14]

The TRICO was left in place, and the scientists at the centre—unaware of the threat from the CIA—quietly continued their work.

* * *

BUT THE TRICO WAS not the main atomic-related matter in the Congo of interest to the US. That was the Shinkolobwe mine.

There had been a change of policy in relation to Congolese uranium: it was decided in October 1959 not to import the uranium oxide stored aboveground at Shinkolobwe. This decision was confirmed at the highest levels of the US government on 25 July 1960, at a meeting of the National Security Council. John McCone, the chairman of the US Atomic Energy Commission, told President Eisenhower and his senior security advisors that the Congo was no longer considered an essential source of uranium for the US.

Then there was a dramatic turnaround, triggered by an unexpected speech given by Lumumba in which he accused the US of supporting the Katanga secession in order to prevent the Soviet Union from getting its hands on the Shinkolobwe uranium. The speech was delivered on 2 October 1960 at the fashionable Restaurant du Zoo in Leopoldville, at a high-profile dinner hosted by the commander of Guinea's contingent in ONUC. An account of the speech and the dinner appeared the following day in the *New York Times* under a striking headline: 'Lumumba Assails US on Uranium: Ousted Congo Premier Says Katanga Gets UN Aid Because of Its Mines'.

The newspaper reported that Lumumba had left his official residence, where he was protected by Ghanaian soldiers, in a limousine;

he was escorted to the restaurant by a jeep-load of Guinean soldiers, who were armed with machine guns to ensure his safety. At the restaurant, Lumumba had told a cheering crowd of dinner guests that the secession of Katanga had been a Belgian-American plot to prevent the Congo's uranium from falling into Soviet hands. According to the *New York Times* article, Lumumba claimed he could have had millions of dollars from the US if he had been willing to 'mortgage the national sovereignty'. He continued, 'They were only interested in Katanga, our only wealth'. Who will get the Katanga uranium? his listeners asked. 'Maybe it will go to the Russians', Lumumba replied. 'We must prevent that at all cost. That is the real truth of it'.

Lumumba was referring, added the *New York Times*, 'to the Shinkolobwe uranium deposits in Katanga which supplied uranium for the Hiroshima and Nagasaki bombs, but have fallen into disuse with the discovery of richer deposits in Canada and elsewhere'.[15]

The reference to 'richer deposits in Canada and elsewhere' was inaccurate, since deposits richer than the Shinkolobwe uranium had not been found anywhere else in the world. Further false information was given in the caption to the photograph illustrating the article, which showed Mobutu in his army uniform and sunglasses. The caption stated: 'Ignored by Lumumba', suggesting that Mobutu had been rejected by Lumumba. The truth was that Lumumba had been at pains to work with Mobutu since 1959, but was betrayed by him.

What happened next proved Lumumba to be largely right in his assessment of US concerns.

* * *

IF THE SOVIETS HAD been under any illusions about the richness of the Shinkolobwe uranium, those illusions would have been shattered by Lumumba's public speech. Washington's position started to shift substantially, and consideration was given to the purchase of the uranium ore stored aboveground at the mine.

Burden records in *Peggy and I* that in the 'autumn' of 1960—he does not specify the day or month—he flew to Washington, where he had a 'big meeting' with Douglas Dillon, the undersecretary of

state, on future plans for the Congo. These, he wrote, were 'principally financial'; most likely, they related to the purchase of Congolese uranium. The discussions resulted in advantages to both
sides—'thanks to the confidences' he had received from André de
Staercke, the Belgian ambassador to NATO, and from Baron Jean
van den Bosch, the Belgian ambassador to the Congo until early
August 1960, when the Congolese government accused him of fostering unrest and deported him. 'Gaining the trust of the "insid-
ers"', commented Burden with self-satisfaction, 'is the touchstone
of diplomacy'.[16]

A meeting of the National Security Council was held on 6 October to discuss the Congo. Allen Dulles noted that Mobutu had
expelled Soviet technicians, planes and equipment after his military takeover; Soviet-bloc diplomats had also left, but were now
in Accra and Conakry. A Soviet freighter, he added, believed to be
carrying equipment for Lumumba, was still off the African coast.

Then the discussion turned to the matter of the uranium stored
at the Shinkolobwe mine. McCone reported that the US was considering purchasing the stocks: 'Mr. McCone said 1500 tons of
uranium-oxide was above ground in Katanga. The U.S. was considering preclusive buying of this material to prevent it falling into the
hands of the Soviets'.[17]

The next day, McCone distributed a memorandum on Congolese uranium to members of the NSC. In a cover letter to Douglas
Dillon, McCone reported, 'Bill Burden dropped in on me today
and I gave him a copy of the memorandum'.[18]

'Thank you for your note of October 7 enclosing the paper on
Belgian Congo uranium', wrote Dillon to McCone three days later.
'In view of its importance I have made it available on a limited basis
to the interested offices in the [State] Department'.[19]

McCone also sent the memorandum to Gordon Gray, President
Eisenhower's special assistant for National Security Affairs. In his
cover letter, McCone referenced Lumumba's speech in Leopoldville at the Restaurant du Zoo. The facts in the memorandum, Mc-
Cone told Gray, refuted Lumumba's statements and could be used
to release a statement if that seemed appropriate.[20]

The memorandum was sent 'in multiple copy' to Gray, for circulation to members of the Operations Coordinating Board (OCB), which had discussed the matter some days before.[21] The OCB comprised Allen Dulles, as the director of Central Intelligence, the deputy secretary of defence, and ad hoc members at the undersecretary level. The board was of 'very special interest to the Agency', explains Philip Agee in *Inside the Company: CIA Diary*, 'because its function is to review and approve CIA action operations (as opposed to collection of information) such as propaganda, paramilitary operations and political warfare'.[22]

Eisenhower relied heavily on Gordon Gray, a weighty figure who had been the first chairman of the Special Group, the National Security Council subcommittee responsible for the planning of covert operations. He had already served Eisenhower's predecessor, President Truman, in several capacities: as secretary of the army, as first director of the Psychological Strategy Board (which evolved into the OCB), and as chairman of the Atomic Energy Commission's Personnel Security Board during its investigation of J Robert Oppenheimer.

Gray was closely involved in America's plans for the Congo and had been present at the meeting of the Special Group in mid-August, when Eisenhower effectively authorised the assassination of the Congolese prime minister. Gray was the key insider: if there had been a discussion with anyone in the Eisenhower administration on plans to assassinate Castro, said Richard Bissell, 'it would have been with Gordon Gray'.[23]

On 14 October 1960, Karl G Harr Jr, special assistant to the president, wrote from the White House to McCone, to report that McCone's material on Congolese uranium had been made available to the State Department. It had been used by them, he said, to prepare a circular telegram 'containing information for local use as appropriate in respect to future charges similar to that made by Lumumba on October 3'.[24]

It is hard to push further on these developments, since key material in the relevant file at the US national archives—including the memorandum itself—is classified.[25] Despite the barriers, it is reasonable to assume that—led by the powerful McCone, with the support of President Eisenhower and Burden—an agreement was made to purchase fifteen hundred tons of Shinkolobwe ore offered for sale by Union Minière.

* * *

IT WAS AN IMMENSE quantity of uranium ore—well over half the amount that was freighted during World War II from the Congo to the US for the Manhattan Project. Shipping this quantity of ore during the years of war and the early postwar period had been a substantial challenge. And in the last months of 1960, the upheaval and instability in the Congo presented fresh kinds of obstacles.

During the war and into the 1950s, the ore destined for the US had been freighted to Matadi, on the Congo's Atlantic coast, via the railroad known as the Route Nationale.[26] But by the end of 1960, railroad bridges had been damaged, making the route insecure and difficult, if not impossible, in places. There was also a high level of instability in the country. Consequently, export-import traffic from Katanga was routed over the Angolan railroad to the Atlantic Ocean port of Lobito, in Angola, while other, small quantities of freight from Katanga were moved over the Rhodesian railroads to Indian Ocean ports.

Moving freight by airplane was more reliable than doing so by rail. But the logistics involved in carrying 1,500 tons of ore were daunting. To use a cargo plane like the Lockheed C130 Hercules, which had a maximum cargo load of 22.5 tons, would require sixty-seven flights. With one flight a week, this would take close to a year and a quarter. The freighting of such a massive quantity of uranium ore to the US would be a major operation, steeped in risk and danger.

* * *

AFTER THE INDEPENDENCE OF the Congo, the official line of Union Minière and of US authorities had been that exports of Congolese uranium had come to an end—that the Shinkolobwe mine was depleted and had been sealed with concrete in April 1960, before independence.

The message was repeated with more publicity and more force after Lumumba's speech on 2 October 1960. On 13 October, L K Olson, the commissioner of the US Atomic Energy Commission, gave an address to the American Mining Congress at Las Vegas in which he specifically tackled Lumumba's speech, describing its claims as false. 'I would like', said Olson, 'to make a comment regarding a statement in a recent news dispatch attributed to Mr. Lumumba. He is reported to have said that some of the problems arising between mineral-rich Katanga Province and the Central Government are due to the United States' interest in preventing the Soviet Union from obtaining Katanga uranium'. Lumumba's statement was absurd, suggested Olson, because the Shinkolobwe mine had been closed: 'The fact of the matter is that the Shinkolobwe mine has been exhausted and was closed in April, some months before the Congo attained independence'.

He continued, 'We understand that the mill was still operating at the time of the disturbances in order to clean up surface stocks. These clean-up operations, however, would have been completed in a few months. Despite extensive exploration no other economically exploitable deposits have been turned up'.[27]

Some geologists working for the British government were perplexed by Olson's statement that Shinkolobwe was exhausted. One official at the Metals Branch wrote a memorandum a year later raising questions about what Olson had said. In the memo, titled 'Congo Uranium', he noted that that the 'opinion of our geological advisers, the Atomic Energy Division of the GSM [Geological Survey and Museum], is to some extent at variance with Olson's statement'. He went on: 'Although our information about Congo reserves is meagre, certainly the evidence available to our Geological advisers makes us doubt the validity of Olson's categoric statement that there is no Congo uranium left'.[28]

Smith Hempstone, a well-informed American journalist working in the Congo in 1960, also questioned the official message that Shinkolobwe had been closed and its uranium depleted. 'Two months before independence', he wrote in *Katanga Report*, Union

Minière 'said that the mine was exhausted and had been closed down, its machinery dismantled'. In matters relating to economic affairs, he added, one would be inclined to believe the company's word. 'But the Belgian mania in regard to atomic matters, the obvious fear that uranium will make Katanga attractive prey for both Russia and America', he reflected, 'makes one wonder if the country's uranium is exhausted'.[29]

*　*　*

SIMILAR DOUBT HAD BEEN felt for some time among senior military personnel at NATO. At a restricted meeting of the NATO Standing Group in the Pentagon on 18 July 1960, General Burniaux, the Belgian military representative, stated that the situation in Katanga needed to be seen in the context of its mineral resources, including diamonds and cobalt. Then he added, almost coyly, 'I won't mention uranium'.

Air Chief Marshal Sir George B Mills, the UK representative, warned of the risk that the Russians might get hold of Katanga's mineral resources, or prevent the West from having them. 'And uranium too', added Burniaux darkly. 'Everything going under uranium', he said, 'is so secret I can't even know the figure myself. But still, although there [are] a lot of mines where you could find uranium, the Belgian Congo is one of the main producers'. General Clark L Ruffner, the US representative and chair of the meeting, shared his concern. 'I think it would be interesting', he said, 'to know what the political implications are behind this entire matter'.[30]

*　*　*

ANICET KASHAMURA FEARED THAT the prime minister was making a mistake when he made explicit his wish for the Congo to take control of its strategic resources. 'To be candid', he reflected with regret in 1966, six years after independence, Lumumba believed that 'the United States would not make him suffer the blow of Mossadegh if he persisted in wanting to sell raw materials to the countries of the East as well as to the West'. America, he added, was afraid of losing its exclusive monopoly to purchase strategic minerals—and would do anything to stop the loss.

The reference to Mohammad Mossadegh, Iran's prime minister in 1951–1953, was intended by Kashamura to spotlight the danger to Lumumba. Mossadegh had been overthrown in a coup orchestrated by the CIA and MI6 after he nationalised the Iranian oil industry previously owned by the Anglo-Persian Oil Company (now known as BP). Like Lumumba, Mossadegh had been democratically elected and was a champion of secular unity in his country.[31]

Decades later, in 2014, Jean Omasombo, a Congolese political scientist, commented on the importance of the Shinkolobwe mine at independence. 'The great powers', he said, 'were interested in the natural resources, the uranium in Congo. Neither the East nor the West wanted to give up the Congo'.[32] But only the West—in the shape of the United States—actually had something to give up.

PART VIII

CARROT AND STICK

24

Third-Country Agent QJWIN

O N 10 OCTOBER, MOBUTU TRIED once more to get Lumumba arrested. But when Mobutu's troops arrived at Lumumba's official residence with an arrest warrant, the Ghanaian guard ordered them to leave. Mobutu turned to Rajeshwar Dayal to ask for assistance in extracting Lumumba—but Dayal refused. Instead, Dayal reinforced Lumumba's guard.[1]

This frustrated Mobutu's aims—and the aims of the CIA station in Leopoldville. For, as Larry Devlin explained in a cable to Washington, he had been pushing the Binza group to arrest Lumumba: 'STATION HAS CONSISTENTLY URGED [CONGOLESE] LEADERS ARREST LUMUMBA IN BELIEF LUMUMBA WILL CONTINUE BE THREAT TO STABILITY CONGO UNTIL REMOVED FROM SCENE'.[2]

The following day, two hundred ANC paracommandos surrounded Lumumba's residence. The UN responded immediately with an equal show of strength, driving them away. But Mobutu's forces returned, taking up positions around the house.[3] The prime minister was now effectively a prisoner. It was no longer possible for him to visit friends, go to a bar or attend a meeting.

Luis López Álvarez, Lumumba's Spanish friend in Brazzaville, crossed the Congo River to see him and was horrified to find the house barred by Mobutu's soldiers. He had been friendly with Mobutu during the Round Table in Brussels, so decided to visit him to press his wish to see Lumumba. With a Chilean friend, López Álvarez took a taxi to Mobutu's villa outside Leopoldville, and after a long wait they were admitted inside.

Mobutu invited them to lunch, and throughout the meal spoke of his hopes that Lumumba would be reconciled with Kasavubu; he said, too, that he had no personal ambition and that he was suffering from hypertension and needed rest. Perhaps Mobutu was genuinely stressed and hoped to elicit sympathy from López Álvarez. More likely, this was an act, aimed at keeping López Álvarez on his side. If so, it didn't work; López Álvarez pressed Mobutu to let him see Lumumba. Mobutu told him to wait a few days—that he would shortly withdraw his soldiers from Lumumba's house. López Álvarez listened in dismay; it was clear that Mobutu had no intention of letting him see his friend.[4]

Meanwhile, Devlin was working hard to find a way to obtain access to Lumumba—to kill him. On 15 October, he cabled a new plan to headquarters: 'POSSIBLE USE COMMANDO TYPE GROUP FOR ABDUCTION [LUMUMBA] . . . VIA ASSAULT ON HOUSE'.

This quickly proved impossible. Two days later, Devlin asked for a sophisticated rifle to be sent by diplomatic pouch to Leopoldville: 'NOT BEEN ABLE PENETRATE [LUMUMBA'S] ENTOURAGE . . . RECOMMEND HQS POUCH SOONEST HIGH POWERED FOREIGN MAKE RIFLE WITH TELESCOPIC SCOPE AND SILENCER. HUNTING GOOD HERE WHEN LIGHTS RIGHT'.[5]

Devlin was getting his hands dirty. This was not the case with George Wittman, whose mission appears to have been a matter of business, rather than assassination. But his warnings of the threat posed by Lumumba were becoming urgent. 'Make no mistake', insisted Wittman, 'there is no real question of doing business with Lumumba. Whether he puts on the good face in the beginning or not, any country headed by Lumumba is only in a matter of time some form of African stronghold for the Soviets. . . . If Lumumba regains power, the only alternative is to work to deny access to the areas of strategic materials, as has already been done in Katanga'.[6]

The CIA's plans for the Congo were supported by the highest level of the government. On 27 October, the NSC Special Group approved the allocation of $250,000 for the CIA to use to influence parliamentary support for a Mobutu government.[7]

* * *

LUMUMBA WAS SURROUNDED BY two concentric circles: UN soldiers protecting him, and ANC soldiers on the alert for an opportunity to seize him. On the one hand, this was reassuring to Devlin, since it meant there was no further risk of Lumumba accepting invitations to dinners where he might give public speeches, as he had done at the Restaurant du Zoo on 2 October. On the other hand, it was very difficult to enter the residence and get close to Lumumba in any useful way, in order to implement Sid Gottlieb's plan to poison him or, indeed, employ any other method of assassination.[8]

A new direction was needed. This took the form of Justin O'Donnell, a senior CIA officer in his mid-forties who was in the Directorate of Plans—the department of clandestine operations. In October 1960 he was asked by Dick Bissell, the deputy director of plans, to go to the Congo to assassinate Lumumba. O'Donnell refused. He discussed the matter twice with Bissell, explaining that he was not willing to kill. He then met with Richard Helms, Bissell's deputy, to put this position on record.[9]

O'Donnell gave a reason for this to the Church Committee in 1975.[10] In the agency, he said, 'since you don't have documents, you have to be awfully canny and you have to get things on record, and I went into Mr. Helms' office, and I said, Dick, here is what Mr. Bissell proposed to me, and I told him that I would under no conditions do it, and Helms said, "you're absolutely right"'.[11]

O'Donnell was unwilling to participate in outright murder—at least, that is what he told the Church Committee. The matter of O'Donnell's testimony is problematic, however, because—like Gottlieb's testimony—it is missing.[12] The only related record available is a brief and redacted 'Summary of Expected Testimony [sic] of Justin O'Donnell', dated 9 June 1975, which was declassified in April 2018 under the JFK Assassination Records Collection Act.[13] The missing transcripts may contain important information that is not reflected in the Church Committee's report.

According to the report, O'Donnell explained he was not opposed to capital punishment, but wasn't prepared to be the executioner. He believed there was a 'very, very high probability' that if Lumumba was captured, he would receive capital punishment at the hands of the Congolese authorities, but he 'had no compunction about bringing him out and then having him tried by a jury of his peers'. He therefore agreed on a compromise: to draw Lumumba away from the protective custody of the UN guard and place him in the hands of Congolese authorities.[14]

The mission was urgent. Within forty-eight hours of his second discussion with Bissell, O'Donnell departed for the Congo. For the purpose of cable traffic and other communications, his pseudonym was Oliver B Altman. He arrived in Leopoldville on 3 November and met with Devlin. Much to his surprise, he learned there was a virus locked away in the CIA station safe. O'Donnell said he assumed it was a 'lethal agent', although the station officer was not explicit. Still, O'Donnell 'knew it wasn't for somebody to get his polio shot up to date'. O'Donnell had known of no other instance when a CIA station had possessed lethal biological substances. He assumed that its purpose was assassination, probably targeting Lumumba. 'My feeling definitely', he stated to the Church Committee, 'is that it was for a specific purpose, and was just not an all-purpose capability there, being held for targets of opportunity, unspecified targets'.[15]

After his arrival, O'Donnell formulated a plan for 'neutralizing' Lumumba by drawing him away from the custody of the UN guard around the prime ministerial residence: 'What I wanted to do was to get him out, to trick him out, if I could, and then turn him over [redacted] to the legal authorities and let him stand trial. Because he had atrocity attributed to him for which he could very well stand trial'. To implement the plan, O'Donnell made arrangements to rent 'an observation post over the palace in which Lumumba was safely ensconced'. He also carefully made the acquaintance of a UN guard, in order to recruit him to lure Lumumba outside the building. He cabled progress reports to CIA headquarters and kept Devlin informed about his activities.[16]

Before leaving the US for the Congo, O'Donnell had arranged for a third-country agent, Jose Moise Czeschlak, to come to Africa to work with him. Czeschlak was a Luxembourg citizen of

Basque origin who went by the name of Jose Marie Andre Mankel.[17] He was forty-seven, two years older than O'Donnell, and a heavy smoker.

Mankel was given the cryptonym of QJWIN/1 by the CIA. The use of the prefix 'QJ' is consistent with the CIA procedure of using a two-letter digraph to designate a geographical or functional area. 'QJ' appears to have designated Luxembourg: the chief of the CIA station in Luxembourg was Arnold M Silver, whose cryptonym was QJBANNER/1. QJWIN was a programme headed by Silver that aimed to spot and recruit agents for sabotage and covert intelligence activities. QJWIN/1, or Mankel, was frequently referred to as QJWIN, without the digit '1'.

O'Donnell gave an account of his dealings with QJWIN in his testimony to the Church Committee. 'What I wanted to use him for', said O'Donnell, 'was [redacted] counter-espionage. [redacted] I had to screen the US participation in this [redacted] by using a foreign national whom we knew, trusted, and had worked with. [redacted] the idea was for me to use him as an alter ego'. In other words, QJWIN's role was to implement O'Donnell's plans without any association being attached to the US.

'I would say', added O'Donnell, 'that he would not be a man of many scruples'. He would be capable, O'Donnell thought, of doing anything. When asked if that would include assassination, he said, 'I would think so'.[18] Much of the CIA correspondence involving this operation was RYBAT—high-level secrecy, with photocopying forbidden. Some of the correspondence was KAPOK, the cable indicator for the highest level of document sensitivity.

* * *

FACILITATING THE EXTRACTION OF Lumumba from his residence was not Mankel's sole task, however. Records released in 2017–2018 under the JFK Assassination Records Collection Act suggest there was far more going on.

Mankel's professional career was that of smuggler. He had been involved in 'East/West nickel smuggling' and 'the clandestine shipment of atomic devices from Poland to the US', as well as the smuggling of large amounts of opium from China to the US. He had 'smuggled narcotics before and after the war from North Africa' and been convicted three times. He had also smuggled cobalt in 1957 and 1958. In the past, he had worked for French, Luxembourgian, Belgian and West German intelligence.[19]

He was a perfect fit for a mission that involved smuggling. And there was an urgent need for a highly qualified person to participate in a top-secret operation that required the skills used in smuggling: the removal to the US of fifteen hundred tons of uranium at Shinkolobwe.

On 19 and 20 October 1960, two CIA officers met Mankel in Luxembourg and asked him if he would be willing to undertake a trip to Africa, probably Dakar, the capital city of Senegal. 'He was not given the true objective of his mission', it was reported, 'because of its extreme sensitivity and pending a final decision to use him'.

A plan was made for O'Donnell to meet Mankel on 30 October in France, when O'Donnell was en route to the Congo. Dulles sent instructions to Luxembourg, using the pseudonym 'Altman' to refer to O'Donnell: 'Instructions for meeting Fran[ce]: at 1400 hours 30 October Mankel to enter lobby hotel Carlton. Will be approached by Altman using name Mr Black. Altman will ask Mankel "Are you the salesman from Luxembourg?" Mankel to answer "Yes, I am the Arbed representative". Describe Altman to Mankel as 181 cms tall, fat, red-faced, tortoise-shelled glasses, smoking cigar. Do not reveal Altman true name'. Mankel was instructed to arrange a commercial-type cover for the trip.

The meeting ended up taking place a few days later, on 2 November. The precise mission was not conveyed to Mankel; he was only informed that it 'might involve a large element of personal risk'. When he was told that the destination would be Leopoldville, Mankel agreed. O'Donnell thought that Mankel was 'qualified to handle a potential operation' in the Congo.[20]

In mid-November, two cables from Leopoldville urged CIA headquarters to send Mankel to the Congo urgently. Along the way, Mankel 'spotted' and recommended two French contacts—Jacques Santelli and Edmond Perroud—'who agree undertake unspecified job'. Meanwhile, the allocation of funds to the CIA to persuade lawmakers in the Congo to support a Mobutu government—as approved by the NSC Special Group—had failed utterly. Parliament remained closed. The Special Group then took a different track: it authorised the CIA to provide arms, ammunition, sabotage materials and training to Mobutu's military.[21]

* * *

QJWIN ARRIVED IN THE Congo on 21 November. He stayed at the Regina Hotel, the same rundown hotel in which Washington Okumu had stayed in August. He started work on a plan to 'pierce both Congolese and UN guards to enter Lumumba's residence and 'provide escort out of residence'. O'Donnell directed QJWIN to make the acquaintance of a particular member of the UN force.[22]

But QJWIN's activities were not limited to Leopoldville. QJWIN cultivated 'a close personal relationship' with Major Djurorie Dujare Djurovic, a Yugoslav air force pilot on UN duty at the huge Kamina base who transported UN supplies into the interior of the Congo. Djurovic, about forty-one years old, was from Belgrade and spoke some English. Though married and with a seven-year-old daughter, a CIA report noted, he was 'inordinately fond of women and complains about lack of sufficient funds'. He was believed to be 'of high class family'. He was given the cryptonym DMLIVID-1 (the digraph 'DM' referring to his Yugoslav origin).

A test was planned by the CIA to assess DMLIVID. QJWIN reached an agreement with him to smuggle worthless industrial diamonds to Rome, where he would make contact with a CIA officer. The Rome contact would represent himself as a QJWIN associate and would not appear to be American. A cable was sent: 'After turnover diamonds completed (turnover should be photographed) and assessment by Kubark [CIA] officer, decision could be made whether try recruit IDEN[TITY] A'—that is, DMLIVID.[23]

Mankel was also briefed on a 'Dakar mission', which was linked to the Leopoldville operation. Plans for the mission were being developed by his CIA case officer in Europe, Arnold Silver, the chief of station in Luxembourg. It was anticipated that Mankel would go directly from Leopoldville to Dakar in Senegal, a former French colonial territory.

Dakar had a well established airport that handled large volumes of freight; it was also a major seaport with links to many parts of the world, including North America. If the Congolese uranium could be airfreighted to Dakar from Katanga, it would be easy to ship out of Africa.

It is reasonable to speculate that the role the CIA had in mind for Djurovic was to freight uranium to Dakar. As a pilot based at Kamina air base, he was in a situation that would facilitate the mission. Flying heavy amounts of ore would require a long runway, which was available at Kamina. As Bill Burden noted, after spending two nights at Kamina, the air base was 'very large and well manned, with 11,000 foot runways and . . . a substantial number of C-119s and C-47s [military transport aircraft]'.[24]

* * *

'VIEW DELICATE NATURE OP', reported Devlin to headquarters, 'Station did not surface [QJWIN] to [Mobutu]'.[25]

One of the files relating to Mankel, headed 'ZRRIFLE', includes a dispatch dated 1 November 1960. At the time, ZRRIFLE was the official cryptonym assigned to a programme to recruit foreign criminal assets for illegal activities such as burglary, wiretaps and other tasks to support ZR—that is, Division D intelligence. ZRRI-FLE was the creation of William 'Bill' Harvey, the head of Division D of the Foreign Intelligence Staff. Harvey, who was O'Donnell's immediate superior, has been described as a 'gruff, bulbous man with a frog-like voice' and 'none of the cosmopolitan polish of his Ivy League bred CIA colleagues'.[26] But he was widely respected in the agency for his successful field operations, including the exposure of Kim Philby, a British intelligence officer, as a double agent working for the Soviets.

At the beginning of 1961, Harvey was asked by Dick Bissell to explore the possibility of setting up an executive action assassinations capability within the CIA. He duly established this programme, hiding it under the existing cryptonym of ZRRIFLE; later that year, the area of executive action was applied to the specific target of Castro. Mankel's mission in Africa was initiated in 1960, therefore predating Bill Harvey's creation of the 'executive action' capability under ZRRIFLE. The fact that a file relating to Mankel was slugged ZRRIFLE, therefore, does not necessarily mean that it involved an assassination.[27]

'I was kept informed of the arrangements for QJ/WIN's trip to the Congo and, subsequently, of his presence in the Congo', Harvey later stated. 'I do not know specifically', he added, 'what QJ/WIN did in the Congo. I do not think that I ever had such knowledge [redacted]. If QJ/WIN were to be used on an assassination mission, it would have been cleared with me. I was never informed that he was to be used for such a mission'. He recalled, he said, that QJWIN might have been sent to an African country other than the Congo, but he was 'almost certain that this was not connected in any way to an assassination mission'.[28]

The Church Committee was given a set of files about Mankel, in which there was nothing that referred 'explicitly or implicitly to assassination or "executive action" in any form'. But it was noted that 'clandestine operatives of the type who wrote the documents contained in these files would never commit to writing anything having to do with the subject of assassination'.[29]

The financial memoranda in the Mankel files seemed to indicate a 'one-shot purpose', noted the Church Committee. This would be consistent with a plan to use him for a 'one-shot assassination attempt in the Belgian [sic] Congo', but not with 'an ongoing relationship with QJWIN for the purposes of recruiting safecrackers and burglars'. Furthermore, the cable traffic between Mankel and headquarters was handled at the very highest levels of the CIA; this was unlikely in a case involving safecracking and burglary.

The Church Committee was baffled: 'We do not know and at present are unable to determine what the assignment was'.[30]

* * *

WHILE THE CIA WAS inserting O'Donnell and Mankel into the Congo, Antoine Gizenga was developing plans to leave Leopoldville for Stanleyville. He and other Lumumbists were determined to establish a new capital of the Congo there, as a centre for the legal government of Lumumba. Gizenga left the capital city in disguise, like a fugitive, arriving quietly in Stanleyville in the afternoon of 14 October. The next day, everyone there was surprised to see him, but he was welcomed with warmth and enthusiasm.[31] He sent word to Andrée Blouin that he had taken power in Stanleyville in Lumumba's name and the people were awaiting Lumumba's arrival.[32]

In November, Mobutu ordered Blouin's expulsion from the Congo. She was heartbroken. Her husband and children were not allowed to leave with her, as a form of blackmail to ensure her silence in Europe. When a representative of the Ministry of Interior came to collect her, he apologised: 'Excuse us, these are our orders. We have to carry them out. It's not our fault'.[33]

In the month before Blouin's expulsion, on 13 October, she was among the subjects mentioned at a meeting of the US National Security Council. 'We had succeeded', said Allen Dulles, 'in neutralizing Mme. Blouin who now wants to come to the U.S. She is writing her memoirs which . . . should make interesting reading'.[34] He did not explain what he meant by 'neutralizing', nor did he flesh out the news that Blouin was writing her memoirs, but his statement indicates that the CIA claimed some responsibility for this development.

Blouin *did* eventually produce a memoir, written in English with the collaboration of the American writer Jean MacKellar; it was published as *My Country, Africa* in 1983 by Praeger. Intriguingly, Praeger was a regular publishing partner of the CIA. Frederick A Praeger defended this involvement in 1967, following its exposure. 'Whatever cooperation I have given to any government agency was voluntary and enthusiastic', he said. 'I cooperated in projects because I thought that their aims were for the good of the country'. He added that the CIA had no editorial control over the books they sponsored.[35] Some years later, however, during the Watergate hearings, Praeger's claims that his press had only limited involvement with the CIA were revealed to be false.[36]

Blouin was unhappy with the manuscript of *My Country, Africa* and sued MacKellar in order to block its publication, but without success.[37] No evidence is available to suggest that the CIA was involved in the publication or that Blouin suspected this, but it is a reasonable speculation, given the vast scale of CIA-sponsored publications.

* * *

ALSO IN NOVEMBER 1960, when Blouin was expelled from the Congo, Richard Wright died in Paris; he was only fifty-two.

Increasingly angry at what he called 'the CIA's vacillating between secretly sponsoring and spying', he had lost faith in anticommunism. 'My attitude to Communism', he said shortly before his death, 'has not altered but my position toward those who are fighting Communism has'. When he lifted his hand to fight communism, he pointed out, 'I find that the hand of the Western world is sticking knives into my back. The Western world must make up its mind as to whether it hates colored people more than it hates Communists or . . . Communists more than . . . colored people'.[38]

Wright had also become depressed about the role of the US in Africa, according to his biographer Hazel Rowley: 'He listened to the Voice of America and the Voice of Peking and tried to make sense out of the world. The African countries, one after the other, were proclaiming their independence. Wright worried that America would bring the Cold War to Africa, and he did not underestimate the role of western secret agents. "The Americans have their fingers everywhere." '[39]

At the beginning of September 1960, Dorothy Pizer, George Padmore's widow, passed through Paris and visited Wright. She was 'shocked' to see the writer's exhausted appearance, notes Rowley, 'and privately thought he looked just like her husband in the last weeks of his life'. Padmore had died earlier that year at age fifty-six. Wright took Pizer to his doctor's apartment, and the three of them went to a restaurant for dinner. Pizer did not understand how the doctor could live in such lavish surroundings when he had so few patients; she also thought it bizarre that he encouraged Wright to take a trip to Africa with himself and his father. Pizer did not tell Wright, but she was suspicious of the doctor.

Wright died of a heart attack a couple of months later. Some nursed suspicions that his death was sinister—linked to the FBI or CIA. Those suspicions have never gone away.[40]

25

'The Big American Stick'

T HE UN's RAJESHWAR DAYAL BELIEVED that the Western powers 'were firmly opposed to a return to constitutional rule' in the Congo because this would mean only one thing, so far as they were concerned—the return of Lumumba. But they could not openly take a stand against the restoration of the legitimate government, nor could they formally support the illegal regime of Mobutu. And so, Dayal explained in *Mission for Hammarskjöld*, in November 1960 they seized 'on the figure of Kasavubu to make their point by bringing him over in person to New York as head of the Congolese delegation. As the undisputed Head of State, he had the right to address the general assembly'.[1]

Thomas Kanza, who had been appointed by Lumumba as UN ambassador, analysed the situation in the same way as Dayal. 'The American game', he said, 'was all too obvious. In the constitutional confusion reigning in the Congo, they needed a "legal" and Congolese entry to permit their maneuvers and to confound their critics all over the world'. Accordingly, noted Kanza, 'They decided to get Kasavubu into the UN, as an individual who could embody the Congo as a nation. Once recognized by the UN, Kasavubu could ratify every initiative from Washington which was then, in the eyes of the world, acting fully in conformity with the wishes of the president of the Republic of the Congo, and in collaboration with the UN authorities there'.[2]

But the 'game' was not straightforward: the Western powers were resisted at every turn by a group of nonaligned African and Asian member states. The lines of battle at the UN were growing more and more sharply defined.

* * *

So, on US advice, Kasavubu appointed a delegation to take to the United Nations and flew to New York in November. 'He had been literally rushed there by the Americans', writes Kanza, 'who wanted to get him accepted internationally'.[3]

When Lumumba heard of Kasavubu's departure, he, too, tried to leave for New York. But he was prevented by the Armée Nationale Congolaise, which reinforced its guard around his house. In any case, as the UN leadership in the Congo reported to headquarters, Lumumba would not have been granted a visa by US ambassador Timberlake.[4]

Kanza approached the US embassy for a visa, but it was refused. He was told that the commissioner for the interior had withdrawn his passport. This greatly concerned Special Representative Dayal. He wired New York to object, pointing out that Kanza was the accredited Congolese ambassador to the UN. Timberlake, Dayal complained bitterly, was 'determined not to allow any Lumumbist to enter New York to ensure that Kasavubu has all the advantages'.[5]

Hammarskjöld wired back. UN policy, he pointed out, was to facilitate the exit of leading personalities from Leopoldville to New York, but the issue of passports was unfortunately beyond its competence. 'On a strictly personal basis', added Hammarskjöld sombrely, 'we regret the situation facing Kanza'.[6] His regret was not simply official; he also felt it as a friend. He had a deep respect and affection for Kanza—who, like him, was erudite and hardworking, with a strong sense of justice.

Without Lumumba's or Kanza's presence at the UN, Kasavubu's plan to represent the Congo was greatly facilitated. But the seating of his delegation still had to be approved by the Credentials Committee. The Congo had been formally accepted as a UN member state in September, and the issue of accreditation was still outstanding. Kasavubu did not anticipate any serious difficulties: the committee was heavily weighted in favour of the Western powers. He hoped, too, that his forthcoming appearance in the General Assembly would tilt the issue of seating in his favour.

But a formidable challenge lay ahead. President Sékou Touré of Guinea proposed a draft resolution recommending the seating of a delegation representing Lumumba's government. The draft resolution had been cosponsored by eight member states, including India.

Kasavubu addressed the General Assembly on 8 November. He announced the composition of his delegation, describing it as representative of the Congolese people. Then he asked for a meeting of the Credentials Committee to be convened, to admit him and his delegation. It prompted a fiery debate. Guinea's UN ambassador referred to the motion introduced by Touré and called for the restoration of the Congo's democratic institutions. Support for the Guinean draft resolution was presented by Valerian A Zorin, the chief Soviet envoy to the UN. Charming and affable, Zorin commanded respect from his peers in the UN community; according to the *New York Times*, his 'craggy face . . . betrayed a keen intelligence. He often looked more like a college professor than the tough-minded diplomat he was'.[7] His words of support for the draft resolution were listened to attentively.

There was criticism of Belgian activities in the Congo and of the secretary general's doctrine of nonintervention, which, argued some, supported the foreign-backed military coup that had taken place. Then Dr Alex Quaison-Sackey, Ghana's energetic ambassador to the UN, 'sprang to the floor on a point of order', asserting that the debate should be suspended until the Conciliation Commission that had been sent to the Congo by the UN had completed its work. He reminded the assembly of the importance of the commission, which had been set up on 5 November. It was composed of African and Asian representatives of countries with troops in the Congo and was intended to assist in 'decisions being reached with a view to the speedy restoration of parliamentary institutions'.[8] A number of diplomats were arranging to go to the Congo in order to interview the key people involved.

The plan was firmly opposed by Mobutu—especially the commission's aim to organise a national Round Table, which would bring together the legitimate government under the elected prime minister, Lumumba, with president Kasavubu. It was also opposed by the US and other Western states. Still, Quaison-Sackey's argument was persuasive to many member states, who agreed that holding the debate before the report of the Conciliation Commission had been completed would be premature. The case had been well made by a man who carried a natural authority among his peers. 'Even as an Oxford undergraduate', noted the *New York Times*, the highly educated Quaison-Sackey 'displayed an aggressiveness of purpose that could not be overlooked'. He was also very likeable. In the previous summer, he had surprised some of his more staid colleagues by becoming the patron of a jazz festival in Central Park, 'inviting fellow diplomats to pass up "cold war" talk to attend what he promised would be a "cool, cool war"'.[9]

A vote was taken by roll call on Quaison-Sackey's motion of adjournment. The Western powers and their followers voted against it, and there were eighteen abstentions. But his point of order was carried—by forty-eight votes to thirty.

The US was alarmed. First, there was a risk that the Conciliation Commission would be given a chance to do its job—and if this were to happen, it was bound to advocate a reconciliation between Kasavubu and Lumumba. And second, the passing of the motion potentially undermined the plan to get Kasavubu's delegation accredited as swiftly as possible.

As a general rule, the Credentials Committee met towards the end of the session, but the US pressed for a meeting within days. It duly took place, and the US proposed that the committee accept the credentials of Kasavubu's delegation, a plan that was adopted by six votes to one. The committee presented the recommendation to the General Assembly on 10 November.

The General Assembly had already decided to adjourn the discussion, on the basis of a majority vote. So when the assembly was asked to accept the recommendation of the Credentials Committee, the proposal was firmly opposed by Quaison-Sackey on a point of order, with support from India. The president of the assembly put the issue of adjournment to the vote. But it was evident that many delegations had switched their votes since the previous debate. The tide had turned.

'It was common knowledge in the corridors and lounges', recorded Dayal, 'that the intensest pressure had been applied to force

countries to change their votes—if not their convictions—from af-
firmation to abstention and from abstention to negation'.[10]

A large measure of responsibility for the accreditation of
Kasavubu and the effacement of Lumumba was claimed by Howard Imbrey—the CIA agent under nonofficial cover who had exerted a powerful influence in the Congo in favour of American
interests. Imbrey was now in New York, based at the headquarters
of his public relations office, Overseas Regional Surveys Associates,
just a few minutes' walk away from the UN.

In his interview with Charles Stuart Kennedy in 2001, Imbrey
touted the success of his lobbying:

> There was a fight between President Kasavubu and Lumumba.
> Lumumba was Prime Minister, Kasavubu the president. Each one
> could seek a delegation at the United Nations, but there could only
> be one delegation; they both had the right to seek it.
>
> Now, we figured that if Kasavubu seated his delegation at the
> United Nations it would be a pro-American one and if Lumumba
> seated his, God knows what it would be.
>
> So, Ambassador Timberlake, who is very good friend of
> mine . . . knew that I had this public relations office and he asked
> if I would take on the job of taking on Kasavubu, which I would
> get paid for by my organization and the expenses would be met.
>
> So, I agreed to do that and they sent over Kasavubu and with a
> little bit of engineering we got Kasavubu into the United Nations
> and seated his delegation.

Kennedy asked Imbrey, 'How do you work this sort of thing?'
Imbrey explained, 'Well, we knew the people in the delegations
and we had on our side Morocco and a number of heavy hitters,
France, England. It just was a matter of explanation getting their
support for the Congo delegation under Kasavubu and we heralded
non-communist delegations and at any rate we got him in. Then
Kasavubu went home'.[11]

In his interview a few months earlier with a high school student,
Imbrey described the process less formally. Working with Clare

Timberlake, he recalled, 'through a series of operations, we managed to, uhh . . . The word is nobble, to make it difficult, to make difficulties for Lumumba and to promote the case of Kasavubu. Kasavubu eventually named his delegation to the United Nations. So that's what I was doing for a long time'.[12]

US lobbying was taking place not only in New York, but also in the cities of member states. Francis H Russell, who was appointed US ambassador to Ghana in January 1961, gave an account of how this worked. When you want to exert leverage, he said, 'you do it as a friend who had money in the bank, someone who has talked over all kinds of problems, who has given the impression that he would accurately convey to Washington what they thought about a problem. If there was an issue coming up in the United Nations, we always made it a point to let them know how we were going to vote, and in fact how we hoped they would vote'.

This didn't work with Nkrumah. 'Well', said Russell regretfully, 'I never exerted successfully any leverage on Nkrumah'. And on a matter like the Congo, he added, 'Nkrumah was going to be an African radical first and always'.[13]

* * *

ONE LAST ATTEMPT WAS made by an Indian delegate to secure an adjournment of the debate on the accreditation of the Congolese delegation, but it was overruled by the president of the General Assembly. The recommendation of Kasavubu by the Credentials Committee was presented, triggering a debate for six days.

The debate ended on 22 November, with a vote in favour of seating Kasavubu's delegation: fifty-three to twenty-four, with nineteen abstentions.[14] 'Not surprisingly', observed Nkrumah drily, 'Belgium, France, South Africa, the United Kingdom and the USA were among those who voted in favor of Kasavubu's delegation'.[15] But so were African member states who had accepted Imbrey's 'explanation' or had been offered other forms of persuasion. 'The Western powers sat back', Dayal wrote, 'to watch the spectacle of African against African, secure in the knowledge that they had got the votes they needed'.[16]

That night, Hammarskjöld anxiously reviewed the situation in his suite on the thirty-eighth floor of the UN secretariat building.

'He was appalled', said Dayal, 'at the methods used and depths to which the Assembly had fallen'. He knew, too, that the difficulties ahead had increased massively: 'He would now be under pressure to come out more actively in support of Kasavubu and the illegal regime which [Kasavubu] had fathered'.

For Kasavubu in New York, noted Dayal, 'there was no lack of the kind of advice and encouragement he wanted. Representatives of powerful countries sought his favors in his sumptuous suite at the Waldorf Astoria'. Dayal succeeded, with some effort, in paying him a call himself, but found him 'more uncommunicative than ever'.[17]

The vote in favour of Kasavubu, reported *Le Monde*, was 'a success of the American big stick'.[18]

* * *

YET, THE US PAID a high price for this ruthlessly enforced victory. 'The vote drove a deep wedge between the West and the Africans', observed Wayne Morse, a liberal US senator from Oregon, to the Senate Foreign Relations Committee. 'Every major troop contributor sided with the Soviet Union in opposing the seating of the Kasavubu delegation. . . . You can buy your Kasavubus, you can buy a few stooges in Katanga, but it is only temporary, and you are building on quicksand'.[19]

The historian Richard Mahoney has made a similar point. By forcing the credentials issue, he argues, the US and other Western powers 'may have driven a nail into Lumumba's political coffin, but their action also gave his followers no choice but to secede'.[20]

Gizenga was strengthening the Lumumbist government in Stanleyville, as a rival to the Leopoldville government. Meanwhile, two territories had seceded from the Congo and were ruled by self-styled presidents: Tshombe in Katanga, and Albert Kalonji in South Kasai. There were now four different governments in the Congo, all hostile to each other.

Lumumba was at the centre of the growing enmities. When he learned of the accreditation of Kasavubu's delegation at the UN, he became convinced there were serious threats to the safety of his family. He had become close friends with the Egyptian ambassador in Leopoldville, Abdel Aziz, and asked him to convey an important message to President Nasser: a request for sanctuary in Egypt for his two oldest children, François, the son from a previous relationship, and Patrice, the eldest child of himself and Pauline Opango. If Nasser agreed, Lumumba hoped that Aziz would take responsibility for the mission. Both Nasser and Aziz agreed to Lumumba's requests.

A few days later, François and Patrice were put on a Sabena flight for Brussels, where they would change planes for Cairo. The children travelled under the last name of Abdel Aziz and were passed off as members of his family. It was a late flight, and the children, wrapped in blankets, were fast asleep when they were taken to the airport. Thomas Kanza, who greatly admired the courage of Aziz in taking on this heavy—and dangerous—responsibility, wrote down what happened: 'Two Egyptian diplomats took them from the car to the plane where they were laid to sleep on reserved seats in the back row. The Belgian air hostess wanted to unwrap them from their blankets, but did not insist when it was explained to her that they were exhausted and deeply asleep'.

The children arrived safely in Cairo. President Nasser met them personally several times and made a commitment to protect them from their father's enemies.[21]

* * *

THE PATIENT WORK OF the UN mission in the Congo 'to hold the scales even, and by insulating the situation to make it more amenable to correction by legitimate parliamentary means', judged Dayal, 'was undone'. He surveyed with sorrow 'the harvest reaped by the manoeuvre to force the seating of Kasavubu's delegation. The seeds carried by the winds from New York produced an even more bitter crop of violence, disorder, and bloodshed in the Congo'.[22]

But for Imbrey it was a success, for which he was amply rewarded. 'I was named public relations counselor through the government of the Congo', he recalled later. 'A very nice title you see. So, they began calling on me, they said, "Well, we're having trouble in Zambia, why don't you go there and tell them what it's all about. We're having trouble in West Africa." Well, I went to every country in Africa, explaining what the Congo was up to and that took at least two or three years out of my life. I was all over the place'.[23]

26

Ambassador Satch

I N OCTOBER 1960, LOUIS ARMSTRONG left America for a two-month tour of Africa in the role of jazz ambassador. With him were his wife, Lucille, and his band, the All Stars. His doctor went, too, because the world-famous trumpeter, then sixty years old, had suffered a minor heart attack the year before.[1] The tour was sponsored by the United States Information Agency in collaboration with Pepsi-Cola. The State Department took a keen interest: cables and memoranda from US embassies in the capital cities of Africa were exchanged with senior members of the department, right up to the levels of Secretary of State Christian Herter and Undersecretary Douglas Dillon.[2]

Three years earlier, Armstrong had suddenly refused to go on a trip sponsored by the State Department. It was a tour of the Soviet Union to which he had initially agreed. But then, on 2 September 1957, the governor of Arkansas ordered the National Guard to surround a high school in Little Rock to block the entry of African American students. Armstrong, deeply upset, became furious when the US government refused to enforce the integration of the school, as required by a federal court order. He denounced Eisenhower as being 'two-faced' on civil rights and having 'no guts'. 'It's getting so bad', he protested, 'a colored man hasn't got any country'.[3] Armstrong refused to represent America. 'The way they are treating my people in the South', he said bitterly, 'the government can go to hell'.

In 1960, Armstrong—known as 'Satchmo', 'Satch' and 'Pops'—agreed to a tour of twenty-seven cities in Africa, starting in Ghana. It would be his second visit to the West African nation. His first, in

1956, had affected him deeply and given him a strong sense of connection with the Ghanaian people. During an open-air display of dancing and drumming, he saw a woman who looked just like his mother, who had died twenty years earlier. This convinced him that his ancestors must have originated from Ghana. 'I came from here, way back', he cabled from Ghana to a friend in the US. 'At least my people did. Now I know this is my country too'.[4]

When his plane landed at the Accra airport in 1960, a vast crowd was waiting to welcome him and the All Stars back. As the musicians emerged into the sunshine, they were greeted with cries of joy and serenaded by two Ghanaian bands playing Highlife music. Beaming broadly, Armstrong and the band responded immediately with 'When the Saints Go Marching In'. According to the *New York Times*:

> The Lord Mayor of Accra, dressed in gold and green robes, poured a pint of Scotch whisky on the ground as a libation to the gods. He chanted 'Akwaaba' [Welcome].
>
> Mr. Armstrong responded by pouring a fifth of Scotch on the ground. The Lord Mayor repeated: 'Akwaaba'.
>
> 'Yeah', said Mr Armstrong.[5]

Armstrong and his band played to an audience of about a hundred thousand at Accra's Old Polo Ground, where independence had been celebrated two years before. They also played in more intimate venues and hung out with local musicians in the capital city and up country. In Ghana, as in many of the nations they visited, Armstrong's picture was plastered on billboards and advertisements everywhere, with the message 'Pepsi brings you "Satchmo"'. The admission fee to his concerts was five Pepsi-Cola bottle tops and two shillings and sixpence.[6] The war, said the *New York Times*, was 'between Coca-Cola and Pepsi-Cola. The prize is the African market'.[7]

From Ghana, Armstrong went to Nigeria, where he joined in the celebrations of Nigeria's independence from Britain.

* * *

SEVERAL WEEKS LATER, ON the morning of 28 October, Armstrong and the All Stars arrived in Leopoldville, on a leg of the tour that was not used to advertise Pepsi but was sponsored entirely by the US State Department. Dillon had pressed the importance of Pepsi-free events in the Congo to Ambassador Timberlake. 'The Department', he cabled, 'strongly opposed commercial sponsorship Armstrong'.[8]

Arriving by ferry from Brazzaville, Armstrong was escorted from the Leopoldville dock by a jeep-load of Ghanaian UN troops and greeted by a huge crowd. He was formally welcomed by the Congolese director of Cultural Affairs, the playwright Albert Mongita.[9] An American newsreel described his enthusiastic reception: a 'mellow cat the Congolese find right on the beam'.[10] African Jazz, the group headed by Le Grand Kallé—Kabasele Tshamala—performed for him. Kabasele sang a song in Lingala, which he had written as a tribute: 'Satchmo Okuka Lokolé'.[11] 'Local talents, inspired by the story of Okouka Lokole, a legendary figure with powers to charm wild beasts with his music', noted a local newspaper approvingly, 'composed a song in Armstrong's honour with the words: "They call you Satchmo, but to us you are Okouka Lokole"'.[12]

The following day, Armstrong was carried into the King Baudouin stadium on a chair mounted on poles. The stadium was filled to capacity; ten thousand people were on their feet, cheering.[13] 'Finally', wrote an American journalist, 'Satchmo raised his hand for silence. Then he put his trumpet to his lips':

> The first cool, clear, wild notes echoed over Léopoldville and, for a while, jazz succeeded where diplomacy had failed and the city knew peace. When he had finished, the silence hung for a moment, and then there was a thunderous ovation.
>
> Three encores later the ovation was still going on and there was no doubt that the Congolese dug Satchmo the most. Why wouldn't they? He'd spoken to them in the universal language, the one cultural tongue of America, a lingo sprung from Africa itself. It was cool, man. Real cool![14]

Asked how the African climate was affecting his playing, Armstrong said, 'I perspire a little when I blow, but I never faint or anything like that because I'm cool all the time'.[15]

* * *

THE NEXT STOP ON Armstrong's tour of the Congo was Elisabethville. It was an odd arrangement since the secession of Katanga had
not been recognised by the US. 'For reasons that escaped us in the
embassy', wrote the CIA station chief Larry Devlin in his memoir,
'the USIA decided to have him play in Elisabethville, capital of the
so-called Independent State of Katanga, a political entity that our
own government did not recognize'.

For Devlin to suggest that he and his colleagues at the embassy had no idea why Armstrong was sent to Elisabethville is
deeply disingenuous. If they really had no idea why, they would
have made great efforts to find out. This is one of many examples
of claims made by Devlin in his memoir that do not hold up to
scrutiny.

Ambassador Timberlake decided to go to Elisabethville for the
event, claimed Devlin, to make the best of a bad situation. 'The object was to talk to Tshombe, the elected president of the Congolese
province of Katanga, without recognising him as the president of
an independent state'.[16] In fact, many of the embassy went to Katanga, including Devlin and his wife. So, too, did Loy Henderson,
the deputy undersecretary for administration in the State Department, who arrived in Leopoldville on the day of the concert and
flew to Elisabethville in his official aircraft, a C-47, flown by his air
attaché.[17]

Armstrong and the All Stars gave a gala performance at the
Théâtre de la Ville in Elisabethville on the night of Sunday 20 November. It was attended by Tshombe and Ambassador Timberlake,
along with all the US officials and their wives who had travelled to
Katanga from Leopoldville. The performance was recorded and subsequently sold as a gramophone record with the title 'What a Wonderful World': The Elisabethville Concert. The lyrics of the song after
which the album was named were full of optimism—an optimism
that struck a discordant note in the context of the crisis in the Congo:

I see skies of blue, clouds of white . . .
And I think to myself, what a wonderful world.

The last song of the concert was 'When the Saints Go Marching In'. But the visit of the American party to Elisabethville was
less a case of 'saints' marching in than of the CIA and high-level
State Department officials using the event as a kind of Trojan horse
to visit Katanga.

Armstrong's visit to Katanga lasted four days. He and the All
Stars also performed outdoors at the Albert Stadium, and again at
the Theatre de la Ville. Armstrong kept records of his visit, including a programme. They reveal that, far from avoiding the risk of
giving an impression that the US recognised the secession of Katanga, Ambassador Timberlake and his party behaved as if the self-
styled president of Katanga and his ministers were the legitimate
government. They were met at the airport by Tshombe and other
Katanga dignitaries. Over the next few days, they participated in
a series of official luncheons, receptions, suppers and dinners, all
involving Tshombe and Timberlake and their respective officials.

After one luncheon, according to the programme, there was a
'visit of the city and the installations of Union Minière du Haut
Katanga'.[18] The nature of the 'installations' is not specified, but this
would have been an ideal opportunity for secret meetings between
American officials and Union Minière executives, to discuss the
matter of the fifteen hundred tons of uranium ore at Shinkolobwe.

* * *

AMERICAN INTELLIGENCE WAS WELL represented during Armstrong's visit to Katanga. Devlin attended the concerts, and David
Doyle, the chief of the CIA's Elisabethville base, along with his
small staff, enjoyed the jazz and acted as chauffeur for the All Stars
when needed.

An intriguing file in the UN archives in New York contains
a set of photographs found by an Ethiopian soldier in the 'area
[of] Union Minière, Eville [Elisabethville], on 19 December 1961'.[19]
The file bears the stamp of the UN Military Information Branch
in the Congo, which was established as a part of ONUC to support
the security of UN personnel and to collect intelligence.

At the end of the file is a copy of a letter to Carlos Huyghe (also
known as Carlo and Charles), the Belgian *chef de cabinet* to the

Katangan minister of defence, who was also involved in a South African–based recruitment agency that sent mercenaries to Katanga.[20] Such agencies provided Moise Tshombe with many of the white soldiers of fortune—mainly from South Africa, Rhodesia and Britain—that he needed to maintain the secession of Katanga.

The letter to Huyghe is apparently from a woman, who refers to an affair between Huyghe and another woman. She writes, 'I enclose the snaps you took'. There are anomalies in the letter which may indicate that it is laden with encryptions. Even so, the note suggests that Huyghe took at least some of the photographs in the file; any others in the file may have been collected by him or under his instruction.

A number of the photographs give the impression of visual surveillance. One shows the guests who had arrived from the US embassy in Leopoldville in a marquee; the crest in front of the marquee, which contains the letter 'E', for Elisabethville, confirms the venue.[21] The man who is second from left in the photograph resembles Larry Devlin. There are two larger men, one of whom may have been Justin O'Donnell (described as 'fat' in a CIA document), who had arrived in the Congo on 3 November. The woman at the far right is Alison Palmer, the US vice consul based in the Leopoldville embassy. Close-ups of people in the photograph are also in the file; evidently the American party was being carefully watched.

* * *

A FURTHER OPPORTUNITY FOR CLANDESTINE meetings under the cover of Armstrong's tour of the Congo was enabled by a concert at the huge Kamina airbase on the evening of 23 November. Curiously, on 9 November—a week after O'Donnell's arrival in Leopoldville—the performance schedule was suddenly changed to include a concert at Kamina. A week later, the new arrangements had still not been confirmed. 'Communications in Africa are so difficult', complained the embassy in Leopoldville wearily to Washington.[22]

But the plans finally went ahead. This meant that instead of going directly to Leopoldville after the Elisabethville visit, Armstrong and his band left Elisabethville after lunch on 23 November, arriving in midafternoon at Kamina, where they performed in a double airplane hangar to an audience of six thousand UN soldiers. They departed for Leopoldville the following day.[23]

Once Armstrong was back in Leopoldville, he made one more public appearance, which had been planned by the public affairs representative at the American embassy for 'real Satch cats'. One of these cats was Larry Devlin, a great fan, who attended the show with his family. Afterwards, they took Louis and Lucille Armstrong out for dinner.[24] The Armstrongs spent their last evening in the Congo with the CIA station chief, who hosted them under his cover at the embassy as political officer. They did not meet the legitimate prime minister of the Congo, Patrice Lumumba, who was being kept captive in his official residence on Avenue Tilkens, not far away.

Louis Armstrong was conflicted about representing the US on cultural missions abroad. He later tried to justify his trip to the Congo, claiming that his arrival had stopped a civil war—that a truce was called so that both sides could hear him perform.[25] But the situation in which he found himself in the Congo was far more sinister than he could have possibly realised. He would have been appalled to know that the man from the embassy with whom he dined was actually a CIA official who was cold-bloodedly plotting the death of the democratically elected prime minister of the country.

Armstrong's visit to the Congo was a success for the US in several ways. It took the spotlight away from the crisis triggered by Mobutu's coup and the confinement of Lumumba. It also showcased America in very positive, appealing terms, which was appreciated by the US ambassadors in all the cities included on Armstrong's tour. 'No other American attraction could possible [sic] elicit same goodwill and publicise our interests this area!' exclaimed the US ambassador in Freetown, as he anticipated Armstrong's arrival in Sierra Leone.[26] 'Pressure excessive, programme value Armstrong tremendous', enthused the US ambassador in Kenya.[27]

* * *

AFTER ELEVEN WEEKS OF touring Africa, an exhausted Armstrong arrived in Paris in early December. After his last three concerts, which had been performed in Abidjan in the Ivory Coast, he was suffering from 'intense fatigue'.[28] He returned to Africa in January 1961, going first to Dakar. By the end of the tour, he and the All Stars had played in Ghana, Cameroon, Congo Brazzaville, Congo Leopoldville, Uganda, Kenya, Tanzania, Northern Rhodesia, Southern Rhodesia, Nyasaland, Togo, Ivory Coast, Senegal, Mali, Sierra Leone, Liberia and Sudan.

Armstrong enjoyed many aspects of the tour. But he was deeply ambivalent about the ambassadorial role in which he was used by the State Department—a role that, he believed, amounted to support for segregation in America. He spotlighted this issue in *The Real Ambassadors*, a musical that he and the All Stars developed with Dave and Iola Brubeck, which was performed and recorded as an album in 1962. Dealing with civil rights and related issues, it was set in a fictional African nation and its central character was based on Armstrong and his role as a jazz ambassador. 'Though I represent the government', said Armstrong in the musical, 'the government don't represent some of the policies I'm for'.[29]

The lack of trust was mutual: Armstrong had been spied on by the FBI since 1948.[30]

PART IX

THE TURNING POINT

27

Trick or Escape?

L UMUMBA'S SONS, FRANÇOIS AND PATRICE, were in Cairo under the care and protection of President Nasser. Lumumba and Opango's daughter, Julienne, was safe with relatives, and Roland, their youngest child, was with them. Early in November 1960, Pauline had given birth prematurely to a baby, Marie-Christine, who was extremely frail. The Red Cross arranged for her to be taken to Geneva for intensive medical care, where she died on 18 November. Her tiny body was flown to the Congo.[1] Lumumba was devastated by the loss of Marie-Christine, whom he had never been able to see or hold. He and Pauline wished to take her to Stanleyville, their home region, to hold a funeral and bury her. Permission was not granted.

Stanleyville also beckoned because Gizenga was successfully setting up a base there for Lumumba's ministers and advisers.[2] Lumumba stayed in contact with Kanza, Kashamura and his other supporters in Leopoldville by telephone. His own telephone had been cut off by the Sûreté, but the UN soldiers guarding his residence allowed him to use the phone that had been installed for their own use.

Lumumba had a high degree of hope for a resolution of the crisis. He had faith in the UN Conciliation Commission, which planned to organise a national Round Table to reconcile the different factions and to restore the legitimate government. The Round Table in Brussels—less than a year earlier—had resolved many huge conflicts; perhaps a second one, this time under the aegis of the United Nations, would also lead to a satisfactory outcome.

Meanwhile, the CIA Station in Leopoldville was finding it difficult to make any headway with the operation to kill Lumumba. He was not far away, but out of reach. On 14 November, Devlin cabled Tweedy:

Target has not left building in several weeks. House guarded day and night by Congolese and UN troops [redacted]. Congolese troops are there to prevent target's escape and to arrest him if he attempts. UN troops there to prevent storming of palace by Congolese.

Attempting get coverage of any movement into or out of house by Congolese [redacted]. Target has dismissed most of servants so entry this means seems remote.

The cable added that a CIA agent had learned that Lumumba's 'political followers in Stanleyville desire that he break out of his confinement and proceed to that city by car to engage in political activity'. A decision 'on breakout will probably be made shortly': 'Station expects to be advised by [agent] if decision was made [redacted]. Station has several possible assets to use in event of breakout and studying several plans of action'.[3]

Fresh light was cast on the CIA's plans in 2013, when the US State Department released a substantial set of classified documents relating to the Congo.[4] One of these is a short report cabled by Devlin to headquarters in Washington on 29 November 1960, detailing critical events from the previous days. It discloses that QJWIN, who had shown 'great initiative, imagination and courage since arrival', was focussed on developing ways to get Lumumba out of his residence and into the open, where he would lose the protection of the UN.

'Unilaterally and on own initiative', wrote Devlin approvingly, QJWIN 'made contact with Iden[tity]'. This 'Iden', explains the cable, 'agreed 26 Nov in following plan against target: . . . . Iden to supply four UNO vehicles and six Congolese soldiers with UNO brassards and berets. QJWIN posing as [redacted] officer would enter target's home and provide escort out of residence. Iden said could easily provide vehicles and men. (UNO announced fifty-five of its vehicles have been stolen and Station knows where [*less than* 1 *line not declassified*] uniform available.) Iden organization needed to pierce both Congolese and UNO guards'. The cable added that QJWIN had 'identified self to Identity as German'.[5]

It is reasonable to assume that 'Identity' had close contacts with the UN mission in the Congo, given his ability to obtain and supply UN vehicles, brassards and berets. He may have been a genuine member of the UN mission. Another possibility is that Identity was able to pass himself off as a member of ONUC and to infiltrate UN circles. Sully deFontaine's account of being issued an 'ONU' armband may not be true, but it does suggests that obtaining one was possible. There is also an outside chance that deFontaine was the 'Identity' in Devlin's reports to Washington—that deFontaine remained in the Congo after receiving an instruction by Timberlake on 21 August 1960 to leave the following day on a flight out of Leopoldville. In any case, the only source for this instruction is deFontaine.[6]

* * *

THE DAY AFTER THE plan had been agreed between QJWIN and Identity, 'the target' *did* leave his residence. 'The night of November 27, 1960', wrote Devlin in his memoir, 'changed the entire political situation in the Congo'.[7]

Earlier that day, Kasavubu had returned from the UN in New York to Leopoldville. He was received at the airport 'with pomp and ceremony', wrote Rajeshwar Dayal, unimpressed. The president 'took a long time to emerge from the plane', Dayal noted, 'while he donned a brand new Field-Marshal's white uniform, complete with epaulettes, gold braid, and sword, which we watched being carried across the tarmac to the waiting plane'.

That night there was a banquet at the president's residence on Mont Stanley. It was a lavish event, attended by two hundred guests, to celebrate the UN accreditation of Kasavubu's delegation. Dayal, who was bitterly dismayed by this development, contemptuously referred to the banquet as a 'junketing'.[8]

Not far away, a very different drama was in progress: Lumumba left his residence, in the midst of a torrential rainstorm beating down on the Congolese capital. His departure was not discovered until the following day, according to a UN report. The Moroccan guard posted at the residence ordered a search of the house, which was found to be empty.[9]

Varying accounts emerged of what had happened. The UN guard noted the approach of a large black car, which he and his fellow soldiers stopped. But they 'recognized the car and no suspicion was raised as they had seen that car go in and go out a number of times with the same driver'. It was not Lumumba's personal car, which was a Chevrolet station wagon, but 'a car which frequently came into the residence and left with various other passengers; so they let the car in, and after a short while the car left with three passengers—all men'.[10]

Mobutu gave the press an entirely different story: that Lumumba had slipped down to the river facing his house and had then been rowed some miles upstream, where he was picked up by a convoy of cars.[11]

The details that are available are sparse and contradictory. Even so, they are consistent with QJWIN's plan, arranged with Identity the day before—according to which QJWIN would pose as an officer of some kind (which it is impossible to establish, as that information is still classified), who was already known to Lumumba and his guards. He would escort Lumumba out of his home, presumably with the assistance of Congolese soldiers in UN uniforms, in a car with UN markings.

'In all likelihood', wrote Devlin in his memoir, Lumumba 'received some assistance from the UN peacekeepers assigned to protect him'.[12] This was disingenuous, given that Devlin was overseeing an operation in which—as he knew full well—a deliberate attempt was made for the visitors to Lumumba's residence to masquerade as UN officials.

In his testimony to the Church Committee in 1975, Devlin protested that he was 'quite certain that there was no Agency involvement in any way' in Lumumba's departure from UN custody, and that he had no advance knowledge of Lumumba's plan. He noted the variety of stories explaining what had happened. But, he said,

'I have never believed it worthwhile to determine which, if any, was correct'. He added, 'Just how he managed his escape is of little importance'.[13]

His protestation is defensive. This is hardly surprising, since the manner of Lumumba's departure from his residence is of huge, instrumental importance to any assessment of America's role in Lumumba's fate. If the CIA secretly conspired in Lumumba's departure, they were responsible for his ultimate delivery into the hands of his enemies. This had been O'Donnell's plan from the beginning, as was recorded in a cable from Leopoldville to Washington: 'What I wanted to do', said O'Donnell, 'was to get him out, to trick him out, if I could'.[14]

* * *

Given the thick band of ANC troops around his official residence, Lumumba could not have left without the connivance of at least some of them. The aggressive nature of the troops is apparent from an episode that had occurred just over a week earlier, on 15 November, when Lovelace P C Mensah, a second secretary of the Ghanaian embassy in Leopoldville, had entered the residence and been seized by Mobutu's troops. Mensah, a resident of Leopoldville for the previous fifteen years, was a trusted friend both of Prime Minister Lumumba and of President Nkrumah—and a safe intermediary between them.

A memoir by Mensah's son gives an account of the episode; it explains that Mensah went through all the security checks and finally arrived in the section of the residence where Lumumba lived. He had brought with him a two-page handwritten letter from Nkrumah, with a rescue plan. Before his arrival, Mensah had wrapped it in rubber and 'hidden it in a secure part of his body'. Then, after briefing Lumumba, he 'carefully took out the letter from President Nkrumah and handed it over for him to read'.

But suddenly, there were loud shouts and a 'mad rush of feet', as soldiers loyal to Mobutu ran towards them. Mensah 'snatched the two-page document from Lumumba, chewed it, and had just swallowed it when he found himself in the grip of macho soldiers and security guards, all armed with guns and truncheons'. They shoved their fingers down Mensah's throat and slapped him hard, in an effort to get hold of the chewed-up letter. But it was too late.

Mensah had been 'prepared to die rather than give away a hand-written letter of such political significance to the "enemy"'. He paid for this severely. He was arrested on allegations that he was carrying plans for an invasion of Katanga and money for Lumumba. He was placed in the Leopoldville army camp, where his arms and legs were tied to his chair and he was blindfolded. He was tortured for two days, and the torment, according to his son, 'was so gruesome that it could not be repeated in print'. But Mensah gave no information to his captors.[15]

Mobutu, Justin Bomboko and Victor Nendaka were furious when they heard of Mensah's visit to Lumumba. They were already angry at the Ghanaian embassy: they believed that the Ghanaian chargé d'affaires, Nathaniel Welbeck, who had replaced Ambassador Djin (and was waiting for his diplomatic credentials to be formally signed by Kasavubu), was spreading pro-Lumumba propaganda in the cité. Welbeck spoke fluent French and was now serving, noted the New York Times, as 'Ghana's Man in Leopoldville'.[16]

It occurred to Mobutu that the incident involving Mensah offered an ideal opportunity to throw Ghana's diplomatic representative out of the Congo. He immediately issued an expulsion order to Welbeck—which was disregarded. He then turned to Devlin for advice, who was also eager to see the departure of the troublesome Ghanaian. Devlin suggested they send a formal letter from Kasavubu to President Nkrumah, asking him to recall his ambassador. Nkrumah refused to see the Congolese envoy or to accept the letter from Kasavubu.[17] Welbeck stayed on in Leopoldville.

The crisis escalated. On 19 November, Gilbert-Pierre Pongo, the deputy to Victor Nendaka, the head of the Sûreté—and the brother-in-law of Kasavubu—served a forty-eight-hour notice of departure on Welbeck and sent soldiers to the embassy. Dayal was told about the notice but refused to accept its validity—a position with which Hammarskjöld and Bunche fully agreed, upholding the doctrine of the inviolability of embassies. At lunchtime on 21 November, Brigadier Rikhye sent Tunisian UN soldiers to guard the

Ghanaian embassy; the soldiers refused to hand over Welbeck and took up positions in the garden to protect him.

After three days, the strained relations between the two groups of soldiers exploded. Ghana's newspaper, the *Daily Graphic*, gave an account of the episode:

> The tension rose throughout the sweltering afternoon, and after dark the shooting started. The first shooting lasted for an hour then, after a break of half an hour, it began again sporadically.
>
> Shots were fired from armoured cars, machine guns and rifles.
>
> Journalists were shot at as they tried to get near the scene and were prevented from getting close by the Congolese. Flashes could be seen all over the town.[18]

Finally a ceasefire was agreed, but by that time two people had died: Colonel Kokolo, a popular leader of the Armée Nationale Congolaise, and a Tunisian UN soldier. Their bodies were taken to the UN hospital, along with four wounded Tunisians. Sporadic fighting continued until the next morning, leading to yet more injuries. Tensions between Mobutu's troops and the UN spread throughout the city.

The following morning, General Alexander intervened; he had flown to Leopoldville a few days earlier to investigate the expulsion order. He went to the Ghanaian embassy, indicating to Welbeck that Nkrumah had ordered the entire Ghana staff, including Lovelace Mensah, to leave the Congo. Alexander took them to the airport, from where they were flown home on Tuesday 22 November on a Soviet aircraft.[19] Also on the plane were Richard Quarshie of the Ghanaian Ministry of Foreign Affairs, who had flown to Leopoldville with Alexander, and eighteen Ghanaians, who had been sent to the Congo to assist the new nation with technical expertise. They received a heroes' welcome at Accra airport. Welbeck's wife and daughter were waiting for him on the tarmac, along with high-ranking state officials.[20]

After the euphoria of his safe arrival home, Lovelace Mensah sought to recover from his ordeal. He found it painfully difficult to move his limbs, and his vision was blurred. He also suffered 'spasmodic panic attacks from mental recall of guns pointed at his head, voices of soldiers barking threats and obscene orders at him, and nightmares about some of the unimaginably grisly torture'. President Nkrumah offered personal words of solace and encouragement.[21]

There was relief in Ghana that the embassy staff were safe. But there was also outrage when it became known that Nkrumah had never, in fact, issued an order to General Alexander to withdraw Welbeck. On the contrary—as Nkrumah noted in *Challenge of the Congo*—he had written a letter to Welbeck on 21 November, which Alexander was supposed to hand over. The letter contained a clear instruction to Welbeck to stay in the Congo: 'I am writing to order you to remain at your post in Léopoldville. I am aware of the deterioration of the situation in Léopoldville but I expect you to rise to the occasion. The Ghana Government does not take notice of the expulsion order emanating from certain quarters in Léopoldville; nor does it recognise the so-called Mobutu Government which is usurping the powers of the legally appointed Government'.

The Mobutu gang, added Nkrumah, was 'propped up by imperialist and colonialist powers' and, with the tacit connivance of these powers, was deliberately creating confusion. He emphasised that the position of the Ghana government was to support the Lumumba government, and that he would be demanding that Secretary General Hammarskjöld order the UN to provide adequate protection for all Ghanaian personnel. He would also be asking the UN to secure Mensah's release.

His concluding paragraph emphasised his order to Welbeck to remain in his role at the embassy: 'I expect you to stand up to the situation. Report regularly on the situation to me'.[22]

Alexander had failed to give the letter to Welbeck, as he had been instructed to do. In a rather defensive record written on 27 November, he explained that when he went to see Welbeck, he had forgotten to take the letter from the hotel. It was a weak excuse, since he was well aware of the message in the letter and could have conveyed it to Welbeck in his own words. He added in the record that, in any case, Welbeck had asked to be rescued during the crisis.[23]

Welbeck said afterwards that he would certainly have stayed in the Congo had he known that his president wished him to do so.[24]

It is unclear whether Alexander, in ignoring the orders of his superior—namely, President Nkrumah—was acting on his own initiative or was being directed by others. It does not seem likely that any orders came from the British government. For although he was seconded from the British Army, he does not appear to have been in communication with the British government at that time. Indeed, British official files reveal repeated frustration with Alexander during that period.

General Alexander's chief ally in Leopoldville was Ambassador Timberlake, with whom he had established a good relationship from the first day of his arrival in mid-July.[25] Alexander's value as a source to the US embassy was frequently mentioned in the Central Intelligence Bulletin, President Eisenhower's daily intelligence digest. In any case, Devlin himself had recommended to Mobutu that the Ghanaian embassy staff be expelled; he and Timberlake welcomed Alexander's action.

Ghana's embassy was not the only one to be closed down. The diplomats and staff of the United Arab Republic were also expelled. President Nasser immediately responded by breaking off diplomatic relations with Belgium; Nkrumah wrote to Nasser to express his appreciation of the stand he had taken.

The battle between Mobutu's forces and ONUC had dire repercussions for the UN. 'Whatever remained of the professional bonds between the military officers on both sides', observed Dayal sadly, 'was shattered'. Life for UN personnel became increasingly dangerous, and in New York, the Conciliation Commission decided to defer its departure for the Congo.[26]

* * *

THERE WAS WIDESPREAD INCREDULITY that on 27 November Lumumba managed to leave his residence, given the vigorous guarding by Congolese troops. 'It seems incredible', observed Nkrumah, 'that he was undetected by Mobutu's soldiers'. But 'obviously', he reflected, 'they were totally unsuspecting when the car containing Lumumba drove away from the house. Even Lumumba's own colleagues, when told of the escape the following morning, could scarcely believe that he would be so foolhardy as to leave without taking any precautions'.[27]

In Stanleyville, some twelve hundred miles from Leopoldville, Antoine Gizenga heard the news on Radio Katanga the morning after Lumumba's departure. 'Lumumba committed a monumental error', he commented with regret, 'in precipitating his departure from Léopoldville—a departure which I learned on the radio at the same time as the entire world'.[28] Gizenga, who had been working hard on a plan to safely transfer Lumumba to Stanleyville, was bitterly disappointed.

It does not appear to have occurred either to Nkrumah or to Gizenga that Lumumba's departure may have been inspired by an enemy. Rajeshwar Dayal, however, who was nearby and closely monitoring the situation, was deeply suspicious. How Lumumba managed to elude the ANC guard, he suggested to New York, showed the resourcefulness of his supporters—'*unless* his escape was actually encouraged to get rid of an inconvenient element'. Dayal had good reasons for his suspicions: 'How Lumumba was able to slip through both the UN guards—whose duty it was to keep out unwanted visitors—as well as the ANC troops, who were there to prevent his escape, remains a mystery. Normally, the UN guard would not concern itself with an outgoing vehicle, but had the Congolese troops been bribed or were they caught napping?'[29]

No doubt the banquet at President Kasavubu's official residence on Mont Stanley, which was taking place at the time of Lumumba's departure, helped to keep the spotlight away. It meant that numbers of VIPs, living in the same neighbourhood as Lumumba's official residence, would be far enough away as to be oblivious to any unusual activity. Ian Scott, the British ambassador, who lived next door to Lumumba, is likely to have been at the banquet; Scott had gone to the airport to welcome Kasavubu and, Dayal observed disapprovingly, cheered him enthusiastically.[30] One building in the neighbourhood, which would have been staffed with people looking out for Lumumba's welfare at all times, was empty—the villa of Nathaniel Welbeck, the Ghanaian chargé d'affaires, who had been deceived into leaving his post and returning to Ghana.

In *Queen of Spies*, a biography of Daphne Park, Paddy Hayes records that Park flew to Stanleyville on the morning of 27 November 1960, the day that Lumumba left Leopoldville. He quotes from a memoir by Ian Scott, which refers to 'a woman member of my staff who happened to arrive in the airport that morning'; the date provided by Scott is 27 November. This 'woman member', argues Hayes, 'was undoubtedly Park'; he suggests that her journey to Stanleyville was directly connected to the expectation that Lumumba would arrive there shortly.[31] If that is so, she is likely to have been aware of Lumumba's forthcoming departure from his residence.

* * *

THE WORD 'ESCAPE' TO describe Lumumba's departure has dominated most accounts of the episode. But Lumumba himself was clear that it was not an 'escape', as Anicet Kashamura explained in *De Lumumba aux Colonels* (1966). Before Lumumba left his residence, wrote Kashamura, he placed a letter of explanation on a table. It read:

> I never considered my departure from Léopoldville as a flight. I asked the UN authorities to facilitate my trip to Stanley[ville] in order to proceed with the burial of my daughter, who died on the 18 November in Switzerland, where she had been sent under the care of Doctor Beck.
>
> To this I add the fact that since her birth, I did not have—and I will never have—the possibility to see my daughter.

'My trip', said Lumumba 'has a strictly family character'. Then he added:

> It is of limited duration; I will return to Léopoldville where I am awaiting the arrival of the [UN] commission of conciliation. Besides, I hope soon to meet Monsieur Kasavubu who has supported since New York the idea of organizing a National Round Table,

to which I must assist as the prime minister of the only legitimate government, at the same time as Monsieur Tshombe, president of the province of Katanga.

With these words, Lumumba set down in writing that he expected to return to his residence.[32]

Lumumba appears to have had great faith in the outcome of the Conciliation Commission. For several of his ministers and senior members of the MNC, however, the future looked bleak. The UN vote in favour of Kasavubu earlier that month had convinced them that they could no longer rely on UN troops to protect them from arrest, torture and even murder.

Discussions about going to Stanleyville had been taking place in Leopoldville among the core of Lumumba's supporters, including Antoine-Roger Bolamba, secretary of state for information and cultural affairs; Cléophas Kamitatu, president of the Leopoldville provincial government and provincial president of the PSA; Joseph Okito, the highly respected vice president of the Senate; Maurice Mpolo, minister of youth and sport; Joachim Masena, minister of labour; Anicet Kashamura; Georges Grenfell, minister of state; and Joseph Mbuyi, minister of the middle classes.

At midnight on 24 November, Kamitatu went to see these colleagues to report on a new development: he had received a sum of money from Lumumba to enable them to leave for Stanleyville. Their response was mixed. Okito, the eldest in the group, was concerned they would be massacred; Mpolo, the youngest, was excited.[33]

The next morning, Lumumba told Kashamura over the telephone not to be concerned about him and not to stay with him—he was happy to see them leave, believing they would be saved. On the morning of Saturday 26 November, the first convoy left: Masena, Mpolo, Okito, Grenfell, Mbuyi and Kashamura. Mpolo did not stay with the group but decided to travel to the district where he had grown up, to see his family; he was spotted by Mobutu's soldiers and arrested.

Lumumba left Leopoldville the following night, with a second convoy: Pierre Mulele, minister of education and culture; Rémy

Mwamba, minister of justice; Gabriel Yumbu, deputy chairman of the PSA; Christophe Gbenye, minister of the interior; Jérôme Mutshungu of the MNC-L; and Barthélemy Mujanay, governor of the Central Bank of the Congo.

Between the departures of the two convoys, Kamitatu issued an announcement to the press in which he attacked Kasavubu and declared his support for Lumumba. A political presence such as Lumumba, he asserted, could not be destroyed; his supporters and followers were too many. It was necessary, he said, that there should be a reconciliation between Kasavubu and Lumumba.[34] It was exactly what Lumumba had said in his letter.

* * *

DEVLIN HAD BEEN SCHEDULED to go to Rome to attend a meeting of the CIA chiefs of station working in Africa. Following Lumumba's departure from his residence, Devlin wrote in his memoir, he cabled his superiors to say he would not go. But he received an immediate response, asking him to go to Rome, if only for twenty-four hours, so that he could discuss the Congo situation with Dick Bissell.

When Devlin arrived in Rome at about six in the evening, 'John', a senior administrative officer and old friend, met him and drove him to the home of Tom Karamessines, who was the CIA station chief for Italy, under official cover as a political officer at the US embassy in Rome. They were joined for dinner by their Washington superiors, Bissell and Bronson Tweedy.

They talked Congo, Devlin reported in *Chief of Station, Congo*, 'until nearly one in the morning', when he left for his hotel, 'happy to find that they very much appreciated the success of the station's operations and fully supported our efforts'. All of Devlin's operations were apparently discussed at length—'with one exception, the [YQ]PROP operation' to kill Lumumba. To his surprise, Devlin claimed, Bissell did not mention it.[35] If that was so, it is odd that Devlin himself did not bring it up—since it was his major concern at the time.

But it would be a mistake to rely on Devlin's memoir for any kind of truth. It is candid about those parts of the plot to kill Lumumba that were already in the public domain at the time of writing, but it omits developments that have emerged since publication. The series of anecdotes it presents are frequently in conflict with the cable traffic between Leopoldville and Washington.

According to the memoir, Bissell and Tweedy took Devlin to lunch the day after their late-night conversation, for two more hours of Congo talk. Afterwards, Devlin rushed to the airport. 'I was settling into my seat', he wrote, 'when my eye caught the headlines of a newspaper someone in front of me was reading: "LU-MUMBA CAPTURED"'.[36] He presents the news as a surprise. Most likely, he was kept informed throughout the search and was told the moment Lumumba was seized.

Manhunt for Lumumba

A N INTENSIVE SEARCH FOR LUMUMBA followed swiftly upon his disappearance on Sunday 27 November. Gilbert-Pierre Pongo of the Sûreté, Nendaka's deputy, asked the UN for air and road transport to facilitate the hunt, but it was adamantly refused by Dayal, who issued clear orders to the UN military command.[1] It was 'no part of ONUC's functions', instructed Dayal, 'to provide or transmit intelligence to either side concerning the movements or whereabouts of pursued or pursuers'.[2] Ambassador Timberlake then asked Abbé Youlou, the president of Congo Brazzaville, for a helicopter, which was immediately provided and made available to Pongo.[3] Meanwhile, no other aircraft were allowed to take off from Ndjili, Leopoldville's airport.

Lumumba was making his way to Stanleyville. Details of the journey vary, but it appears that the prime minister left the rain-drenched streets of Leopoldville in a Peugeot belonging to Cléophas Kamitatu. It was driven by Bernardin Diaka, minister of defence. They headed east, passing Ndjili airport. They were joined by Lumumba's chauffeur in his powerful black Chevrolet, who had stopped to pick up Pauline and two-year-old Roland from the cité, where they were staying. By four o'clock the following morning, they had reached the ferry station on the Kwango, one of the tributaries of the Congo River. There a third car was waiting for them, with some of Lumumba's ministers, deputies, and other supporters.[4]

A message had been sent ahead of time by Kamitatu to the ferrymen, telling them of their forthcoming arrival. But the ferrymen knew nothing of the plan. This caused difficulties, since no one in

Lumumba's party could speak their language. Finally, they were able to persuade the ferry captain to transport them and their cars across the river.

The next morning they continued their journey. It was tough going: heavy rain had washed away the surface of some roads, leaving thick and sticky mud. Two cars went ahead of the party, but the men in those cars were taken prisoner by policemen loyal to Lumumba, who mistakenly suspected they were supporters of Mobutu. The men were locked up in the town of Kenge, and all were beaten except Diaka, who was treated with respect because he was carrying Lumumba's ivory baton. When Lumumba arrived and explained the situation, the captives were instantly released. The police expressed heartfelt apologies and sought to assist Lumumba's progress, providing a truckload of gasoline and an escort for part of the way.[5]

They reached Masi-Manimba, an administrative centre, where they rested for a while so that Pauline and little Roland could eat; Lumumba ate nothing. 'Crowds of people barred our way', said one of Lumumba's supporters later. 'They brought us chicken, eggs and bananas to show that they were kindly disposed towards us. In many villages the people came out with weapons, thinking that Lumumba was mustering volunteers against the rebels'. But he urged them to put their weapons away.[6]

Then they drove through the night and reached Bulungu, where—as soon as Lumumba was seen—local people rushed out. He spoke to them, promising to continue the fight for freedom. Lumumba's journey was turning into a triumphal procession, wrote the historian Robin McKown: 'Word spread ahead. From then on, the inhabitants of even the tiniest villages lined up to wait for them'.[7] One night, travelling through deep forests, they were stopped by soldiers who, when they recognised their prime minister, waved the party on.

On the morning of Wednesday 30 November—five months exactly since the joyous day of independence—the convoy reached Mangai on the Kasai River, another Congo River tributary. They crossed the border into northern Kasai and reached the town of

Brabanta (now Mapangu), which was steeped in the painful history of forced labour in the palm-oil plantations established by the British peer Lord Leverhulme in 1911.[8]

In the evening, they were joined by Pierre Mulele, the minister of education, and Rémy Mwamba, the minister of justice. But they had been sighted by the Sûreté's Pongo from his plane, which had reached Kasai. It landed at Kikwit, the bailiwick of the Parti Solidaire Africain, where Pongo went to the local offices of the UN to demand road transport from the UN. He was refused.

The UN troops in Kasai were from Ghana. The Ghana contingent as a whole had been moved from Leopoldville to Luluabourg (now Kananga), the capital of Kasai, some months after independence. The Ghana Brigade, commanded by General Alexander, became responsible for UN tasks in Kasai.[9]

* * *

UNAWARE THAT THEY HAD been seen by their pursuers, Lumumba's convoy drove to Port Francqui, the large commercial port on the Sankuru River. One member of the convoy, a twenty-five-year-old Congolese man, provided an account of the journey to a Soviet journalist later that year; he gave his name to the journalist as Jacques N.[10] At Port Francqui, said Jacques N, many people came out to greet Lumumba and milled around him. But suddenly, a lorry full of ANC troops drove up, and the sergeant in charge ordered Lumumba to follow them.

Jacques N ran to a nearby UN post to ask for help but was turned away. The 'officer, an Englishman', listened to him coldly and replied, 'We do not interfere in Congolese affairs'. The officer would have been a member of Ghana's UN troops; the only British officers in the UN forces were serving in the Ghana contingent, led by General Alexander.

The Ghanaian soldiers serving under the British officer had other ideas: they were determined to rescue Lumumba. Paying no attention to their officer, they quickly got their guns and forced the ANC soldiers to leave. 'That decided the issue', said Jacques N. 'The rebels departed. The UN troops, riding in a lorry, accompanied us for about fifty kilometers and then waved us on'.

They drove on to the small town of Mweka, where several thousand people had assembled on the square to welcome their prime minister. He spoke to them, but as the rally was ending, the ANC soldiers reappeared in cars that had been provided by Belgians in Port Francqui. With quick thinking, Jacques N jumped into Lumumba's Chevrolet and sped along the highway, to draw the ANC soldiers away. They promptly gave chase, but Jacques N soon lost them, the Chevrolet being much faster than their cars.

On Thursday 1 December, Lumumba and his group reached the tiny village of Lodi, where there was a ferry across the Sankuru River. But the ferry boat could not be found. Lumumba and three of his companions decided to abandon the cars and cross the river in a canoe, while Pauline and the rest of the group waited for the ferry. Lumumba's party reached the opposite bank, where they found the ferrymen and asked them to cross the river to collect the others.

But the convoy had been spotted by ANC soldiers in the helicopter. They immediately alerted the Luluabourg solders, who rushed to the ferry landing and seized the boat. They sailed across the river to where Lumumba and his companions—unsuspecting—were waiting patiently for the rest of their party. As the boat emerged from the darkness, the soldiers jumped out and grabbed Lumumba.

Lumumba was taken to Mweka. 'I was there', recorded Jacques N. He had already saved Lumumba's life once, by using the Chevrolet to outwit the ANC soldiers; he was determined to do so again. He saw a truck with troops stop at the UN post on the town's outskirts at six o'clock in the morning: 'Lumumba, his hands tied behind his back, was standing in the lorry, and beside him were his wife, son, a Minister and several MPs'.

Jacques N ran to the British lieutenant at the UN post and shouted, 'It's Lumumba, save him'. Then Lumumba himself said 'clearly and loudly' from the lorry, 'Lieutenant, I am the Prime Minister. I request United Nations protection'. But the premier's request was denied. 'The lieutenant looked indifferently at him, crushed his cigarette and went into the house without replying.

The rebel soldiers, who had watchfully waited for the results of Lumumba's appeal, seized Lumumba, dragged him out of the lorry
and pushed him into a small red Opel that had come from Port
Francqui'. Jacques N ran to the UN African troops, who raised the
alarm and gave chase. But the red Opel was already too far away.[11]

The Ghanaian soldiers were incensed with anger at their lieutenant. They set the other prisoners free, including Pauline and
Roland.[12]

*   *   *

TWICE, THEREFORE, BRITISH ARMY officers serving the UN refused
to save Lumumba from his pursuers. 'Whenever people now
say that the UN could do nothing to prevent Lumumba's arrest and
that its representatives did their utmost to stop his illegal detention', said Jacques N bitterly, 'I remember that UN lieutenant, his
haughty, indifferent face and the boot slowly crushing a smoking
cigarette'.[13]

The British officers in the Ghanaian UN contingent worked in
a tight group with General Alexander. At the time, there were 230
British officers in Ghana's army, many of whom were sent to the
Congo.[14] 'It was they, rather than the few Ghanaians at the top of
the army', noted the historian Jitendra Mohan in 1969, 'who commanded and controlled the large majority of Ghanaian soldiers in
the Congo on routine operations'. On the whole, adds Mohan, the
British officers in the Congo were 'more pro-Belgian, just as the
Ghanaian officers were on the whole more pro-Congolese'. This
produced mutual suspicion and tension, which extended through
the ranks.[15]

*   *   *

LARRY DEVLIN TOLD THE Church Committee that he was 'not a
major assistance' in tracking Lumumba down; his contribution, he
suggested, was limited to consulting with Congolese officers about
the possible routes Lumumba might take to Stanleyville. But a
rather different impression emerges from a cable he sent to Washington the day after Lumumba's departure: '[Station] working with
[Congolese government] to get roads blocked and troops alerted
[block] possible escape route'.[16]

On Tuesday 29 November, he sent a cable concerning QJWIN. 'View change in location target', he wrote, presumably referring to Lumumba, 'QJ/WIN anxious go Stanleyville and expressed desire execute plan by himself without using any apparat[us]'. The nature of QJWIN's plan is unclear, but its meaning was evidently understood by Devlin and by his seniors in the Africa Division. They were in favour but wanted to ensure that no fingerprints left behind could be traced to the US. On 30 November, Tweedy responded to Devlin: 'Concur QJ/WIN go Stanleyville [redacted]. We are prepared consider direct action by QJ/WIN but would like your reading on security factors. How close would this place [United States] to the action?'[17]

In the event, Lumumba did not reach Stanleyville, making this particular 'direct action' redundant. QJWIN may, however, have taken actions of a different nature.

The role of Justin O'Donnell at this stage of events is not mentioned in the report of the Church Committee. It is likely, however, that his participation was explored in the course of his testimony, which makes it all the more frustrating that the transcripts are missing. Given that O'Donnell described QJWIN's stay in the Congo as 'coextensive with my own', it is reasonable to assume that O'Donnell was involved in some way in the search for Lumumba. In any case, O'Donnell had been specifically sent to the Congo to facilitate Lumumba's murder, so it is reasonable to assume that he did play a role. But when he was asked by the Church Committee if he and QJWIN were responsible for Lumumba's departure and subsequent capture, he replied, 'Absolutely not'.[18]

On 14 December, a cable from CIA headquarters to Devlin and O'Donnell instructed the Leopoldville station to 'restrict QJWIN to activity directly pertinent his mission Leopoldville or forthcoming mission Dakar and possibly elsewhere (e.g., Milan) for KUTUBE/D purposes'. (KUTUBE is the Foreign Intelligence Division.) The cable does not specify the nature of the missions in Leopoldville, Dakar and elsewhere, but it implicitly suggests that the mission in Leopoldville was ongoing. It may have been the transport of uranium to the US.

The cable adds:

1. He our only asset of this type and we wish keep him clean of any operational involvement other than that originally planned for him.

2. Above does not necessarily preclude taking advantage any lead offered by QJWIN on high priority target (Soviet or Chicom [Chinese Communist]) but target refs appear marginal when considered against framework of plans for QJWIN.

'If action . . . not already taken', the cable adds, 'please instruct him desist'.

The cable also bears the instruction to 'pls add ZRACORN slug to command channel traffic on QJWIN. Released by William K. Harvey'.[19] The digraph 'ZR' denoted Division D intelligence, which was headed by Bill Harvey, but this did not necessarily suggest a plan for the assassination of Lumumba, since Harvey did not set up the Executive Action programme within ZRRIFLE until the start of 1961.

Later that month, QJWIN left the Congo. A cable dated 19 December authorised his return to Luxembourg on 21 December; the Luxembourg station was instructed to pay him $1,000 for his December salary, as the final payment for his services on this operation.[20]

QJWIN's operation was regarded as a success by the CIA. In a memorandum to arrange the financial accounting for QJWIN's activities in the Congo, Bill Harvey noted that 'QJ/WIN was sent on this trip for a specific, highly sensitive operational purpose which has been completed'.[21] This 'operational purpose' had been to act as Justin O'Donnell's 'alter ego': to draw Lumumba away from the protective custody of the UN guard and place him in the hands of Congolese authorities. But what other purpose had been assigned to QJWIN is not reflected in the available documentation.

QJWIN was a proven and valuable agent. In 1962 the CIA discovered that he was about to go on trial in Europe on smuggling charges. Headquarters suggested, 'If [redacted] information true we may wish attempt quash charges or arrange somehow salvage QJ/WIN for our purposes'.[22]

* * *

AFTER HIS CAPTURE IN Kasai, Lumumba was flown in the Air Congo plane to Leopoldville, four hundred miles away, landing at Ndjili airport at five o'clock in the afternoon of 2 December. On arrival, he was forced out by Pongo's men, with his arms bound tightly behind him with a long rope. His glasses had been removed; without them, he could see little.

The international press, having been alerted, was there in force. As the photographers started to snap pictures, one soldier seized the prime minister by his hair and jerked his head up. Then Lumumba was dragged roughly towards a truck filled with soldiers; he walked with considerable difficulty and his face showed signs of heavy blows. He was pushed into the truck, which drove off in a convoy of other, armed trucks; the cars of the reporters and television cameramen followed. The long procession made its way to a villa that had been converted into a prison in Binza, the neighbourhood beyond Leopoldville where Mobutu and Devlin lived.

Photos and films of the scene caused worldwide shock. An Associated Press correspondent reported, 'Colonel Mobutu, his arms crossed, watched calmly while the soldiers slapped and pushed the prisoner and pulled his hair'.[23]

Less than two years earlier, Lumumba and Mobutu had shared a friendship and an alliance at the Round Table in Brussels; a few months later, they both attended the conference sponsored by the Congress for Cultural Freedom at University College, Ibadan. At independence, Lumumba had appointed Mobutu secretary of state for defence and, subsequently, army chief of staff. When Gizenga and Kashamura sought to dismiss Mobutu from this position, Lumumba protected and defended him.

But now, Mobutu was his nemesis.

Frank Carlucci witnessed Lumumba's suffering. Had Lumumba stayed in his residence, he reflected later, he would probably not have been captured. 'As it was', he said, 'I was probably—I and then Senator Gale McGee—were probably the last two westerners to see him alive. We were having a drink about mid-afternoon at a sidewalk café and a truck went by. Lumumba had his hands tied behind his back and was in the rear part of the truck'.[24]

On arrival at the villa in Binza, a Congolese soldier read out a statement by Lumumba that pronounced him as the head of the legitimate government of the Congo. The soldier then crumpled up the paper and tried to shove it into Lumumba's mouth. The prime minister did not flinch and his expression did not change. The appalling scene was captured on a newsreel, which was viewed by millions worldwide.[25]

The following day, Lumumba was taken out of the villa to be transferred to the military Camp Hardy at Thysville (now Mbanza-Ngungu), down the river from Leopoldville. His face showed signs of beatings, and he climbed into the waiting truck with great difficulty.[26]

Rajeshwar Dayal was horrified. He sent a protest to Bomboko, president of the College of Commissioners, who responded by saying that Lumumba would be treated with human dignity and 'conforming to the requirements of the Universal Declaration of Human Rights'. Dayal was by no means reassured. He sent an urgent report to UN headquarters in New York.[27] Hammarskjöld wired back, 'The emotional tension here around the Lumumba case is considerable and if things run wild or summary justice executed, consequences may be very bad also for the Organization and its Operation. We are in the middle of an extraordinarily complicated and indeed politically dangerous situation'. He knew, he said, that Dayal would use all his 'diplomatic means, as on previous occasions, to see that civilized rules of law are upheld'.[28] But it was becoming increasingly difficult for Dayal to see his way forward wielding any kind of diplomatic influence.

Hammarskjöld wrote a message of protest to Kasavubu. The president, however, dismissed it. He said that he was surprised by the importance attached to Lumumba's arrest by 'a certain number of Afro-Asian and East European delegations'.[29]

* * *

For the first three days of Lumumba's confinement in Thysville, Kashamura reported, he was left in his cell with his hands tied behind his back and with nothing to eat or drink. UN troops in Thysville, who sought to monitor his captivity, also found conditions of severe abuse: 'His head has been shaven and his hands remain tied. He is being kept in a cell under conditions reported to be inhuman in respect of health and hygiene'.[30]

In addition to Lumumba, a number of his ministers and supporters were being held at Camp Hardy, including Maurice Mpolo, Joseph Okito and Georges Grenfell. Mpolo and Okito had been making their way to Stanleyville to join Gizenga when they were arrested in Mushie, on the northern bank of the Kasai River.

Several journalists managed to interview Lumumba in his prison and to record his words. The Italia Canta Company of Rome produced a record titled 'Songs of the Independent Congo and Patrice Lumumba's Last Speech'. In this last spoken message, Lumumba drew attention—as in earlier speeches—to the success of America's struggle against colonial oppression: 'All peoples have had to fight for their freedom. . . . The former colonies of America were liberated in this way. I remind you here of the Declaration of Independence adopted by the Congress of the United States in 1766 [sic], which proclaimed the overthrow of the colonial regime, the united colonies' liberation from the British yoke, and their transformation into a free and independent state'.

He urged, 'We have chosen only one weapon for our struggle: nonviolence. The only weapon that would bring victory in dignity and honor'. He called on the Congolese to continue the struggle:

> Onward, men and women citizens, to the building of a united, proud, and prosperous Congo.
>
> A radiant future is dawning on our horizon.
>
> Long live the independent and sovereign Republic of the Congo![31]

* * *

THE HOPEFULNESS VOICED BY Lumumba—despite the horror of his situation—was nourished by the election on 8 November 1960 of John F Kennedy as president of the United States. Kennedy, the Democratic candidate, had beaten Vice President Richard Nixon,

the Republican nominee. His election was seen by the newly independent nations of the world—and those still struggling against
colonial occupation—as a great opportunity for hope.

Kennedy had taken a public stand against French colonialism,
notably France's war against Algeria's independence movement—
'which again found the Eisenhower administration on the wrong
side of history', David Talbot comments in *The Devil's Chessboard*.[32]
Eisenhower's position had been perceived by many people in Africa as siding with the colonial powers, against the interests of the
colonised.[33] This stance, declared critical African leaders, did not reflect the lessons of freedom engrained in US history. But Kennedy, it
seemed, had understood those lessons. In July 1957, two days before
America's Independence Day, he had risen on the floor of the Senate
and given a powerful speech that generated hope across the world:
'The most powerful single force in the world today is neither communism nor capitalism, neither the H-bomb nor the guided missile—it
is man's eternal desire to be free and independent. . . . Thus, the single
most important test of American foreign policy today is how we
meet the challenge of imperialism, what we do to further man's desire to be free. On this test more than any other, this nation shall be
critically judged by the uncommitted millions in Asia and Africa'.[34]

* * *

IN THE SAME MONTH that Kennedy won the presidential election,
a US naval task force called Operation South Atlantic Amity—
designated SoLant Amity—left for Africa. Undertaking what was
described as a goodwill tour, the vessels visited various countries
along the western coast of Africa, from Dakar in Senegal to Cape
Town in South Africa, to show the American flag. This was a much
larger operation than the reconnaissance tour of July 1960, when
marines had photographed and mapped portions of the coast of the
Congo as a basis for potential amphibious landings. The vessels involved included the landing ships *USS Hermitage* and *USS Graham
County*, the destroyers *USS Vogelgesang* and *USS Gearing* and the
small tanker *USS Nespelin*.[35]

The goodwill tour was a cover for a military exercise. William C
Daley, a marine serving on the *USS Graham County*, later recalled

his preparations before leaving: 'All that "extra" training we received stateside: "jump" [from five-foot-high platforms to the soft sand below] school and rubber boat excursions at the Onslow Beach Recon facility where we were ordered to deliberately overturn, then upright and re-board the craft'.[36]

Marines were also taken to 'the Kunai grass shrouded hill-and-dale complex of Vieques' in Puerto Rico, where they were provided with 'staggering amounts of expensive ammunition and explosives for live fire training. As well as still more helicopter drop-zone and amphibious tractor landing exercises'.[37]

This was practise for a possible landing operation in the Congo. 'In the course of this mission', notes the SoLant Amity website, which is carefully maintained by veterans of the task force, 'our Marines and sailors of our US Navy were trained in all manner of assault landings, rubber rafts, parachute assaults, and AMTRACS [amphibious tractors]'.[38]

The task force sailed via Trinidad, Brazil and the Canary Islands. After that, writes Daley, 'we . . . all of us this time, wound up where the US Navy Department and the Marine Corps wanted us to be, the west coast of Africa. There we stayed for most of the next few months in the Gulf of Guinea, within striking distance of the former Belgian Congo and its ongoing revolution'. They landed at Matadi, the Atlantic port of the Congo, and at Pointe Noire, the port of Congo Brazzaville, which is two hundred miles north of Matadi.[39]

'The Belgian Congo', recalled Thomas DeLange, who was serving on the destroyer USS Gearing, 'was where I got to go ashore and play Marine. It seems that the Corps' radio equipment could not contact the naval radio equipment aboard the ship. I was issued a portable radio, MI and .45 cal pistol. A grunt [infantry soldier] was assigned to me to turn the hand cranked generator for the radio when I needed to contact the ship and relay the Marine's traffic'. Shortly after they landed on the beach, 'there was a virtual snowfall of paratroopers (well over a hundred) dropped to the west of our location'.

DeLange was 'never made privy to who the troops were or why they were dropping in for a visit'. Shortly thereafter they withdrew to the ship. 'I know it was the Congo', he adds, 'as we stood off the African coast for roughly thirty days, and the landing was done in this time period'. During the time they were on the beachhead, 'several Marines moved inland, but the group I was with stayed at the landing site and waited for their return'. The only radio traffic that he passed was a request for the whale boat to come back to pick them up. 'Again', DeLange said, 'no answers were provided and questions were discouraged'.[40]

John Stockwell, who resigned from the CIA in December 1976 because of his moral objections to its covert interventions, was involved in SoLant Amity as a marine. 'Early 1961', he wrote in his memoir, *In Search of Enemies*, 'as reconnaissance officer on a navy cruise, which President Kennedy called SOLANT AMITY, I had run covert hydrographic surveys of beach gradients and sand composition up and down the western coast of Africa, in Monrovia, Lome, Conakry, Pointe Noire, and Bathurst'. He and his men would take a 'Peter' boat—a navy landing craft—and 'fake a beer party while we dived and took soundings. None of us, though highly trained reconnaissance marines, had much stomach for the murky depths a hundred yards from the beach'.[41]

Ed Gullion, a US diplomat who in 1961 replaced Clare Timberlake as Kennedy's choice of ambassador to the Congo, was clear about the purpose of SoLant Amity. 'It was touring African harbors on a "goodwill tour"', he commented in an interview some years later, 'barely concealing its character as a force ready for potential intervention (500 marines, tanks, six helicopters) and its intelligence gathering function'.[42]

* * *

THE SoLANT AMITY FORCE reached Dakar in Senegal at the same time as another American 'goodwill' tour of Africa—Louis Armstrong and the All Stars. 'I don't know who was responsible', wrote Paul Kelly, who was serving on *USS Gearing*, 'but it was a brilliant move. . . . I believe we were in Senegal (Dakar), and at about 11:00 two French Army trucks come out on the pier and in them is Louis Armstrong and his band!' Armstrong played for two hours in the blistering heat, then went on board to share a meal with the crew on the mess decks. 'What a guy!!!!' enthused Kelly with deep pleasure at the memory.[43]

The SoLant Amity operation made a contribution to UN efforts in the Congo. On 1 February, *USS Hermitage* picked up Guinean UN soldiers from Matadi and disembarked them at Conakry a week later. But, notes Ed Shea, a marine serving in Operation SoLant Amity, 'UN documents do NOT [*sic*] reflect our presence'. He and other marines who served in the operation regret that this made them ineligible for the UN Medal, which was awarded to any member of the US Armed Forces for their service in a UN military operation or disaster relief.

'Like a shipload of James Bonds', Shea notes sadly, 'We were "never there"'.[44]

29

Deep Cover Agent WIROGUE

I N NEW YORK, ON 14 December 1960, the UN General Assembly
adopted Resolution 1514 (XV), which stated that the subjection
of peoples to alien domination constituted a denial of fundamental human rights and was contrary to the UN Charter. It asserted
that all peoples had the right to self-determination and urged that
immediate steps be taken in territories that had not yet attained
independence to 'transfer all powers to peoples of those Territories,
without any conditions or reservations'.

The resolution was 'one of the greatest achievements of the anticolonial forces in the United Nations', comments Wellington W
Nyangoni in a study of Africa and the United Nations. Sponsored by
forty-three African and Asian countries, it was adopted by a vote of
eighty-nine to none, with nine abstentions. The abstentions included
Belgium, France, Britain, South Africa and the United States.[1]

The resolution referred specifically to territories that had not
yet attained independence. But the subjection of peoples to alien
domination did not happen only under colonialism, argued Nkrumah; it happened under neocolonialism too. 'The essence of neo-
colonialism', he explained in 1965, 'is that the State which is subject
to it is, in theory, independent and has all the outward trappings of
international sovereignty. In reality its economic system and thus
its political policy is directed from outside'.[2]

And this, Nkrumah believed, was the threat faced by the Congo.

On the same day that the resolution was adopted, Nkrumah
wrote to British prime minister Harold Macmillan to express his
deep concern about events in the Congo. Lumumba was considered

to have ceased to be prime minister, Nkrumah objected, merely because of an announcement made by President Kasavubu. Nkrumah asked, 'Who ratified this decision?' He pointed out that 'neither the elected parliament nor the people as a whole had been consulted'.[3]

* * *

TWO DAYS BEFORE THE passing of Resolution 1514 (XV), Antoine Gizenga proclaimed Stanleyville, the capital of Orientale province, the seat of the legitimate government of the Congo and its provisional capital. Gizenga's government was joined by the ministers and members of Parliament who had managed to reach Stanleyville safely. Some of them, as Thomas Kanza recorded, reached there after 'most hair-raising adventures'. The pragmatic General Lundula, who had been jailed for two months and was released in November, had disguised himself as a woman to get out of Leopoldville. Pierre Mulele and Rémy Mwamba, members of Lumumba's escort, spent days and nights in the bush. Other ministers, including Anicet Kashamura, Joseph Lutula and Christophe Gbenye, reached Stanleyville without mishap. Kanza himself fled to Guinea, where he sought asylum and was treated as a minister officially representing Lumumba's government.[4] Mulele went on to Cairo to serve as Gizenga's representative.

Barthélemy Mujanay and Joseph Mbuyi did not make it to Stanleyville. They were separated from the convoy and murdered in Kasai; Mbuyi's body was cut into pieces. Maurice Mpolo and Joseph Okito were prisoners in Thysville with Lumumba.

The proclamation of Gizenga's provisional government was followed by a declaration that if Lumumba was not released within forty-eight hours, all Belgians would be arrested and some killed. This was then reduced to twenty-four hours, triggering a panic among Belgians in the region. Dayal feared an outbreak of civil war and, after swift consultation with Hammarskjöld, intervened to advise the repatriation of Europeans in Orientale province. Western envoys agreed, despite their concern about a huge economic loss to foreign firms. The crisis was over.

The official proclamation of the Free Republic of the Congo was welcomed enthusiastically by Nkrumah, Nasser and the Soviet bloc, who regarded it as the only legitimate government. But the US was appalled. A CIA document described Gizenga as 'a shifty and somewhat taciturn person, an extremist', who was leading a 'red-tinged (if not Communist) regime'. It warned of his association with Andrée Blouin, 'a mulatto West African woman . . . who was present in Léopoldville and had much influence during the Lumumba regime, [who] was reportedly his mistress until forced to leave the Congo Republic'.[5]

In the midst of these dramatic developments, an American fact-finding tour of African countries—an initiative of the Senate Foreign Relations Committee—arrived in Leopoldville. The tour included Edward M Kennedy, the younger brother of President-elect John F Kennedy. The tour was headed by Senator Frank Church of Idaho, the Democrat who in 1975 would chair the Senate Select Committee investigating American intelligence.

Senator Church was accompanied by his wife, Bethine Church, who was appalled by Clare Timberlake, whom she described as 'an absolute case'. He and Mrs Timberlake, she complained, 'wanted us to think that everything was going along just as normally as could be, despite the UN troops. He insisted we take a shopping trip, as if we were in the middle of Paris, although we had to have an escort'. Very few people were in the marketplace, she added, 'and you could tell things were amiss'. The Churches compared Timberlake most unfavourably with Rajeshwar Dayal—'Frank and I liked him much better than our ambassador in Leopoldville'.[6]

On a sightseeing tour of the area around Leopoldville, which included Lovanium University, Frank Church was surprised to come across the TRICO: 'we found ourselves inspecting an atomic reactor!'[7]

* * *

ON 20 DECEMBER, THE Leopoldville government launched an economic blockade against Orientale province along the Congo River. The Stanleyville government of Gizenga immediately sent out a call to its allies for food and medical supplies, to which Nkrumah and Nasser responded supportively. However, the logistics involved in providing this assistance were considerable. The ideal method would be to send supplies via Sudan, but Khartoum was concerned with maintaining cordial relations with the US.

The Central Intelligence Bulletin expressed suspicions that the 'USSR may be preparing to supply material aid to [the] Gizenga group'.[8] This was correct. But for the Soviet Union, too, logistics were a huge challenge. Nasser suggested dropping aid into the Congo by parachute.[9]

Thomas Kanza returned to New York to join his delegation at the UN. 'We were allowed to act', he recorded later, 'as the official representatives of the Stanleyville government, which was recognized by something like a third of the UN member states'. They received financial help from the governments that supported Lumumba and also via Mulele in Cairo. Despite the fact that Kasavubu had been accredited by the UN Credentials Committee, Kanza's delegation was much sought after by American groups 'of all political shades, anxious to learn about the Congo'. Kanza was especially appreciative of the moral support of Eleanor Roosevelt, the influential widow of President Franklin D Roosevelt. The State Department, however, was none too pleased by the presence at the UN of Kanza's delegation.[10]

Nkrumah was increasingly concerned that the UN peacekeeping force in the Congo was being manipulated by the big powers, against the interests of the Congolese people and of Africa as a whole. The best way to deal with this problem, he thought, was to set up an African High Command, with a military planning headquarters in Africa.[11] In December, he set about selling his idea to the other leaders of independent African states, including Nasser, Touré, President Modiba Keita of Mali, Emperor Haile Selassie of Ethiopia, President William Tubman of Liberia, President Habib Bourguiba of Tunisia, President Aboud of Sudan, King Mohammed V of Morocco and King Idris of Libya. He invited them to send their nation's military experts to Accra for joint planning. If this was not possible, he said, he was prepared to send Ghanaian military experts to Cairo for the same purpose.

At the All African People's Conference in Accra, held two years earlier, Nkrumah had energetically supported the pathway of Gandhian nonviolence in order to achieve freedom. No longer. He now shared the view, expressed so eloquently at the conference by Frantz Fanon, that when attacked with violence, it was necessary to retaliate. This was the only way forward to attain national independence and freedom for the people of Africa.

It was essential, Nkrumah argued, 'to nip in the bud the kind of evil being perpetrated by the Colonialists, Imperialists and their Agents in the Congo'.[12]

*　*　*

By 'Agents', Nkrumah most likely meant Mobutu and other politicians acting in partnership with the US. But there were other types of agents in the Congo, too, inserted by the CIA—not only men operating under the cover of diplomatic status, like Devlin and Doyle, or under nonofficial cover, like Imbrey, but third-country agents like QJWIN.

A new third-country agent arrived the day before Lumumba was taken to Thysville: David Tzitzichvili. He had already worked for the CIA, participating in preparations for a mission in the REDSOX program, which targeted the Soviet Union. The mission was eventually cancelled, and the agency was planning to resettle Tzitzichvili, possibly in Mexico. But on 19 September 1960, two members of the CIA Africa Division met with him to discuss 'an operational assignment in Africa Division'. In connection with this assignment, he was to be trained in 'demolition, small arms and medical immunization'.[13]

Tzitzichvili was a stateless man of forty-two who had been born in Georgia, USSR. He moved to Western Europe as a small child, living in Paris from 1922 until the outbreak of World War II. He served in the French Foreign Legion and volunteered in 1942 for work in Germany, where he spent time in German prisons and concentration camps, after being arrested for forgery. He was liberated by the US Army in 1945 and returned to Paris, where he robbed a bank of a large sum of money, for which he received a prison sentence; he was released five years later for good behaviour. Standing five feet six, he was of slight build, with a long face, long nose, dark brown hair that was balding in front and a 'swarthy complexion'. He was 'extremely agile and in perfect health'.[14]

His CIA handlers noted that he spoke native French and fluent Georgian, German and English. He had skills that were identified as useful. 'He has a schooling and experience in mechanical engineering, as a camera technician and in commercial photography'. He was characterised as a man who 'learns quickly and carries out any assignment without regard for danger'.[15]

For the REDSOX programme his cryptonym had been AEASPIC (the digraph 'AE' designating the Soviet Union). For his new mission, he was given the cryptonym of WIROGUE/1, which identified him as an agent in WIROGUE, a programme in 'the Congo and adjacent areas in order to build a covert net in support of operational activities and to provide an asset for utility support for KUBARK [CIA] personnel under official cover'.[16]

The digraph 'WI' designated the Congo. As was the case for QJWIN/1, WIROGUE/1 was frequently referred to in CIA communications simply as WIROGUE; at times this was abbreviated to W/1. The cryptonym for Lumumba was WIROAK. Mobutu was WIFLAT/3. WIFLAT operations included individuals numbered from WIFLAT/1 to WIFLAT/7.[17]

WIBOTTLE was a 'genuine third national asset on ground' who was considered for operations before the arrival of QJWIN.[18] Other CIA cryptonyms using the digraph 'WI' in the early 1960s included WIBOTHER, WICLAM (with one person 'with Belgian connections' given the cryptonym of WHITECLAM), WIFLAP, WILCO, WILDCAT, WIROOT and WIZARD.[19] The blending of the digraph into a 'pronounceable' word (like WIZARD) or phrase (like WIBOTHER), notes John Stockwell, was the work of 'the young women who assign cryptonyms'.[20] They had their work cut out for them in relation to the Congo at this time, judging by the alphabet soup of cryptonyms in the documents released under the JFK Assassination Records Collection Act in 2017–2018.

Some of the cryptonyms in CIA cables between Washington and the Congo used a digraph that was not WI. One of them was CA, as in CAJEEP/2 and CAECLIPSE; the digraph 'CA' designated covert action staff in the Directorate of Plans. YQ was used to form YQPROP and YQNECTAR; the designation of YQ is unclear.[21]

The importance of the digraph is underlined by the fact that in the initial release of Bronson Tweedy's testimony on 9 October 1975 to the Church Committee, all digraphs—for example, WI and YQ—were redacted, both in the record of the testimony itself and in the documents that were attached. In the case of the cryptonym WIBOTTLE, 'BOTTLE' was declassified, but 'WI' was blacked out. Larry Devlin's memoir, *Chief of Station, Congo*, refers to the 'ultra-secret PROP operation' under his direction on several occasions, but always without the digraph 'YQ'.[22]

In the most recent release of Tweedy's testimony, in 2018, many of these digraphs have been revealed (although not all, and much of the document is still classified).

* * *

IN OCTOBER 1960, JUST two months before Lumumba's capture, CIA headquarters informed Devlin that an agent with the cryptonym of WIROGUE/I was being prepared for a 'deep cover' assignment in the Congo. He would arrive in late November. His role would be that of a utility agent, in order to: 'a) organize and conduct a surveillance team; b) intercept packages; c) blow up bridges; and d) execute other assignments requiring positive action'. As in the case of QJWIN, his mission in Africa was not intended to be limited to Leopoldville: 'His utilization is not to be restricted to Leo. Indeed, he may be subject to call by other African stations although it is expected for him to be resident in Leo'.[23]

Africa Division described WIROGUE to Devlin in the following terms: 'He is indeed aware of the precepts of right and wrong, but if he is given an assignment which may be morally wrong in the eyes of the world, but necessary because his case officer ordered him to carry it out, then it is right, and he will dutifully undertake appropriate action for its execution without pangs of conscience. In a word, he can rationalize all actions'. A psychological study organised by the agency described him as 'like a man who wants to kill an elephant—all he wants from us is a high-powered rifle—then he feels he would be equal to the elephant'.[24]

Before sending WIROGUE to the Congo, the CIA arranged for him to undergo plastic surgery on his nose. He also started

to wear a toupee—all to ensure that Europeans travelling in the
Congo would not recognise him.[25] His cover would exploit his
skills as a camera technician and in commercial photography; he
would establish 'a small photo or repair shop, which will give him
a degree of latitude in movement and cover for covert contact'. His
mission would take place in the Congo 'and adjacent areas in order to build a covert net in support of operational activities and to
provide an asset for utility support for KU [CIA] personnel under
official cover'.[26]

WIROGUE, like QJWIN, stayed at the Regina Hotel in Leopoldville. Neither agent knew of the other's CIA connection, although QJWIN suspected that WIROGUE was a spy of some
sort, from the first day of his arrival. He thought it was odd that
WIROGUE claimed to be Austrian and was carrying an Austrian
passport, but his German was not very good. Furthermore, he spoke
French with a Parisian accent, and his English was only fair, even
though he said he had spent a number of years in the US. QJWIN
reported on his suspicions to the Leopoldville station; he said that
the other man 'smells as though he is intel business'.

On 14 December, WIROGUE approached QJWIN with an
offer of $300 per month to participate in an intelligence net and
to be a member of an 'executions squad'.[27] When QJWIN said he
wasn't interested, WIROGUE added that there would be bonuses
for 'special jobs'. Eventually, WIROGUE told QJWIN that he
worked for 'P.B.PRIME SERVICE'—that is, the CIA. He said
he could get Polaroid cameras into the country via the diplomatic
pouch. To impress on QJWIN the veracity of what he was saying,
WIROGUE telephoned 'an Embassy' in the presence of QJWIN
and made some appointments. He said he met his contact sometimes at the central post office—'so if he, QJWIN, ever happened
to see him there talking to someone, just pretend not to know him'.

WIROGUE, who was keenly interested in cars, told QJWIN
that he had purchased three cars since his arrival in Leopoldville—
a Chrysler, a Citroen and a Triumph. He told QJWIN that he had
sold the Citroen, but it was still parked near their hotel.[28]

By approaching QJWIN in this way, without checking first with the Leopoldville station, WIROGUE was grossly exceeding his instructions.[29] QJWIN reported on the bizarre episode to the station, and when the news reached headquarters they were greatly concerned—at the evident freewheeling of WIROGUE, his lack of security, his inability to handle finances and his failure to follow instructions. Furthermore, he was revealing a flamboyant side that was disturbing.

When the Church Committee investigated WIROGUE's role in the Congo, they found it impossible to identify its exact nature. Burt Wides, an advocate who was chief of the investigations of the CIA for the Church Committee, pressed as hard as he could. He was especially concerned about one particular aspect of the documentation on WIROGUE—that he had received 'inoculation training' before going to the Congo: 'Mr. Wides then harked back to the "inoculation training"'. The reason for his concern, explained Wides, was that he had seen 'sworn statements that the use of biological warfare was contemplated in the Congo and wanted to know if WIROGUE was trained in these techniques'.[30] Wides was unable to obtain any clarification on the matter.

These 'sworn statements' about a plan to use biological warfare in the Congo are not listed in any catalogue of US official documents; they cannot be found. Possibly they were in the set of MKDelta records—relating to the use overseas of MKUltra toxins—that was wholly destroyed.

A memorandum of a meeting of the National Security Council in early October 1960 records an intriguing statement by Allen Dulles: 'Moreover, the water supply of Leopoldville may soon be contaminated'.[31] This may have been simply an expression of concern about the water at a time of great upheaval. But it is possible—given the 'sworn statements' seen by Wides—that it was a reference to a plan to weaponise the city's water supply as an act of biological warfare. The deliberate poisoning of a water supply as an act of sabotage has many precedents in history.[32] In the case of the Congo in the 1960s, the CIA may have developed such a plan as a contingency against their possible failure to neutralise Lumumba and his influence.

Mr Wides's questioning about 'inoculation training' is likely a reference to the instruction that WIROGUE was given in 'medical immunization' before going to the Congo. This training was not limited to the Congo mission; indeed, the CIA planned to use WIROGUE elsewhere in Africa: 'His utilization is not to be restricted to Leopoldville. Indeed he may be subject to call by other African stations although it is expected for him to be resident in Leopoldville'. It is not possible to establish what the agency anticipated regarding 'other African stations'.[33]

* * *

ON CHRISTMAS DAY 1960, Gizenga's army, led by General Lundula, marched south to Kivu, a province adjacent to Katanga. There they joined with dissident members of the ANC and took control of the province. The provincial president, who sided with Mobutu's regime, was taken prisoner, and Anicet Kashamura—who was himself from Kivu and popular there—took his place in the capital, Bukavu.

This put Stanleyville in a powerful position—a serious threat to the Leopoldville government of Kasavubu and to the seceded province of Katanga. Justin Bomboko, who was the chairman of the College of Commissioners and also served as its foreign minister, met with NATO ambassadors in Paris to discuss the situation. He requested money and military equipment to remove what was described as the 'cancer' of Stanleyville, 'metastasizing' across the Congo.[34]

At the end of December, the CIA was in discussions with the State Department to develop a strategy to eradicate this 'cancer'. Ambassador Timberlake had presented options, but they were perceived as muddled. He advocated a political settlement, but at the same time was asking for assistance to support a military campaign against Gizenga. In any case, State Department officials were hesitant about the prospect of military action, on the grounds that it would trigger a conflict with UN troops and force the UN to fight on Gizenga's side. As well, the Belgians would be likely to get involved in such a campaign, which could 'turn [the] entire Afro Asian world violently against Kasavubu-Mobutu'.

The State Department sent queries to Timberlake on 30 December. He responded with a message of reassurance: a clash between UN troops and Mobutu's forces was unlikely, and Belgium would exercise maximum discretion. The communications between the ambassador and the State Department were transmitted through CIA channels.[35]

The next day, Tweedy cabled clear instructions to Devlin: he should 'advise Congolese we prepared in principle to support financially their efforts to topple Gizenga regime'. The cable added that the Africa Division would prefer to avoid full-scale fighting and bloodshed, but wanted to see a show of force to produce the desired political end. They asked for an indication of the 'arithmetic' regarding the financial support that would be required by the Leopoldville government. Tweedy emphasised the need to minimise the risk of any leak about US involvement in the planned military campaign.[36]

He concluded by saying that the State Department was sending a parallel cable via its own channels. The message of this cable— sent to Timberlake by Livingston Merchant, the undersecretary of state for political affairs—was substantially the same as the one sent by the agency to Devlin, but with less detail; it gave support for military action, but in a weaker and more qualified way. It expressed a wish that the 'Gizenga regime can be overthrown or neutralized by political means backed by economic pressure'.[37]

The US-backed military operation began on New Year's Day. Mobutu sent the Sûreté's Pongo to reoccupy Kivu with troops from Leopoldville. To do this, Pongo used an airport in Ruanda-Urundi, a neighbouring territory ruled by Belgium (which became the two separate states of Rwanda and Burundi after independence in 1962). This move was met with international condemnation.

In any case, Pongo's attack on Kivu failed, and he was taken prisoner. He sent numerous messages to Leopoldville, pleading to be exchanged for Lumumba, but they went unheeded. Meanwhile, General Lundula's men had joined forces with the Baluba people—who were enemies of Tshombe—in northern Katanga; together they occupied Manono, the largest town in the region. Other Lumumbist troops moved into the north of Equateur province, where there was considerable support for the Stanleyville government.[38]

Thus far, the American strategy to topple the Lumumbist government in Stanleyville was failing dismally. Far from being defeated and diminished, Gizenga—in his role as the deputy of the democratically elected prime minister—was gaining ground and influence across large parts of the Congo.

Significant areas of the Congo were now outside the control of Leopoldville: the territory supporting Gizenga, Katanga under Tshombe and South Kasai under Kalonji. No more than one-third of the country, noted Dayal, remained loyal to the Kasavubu regime.[39]

On the same day that Gizenga's forces marched south to Kivu—25 December—the presidents of Ghana, Guinea and Mali announced a political union, following a two-day meeting in Conakry. The Central Intelligence Bulletin noted the development shortly afterward. But the bulletin did not regard it as a serious threat, on the grounds that a genuine union was unlikely. A staff memorandum prepared in early February by the Office of National Estimates at the CIA took the same view, noting that the three nations had separate currencies and different colonial histories. The leaders of all three, it added, were 'unwilling to sacrifice their power in a real union, disagreeing on foreign policy initiatives, and are basically suspicious of one another's political ambitions'. The Ghana-Guinea-Mali union, it argued, 'remains a paper amalgam'.[40]

But the authors of the CIA memorandum had failed to understand the basis of the union: the shared determination, against all odds, to build at last a future of unity, peace and prosperity in Africa, free of imperial and colonial occupation and exploitation. This determination was the hallmark of a message written from the Thysville army camp by Patrice Lumumba to his wife, Pauline:

We are not alone. Africa, Asia and the free liberated people from all corners of the world will always be found at the side of the millions of Congolese who will not abandon the struggle until the day when there are no longer any colonialists and their mercenaries in our country.

As to my children whom I leave and whom I may never see again, I should like them to be told that it is for them, as it is for every Congolese, to accomplish the sacred task of reconstructing our independence and our sovereignty: for without dignity there is no liberty, without justice there is no dignity, and without independence there are no free men.

Then Lumumba expressed his bitter disappointment in 'certain high officials of the United Nations':

But what we wished for our country, its right to an honorable life, to unstained dignity, to independence without restrictions, was never desired by the Belgian imperialists and the Western allies, who found direct and indirect support, both deliberate and unintentional, amongst certain high officials of the United Nations, that organization in which we placed all our trust when we called on its assistance.

Lumumba ended his letter with a call for hope:

Do not weep for me, my dear wife. I know that my country, which is suffering so much, will know how to defend its independence and its liberty.

'Long live the Congo! Long live Africa!'[41]

30

Baking a Snake

W HILE SENIOR OFFICIALS IN WASHINGTON were developing plans to topple Gizenga, the leaders of neutralist countries in Africa were preparing for a meeting, called at short notice, to find a way to support the Lumumbist government-in-exile. Known as the Casablanca Conference, it met between 3 and 9 January 1961 in the Moroccan city after which it was named.

The chair was King Mohammed V of Morocco, who had successfully led that nation's struggle for freedom against French colonisation. He was respected worldwide for the stand he had taken against the Nazis and Vichy France during World War II, when he refused to allow Moroccan Jews to be sent to concentration camps. 'I absolutely do not approve of the new anti-Semitic laws and I refuse to associate myself with a measure I disagree with', he said. 'I reiterate as I did in the past that the Jews are under my protection and I reject any distinction that should be made amongst my people'.[1]

President Nasser, the leader of the United Arab Republic, sailed to Morocco on his yacht, via the coasts of Libya, Tunisia and Algeria. He was welcomed with visible pleasure by King Mohammed and by huge crowds at the dock. When President Nkrumah arrived on a Ghana Airways plane, his face broke into a broad smile when he saw the king. They shook hands firmly.

Ferhat Abbas, the prime minister of the provisional government of the Algerian Republic, flew to Morocco from its current base in Tunisia. This was a critical time for the National Liberation Front (FLN) as it was just days before De Gaulle's referendum on the self-determination of Algeria, scheduled for 8 January (which was approved by 75 per cent of the populations of both Algeria and France). Abbas was greeted at the landing field by tumultuous crowds, many of them waving Algerian flags in a vigorous show of support.[2]

Also at the Casablanca Conference were the presidents of Guinea and Mali, the foreign minister of Libya, and the foreign minister of Ceylon (Sri Lanka). Ceylon was one of several nations in Asia to be invited because it had a UN contingent in the Congo and supported its legitimate government.

The nations represented at the conference, subsequently known as the Casablanca Group of Powers, were neutralist and anticolonial. This distinguished them from the Brazzaville Group—twelve former French territories (Congo Brazzaville, Ivory Coast, Senegal, Mauritania, Upper Volta, Niger, Dahomey, Chad, Gabon, the Central African Republic, Cameroun and Madagascar) that had formed a union in October 1960 and met in Brazzaville in December. Essentially conservative, their approach was to favour close cooperation with France and the West.[3]

The existence of two rival groups was a far cry from the Pan-Africanism that had imbued recent conferences in Africa, starting with the All African People's Conference in Accra, two years before. The spirit of inclusion—which envisioned that all the people of Africa would come together—had fractured.

But Nkrumah was undeterred. For him, the unity of Africa remained the only vision that would secure the autonomy of individual African nations.

* * *

ALL THE STATES REPRESENTED at Casablanca wanted to see the transfer of their troops in ONUC to Gizenga—except for Nkrumah, who pushed for a moderate approach. He advocated continuing to work with the UN, especially at a time when the UN Conciliation Commission was starting its work. The commission members arrived in the Congo on 5 January 1961; they planned to meet with all the political leaders of the Congo, including Lumumba, and to make arrangements for a Round Table. An encouraging sign was that Kasavubu had proposed to hold a round-table conference later in the month.

The Casablanca leaders agreed to withdraw their troops from the UN command unless Lumumba's legitimate government and the Congolese Parliament were restored immediately. In addition, they demanded the disarming of Mobutu's army and the expulsion of Belgians from the Congo. They hoped to put pressure on Sudan to open up transit rights to the eastern provinces of the Congo, in order to break the blockade on Orientale province and to enable the Soviets to send in supplies. But this would be problematic, given heavy American pressure on Sudan.[4]

An 'African Charter of Casablanca' was agreed on, setting out the delegates' shared vision for the future of Africa. In addition to matters relating to the Congo, the delegates agreed to continue to impose transport bans and boycotts on South Africa, and to oppose the French testing of atomic bombs in the Sahara. In the judgement of a newsreel covering the conference, it was a call for an African NATO to consolidate liberty in the continent.[5]

After five days of intense discussion, Nkrumah gave the closing speech. 'I can see no security for African states', he urged with energy, 'unless African leaders, like ourselves, have realized beyond all doubt that salvation for Africa lies in unity . . . for in unity lies strength, and as I see it, African states must unite or sell themselves out to imperialist and colonialist exploiters for a mess of pottage, or disintegrate individually'.[6]

Rajeshwar Dayal welcomed the charter. The fact that all the Casablanca powers had contributed troops to the UN forces in the Congo, he believed, gave their recommendations authority.

The challenges facing the Congo and Africa generally were immense. But despite this, the Casablanca Conference ended on a note of hope. For in just one and a half weeks, on 20 January, John F Kennedy, who had spoken so clearly in support of the self-determination of colonial states, would take office as president of the USA. The Casablanca powers hoped that Kennedy's presidency would save Lumumba from death—and might help to solve the political crisis in the Congo. Officials in the UN secretariat took a similar view. They hoped, Dayal wrote later, for 'a holding operation until the new American president took over, when we might be able to reverse the tide'.[7]

But as Sean Kelly notes in *America's Tyrant*, the timing of Kennedy's inauguration had no doubt occurred to Lumumba's opponents as well.[8]

* * *

LARRY DEVLIN WAS GROWING increasingly apprehensive that Lumumba might return to power—a concern, he informed Washington, that was shared by the Leopoldville government. A crisis was brewing, fuelled by the anger of the Congolese army and police over their low pay.

Devlin asked his superiors in Washington to consider an urgent response to the crisis. 'Station and embassy', he reported, 'believe present government may fall within few days. Result would almost certainly be chaos and return [of Lumumba] to power'. The reopening of the Congolese Parliament—which was a specific demand of the Casablanca group—was not an acceptable strategy because of the popularity of Lumumba: 'The combination of [Lumumba's] powers as demagogue, his able use of goon squads and propaganda and spirit of defeat within [government] coalition which would increase rapidly under such conditions would almost certainly insure [Lumumba] victory in parliament [redacted]'. He added, 'Refusal take drastic steps at this time will lead to defeat of [United States] policy in Congo'.[9]

Then the situation exploded: a mutiny broke out at Camp Hardy in Thysville, where Lumumba was incarcerated. It was the second mutiny at the garrison since independence: in July, soldiers had demanded to be paid immediately. Their second protest took on an added dimension; many were angry that Lumumba was a prisoner and wanted him to be set free.[10]

Mobutu, Kasavubu, Justin Bomboko and Victor Nendaka flew urgently to Thysville to calm things down and to offer a raise in pay. When they arrived, many of the prisoners rioted. A soldier opened the door to Lumumba's cell and said he was now a free man. But Lumumba remained, in case it was a trap. 'And he was right to do so', noted his friend Jean Van Lierde, 'for European agents, adopting a cruel trick that had taken many innocent lives in Algeria, had set things up so that there would be an "attempted escape" during which Lumumba would be shot'.[11]

The Mobutu regime decided to move Lumumba out of Thysville as soon as possible. On 14 January, less than a week before Kennedy's inauguration, Devlin was told that Lumumba would be transferred from Thysville to a prison in Bakwanga (now Mbuji-Mayi), the capital of South Kasai. Bakwanga was the third-largest city of the Congo and the base of Albert Kalonji, who had declared the secession of South Kasai on 8 August 1960. Kalonji led MNC-K, the wing of the MNC that had broken away from Lumumba's faction in 1959. Howard Imbrey, the CIA agent under nonofficial cover who had been passing out money to selected Congolese politicians, had described Kalonji as one of 'my people'. Kalonji hated Lumumba with a passion.

On the morning of 17 January 1961, Victor Nendaka, chief of the Sûreté, flew to Thysville to extract Lumumba from the camp. He told Lumumba, Mpolo and Okito that a coup d'état was about to take place in Leopoldville and offered to escort them to the city to take power. According to a UN report in 1961, which looked into the circumstances of this episode, Lumumba agreed to leave Thysville and go to the airfield at Lukala, where 'he was apparently put on a small plane belonging to the Belgian company Air-Brousse'. Mpolo and Okito went with him.[12]

'It has been difficult, and indeed almost impossible', observed the UN report, 'to obtain precise information regarding the circumstances in which the prisoners left the garrison at Thysville'.[13] It appears, however, that after a flight to the airport of Moanda, a small town on the Atlantic coast, the three men were told the truth: that they were still captives and were being transferred to another prison. They were tied up and forced aboard an Air Congo DC-4. The Belgian pilot—Piet Van der Meersch—had been expecting to fly to Bakwanga, the capital of Kalonji's South Kasai. But just before departure, he was ordered to take the prisoners to Elisabethville, Katanga, eleven hundred miles away.

There are serious doubts about this account. Since 4 January, Mobutu's Belgian advisor Colonel Louis Marlière and a Belgian intelligence officer named Andre Lahaye had agreed that Lumumba should be transferred out of Thysville. They had been in talks with Katanga's leader, Moise Tshombe, to get him to agree to accept Lumumba.[14] Katanga was likely the destination all along.

* * *

THROUGHOUT THE LONG FLIGHT to Elisabethville, Lumumba, Mpolo and Okito were tied together and beaten. The actions of the soldiers were so violent as to make the aircraft unstable. Van der Meersch and the crew—Jean-Louis Drugmand, Robert Fau and Jack Dixon—tried to calm the soldiers down. They were appalled by what they saw, and the radioman vomited; they returned to the cockpit and locked the door.

At 4.45 in the afternoon, the aircraft arrived at Luano, Elisabethville's airport. It taxied directly to the hangars of the Katangese air force, which were separate from the UN area of the airport. Waiting for the arrival of the plane were fifty police and two platoons of the military police of the Katangan army, another sixty men. The three victims were dragged roughly into a military van on the orders of Captain Julien Gat, the head of the military police.[15]

The jeep drove at high speed to a nearby bungalow, which had recently been built for a Belgian farmer, Lucien Brouwez, and his wife, who were planning to move into it shortly. The Villa Brouwez was on a side road off the airport highway, not far from Elisabethville; the Sabena Guest House, owned by the Belgian airline, was close by. The villa had been 'requisitioned' by the Katanga government as a place to take the prisoners. Waiting in the house for the prisoners were Belgian officers and some of Tshombe's ministers, including Godefroid Munongo, the cruel and sinister minister for the interior and the strongman of the secessionist regime.

Then began the torture of thirty-five-year-old Patrice Lumumba, thirty-three-year-old Maurice Mpolo and Joseph Okito, in his early fifties. It continued unabated.

At 8.00 pm, Tshombe arrived at the house, coming directly from a ministerial conference; with him was Frans Verscheure, the

Belgian police commissioner, who—almost exactly a year earlier—had taken Lumumba to the jail in Jadotville. The ministers left, and at about 8.30, Verscheure forced the three prisoners into the backseat of a car.

The prisoners were driven to a remote spot thirty miles away, on a dirt track off the road to Jadotville, the town closest to Shinkolobwe. There, they were forced out of the car. In the darkness of the early night, illuminated by the lights of military vehicles, they were executed. In turn, they were led to a tree, where they faced a firing squad of two soldiers and two policemen. Each man was riddled with bullets: first Okito, then Mpolo, finally Lumumba. The bodies were rolled into a pit and covered with dirt. When the murderers left the scene, an arm was still visible above the ground.

Lumumba was killed between 9.40 and 9.43 pm, within five hours of his enforced arrival in Katanga.

Much of what is reported about this terrible episode is based on the recollections of the Belgians involved. Gerard and Kuklick in *Death in the Congo* express regret that these recollections 'furnish almost our entire knowledge of Lumumba's demise'. Every detailed narrative, they say, 'makes unsubstantiated assumptions'. The only documentary evidence is a date book kept by Verscheure, which noted, '9.43. L. dead'.[16]

* * *

THE NEXT DAY, THE bodies were exhumed by a group of men led by Gerard Soete, the adviser to the chief commissioner of the Katangan police. They were buried again, about 150 miles away. On 26 January, Soete exhumed the bodies once more, this time with a plan to obliterate them. He and an assistant spent two days cutting up the bodies with a hacksaw and inserting the pieces of flesh into sulphuric acid, obtained from Union Minière, in order to dissolve them. 'We did things an animal would not do', said Soete later.[17] In an interview on German television in 2000, he felt no compunction in displaying two teeth, which he claimed to have saved from Lumumba's body.[18]

'Eventually', wrote John Stockwell in an open letter on 10 April 1977 to the director of the CIA, 'we learned Lumumba was killed, not by our poisons, but beaten to death, apparently by men who were loyal to men who had Agency cryptonyms and received Agency salaries'.[19] Stockwell linked a specific CIA official with the death of Lumumba. 'A man I felt I understood, despite our differences', he wrote, 'was an officer who had addressed my training class at the "Farm" [a clandestine CIA training facility near Williamsburg, Virginia] in 1965. Afterwards, he had opened up a surprisingly long way, referring to an adventure in Lubumbashi [as the former Elisabethville is called today], driving about town after curfew with Patrice Lumumba's body in the trunk of his car, trying to decide what to do with it'.

Five years later, in 1970, Stockwell found this officer in an Asian post, as the CIA chief of station, 'sitting at a desk mounted on a platform a foot higher than the rest of the room. His chair was a tall, straight-backed Victorian antique, behind it was a background of flags and drapes. He was glisteningly bald, and stared down at me through half-closed, puffy eyes, as I tried to brief him about my mission'. In 1974, Stockwell found him again, in a European station, 'still playing at "Goldfinger" in his antique chair, the same one as far as I could tell. We dined in the palatial "safehouse" apartment which the US taxpayer maintained for him in the city. (His other home was a residence thirty miles away.) Twice during dinner he went to the tiled lavatory where he spent fifteen minutes scrubbing and drying his hands, cleaning his fingernails, and staring at himself in the mirror'.[20]

Stockwell does not identify this individual. 'I have no desire', he wrote in the introduction to *In Search of Enemies*, 'to expose or hurt individuals'. He added, 'Since my resignation, I have revealed no covert CIA employee or agent's name'.[21]

After the murder, according to Gerard and Kuklick, rumours spread in the CIA that Devlin had driven Lumumba's body around Elisabethville in the trunk of a car.[22] To some extent, Devlin's history matches Stockwell's account of the CIA officer who played at 'Goldfinger'. First, Devlin was based in the US for much of 1965, until the month of July, so he could have addressed the training class at the 'Farm' to which Stockwell refers. Second, Devlin was chief of station in Laos between 1967 and 1971, which fits the chronology set out by Stockwell. But he was not 'glisteningly bald' at any time in his life. Nor does the reference to the European station in 1974 fit, since Devlin was based in Washington as head of the CIA's Africa Division between 1971 and 1974, when he retired from the CIA.

David Doyle could not have been the CIA officer described by Stockwell, since photographs show he had a full head of hair late into his life. Gerard and Kuklick comment that 'the hearsay about the murders usually contained a kernel of truth, if not the entire story'. They wonder if Gerard Soete worked for the CIA.[23] It is possible that Soete was working as a local asset for Doyle. However, it is unlikely that Soete, a Belgian policeman, was the CIA officer referred to by Stockwell who gave a talk at the 'Farm'.

* * *

'THE FIRST HARD INFORMATION' about Lumumba's death, wrote Devlin, 'came to me from the CIA officer in Elisabethville'. Two days after Lumumba was flown to Katanga, the CIA base chief in Elisabethville, David Doyle, sent an unusual message to Leopold-ville, copied to headquarters in Washington: 'Thanks for Patrice. If we had known he was coming we would have baked a snake'. The cable stated that the base's sources had provided 'no advance word whatsoever' of Lumumba's flight to Katanga.[24]

The report of the Church Committee referred to this cable as an indication that the CIA had no knowledge of the Mobutu regime's decision to transfer Lumumba from Thysville into the hands of his enemies. The cable showed, it said, that the base did not expect Lumumba's arrival.[25] This would be consistent with the repeated account that the place to which the three victims were taken was changed at the last minute—from Bakwanga to Elisabethville.

But the words 'if we had known he was coming' cannot be regarded as any kind of proof that the base did not expect Lu-mumba's arrival in Elisabethville. They are a playful reference to an immensely popular American song from the 1950s—'If I Knew You Were Comin' I'd've Baked a Cake'—and could have been a meaningless attempt at a clever comment on events. Furthermore, the fact that the cable gives thanks for the delivery of Lumumba is a sign that Doyle welcomed his arrival in Katanga; he expressed no outrage at the fact that Lumumba, Mpolo and Okito had visible signs of being very badly beaten.

There is an outlying possibility that 'snake' refers in some way to Captain Clement, the Green Beret pilot who was sent to the Congo the summer before on a mission to rescue Americans and whose nickname was 'Snake'. According to Jack Lawson in *The Slaver's Wheel*, Clement left the Congo at the end of July 1960, but he may have stayed secretly or returned.

On 7 February, the CIA in Washington circulated to relevant departments a report on the death of the three men. 'A Belgian officer of Flemish origin', it noted, 'executed Lumumba with a burst of submachine gun fire at 2300Z 17 Jan'. It added a gruesome note: 'An ear was severed from Lumumba's head and sent to Albert Kalonji, President of South Kasai'.[26] Kalonji, who loathed Lumumba, was presumably delighted by this proof of his death.

On 10 February, the Elisabethville base cabled headquarters that 'Lumumba fate is best kept secret in Katanga'.[27] The cable set out different versions from several sources about Lumumba's death. Devlin testified to the Church Committee that the cable confirmed his recollection that the CIA 'did not have any hard information' about Lumumba's fate after his arrival in Katanga. He added, 'At least to my recollection we did not. We may have obtained it later but at the time we did not—which would I think substantiate the fact that we did not participate in it nor did we have an agent doing it for us what have you'.[28]

In his own testimony, Tweedy denied that the CIA had a role in the events leading up to Lumumba's death. Tweedy's words were unqualified: 'none whatsoever'. He added that 'the fate of Lumumba in the end was purely an African event'.[29]

O'Donnell, too, was clear that the CIA was not involved, according to a quotation from his testimony in the Church Committee's report: 'CIA had absolutely no connection, to my certain knowledge, with the death of Patrice Lumumba'.[30] O'Donnell's testimony is missing, but the 'Summary of Expected Testomony [sic] of Justin O'Donnell' that was declassified in April 2018 suggests that

O'Donnell was rather more cautious at another stage of the hearings. 'He does not *know* if we had anything to do with Lumumba's actual death', notes the summary, 'but does not think we did'.[31]

QJWIN, O'Donnell's 'alter ego', left the Congo on 21 December 1960, and O'Donnell stayed on. According to the summary of his expected testimony, he was in the Congo for three months, which suggests that he departed in early January.[32] But an early version of the Church Committee's report, which was also declassified in April 2018, reveals that O'Donnell stayed until Lumumba's death, about three and a half months after his arrival. This early draft states, 'O'Donnell said he left the Congo around the time of Lumumba's death in Katanga at the hands of Congolese authorities'.[33] This information was removed from the report before its finalisation.

The departure of O'Donnell, who was sent to the Congo to oversee the elimination of Lumumba, 'around the time of Lumumba's death', which occurred on 17 January 1961, is an important finding. O'Donnell may have been working on this CIA operation right up to the death.

The early draft of the Church Committee report also reveals that Arnold Silver, the chief of station in Luxembourg who 'lent' QJWIN to O'Donnell, was in the Congo in the period leading up to Lumumba's death, on 'a counter-intelligence mission'. It quotes a statement from Devlin's testimony that Silver arrived during Devlin's tenure, but that 'they did not discuss the plan to assassinate Lumumba'; this indicates that he came during the period before the murder. Silver became involved in early 1961 with William Harvey in discussions regarding the plan to develop a 'standby assassination capability'. QJWIN, who was managed by Silver, was used as part of this programme.[34]

Bronson Tweedy, head of the Africa Division, also apparently arrived in the Congo during this period. Although none of the Church Committee records reveal that Tweedy visited the Congo, the memoirs of both Larry Devlin and David Doyle say that he did. According to Devlin, Tweedy 'was making a tour of his African parish'; he collected him from the airport not long after the Louis Armstrong concert.[35] Doyle recorded that Tweedy 'came to visit the Katanga, an occasion that was both useful professionally and a pleasure socially'.[36]

* * *

IN HIS MEMOIR, DEVLIN stated that on 13 January 1961, Mobutu, Nendaka, Kasavubu and several others in the Binza group went to Thysville. But he himself, he insisted, had no idea what was going on. He heard 'many rumors' about the Thysville mutiny and the subsequent removal of Lumumba, but he did not get involved.

Devlin was lying. A newly released document reveals that he sent WIROGUE to Thysville in January. The records released in 2017–2018 under the JFK Assassination Records Collection Act contain a financial report sent by Devlin in Leopoldville to the chief of the CIA's Finance Division on 27 July 1961, headlined 'Transfer of Accountability'. The report reveals that WIROGUE was ordered by Devlin to drive from Leopoldville to Thysville: 'In January 1961 WIROGUE was ordered to Thysville by the Station and was authorised $0.10 per mile for use of his personal car, therefore 312.5 miles times $0.10 equals $31.99 leaving WIROGUE a credit of U.S. $1,111.23. (See attachment)'.[37]

The distance between Camp Hardy, which is near Thysville, and Leopoldville is ninety-four miles. The details regarding the expenditure on gas are therefore consistent with the mileage involved.

But the significance of this financial report lies not in the number of miles or the cost of the gas. Rather, it lies in two key points: first, that WIROGUE was ordered to go to Thysville when Lumumba was imprisoned there; and second, that he was ordered to do so by Devlin, the CIA chief of station. These points expose Devlin's claim—to have had no involvement whatsoever in the brutal treatment and rendition of Lumumba—as highly likely to be deliberate misinformation.

The financial report refers to an attachment, which is listed at the bottom of the report as 'Thysville certification by Guthman [Devlin's cryptonym], h/w'. The attachment was not released with the report. (There are two copies of this financial report in the set of JFK Assassination Records released in 2017–2018; each has different redactions. Looking at them together, it is possible to build a full document, which refers to WIROGUE under one of his pseudonyms: Ernest C Maycrink.) The CIA was therefore involved in events at Thysville in January 1961, a fact that Devlin frequently denied.

* * *

SINCE 1961, REPEATED AND concerted efforts have been made to identify who was responsible for the deaths of Lumumba, Mpolo and Okito. The UN set up a dedicated commission in 1961, which issued a report in November of that year. 'President Kasavubu and his aides, on the one hand, and the provincial government of Katanga headed by Mr. Tshombe on the other', affirmed the report, 'should not escape responsibility for the death of Mr. Lumumba, Mr. Okito, and Mr. Mpolo'. Kasavubu and his aides, it added, had handed over Lumumba and his colleagues to the Katanga authorities 'knowing full well, in doing so, that they were throwing them into the hands of their bitterest political enemies'. In turn, the government of the province of Katanga had, by its action, contributed directly or indirectly to the murder of the prisoners.[38] Suspicions were presented about several individuals, including Carlos Huyghe.

The 1975 report of the Senate Select Committee that had been set up in the US under the chairmanship of Senator Frank Church to study governmental operations with respect to intelligence activities acquitted the CIA of any responsibility in Lumumba's death. It judged that in spite of CIA activities in late 1960 aimed at bringing about Lumumba's demise, agency representatives in the Congo were not involved in his death and had no certain information concerning his fate after his arrival in Katanga.[39]

In 1999, Ludo De Witte, a Belgian sociologist and writer, published the pathbreaking study *De Moord op Lumumba*, which appeared in English translation as *The Assassination of Lumumba* in 2001. De Witte challenged standard assumptions about Belgium's role in the Congo, setting out new and original findings in thorough detail. Unlike many earlier studies, De Witte did not flinch from uncomfortable facts that clearly pointed a finger at the Belgian government's complicity in Lumumba's death. He showed, too, that King Baudouin and his inner circle were kept informed of the plot to kill Lumumba and gave it a veiled blessing. The book was explosive, triggering a storm of controversy and debate in Belgium. And although it focussed largely on the role of Belgium, it did not exculpate the actions of the US and Britain.

As a direct consequence of De Witte's book, a Belgian parliamentary commission of inquiry was set up in 2000. Its final report, issued on 16 November 2001, confirmed De Witte's major findings.[40] The report found that 'no document nor witness' indicated that the Belgian government 'or any of its members gave the order to physically eliminate Lumumba'. Nor, it states, did it find any evidence on the part of Belgian authorities of 'premeditation to assassinate Lumumba or to have him assassinated'. However, the report said, it was 'manifestly clear that the government was unconcerned with Mr. Lumumba's physical integrity'. It acknowledged that Belgium had 'an irrefutable portion of responsibility in the events that led to the death of Lumumba'.

Responding to allegations that King Baudouin had prior knowledge of the plot to assassinate Lumumba, the commission acknowledged that the king 'did not inform the government of important facts in his possession'. Belgium, judged the report, bore a 'moral responsibility' for the assassination of Patrice Lumumba.

The inquiry also pointed a finger at the role of the USA, questioning the conclusions of the Church Committee. A study of Belgian government files, it stated, did not support the modest role claimed by CIA officials in their testimony before the Church Committee. It suggested that the Church Committee's findings were weakened by their reliance on the testimony of CIA officials. On the subject of the hunt for Lumumba after his disappearance from his residence, it added, 'Indirectly, we can equally confirm that the CIA played, in this hunt, a more important role than the Church Committee report, presented in 1975 by the American Senate, was willing to admit'.[41]

The scepticism of the Belgian parliamentary inquiry regarding America's role in the assassination is supported in numerous ways, argues Stephen Weissman in his 2002 review of the Belgian committee's report. 'The full extent of what one U.S. document calls the

"intimate" relationship between the CIA and Congolese leaders',
notes Weissman, 'was absent from the Church Committee report'.[42]

A major plank in Devlin's defence was that by the time Lumumba was sent to Thysville, the hands of the CIA were off the
whole affair; he said he consulted with Congolese authorities about
possible routes Lumumba might take to Stanleyville, but he was
'not a major assistance' in tracking him down.[43]

For this reason, the discovery of the financial report showing
that Devlin sent his third-country agent, WIROGUE, to Thysville
in January is a major development. On the one hand, it is a small
detail of expenditure; on the other, it suggests that Devlin's claims
were a tissue of lies.

* * *

AT ALMOST THE EXACT moment that Lumumba was murdered,
President Eisenhower delivered his farewell address to the American people.[44] He warned of the rise in power of the 'military-
industrial complex': the 'conjunction of an immense military
establishment and a large arms industry' that, he said, was new in
the American experience. 'We must never', he insisted, 'let the
weight of this combination endanger our liberties or democratic
processes'.

Three days later, John F Kennedy was inaugurated as the thirty-
fifth president of the USA. 'To show new states whom we welcome
to the ranks of the free', he promised, 'we pledge our word that one
form of colonial control shall not have passed away merely to be
replaced by a far more iron tyranny'. This 'iron tyranny' was communism. Kennedy sought to reach out to the newly independent
nations of the world. 'We shall not always expect to find them supporting our view', he acknowledged. 'But we shall always hope to
find them strongly supporting their own freedom'.[45]

31

Sunk Hope

Once Patrice Lumumba, Maurice Mpolo and Joseph Okito had disappeared after their arrival at Elisabethville airport, Moise Tshombe was under pressure to say where they were. He announced that they had been taken to a model prison farm, to be given medical care. Meanwhile, the UN Conciliation Commission, which had arrived in the Congo in early January, went to Elisabethville to speak with Lumumba. They made an immediate request to Tshombe to see him, which was refused, as were any formal discussions. They left for Leopoldville the following day. 'Peace Men Fail to See Lumumba' read a headline in Ghana's *Daily Graphic* on 24 January 1961.

On 10 February, Godefroid Munongo called a press conference. The prisoners, he announced, had made a large hole in a wall and escaped through it. They had apparently overpowered two guards and stolen a Ford car that had been left near the prison farm. Munongo fleshed out minute details, saying that the captives had tied up their guards with 'pieces of the curtains which were of white cotton', and had left behind 'a twisted door, a dented bumper and a broken rear-view mirror'.[1] The story was illustrated with photographs.

Three days later, Munongo summoned the press again. This time, he said that Lumumba, Mpolo and Okito were dead—that they had been killed by hostile villagers. 'I would be lying', added Munongo, 'if I said that the death of Mr Lumumba makes me sad'.[2]

Across the world, people were stunned with shock and anger at the news of the deaths; few people anywhere believed Munongo's explanation.

Although Lumumba's murderers had sought to dissolve his body with acid—to eradicate any physical mark of the man—they were unable to destroy what he meant and signified to the people of the Congo and of the world. Protests broke out on the streets of the world's cities, including Lagos, New Delhi, New York, London, Paris, Vienna, Warsaw, Moscow, Damascus and Shanghai. In Belgrade, a mob stormed the Belgian embassy. In Cairo, protesters tore down a portrait of King Baudouin inside the Belgian embassy and replaced it with one of Lumumba, then set the building on fire. Not only was the Belgian embassy attacked in a number of cities, but so were the French and American embassies and UN offices. In Cuba, Castro announced three days of mourning, and flags were flown at half staff on all public buildings. In the Soviet Union Khrushchev announced that the People's Friendship University in Moscow would be renamed Patrice Lumumba University, to honour the Congolese leader.

* * *

A FUNERAL PROCESSION MARCHED SLOWLY through the streets of the cité of Leopoldville on Wednesday 15 February, led by Pauline Opango, a widow at only twenty-eight, marching bare-breasted and barefoot in her grief, and carrying her two-year-old son, Roland. She had heard the news about her husband on the radio the night before.

Opango was accompanied on her march by women who were bare-breasted and by men with their heads bowed. Due to the culture of fear created by Mobutu's regime in the city, they carried two white flags to give the message that they were walking in peace. They walked from the Lumumba family home in the cité to ONUC headquarters in the Royal Building, where Opango spoke with Dayal for an hour; she begged him to arrange for Lumumba's body to be exhumed and sent to her for a Christian burial by his family.[3] Dayal argued strenuously with Tshombe to return the body, but the self-styled president refused, on the grounds that local customs prevented it. Of course there was no body to return.

A wake was held in Opango's grief-stricken home. The *New York Times* correspondent in Leopoldville reported that women wailed and sobbed, while men were silent, sullen and motionless under the tropical sun.

Without even the solace of a burial, Opango continued to protest the murder. At one point she was forced to take shelter in a UN refugee camp in Leopoldville with her children. Later she moved to Cairo, where the family settled down together under the protection of President Nasser.[4] She never saw for herself the letter Lumumba had written to her from prison in Thysville. 'I only read the text later in newspapers', she said sadly, decades later. 'It was a journalist who got hold of it and told me that he had given it to François [Lumumba's son from a previous relationship]. I have never seen it myself'.[5]

Gizenga recorded in his memoir the reaction in Orientale Province to Lumumba's death: 'As the assassinations of Patrice Lumumba and his companions Maurice Mpolo and Joseph Okito were announced and confirmed, the whole population of Stanleyville started making an uproar. They threatened to raid the city and cut the heads of some of the whites, if not all of them, in retaliation. Even the soldiers, in their overwhelming majority, were driven by those intentions'. Gizenga attempted to calm the people: 'Let us cry peacefully for our hero', he urged, 'and wish him a good journey to his ancestors'.[6]

Le Grand Kallé wrote a tribute to Lumumba, 'Matata Masila Na Congo', which recalled the moment in 1958 when Lumumba returned to the Congo from the All African People's Conference in Accra, bringing with him the vision of a united Africa.

The only songwriter who dared to openly condemn Lumumba's assassination was Franco Luambo Makiadi, the leader of OK Jazz. Franco composed 'Liwa Ya Emery', also known as 'Liwa Ya Lumumba':

Oh Mawa Vraiment
Oh Ndenge nini tokolela ye
Tango Ekokaki te
Ba Nationaliste balati pili.

This is really sad
How shall we mourn Lumumba

His time here was not enough
The Nationalists are in mourning.[7]

Franco 'stood up for Lumumba's followers', commented the historian Malambu Makizola, 'in a period of terror in which demonstrating your support for Lumumba could cost you your head. Franco took an enormous risk with this song, nobody dared to imitate him'.[8]

* * *

LUMUMBA'S DEATH WAS FELT 'in a very keen and personal way by Nkrumah', observed June Milne, Nkrumah's British research assistant. He had regarded the younger man 'as a son and freedomfighter, and had recognised in him exceptional ability which could be harnessed to the African revolutionary struggle'.[9]

The day after Lumumba's death was announced by the Katangan government, Nkrumah spoke over the radio to the people of Ghana with great emotion. 'Three of our brother freedom fighters', he said sorrowfully, 'have been done to death'. He blamed the UN for not protecting them, even though the world organisation had been invited to the Congo by Lumumba to preserve law and order. The US and the Western powers, he said, were culpable. 'In Ghana', he added, 'we realise the great financial stakes which some Great Powers have in the Union Minière and other industrial and commercial undertakings in the Congo'. But his faith in the possibility of African freedom and unity was undimmed: 'The colonialists and imperialists have killed them, but what they cannot do, is to kill the ideals which we still preach, and for which they sacrificed their lives. In the Africa of the future their names will live forever more'.[10]

The president's outrage was shared by Ghanaians. A large crowd invaded the US embassy in Accra, causing damage; elsewhere in the city, the UN flag was torn down. In one demonstration, women carried a large picture of Lumumba as well as posters declaring, 'Dag Hammarskjöld must be sacked at once', 'Down with Kasavubu the traitor', 'Down with Mobutu the traitor' and 'The evil that men do lives after them'.

The Ghanaian press devoted many pages to the tragedy through-out the week. On its front page, the *Daily Graphic* published a photograph of eight-year-old Patrice Lumumba and five-year-old Julienne Lumumba in Cairo with Fathia Nkrumah, who was visit-ing Egypt at the time of the terrible news. She was evidently dis-tressed and can be seen giving a hug and a kiss to young Patrice.[11]

Radio Ghana broadcast news bulletins and programmes about the tragedy through its Voice of Africa transmissions to the peo-ple of Ghana, greater Africa and the world. Meanwhile, Aloysius K Barden, director of the Bureau of African Affairs, prepared to leave for the Congo with a colleague to discuss the new situation with An-toine Gizenga and to offer additional support. The BAA published the letter Lumumba had written to his wife in the form of a pam-phlet; the letter was also reproduced in its magazine, *Voice of Africa*.[12]

The son of Maurice Mpolo, Alfred Maurice Mpolo, was taken to Ghana for safety. The records of the Bureau of African Affairs contain some receipts for the maintenance of Mpolo, who is refer-enced as a 'Freedom Fighter from Congo'. The receipts cover a sub-sistence allowance, clothing and funds to purchase French books and papers.[13]

Later that year, Denis Prosper Okito, the son of Joseph Okito, also moved to Ghana, helped by Cameron Duodu. At the time, Duodu was the editor of *Drum* and had been invited by the Ghana army to go to the Congo to cover the visit of a Ghanaian dance troupe, the Heatwaves, which the army was sending to the Congo to entertain the Ghanaian troops. One day in Luluabourg, Duodu was told that a Congolese man wanted to see him. He later recalled the episode:

I said I would see the guy, and he turned up. He was a young man of about twenty-plus. He looked a bit uneasy.

I put him at his ease and offered him a drink.

After taking one sip of the drink, he looked straight into my eyes and announced: 'I am the son of Joseph Okito!'

Goosepimples broke out all over me when I heard the name 'Joseph Okito'. . . .

There were tears in the eyes of Okito's son as he told me the sad tale of how he and members of his family had gone into hiding after his father's arrest, how they had waited for news of his fate and how they had heard, from the Katanga government, the lie that the prisoners had been brought to Katanga under guard but had 'escaped' and had been murdered by 'villagers' who had recognised them and killed them because they didn't like their politics.

'We don't believe Tshombe's government', the young Okito told me. 'But we still don't know the full truth of what happened to my father, Mr Lumumba and Mr Mpolo'.

Denis Okito asked Duodu to take a letter to President Nkrumah for him, because he needed help to care for his widowed mother and his siblings. Duodu agreed but gave him careful advice to ensure the safety of the letter: 'I asked him to write a letter but not to put Dr. Nkrumah's name on the envelope. He understood what I was saying: if I was ever searched by Congolese security agents and was found with a letter addressed to the president of Ghana on me, it would be read, and that would make matters difficult for the young Okito'.

Okito went home and wrote the letter, which he delivered to Duodu in a plain envelope. When Duodu returned to Accra, he took it not to the office of the president but to the office of the Bureau of African Affairs. There, Barden listened attentively to Duodo's explanation of what had happened and agreed to carry the letter to Nkrumah.

'I was confident', observed Duodu, 'that Okito would receive a scholarship to study abroad, or a monthly stipend, or both'.[14]

In July 1961, *Voice of Africa* published an interview with Denis Prosper Okito, in which he praised a Ghana that 'so selflessly' had 'devoted itself to the welfare of the Congo' and had offered 'technicians, health personnel and administrative officers'.[15]

* * *

ON THE DAY THE news of Lumumba's death was announced, Leonid Brezhnev, the leader of the Soviet Communist Party, was in Guinea. Nkrumah invited him to visit Accra, to discuss the situation in the Congo. The invitation was immediately accepted, and the two leaders issued a joint press release setting out their united points of view.

On 14 February 1961 the United Arab Republic recognised the Stanleyville government as the legitimate government of the Congo. The next day, Ghana, Guinea, East Germany, Yugoslavia, the Soviet Union, Czechoslovakia and the People's Republic of China followed suit. Moscow pledged 'all possible help' to the 'lawful' government of the Congo that was led by Gizenga. 'Suddenly a specter haunted Washington', notes Stephen Weissman. 'The Communists and radical Africans would support a "war of liberation" against the Central Government'.[16]

Frantz Fanon, who had been appointed the provisional Algerian government's ambassador to Ghana in March 1960, returned briefly to Accra after Lumumba's death. He was appalled by the tragedy. He had now lost—to murder—both of the special friends he had made at the All African People's Conference: Félix-Roland Moumié and Patrice Lumumba.

The Congolese leader's fault, Fanon argued in an article written in response to his death, was initially to believe in the impartiality of the UN. 'If we need outside help', he insisted, 'let us call on our friends. Our friendship with them is one born of struggles. . . . If we decide to support Gizenga, we must do so resolutely'. He added, insistently, 'Because nobody knows who the next Lumumba will be. There is a trend in Africa that is displayed by certain men. That trend can threaten imperialism and that's what's at stake. For let us never forget: Our fate is being played out in the Congo, the fate of all of us'.[17]

Fanon was distilling the lessons of the Congo into what would become *The Wretched of the Earth*, which advocated violence when necessary to achieve freedom.[18] Unlike Fanon (but like Gandhi, whom Lumumba admired deeply), Lumumba had never lost his faith in nonviolence. 'Patrice was always hoping', wrote his friend Luis López Álvarez, 'to win the day without resorting to violence'.[19] But Lumumba was killed—viciously and brutally—by the terrible violence he so opposed.

* * *

ONLY FIVE MONTHS EARLIER, in New York, Nkrumah had given a powerful speech at the UN General Assembly in support of the legitimate government of Patrice Lumumba. Then, the Congo was the main focus of interest. In February 1961, the Congo was the central issue once again but this time with newfound sorrow and bitterness. Many Americans went to UN headquarters in New York on 15 February to express their outrage to Adlai Stevenson, the new US ambassador to the UN, who was due to speak to the General Assembly.[20] Maya Angelou was one of the protesters who showed up at the UN to interrupt his speech. She wrote about the episode in *The Heart of a Woman*:

The little white man so far away leaned toward his microphone, his bald forehead shining-white. Dark-rimmed glasses stood out on the well-known face.

A scream shattered his first word. The sound was bloody and broad and piercing. In a second other voices joined it.

'Murderers'.

'Lumumba. Lumumba'.

'Killers'.

'Bigoted sons of bitches'.

The scream still rode high over the heads of astounded people who were rising, clutching each other or pushing out towards the aisle.

The houselights came on. Stevenson took off his glasses and looked to the balcony. The shock opened his mouth and made his chin drop.

The diplomats rose and filed out of the assembly hall. 'When the piercing scream stopped', wrote Angelou, 'I heard my own voice shouting, "Murderers. Killers. Assassins"'.

Angelou was shaken. She had come to protest and had not anticipated a riot. That night, she watched the evening news: 'The cameras caught black bodies hurtling out of the UN doors, and marchers chanting along 46th Street'.

Many of those mourning Lumumba held the United Nations responsible. Angelou quoted one of the protesters as saying, 'This ain't no United Nations. This is just united white folks'.[21]

There was anger at Hammarskjöld for not intervening militarily in the Congo to expel the Belgian troops and end the Katanga secession. This had been Lumumba's urgent demand, to which Hammarskjöld responded by insisting that the UN must rely on negotiation, not on force; he pointed out that he had to operate within the mandate of the resolutions passed by the Security Council. But many, including Nkrumah, believed that Hammarskjöld should have found a way to force the Belgians out.

'History proved that Lumumba's analysis that it would take force to end Katanga secession was correct', comments Herbert Weiss. 'Hammarskjöld's view that it could be done diplomatically', he adds, 'turned out to be wrong'.[22]

What is clear is that among the UN representatives in the Congo, there was a powerful strand of opposition to Lumumba that was instrumental in his fate. A significant opponent was General Alexander, the British commander of the UN Ghana contingent, who collaborated with the US embassy in Leopoldville.

Many Americans were shaken by Lumumba's death and the possibility that the US may have played a role. For the American labour activist Maida Springer, it raised questions about the very nature of her work. Asked if the assassination had affected her relations in Africa, she answered, 'Yes. To many there was the assumption that the United States was implicated in Patrice Lumumba's death. And never mind what I was saying or attempting to do with the labor unions. No, it was difficult! Couldn't explain Patrice Lumumba's death. I couldn't. . . . People smarter than I maybe explained it. I couldn't. I couldn't. I could not accept assertions of US complicity. If I had, I would have raised questions within myself about my role in Africa'.

In Springer's judgment, Lumumba 'was a good person who was challenging. As far as I note, he did *nothing* wrong'.[23]

For Washington Okumu, who by then lived in Massachusetts with his family, Lumumba's murder was a turning point. 'That's when my anger began to show', he told Nancy Jacobs in an interview, 'and my hatred began to develop'. He was 'against white people' and said that whites in the Congo should be killed. But, he added, he saw American whites and European whites differently: 'I separated white people in Europe and Belgium from the United States. The white people in the US, I considered them to be friends, except the ones who discriminated against me. I knew it was a problem in the United States. I just became racialist as I grew up, very strange. I became an intense racialist'.[24]

He continued his relationship with the CIA.

* * *

FOR THOSE WHO HAD plotted and schemed to achieve Lumumba's death, there was much relief. 'When Lumumba was murdered by his Congolese enemies', wrote Bill Burden with satisfaction in 1982, 'the sky began to clear. . . . Today under President Mobutu[,] Zaire [the name given to the Congo by Mobutu in 1971] is one of the most secure of the new nations in Africa'.[25]

Time showed a photograph of Opango, bare-breasted in her grief, with a sneering caption: 'Gone were the Paris frocks'.[26]

The poisons that Sidney Gottlieb had taken to the Congo to deliver to Larry Devlin were no longer necessary. Devlin took them out of the office safe and threw them into the Congo River.[27] 'For those who think we should not have attempted to remove Lumumba from power', commented Devlin in his memoir,

> I can say only that I believed that his lack of understanding of world politics and his dalliance with the Soviet Union made him a serious danger to the United States. We were, after all, involved in a major war, albeit a cold one. Had the Soviet Union succeeded in gaining control of a large part of the African continent and its resources, it could have carried us over the thin red line into a Hot War. In a Hot War, one has to kill one's enemies or be defeated. In the Cold War it was much the same, only one had to remove the enemy from a position of power in which he could contribute to the weakening of the United States' role in the world.[28]

Daphne Park made two different claims about Lumumba's murder: both that the CIA had killed him, and that she herself, as MI6's chief in the Congo, had organised it. In 1989, she gave a long interview to Caroline Alexander for the *New Yorker*, in which she was asked 'Who killed Lumumba?' Her answer was straightforward: 'The CIA of course'.[29]

Twenty-four years later, shortly before her death, Park gave a different answer in a conversation with Lord Lea, a fellow peer in the House of Lords. Lea asked Park if MI6 had had anything to do with Lumumba's murder. This time she said, 'We did. I organised it'.[30]

At first sight, these two responses seem contradictory, but perhaps there is truth in both. In any case, Park was honoured with the Order of the British Empire—OBE—when she returned to Britain from the Congo in October 1961.[31]

* * *

ACUTE DISAPPOINTMENT WAS FELT in Africa and beyond that Lumumba was murdered while Kennedy was president. But in fact, the assassination took place just a few days before his inauguration. A photograph of Kennedy taken by the White House photographer on 13 February 1961, immediately after the president heard the news by telephone, shows him in a state of shock, with his head in his hand.[32]

Whatever the nature of his reaction to the news, it is clear that Kennedy had received highly critical briefings about Lumumba. Averell Harriman visited the Congo in September 1960 as part of a fact-finding mission for Kennedy, then a presidential candidate. Harriman spoke to the leading political figures, including Lumumba.[33] After his return to the US, Harriman reported to Kennedy that Lumumba 'would cause trouble in power, in jail, or upon release'.[34] He described Lumumba as 'a rabble rousing speaker. He is a shrewd maneuverer who has clever left-wing advisers, with the aid and encouragement of Czech and Soviet ambassadors'. Lumumba, Harriman continued, 'counts on full support from the USSR'.[35]

Ulric Haynes Jr, a young African American attorney who accompanied Harriman, later recalled the meeting between him and the Congolese premier:

But it's interesting, Lumumba was very, very conscious of the fact that the Americans were trying to subvert his government. He was very, very suspicious of the activities of the CIA in the Congo at the time. And I'll never forget when Harriman went to his office to speak to him (he was prime minister at the time) about U.S. relations, he ushered us both (I was interpreting) into his bathroom.

He would not speak in his formal study because he was suspicious that it was being bugged. And the gist of his conversation was a complaint about the subversive activities of the American government.[36]

Questions have been asked over the years about the extent to which Kennedy, as president-elect, was informed of US plans to kill Lumumba. There is no clear answer.

David Doyle, the chief of the CIA base in Elisabethville, suggested that Kennedy backed plans to remove Lumumba. 'President Eisenhower and President-elect John Kennedy', he wrote in his memoir, *True Men and Traitors*, 'apparently wanted Lumumba removed from power and had discreetly made that clear to the CIA'.[37] But Doyle does not give his source.

Dick Bissell, who in 1960–1962 was the deputy director of plans, the branch of the CIA responsible for covert operations, gave testimony to the Church Committee about the CIA's plan to assassinate Castro. 'Bissell repeatedly coupled Eisenhower and Kennedy', noted the report, 'when he speculated that the Presidents would have been advised in a manner calculated to maintain "plausible deniability"'.[38] Bissell said he believed that Allen Dulles had briefed both Eisenhower and president-elect Kennedy:

> *Bissell*: I believe at some stage the President and the President-elect both were advised that such an operation had been planned and was being attempted.
> *Senator Baker*: By whom?
> *Bissell*: I would guess through some channel by Allen Dulles.[39]

But Bissell was not asked whether President-elect Kennedy had been briefed about the plot to kill Lumumba.

* * *

ON 20 FEBRUARY 1961, further shocking news emerged from the Congo: six Lumumbists had been deported from Leopoldville to South Kasai, the stronghold of Kalonji, then executed.[40] As Hammarskjöld broke the news to the Security Council, he felt 'revulsion and shock', and subsequently wrote a letter of condemnation to Kasavubu. The UN representative of the United Arab Republic said that Kasavubu's hands were 'dripping with blood'.[41]

Violence was escalating. On 21 February, it was announced that fifteen political prisoners had been shot in Stanleyville, including Pongo, Victor Nendaka's deputy, who had been one of the hunters for Lumumba just a few months earlier. The executions were in retaliation for the killing of the six in South Kasai.[42]

In New York, at the UN, an explosive atmosphere of tension and fury swirled. Nkrumah, along with other leaders who had remained loyal to Lumumba, put pressure on the Security Council to tackle the crisis with a tougher approach. On 20 February, the Security Council adopted a resolution to urge the UN to take immediate steps to prevent civil war and to use force if necessary as a last resort. The resolution, which was passed by nine votes to none with two abstentions (France and Soviet Union), also called for the convening of Parliament and the prompt evacuation from the Congo of all Belgian and other foreign military and paramilitary personnel not under the UN command.

A key demand in the resolution was for an immediate and impartial investigation into the deaths of Patrice Lumumba, Maurice Mpolo and Joseph Okito. The investigation was given the name Project Sunk Hope.[43]

PART X

THE SEEDS ARE SOWN

32

Arming the Skies

A s NEWS OF LUMUMBA'S DEATH sank in across the world, there
were revelations of deepening American involvement in the
Congo. On 17 February 1961, a week after Munongo's announcement, a story broke in the *Daily Telegraph*, a British newspaper, that
an American cargo airline was secretly shipping Fouga Magister
jets to Katanga.[1]

This was shocking news. The French-built Fouga CM.170 Magister was a jet-trainer aircraft that could be used for combat; with a
maximum speed of four hundred miles per hour, it had the capacity
to carry and use rockets, bombs and two machine guns. The delivery of fighter aircraft to Katanga was in violation of UN Security
Council resolutions and contrary to official US policy.

The British press got hold of the story by chance because a US
cargo aircraft was unexpectedly forced by engine trouble to land in
Malta, then a British colony, in the early evening of 9 February 1961.
The aircraft was a Boeing C-97 Stratocruiser, a long-range, heavy,
military cargo plane, on which the words 'Seven Seas Airlines' had
been painted over but were still visible. Otherwise, the only mark-
ing was the registration number on the tail, which started with 'N',
identifying it as a US plane. It had flown from Luxembourg and
was apparently bound for Johannesburg, and it carried three Fouga
jet trainers. The names of the crew members, all Americans, were
given to the US consul general in Malta.

Parts for the engine were flown from the US to repair the cargo
plane; once it was ready to fly again, the aircraft and its sinister
freight left Malta for Entebbe, Uganda, at night on Monday 13

February. While in the air, the captain of the aircraft reported to traffic control that it was short of fuel and needed to alter course for Fort Lamy (now N'Djamena), the capital of Chad; this was a ploy to justify flying in the direction of Katanga. It then flew on to Elisabethville, Katanga's capital.

British colonial authorities in Malta had not appreciated the significance of the stop by this aircraft until the story broke in the British press, at which point they sent a report to the colonial office in London.[2] Seven Seas Airlines was closely linked to the CIA, either as a CIA proprietary company or as a company contracted to the agency.[3] Set up in 1957 by the American brothers Earl J Drew and Urban L Drew, the airline based its fleet at Findel airport in Luxembourg. Its headquarters was in the Lincoln Building, at 60 East 42nd Street, in Midtown Manhattan, opposite Grand Central Station; this was also the registered address of Earl Drew.[4] The Lincoln Building, a 1930s Gothic-style skyscraper, was also the headquarters of International Aviation Consultants, a CIA front involved in operations targeting Castro's Cuba.[5]

In July 1960, Seven Seas had been awarded a contract with the UN for the delivery of relief goods from Europe and some African countries to the Congo. The company's four Douglas DC-4s were mainly used for flights from Europe to Leopoldville; later that year the company purchased two Boeing C-97s from the US Air Force, which were deployed to the Congo to carry UN troops and supplies around the country.

Another American airline operating in the Congo and based in Luxembourg was Intercontinental US Inc, a company formed in New York in 1960 for worldwide charter work. A subsidiary company, Interocean Airways SA, was also engaged in transporting cargo, including vehicles, around the Congo.[6]

Jan Knippers Black, in later years a professor of human rights and international politics, was unexpectedly exposed to this world in 1961, when she 'stumbled upon a nest of Americans' at cocktail hour every evening in the Hotel Dolphin in Luxembourg. She was 'a naive 21-year-old woman from rural Tennessee, vagabonding across Europe'; they were the managers and crew of Intercontinental US and Seven Seas. She was entranced by the 'spectacle of the crews staggering in' and one of them, a Seven Seas pilot—amused by her 'wide-eyed wonder'—offered to arrange for her to fly to Katanga.

It was a 'bizarre adventure' that made her curious about the airlines. Some years later, as she wrote in 1980 in the *Washington Monthly*, 'I ran across the son of the man who had identified himself to me as the manager of Seven Seas. The son confirmed what I already suspected: his father, now retired, was a career CIA officer. Both Intercontinental and Seven Seas had belonged to the CIA, he said'.[7]

Another aircraft company linked to the CIA and operating in the Congo was Southern Air Transport, which flew DC-6 transports. Its CIA cryptonym was ZRCLIFF. According to a 1973 report in the *New York Times*, Southern had begun a connection with the CIA in August 1960; it quoted a Miami-based pilot as saying, 'Everybody knows Southern was doing spook stuff'.[8]

The CIA's involvement with Southern Air became a matter of public record in 1973, when documents relating to a planned purchase of the airline were filed with the Civil Aeronautics Board in Washington, DC. The documents revealed that the CIA proprietary airlines all shared the same Washington address: 1725 K Street NW. Included were Southern Air Transport, Air America (which had been created in 1950 as Civil Air Transport Inc, to support US foreign policy in Indochina), Pacific Corporation and Civil Air Transport Ltd.[9]

Another airline flying in the Congo with links to the CIA was Air Congo, which was managed by Foreign Air Transport Development, a CIA front established in 1954 to operate a number of small airlines overseas.[10] On 1 June 1961, Michael Hathorn, a medical doctor escaping South Africa for exile in Accra, flew to Ghana via the Congo. 'We boarded an Air Congo plane', he recalled later, 'and we were rather disconcerted at first to find that half the seats had been removed and the rear half of the cabin was filled with cases containing bank notes and ammunition!'[11]

Air Congo featured prominently in the brutal treatment of Lumumba in his final weeks of life. When he was taken to Leopoldville on 2 December 1960 from Kasai, where he had been captured, he was flown in an Air Congo plane. Then, when he, Mpolo and Okito were flown to their deaths in Katanga on 17 January 1961, their terrible journey to Elisabethville was on board an Air Congo DC-4.

* * *

ON 16 FEBRUARY 1961, a British official in Katanga reported to the UK Foreign Office on the arrival of the Seven Seas Boeing C-97 at Elisabethville airport. 'A Stratocruiser aircraft registration N9540C', the cable read, 'but with no other markings arrived here 14 February carrying a small jet aeroplane possible a Fouga Magister which was disembarked this morning'.[12] The specification of a single jet is echoed by another cable sent on the same day, which reported that according to the US embassy in London, the C-97 was carrying 'one complete Jet trainer and parts for two others'.[13] However, all other official UK documents relating to this episode refer to three jet trainers, and when the British government was asked about these events in Parliament, the response referred clearly to three crated Fougas.[14]

David Doyle, the chief of the CIA base in Elisabethville, was at the airport when the three Fougas arrived. 'Not long after the Lumumba incident', he wrote in *True Men and Traitors*, 'three Fouga Magisters (French jet fighters) were secretly flown in by US commercial air craft and crew, in direct violation of US policy, to join Tshombe's forces. During a routine airport check-up, I chanced on them being unloaded from a US civilian KC97 pipeline cargo aircraft at night'. When he chatted with the American air crew, it seemed to him that they were mere delivery men, with 'no idea of the situation their cargo was about to make more tense—the aircraft were obviously there to shoot down UN planes'. Years later, Doyle identified the crew as US Air Force personnel.[15]

The three Fougas, Doyle explained in his memoir, were training aircraft, but they were armed and perfectly able to destroy UN piston-driven transport planes. 'The UN was furious', he said, 'and it was suspected that was a CIA operation to help secretly build a stable, pro-Western Katanga in case the rest of the Congo were to fall under communist domination'. But if that was the case, he insisted, 'nobody had told me anything about it—which makes CIA involvement highly unlikely'.[16]

Doyle's version of events cannot be true. Documents show that the CIA had arranged the purchase of the Fougas and their delivery by Seven Seas, a CIA contractor or proprietary company. No doubt Doyle, as head of the CIA base in Katanga, was kept fully informed and was instructed to await the arrival of the planes at the airport. Doyle's claim that he was at the airport that night to carry out 'a routine . . . check-up' is implausible, since he was not responsible in any way for the functioning of the airport, and in any case routine checks rarely happen at midnight. Equally unlikely is his claim that he 'chanced' on the Fougas being unloaded. Presumably Doyle felt obliged in his memoir to acknowledge the Fouga episode, since it had been splashed across the newspapers in February 1961. And in doing so, he contrived, unconvincingly, to dissociate the CIA from it.

* * *

On 17 February the Foreign Office in London sent a telegram to the UK's UN mission in New York, headed, 'Jet aircraft for Katanga'. The American embassy in London, it stated, had received reports that the three French-made Fougas were the first of nine to be delivered to Elisabethville.[17]

The Stratocruiser C-97 that had been carrying the Fougas had previously been owned by US Air Force Air Materiel Command at Kirtland Field, New Mexico, and was used in a project code-named 'Chickenpox', in which its interior was adapted for the mobile assembly of atomic bombs. The C-97 was then assigned to the US civilian registry and 'may have been used to ferry arms to Katangan rebels in early 1960s', according to a flight log.[18] However, it was not registered under the name of Earl J Drew until 16 February, which was two days after it had delivered the Fougas to Elisabethville.

Aware of the flare-up of tensions over the Fougas, the British government hastily sought to distance itself from the incident and to prevent further embarrassments. 'In view of serious political repercussions that could arise out of Aircraft ferrying operations to Katanga', wrote the colonial secretary to the governor of Malta on

18 February, 'I should be most grateful if you would do what you can to prevent use of Malta by such Aircraft'.[19]

*   *   *

WHEN NKRUMAH LEARNED FROM the UK press on 17 February of the delivery of three Fougas to Elisabethville by a US aircraft, he was appalled. Then he learned that the three jet trainers were merely the first of nine to be delivered to Tshombe. Ghana's minister of foreign affairs issued a strong statement to the US ambassador to Ghana on 20 February. If the reports were true, the minister objected, they 'are obviously of most serious nature'. In this regard, he continued, the government of Ghana called attention 'to statement made by president of US on Thursday 16th February to effect that unilateral intervention in Congo by one country [or] one group of countries would endanger peace in Africa'.[20]

Kennedy was embarrassed. He told Nkrumah, 'The United States government did not, in fact, learn of this shipment in sufficient time to prevent a transaction which took place entirely outside the borders of the United States'. He added that Adlai Stevenson, the US ambassador to the UN, had condemned the delivery of the aircraft. Nkrumah was unimpressed—and said so.[21]

The American embassy in London reported to the UK foreign office on 17 February that its government had little control over Seven Seas, which operated entirely outside the USA. The embassy added, 'The French have apparently detained the remaining six Fouga aircraft at Toulouse'.[22]

But there was some confusion about the intentions of Seven Seas. On 27 February 1961, the UK embassy in Luxembourg sent further information to the UK foreign office about the delivery of the Fougas to Tshombe; in turn, the information was cabled to the governor of Malta on 3 March. The message reported that Seven Seas proposed 'to transport to Katanga six more Fouga Magister jet trainers (with machine guns) which were awaiting shipment by them from Toulouse'. According to the US embassy in Luxembourg, however, Seven Seas had now given an assurance that it would not transport any more such aircraft to Katanga, in response to the embassy's 'strong representations' after the shipment the week before.[23]

* * *

THE EXPOSURE OF THE role of Seven Seas Airlines in the delivery of the Fougas came as a shock to the UN, which had a contract with the airline. It grounded the entire fleet of Seven Seas planes in the Congo.[24]

But the UN could not stop the airline from operating in Katanga and working directly for Tshombe's government, or in South Kasai and working for 'King' Kalonji, as he called himself. On 15 March 1961, an American pilot, Bob Williams, flew his first C-46 trip in the Congo, to Bakwanga, the capital of South Kasai. 'Our company (Seven Seas Airlines)', he noted some years later, 'was no longer under contract with the United Nations and now we were flying for the Government of Katanga. . . . We were hauling mostly freight that supported the army financed by the government of Katanga'.[25] Tshombe used a Seven Seas Curtiss C-46 Commando as his personal aircraft.[26]

Once the three Fouga Magister jet fighters had been delivered to Elisabethville, the Katanga Air Force dominated the skies, for the UN had no combat aircraft at all. This superiority in the air was diminished within a few months, when one Fouga was seized by the UN and another was destroyed in a crash. But there was still one operational Fouga Magister left, which continued to wreak havoc on the UN, bombing and attacking its ground forces.

It has been claimed that this Fouga Magister, which was capable of air-to-air attack, shot down the DC-6 carrying UN Secretary General Dag Hammarskjöld on the night of 17–18 September 1961 near Ndola airport in Northern Rhodesia—a death that was separated from the execution of Lumumba by only eight months and less than two hundred kilometres.

Inquiries into the role of the Fouga constitute an important plank in the UN investigation into Hammarskjöld's death led by Judge Othman, which was initiated by the UN secretary general in 2015.[27]

Commander Charles M Southall, a US naval intelligence officer working at the National Security Agency's listening station in Cyprus in 1961, linked the Fouga to Hammarskjöld's death.[28] Giving testimony in 2012 to an independent commission of inquiry into the crash, Southall said that he had heard the recording of a pilot's commentary as the pilot shot down Hammarskjöld's DC-6: 'It was, I was told, a Belgian mercenary, up there in his Fouga Magister. Fougas were built as trainers but later additions of them had gun cannon fitted.

A pilot himself, Southall made the following observation: 'Now mind you, the Fougas only had what we call a loiter time of about 30 minutes at altitude, so he must have been pre-positioned up there'.

Southall said he heard the pilot call out, 'I see a transport coming in low, I'm going to go down and look at it', and then he said 'yes, it's the transport'. Southall added, 'Now whether he said "yes it's the Trans Air", "DC6", or it's just, "yes, it's the plane", I don't remember, but he said "I'm going to make a run on it"'.

Southall continued, 'It's quite chilling. You can hear the gun cannon firing and he said "Flames coming out of it, I've hit it! Great", or "good" or something like that[;] "it's crashed". And that was the end of the recording. I remember the watch supervisors commenting that this recording was only 7 minutes old at the time'.

Asked who he thought was responsible for the crash of the aircraft, Southall replied, 'In my view, and it's a private view, it's not the view of the US Government, it's not a view that is greatly backed up by fact, but in my view there was a CIA unit out there and they had responsibility for fuelling the plane, finding the pilots, coordinating with the Belgian, French mining interests and it was the CIA unit that ensured that the plane would be shot down'.[29]

Southall's testimony is by no means the only suggestion of a connection between the CIA and the deaths of the passengers and crew of Hammarskjöld's DC-6. In 1998, for example, a small set of documents with the letterhead and Johannesburg address of a mercenary-related organization called the South African Institute for Maritime Research (SAIMR) were found in a file examined by the Truth and Reconciliation Commission, just as the TRC investigation was concluding its work. One of the documents states that CIA director Allen Dulles had promised full cooperation with 'Operation Celeste', a plot to kill Hammarskjöld. The murder of

Lumumba is referenced: 'I want his removal to be handled more efficiently than was Patrice [Lumumba]'. The purported plot in the SAIMR documents involved the placing of a bomb on Hammarskjöld's plane, which failed to explode; a pilot was then dispatched to shoot down the aircraft.

These documents have disappeared, and the only copies available are scans of faxes. But the original documents need to be found and analysed forensically in order to make a proper assessment of their authenticity. It 'remains necessary' to obtain them, argues Justice Othman, 'to verify or dispel the hypothesis relating to "Operation Celeste"'.[30]

* * *

HAMMARSKJÖLD'S DC-6 CRASHED WHILE preparing to land at Ndola. This is significant, the author Matthew Stevenson believes, who was curious about the tragedy and visited the crash site. He noted the absence of any serious hills near the location: 'All I saw as I drove up to the crash site in a taxi and as I walked around the memorial were open fields and small clusters of forest land, none of which were very dense'. The plane, therefore, did not crash into a mountain or hilltop, as some people have maintained. 'To me', said Stevenson, 'it felt like an ambush'.

For an expert opinion, he turned to Joseph Majerle III, a pilot and aviation mechanic in Alaska who has visited many crash sites and repaired damaged planes. Majerle has observed major structural repair operations on DC-6 aircraft. In 2017 Stevenson and Majerle wrote an article, 'Who or What Brought Down Dag Hammarskjöld?', that rejected the theory of pilot error. They believed the testimonies of local witnesses who had seen a second plane flying above the DC-6 and shooting at it, which was consistent with Southall's testimony. Majerle speculates,

> I think one of the mercenary aircraft, operating around Ndola on that night, fired a tracer bullet into the fuel tanks of the Hammarskjöld plane, causing the left wing to catch on fire. Fearing that the left wing would fold up into the fuselage of the plane, the pilots did the only thing that was available to them: to configure

the plane for a controlled (so to speak) crash landing in the short amount of time available to them. That action explains the 30 degrees of flaps setting on impact (nine miles out from the Ndola runway!), the relative slow speed at impact (they were just above the stall speed), and the compact crash site. . . . The pilots had no choice but to put the plane 'on the ground . . . now!' and that they did, skillfully, in my mind.[31]

Majerle has identified similarities here with the wartime tactic of 'rat catching': attacking enemy planes on their landing approach, when they are at their most vulnerable.[32] The rat-catching manoeuvre, explains Majerle, 'would be the first thing a pilot would think of', if he aimed to shoot down Hammarskjöld's plane: 'Not knowing the exact route of the rat, and at night, the only possible chance you would have would be to wait near a point where you know it would have to go to. And in this particular situation of the types of planes involved, with the DC-6's very respectable cruise speed and Fouga's short range and endurance, anyone trying to accomplish this would have any previous experience with it in the forefront of their mind, I would think'. If the DC-6 'was in fact hit by a bullet fired from an airborne aircraft, while in an airport traffic area', adds Majerle, 'then that is an absolute definition of a "rat catch"'.

Majerle makes a further point: 'for any pilot flying in the European Theatre of Operations in the last nine months of World War II, the Rat Catch became the "in" thing to do for a fighter pilot'.[33]

A number of pilots who fought the Luftwaffe in World War II were in Katanga in September 1961. One of these was an American veteran of the US Army Air Forces (USAAF): Urban L 'Ben' Drew, 'an extremely handsome and sociable man, who liked women and whiskey, who would make a lot of money just to lose it'.[34] Drew, an ace fighter pilot, had ambushed two Luftwaffe jet-powered Messerschmitt Me 262 aircraft in October 1944, as they sought to take off. It was the first recorded instance of an Allied pilot shooting down two German Me 262 planes in one aerial combat on a single mission.[35]

Ben Drew was closely associated with the Fouga Magisters in Katanga, for it was Seven Seas, the CIA-linked airline that he had set up with his brother Earl, that delivered the planes to Katanga in February 1961. His covert work for the US has been acknowledged by his son, who said that Drew 'was called upon by the U.S. government to work on clandestine bases in the Belgian Congo and Vietnam'.[36] In a 1975 study of arms trafficking, Drew is described as 'an old hand of the CIA with a particularly adventurous past', and with a history of messy gun-running exploits in different parts of the world.[37]

According to a 2014 article in the South African newspaper *The Citizen*, Drew was working in Katanga for Tshombe in 1961. The newspaper reported that following Drew's death in 2013, his widow was seeking to sell an 'African mask' that had been given to him by Tshombe. It also stated that Drew had been suspected of shooting down Hammarskjöld's plane: 'Drew, for example, attracted much controversy because of his alleged gun-running for Tsombe [*sic*] and others, and was even suspected of having shot down an airplane that carried Dag Hammerskjold [*sic*], the UN's Secretary General at the time, killing all on board. . . . In a video-graphed affidavit Drew vehemently denies this, relating in great detail events surrounding his coercion by the CIA in shady cold war deals, [and] his friendship with Tsombe [*sic*]'. The article does not provide a source for its information about the video, which has not been traced.[38]

Drew may have been involved in some way in the attack on Hammarskjöld's plane without necessarily acting as the pilot; there were other pilots in Katanga flying the Fouga who were veterans of World War II. One of these was Jan van Risseghem, a Belgian mercenary who enlisted in the British Royal Air Force in November 1942 and was the commander of the Katangan air force in 1961. Just hours after the disappearance of Hammarskjöld's plane (many hours before the official finding of the crash), the US ambassador to the Congo, Ed Gullion, cabled to Washington that the plane had disappeared near Ndola and may have been shot down by a Belgian mercenary pilot, whom he named as 'Vak Riesseghel'.[39]

It is possible that Drew was a conduit of information about Hammarskjöld's flight details between the CIA and the pilot of the plane that shot down Hammarskjöld's DC-6.[40] There are good reasons to believe that the CIA had access to this information. One of these is the testimony of Commander Southall. Another is the fact that Hammarskjöld's CX-52 cipher machines enabled his secret messages to UN headquarters to be read in real time in the US by American intelligence. As well, USAF air attaché colonel Don Gaylor, who was stationed in Pretoria, had been sent to Ndola on the night of the crash in order 'to be available to help Hammarskjöld, when he arrived'. The crew of a Norwegian UN plane, which had flown to Ndola to help in the search for the crash, were invited on board Gaylor's DC-3 to get some food, and they discovered that the American plane was packed with sophisticated radio equipment.[41]

Seven Seas Airlines went bankrupt in September 1961.[42] But Ben Drew's association with the CIA in Africa continued. After his stint in Katanga, he went on to found and manage Caprivi Airways, which has been identified as a CIA operation.[43]

* * *

THE ROLE OF AMERICAN aircraft and pilots in the Congo was by no means limited to covert operations. In 1960 the US Air Force in the Congo had its own radio and air traffic control station in Leopoldville, which was operated by American personnel and reserved for American military aircraft. It was approximately one mile from the civil Leopoldville Flight Information Centre.[44]

The first USAF air attaché to be posted to the independent Congo was Colonel Benjamin M Matlick, who was stationed there between 1960 and 1962.[45] Matlick flew his own DC-3, which took him to Ndola on 18 September 1961, when he was ostensibly sent by the USAF to assist the Rhodesian authorities with their search for Hammarskjöld's plane. Matlick's assistant air attaché was Major Harris.[46] In July 1960 a C-47 that had been lent to the Leopoldville embassy by the US embassy in Pretoria, South Africa, was used in the Congo for a short period, probably until 1961.[47] In addition to Matlick's DC-3, two other USAF DC-3s were in use in the Congo.[48]

It is unclear to what extent Matlick and Harris knew about, or participated in, CIA air operations in the Congo, which were given the cryptonyms CLAM and WICLAM. Consistent with this code, the US station plane in Leopoldville was registered in the name of YQCLAM/1; possibly this was Matlick or Harris.[49] YQ was the digraph used as a prefix to YQPROP, the special channel with the objective of killing Lumumba. However, YQCLAM operations do not appear to have been involved in the CIA plot against Lumumba. A report from Devlin to Washington in January 1961 states, 'Station acknowledged disadvantage of crossing WIROGUE and YQCLAM operations (YQCLAM was never involved in any assassination schemes)'.[50]

* * *

WIROGUE, THE THIRD-COUNTRY AGENT sent by the CIA to the Congo in late November, had a penchant for fast cars—but he had never flown a plane. Nevertheless, he was flying in the Congo's skies within a few months, as a qualified pilot. In late January 1961, Devlin asked CIA headquarters to give approval for WIROGUE to take flying lessons. A memorandum about the lessons, which is partly redacted, states they were approved so that the 'station plane could be used for clandestine missions'.[51]

WIROGUE took to flying with ease. By March, he had obtained a position as adviser to the Congolese Air Force. By April the air force were trying to use him to obtain arms and instructors in Western Europe, and he was also teaching Congolese men to fly.[52] On instructions from Washington, Devlin asked WIROGUE to set up an air intelligence unit.

Despite WIROGUE's achievements, his unpredictable behaviour was worrying the CIA, which decided to get him out of the Congo. WIROGUE was instructed to leave for Brazzaville in early July 1961 and was then transferred to Washington for meetings in a safe house with Bronson Tweedy. He was given new documents and funds and flown to Frankfurt on a military airplane; his contract with the CIA was terminated on 8 September 1961.

WIROGUE had lost none of his maverick nature, however. He returned to the Congo a couple of weeks later under his own steam. Flying from Frankfurt to Brazzaville, he arrived on 22 September 1961 and crossed the Congo River to Leopoldville the same day.[53] He appears, thereafter, to have maintained his association with the

CIA, which resettled him to keep him out of the way. According to an October 1964 assessment of WIROGUE, he had been turned over to HARVARD, evidently a branch of a CIA program, 'for resettlement in Germany'. The assessment noted that 'Resettling him had turned out to be an enormous problem': 'WIROGUE/1 had an intense desire for intelligence service and enjoyed the role of lower echelon action agent. . . . The assessment indicated there was little flap potential with WIROGUE/1 since he knew little about the Agency'.[54]

It is difficult to flesh out the details of WIROGUE's activities as a pilot and of the air intelligence unit he was instructed to set up in the Congo. The files released in 2017–2018 under the JFK Assassination Records Collection Act contain a wealth of information that is not available elsewhere about his operations in the Congo, but they are heavily redacted. Several files totalling nearly two hundred pages each relating to WIROGUE have been so extensively redacted that almost all the pages are blank.[55] The so-called CIA 'Miscellaneous Files' contain further records on WIROGUE, but as of 2021 they have not yet been listed or described in the JFK Collection database.[56]

This is yet another example of the secrecy that prevents any full understanding of the Congo's history, much of which has been shaped by other nations. The records that *are* available reveal the large extent of the CIA operations in the Congo involving aircraft and pilots. But it is a confusing situation in which the CIA appears to have been riding several horses at once that were going in different directions: it supported Tshombe's war on the UN; it supported the UN mission in the Congo; and it supported the Congolese Air Force, the air arm of the Leopoldville government. All these efforts, however, contributed to the objective of keeping the whole of the Congo under America's influence and guarding the Shinkolobwe mine against Soviet incursion.

33

'A Bride Everybody Wants'

L UMUMBA WAS DEAD. BUT THE American government did not relax its grip on the Congo. Rather, it intensified its efforts to neutralise those who were supportive of Lumumba. One was Rajeshwar Dayal, Hammarskjöld's special representative in the Congo, who had consistently argued that since Lumumba had been elected on a democratic basis, it was the UN's duty to support his government. For him, this was not a personal or sentimental matter, but one of justice and adherence to the UN Charter. He had maintained his position consistently, regardless of the dangers and anger he regularly faced in the Congo.

The Eisenhower administration had already shown its hostility to Dayal. Now, the incoming Kennedy administration resolved to force him out of the Congo. 'Within weeks of the change of administration', write Gerard and Kuklick in *Death in the Congo*, 'the Democrats went after Dayal as the Republicans had not'.[1]

When Dayal went to New York for consultations, Adlai Stevenson pushed hard for Dayal to resign, on the grounds of his health.[2] Dayal politely suggested that this solicitude for his health was unnecessary, which prompted Stevenson to observe that his long absence from Pakistan as India's ambassador was not good for Indo-Pakistani relations. Dayal replied firmly that as a civil servant, he was not indispensable in any post; moreover, he added, this was a matter between Hammarskjöld and Prime Minister Nehru.[3] But the pressure on Dayal to leave the Congo was building inexorably.

Meanwhile, President Kennedy led a public attack on Gizenga and his government in Stanleyville. On 15 February—just two days after the news of Lumumba's assassination—the president went on American television to say that he was 'seriously concerned at what appears to be the threat of unilateral intervention' in the Congo. He denounced the 'purported recognition of Congolese factions as so-called governments'. The only legal authority entitled to speak for the Congo, asserted Kennedy, was the government of Kasavubu.[4]

This infuriated Nkrumah. The next day he summoned the US ambassador to his office, where he handed him an aide-mémoire condemning Kennedy's statement. He told him that he would be issuing a press statement to this effect. Ghana radio carried a 'long, critical and derisory comment' on Kennedy's statement.[5]

Kennedy had used his television appearance to issue a strong warning: 'there should be no misunderstanding of the position of the United States if any government is really planning to take so dangerous and irresponsible a step'.[6] The trigger for this admonition was pressure by the Casablanca group on Sudan to open up transit rights to eastern Congo, in order to break the Leopoldville government's blockade of Orientale province; such a move, Kennedy feared, would render a Soviet supply line feasible. G Mennen 'Soapy' Williams, Kennedy's assistant secretary of state for African Affairs, flew to Khartoum to secure a guarantee from the Sudan government that they would refuse transit for supplies to Stanleyville.

Kennedy said he was reluctant to intervene militarily in the Congo but that if the UN failed to maintain control of the territory, 'a decision on United States participation would await further development'. The Pentagon, according to the *New York Times*, had developed contingency plans for such an intervention. The paper gave details: 'about 900 aircraft would be needed for the first four days and 750 for the next eight days if the United States should want to send an airborne division and an infantry division, plus supporting units, a total of 80,000 men'. It would be a 'limited war' operation.

The newspaper set out figures regarding the four different sets of forces in the Congo. The Leopoldville government, under President

Kasavubu, had about fifteen thousand troops and controlled about half the territory of the Congo, including Leopoldville's port, Matadi, 180 miles down the Congo River. The 'regime of Antoine Gizenga', headquartered in Stanleyville and dominant in Orientale and Kivu provinces, had about six thousand troops; it was believed to have been 'getting some arms from Communist sources, with the assistance of the United Arab Republic'. Other major groupings were Tshombe's government in Katanga, with about five thousand troops, and the government of Albert Kalonji in South Kasai, with one thousand troops.

The challenging terrain of the Congo considerably limited military operations to air transport and some rail and steam navigation. 'Much of the country', noted the *New York Times*, 'is covered with jungle and effective military action of any significant scope is very difficult'. Five American naval ships, it added, were already operating in the vicinity of the Gulf of Guinea, 'ostensibly for goodwill visits to African ports'; these were the ships of SoLant Amity, the US Navy's operation off the coast of the Congo. But, suggested the newspaper knowingly, this task force had more purpose than simply goodwill—it could take 'a possible emergency role in the Congo crisis'.[7]

The new administration did not alter Eisenhower's policy in relation to the Congo; if anything, it strengthened it.

* * *

MANY OF KENNEDY'S ADVISERS, as well as other individuals associated with the Democratic Party, had business interests in the Congo. One of these was Maurice Tempelsman, who was able to profit from the appointment of Adlai Stevenson as Kennedy's ambassador to the UN in 1961. Stevenson's high-profile role offered a rich vein of contacts for Tempelsman: access to Kennedy, access to the delegates of UN member states and access to the UN secretariat.

When questioned about his relationship to Tempelsman in 1963, Stevenson 'became evasive', according to David Gibbs. Stevenson acknowledged that his law firm had represented Tempelsman, but 'never in connection with anything in the Belgian or indep[endent]

Congo'. This statement is false. 'The full details of the Stevenson-Tempelsman relationship', notes Gibbs, 'may never be known, since in at least one instance Tempelsman helped finance the editing of Stevenson's personal papers. In any case, it is clear that the relationship was close'.[8]

In early 1961, Tempelsman urged the Kennedy administration to acquire industrial diamonds from the Congo, justifying the plan in anticommunist terms. This was the scheme that CIA agent George Wittman had been seeking to take forward since his arrival in the Congo in September 1960. The value of the US goods to be imported in exchange for Congolese resources would be $54 million.[9]

A file in the Belgian state archives fleshes out Wittman's negotiations with senior members of the Congolese government in 1961.[10] It contains the transcript of a telex communication (not dated, but evidently early August 1961) between Tempelsman and Wittman.[11] Tempelsman started the discussion with news of a session with President Kennedy: 'Hello Maurice here. I have just had long briefing session with the president on the subject of the continued delays and obstructions involved with the diamond trade project. I reviewed the fact that President Kasavubu had sent a cable to Rusk last February 7 . . . giving approval firmly in principle to our particular project'. This telex discussion was on an open line; if the project involved uranium, it needed the masquerade of diamonds.

Tempelsman asked Wittman to organise a cable to President Kennedy from President Kasavubu or Cyrille Adoula (prime minister from August 1961). The telex reveals that Vice President Lyndon Johnson had already been approached about the project by Wittman: 'The briefing that you had given Vice Pres[id]ent Johnson was very helpful in my being [able] to explain clearly to the White House the political ramifications of a strong support with positive programs of assistance to the new government'. In any case, noted Tempelsman, Kennedy had known about the project even before he was elected, and now that he was president, he was 'annoyed' that no action had been taken.

Tempelsman told Wittman of a conversation with Adlai Stevenson: 'Ambassador Stevenson and I had lunch today and he also is now completely up to date on the project and the need for the soonest possible assistance to the Congo'.[12]

The file with this telex contains a set of related correspondence, including a telegram from Kasavubu to Secretary of State Rusk on 7 February 1961; a letter of approval of the contract with Tempelsman initialled by Albert Ndele on 14 May 1961; a letter from Ndele to Timberlake; a draft of a telegram from Adoula to Kennedy, undated; and a number of courtesy messages between the Congo's minister of mines, Tempelsman and Prime Minister Adoula between September and mid-October 1961. A note about Wittman describes him as a personal friend of Vice President Johnson.[13]

* * *

DAVID GIBBS HAS PUZZLED over the fact that Tempelsman's barter scheme was 'of dubious value' to the US government, since America's strategic stockpile was already amply supplied with industrial diamonds.[14] This book has suggested that 'diamonds' may have been a cover word for uranium and strategic minerals in discussions of the barter plan. Support for this suggestion is supplied by a document in the archives of the John F Kennedy Presidential Library. On 19 October 1961, Tempelsman sent a memorandum to President Kennedy, reminding him that 'on January 18 you considered a memorandum outlining the advantages of using the barter programme to avoid further cash payments for uranium purchase commitments approximating $415,800,000'. The memorandum does not name the country with which Tempelsman was advocating a barter programme. However, its arguments and dating are consistent with the correspondence in which Tempelsman urged the Kennedy administration to purchase industrial diamonds from the Congo.[15]

A copy of the 18 January memorandum was attached to the memorandum of 19 October, wrote Tempelsman. This date of 18 January was two days before Kennedy's inauguration as president, and the day after the assassination of Patrice Lumumba.[16]

On 4 February, a minute sent by McGeorge Bundy, the special assistant to the president for national security affairs, to the secretary of defense, referred to a discussion at the National Security Council on 1 February, when Kennedy requested the secretary of defense to consult with the Atomic Energy Commission about a review of the purchases of uranium from foreign countries. It was hoped, Bundy added, to make early savings of foreign exchange in this area.[17]

The copy of the October memorandum from Tempelsman to Kennedy in the Kennedy Presidential Library is incomplete. Only one page is available, which ends in mid-sentence. The January memorandum is not available.

There is a reference to potential friction with Canada in the October memorandum. This is reminiscent of the warning given by Secretary of State Herter in October 1959 when Burden, supported by President Eisenhower, was pressing for the purchase of fifteen hundred tons of uranium stockpiled at Shinkolobwe. Two years later, Tempelsman gave very different advice from that given by Herter. He reassured the president that 'the Canadian Government recently has sold additional quantities of uranium to the United Kingdom and substantial quantities of agricultural commodities to Communist China on credit'.[18]

The truncated memorandum suggests that Tempelsman's barter scheme was discussed and rejected by the interdepartmental Supplemental Stockpile Advisory Committee in October 1961. But Tempelsman continued to put pressure on the administration.[19] The negotiations appear to have been successful. Writing about the barter scheme to Stevenson on 9 November 1961, Tempelsman declared, 'I think that one can take some pride in . . . a project which is of benefit to everybody (including Tempelsman—I hope!)'[20]

George Wittman took some pride as well. An entry in the 1966 *Alumni Magazine* of Trinity College, in Hartford, Connecticut, where Wittman had studied government, boasts that he had 'worked out a 30-million dollar diamond transaction with the Congo. American dealers will stockpile diamonds here and they will be paid for from the sale of surplus farm commodities'.[21]

The evidence relating to these negotiations is incomplete: a jigsaw puzzle of secret and missing pieces of information. Nonetheless, it reveals an inextricable entanglement of Tempelsman's business interests with US foreign policy directly involving President

Kennedy, Vice President Johnson and UN Ambassador Stevenson, and facilitated by the CIA. Whether the deals were related to the strategic stockpile of uranium or diamonds, or possibly both, they involved a conflation of private business and public policy.

The American people were unaware of these negotiations and their outcome. So, too, were the Congolese.

* * *

THE FIFTH ANNUAL CONFERENCE of the International Atomic Energy Agency was held in Vienna between 26 September and 6 October 1961. It opened under a very dark shadow—the death of UN secretary general Dag Hammarskjöld and those travelling with him, in the plane crash near Ndola in British-ruled Northern Rhodesia. There was a significant development at the conference: in the mid-morning of 26 September, the Congo was formally accepted as the seventy-seventh member of the IAEA. Joseph Kahamba, minister of mines, was the Congolese delegate.

The minister was closely associated with the TRICO Nuclear Centre and in 1962 published a paper about the work of the centre with Monseigneur Luc Gillon, the nuclear physicist who was the rector of Lovanium University. The paper reported on the utilisation of the Triga Mark reactor for research and isotope production.[22]

Kahamba gave a powerful speech to the IAEA, which echoed the spirit of Lumumba's speech at the Restaurant du Zoo in Leopoldville almost exactly one year earlier. 'Since gaining its independence on 30 June 1960', said Kahamba, 'it should be noted that the Congo did not intend to rest content with the role of a producer of raw materials. It did not wish to go on being exploited by foreign interests. It was aware that certain States, which were trying to maintain their political influence in some regions of the Congo, were keenly interested not only in copper but also in uranium'. The Congo, he assured his audience, 'did not intend to expel foreigners from its territory, but they must understand that it was now an independent State that valued its natural resources and wished to manage its own affairs'.

Moreover, he added, 'the Congolese people were convinced that the use of atomic energy for economic purposes could become a reality in the Congo in the near future. Possibilities in that field were unlimited and international co-operation should enable the Congo, like other countries in course of development, to take advantage of the new source of energy'.

Kahamba noted that commitments had been entered into by Belgium before the Congo had become independent, 'by which the latter was still bound'. But, he insisted, the Congo—having become an independent and sovereign country—'felt free to examine and review those agreements. . . . It would conclude other agreements which would be more in keeping with its new status and its national interests'. He emphasised that 'the Congo would never allow its natural riches to be used by any country for non-peaceful purposes'.

His speech concluded with a tribute to Secretary General Hammarskjöld, observing that he had died in tragic circumstances, in the course of his efforts to secure peace in Kahamba's own nation, the Congo.

The Soviet delegate picked up Kahamba's theme with energy, accusing the US of trying to control the Congolese uranium ore. 'The colonizers', he argued, 'had endeavoured to keep in their own hands the Republic's rich natural resources, including its very large deposits of nuclear raw materials. To that end, they had resorted to new forms of colonialism without, however, changing its substance'.[23] This statement revealed beyond any doubt that the Soviet Union was well aware of the rich stocks of uranium at Shinkolobwe.

The US resolved to strengthen the mine's defences. A vast military camp—the Shinkolobwe garrison—was established close by the mine and put under the command of Roger Faulques, the notorious French veteran of Dien Bien Phu and Algeria who was now a mercenary working for Tshombe.

Strenuous efforts were made to cast a veil of secrecy over the garrison and the mine, to diminish the publicity generated by Lumumba and Kahamba. Most people in Katanga still had no idea of the mine's significance. Robert K Mpoyo, who in the 1960s attended secondary school—the Mulungwishi boarding school—in the same district as Shinkolobwe, recalls that 'the role played by this military training camp for the paracommando of "Shinko" confined in the vicinity of the Mine . . . has been and remains just as mysterious'. He added, 'Although everyone living in Likasi [then Jadotville] knew Shinko's name, few really knew what was going on at this site'.[24]

'Although uranium is now available from many other sources in the world', wrote Ritchie Calder, a Scottish science journalist who was sent by the UN on a fact-finding mission to the Congo in 1961, 'the Katanga deposits are naturally an important actor in the international and, indeed, in the internal political concerns of the Congo'. A recognised government, he observed, 'will have a very important say in the present and future of the concession'.[25] 'The Congo', observed Soapy Williams drily in 1961, 'is a bride everybody wants'.[26] It was a bride that was not wanted for her rich humanity, culture, intelligence and beauty—but for her magnificent dowry of strategic resources.

34

Made in America

P RESIDENT NKRUMAH WAS IN NEW York on 7 March 1961 to address the opening meeting of the resumed fifteenth session of the UN General Assembly. Hammarskjöld greeted him in the lobby. The two statesmen stood together quietly, shaking hands slowly, with solemn smiles of respect and shared goodwill.

In many ways Hammarskjöld and Nkrumah were alike: self-disciplined, high-minded and ascetic. 'I have never liked parties', wrote Nkrumah in a letter to a friend. 'I had to stop going to them. Even those I gave I always did so with reluctance. They are horri-ble shows, almost like a circus. And then the "talk about nothing" which goes on there nauseates me'.[1] Hammarskjöld felt the same. In the words of a UN colleague and trusted friend, Hammarskjöld 'was no fan of small talk'.[2]

The focus of Nkrumah's speech was the Congo. Nkrumah said that he deplored the action of the UN in recognizing the govern-ment of Kasavubu and Mobutu, 'which did not even claim to speak for the whole country'. By doing so, and as a result of vacillation and weakness, he warned, the moral authority of the United Na-tions had been 'dangerously weakened'.

On paper, the Leopoldville government had reverted to civilian rule. On 9 February 1961, Mobutu's College of Commissioners was dissolved by Kasavubu and replaced three days later by a provisional government under Joseph Ileo. But it was hardly constitutional; the provisional government had not been approved by Parliament, which had been adjourned by Kasavubu on 11 October 1960.

'The first task of the United Nations', said Nkrumah firmly, 'is to allow the Congolese people to be ruled by a government of their own choice'. In Ghana, he added, 'we support the Gizenga Government because it was chosen by this means'. He proposed that the United Nations should supervise a fresh general election.[3]

* * *

GHANA AND THE OTHER Casablanca powers were providing Gizenga with aid, including munitions and technical assistance, as well as radio propaganda to help popularise the Stanleyville government. Nkrumah received regular reports from members of the Ghanaian mission in Stanleyville, who had arrived there in late February and were working with Gizenga and his cabinet.

By now, almost all the pro-Gizenga countries had withdrawn their UN contingents from the Congo, on the grounds that the Leopoldville government was illegitimate. Ghana, however, did not. 'I felt it was important to support the UN effort', explained Nkrumah in *Challenge of the Congo*, 'while at the same time to continue quietly and effectively to help the legitimate Government of the Congo in Stanleyville'.

But Ghana's support for ONUC reached a crisis point on 28 April 1961, when many Ghanaian soldiers on duty in Port Francqui were killed. The 'A' Company of the 2nd Ghana Regiment were disarmed by Mobutu's troops and then herded into houses, where forty soldiers were shot without mercy. The people of Ghana were heartbroken. As the first nation to send troops, who had been in the country since 15 July 1960, they felt it as a terrible sacrifice.

General Alexander blamed the murders on the military inexperience of the men's officers and on the UN's reliance on persuasion. In Alexander's view, force was more effective. 'Argument from strength', he insisted, 'is the only answer with the Congolese armed man, since, sad to say, this is what the Belgians have taught him to understand'.

Nkrumah disagreed vehemently. In his view, Alexander was simply trying to pass the blame on to others. Nkrumah argued that as chief of defence staff of the Ghana army, Alexander had had a 'duty to see that Ghanaian troops were not placed in the kind of impossible position they found themselves in at Port Francqui'. He noted that Alexander himself did not go to Port Francqui but allowed the platoon to go there, even though he claimed that the officers were inexperienced.

Meanwhile—unknown to Nkrumah—General Alexander was assisting American efforts to keep watch on developments in Stanleyville. The Central Intelligence Bulletin of 17 April 1961 recorded that Alexander had informed the US ambassador in Accra that he would soon be going to Stanleyville. At Nkrumah's request, he was going to leave a radio transmitter-receiver there, to establish a direct link between Gizenga and Accra. According to the bulletin, Alexander 'stated that the traffic on this link would go through his office and that he would monitor it'.[4] The clear implication was that he would pass on details of this traffic to the US. By so doing, he would betray the trust placed in him by President Nkrumah.

Meanwhile, the SoLant Amity operation was continuing its 'goodwill tour' off the west coast of Africa, sailing south to Cape Town. In early March, when fighting broke out at Matadi between Congolese troops and UN soldiers, Ambassador Timberlake asked the task force to reverse course and proceed north. The admiral acquiesced. But this change in plan triggered acute concern at the White House: Kennedy wished to avoid giving the impression that the US had any aspirations to intervene in the Congo.[5] SoLant Amity was swiftly instructed to resume course to Cape Town.[6] 'SoLant forces continued to sail the oceans blue along the African coast until April of 1961', notes the SoLant Amity veteran Ed Shea, 'but well out of sight of observant eyes'.[7]

* * *

RAJESHWAR DAYAL WAS GREATLY saddened by the death of Lumumba. His grief was informed not so much by friendship as by a powerful sense of injustice over the fact that the man who had been democratically elected had been destroyed. 'His cruel end', Dayal believed, 'was a catastrophe for the Congo and a tragedy for Africa'.[8]

Dayal himself was the victim of a savage and vigorous campaign against him—in New York by the Western powers, and in the Congo by Ileo's provisional government and by US officials, especially Larry Devlin.

From the moment Dayal had arrived in the Congo, Devlin complained, he was 'a thorn in the [American] embassy's side'. In Devlin's perception, Dayal had a strong anti-American bias and 'had a way of needling Americans, particularly at one-on-one meetings where there were no witnesses'. He recalled one such incident 'that sent me through the roof': "'Ah, Mr Devlin", [Dayal] said. "I so admire America and Americans. You make the very best air-conditioners, the best refrigerators, so many fine machines. If only you could concentrate on making your machines, and let us *ponder* for you"'.

According to Devlin, Dayal carried this anti-American attitude into his work. And unfortunately, said the CIA station chief with resentment, 'Dayal appeared to be respected and admired by Hammarskjöld'. Devlin believed that the secretary general's reliance on Dayal posed serious problems for American interests.[9]

Even after Lumumba's death, when Dayal was in New York for discussions with Hammarskjöld, he was denounced for his support of the legitimate prime minister of the Congo. But overall, noted Dayal, 'There was no specific criticism of any of my actions or decisions, only vague innuendoes about my being pro-nationalist and even Communist'. Sections of the Western press went on muckraking expeditions but could not find anything specific to use against him. Even so, the *Washington Post* published a cartoon showing Dayal in a jeep, blazing a trail for Khrushchev in the Congo, who was following in a bulldozer. Dayal was taken aback by the virulence and dishonesty of the attacks against him.[10]

At the same time, there was considerable pressure from African and Asian countries for Dayal to return to the Congo and continue his work. In the Indian Parliament, Nehru rose to condemn the campaign against Dayal, and there were widespread demands in India to recall the Indian UN contingent from the Congo.

Dayal was finally forced to resign towards the end of May 1961. He was concerned that if he were to return to the Congo, it would prejudice the UN mission. For the US, Dayal's departure removed a major obstacle to their plans for the Congo. But for Hammarskjöld, it was a terrible blow; he accepted Dayal's resignation with great reluctance. According to an official in Washington, Hammarskjöld was 'obviously sore and unhappy'.[11] He made a public statement in which he emphasised Dayal's 'highest ability and level of performance', as well as his 'unfailing integrity'.[12]

Hammarskjöld's special representative left the UN to return to his office as India's high commissioner to Pakistan. Dayal was possessed of immense courage. Throughout the ordeal of physical intimidation in the Congo and of personal attacks and unjustified smears, he never compromised his principles. He was guided at all times by the tenets of the UN Charter and by the rights of the legitimate government of the Congo.

Meanwhile, Hammarskjöld was growing increasingly uncomfortable about the interference in UN matters by the West, most notably the US, which he regarded as an attack on the integrity of the world organisation itself. 'Wouldn't it be better,' he asked Ralph Bunche, 'for the UN to lose the support of the US because it is faithful to law and principles than to survive as an agent whose activities are geared to political purposes never avowed or laid down by the major organs of the UN?'[13]

* * *

JOSEPH ILEO AND HIS government were failing to establish any real authority outside the Leopoldville and Equateur provinces. Meanwhile, Gizenga was consolidating his power in Stanleyville. Just a few days before the first anniversary of the Congo's independence on 30 June 1961, CIA official George Wittman sent a report warning of the real risk of a Gizenga government. 'This seems a very poor end indeed', observed Wittman pragmatically, 'for the tens of thousands—indeed millions of dollars of both open and under the table assistance that has been given to the Congo since the Mobutu coup last September'.[14]

It was evident to the US and the CIA that a change of direction was required urgently. The Kennedy administration, notes the historian Stephen Weissman, 'decided to bring about a legal parliamentary regime under Cyrille Adoula that would absorb Gizenga and his allies'.[15]

Representatives of Hammarskjöld held discussions with the various authorities in the Congo on the question of convening Parliament; Kasavubu was responsive. At the same time, the UN mission made strenuous efforts to bring about a rapprochement between the leaders. In June 1961, delegations from Leopoldville and Stanleyville met and agreed that Parliament—the lawmakers elected in May 1960—should convene. Under arrangements devised by the UN, members of Parliament assembled at the University of Lovanium in mid-July for discussions. On 1 August, President Kasavubu nominated the labour leader Cyrille Adoula to head the formation of a federal government.

Behind this outcome was the generous hand of the CIA, which in June had decided to set aside $23,000 to support America's choice of politicians in the Congo.[16] 'To avoid a too obvious American involvement, and in the interests of speed and efficiency', noted the *New York Times* in the second of its series of five articles on the CIA in April 1966 (which are discussed in Chapter 5 of this book), 'the Government again turned to the CIA'. The *Times* added, 'Money and shiny American automobiles, furnished through the logistic wizardry of Langley, are said to have been the deciding actors in the vote that brought Mr. Adoula to power. Russian, Czechoslovak, Egyptian and Ghanaian agents were simply outbid where they could not be outmaneuvered'.[17] A local saying, Wittman reported, 'goes that money is flowing like wine, and wine is merely flowing in search of votes for the parliament meeting. The current price quoted by an official in the French Embassy (who certainly should know) for a pledged vote is $3,000, United States'.[18]

On 2 August 1961, Adoula presented his government to the two houses of Parliament, describing it as a government of national unity and political reconciliation. Gizenga was appointed deputy prime minister; Gbenye, a Lumumbist, became minister of the interior. Such a broad-based coalition looked promising, even though Katanga and Kasai remained outside the joint government. The government was approved in the Chamber of Deputies by a unanimous vote, with one abstention, and in the Senate by a unanimous vote.

Dean Rusk, US secretary of state, sent Kennedy a memorandum the next day. 'Adoula's victory', he reassured the president, 'removes any legal basis for Gizenga to claim that his regime is the legal government of the Congo. It is the second Soviet defeat in the Congo'.[19]

The Stanleyville government-in-exile was dissolved. A CIA memorandum observed with satisfaction, 'The UN and the United States, in closely coordinated activities, played essential roles in this significant success over Gizenga'.[20] After the election, Adoula hosted his peers at the Restaurant du Zoo, where, the previous October, Lumumba had given a powerful speech denouncing the US for interfering in Congolese politics.

The US embassy sent a favourable report on the first ten days of Adoula's government to the State Department. It submitted seven key guidelines, including 'Early approval Tempelsman barter deal most desirable'. This was a reference to the trading scheme that Tempelsman had proposed to Kennedy in January 1961, whereby agricultural goods—instead of cash—would be used ostensibly to pay for diamonds, but more likely to pay for uranium.

Since 1959, Adoula had been carefully groomed—and well funded—for his role as the leader of the Congo by Howard Imbrey and other CIA agents. He was an ideal contrast to Lumumba in the eyes of the US: he was closely associated with the pro-Western and CIA-backed International Confederation of Free Trade Unions and was praised by Timberlake as 'an intelligent and well-balanced moderate whose chief interest has been in organizing an independent African labor movement'. Adoula was strongly anticommunist, added Timberlake, and 'has talked openly with the American Embassy in Leopoldville, which long considered him one of the best prospects for top leadership in the Congo'.[21] Adoula's key political supporters, the Binza group, continued to receive CIA subsidies.[22]

Howard Imbrey, who had a good relationship with Adoula, sought to build up his reputation throughout Africa. Imbrey's public relations firm, the New York–based Overseas Regional Surveys Associates, was formally hired by the Adoula government as its public relations coordinator for several years.[23] Imbrey later said, 'To do the, you know, the public relations for the Congo, I had to visit every African country, represent the Congo, and speak for them. They had very few people to do that sort of thing themselves. They had only a few graduates from college and they certainly had other jobs. So for the next three or four years I was in all parts of Africa'. He summed up his role: 'Public relations handler with an office in New York and tired feet in Africa'.[24]

* * *

THE SUCCESS OF US aims in the Congo was matched by the failure of the joyful hopes for freedom that had been felt by millions of Congolese people on 30 June 1960. Despite the new joint government, the promise of reconciliation between the different political and regional groups was swiftly shown to be empty. Adoula's government, wrote Nzongola-Ntalaja, 'was basically a puppet regime, responsive to the pressures of General Mobutu, who had become a veritable kingmaker due to his external ties, and taking its directives from the US Embassy in Kinshasa'. He adds that, having outmanoeuvred the Lumumbists at Lovanium, 'Adoula's tutors and advisers sought to diminish their influence in the new government, before having them dismissed'.

By January 1962, Deputy Prime Minister Gizenga had been arrested on the orders of Adoula and exiled to the lonely island of Bulabembe, at the mouth of the Congo River. 'The first independence had failed', notes Nzongola-Ntalaja. 'It was time to fight for a second independence'.[25]

35

Hands off Ghana!

O N 8 March 1961, the day after his speech to the UN General Assembly, Nkrumah flew to Washington to meet with Kennedy. The American leader was waiting for him at the airport and, despite a heavy downpour of rain, hastened to greet Nkrumah as he stepped from his aircraft. It was an expression of friendship that had been strikingly absent when Nkrumah met Eisenhower at the UN in September 1960.

The two men, both smiling, went into a dry hangar to speak to the press. Nkrumah appeared tired from his travels and negotiations in New York. By contrast, Kennedy—eight years younger and still new to his position—was fresh and energetic. Kennedy spoke first, welcoming Nkrumah to America—'which he knows so well'. Then he quoted President Jefferson—'The disease of liberty is catching'—before adding, 'It has been the object of our guest's life to make sure that that disease spreads around the globe'.

Nkrumah said solemnly, 'We all look forward to a period of continued cooperation and understanding between our two countries'.[1]

At their meeting in the White House, the two men focused on the Congo. They agreed that Belgian military personnel should be removed and that the Congolese should be free to work out their own political situation, without foreign interference.[2] The meeting took place against a large measure of mutual mistrust, rooted in their different views on Gizenga. But it ended on a personal note that gave Nkrumah sincere pleasure: Kennedy took him upstairs to meet Jackie Kennedy and their daughter, Caroline. On the plane back to New York, Nkrumah penned a warm note of appreciation to Kennedy; he told his aides that he believed the meeting 'marked a new era of African-American friendship'.[3]

* * *

NKRUMAH WAS UNAWARE THAT a few weeks earlier, in late February and early March, Komla Gbedemah, Ghana's minister of finance, had spoken against him to American officials in Washington. Gbedemah was there on behalf of the Ghanaian government to work out the details of a contract with the US government and the World Bank to finance the huge Volta River hydroelectric project.

Dean Rusk reported to Kennedy on 7 March that he had been unable to talk privately with Gbedemah because members of the minister's entourage were always with him. But, he added, Gbedemah had discussed matters with other officers of the State Department. He had told them that the Soviets had established a foothold in Ghana, which he deplored, and that he was finding it increasingly difficult to make his voice heard. He delivered a strong message to the United States: it should be more aggressive, or it would lose out in Africa.[4]

* * *

THE AMERICAN GOVERNMENT HAD looked favourably on Komla Gbedemah for some time. In January 1959, Edwin 'Ned' S Munger, a political geographer at the California Institute of Technology who travelled widely through the African continent and lived for a year in Ghana, wrote an enthusiastic report about Gbedemah, *Ghana's Finance Minister, Komla Agbeli Gbedemah: A Study of a Remarkable African Personality, His Problems, and His Policies*. The month before writing the report, Munger had attended the All African People's Conference in Accra, representing the American Universities Field Staff. There he met Lumumba, who Munger thought 'had the attention of the KGB, which supplied him with funds for his campaigning in the Congo'.[5] Munger was a trustee of the CIA-sponsored African-American Institute and was responsible for some time for overseeing its publication, *Africa Report*.[6] It has been suggested that the American Universities Field Staff was also sponsored by the CIA.[7]

Komla Gbedemah, along with Kojo Botsio, was the most powerful figure in the Convention People's Party after Nkrumah. In the years of struggle against British rule, it was Gbedemah who had led the campaign to get the imprisoned Nkrumah elected to the legislative assembly; he was widely regarded as the architect of victory.[8] On the night of Ghana's independence in 1957, at the celebrations on the Old Polo Ground in Accra, Gbedemah and Botsio had stood together with Nkrumah.

Gbedemah was a tall, distinguished-looking man with an upright bearing who, like Nkrumah, had studied at Achimota School. He had great charm and was very clever, a 'first class organiser'. He spoke most major Ghanaian languages perfectly and was also 'a polished and suave negotiator in English'.[9] He was very formal: at independence, he had suggested that the ministers should attend the evening functions in tails. 'Never!' Nkrumah declared. 'An African in tails looks just like a penguin'.[10]

Gbedemah served as Ghana's first minister of finance. But his approach led to disputes with Nkrumah, who thought he was too orthodox. He had failed to introduce effective exchange-control legislation or to do away with the sterling exchange system in Ghana, a remnant of the colonial state.[11] In relation to foreign policy in Africa, Gbedemah took a pro-Western, moderate position and had little tolerance for the extensive support provided by Ghana to freedom fighters and liberation movements.[12] Gbedemah went from being one of Nkrumah's closest friends and associates to being one of his fiercest critics. To the American government, this rupture looked promising.

Since independence, Gbedemah had carved out a number of profitable businesses. According to the American ambassador in Ghana, Francis H Russell, the press had made allegations against Gbedemah of diamond smuggling.[13] As Russell found out after he took up his appointment in January 1961, Gbedemah was linked to the businessman Maurice Tempelsman, whose business was involved in diamonds in Ghana.

Russell asserted that Gbedemah was in discussions with the CIA. 'The CIA was quite active in Ghana', said Russell in an oral-history interview with William W Moss in 1973. 'I had excellent relations with our CIA people. We worked very closely. They made, not complete reports to me of everything that was said or all the meeting[s] they had, but I felt that I was being adequately briefed in general on what they were doing. They had quite a few good contacts in Accra and out around the country'. The CIA officer 'came in quite regularly, almost daily', added Russell, 'and would give me reports on what they had picked up about Nkrumah, about the activities of the Soviets, and other things that would be of interest'.[14]

The level of the CIA presence in Ghana astonished the South African Michael Hathorn, who lived in Accra in 1961. A medical doctor who worked as a researcher, he had been imprisoned by the apartheid government in 1960 and then, unable to obtain a passport, had escaped to Ghana. He saw that Nkrumah had brought over from the US some people from the National Institutes of Health and Medical Research (NIHMR) in Bethesda, Maryland. Some of these men, observed Dr Hathorn, were genuine scientists—but others seemed suspiciously like CIA. Regarding a paediatrician, Hathorn couldn't remember him doing much in paediatrics; rather, he spent most of his time at the US embassy. In a laboratory next door to Hathorn was a biochemist who seemed to know less about biology than Hathorn did. The biochemist spent nearly all his time on a secret radio; his cover story was that he was delegated to set up a radio network to integrate with the medical services—which, Dr Hathorn commented, was unnecessary.[15]

Hathorn discovered that the role of NIHMR was evidently of interest to the Soviets. 'At one of the Cuban diplomatic parties held at the Ambassador Hotel', he noted, 'I had struck up a conversation with one of the people working at the Soviet Embassy in Accra, one Alexei Ivanovitch Savchenko. He was a very likeable young man, living with his wife Rosa and small daughter Sasha'. Savchenko invited Dr Hathorn and his wife to his home for a meal, 'to get to know more about the situation in South Africa'. When the Hathorns arrived, 'there was a small party—we thoroughly enjoyed the ice-cold vodka, drunk neat and immediately followed by sucking a slice of lemon, followed by caviar on black bread. . . . It was a great party'.

Shortly thereafter, Savchenko asked Hathorn if he could see him about a problem; they met at the beach near Accra's Korle Bu hospital the next day. To Hathorn's surprise, the Russian told him that 'the Soviet Embassy was desperately short of information about what was happening with medical research in Ghana, and the role of the NIHMR. . . . Could I help?' Hathorn had no such information to give him. Nonetheless, the two stayed friendly and continued to entertain each other's families. When the Hathorns went to England in 1965, they were never contacted again—'much to my relief'.[16]

It is not surprising that the Soviets were interested in the National Institutes of Health in Bethesda. A Senate investigation in September 1977 named 'Human Drug Testing by the CIA' identified an association between the NIH and the CIA in the development of nonlethal weapons in the MKUltra programme during the 1950s and 1960s. Charles F Geschickter, a professor of pathology at Georgetown University, was closely involved in CIA-sponsored research, which the *Washington Post* described in 1977 as a 'secret, 25-year, $25 million effort to learn how to control the human mind'.[17] Geschickter, giving evidence to the Senate investigation, referred to a range of studies, including one on concussions in which the heads of living animals were rocked back and forth to try to trigger amnesia by concussion of the brain: 'that was for $100,000'. Another study directed radar at the brains of monkeys to put them to sleep.[18]

Dr Geschickter facilitated the funnelling of CIA money to researchers, including himself, by means of a private foundation, the Geschickter Fund for Medical Research. Over thirteen years, the total amount of CIA funding included more than $1 million to Geschickter's institution and well over $2 million to other universities.[19] The construction of a new research wing at Georgetown University Hospital, covertly funded by the Geschickter Fund, enabled the pursuit of agency-sponsored research projects in sensitive fields. The university was unwitting.[20]

In the course of the 1977 Senate investigation, Dr Geschickter stated that one of the by-products of his work was cancer research advancement. A report on this research came to him from Allen

Dulles, who said, 'Thank God there is something decent coming out of our bag of dirty tricks. We are delighted'.[21]

* * *

IN THE EARLY DAWN of 8 April 1961, the people of Ghana were surprised to hear the voice of their president on Radio Ghana. He was speaking to them so early in the day, he said, in accordance with the 'cherished custom of our fathers, whereby advice is given at early dawn'.[22] This 'advice' was a denunciation of financial impropriety by some members of his cabinet, his party and some senior civil servants. He condemned the 'evil of patronage . . . and its twin brother nepotism' and criticised those who used their position to amass wealth and extract bribes. He also denounced high living. Nobody, he insisted, needed more than one car and one house.

'It is most important', insisted Nkrumah, 'to remember that the strength of the Convention People's Party is derived from the masses of the people'. These individuals were 'the unknown warriors—dedicated men and women who serve the party loyally and selflessly without hoping for reward'.[23]

'What became popularly known as the Dawn Broadcast', notes Joseph Amamoo, author of Ghana: 50 Years of Independence, 'had immediate and profound effect'.[24] Ten days after the broadcast, Parliament announced that a Budget Bureau was to be created immediately under the direct control of Nkrumah, to investigate corruption. The bureau would take over budgeting from the Ministry of Finance.

Gbedemah was appalled. He said he would not accept this change and asked to be posted to another ministry; he was transferred to Health.[25] It was a significant demotion.

The creation of the Budget Bureau was followed by the presentation of a bill to Parliament to tighten the movement of private capital out of Ghana. And then, on 7 July, a tough austerity budget was set out by the new finance minister to quell rising inflation. Planned measures included a compulsory savings scheme and additional taxation in the form of income tax, property tax and a purchase tax on luxury goods.

A crisis of conflict arose between the old guard—the conservative right wing of the CPP—and the progressives. The conservatives complained that Nkrumah was lurching to the left, whereas the progressives were pleased with his new initiatives. They converted the independence slogan 'One man, one vote' to 'One man, one house' and 'One man, one car'.[26]

Two days after the announcement of the austerity budget, Nkrumah and a sixty-person delegation embarked on a two-month trip to the Soviet Union, the Eastern European countries and China. The itinerary was noted with pursed lips in the US. At the end of the official tour, Nkrumah's wife and children would join him for a two-week vacation at Khrushchev's dacha on the Black Sea. He would return to Ghana on 16 September. Nkrumah left a three-man presidential commission to govern Ghana in his absence. One of these men was Komla A Gbedemah.

Nkrumah appears to have been unconcerned about leaving the country for so long. His government was popular, and the membership of the CPP had doubled from one to two million people in 1960–1961. An articulate opposition existed, but it did not have widespread support.[27] Overall, Ghanaian citizens felt they were building a modern and successful nation and benefiting from the government's policies and measures.

* * *

WHEN NKRUMAH RETURNED TO Ghana, the nation was in turmoil. On 4 September, a general strike of railway and harbour workers had been declared in Sekondi and Takoradi, located in the western region of Ghana.[28] Nkrumah demanded on national radio that striking workers return to their jobs. But the next day, three thousand skilled and semiskilled workers went on strike in Accra. Workers in Takoradi ignored the order.

Against the background of this instability, Gbedemah invited US Ambassador Russell to his house several times for dinner. Towards the end of the first week of September, Russell was told by Gbedemah of a startling plan—to unseat Nkrumah.[29] 'I had called on Gbedemah on business of some kind', Russell later recalled in his interview with William W Moss. Gbedemah, he told Moss, 'had been unusually frank in telling me how he felt, and kind of looked at me with a questioning look as though he would like to know, well, what did I think about it, you know, what did I think he ought to do? He didn't ask me that question, but put it in terms of how he felt, what his views and policies were. It was a very dangerous thing for him to do'. Russell reported on this conversation to Washington on 6 September.[30]

The next day, Russell sent further information to Washington. Gbedemah, he said, had told him, 'I would be sorry to have to do it but [the] country has had enough of Nkrumah's arrogance, whims and madness'. The plan was provided for by the constitution; the chief justice had remarked a few weeks earlier that 'when [the] time for destoolment comes procedure exists for effecting it'.[31]

Somewhat to Russell's surprise—and much to his approval—he was told by Washington that if he thought ousting Nkrumah was a good idea, he could call on Gbedemah and say 'that the department appreciated the position that he was taking, and they could count on the support of the American government if he should decide to take certain steps'.

Russell told Moss that he did not get involved in discussions about the plot with the CIA. 'I didn't know anything about any conversations between the CIA and Gbedemah', he affirmed. 'All that I knew was that he made this statement to me. . . . I was a bit surprised at the extent to which I was authorised to go in the conversation'. But, he added, he thought it could be 'reconstructed, in view of the extent of the CIA activity in the country, that there were some conversations between our CIA head representative and Gbedemah, and if a statement was made to Gbedemah, that he would receive funds, it must have been made by a CIA representative'. Russell added, 'It may be that Gbedemah was encouraged to make the statement that he did because of some previous CIA conversations with him. It's conceivable that I was authorised to make the statement that I did after consultation between the department and CIA back in Washington'.

During the interview, Moss made an observation to Russell on the role of the CIA: 'This differentiates a little bit between an activist role and a passive reporting role on the part of the CIA'. Russell agreed, replying, 'This is a situation in which it's difficult to draw a very precise line'.[32]

* * *

WASHINGTON WAS READING ITS cable traffic with Ghana with care. The matter of the Volta River hydroelectric project was pressing, and the US needed to respond to Ghana's request for funding. Kennedy discussed the issue over the telephone with George Ball, the undersecretary of state. One option, noted the president, was to back out of supporting the Volta Project and 'immediately commit a good percentage of the money to some other African countries'. Then, at least, 'we wouldn't look like we had pulled the rug out of Africa—just Ghana'. Ball advised Kennedy to sit tight on the decision. 'There was a chance', he said, that 'this fellow might get overthrown in the next couple of weeks and a really solid government come in. The situation is very fluid'.[33] The State Department also wanted 'to see if Gbedemah gets anywhere'.[34]

Kennedy told Ball that he had 'given up' on Nkrumah. 'He's been unnecessarily difficult with us', said Kennedy, 'considering the effort we've really made about him'. Kennedy voiced his strong objection to Nkrumah's wish to send four hundred Ghanaian soldiers to the Soviet Union for training.[35]

There was concern, though, that Gbedemah had 'little aptitude for intrigue'. According to the historian Richard Mahoney, on the basis of confidential interviews he conducted with a Ghanaian CIA operative and a CIA officer in the US embassy, Gbedemah seemed to want the Americans to do all the work for him; he 'spent as much time plotting with the CIA station chief in Accra as he did with other Ghanaian conspirators'.[36]

Gbedemah's conspiring involved the American businessman Maurice Tempelsman and his agent in Accra, one Mr Grosse. It has been impossible to discover any information about Grosse—not even his first name.[37] He is not mentioned by George Wittman in his reports to Tempelsman. Given that Wittman, a CIA official, was working in association with Tempelsman in the Congo and Ghana, it is possible that Grosse was also employed by the CIA.[38]

Russell's cables to Washington show that he was kept informed of dealings between Grosse and Gbedemah. Grosse was to play a key role in Gbedemah's plot.

On 21 September 1961—just five days after Nkrumah's return from his two-month trip—the plot was suddenly blown. Grosse telephoned Tempelsman in New York on an open transatlantic line and told him about a secret scheme against Nkrumah by Gbedemah, involving US support. The telephone line was being tapped by Ghanaian security and intelligence officers, and Nkrumah was immediately informed.

Grosse had 'spilled everything', including the name of the top CIA man in Accra; he had compromised 'everybody'. This was a disaster from the US point of view. McGeorge 'Mac' Bundy, the national security advisor to President Kennedy, suggested that the Ghanaians might not have a record of the conversation. George Ball replied, 'We might be lucky but we didn't deserve that sort of luck'.[39]

Over the next few days, Washington moved swiftly to limit the fallout. On 23 September, Bronson Tweedy, chief of the CIA's Africa Division in Washington, was summoned to Ball's office to attend to the damage. The next day, Ball telephoned Tempelsman and told him firmly that Mr Grosse had been 'quite indiscreet' and should be pulled out of Ghana.[40]

* * *

ON 22 SEPTEMBER, RADIO Ghana announced that the president was relieving General Alexander, the British chief of staff, who had been in the post for twenty-two months, of his duties, with immediate effect.[41] He was instructed to leave within days.[42] Nkrumah also relieved all 230 British officers of their command positions and ordered them back to the UK.

Before Alexander left, he went to say goodbye to the president. After the meeting, Erica Powell, Nkrumah's private secretary, stepped to the door to see him out. But Brigadier S J A Otu, who had been promoted to army chief of staff in place of Alexander and who had gone to the meeting with him, asked her to wait. 'The General had collapsed in bitter tears', Powell wrote. 'It was terrible to see this strong man overcome by such grief'.[43]

'It was politically imperative', stated Nkrumah's formal letter of dismissal to Alexander, that 'direct command of the Ghana Armed

Services should be held by Ghanaians'. Nkrumah added that he was 'greatly disturbed by the attitude which the British Government have taken over the question of Katanga in the Congo, and the assistance which the British Government have given to the secessionist elements in Katanga'.[44]

Nkrumah's disturbance over the attitude of the British had been fuelled by the death just a few days earlier of Secretary General Hammarskjöld in the plane crash in British-ruled Northern Rhodesia. Like many people across the world, Nkrumah was troubled by the details of the crash that emerged and by the lack of transparency about the crash by the British and the Rhodesian governments.

'There have been several theories about the affair, none of them entirely credible', Nkrumah noted five years later in *Challenge of the Congo*, 'and the circumstances of Hammarskjöld's death remain obscure. But as in the case of the murder of Lumumba, there are doubtless people living who can throw light on the tragedy and one day perhaps they may be induced to tell what they know'.[45]

The State Department reported to the US embassy in London that according to the British High Commission in Ghana, the British government was appalled by Nkrumah's 'perfunctory dismissal' of Alexander and his 'accusations [that the UK Government was] culpable [of] death Hammarskjöld and conditions [in] Katanga'.[46] In any case, Nkrumah had been harbouring doubts for some time about Alexander's loyalty to Ghana.

Dean Rusk had predicted to Kennedy that if Nkrumah went through with the plan to send officer cadets to be trained in the Soviet Union, Ghana's British-trained officer corps might depose him.[47] This would have involved Alexander. Furthermore, a report dated 14 September by the director of intelligence and research at the State Department had observed that it was unlikely moderate politicians would attempt a coup without army support. This assessment was based on his sense of Nkrumah's political astuteness and of his popular support.[48]

Alexander was humiliated by his dismissal and bitter with anger at Nkrumah. Once back in London, he gave an interview to a correspondent for the magazine *Topic* in the exclusive White's Club on

St James's Street. He objected to what he described as Nkrumah's 'grandiose schemes'. 'Kwame is finished', he said bluntly. 'It's a tragedy'. Nkrumah's downfall, he added, was 'inevitable', and 'bloodshed seems certain'.[49] Meanwhile, Alexander bought a couple of horses with some of the £2,000 he had received from the Ghanaian government as compensation for his dismissal, which the government was contractually required to pay.

* * *

DESPITE THE EXPOSURE OF his plans to unseat Nkrumah with the help of the CIA and Tempelsman, Gbedemah had not given up. On 25 September, in a top-secret cable to Washington, Ambassador Russell reported that Gbedemah was 'determined to make his last stand'.[50] In Russell's judgement, he had less than a 50 per cent chance of success but should be 'discreetly supported'.[51]

Russell was keeping his finger on the pulse of developments. Grosse had already returned to Accra, and on 27 September a dinner meeting was held at his house for the conspirators: Gbedemah, W A Wiafe (an MP and ministerial secretary in the Volta River secretariat) and Hugh H Cofie Crabbe, the executive secretary of the Convention People's Party. They were apparently functioning as a 'central committee' for a New Ghana National Party, supported by the police commissioner and the minister for trade.

At the dinner, Gbedemah said he was determined to overthrow Nkrumah by peaceful means and through constitutional processes. The men planned to announce the formation of the new party at the opening of the National Assembly on 10 October. Simultaneously, Wiafe would deliver a written resignation to the president at Flagstaff House.

Grosse reported to the conspirators that Washington was especially interested in the attitude of Brigadier S J A Otu and his potential role in the plans. Otu had worked closely with Alexander in the Congo as a senior member of the Ghanaian UN contingent, and had been appointed by Nkrumah to take over Alexander's role as army chief of staff. Gbedemah said he would check him out.

Throughout the meeting, Grosse took an advisory role. He suggested that Gbedemah draft a statement of principles for the new party, which could be released abroad to time with the action in the National Assembly.[52] The principles were entirely consistent with American preferences: one of them required that trade unions should not be tied to any political party or government.[53] Russell noted that although Grosse had said he would bow out of the ongoing conspiracy, he was evidently still playing an instrumental role. Russell asked Washington for advice on how to deal with him.[54]

On 28 September, Nkrumah dismissed Gbedemah from the government, but Gbedemah was still not ready to give up. Grosse and Cofie Crabbe called on Russell to report that Gbedemah wanted the American assistance that had been agreed on, to be provided as soon as possible. They said, 'He plans move [at] any event'.[55]

Nkrumah moved too swiftly for Gbedemah. In September, charges of dereliction of duty and corruption were brought against several of the old guard, including Gbedemah himself, Kojo Botsio (the speaker of the National Assembly), Krobo Edusei and A E Inkumsah. In October they were removed from office. Tafia Adamafio took over the position of minister of information and presidential affairs, with Cofie Crabbe and Ako Adjei as minister of information and minister of foreign affairs respectively. Kwaku Boateng became the executive secretary of the CPP and was later named minister of the interior.[56]

On the day that had been planned for Gbedemah's move against Nkrumah—10 October 1961—Parliament opened; it was peaceful and quiet in Accra and the rest of the nation. Gbedemah proclaimed his innocence in a spirited speech in which he was critical of Nkrumah's 'dictatorial tendencies'. Then he swiftly left the country.[57] Before he departed, somebody from the US embassy approached him and offered him financial assistance.[58]

Gbedemah first went to London, where he met a senior member of the US embassy. Meanwhile, Ball heard that Gbedemah planned to go to New York in November to see Tempelsman.[59] Eugene Black, the president of the International Bank for Reconstruction and Development, received a confidential letter from

Gbedemah, which Black then forwarded to Ball; he also told Ball that Gbedemah was going to talk to someone in the US government.[60] Gbedemah then went to West Germany.

On the same October day that the Parliament of Ghana had opened, an announcement was made that seventy-six Ghanaian cadets had been flown to Moscow to be trained as army, naval and air force officers. The news was noted with strong disapproval in Washington.[61]

* * *

THE CONSPIRACY HAD FAILED. Nkrumah had triumphed over the plotting of his opponents in the US and at home to overthrow him.

In Accra, an official inquiry found that a plot against the government had been started before the budget modifications, but those changes had been seized on by the conspirators as an excuse for creating disorder 'and so covering the first stage of their far more serious intrigue'.[62]

The inquiry report said that the conspirators had come from within the leadership of the United Party, but were joined by certain members of the CPP who felt threatened by the government's campaign against corruption. The report added that the conspirators had the sympathy and the financial support of 'certain expatriate interests', and that 'certain colonial and imperialist powers intervened, directly or indirectly, by fomenting plots and conspiracies because of vested financial interests'. It also raised questions about General Alexander and senior British officers in the army.[63]

Nkrumah ordered eight arrests under the Preventive Detention Act of 1958, which allowed for the imprisonment of people without trial for five years. The detainees included Dr J B Danquah, the lawyer and politician who had stood unsuccessfully as a presidential candidate against Nkrumah in 1960. The American lawyer Pauli Murray, who had joined Ghana's School of Law at the urging of Maida Springer, worked secretly with another American lawyer to assist Danquah in preparing a defence.

While Danquah was in prison, his family received support from the CIA. This was exposed when Danquah was released the following year. In November 1962 he went to see the new US ambassador to Ghana, William P Mahoney, who had taken over from Ambassador Russell. Danquah asked Mahoney why the funds his family had been receiving had been cut after his release. Mahoney, who had known nothing about the arrangement, was highly displeased, since his authority was supposed to extend to all forms of embassy decision-making. He summoned the CIA chief of station to ask for an explanation, and he flew to Washington two days later to inform President Kennedy of the affair. The president sent Ambassador Mahoney to CIA headquarters for discussions with John McCone, who assured him that such unilateral activity by the CIA in Ghana would not happen again.[64]

* * *

GBEDEMAH'S ATTEMPT TO REMOVE and replace Nkrumah was a political act and parliamentary in scope; it was not an effort to overthrow a government by force. It was not, therefore, reminiscent of the actions taken by Joseph-Désiré Mobutu and his accomplices in the Congo to overthrow Lumumba. All the same, the two schemes shared a common feature: the secret involvement of the US government and its foreign intelligence service in a conspiracy to remove and replace a legitimate government. And in Ghana, as in the Congo, many American dollars were involved. Again in Ghana, as in the Congo, a powerful businessman participated in the plot: in the case of Ghana, Maurice Tempelsman, and in the Congo, Bill Burden.

At the State Department in Washington, George Ball and McGeorge Bundy wondered about Tempelsman, whose name had been cropping up not just in connection with the plot to depose Nkrumah, but also as the backer of the barter scheme to avoid cash payments for Congolese uranium. Bundy asked Ball in a telephone conversation about 'this fellow Tempelsman who keeps slipping things through the back door'. Ball told him that Tempelsman was 'a rather dubious fellow . . . smooth, soft-spoken . . . a manipulator', who had been a generous donor to the Republican Party during the Eisenhower administration. 'Now', added Ball, 'he emerges as a Democrat and a great friend of the New Frontier'.[65]

Kennedy was rather more appreciative and said that Tempelsman should not be 'downgraded'.[66] This was a strange thing to say,
given that a telephone call between Tempelsman and his agent in
Accra had exposed the role of the US administration in a conspiracy against a foreign government.

36

'America's Angolan'

T HE INSTALLATION OF CYRILLE ADOULA as the prime minister
of the Congo in August 1961 was good news for the Angolan
freedom fighter Holden Roberto. Living in Leopoldville, Roberto
was a long-standing friend of Adoula, with whom he had played
football in the 1950s for the Daring Club, the top soccer club in the
Congo.¹ Both politicians were backed and heavily financed by the
CIA.

Roberto depended increasingly on the hospitality and assistance
of Adoula's government, observes Stephen Weissman. 'Of course',
he adds, 'top [Congolese] leaders were on the CIA payroll and their
relationship with Roberto could only be enhanced by the sense of
a common benefactor'.²

The União das Populações do Norte de Angola, Roberto's political party, had been created in exile in 1954 in the Congo, in resistance
to Portuguese colonial rule. It identified with the ethnic group of
the Bakongo, who lived on both sides of Angola's northern border
with the Congo. At the All African People's Conference in Accra
in 1958, however, Roberto discovered that Kwame Nkrumah, Sékou
Touré and other leading African nationalists had no sympathy for
ethnic separatism. He therefore dropped 'Norte' from the name of
the party. It became the União das Populações de Angola (UPA),
and it had the aim of liberating the whole of Angola.

Once the AAPC came to an end, Roberto stayed in Ghana
for most of the following year, living at the African Affairs
Centre established by George Padmore. He then obtained a Guinean passport from Sékou Touré, which enabled him to go to New

York to campaign at the UN for international support for Angolan freedom.

Roberto returned to the Congo after its independence from Belgium at the end of June 1960. He received backing from Lumumba, who—mistakenly—considered Roberto a friend, as Larry Devlin noted to Washington.[3] Roberto's relations with Kasavubu became increasingly difficult. They were both from the Bakongo ethnic group, but they disagreed in their political aspirations for the Bakongo.

Roberto decided to leave the Congo and return to Accra, only to find that his relations with Nkrumah had cooled. The Ghanaian president charged him with being too close to the US and with refusing to join a united front with the Movimento Popular de Libertação de Angola (MPLA), the other principal party dedicated to the liberation of Angola, which had been set up in 1956.[4] The common-front policy was supported energetically by the Casablanca powers as the only way forward for Angola to free itself from Portuguese occupation.

The MPLA, which described itself as anti-imperialist, received funding from the Soviet Union and the Eastern bloc; consequently, it was perceived as an enemy to America. The MPLA actively favoured a union with other Angolan freedom fighters, a stance that the US firmly resisted.

In January 1961 Roberto returned to the Congo, where he successfully opposed demands from many of his supporters to form a union with the MPLA. Importantly, from April 1961 he was in close contact with the American embassy in Leopoldville.[5]

In February and March 1961, the UPA led a violent revolt in Luanda, the capital of Angola, and also in the northern region of the Portuguese colony. Attacks were made on farms, government outposts and trading centres, leading to the deaths of an estimated two hundred white people. 'This time', Roberto later stated, 'the slaves did not cower. They massacred everything'.[6]

The Portuguese responded 'with a veritable blood bath', writes Weissman.[7] Fleeing villagers were strafed and napalmed. Between twenty thousand and thirty thousand people were killed. Hundreds of thousands of refugees fled Angola, walking long distances to reach the Congo.

A range of new strategies was developed by the Portuguese in order to suppress the Angolan freedom struggle. One was an industrialisation policy for the colony, which included plans to greatly increase and support white immigration. Another was to send a massive number of troops to Angola, which was observed by G Mennen Williams, Kennedy's assistant secretary of state for African Affairs, on a visit to Angola in 1961: 'We could walk nowhere downtown without passing a dozen or so Portuguese soldiers, walking in groups of three or four. On the outskirts of Luanda, I saw sizable military encampments, and trucks rolled through the countryside. Angola is on a military footing'.

The revolt has been described as the beginning of the War of Independence against Portuguese colonial rule.[8]

* * *

FOLLOWING THE REVOLT, SOME in Washington expressed doubts about backing Roberto, since Portugal perceived American support of the UPA as a hostile act. There was concern, too, that America's publicly stated opposition to Portuguese colonisation was creating difficulties for the US, since Portugal was a member of NATO. Another factor was America's wish to continue its use of the Portuguese Azores as a military base.[9]

In April 1961, Roberto visited the US to campaign for American support, and on the 25th of that month, he had a successful meeting with President Kennedy.

Angola was of central significance to the US by reason of its geographical position, its mineral resources and the discovery of oil there in the mid-1950s. Additionally, the Benguela railroad, which carried freight from Katanga across Angola to the Atlantic Ocean for shipment onwards, was a key trade route. It was the same passage used by the US to freight uranium to the coast in World War II, before concerns about Portugal's association with Nazi Germany led to use of the (far more complex and difficult) route to Matadi. The Benguela railroad returned to use in the 1950s. 'It was the importance of the Shinkolobwe uranium, not a desire to work with black nationalists', notes Alexander Joseph Marino in his study of America's role in Angola, 'which brought Holden Roberto on the CIA payroll in 1955'.[10]

Roberto's successful visit to the US in April 1961 led to arrangements for him to receive an estimated $6,000 retainer through the CIA station in Leopoldville. The Portuguese objected when they found out about the arrangement, but they were told it was simply to tap Roberto as a source of intelligence. The funding increased to $10,000 in 1962 and continued to rise over subsequent years. Marino writes, 'Holden Roberto became America's Angolan', representing the US's plan for postcolonial Angola and for the southern Africa region.[11]

Time magazine, ever ready to support the role of the CIA in Africa, portrayed Roberto in April 1961 as 'a determined, soft-spoken, exiled African Angolan'.[12] However, his appearance was off-putting to some. 'Roberto wore dark glasses indoors. Very dark', observed a senior American official visiting the Congo. 'We couldn't see his eyes'.[13] His manner was described as 'conspicuously charm-free' and extremely arrogant.[14]

* * *

IN JUNE 1961, THE South African writer and activist Patrick Duncan went to the Congo on his way home from the US. He wrote an article about the visit in *Contact*, the Liberal Party journal he edited, which had a funding source associated with the CIA.[15] Duncan, who thought Angola was the key to the liberation of southern Africa, wrote an article setting out his approval of Roberto. Both Roberto's UPA and the MPLA—which were 'not on good terms'—were neutralist, he wrote, 'but the MPLA has shown itself prepared to accept help from the communists, while the UPA has refused it'.[16]

The MPLA was based in Guinea until late 1961, when it moved to Leopoldville to establish its first major headquarters. This was a logical choice for the MPLA, just as it was for the UPA, because of the proximity of the Angolan border; furthermore, the area sheltered a large community of Angolan refugees, greatly increased by the UPA-led revolt within Angola in February and March of that year. The MPLA continued to petition for a union of all Angolan liberation movements, a position that was firmly opposed by the UPA.

Roberto was closely associated with the American political scientist John A Marcum, whom he had met at the All African People's Conference in Accra. As discussed in an earlier chapter of this book, Marcum claimed to have acted at the conference as Lumumba's interpreter—a role that was filled, Nkrumah said later, by a CIA agent. Marcum was supported financially by the CIA via foundations and pass-throughs, which enabled his travels, research and publications; he also wrote for journals that were covertly subsidised by the CIA. However, it is unclear whether or not he was aware of this financial backing.

A few weeks after the AAPC, Marcum travelled to the Belgian Congo, just before the freedom riots swept the colony. He also went to Brazzaville, where he met other Angolan nationalists. These activities began a strong personal connection with the nascent political movements in Portuguese-ruled Angola and Mozambique.[17] Funded by the Ford Foundation, Marcum travelled widely through Africa. In January 1962, he travelled in Angola with Roberto and George M Houser, the executive director of the American Committee on Africa (ACOA), who had also been at the AAPC. The association created problems for Houser because it was widely known that Roberto received aid from the CIA; many assumed that for much of the 1960s, funding from the CIA was delivered through the conduit of the ACOA, which functioned as a pass-through. Houser strenuously resisted the allegation.

Marcum, who became established in the US as an expert on Angola, wrote *The Angolan Revolution*, a two-volume history of the Angolan struggle between 1950 and 1976. The publication in 1969 of the first volume, as well as a research grant to complete the second volume (published ten years later), was sponsored by the Center for International Studies at MIT, which was funded by the CIA.[18] The assistance, states Marcum in his first volume, was made possible by a grant to MIT from the Ford Foundation.[19]

Marcum acknowledged that Roberto was financed by the CIA. But he did not hold the CIA and the US government responsible for Roberto's implacable resistance to the goal of a common front against Portugal. In fact, argued Marcum, what looked like American influence was instead a function of Roberto's character, which was stubborn and arrogant.

But the US influence was real. Washington put pressure on Adoula to foster division between Roberto, who was seen as a 'bona fide nationalist', and the communist-backed MPLA. In October 1961, Secretary of State Dean Rusk cabled the US embassy in Leopoldville to express concern over intelligence that Roberto was in danger of losing control of the Angolan nationalist movement. The CIA, added Rusk, 'reports that the MPLA organization is moving into Leopoldville and that they are being supported by Gizenga elements, with [the] intention of throwing out Roberto. Dept considers Roberto genuine non-Communist nationalist and believes his continued control of Angolan nationalist movement in our best interests'. The State Department advocated the strengthening of Roberto's position, to avoid the risk of 'some accommodation' being reached between the UPA and MPLA.

Rusk recommended that the US embassy in Leopoldville make a discreet approach to Adoula, to ensure his opposition to any union of the UPA and MPLA. 'We believe', he explained, 'that MPLA takeover of Angolan nationalist movement would not be in Adoula's interest. Dept considers it would be helpful to Roberto and Adoula if latter informed US regards Roberto as the leader of the genuine Angolan Nationalist Movement'.

He continued, 'Unless you perceive objection, Dept requests approach be made on above lines, pointing out to Adoula need for extreme secrecy in order to avoid word of our approach getting back to Portuguese authorities. Presumably Adoula may wish to inform Mobutu of our approach'.[20]

* * *

THE TRINITY IN THE Congo of Roberto, Adoula and Mobutu— each one backed, funded and guided by the CIA—destroyed any possibility of a union between UPA and MPLA, which had been urged by the Casablanca powers. Nkrumah's passionate vision of a United States of Africa was fading further away.

Roberto divorced his wife and married the sister-in-law of Mobutu, which strengthened the two men's personal bond. But his position was weakening. His organisation—known as the FNLA since 1961—was unable to appeal as widely to Angolans as the MPLA, which was led from 1962 by the doctor and poet Agostinho Neto. The CIA decided to sideline Roberto; instead, it backed Jonas Savimbi, who had left the FNLA in 1966 to form the pro-Western Unita movement. In November 1975, after the Portuguese finally withdrew, the MPLA was recognized as the legitimate government of Angola.

When John Stockwell was assigned to the Congo (then Zaire) to command the CIA's Angola Task Force in 1975, he was appalled by the stupidity of America's policy for Angola. The CIA, he pointed out, had singled out the MPLA as an enemy, even though the MPLA wanted relations with the US and had not committed a single act of aggression against the country.

A bitter civil war between the MPLA and Savimbi's Unita ensued, lasting twenty-seven years and killing more than five hundred thousand people. South Africa and Mobutu's Congo intervened on the side of Unita, backed by the US. Cuba sent fifteen thousand combat troops to support the MPLA, which finally prevailed.

John Marcum became increasingly unhappy about American policy in Angola. He warned publicly that the US should avoid 'the trap of overreacting to hostile rhetoric and socialist advocacy and of identifying potential "enemies"'.[21]

In Stockwell's analysis, the US 'led the way at every step of the escalation of the fighting':

We said it was the Soviets and the Cubans that were doing it. It was the U.S. that was escalating the fighting. There would have been no war if we hadn't gone in first. We put arms in, they put arms in.

We put advisors in, they answered with advisors. We put in Zairian para-commando battalions, they put in Cuban army troops. We brought in the S. African army, they brought in the Cuban army. And they pushed us away.

They blew us away because we were lying, we were covering ourselves with lies, and they were telling the truth.

And it was not a war that we could fight. We didn't have interests there that should have been defended that way.[22]

In 1992, Holden Roberto ran for the presidency of Angola and won a mere 2.1 per cent of the vote. The power he had worked so hard for, and which had been so generously funded by the CIA with American taxpayers' money, had come to nothing. In the opinion of the Ghanaian writer Cameron Duodu, Roberto 'was a traitor to African liberation'.[23]

DARK DAYS

37

'The CIA Reptilian Coils'

ASSASSINATION, OVERTHROWING ELECTED GOVERNMENTS, SOWING conflict between political groups and bribing politicians, trade unionists and national representatives at the UN were some of the clandestine and coercive strategies used by the CIA to support American plans for the African continent. Other strategies took the form of soft power initiatives: the secret sponsorship and infiltration of educational facilities, artistic endeavours, literature and Africa-focused organisations.

On 13 February 1961—the same day that news of Lumumba's assassination was revealed internationally—a new institute, sponsored by the CIA, opened its doors in Leopoldville. This was the École Nationale de Droit et d'Administration (ENDA)—the National School of Law and Administration—which had been backed by Mobutu's College of Commissioners.[1] In March, the Ford Foundation announced a $228,000 grant for ENDA. The school's purpose, notes the historian Hugh Wilford, was 'to train local politicians in western administrative techniques (and, probably, channel CIA subsidies to them)'.[2] Its graduates were expected to move into careers in law and the civil service, taking over roles previously held by Belgians.

The rector of ENDA was Congolese: Étienne Tshisekedi, who was awarded the Congo's first doctorate in law from Lovanium University in 1961. Formerly an advisor to the MNC under Lumumba, Tshisekedi had shifted his alliance to Albert Kalonji and became a minister of justice in the seceded South Kasai.

But the running of ENDA was largely in the hands of its American director, James Theodore (Ted) Harris Jr, who was directly employed by the CIA and had been president of the CIA-backed US National Student Association in the late 1940s. In 1958, Harris had been appointed assistant executive director of the CIA front the American Society for African Culture, when he had taken an interest in the All African People's Conference in Accra. A tall African American, he frequently sported a goatee.[3] One of Harris's colleagues in the Congo described him as 'just one of those extraordinary brilliant guys' who had been singled out as a 'comer' by someone in the hierarchy of the white establishment. And 'as things were going to change', she added, 'they knew that they were going to have him in places; one of their black guys. You know. He was targeted. He was just extraordinarily talented, he spoke fluent French . . . he was a bon vivant'.[4]

The faculty of ENDA were mostly expatriates from the US, France and Belgium, with little knowledge of Congolese concerns. Tensions arose with the University of Lovanium over the types of degrees that ENDA was entitled to award.[5]

* * *

IN BRAZZAVILLE, THE INSTITUT d'Études Congolaises had been established in 1959 through the determination of Luis López Álvarez, Lumumba's friend, whose vision for the organisation was passionately shared by Lumumba himself. The institute continued to appeal to young adults on both sides of the Congo River. It was still sponsored by the CIA front the Congress for Cultural Freedom, which increased its funding from year to year. Its projected budget for 1961–1962, covering the costs of professors, scholarships and the library, was US$37,180, according to a report prepared by the CCF for the Charles E Merrill Trust, a CIA pass-through.[6]

Glowing testimonials of the institute's success were provided by recognised politicians and intellectuals; a well-known French journalist spoke of it 'in the most laudatory terms', observing that the institute was already exercising 'an influence which, in the future, could not but grow even greater'. One student warned in February 1961 that if the institute were to continue to accept other students, 'the room would be too small'. The CIA was feeding this approval; one of the testimonials was written by the editor of *Cuadernos*, the CCF-funded journal to which López Álvarez contributed a number of articles. Another testimonial was written by a representative of the International Commission of Jurists, which received money from the American Fund for Free Jurists, a conduit for CIA financing.[7]

López Álvarez was expelled from Congo Brazzaville in early 1961. In Paris, members of the Congress for Cultural Freedom were dismayed by the news. For without López Álvarez, the institute would no longer be managed by a CCF member. John C Hunt, the CIA-salaried executive director of the CCF, sent a letter to the institute in June, asking why López Álvarez had been expelled. The director replied with a detailed report that gave a list of reasons; the primary one was López Álvarez's warm friendship with Lumumba, which had apparently encouraged some students to talk of founding a branch of MNC-L in Brazzaville. Furthermore, López Álvarez's grief over Lumumba's death had affected students in Leopoldville, which was not to the liking of powerful people in the Congo. A rumour, rooted in fact, circulated that López Álvarez was preparing to write a book on Lumumba.

At the end of 1961, nine lecturers—from France, Switzerland, the Cameroons and French Guiana—received funding organised by the CCF to travel to Brazzaville to teach at the institute. Thirty students received financial support, and some 'scholastic leaders' were given small grants for study visits to Europe. Other contributions included the monthly publication of a periodical, *Buatu Ya Congo*; the purchase of subscriptions and books, in association with the African Section of the CCF; and the support of programmes in music, theatre and cinema.

* * *

THE INSTITUT D'ÉTUDES CONGOLAISES was the first cultural centre sponsored in Africa by the Congress for Cultural Freedom. The model was copied with the creation of the Mbari Artists' and Writers' Club in the commercial centre of Ibadan in 1961, in the early months after Nigeria's independence; its name was suggested by the writer Chinua Achebe.[8] According to a Peace Corps volunteer, it provided 'theatrical productions, art exhibits, art schools, and publishing', as well as library resources, for a membership fee of one pound.[9] The first president of the Mbari Club was the South African writer Ezekiel Mphahlele, who was living in exile and had been galvanised by the All African People's Conference in 1958. 'Inspired by Nkrumah', Mphahlele wrote in his memoir, 'we heard the rumble of wheels of freedom's chariot just around the corner'.[10]

The success of the original Mbari Club prompted the establishment of additional Nigerian branches in Osogbo and Enugu, all sponsored by the CCF. The club also became a publisher, producing books written by the Ghanaian poet J P Clark, the Nigerian poet Christopher Okigbo and Wole Soyinka. 'The historical irony', comments one analyst, 'is that as the Mbari writers sought to escape the orbit of the colonial university, the local publication venues to which they turned were surreptitiously funded by another global power: the United States'. Mbari Publications, he adds, 'was positioned within a complex network of cultural institutions, many of them supported by covert CIA funding, which helped to distribute its titles; it had a symbiotic relationship with [the journal] *Black Orpheus*'.[11] The system was incestuous: some of the titles were reviewed positively in *African Forum*, which was covertly funded by the CIA's AMSAC.

Members of the Mbari Club had no idea that it was the brainchild of the CIA. Most of them 'were distinctly unenthusiastic about American foreign policy', noted Gerald Moore, the British director of the Extra-Mural Studies Department of Makerere University in Kampala, Uganda, in the early 1960s; Moore coedited *Modern Poetry from Africa* (1963) with Ulli Beier, the Mbari Club founder. The club's members, said Moore, 'would have been horrified to know that the funds that built their premises in Ibadan came from the same courses that were busy toppling "unfriendly" elected governments from Greece to Chile and Guatemala, or sending exploding cigars to Fidel Castro'.[12]

Mphahlele had met Mercer Cook, who became director of the Africa programme of the Congress for Cultural Freedom, in Accra in 1958. A couple of years later, Cook proposed to Mphahlele that he succeed him as the director of the Africa programme, as he was about to leave for Niger as US ambassador. He invited Mphahlele to Paris for an interview with John Hunt, the undercover CIA officer who was the executive director of the CCF. The meeting with Hunt was a success, and Mphahlele moved with his family to Paris in August 1961.

'Our apartment', wrote Mphahlele in his autobiography, *Afrika My Music*, 'was to become a kind of crossroads for writers and artists'.[13] He was proud of the work of the congress, which he described as 'an international organization in Paris which encourages the arts, literature, music and scholarship all over the world. It organises conferences, music festivals, or sponsors them, and also assists individuals who pursue any of these branches of cultural activity'.[14] In his role as director of the Africa programme, Mphahlele travelled through large parts of Africa in 1962. 'Throughout the tour', he recorded, 'I was dispatching reports to John Hunt, Executive Director of the Congress, to give him a sense of the potential in each country'.[15] This was an ideal method for the CIA to obtain up-to-date and accurate intelligence about developments in African nations.

John Hunt suggested that an arts and culture centre be established in Nairobi. Mphahlele was sent from Paris to set it up in August 1963, a few months before Kenya's independence. It was named the Chemchemi Creative Centre, after the Kiswahili word *chemchemi*, meaning 'fountain', and was conceived as 'a sister to the three Mbari writers' and artists' clubs in Nigeria'. Its resources included an art gallery, a large arts and crafts studio, a conference room seating one hundred people, with a stage for experimental theatre, two offices and a reference library. The Farfield Foundation provided additional funds for special projects.[16]

* * *

IN THE UK, THE CCF developed an organisation similar to the Mbari Clubs: the Transcription Centre, which opened in Dover Street in London in February 1962 under the directorship of Dennis Duerden, a British man who had previously worked for the BBC African Service. Its brief was to record interviews with African and Caribbean writers, artists and intellectuals and to make the recordings available to radio stations in Africa.

Even as the plans for the centre were being developed, Duerden was being asked difficult questions about the CCF. After a tour of parts of Africa in 1961, he wrote, 'I had to explain how I came to be seconded to the Congress and what the Congress was doing sponsoring an enquiry into broadcasting. They know what the BBC stands for, but what does the Congress stand for? Where does its money come from? It must be a subtle instrument of American politics and he [his Nigerian interlocutor] would prefer it to come out in the open and admit what its politics are'.[17]

Nonetheless, Duerden went ahead with the centre, determined to maximise the opportunities it afforded for intellectuals and artists from Africa. The centre broadened its scope to include the making of television films, radio plays and music recordings, as well as the sponsorship of exhibitions, stage productions and discussion meetings. Gerald Moore comments that it became something of an informal club for all Black artists visiting London, as well as providing a flat for visitors.

The centre organised the performances of plays by Wole Soyinka and a fifteen-minute weekly radio programme called *Africa Abroad*, edited by the South African journalist Lewis Nkosi, who had worked on *Drum*. The centre also distributed the books published by the Mbari Club in Nigeria, and in 1964 Duerden published a periodical titled *Cultural Events in Africa*.

Exposure of the congress as a CIA front in 1966 created serious financial difficulties for the Transcription Centre. Sponsorship was switched from the CCF to the Farfield Foundation, yet another CIA front, which only made matters worse. 'The first unfortunate result', writes Gerald Moore, 'was the move from the chic and central Dover Street . . . to the back streets of Paddington. The West End premises . . . were essential to Duerden's vision of a virtual writers and artists club in a location where everyone could find it. . . . No one "drops in" to a place in the back streets of Paddington!'[18]

* * *

EZEKIEL MPHAHLELE'S LITERARY AND academic career went from strength to strength. In 1959, the year after the AAPC in Accra, he published a powerful memoir of his experience of apartheid, *Down*

Second Avenue. In 1966–1968 he was sponsored by the Farfield Foundation to study for a PhD in creative writing at the University of Denver. His thesis, a novel titled *The Wanderers*, won first prize for the best African novel in a competition organised by *African Arts* magazine at the University of California, Los Angeles.

When the source of the funding of the CCF and the Farfield Foundation was revealed in the mid-1960s, Mphahlele's response was one of anger. In a letter to the editor of *Transition*, he gave what he called 'my side of the story':

> Yes, the CIA stinks. . . . We were had. But in Africa, we have done nothing with the knowledge that the money came from the CIA; nor have we done anything we would not have done if the money had come from elsewhere. . . .
>
> We must naturally bite our lips in indignation when we learn the CIA has been financing our projects. But it is dishonest to pretend that the value of what has been thus achieved is morally tainted. . . .
>
> We attend a number of conferences abroad without ever asking ourselves the ulcer-promoting question where the organisers got the money from. We sit in hotel bars and get boozed up between conference sessions without asking ourselves such questions. . . . And it would be stupid to ask such questions, as long as one is satisfied that one is not compromising one's intellectual and moral integrity.

Then he insisted, 'I firmly believe that those who have, have the moral duty to give to those who haven't. . . . I know what poverty is. The rich must support worthy causes. It is a fiction to think that the poor must necessarily lose their self-pride when they are being helped'.[19]

Mphahlele continued his argument in *Afrika My Music*: 'A gong went. Someone blew the whistle. . . . Several of our accusers should also remember, I concluded, the conferences they had attended abroad and locally, where they were accommodated in posh hotels, and dined and wined on money which, for all they knew, might have come from a contaminated source'.[20]

Wole Soyinka was outraged by the discovery. 'Nothing, virtu-ally no project, no cultural initiative', he noted in fury, 'was left unbrushed by the CIA reptilian coils'. One such project, he com-plained bitterly, was the first Congress of African Writers and In-tellectuals, which was held at the University of Makerere in June 1962 and was sponsored by the Congress for Cultural Freedom. Or-ganised by Mphahlele, it brought together many of the best-known writers at the time from Africa and the African diaspora, including Soyinka, Ngugi wa Thiong'o (then using the name James Ngugi) and Chinua Achebe. Writers for *Drum* came, too, including the South Africans Lewis Nkosi, Nat Nakasa and Bloke Modisane, and the Ghanaian Cameron Duodu.

Yet more conferences in Africa were sponsored by the Congress for Cultural Freedom and other CIA pass-throughs, such as a sem-inar on French African Literature at the University of Dakar in 1963 and the Freetown Conference of African Literature and the University Curriculum held at Fourah Bay College, also in 1963. The papers given at these conferences were edited by Gerald Moore and published as a book by the CCF.

'Not one of us', lamented Soyinka about his fellow African in-tellectuals, 'had the slightest suspicion that a Farfield Foundation of America, which so lavishly expended its resources on the conti-nent's post-colonial intellectual thought and creativity, was a front for the American CIA!'[21]

Nevertheless, the reputations of some of these writers were af-fected by the revelations, because it was assumed they had been witting. They were yet more casualties of the injustice inflicted by the masquerades of the CIA.

* * *

THROUGH THE CIA's LAYERED and extensive network of connec-tions, writer Lewis Nkosi met John 'Jack' Thompson, the CIA-salaried executive director of the Farfield Foundation. Encouraged and aided by Thompson, Nkosi obtained funding for a year's fel-lowship at Harvard. 'One pearly-white evening in January of 1961', wrote Nkosi in *New African*, 'we were winging down over New York. Jack Thompson, the executive director of Farfield Foundation, and the man most instrumental for my coming out to America, was waiting on the balcony of the airport lobby. Jack Thompson and I had our first drink at the airport bar. The last time we had had a drink together was at Western Native Township on one incredibly hot night'. As Nkosi shows, Farfield hospitality was generous.[22]

Nathaniel 'Nat' Nakasa was also brought to Harvard by Jack Thompson in 1965, on a fellowship funded by the Farfield Foundation.[23] He had already been funded by Farfield to establish a literary magazine called *The Classic*, which featured writers such as Mphahlele and Can Themba. Soon after his arrival in the US, he became the subject of surveillance by South African intelligence and the FBI.

On one of his student assignments, he stayed at the Hotel Theresa in Harlem. When a Harlem shopkeeper showed him a photo of the burned body of a lynching victim surrounded by a crowd of grinning whites, he was shocked. 'I had never known such personal fear, not even in South Africa', he told *The Harvard Crimson*.[24]

One night, Jack Thompson invited Nakasa to spend the night at his Central Park West apartment. The next morning, the twenty-eight-year-old writer was found dead on the street, seven stories below Thompson's apartment. The death was reported as a suicide, and it was noted that Nakasa had been depressed at the time. However, many questions have been asked about what happened that night, and members of his family are convinced it was not a suicide.[25] The fact that he had spent the night in the apartment of a CIA official suggests that any sinister explanation for the death would point to the agency, but it is unclear why the CIA would wish him dead. The apartheid government of South Africa had identified Nakasa as a communist, but this had not prevented Thompson from facilitating his move to the US. One can speculate that Nakasa had discovered the source of his financial support and was planning to expose it.

The nature of Nakasa's death recalls the method of killing advocated in the 1950s CIA manual referred to in Chapter 20 of this book: 'the contrived accident', the most efficient of which was 'a fall of 75 feet or more onto a hard surface. Elevator shafts, stairwells, unscreened windows and bridges will serve'. Grabbing the victim by the ankles and 'tipping the subject over the edge' was recommended.[26]

Similar questions were asked about the death of Frank Olson, an American scientist working in the CIA's secret biological-warfare laboratories at Fort Detrick who fell from the thirteenth-floor window of a hotel in New York in 1953. The death was ruled a suicide, and he was labelled as depressed. However it emerged in 1975 that his drink had been covertly laced with LSD at the direction of Dr Sidney Gottlieb, the head of the Technical Services Division at the CIA, who ran the MKUltra programme—the same biochemist who went to the Congo to deliver poison to Larry Devlin to kill Patrice Lumumba.[27]

There are similarities between the tragic deaths of Frank Olson, of Abraham Feller, the chief legal counsel of the UN, in 1952, and of Nat Nakasa: all three were described officially as suicides; all three men were described as depressed; and all three fell from the balconies of New York high-rises.

* * *

IN THE LATE 1970s, Mphahlele changed his first name from Ezekiel to Es'kia. In 1990, he and Alf Kumalo cowrote *Mandela: Echoes of an Era*, which gives an account of Nelson Mandela's life, intertwined with a chronicle of forty-one years of the African National Congress. Four years later, in South Africa's first free elections, the ANC was voted into power and Mandela became president. Mphahlele returned home, and Mandela awarded him the Order of the Southern Cross, which at the time was the highest form of recognition in South Africa.

The lives of both Nelson Mandela and Es'kia Mphahlele were profoundly influenced by the CIA, but in markedly different ways. Mandela was a target of the agency's surveillance and covert operations, which led directly to his arrest in 1962, after CIA agent Donald Rickard gave the apartheid government information about Mandela's whereabouts and his disguise. For Mphahlele, the agency was a source of generous funding, international travel and contacts, and facilitated the publishing and positive reception of his work. It was also a source of anguish after the revelations about the role of the CIA in the Congress for Cultural Freedom.

Together, their histories illustrate the spider's web of the CIA's covert interference in Africa. It was a vast and spreading web, glued by money, violence and betrayal, collaboration with racist governments, propaganda projects and the hijacking of sincere artistic aspiration in a battle for hearts and minds.

Covert action of any sort, said Frank Church, the Idaho Democrat who chaired the 1975 Senate Select Committee investigation into the abuses of the CIA, was nothing more than 'a semantic disguise for murder, coercion, blackmail, bribery, the spreading of lies, whatever is deemed useful to bending other countries to our will'.[28]

38

Closing In on Nkrumah

B EGINNING WITH THE MURDER OF Patrice Lumumba, the year
1961 had taken a heavy toll on the Ghanaian president. By October, there was a new source of grief. Frantz Fanon, Nkrumah's
close and trusted friend and the ambassador to Ghana for the Algerian provisional government, became acutely ill. Fanon had received medical care for leukaemia earlier that year in the Soviet
Union, but his recovery was short term. In a desperate bid for life,
he agreed to be taken urgently to the US, to receive specialised
treatment at the National Institutes of Health and Medical Research in Bethesda, Maryland.

'Flying Fanon to the United States', comments Fanon's biographer David Macey, 'obviously involved some delicate politics'.[1]
The CIA appointed a case officer for Fanon for the duration of his
visit: Oliver Iselin, who had already been in contact with Fanon and
the Front de Libération Nationale while operating under cover as
a diplomat for the State Department in North Africa. Fanon does
not appear to have suspected that he was a CIA official.

Iselin described Fanon's arrival in the US to the American historian Thomas Meaney in 2016: 'He accepted to come to the States,
obviously with a lot of qualms because of his views and whatnot.
I went to New York and met him on the plane, got him down to
Washington and then put him in a hotel. He was a sick man. Oh,
he was hurting. He was tired'.

Iselin stayed with Fanon through his last days and sought to
assist his wife and son, who were guests of the Guinean embassy
in Washington. It was an opportunity for Iselin to extend and

strengthen his contacts in Africa. One of the visitors to Fanon's hospital room was Holden Roberto, who subsequently became a contact for Iselin in Angola.[2]

Fanon died on 6 December 1961, aged just thirty-six. 'Moumié, Lumumba and Fanon all died in their thirties', noted the Cameroonian freedom fighter Ndeh Ntumazah, recalling the time they had spent together at the All African People's Conference in Accra in 1958. 'I remember them all', he added sadly, 'being full of life and looking forward to enjoying it. Lumumba was tall and slim with his goatee beard. Fanon was of medium height, slim, with a fair complexion and very thoughtful. Moumié was shorter but also thin, with a big head'.[3]

Moumié and Lumumba had been assassinated in clearly violent acts. Many harboured suspicions about the pattern of early deaths of other men, too, even though they were certified as having natural causes.[4] Fanon died of leukaemia; Padmore died of a liver ailment in 1959 at age fifty-six. The following year, Richard Wright died at fifty-two from a heart attack; a few months before his death, his appearance had shocked Padmore's wife, who thought he resembled the way her husband had looked shortly before he died.

* * *

Nkrumah decided to hold a Freedom Fighters Conference in Ghana in late May 1962. But Tawia Adamafio, minister of information and presidential affairs, was apprehensive. As he related years later in his book *By Nkrumah's Side*, he warned the president that 'we were going to fish in troubled waters and draw to Ghana more CIA agents and imperialist spies. They would troop in as reporters and observers to collect information about freedom fighters to be used against them later'. Already, he wrote, 'Accra was filled to the brim by CIA agents and other spies. They had come in their numbers as reporters and observers'.

But Nkrumah believed it was a risk worth taking. 'The spies swarmed around us already', he said. 'We were swimmers and need not fear getting wet'.

All the same, the minister's warning troubled Nkrumah. Shortly before the scheduled start of the conference, he summoned

Adamafio at 12.45 am to tell him of a ruse he was planning. He proposed to cancel all hotel bookings for the delegates and instead to house them at the Ideological School at Winneba. While the change was being organised, the conference would begin immediately. Nkrumah and his team would travel daily to Winneba for the meetings without any motorcade or escort of any sort. Meanwhile, publicity would be arranged to mislead the spies by giving out the message that the opening of the conference would be postponed.

'When we have finished with the conference work', explained Nkrumah, 'we will appoint a day for the public opening of the conference and I will declare the conference closed that day'.

The plan went ahead. Adamafio waited until all the delegations had arrived and the 'international reporters, spies and poisoners were fluttering around Accra in droves', then he announced that the conference was postponed.[5] The secret conference proceeded, marred only by conflicts between the Angolan freedom fighters. 'All Freedom Fighting Africa was there', reported *New Age*, a South African left-wing newspaper, the following month.[6]

Shortly before the end of the conference, Adamafio announced that it would open at Parliament House on a fixed date. He later recalled: 'The attendance overflowed and there was no elbow room. We came in great style with a big motorcade. I had directed the various Party sections to their assigned places in Parliament Yard and the pressmen surged around us with their cameras and other devices like hungry wolves around their victim. We entered the House to a great ovation'.

Nkrumah gave a speech in which he 'lashed the oppressors of Africa'. At the end, he announced that the conference had been a great success and that all the work had been done at Winneba. At this, 'The crowd rose to a man, and roared. The roof nearly tumbled in'.

Then Kenneth Kaunda of Northern Rhodesia, dressed in Kente cloth, stood up, 'tall and stately', to deliver thanks, pronouncing Nkrumah 'the greatest son of Africa'. So far as the organisers could tell, the conference had not been infiltrated by foreign spies. 'Kaunda was given a standing ovation and Kwame declared the conference closed to the dismay of the spies and international detractors'.[7]

* * *

NKRUMAH'S TRIUMPH WAS SHORT-LIVED. On 1 August 1962, an attempt was made on his life. It occurred in the village of Kulungugu, in the northeastern corner of Ghana, when he was returning to Accra from talks with the president of Upper Volta (now Burkina Faso). As a child approached the president with a bouquet, a bomb hidden within the flowers exploded. Nkrumah's bodyguard pushed him out of the way, and the two men survived, with injuries. But the child was killed, and several others were injured.[8]

Nkrumah was horrified, especially by the killing of a child and the maiming of others. He was hospitalised for two weeks to remove the shrapnel from his back. Swiftly, arrests were made under the Preventive Detention Act of several associates of the president, including Tawia Adamafio, Foreign Minister Ako-Adjei and H H Cofie Crabbe. All three men were acquitted, but in 1964 they were sentenced to death for treason. The sentence was commuted to imprisonment (no political executions took place during the period of Nkrumah's rule).[9]

Following the assassination of Lumumba, it was reasonable for Nkrumah to assume that he might be next. He was aware, too, of violent attacks against other national leaders, notably the failed Bay of Pigs invasion of Cuba in April 1961. In all these disturbing events, he saw the menacing hand of the CIA.

Nkrumah suspected that some of his enemies, particularly those in neighbouring Togo, were plotting with Komla Gbedemah and the CIA. According to an analysis by the historian Mary E Montgomery, CIA reports and message traffic between US officials in Accra and Washington after the attack at Kulungugu refer to the likelihood that attempts to assassinate Nkrumah came from Togo, where the US was in active contact with Ghanaian exiles. In Montgomery's view, 'This suggests the possibility of US involvement in, or at the least, prior knowledge of, the assassination attempt'.[10]

More and more, commented the *New York Times*, Nkrumah believed that Ghanaian exiles were being trained and financed by the 'imperialists'. His fears had been reinforced by Andrew Tully's 1962 book, *CIA: The Inside Story*, which offered a disturbing account of the agency's destructive interference in foreign nations. Nkrumah reportedly bought five hundred copies of the book to distribute to friends and visitors. To Nkrumah, the book 'seemed confirmation that the CIA was really a "reactionary" state-within-a-state which often operated on its own, without White House bidding'.[11] The Accra newspaper *Evening News* began making attacks on US Ambassador William P Mahoney and accused the Peace Corps of being a front for the CIA.

The American writer Maya Angelou, who was still living in Accra, was appalled by the sudden change in daily life after the attack in Kulungugu. 'One day', she wrote later, 'the springs burst and the happy clock stopped running. There was an attempt on the President's life, and the spirit of Ghana was poisoned by the news'. Government officials, she added, 'began to search for spies everywhere. There were denunciations of American capitalism, American imperialism, American intervention and American racism'. This was a view she shared. 'At last', she thought, 'the average Ghanaian would realize that we, the band of disenchanted blacks, were not fabricating the tales of oppression and discrimination. Then they, not the politicians or intellectuals, they, the farmers and tradespeople and clerks and bus drivers, would stop asking us, "How could you leave America? Don't you miss your big cars?"'

But before she could 'really sit down and enjoy the feast of revenge, the shadow of the pointing finger moved' to the African American community in Accra: 'A high-ranking pundit said, "America can use its black citizens to infiltrate Africa and sabotage our struggle because the Negro's complexion is a perfect disguise". . . . He suggested finally, that Africa should approach all American blacks with caution, "if they must be approached at all"'.

As Angelou drove to her office at the university, 'Roadblocks delayed progress. They were manned by suddenly mean-faced soldiers, their guns threatening and unusual in a country where policemen were armed only with billy sticks'. Some suspects were imprisoned, and rumours flew about. 'None of the Revolutionist Returnees had been directly accused, and we were still grateful to be in the motherland', she recalled later, 'but we had been made a little different, a little less giddy and a lot less sure'.[12]

The security concerns of Ghana were not overreactions: in September 1962, a hand grenade exploded fifty yards from Flagstaff House, the president's residence, killing one person and injuring others. It was followed by four more bombings in the next four months.[13]

Kulungugu was 'the beginning of the end for Nkrumah', observed Ambassador Mahoney in a 1975 interview with William W Moss for the John F Kennedy Library Oral History Program. It was the 'beginning of a kind of a paranoid condition', added Mahoney—'a kind of paranoia on his part about the people around him and the West and the CIA and capitalists. . . . He was never the same after that'.[14] The same criticism had been levelled at Lumumba during the period up to his assassination and even afterwards. 'Critics then and later', note Gerard and Kuklick, 'saw paranoia in Lumumba's fevered complaints about his enemies'.[15]

But there is a difference between paranoia and a reasonable response to a genuine threat to one's life. It would have been foolish of Nkrumah to deny the dangers he faced after the assassination attempt at Kulungugu. As Genoveva Marais pointed out, 'he had great reason' for his distrust.[16] In fact, Nkrumah may have underestimated the full extent of the threats he faced: British government files at the time are riddled with references to plots against him. 'About every two years', reported the British High Commission in Accra to London, 'we are asked to help Ghanaian plotters to get rid of Nkrumah'.[17]

Fathia Nkrumah became increasingly worried about her husband's safety and that of their children and herself. She advised him to be careful not to accept bad advice from his associates.[18]

Nkrumah took careful measures. 'He became so suspicious', recorded Genoveva Marais, 'that he took sealed water with him everywhere; even when he came to my house he brought his own sealed water. On occasion, when he came to dine, he would cleverly make me start eating first, saying, "You go ahead, I'll sip my water first". He thought I had not noticed but I had'. Marais was shocked to witness his suspicions, even of her.[19]

Erica Powell, his private secretary, saw a dramatic change in her boss. 'I saw what seemed a shrunken, smaller version of himself seated at that enormous desk', she wrote later, 'his eyes gazing sadly into the distance'. She noticed that documents she should have been privy to were bypassing her desk.[20]

* * *

ON 31 JANUARY 1964, a referendum was held in Ghana proposing amendments to the constitution that would turn the nation into a one-party state, with the Convention People's Party as the sole legal party. Nkrumah maintained that a multiparty system was divisive and therefore unfit for the newly independent African states, which needed a unified energy in order to move forward. In 1960, Sékou Touré had declared Guinea a one-party state, and various other African countries followed this path after independence, including Kenya, Zambia, Mali, Senegal and Tanzania.[21]

The referendum was won. Nkrumah declared himself president for life of both the CPP and the nation, and gave himself expanded powers, including the power to remove members of the Supreme Court. 'Ghana was not a Western-style democracy', argues a study of America's role in Ghana in relation to Nkrumah, 'but neither was it a tyrannical despotism'.[22] All the same, the move did 'immense damage' to Nkrumah's image and reputation, comments Joseph Amamoo in *Ghana: 50 Years of Independence*.[23] It was widely condemned by the West as a further sign of Ghana's shift to communism.

The CIA was concerned that a one-party state rendered Ghana more difficult to infiltrate with Western personnel and interests. The lack of an opposition reduced opportunities for intervention and influence and created barriers to attempts to foster division. A CIA report commented that barring a successful coup against Nkrumah's government, it would be increasingly difficult for the West to maintain an effective presence in Ghana.[24]

The tension between Ghana and the US was growing more intense. Senator Thomas J Dodd, a Democrat who was vice chairman of the Internal Security Subcommittee of the Senate Judiciary

Committee, in 1963 pointed an accusing finger at Ghana, calling it 'the Cuba of Africa'. He claimed that Ghana, under Nkrumah, was 'the first Soviet satellite in Africa' and was 'the focal point for the subversion of Africa as Cuba is the focal point for the subversion of the Americas'.[25] The State Department moved swiftly to dissociate itself from Dodd's accusations, but many officials shared this view.

One of the reasons for the US mistrust of Nkrumah was Ghana's reactor project, which had gone ahead despite American opposition. The development of the Kwabenya Atomic Project, which lay about fifteen miles north of Accra's centre, was on track, and in 1962 Dr Robert Baffour, its head, was elected president of the IAEA. The Ghana Atomic Energy Commission was established the following year, and the construction of the reactor was officially launched soon thereafter.

American concern about Kwabenya turned to horror when Nkrumah invited Alan Nunn May, a physicist and former atomic spy, to Ghana in 1961, to work at the University of Ghana. May, a British communist who had worked on a nuclear reactor in Montreal for the Manhattan Project during World War II, had passed information to his Soviet case officer and then, three days after Hiroshima, two samples of uranium. Shortly afterwards he was betrayed by Igor Gouzenko, a Soviet defector at the Russian embassy in Ottawa.

For May, his acts of espionage were a moral imperative. He considered it necessary to give the USSR, who fought with the Allies against fascism, information it might need against a potential atomic attack. He judged the US to be morally wrong to keep the technology secret. In any case, he believed—as did Albert Einstein and many others—that nuclear information should be available to more than one country. He only embarked on espionage, he explained later in life, 'because I felt this was a contribution I could make to the safety of mankind'. He *did* feel remorse, he said, but not for sharing secrets; his regrets were for his participation in the atomic weapon project.[26]

May was prosecuted by the British government in 1946 and convicted. After his release from prison in 1952, the government tried, but failed, to prevent him from obtaining a British passport—and, later, from moving to Ghana. In an article titled 'Atom Spy to be Professor in Ghana', the *New York Times* linked the news closely with the fact that 'Ghana University was to be equipped by the Soviet Union with a nuclear reactor for research purposes'. The newspaper added that a spokesman at the Ghana High Commission in London 'did not know if Dr. May would have any connection with the reactor'.[27]

In Ghana, May set up the Solid State and Metal Physics Research Group in 1962 to train young scientists in the physics of solids; he also established a museum. May was eager to contribute to the development of Ghana, as was his wife, Hildegard, a dedicated doctor who cared for over two hundred mothers with their sick infants at a clinic in Accra's main hospital.[28]

The wish of the Mays to support the development of Ghana had been shared by Hildegard's first husband, Engelbert Broda, who was sent by the IAEA as a visiting professor to the TRICO Centre in Leopoldville in 1960. Aware that Broda had supplied the Soviet Union with atomic secrets in World War II, MI5 suspected that it was Broda who had recruited May when they were colleagues at Cambridge.[29] May had refused to give the name of his recruiter to the British, but Broda fit his profile.

* * *

MAY WAS NOT THE only well-known figure invited by Nkrumah to join the faculty of the University of Ghana, to the annoyance of the US government. Another was his friend Paul Robeson, to whom he offered a visiting professorship in April 1962. The Ghanaian government was told that such an appointment 'would have very unfavourable repercussions in the US'.[30]

As it turned out, Robeson's health prevented him from taking up the appointment. For just over year he had been suffering from a strange bout of mental illness, which his son suspected was caused by MKUltra, the mind-altering experimental programme created and implemented by the CIA. In early 1961, Robeson lived in London but was concerned about his security there following the assassination of Lumumba, which had made him conscious of the prevalence of CIA activity abroad. He therefore planned trips to countries where he believed he would be safe, including the Soviet Union, Cuba and—as the highlight—Ghana, at the personal invitation of Nkrumah.

But Robeson never made it to Cuba or Africa. While he was in Moscow in March 1961, a surprise party was arranged for him in his hotel suite without the knowledge of his official hosts; distressed by the raucous behaviour of the guests, Robeson locked himself in his bedroom. He was later discovered in the bathroom in a paranoid and incoherent state and with his wrists superficially cut. He recovered but suffered recurrent anxiety and depression.

A few months after the episode in Moscow, on 21 July 1961, an FBI memorandum was sent to J Edgar Hoover, the director of the FBI, by the bureau's London legal attaché regarding Paul Robeson, his wife and his son. A copy of this document is in the public domain, but it is largely redacted. There is a handwritten note under the last paragraph, signed with Hoover's initials, which reads, 'Info Re. Robeson's Health Status previously furnished State, CIA, AG [Attorney General] & White House under "Top Secret" classification'. Evidently Robeson's health was of serious interest at that time to powerful individuals and departments in the US.

Robeson continued to feel distressed, and his wife, Eslanda, sought medical care for him. This led to his being admitted in September 1961 to the Priory, a private London mental hospital. Refusing to enter the facility voluntarily, he was forced to do so under Section 25 of the UK Mental Health Act. This was the start of a brutal, punitive course of treatment: for over twenty-three months, Robeson was given fifty-four administrations of electroconvulsive therapy (ECT), about ten days apart, as well as highly potent psychiatric drugs. Paul Robeson's son obtained his father's records from the Priory several decades later. According to details of his treatment, one doctor commented that Robeson 'is friendly, although I have no doubt that some justifiable paranoid ideation might emerge if the question of the "colour bar" were raised'.

Paul Robeson Jr believed that the CIA was behind this terrible ordeal from the very beginning. He speculates that the agency organised the party in Moscow and slipped something into his father's drink. His father told him the day after the party that he had felt trapped in a real-life 'James Bond nightmare', with the walls closing around him.

Robeson Jr suspected that after this initial event, the CIA directed Robeson's treatment at the Priory, and that his father was subjected to the MKUltra 'mind depatterning technique', which combined a massive administration of ECT with drugs.[31] Since most of the records relating to MKUltra were destroyed in 1973, it is difficult to take this investigation further. But according to a 1999 article in London's *Sunday Times*, an MKUltra historian with close contacts in American intelligence, Mike Miniccino, has said that it is 'entirely plausible' that Robeson was targeted by the CIA.[32]

The treatments did not end until Paul Robeson Jr transferred his father to a clinic in East Berlin. But the experience had a long-term effect on Robeson, sapping his energy, strength and well-being.

The CIA, suggested Robeson Jr, had been concerned to prevent a high-profile visit by Paul Robeson to Havana shortly before Cuban exiles landed in the Bay of Pigs on 17 April 1961 in the abortive attempt to overthrow Castro that was orchestrated by the CIA. Perhaps, though, Robeson was seen as a problem by the CIA more broadly. John Stockwell told Robeson Jr that the CIA had viewed his father as a dangerous 'badman'.[33] Robeson's role as a prominent African American intellectual and celebrity who cultivated his contacts in Africa and specifically in Ghana was effectively neutralised, as was his energetic campaigning for civil and human rights in America and in Africa.

Between April and June 1961, the FBI kept a 'status of health' file on Robeson, with plans to prevent the communist movement from exploiting Robeson's 'imminent' death. 'The fact that such a file was opened at all', comments Robeson Jr, 'is very sinister in itself'. It also indicated prior knowledge that something bad was about to happen to his father—possibly a murder plot that went wrong.[34]

* * *

ON 22 NOVEMBER 1963, President John F Kennedy was assassinated. Kennedy's sudden and shocking death was a bitter blow to

President Nkrumah, who had believed in Kennedy's good faith even when he strongly disagreed with him.

According to the historian Richard D Mahoney (the son of Ambassador William P Mahoney), Nkrumah 'had no doubts about who was behind the assassination'. When Ambassador Mahoney handed Nkrumah a copy of the Warren Report, the outcome of an investigation set up by Lyndon Baines Johnson, Kennedy's successor, Nkrumah made this clear. He opened the report 'and pointing to the name of Allen Dulles (a member of the Warren Commission), handed it back to Mahoney saying simply, "whitewash"'.[35]

Under Kennedy, the leadership of the CIA had changed. Dulles had been forced to resign as director following the Bay of Pigs fiasco. He was replaced in November 1961 by John McCone, who moved to the CIA from his role as chairman of the Atomic Energy Commission. Under President Johnson, McCone took a keen interest in potential replacements of Nkrumah as the leader of Ghana. His overthrow seemed increasingly likely after yet another attempt on his life on January 1964, when a policeman on guard duty at Flagstaff House fired five rounds from his rifle at the president. The president's bodyguard, Salifu Dagarti, heroically shielded Nkrumah with his own body and was killed.

In a meeting with McCone on 11 February 1964, US Secretary of State Dean Rusk suggested the possibility of General Joseph Ankrah taking over the presidency of Ghana—the same Ankrah who had been close to General Alexander as a brigade commander in the Ghanaian contingent of ONUC. It was Ankrah who had physically prevented Lumumba from speaking to the people of the Congo over the radio on 11 September 1960 to challenge his dismissal by Kasavubu. Ankrah was also serving in Luluabourg, Kasai, at the time that Lumumba was being hunted in the region before his final arrest and murder. He became the first Ghanaian commander of the Ghana Army in 1961.

When Alexander published *African Tightrope*, an account of his two years as Nkrumah's chief of staff, in 1965, he drew attention to his support for Ankrah in an appendix titled 'A Cry from the Heart'. The appendix is a reproduction of a letter written to Ankrah by Alexander on 22 September 1961, at the time of Alexander's dismissal by President Nkrumah, and it warned of the harm that would be incurred by Nkrumah's plan to send Ghanaian soldiers to the Soviet Union.[36]

At the meeting in February 1964 between McCone and Rusk, McCone expressed doubt that Ankrah had sufficient 'political ambition'. But the two men agreed that it might be possible to develop a joint programme involving Ankrah and the British; plans were made to pursue the option.[37]

* * *

THE AMERICAN PRESS WAS increasingly critical of Nkrumah, who in any case had lost faith in the possibility that he would be covered honestly and fairly in the US. When the *New York Times* correspondent in Accra, Lloyd Garrison—a friend and confidant of Pauli Murray—requested an interview with Nkrumah, the president refused. 'I know you', he told Garrison, 'but I don't know your masters and how they might change what you write. The lies I read about me, about Ghana. It's hopeless. I've turned my back on the Western press'. Garrison wrote about this conversation as if it had been an interview.[38]

Nkrumah's reputation was smeared by writers associated with the CIA. Melvin Lasky, the witting editor of the CIA-funded *Encounter*, travelled through some African countries after Lumumba's death and in 1962 published *Africa for Beginners*, using pieces first written for *Encounter*. With a condescending urbanity, the book is routinely critical of Nkrumah, at one point insinuating that he has a cult of personality reminiscent of Hitler and Stalin. Ghana is compared unfavourably with Nigeria, a country seen by Lasky to have the potential to become 'a profoundly constructive influence in Africa'.

Africa for Beginners was reviewed enthusiastically by Gary Gappert, an American writer and academic who was involved in the American Committee on Africa and worked for *Transition* in Uganda—a magazine that, again, was sponsored by the CIA. In his review, Gappert revealed his prejudice—as did Lasky—by referring to Africa as 'the Dark Continent'.[39]

The US government stepped up efforts to demonise Nkrumah. A 'Proposed Action Program for Ghana' was sent on 11 February 1964 from the director of the Office of West African Affairs to G Mennen Williams, the assistant secretary of state for African Affairs. 'Intensive efforts', it instructed, 'should be made through psychological warfare and other means to diminish support for Nkrumah within Ghana and nurture the conviction among the Ghanaian people that their country's welfare and independence necessitate his removal'. In addition, argued the document, 'We must bring home to other African leaders that Nkrumah is a problem which they must face up to in their own national interest'.[40]

The British government was planning its own campaign to discredit Nkrumah. 'We have the S/S's [Secretary of State's] approval in general', noted a senior official in the British Commonwealth Relations Office in 1964, 'to covert and unattributable attacks on Nkrumah'.[41]

The Information Research Department, which has been described as the UK Foreign Office's 'secret propaganda unit', had some ideas on how to smear Nkrumah.[42] It suggested to the Commonwealth Relations Office 'that it would be useful to have a book published which would show up the nature of Nkrumah's activities in Black Africa generally and in particular in East Africa'. The promotion of such a book 'would be strictly unattributable. . . . There would be no indication of any official connection with it'.[43]

* * *

IN MAY 1964, MALCOLM X—in his late thirties—went to Ghana during a tour of African nations. He had recently split with the Nation of Islam and felt happy to be in Africa. During a lecture at Ibadan University in Nigeria, he sought to give 'the true picture' of the plight of African Americans in the US and 'of the necessity of the independent African Nations helping us bring our case before the United Nations'. Politically, he argued, the highest priority was building 'unity between the Africans of the West and the Africans of the fatherland [which] will well change the course of history'.

This was the beginning of his identification with the Pan-Africanist vision espoused by Nkrumah. At the University of

Ghana he gave a speech in which he praised Nkrumah as one of the African continent's 'most progressive leaders' and described his own feeling of connection: 'I don't feel that I am a visitor in Ghana or in any part of Africa. I feel that I am at home. I've been away for four hundred years, but not of my own volition, not of my own will. Our people didn't go to America on the *Queen Mary*, we didn't go by Pan American, and we didn't go to America on the *Mayflower*. We went in slave ships, we went in chains'.

Malcolm had an hour's meeting with Nkrumah at Christiansborg Castle and later spoke to the students at the Kwame Nkrumah Ideological Institute in Winneba.[44]

In his autobiography, as told to Alex Haley, Malcolm X later recalled the distress he felt in the dining room of his Accra hotel, when he had heard American whites 'discussing Africa's untapped wealth as though the African waiters had no ears. It nearly ruined my meal, thinking how in America they sicced police dogs on black people, and threw bombs in black churches, while blocking the doors of their white churches—and now, once again in the land where their forefathers had stolen blacks and thrown them into slavery, was that white man'. He resolved that he was going to 'make things hot' for that white man, who wanted 'to exploit Africa again—it had been her human wealth the last time, now he wanted Africa's mineral wealth'.[45]

Malcolm X was deeply moved by his reception in Ghana; he was astonished that members of the press, including Kofi Batsa of *Spark* and Cameron Duodu, had arranged to pay his hotel expenses.[46]

The CIA, unsurprisingly, was not happy about Malcolm X's visit to Ghana. Coupled with the assassination of Kennedy, Malcolm X's trip was giving a negative impression of the US to African countries. To counter this impression, the American Society of African Culture (AMSAC), a CIA front, arranged for James Farmer, the civil rights leader and advocate of nonviolence, to travel to Africa and foster an alternative view. Farmer had cofounded the Congress of Racial Equality (CORE) in the early 1940s and had organised the Freedom Rides in 1961 to challenge racial segregation on buses in the southern states. Farmer arrived in Africa in January 1965 and visited nine countries, meeting heads of state, members of Parliament, students and representatives of trade unions.

Farmer was unaware of the CIA's involvement in the funding and organisation of the trip, which was carefully managed by John Aubrey Davis, the executive director of AMSAC. Farmer was yet another victim of the CIA's deceit.

* * *

ON 11 MARCH 1965, US Ambassador Mahoney met in Washington with McCone and the deputy chief of the CIA's Africa Division. The memorandum of the meeting reveals that Mahoney was well informed about plots to remove Nkrumah. He was not convinced, he said, 'that the coup d'état, now being planned by Acting Police Commissioner Harlley and Generals Otu and Ankrah, would necessarily take place'. But he did feel that 'one way or another', Nkrumah would be out within a year. In response to McCone's queries as to who would most likely succeed Nkrumah in the event of a coup, Mahoney stated that 'initially, at least, a military junta would take over, headed perhaps by Acting Police Commissioner Harlley'.[47]

The British were on America's side. 'On the whole', stated British high commissioner A W Snelling in Accra in March 1965, 'it is in the interest of Britain that Nkrumah should cease to rule Ghana'.[48]

On 27 May, R W Komer, a National Security Council staffer, briefed McGeorge Bundy, the president's special assistant for National Security Affairs, on plans to overthrow Nkrumah:

> FYI, we may have a pro-Western coup in Ghana soon. Certain key military and police figures have been planning one for some time, and Ghana's deteriorating economic condition may provide the spark.
>
> The plotters are keeping us briefed, and State thinks we're more on the inside than the British. While we're not directly involved (I'm told), we and other Western countries (including France) have been helping to set up the situation by ignoring Nkrumah's pleas for economic aid.

The report concluded with satisfaction, 'All in all, looks good'.[49]

By that year, Nkrumah was hearing of more and more plots against him. One of the rumours he heard wrongly implicated Genoveva Marais. He was told, she wrote in her memoir, 'that I, the one nearest to him, was actually conspiring against him'.[50]

An account of this plot was sent by the British High Commission in Accra to London. It did not refer to her by name, but as an 'un-named mistress of President Kwame Nkrumah's, of African nationality, but not a Ghanaian'. The plan originally 'intended that the mistress should herself arrange for the murder of Nkrumah in bed', but it was revised. Under the new scheme, Nkrumah would be ambushed when his car entered the main road near where Marais lived. General Ankrah, hiding in the bush with twelve men, would accost him, and he would be driven by Land Rover to Togo. No trouble was expected from the people of Accra, but should any develop, the city would be plunged into darkness at the power station while the armed forces dealt with it. The CPP would fall to pieces, and Nkrumah's loyal supporters, such as Nathaniel Welbeck, would be seized.[51]

The Commonwealth Relations Office in London was not impressed with the scheme. On the one hand, noted A W Snelling, 'it is in the interest of Britain that Nkrumah should cease to rule Ghana'. But, he warned, 'in the African whispering gallery the chances of not being found out if we do become involved are remote'.[52]

When Marais was told by Nkrumah of this plot, she challenged his mistrust of her and threatened to leave Accra. She was horrified to learn that the Ghanaian consul in Germany had spoken against her. 'Gladly, however', said Marais, 'Kwame believed me rather than this man'.[53]

* * *

RELATIONS BETWEEN GHANA AND the US deteriorated yet further in October 1965 when Nkrumah published *Neo-colonialism: The Last Stage of Imperialism*. The book launched a powerful attack on the workings of American capitalism in Africa, supported by a mass of factual detail.

'Africa's possession of industrial raw materials', argued Nkrumah in *Neo-colonialism*, 'could, if used for her own development, place her among the most modernised continents of the world without recourse to outside sources'. Instead, this was prevented by the greed and dishonesty of US capitalism. American interest in the Congo, he insisted, 'is motivated by very substantial investments', which were frequently hidden by 'engaging leading personalities in United States political affairs'.

Adlai Stevenson, 'representing his government at U.N.O.', Nkrumah wrote, 'presided over the firm of Tempelsman & Son, specialists in exploiting Congo diamonds'. Arthur H Dean, 'who leads America's delegations to disarmament conferences', he added, 'was vice-president and still is a director of American Metal Climax, a huge consumer of uranium, since it provides 10 per cent of United States production'.[54]

The US government was incensed by the book. Robert P Smith, who was desk officer for Ghana in the State Department at the time, spoke about the department's response in a 1989 interview with Charles Stuart Kennedy. 'I think Nkrumah dropped the straw that broke the camel's back, so to speak', said Smith, 'in that he published a new book called *Neo-Colonialism*. I've forgotten the subtitle, which was simply outrageous. It accused the United States of every sin imaginable to man. We were blamed for everything in the world'.[55]

The assistant secretary, G Mennen Williams, summoned the Ghanaian ambassador to the State Department. Williams 'was shaking his finger in the ambassador's face', recalled Smith. 'And it was a very painful, hour-long interview. To put it mildly, he protested vigorously the contents and publication of this book'.[56]

A stiff note was sent by the State Department to Nkrumah, and American aid to Ghana was instantly cancelled.

39

'One Step Backward. We Shall Take Two Forward'

T HE GHANAIAN ATOMIC REACTOR AT Kwabenya was on target
to reach criticality by the end of 1966.[1] But it never happened.

In the early morning of Thursday 24 February 1966, Nkrumah was overthrown in a military coup dubbed 'Operation Cold Chop' by its instigators. While the Ghanaian president was in Beijing, on his way to Hanoi with proposals for ending the war in Vietnam, the military and the police toppled Ghana's civilian government.

Major General Charles M Barwah, who was in command of Ghana's army, was woken from his sleep by the arrival at his house of a platoon of soldiers led by Colonel Emmanuel Kwasi Kotoka, the commander of the Second Army Brigade stationed in Kumasi. General Barwah was asked to join the coup, and when he refused he was shot dead in front of his wife and children.

Several leading conspirators of Operation Cold Chop were former members of the Ghanaian contingent in ONUC who had been close to General Alexander: General Ankrah, who had been dismissed by Nkrumah the year before on suspicion of plotting a coup; Colonel Kotoka, who had been the company commander in the Second Battalion of the Ghana Army in Leopoldville in 1960; General A K Ocran; and Colonel Akwasi Amankwaa Afrifa. Police Commissioner Harlley was also a leader of the coup, as predicted by Ambassador Mahoney, as was A K Deku, the head of the Criminal Investigation Department.

Ankrah provided a close link between the overthrow of Lumumba in 1960 and the overthrow of Nkrumah in 1966: it was Ankrah who prevented Lumumba from speaking over the radio to the people of the Congo to challenge his dismissal by Kasavubu.

Five weeks before the coup, Mahoney had been replaced as American ambassador in Accra by Franklin Williams, an African American who, like Nkrumah, had studied at Lincoln University. Ambassador Williams welcomed the military regime with the same spirit of enthusiasm with which his colleague, Ambassador Timberlake, had welcomed the overthrow of the legitimate government of Patrice Lumumba in the Congo. 'It is particularly disgraceful', lamented Nkrumah, 'that it should have been an Afro-American ambassador who sold himself out to the imperialists and allowed himself to be used in this way. It was this same man who deliberately lied when he publicly described the coup as "bloodless"'.[2]

Robert P Smith, the State Department desk officer for Ghana, believed that the publication of *Neo-colonialism* might 'have contributed in a material way to [Nkrumah's] overthrow shortly thereafter'. Smith recalled the response in Washington to the news of the coup:

> I got the call about 2 a.m. here at the house and went into the Department and immediately set up a little task force in the Operations Center. Later in the same morning, about 8 or 8:30, Secretary Rusk wandered down the hall and came in and said, 'I've seen the early reports, but I just want to hear it firsthand. What's going on in Ghana?' When I related how Nkrumah had landed in Peking and had been informed by his Chinese hosts of what had happened in Ghana, Dean Rusk broke into an ear-splitting grin. I've never seen him look so happy.[3]

Fathia Nkrumah fled to the Egyptian embassy with her three children, her fear of her husband's enemies tragically vindicated. President Nasser sent an aircraft to transport them to Cairo. They never saw Nkrumah again.

Genoveva Marais was arrested and imprisoned by Ghana's new rulers, who alleged that Nkrumah had bought for her a Thunderbird convertible—an expensive luxury car—with government funds. America's *Life* magazine supported the claim; it published a nasty article about her on 18 March 1966, which described her as 'Nkrumah's slender mulatto mistress' and was illustrated with a photograph of her sitting in the Thunderbird. In fact, Marais had bought the car for herself, with money from her wealthy father in South Africa. Marais was repeatedly raped in prison. After her release, she was forced to leave Ghana.[4]

A ruling council calling itself the National Liberation Council (NLC) was established to govern the country. The chair of the NLC was General Ankrah, who became the second president of Ghana. Diplomatic relations with Russia, China and Cuba were immediately ceased and their embassies were closed.

The leadership of the Convention People's Party were rounded up and arrested, and Colonel Kotoka announced over the radio that it was illegal to belong to the CPP. The British press reported that the coup was bloodless. But in reality the death toll was in the region of sixteen hundred, with many more injured. There was no popular participation in the coup; ordinary people, wrote June Milne, Nkrumah's researcher, 'were initially stunned by the military/police seizure of power, and were powerless to stop it'. Without guns, resistance was out of the question.[5]

Almost as soon as Operation Cold Chop had taken place, the British government sent the atomic physicist Sir John Cockcroft to Accra to assess the Kwabenya atomic project. Cockcroft knew Alan Nunn May, whom he had supervised in the Manhattan Project. The Ghanaian scientists argued earnestly for the continuation of the project. But on Cockcroft's advice, the reactor was dismantled and the project brought to a swift conclusion.

State corporations were privatised, and many state-run projects were abandoned. Foreign multinationals, which had been held firmly at arm's length by Nkrumah, swiftly took control of much of the production sector.

* * *

'THE COUP IN GHANA', observed the National Security Council staffer R W Komer to President Johnson on 12 March 1966, 'is another example of a fortuitous windfall. Nkrumah was doing more to undermine our interests than any other black African. In reaction to his strongly pro-Communist leanings, the new military regime is almost pathetically pro-Western'.[6]

But in the view of John Stockwell, the events unfolding in Ghana were by no means 'fortuitous' in terms of the US government. Stockwell put the CIA firmly at the centre of Nkrumah's 'ouster' in an extensive footnote in his memoir. The Accra station, he noted, 'was given a generous budget, and maintained intimate contact with the plotters as a coup was hatched'. So close was the station's involvement, he adds, 'that it was able to coordinate the recovery of some classified Soviet military equipment by the United States as the coup took place. The station even proposed to headquarters through back channels that a squad be on hand at the moment of the coup to storm the Chinese embassy, kill everyone inside, steal their secret records, and blow up the building to cover the fact'.

This proposal 'was quashed', Stockwell writes, 'but inside CIA headquarters the Accra station was given full, if unofficial credit for the eventual coup, in which eight Soviet advisors were killed. None of this was adequately reflected in the agency's written records'.[7]

The American investigative journalist Seymour Hersh fleshed out Stockwell's account. At the height of the operation in Ghana, he wrote, the CIA in Accra had grown to ten officers, all operating under cover. The CIA chief of station was Howard Bane, who worked under cover as a political officer at the US embassy.[8] A short man with a florid complexion and a temper, Bane has been described as 'a phenomenally good spy'.[9]

* * *

NKRUMAH WAS FORCED INTO exile. He was given a home in Conakry by President Sékou Touré of Guinea, who welcomed him at the airport with a large crowd on 2 March 1966. The next day, at a mass rally, Touré declared, 'The Ghanaian traitors have been mistaken in thinking that Nkrumah is simply a Ghanaian. . . . He is a universal man'. He then called Nkrumah president of Guinea, to cheering crowds. At the time, Nkrumah's knowledge of French was almost nonexistent, so he had no idea of the honour that had been accorded him. When it was explained to him afterwards, he was deeply moved, but he declined the role. He agreed, however, to become copresident, as an expression of practical Pan-Africanism.

In Guinea, Nkrumah continued to argue and to campaign tirelessly for African unity. It was 'one of the most fruitful and happiest periods of my life', he wrote in *Dark Days in Ghana*, which was published during his exile in 1968. He was able to do many of the things he had longed to do but for which he had never had time—reading current books on politics, history, literature, science and philosophy, reflecting, learning French, playing chess and tennis and taking long brisk walks.

As always, his days were disciplined and started when most people were still in bed. 'I am already up and it's 4.30 am', he wrote to June Milne with characteristic enthusiasm in 1967. 'I love to work in the early hours of the morning'. He reported to her that he was thriving physically: 'I feel very fit. Health really excellent. I was dancing the Ghanaian high life in my room this morning—all by myself'.[10] He also completed a course of military training. President and Madame Touré were in regular touch with him and on many occasions ate with him.

'From the seafront villa where I stay', wrote Nkrumah, 'I can see the hills of Sierra Leone, and in the other direction, the distant shores of so-called Portuguese Guinea, where a fierce liberation struggle is going on'.[11] Nkrumah frequently received visitors at his villa, including Kenneth Kaunda of Zambia, who went to Guinea on a state visit, and Amilcar Cabral, a leader of the freedom struggle against colonial rule in Portuguese Guinea (now Guinea Bissau) and Cabo Verde, who was living in Guinea under the protection of Touré.

Genoveva Marais visited Nkrumah too. The last time she had seen him was the evening before he left for North Vietnam. 'Yes', she wrote, 'they eventually deposed him—and that they had to do while he was away on a mission of peace'.[12]

However, Nkrumah would not allow Fathia and their children to visit him. As Mrs Nkrumah explained in an interview with Ghana's *Daily Graphic* on 14 July 1972, he feared that they might be hijacked on their way to or from Guinea. For the sake of their children, therefore, the two decided not to see each other—but to wait for his return to Ghana. In the meantime, they wrote to each other and sent photographs.[13]

As he had done throughout his life, while in exile Nkrumah drew deep pleasure from growing his beloved roses and other flowers, and from animals and all forms of wildlife. On one occasion, two members of his entourage returned from a fishing expedition with a large turtle, which they presented to Nkrumah, assuming it would be made into soup. But he instructed them to place it in a small pool on the veranda, to live there until his hopeful return to Ghana—when the turtle would be returned to the sea.[14]

Nkrumah's chief occupation was writing. Before the coup, many of his books had been published by Thomas Nelson and Heinemann. But following the coup, his publishers simply dropped him. Nkrumah, who never accepted defeat, worked with June Milne to create Panaf Books to publish his many new books (twelve between 1966 and 1970) and to keep his existing works in print. June Milne was assisted by her husband, Van Milne, who by then had founded the Heinemann African Writers series, publishing major authors such as Chinua Achebe, Wole Soyinka and Ngugi wa Thiong'o. June Milne visited Nkrumah in Conakry sixteen times to assist him in his work, taking him books and his favourite chocolates and biscuits.

Milne's notebooks record her observations of Nkrumah's spirit: 'Quicksilver moods, the shadow boxing, the breaking into a skip along the verandah. Then suddenly a change to a heavy, brooding, thoughtful mood. Then a quick change back again. Very occasionally a sudden outburst of impatience or anger at some inefficiency or incompetence. Quickly passes'.[15]

Invariably, optimism triumphed over disappointment. In one letter to Milne, he noted that the magazine *Transition* 'stinks' (he was not aware that it was sponsored by the CIA): 'It is pornographic and sadistic. Apart from the stupidities and the infantilism of the articles, just have a look at the pictures. Dirty and foul. I wonder what is becoming of the so-called intellectuals in Africa. . . . No wonder American neo-colonialism is running wild all over the place'. But this bleak assessment was immediately followed by an expression of confidence in the future: 'One thing I do know. The day of reckoning is in the offing. It won't be long and the rays of the sun shall burst through the clouds of shame over the continent'.[16]

All the time he was in Guinea, said Milne later, his life was in danger despite the strict security measures taken by the Guinean government. 'The Ghanaian military regimes never ceased to plot against him', she wrote, 'doubtless assisted by staffs of Western embassies in Guinea, who were no friends of Nkrumah'.[17]

The presence in Guinea of Amílcar Cabral aggravated the dangers. Cabral was seen as a troublemaker across the Western nations, including the US. After the 1965 riots in the Black neighbourhood of Watts in Los Angeles, Cabral gave a speech in which he emphasised the links between Pan-Africanism and the struggle of African Americans for civil and political rights: 'We are with the blacks of the United States of America, we are with them in the streets of Los Angeles, and when they are deprived of all possibility of life, we suffer with them'.[18]

* * *

For Nkrumah, the Congo was always at the centre of Africa's struggle. The year after his overthrow, he published *Challenge of the Congo* with a clear statement in its subtitle: *A Case Study of Foreign Pressures in an Independent State*. Like all the books he wrote during the Conakry period, it received bad reviews in the Western mainstream press. But Nkrumah believed that 'the readers are no fools. Otherwise, how can I be "the hero of African nationalists" and at the same time "a tedious bore"?'[19]

In 1969, Nkrumah wrote a preface to a new edition of the book, setting out the journey he had made from his earlier commitment to nonviolence. 'A point has now been reached', he wrote, 'where armed struggle is the only way through which African revolutionaries can achieve their objectives'. Recent events, he continued, 'have exposed the fallacy of trying to banish imperialism, neo-colonialism and settler regimes from our continent by peaceful means. The aggression of the enemies of the African masses continues, and has become more ruthless and insidious'. He added in sorrow, 'The evidence is all around us'.

But Nkrumah's spirit and determination were not broken. 'We must', he urged, 'combine strategy and tactics, and establish political and military machinery for the prosecution of the African revolutionary war. It is only in this way that the aspirations of the African masses can be achieved, and an All-African Union Government be established in a totally free and united Africa'.[20]

'These dark days will pass', he believed. 'Nothing can stop the progress of the African revolutionary struggle. On 24th February 1966 Ghana was forced one step backward. We shall take two forward'.[21] But he was starting to feel unwell. 'Dearest', he wrote to his faithful friend June Milne in September 1970, 'my health is not as it should be since the lumbago attack. . . . I feel I am not my usual self. . . . I will rise above it all; and as the night follows the day, we shall be in Ghana'.[22]

* * *

NKRUMAH DIED ON 27 April 1972 in Bucharest, the capital of Romania, where he had gone to seek medical treatment. A specialist doctor had diagnosed his illness as cancer of the spine that had spread from the prostate and into his blood, resulting in leukaemia.[23]

Throughout his illness, he and his associates maintained acute concern about security. In written communications between those caring for him in Bucharest and his friends elsewhere, he was given the pseudonym Diallo. On one of June Milne's three visits to Bucharest, Nkrumah instructed her firmly to be vigilant and careful, as he could not protect her. Nkrumah's bodyguard and his nephew stayed with him at all times, 'on constant duty day and night', sleeping in the same room. Milne realised that they never left Nkrumah's side from the moment they arrived in Bucharest in August 1971: 'They dressed all the time in pyjamas, their underclothes underneath, sandals on their feet. On top they wore thin, wool dressing-gowns provided by the hospital'.[24]

Milne was shocked to see how frail and thin her friend was. He 'passed through hell' because of the pain he was suffering, he told her, although he was given every possible care by the hospital staff.

His last wish, above all, was to return to Ghana—to be on Ghanaian soil and to see his mother, by then in her nineties and almost blind. But he died far from home, with a chill wind blowing outside.[25] He was only sixty-two.

The funeral ceremony in Conakry, recorded in newsreel footage, captures the sorrow of Fathia Nkrumah, dressed in black. Sékou Touré was visibly distressed as he delivered an oration, ending with 'Vive la Révolution!'[26] He listed the men 'assassinated' by the enemies of the African revolution, such as Patrice Lumumba, and included Nkrumah's name. Amílcar Cabral also gave a speech in which he used the term *assassiné* to describe Nkrumah's death.

Too many great men had died prematurely, Milne believed, 'for there not to be questions raised about the now well-known employment of insidious ways of silencing those who threaten the established order'. The body of Kwame Nkrumah did not receive a postmortem.[27]

Cabral was shot dead in an assassination in Conakry in 1973. Touré died at age sixty-two in 1984 'in suspicious circumstances', according to Milne, on the operating table in Ohio, after an apparent heart attack.[28]

The Cameroonian freedom fighter Ndeh Ntumazah lamented that Nkrumah 'did not have time to plant the tree of freedom, which would have borne new flowers'. Nkrumah, Nasser and Touré, Ntumazah added, 'were good men in the world where few had the strength to resist the corroding influence of power, wealth and vanity at the expense of the weak and helpless'.[29]

'I still recall', said Julius Nyerere, the first president of Tanzania, in 1997, 'arguing with Nkrumah in occasional instances, where I told him that his idea of African unity was not going to work because he was doing things for propaganda purposes'. But long after Nkrumah's overthrow and subsequent death, Nyerere added, 'it took me ten years of consistent study, to get the full import of what Kwame was talking about. In fact, Kwame Nkrumah is the greatest African ever'.[30]

In July 1972, Nkrumah's body was flown to Ghana and taken to the village of Nkroful, where it was placed in a tomb on the site of the dwelling where he had been born. Twenty years later, his body was reinterred in a dedicated Memorial Park in the Old Polo Ground in Accra, close to the breaking waves of the Atlantic Ocean—the very place where Nkrumah had hailed the freedom of Ghana from British rule on 6 March 1957. On a pedestal stands a statue of Kwame Nkrumah with his right hand outstretched, pointing the way forward.

40

The Dead Hand

K WAME NKRUMAH HAD NO ILLUSIONS about the extent of the CIA's involvement in Africa in the middle years of the twentieth century. 'Examples of CIA activity in Africa . . . would provide material for a book of their own', he wrote with bitterness in *Dark Days in Ghana*, two years after his overthrow.[1]

But the extent of these covert operations is challenging to unearth because of the agency's extreme secrecy and the fact that sensitive information was not put in writing. Often, explains John Stockwell, the CIA whistleblower, 'CIA business is communicated to and from the field by the "back channel"—hand-carried notes, pouched single copy, official-informal letters, and verbal messages'. This is a tactic to minimise the number of people inside the CIA who know of a given operation or situation and to communicate ultrasensitive messages without leaving a written record.[2]

Justin O'Donnell, the senior CIA officer in the Directorate of Plans who was sent to the Congo to implement the plot to eliminate Lumumba, made a similar observation—though implicitly. In his testimony to the Church Committee in 1975, he stated that 'you have to be awfully canny and you have to get things on record' because of the reliance on the back channel—'since you don't have documents'.[3] The avoidance of written records is a barrier not only to public knowledge, but also to the US government's own institutional memory—almost guaranteeing that mistakes of the past will be repeated. Worse, it is a monumental problem for the people living in the countries that were infiltrated by the CIA who wish to know and understand their history to its fullest extent.

Even when records *were* produced in the course of operations, they might have been destroyed. In an early draft of the Church Committee report, Larry Devlin is quoted as testifying that 'sometime before leaving the Station, he [Devlin] destroyed all cable traffic relating to the assassination mission'. His 'best recollection' was that he had received instructions to destroy those cables, because of their extremely sensitive nature. 'Eventually', he said, 'I destroyed a great deal of traffic, because the Congo was a highly sensitive area in which—at one period I recall we had all of our files in the burn barrels. I mean, when you wanted a file, you went over and dug it out of the burn barrel'. In a footnote to this section, the report adds, 'It is possible that copies of cables dealing with such a sensitive operation were also destroyed at CIA headquarters'.[4]

The lack of records to scrutinise presents a serious obstacle for many countries in Africa, on which Georges Nzongola-Ntalaja has cast a powerful spotlight in relation to his own country, the Democratic Republic of the Congo. 'The people of the DR Congo', he argues, 'are concerned to concentrate on their future rather than their past, but they need to understand that past in order to plan for the future. One particular handicap for my country is that so much of its history has been determined by external powers—and that the documents representing that history are held by those external powers'.

As someone who was born in the former Belgian Congo, Nzongola-Ntalaja feels keenly the deep scars left by Belgian occupation and then by the Cold War and neocolonialism. For him, the full disclosure of relevant documentation by the foreign powers that menaced the birth of his nation is an urgent necessity.[5]

At the end of 2013, a new volume (no. XXIII) of records relating to the Congo was released in the *Foreign Relations of the United States* (*FRUS*) series, covering the years 1960–1968. It was intended to supplement a previous volume published in 1994, which has been heavily criticised by historians for its virtual exclusion of documents relating to Lumumba's death and American covert operations.[6] Newly declassified material appeared in the 2013 *FRUS* volume. But as the historian Lise Namikas points out in a comprehensive review, 'the extent of redaction is perplexing', and much is still missing.[7]

* * *

THE 1975 CHURCH COMMITTEE investigation into the assassination of Lumumba was rightly hailed as a major breakthrough in the accountability of the CIA. Nevertheless, the outcome has not been entirely positive; in some ways it has distorted knowledge of events in the Congo in 1960–1961. The findings were shocking, but they appeared to absolve the CIA from responsibility. This conclusion was severely criticised in the 2001 report of the Belgian parliamentary inquiry into Lumumba's murder, on the grounds that Belgian government files did not support the modest role claimed by CIA officials—and that the Church Committee's findings were weakened by its reliance on the testimony of CIA officials.

Furthermore, the focus of the Church inquiry created the misleading impression that CIA operations in the Congo were limited in scope and run by a small number of officers in the field and in Washington. This impression casts a fog of invisibility over many of the operations, such as those conducted by CIA agents Howard Imbrey and George Wittman. It is difficult, when reading the Church Committee report, to avoid the conclusion that the plan to kill Lumumba was the sole object of the CIA's intervention in the Congo. But this was clearly not the case. And because of its narrow focus, the Church Committee largely neglected CIA operations elsewhere in Africa.

Dr Sidney Gottlieb's work may have included plans not only to assassinate Lumumba but also to physically neutralise other individuals in or from Africa. In his testimony to the Church Committee, Gottlieb referred to an inquiry from Dick Bissell, the deputy director of plans, 'generally about technical means of assassination or incapacitation that could be developed or procured by the CIA'. To this, Gottlieb replied that the CIA 'had access to lethal or potentially lethal biological materials that could be used in this manner'. Gottlieb then discussed assassination capabilities with Bissell in the context of 'one or two meetings about Africa'.[8]

The framework for CIA assassinations in Africa was broader, then, than within the borders of the Congo.

In any case, the CIA operation in the Congo was linked to plans for other African territories. 'Part of the purpose in dispatching QJWIN to Africa', noted an early draft of the Church Committee report, 'was to send him from the Congo to another African country for an unspecified mission'. This country was Senegal, according to a recently released cable. It is speculated earlier in this book that QJWIN's 'unspecified mission' may have involved the removal of uranium from Katanga to the US. Whatever the precise nature of his mission, clearly it was not limited to efforts to remove Lumumba from Leopoldville into the hands of his enemies.

The CIA planned that WIROGUE, too, would be used not only in the Congo, but in other regions of Africa: 'His utilization is not to be restricted to Leopoldville. Indeed he may be subject to call by other African stations although it is expected for him to be resident in Leopoldville'. For the purpose of this utilisation, he was trained in 'demolition, small arms and medical immunization'.[9] Like Mr Burt Wides of the Church Committee, the author of this book argues that the US government owes it to the countries of Africa to discover and put into the public domain all information about the purpose of training in medical immunisation and about the plans for other countries in Africa.

The CIA's broader areas of concern about Africa are troubling, given the premature deaths of men involved in Africa's struggle for freedom in the 1960s. Nkrumah died from the same illness as Fanon: leukaemia. Padmore and Wright both died of liver ailments. Given that America's wish to kill Lumumba and Castro, to name just two of the country's known targets, is well documented, it is reasonable to ask questions about the premature deaths of others who were perceived as enemies to the US. All the more so since the CIA in this period was experimenting with toxins of various kinds under the leadership of Gottlieb.

The Church Committee was told that the documentation of MKDelta—the overseas operations conducted under the umbrella of the sinister MKUltra drug and mind-control programme led by Gottlieb—had all been destroyed. But it did not investigate or follow up on this claim.

Testimony was taken from many people, and the Church Committee collected many volumes of files from the CIA, FBI, National Security Agency and other federal agencies. It issued fourteen reports in 1975 and 1976, all of which quote extensively from their sources. Since the passage of the JFK Assassination Records Collection Act of 1992, over fifty thousand pages of Church Committee records have been put into the public domain, including records released in 2017–2018. But many of them have redactions, in some cases very extensive ones.

A serious obstacle to uncovering the truth is the fact that the transcripts of the testimonies of Sidney Gottlieb and Justin O'Donnell, two key players in the events surrounding Lumumba's murder, are missing. Without access to these records, it is not possible to assess the findings of the Church Committee's report. The report's many quotations from the missing testimonies cannot be seen in context, and the conclusions cannot be properly evaluated.

Also missing and of potential relevance are depositions relating to assassination plots, including those of Richard Helms and of Thomas Karamessines, with whom Devlin met in Rome in November 1960 during the hunt in the Congo for Lumumba. Furthermore, as Rex Bradford, president of the Mary Ferrell Foundation, has observed, 'The full number of missing Church Committee transcripts, let alone other relevant Committee documents, is unknowable'.[10]

In the course of research for this book, a number of requests for the release of files relating to CIA operations and officials in Africa in the late 1950s and early 1960s have been submitted to the CIA, under the provisions of the US Freedom of Information Act (FOIA). They have been largely unsuccessful. Most of them received responses that 'neither confirm nor deny' the existence of the information requested. In the case of a Freedom of Information request for information about CIA officer Howard Imbrey, for example, the response states, 'The CIA can neither confirm nor deny the existence or nonexistence of records responsive to your request. The fact of the existence or nonexistence of such records is itself currently and properly classified and is [*sic*] intelligence sources and methods information protected from disclosure'.[11] Given that Imbrey put information about his CIA career into the public domain towards the end of his life, this response is disingenuous at best.

* * *

NEVERTHELESS, PRESSING ON a range of sources has produced some extraordinary findings in relation to the Congo, Ghana and other African territories during their transformation from the status of colony, occupied by a European power, to independence. The best sources have been university archives and individuals who decided to speak about their past involvement with the CIA in Africa, most notably John Stockwell. It appears that the years of finding freedom—between the independence of Ghana in 1957 and the CIA-backed overthrow of Nkrumah in 1966—were also the years of an intense and rapid infiltration into Africa by the CIA. The agency's operations took place in the territories themselves and at the UN in New York.

The uncovered information reveals an extent and breadth of CIA activities in Africa that beggars belief. These activities took various forms and were performed by an extensive network that included Americans at agency headquarters in Washington; American agents operating under cover; American agents under non-official cover in the field and at the UN; Africans brought to the US and then recruited for use in various countries and situations, such as the Kenyan Washington Okumu; African assets recruited and used locally; third-country agents such as QJWIN and WIROGUE; and cultural patronage through Paris and elsewhere.

Underpinning the success of these activities were dollars. 'Money ran the game', notes Namikas. 'Even by 1960 standards the CIA had a reputation for spending'.[12] Estimates of how much the CIA spent, she adds, are hard to gauge. In 2014, Stephen Weissman wrote that between 1960 and 1968, CIA activity in the Congo 'ranked as the largest covert operation in the agency's history, costing an estimated $90–$150 million in current dollars'. But this did not include the cost of 'the aircraft, weapons, and transportation and maintenance services provided by the Defense Department'.[13]

CIA money was distributed, both within the US and in Africa, through a range of conduits, including dummy organisations and pass-throughs such as the Farfield Foundation. Bribes were handed out to selected politicians, to union leaders and to diplomats at the UN. CIA funds were used to pay for soldiers' wages and for weapons. They paid for front organisations, such as Imbrey's public relations office in New York, Overseas Regional Surveys Associates. The funds were used to set up airlines under cover and to buy and deliver aircraft, including the Fouga that may have shot down the plane carrying UN Secretary General Dag Hammarskjöld.

Active intervention fostered division between different political groups, such as Holden Roberto's UPA, heavily backed by the CIA, and the MPLA—both of which were fighting for the freedom of Angola from Portuguese rule. The consequent strife sowed the seeds for decades of suffering in Angola.

Plans were implemented for assassinations. Governments were overthrown. The UN secretary general's communications were accessed in real time in Washington, when he was on a flight in any part of the world, courtesy of the cipher CX-52 machine.

Propaganda and covert influence operations formed a thick web, frequently facilitated by CIA fronts dedicated to Africa, which were set up with the collaboration of powerful businessmen with interests in Africa. The fronts included the African-American Institute, with its headquarters conveniently located just minutes from UN headquarters in New York, and the American Society of African Culture. Both organisations published Africa-focused journals, perfect for covers and heavy with propaganda. Highly respected organisations such as the American Fund for Free Jurists were penetrated by CIA officials using false pretences and were used to funnel funds secretly.

Cultural and educational centres, such as the Mbari Centres in Nigeria and the Institut d'Études Congolaises in Brazzaville, were set up. They organised conferences and events, such as the seminar in Ibadan, Nigeria, attended by an unwitting Lumumba, and the first Congress of African Writers and Intellectuals at the University of Makerere, Uganda. Underpinning all these activities was the

hand of the Congress for Cultural Freedom, a CIA front with an
Africa programme based in Paris and with fingers in most parts of
the world.

* * *

EXPLANATIONS BY THE CIA for American covert intervention
were invariably framed in terms of the Cold War: the need to resist
communism and the aggression of the Soviet Union. 'My responsibilities as deputy director for plans', wrote Richard Bissell in 1996,
'encompassed crises all over the globe. Africa was one field in which
the forces of East and West were destined to clash; the Congo . . .
was on the verge of civil war'. He added, 'In all of underdeveloped
Africa, which really meant southern Africa up to the Sahara, the
Congo was the most important prize in the contest between the
Soviet Union and the United States'.

Bissell believed that 'from today's perspective, many episodes
might be considered distasteful, but during the Eisenhower and
Kennedy years the Soviet danger seemed real and all actions were
aimed at thwarting it'.[14]

It has been established that President Eisenhower authorised
the assassination of Lumumba. It is unclear to what extent President Kennedy knew about and authorised covert activities in Africa
between his election and premature death. However, it is likely that
he did. In *The Spymasters* (2020), a study of every director of the
CIA since its inception in 1947, Chris Whipple notes that the CIA
reports to the president. 'If you know what the CIA is doing', he
writes, 'you know what the president wants; and if you know what
the president wants you know what the CIA is doing'.[15]

The same point was made by Philip Agee, a former CIA case
officer and author of *Inside the Company: CIA Diary* (1975), which
gives details of operations in Latin America. 'CIA operations', he
states, 'are undertaken on instructions from the President himself
and are approved at the Under-Secretary level or higher, outside
the Agency'.[16]

* * *

INTRINSIC TO THE COLD War struggle was America's wish to
maintain absolute control over the uniquely rich uranium at the

Shinkolobwe mine in the Congo. The aim was achieved in the 1960s and maintained until at least the expulsion in 1997 of Mobutu Sese Seko (as he called himself from 1972).

It was also considered necessary to prevent newly independent African countries from obtaining an atomic reactor. The need appears to have been rooted in a fear that a Black government might use such a reactor to support an atomic weapons programme. This worry was inflamed by the racist assumption that people with Black skin were incapable, in any case, of managing an atomic reactor safely.

When Nkrumah was overthrown in 1966, the Kwabenya atomic reactor project was immediately shut down—just as it was on the verge of becoming critical. Meanwhile, the US supplied apartheid South Africa with enriched uranium for its atomic reactor, known as SAFARI, which achieved criticality in 1965.

The racial dimension of this question has been explored by Joseph Amamoo, who was Ghana's permanent representative to the International Atomic Energy Agency in Vienna in 1962–1964. He pointed out in 2013 that in the late forties and early fifties, 'only a dozen or so white nations, initially, possessed the know-how of nuclear technology'. But this changed as other nations acquired such knowledge—'India, Pakistan, China, Brazil, Egypt, Algeria, Iraq (and the list is growing)'.

The 'exclusive monopoly' of white nations 'over scientific, especially nuclear, knowledge', Amamoo adds, 'has been broken'. He was delighted that in 1963, during the period of his appointment in Vienna, an eminent Ghanaian scientist, Dr R P Baffour, became the first Black person to be elected chairman of the IAEA's annual conference. But there was ongoing resistance, notes Amamoo: when President F W de Klerk prepared South Africa for majority rule in the early 1990s, the country's nuclear weapons were dismantled.[17]

Along with racism and Cold War concerns, America's interest in Africa was motivated by a determination to open up European investments in Africa to US influence and exploitation. There were many connections between CIA activities and American businessmen with operations in Africa, such as Harold Hochschild, the chairman of the board of trustees of American Metal Climax.

Another powerful American businessman, Maurice Tempelsman, exploited the process of decolonisation to push his way into Ghana and the Congo. After Larry Devlin retired from the CIA in 1974, he went to the Congo to work for Tempelsman for the subsequent thirteen years as director of operations.[18] This was a very different role from that of George Wittman in the early 1960s; it is possible, though, that Devlin continued to work for, or at least share information with, the CIA.

Tempelsman's selection of Devlin, writes John Stockwell in *In Search of Enemies*, was 'based on the fact that he alone of all Americans still had an intimate friendship with and ready access to President Mobutu. At stake was a half-billion-dollar investment in Zairian [Congolese] mineral resources'.

Stockwell and Devlin had been CIA colleagues with a long history of fellowship: in Addis Ababa one night in 1970, they had drunk whiskey together from midnight to dawn. In 1975, Stockwell lunched with Devlin in Kinshasa. Devlin was bored with his new job for Tempelsman, noted Stockwell, and was nervous because he had been summoned back to Washington to testify to the Senate's Church Committee about the Congo programme.

'He admitted his physical fitness was not up to par', wrote Stockwell, 'and I scolded him, urging him to start jogging again. What would he tell the Senate about Lumumba?'

Stockwell was confident that Devlin 'would never perjure himself, his testimony would be consistent with any written record and provable facts'. At the same time, he guessed that only Devlin and President Mobutu would ever know 'the complete truth' of Patrice Lumumba's assassination in 1961.

'Over whiskey', said Stockwell, 'other agency supergrades had bragged to me about their careers, disclosing remarkable operational secrets. Larry would brag too, but when it got to Lumumba he never had much to say'.[19]

* * *

THE REPUTATIONS OF BOTH Nkrumah and Lumumba were deliberately traduced by the officials of Western governments, both locally in their own territories and globally. Nkrumah was portrayed as paranoid—a portrayal that persists. But he would have been a fool not to take every precaution against the evident threats to his life and the lives of his family. He was also accused of unrealistic and excessive ambition for Ghana, based, for example, on his plans to rapidly increase educational and health facilities. But the accusers lived in countries that already had these services, which were acutely needed in Ghana following colonial rule. The accusers were content to keep African nations—with the exception of apartheid South Africa—out of the modern world.

Patrice Lumumba was presented as fiery, emotional and volatile—the kind of person who might have become one of Africa's stereotyped 'Big Men'. But, if anything, Lumumba's tragic flaw was being too trusting; far from being a ruthless, cunning operator, he found it difficult and distressing to accept that people might behave without decency. This flaw led him to trust Mobutu, even against the warnings of his advisors. 'Lumumba's personal integrity', Rajeshwar Dayal believed, 'shone like a light in the darkness of the prevailing corruption'. Dayal regarded Lumumba's bravery as exceptional: 'A man who could stand up to his gaolers at Thysville and refuse to compromise to save his life was possessed of no ordinary degree of courage'.[20]

The vilification of Nkrumah and Lumumba, as well as other African leaders, has contributed powerfully to the distorted and negative views of Africa that prevail today. 'In the West', claimed the American philosopher Molefi Kete Asante in 2007, in his *History of Africa*, 'the ignorance of Africa is palpable, like a monster that invades our brains with disbelief, deception, and disinterest, yet is everywhere around us. We are victims of probably the most uninformed educated people in the world on the subject of Africa'. Yet the continent 'is ancestral home', he points out, 'to more than forty million citizens of the United States, nearly seventy million Brazilians, another fifty million South Americans, five to seven million who live in Europe and the Pacific, and about forty million people of the Caribbean, as well as the nearly one billion Africans who live on the continent'.[21]

Barack Obama, the first Black president of the USA, has also deplored the prejudice and ignorance in the West about the people who live on the continent of Africa. His frustration emerges powerfully in his 2004 memoir, *Dreams from My Father*, where he records travelling in 1988, at age twenty-seven, to Kenya, the land of his father, for the first time. He recalls that on the flight to Nairobi, he read a portrait of several African countries by a Western journalist who was 'an old Africa hand'.

The first few chapters of the book gave an account of colonialism: 'the manipulation of tribal hatreds and the caprice of colonial boundaries . . . the indignities large and small'. The early heroism of independence figures like Kenyatta and Nkrumah was 'duly noted, their later drift towards despotism attributed at least in part to various Cold War machinations'. But by the third chapter, Obama writes,

> images from the present had begun to outstrip the past. Famine, disease, the coups and counter-coups led by illiterate young men wielding AK-47s like shepherd sticks—if Africa had a history, the writer seemed to say, the scale of current suffering had rendered such history meaningless.
>
> Poor buggers. Godforsaken countries.

Obama continues, 'I set the book down, feeling a familiar anger flush through me, an anger all the more maddening for its lack of a clear target'.[22]

The target was unclear to Obama because many of the causes of these terrible developments had been covertly orchestrated by the CIA.

And they have continued. In 2019, Mike Pompeo, who was CIA director under President Donald Trump from January 2017 to April 2018, celebrated the agency's immorality. 'I was the CIA Director', he said. 'We lied, we cheated, we stole. We had entire training courses. It reminds you of the glory of the American experiment'.[23]

* * *

AT A CONFERENCE AT the University of Ghana in 2018 to mark the
sixtieth anniversary of the All African People's Conference in Accra, the keynote address was given by Georges Nzongola-Ntalaja.
He reminded his listeners that it was at the groundbreaking 1958
conference that Nkrumah and Lumumba met for the first time.
Referring to Lumumba as 'our country's national hero', he explained
that the young Congolese leader was transformed at the conference
by Nkrumah's powerful vision of a United States of Africa.[24]

At a time of great change in Africa, when everything seemed
possible to millions of people who had suffered occupation by foreign rule for so many long years, the call of the 1958 conference
inspired joy and hope: 'Peoples of Africa, Unite! We have nothing
to lose but our chains! We have a continent to regain! We have
freedom and human dignity to attain!'[25]

Looking back over the past sixty years, Nzongola-Ntalaja in
2018 drew attention to the 'failure of our continent to implement
the Pan-African project of democracy and development'. He asked,
'What went wrong, and what can be done to resurrect and implement the pan-African project?'[26]

Cameron Duodu, too, has looked back and asked what went
wrong. As a Ghanaian rookie reporter, he witnessed the celebrations of freedom on 6 March 1957; a few years later, he reported to
Ghana from the crisis in the Congo. For him, the Congo's tragedy
illustrates Africa's problem with the Western world, whereby the
Congo 'is still not stable and able to relieve the poverty of its people'. Lumumba, writes Duodu sadly, 'lost power, he lost his country,
and in the end, his very life'. The 'amazing thing', he adds, 'is that
Lumumba had *done* absolutely nothing against the combination of
forces that wanted him dead! They just saw him as a threat to *their
interests*; interests narrowly defined to mean, "His country has got
resources. We want them. He might not give them to us. So let us
go get him"'.

'All this was done', Duodu observes, 'to achieve the selfish end
of continuing to control the Congo's rich mineral resources'. But it
wasn't only the Congo they wished to control: 'They wanted to gulp

down the entire African continent'. Duodu adds in dismay, 'Some still do'.[27]

Mutombo Nkulu-N'Sengha, a Congolese philosopher and scholar of religious studies, has noted that Pan-Africanists, in their struggle for freedom, have been guided by the fundamental notion of human dignity called *Bumuntu* (known as Ubuntu in southern Africa). It is a belief in a bond of sharing that connects all humanity: 'I am because we are'. Patrice Lumumba celebrated Bumuntu in his speech at the proclamation of independence on 30 June 1960, in which he articulated the belief that one is a human being first of all, and as such deserves the right to live and pursue happiness in unity with all others. Lumumba was deeply committed to these values and opposed to violence in all its forms.

There has been an assumption in the West, Nkulu-N'Sengha states, that African dictators followed an African tradition of tyrannical chiefs, and that the fundamental cause of the lack of democracy and socioeconomic development in Africa is tribalism. But, he argues, this is 'a colonial habit of mind, which is contradicted by historical evidence'.[28]

Such historical evidence is marbled throughout this book. It reveals America's deliberate violation of democracy in African nations where people had struggled against all odds to free themselves from colonial occupation and to achieve majority rule. This violation was accomplished in the name of American democracy. 'Many criticisms', wrote Dick Bissell in a 1996 memoir, 'have been levelled at the CIA for its activities during the 1950s and 1960s, especially in the field of covert action. Having rethought this policy many times since then, I am convinced that *the agency acted in the government's best interest in attempting to preserve the highly desired principle of democracy*'.[29]

The destruction of the Congo's hard-won democracy was pitiless, despite powerful popular resistance. The expulsion of Lumumbists from government, despite their electoral victory, led to the 'second independence' movement—a major event in the struggle for democracy in the Congo. 'By rising up, arms in hand, against an externally backed regime of corrupt and self-serving leaders', writes

Nzongola-Ntalaja, 'the people sought to uphold the egalitarian and developmentalist ideals of independence, together with the political legacy of Patrice Lumumba'.[30]

The uprisings were met with brutal repression, fuelled by American interference. It has been estimated that the conflict in the Congo between 1961 and 1965 led to the deaths of one million people.[31]

In November 1965, Joseph-Désiré Mobutu once again overthrew civilian rule in a coup backed by the CIA. Six months later, he ordered the public execution of four politicians by hanging. This grotesque event took place on 2 June 1966 in a large open space in Leopoldville close to Matonge, an area considered sacred to the memories of the independence movement.[32] The four men were accused of orchestrating a plot to overthrow Mobutu on Pentecost Sunday; no single piece of evidence was offered, and no legal defence was allowed. The jury, selected by the government, took five minutes to deliberate and found the men guilty.[33]

The day of their executions was declared a holiday, and a military brass band played near the gallows, placed on a wooden podium that had been built for the purpose. More than one hundred thousand people jammed the area and watched in shock and silence. The first condemned man, Evariste Kimba, was taken to the platform wearing only soccer shorts; he made his last confession to a priest at the foot of the platform. His death throes lasted more than twenty minutes. During the hanging of the final, fourth victim, 'the people began running, knocking down the soldiers as they went. Children and adults stumbled and fell in the stampede. Within only a few minutes, tens of thousands of people ran away. When it was over, the field was dotted with groaning bodies and lost shoes. A little farther away a fourth coffin was being nailed shut'.[34]

These terrible killings are remembered as the Pentecost hangings. They were the first public executions to take place in the Congo since the 1930s, when the Belgian colonial government brought the brutal practice to an end. For the next thirty-one years, the Congo was ruled with an iron fist by Mobutu—a dictator chosen by the US government and installed by the CIA.

ACKNOWLEDGEMENTS

WRITING THIS BOOK WOULD HAVE been impossible without the generosity and expertise of many people across the world—all the more so, in the era of Covid. It is an honour to thank them.

My research has been enriched by my academic home at the School of Advanced Study, University of London, and I pay tribute to colleagues at the Institute for Commonwealth Studies, notably Mandy Banton, James Chiriyankandath, John Cowley, Oku Ekpenyon, Howard Jones, Philip Murphy, Sue Onslow, Chloe Pieters and Martin Plaut.

In December 2018, the Institute and the United Nations Association Westminster Branch, chaired by David Wardrop, convened the conference 'Hands off Africa!' to mark the sixtieth anniversary of the All African People's Conference in Accra. Three of the speakers had participated in the 1958 conference: Bereket Habte Selassie from Ethiopia; Cameron Duodu from Ghana; and Kenneth Kaunda from Zambia. Other contributors were Hakim Adi, Joseph Amamoo, Dan Branch, Knox Chitiyo, Koffi de Lome, Salem Mezhoud, Bishop Trevor Mwamba, Marika Sherwood and Leo Zeilig. The Round Table was presided over by Lord Boateng, whose father, Kwaku Boateng, served in Ghana's first government.

The Institute of African Studies at the University of Ghana also marked the sixtieth anniversary with a conference. The keynote speech was given by Georges Nzongola-Ntalaja, whose scholar-activism is an inspiration to so many, including me.

For their sharing of documents, recollections and insights, I thank Joseph Amamoo, Dan Branch, Gabriel Banda, Luc Barbé, Paul Broda, Hans Buser, Gideon Calder, Ludo De Witte, Cameron Duodu, Carol Fouke-Mpoyo, Torben Gülstorff, Michael Hathorn, Fidèle Kalombo, Nina Kann, Wren Mast-Ingle, Isaiah Mombilo, Robert Mpoyo, Mutombo Nkulu-N'Sengha, Ruth Nkulu-N'Sengha, Georges Nzongola-Ntalaja, Lars Öhrström, Mohamed Chande Othman, Avinash Paliwal, Beatrice Anne Pizer, Stephanie Postar, Ricky Riccardi, Chris Saunders, Sixten Svensson, Simon Thomas, Olivier Tshinyoka, Herbert Weiss, Cynthia Zukas and Simon Zukas.

Jim Lesar and Dan Alcorn discussed with me the significance of the 1992 John F Kennedy Assassination Records Collection Act and sent me newly released records, along with their analysis. I also benefited from the database of the Mary Ferrell Foundation and thank Rex Bradford, the president, for our exchanges about the missing Church Committee transcripts.

Hans Kristian Simensen shared his tireless and excellent research. Matthew Stevenson and Joe Majerle III contributed expert analysis of matters relating to aviation. I value discussions with Beatrice Randall about voice and freedom.

I am grateful to Daniel B Domingues da Silva, comanager of the important database at Emory University, 'Voyages: The Trans-Atlantic Slave Trade Database'. K James Myers assisted my use of the database with care and precision.

I have had valuable discussions with many of those mentioned above and also with Richard Aldridge, Amma Asante, Kobby Asmah, Margaret Bluman, Peter Coe, Mary Curry, KG Hammar, Victor Kwawukume, Joe Lauria, Edward Nahem, Margaret O'Callaghan, Neil Parsons, Walt Patterson, Judy Seidman and Stephen Williams.

I have spent long and happy days in the quiet of the British Library in London and have missed this space so much during the Covid lockdowns. Another special space is the George Padmore Research Library in Accra, surrounded by a beautiful garden and birdsong.

Mark Iverson conducted outstanding research for me in the Frank Church archive at Boise State University. Lynn Farnell conducted important research for me in the John F Kennedy Presidential Library. I continue to benefit from Jean-Louis Moreau's kind introduction to the Sibéka papers held by the Royal Archives in Brussels. Svetlana Chervonnaya conducted archival research for me in Moscow.

I am grateful to the archivists at the UN Archives and Records Management Section in New York. I thank Aleksandr Gelfand, Stephen Haufek and Amanda Leinberger for their special help, as well as Remi Dubuisson, Paola Casini, Shelley Lightburn and Cheikh Ndiaye. I also thank the UN Photo Library.

Thanks are due to many archivists and librarians all over the world, including: Esther Adomako; Nuno Costa Branco; Christine Colburn and Elayne; Phillip Cunningham; Joachim Derwael; Joellen ElBashir; Barbara Gilbert; Marc Haegeman; Anna Hocker; Tim Hodgdon; Richard Knight; Coretta Lamptey; Peter Laroy; Lopez D Matthews; Gabriele Mohale; Tom Morren; Tim Noakes; Cheryl Oestreicher; David A Olson; Lise Oomen; Julie Parry; Sarah Patton; Blake Spitz; Amy Staples; Jennifer Tran; Darren Treadwell; Alexa Tulk; Lore Van De Broeck; Hannah Weinberg; Alan Wierdak; and Sonja N Woods.

Amanda Rice has a gifted artist's eye for the significance of an image, combined with technical skill. Her role as image researcher made a valuable contribution to the photo insert. I remember with pleasure our analysis of many photographs.

Jeremy Bigwood conducted crucial research for me in the records of the US National Archives and Records Administration. He pushed on every front possible to get access to closed files and submitted FOIA requests on my behalf. It has been a real pleasure to discuss sources and documents with him.

I am indebted to Carole Steers for her research in the UK National Archives and elsewhere, and for submitting FOI requests. Carole is a document detective who never gives up: when all the libraries and archives were closed by Covid, she found ways online to unearth badly needed information. She has supported this book in many wonderful ways.

Emmanuel Barrault translated passages from French with sensitivity and introduced me to the magnificent musicians who accompanied my days of writing. I am grateful beyond measure to Leanne Simoncelli and to Ahmed Yousseif. Stanislav Gerov solved my computer problems. Yajun Yang deserves a special debt of thanks.

A number of people read drafts of the book in whole or in part and offered valuable suggestions: Joseph Amamoo, Mandy Banton, Jeremy Bigwood, Paul Broda, Cameron Duodu, Michael Dwyer, Michael Hathorn, Gervase Hood, Joseph Majerle III, Robert Mpoyo, Mutombo Nkulu-N'Sengha, Georges Nzongola-Ntalaja, Lars Öhrström, Martin Plaut, Clive Priddle, Amanda Rice, Anupama Roy-Chaudhury, Chris Saunders, Hans Kristian Simensen, Carole Steers, Matthew Stevenson, Karolina Sutton, David Wardrop, Herbert Weiss, Lara Weisweiller-Wu, Peter Willetts, Myfanwy Williams and Simon Zukas. I am indebted to these generous people.

My agent, Karolina Sutton at Curtis Brown, is always supportive, perceptive and judicious. I am also grateful to Caitlin Leydon.

Clive Priddle, my editor at PublicAffairs, played a critical role in shaping the direction of this book. It was exciting to discuss with him the implications of new findings and to take them forward. His insightful reading of the manuscript improved it immeasurably. Anupama Roy-Chaudhury read the manuscript with care and made valuable suggestions. She organised many stages of the publication with admirable efficiency. Working with Kelley Blewster, the copyeditor, was a genuine and delightful collaboration. I am grateful to Michelle Welsh-Horst for her kindness, her professionalism and her steady hand.

Michael Dwyer has walked the road with me ever since our first book together in 2011, and we have had many stimulating conversations about Nkrumah and Pan Africanism. I thank Michael sincerely and the team at Hurst.

I treasure the friendship—on both a personal and an intellectual level—of a special group: Mandy Banton, John Y Jones, Roger Lipsey, Henning Melber, Maurin Picard, Sir Stephen Sedley, Hans Kristian Simensen and David Wardrop.

I pay tribute to the influence of people who are no longer with us: Dr Joe Appiah, Lilian Bloom, David Bloom, Monica Ede, Ferelith Hood, Mama Chibesa Kankasa and Charles M Southall.

Joan Williams and Myfanwy Williams deserve special thanks. My daughter Tendayi Bloom is blessed with an original mind and a powerful sense of justice; I am grateful for her insights, as well as her gentle humour and loyal support.

I could not have written this book without Gervase Hood: he is my partner in everything and my best friend. I dedicate the book to him.

LIST OF ACRONYMS

AAI	African-American Institute
AAPC	All African People's Conference
AATUF	All African Trade Union Federation
Abako	Alliance des Bakongo
ACOA	American Committee on Africa
ADST	Association of Diplomatic Studies and Training
AFIO	Association of Former Intelligence Officers
AFL-CIO	American Federation of Labor and Congress of Industrial Organizations
AMSAC	American Society of African Culture
ANC	African National Congress, South Africa
ANC	Armée Nationale Congolaise (formerly Force Publique)
BAA	Bureau of African Affairs
BOSS	Bureau of State Security, South Africa
CCF	Congress for Cultural Freedom
CDA	Combined Development Agency
CIA	Central Intelligence Agency
CONAKAT	Confédération des Associations Tribales du Katanga
CORAC	Council on Race and Caste in World Affairs
CORE	Congress of Racial Equality
CPP	Convention People's Party
CS	Clandestine Services, CIA
DDP	Deputy Director, Plans, CIA
DRC	Democratic Republic of the Congo (also RDC)
ENDA	École Nationale de Droit et d'Administration
EURATOM	European Atomic Energy Community
Eville	Elisabethville
FBI	Federal Bureau of Investigation
FLN	Front de Libération Nationale/National Liberation Front (Algeria)
FOI	Freedom of Information
FOIA	Freedom of Information Act
FRUS	*Foreign Relations of the United States*
HUAC	House Un-American Activities Committee
IAEA	International Atomic Energy Agency
ICFTU	International Confederation of Free Trade Unions
ICJ	International Commission of Jurists
ILGWU	International Ladies' Garment Workers Union
INR	Bureau of Intelligence and Research, State Department

JFK	John F Kennedy
KGB	Committee for State Security, Soviet Union
Leo	Leopoldville
MI5	Security Service, UK
MI6	Secret Intelligence Service, UK
MIT	Massachusetts Institute of Technology
MNC	Mouvement National Congolais
MNC-K	Mouvement National Congolais, led by Albert Kalonji
MNC-L	Mouvement National Congolais, led by Patrice Lumumba
MoMA	Museum of Modern Art
MPLA	Movimento Popular de Libertação de Angola
NATO	North Atlantic Treaty Organisation
NCL	Non-Communist Left
NGO	nongovernmental organisation
NIHMR	National Institutes of Health and Medical Research
NLC	National Liberation Council
NOC	nonofficial cover
NSA	National Security Agency
NSA	National Student Association
NSC	National Security Council
OCB	Operations Coordinating Board
ONUC	Organisation des Nations Unies au Congo/UN peacekeeping operation in the Congo
ORSA	Overseas Regional Surveys Associates
OSS	Office of Strategic Services
PAC	Pan Africanist Congress
PSA	Parti Solidaire Africain
RAC	Royal African Company
RDC	République Démocratique du Congo (also DRC)
SAC	Société Africaine de Culture
SAIMR	South African Institute for Maritime Research
SIBÉKA	La Société Minière du Bécéca
SSCIA	Senate Select Committee on Intelligence Activities
TRC	Truth and Reconciliation Commission, South Africa
TRICO	Atomic reactor delivered to the Congo in 1959 (TRIGA + Congo)
TRIGA	Training, Research, Isotopes, General Atomics
TSD	Technical Services Division, CIA
UPA	União das Populações de Angola
UPI	United Press International
USAAF	United States Army Air Forces
USAF	United States Air Force
USIA	United States Information Agency
USSR	Union of Soviet Socialist Republics
WFTU	World Federation of Trade Unions

LIST OF ARCHIVES

Archive and Manuscript Repositories: Paper and Digital

AUSTRIA
International Atomic Energy Agency (IAEA), Vienna
    Digital: www.iaea.org/resources/archives

BELGIUM
Archives Générales du Royaume de Belgique (AGRB), Brussels
    Paper: La Société Minière du Bécéca Papers (Sibéka)
    Paper: Union Minière du Haut Katanga Papers
CegeSoma, Anderlecht
    Paper: Collection Edouard Pilaet
Belgian Parliamentary Documents, Brussels
    Digital: www.lachambre.be/kvvcr/index.cfm
North Atlantic Treaty Organisation (NATO) Archives, Brussels
    Digital: https://archives.nato.int/

GHANA
George Padmore Research Library on African Affairs, Accra
    Paper: Bureau of African Affairs Collection (BAA)
Ghana Atomic Energy Commission (GAEC), Accra
    Digital: https://gaecgh.org/

INTERNET ONLY
Kinshasa Then and Now, curated by Mwana Mboka
    Digital: http://kosubaawate.blogspot.com/
SoLant Amity Blog
    Digital: SoLant Amity records and testimonies, https://solantamity.com/

THE NETHERLANDS
African Studies Centre Leiden (ASCL) Library, Leiden
    Paper: Jan-Bart Gewald Papers

PORTUGAL
Arquivo Nacional da Torre do Tombo, Lisbon
    Paper: Polícia Internacional e de Defesa do Estado (PIDE)
    Digital: https://digitarq.arquivos.pt/details?id=4279956

PRIVATE PAPERS
    Paul Broda, Edinburgh
    Michael Hathorn, London

Jim Lesar, Silver Spring, Maryland
Robert K Mpoyo, New York
Hans Kristian Simensen, Gothenburg
Bo Virving; held by Björn Virving, Stockholm
Susan Williams, London

SOUTH AFRICA

Historical Papers Research Archive, William Cullen Library, University of the Witwatersrand, Johannesburg
 Paper and Digital: Nathaniel Nakasa Papers, 1963–1984, A2696, www.histor
  icalpapers.wits.ac.za/index.php?inventory/U/collections&c=A2696/R/6355
The South African History Archive (SAHA), Constitution Hill, Braamfontein, Johannesburg
 Paper: De Wet Potgieter collection
 Digital: Digital Innovation South Africa (DISA), www.disa.ukzn.ac.za/

UK

The Bodleian Library, Archive Collection, University of Oxford
 Paper: Sir Roy Welensky Papers
Churchill Archives Centre, Churchill College, University of Cambridge
 Paper: Sir John Douglas Cockcroft Papers
The National Archives UK (TNA), London
 Government records (Paper; some Digital):
  AB (Atomic Energy Authority)
  BT (Board of Trade)
  CAB (Cabinet Office)
  CO (Colonial Office)
  DO (Dominions Office/Commonwealth Relations Office [CRO])
  FCO (Foreign and Commonwealth Office)
  FO (Foreign Office)
  HW (Government Communications Headquarters/GCHQ)
  KV (Security Service/MI5)
  PREM (Prime Minister's Office)
United Nations Association (UNA), Westminster Branch, London
 Digital: www.Hammarskjöldinquiry.info/

UNITED NATIONS

UN Archives and Records Management Section (ARMS), New York
 Paper: United Nations Archives
 Digital: Digital Library, https://digitallibrary.un.org/?ln=en

USA

African Activist Archive Project, Michigan State University Libraries, East Lansing
 Digital: https://africanactivist.msu.edu/
Albertsons Library, Boise State University, Idaho
 Paper: Frank Church Papers
Amistad Research Center, Tulane University, New Orleans
 Paper: James H Robinson Papers

Digital: American Committee on Africa (ACOA) Records, http://voy ager.tcs.tulane.edu/vwebv/holdingsInfo?searchId=203&recCount=10&rec Pointer=1&bibId=3929499

The Avalon Project: Documents in Law, History and Diplomacy, Lilian Goldman Law Library, Yale Law School, New Haven, Connecticut
Digital: https://avalon.law.yale.edu/

Central Intelligence Agency (CIA), Freedom of Information Act (FOIA) Electronic Reading Room
Digital: Files released through the FOIA and other programmes, including CREST (CIA Records Search Tool), www.cia.gov/readingroom/

University of Chicago, The Hanna Holborn Gray Special Collections Research Center
Paper: John Gunther Papers

University of Chicago Library, Special Collections Research Center
Paper: International Association for Cultural Freedom (IACF), Records 1941–1978, including those of the Congress for Cultural Freedom (CCF)

Columbia University Rare Book and Manuscript Library, New York
Paper: Oral History Archives

Du Bois Library Special Collections and University Archives (SCUA), University of Massachusetts Amherst (Paper and Digital)
W E B Du Bois Papers, https://credo.library.umass.edu/view/collection/mums312
Horace Mann Bond Papers, https://credo.library.umass.edu/view/collection /mums411
Africa American Institute Records, including those of the African American Institute (the name of the organisation until 1998), http://findingaids.library .umass.edu/ead/mums849#scopecontent

Emory Libraries and Information Technology, Emory University, Atlanta
Digital: Slave Voyages, www.slavevoyages.org/

FB Eyes Digital Archives: FBI Files on African American Authors and Literary Institutions Obtained through the US Freedom of Information Act, Washington University, St Louis
Digital: FBI documents on St Clair Drake, 1961–1971, http://omeka.wustl .edu/omeka/exhibits/show/fbeyes/drake

FBI Records: The Vault
Digital: J Edgar Hoover Office and Confidential (O&C) Files, https://vault .fbi.gov/j.-edgar-hoover-official-and-confidential-o-c-files

George Meany Labor Archive, University of Maryland, College Park
Paper: AFL and AFL-CIO International Affairs Department, Irving Brown Papers

Gerald R Ford Library, Ann Arbor, Michigan
Digital: Richard B Cheney, Deputy Assistant to the President; Assistant to the President for White House Operations: Files, 1974–1977, www.ford librarymuseum.gov/library/guides/findingaid/Cheney,_Richard_-_Files .asp#FTL

Hoover Institution Library and Archives, Stanford University, Stanford, California
Paper: Elizabeth Churchill Brown Papers
Paper: Jay Lovestone Papers

John F Kennedy Presidential Library and Museum (JFKL), Boston, Archives, https://www.jfklibrary.org/archives/about-archival-collections (Paper; some Digital)

    George W Ball Personal Papers, including telephone conversation (Telcon) records

    Papers of John F Kennedy: Presidential Papers, President's Office Files (POF)

    National Security Files (NSF)

Louis Armstrong House Museum, Queens, New York

    Digital: Louis Armstrong Archives, https://collections.louisarmstronghouse.org/

Louis Round Wilson Special Collections Library, University of North Carolina, Chapel Hill

    Paper: Charles Mills Papers

The Martin Luther King, Jr, Research and Education Institute, Stanford University, Stanford, California

    Digital: Martin Luther King, Jr, Papers Project, https://kinginstitute.stanford.edu/king-papers/about-papers-project

Moorland Spingarn Research Center, Howard University, Washington, DC

    Paper: American Society of African Culture (AMSAC)

    Paper: The Dabu Gizenga Collection on Kwame Nkrumah

National Archives and Records Administration (NARA), Washington, DC

    Paper and Digital: Multiple and various government records

    Paper and Digital: Documentation released under the President John F Kennedy Assassination Records Collection Act

Schlesinger Library, Radcliffe Institute, Harvard University, Cambridge, Massachusetts

    Paper: Maida Springer Kemp Papers

    Paper: Pauli Murray Papers

Schomburg Center for Research in Black Culture, Manuscripts, Archives and Rare Books Division, New York Public Library, New York

    Paper: Etta Moten Barnett Collection

Stanford University Libraries: Special Collections Manuscripts Division, Stanford, California

    Paper: John Marcum Papers

Tamiment Library and Robert F Wagner Labor Archive, Elmer Holmes Bobst Library, New York University

    Paper: American Committee for Cultural Freedom Records

The Woodrow Wilson International Center for Scholars' Cold War International History Project and Africa Program, Washington, DC

    Digital: Digital Archive, International History Declassified, http://digitalarchive.wilsoncenter.org/document/155185

NOTES

Many of the archive collections cited as sources are referred to in the notes by abbreviated references. Each such reference corresponds to an entry in the List of Archives, where more information about the collection can be found.

1. Freedom at Midnight

1. Information given in this chapter about the independence celebrations is drawn from a range of sources, including: Raymond, *Black Star in the Wind*; Powell, *Private Secretary*; I M R Maclennan to the Earl of Home, 1 May 1957, TNA, DO 35/9203; Cameron Duodu, '6th March 1957—You'd Simply Have Loved to Have Been There!', *Modern Ghana*, 6 March 2018, www.modernghana.com/news/839638/6th-march-1957-youd-simply-have-loved-to-have.html.

2. Duodu, '6th March 1957—You'd Simply Have Loved to Have Been There!'

3. The author is grateful to John Cowley for sharing his research on the Highlife.

4. 'The Birth of a New Nation', sermon delivered by Martin Luther King Jr at Dexter Avenue Baptist Church, 7 April 1957, The Martin Luther King, Jr, Research and Education Institute, Stanford University, King Papers 4:1604:160.

5. I M R Maclennan to the Earl of Home, 1 May 1957, TNA, DO 35/9203.

6. Nkrumah, *Africa Must Unite*, p 32.

7. *Ibid*, p 35.

8. Powell, *Private Secretary*, pp 31–32.

9. *Ibid*, p 31.

10. *Ibid*, p 76.

11. Frederick, *Ten First Ladies of the World*, pp 128–129.

12. Quoted in Charles Leonard, 'The Nkrumahs' Marriage Was No Match Made in Heaven', *Mail and Guardian*, April 14, 2020.

13. Nkrumah, *Africa Must Unite*, p 59.

14. Raymond, *Black Star in the Wind*, p 277.

15. Powell, *Private Secretary*, p 103.

16. Raymond, *Black Star in the Wind*, p 276.

17. *Ibid*, p 279.

18. *Ibid*, pp 279–280. The description of Benedictov as 'handsome' was made by Powell in *Private Secretary*, p 106.

19. *Ibid*, pp 271–272.

20. Urquhart, *Ralph Bunche*, pp 277 and 283.

21. Quoted in James, *George Padmore and Decolonization from Below*, p 181.

22. Raymond, *Black Star in the Wind*, p 276.

23. See, for example TNA, KV 2/1849, and TNA, KV 2/1851.

24. Ray, *Crossing the Color Line*, pp 212, 215–217.

25. Powell, *Private Secretary*, p 103.

26. *Ibid*, pp 108–109.

27. Gaines, *American Africans in Ghana*, p 82.

28. Marais, *Kwame Nkrumah*, pp 9, 88, 97, and 12.

29. Vincent Djokoto, 'Genoveva Esther Marais: The Woman Rumored to Be Nkrumah's Secret Lover', *GhanaWeb*, 28 June 2020, https://www.ghanaweb .com/GhanaHomePage/NewsArchive/Genoveva-Esther-Marais-The-woman -rumoured-to-be-Nkrumah-s-secret-lover-992371.

30. Radio interview with Martin Luther King Jr by Etta Moten Barnett, Accra, 6 March 1957, The Martin Luther King, Jr, Research and Education Institute, Stanford University, King Papers, 4:146.

31. King, *The Papers of Martin Luther King, Jr.*, vol 4, p 9.

32. Quoted and discussed in Garrow, *Bearing the Cross*, p 91.

33. Raymond, *Black Star in the Wind*, p 279.

34. Powell, *Private Secretary*, p 106.

35. Batsa, *The Spark*, pp 31–32.

2. 'My Home is Over Jordan'

1. Frederick, *Ten First Ladies of the World*, p 130.

2. Davidson, *Black Star*, pp 25–30.

3. FBI report on Kwame Nkrumah, 29 May 1945, FBI 100-21745, reproduced in Rahman, *The Regime Change of Kwame Nkrumah*, pp 76–77.

4. Alden Whitman, 'Nkrumah, 62, Dead: Ghana's Ex-Leader', *New York Times*, 28 April 1972; Sherwood, *Kwame Nkrumah*, pp 51, 75, 79.

5. Davidson, *Black Star*, p 32.

6. Milne, *Kwame Nkrumah: A Biography*, pp 11-12.

7. Nkrumah, *The Autobiography*, pp 42–43.

8. Andrew Glass, 'Eisenhower Apologizes for Racial Insult, Oct. 10, 1957', *Politico*, 10 October 2018, www.politico.com/story/2018/10/10/eisenhower-apologizes -racial-insult-1957-880971.

9. Meriwether, *Proudly We Can Be Africans*, p 172.

10. 'Portrait of Nkrumah as Dictator', *New York Times*, 3 May 1964, p 10.

11. Quoted in Meriwether, *Proudly We Can Be Africans*, p 174; emphasis in the original.

12. Meriwether, *Proudly We Can Be Africans*, p 174.

13. Nesbitt, 'Race for Sanctions', pp 84–85.

14. Powell, *Private Secretary*, p 136.

15. 'Year of Return Tour', Ghana Tech Summit, London, 1 November 2019, Movemeback, www.movemeback.com/about/.

16. 'Beyond the Return', Visit Ghana, https://visitghana.com/beyond-the-return/, accessed 15 March 2021.

17. Myers refers to Fage and Oliver, *The Cambridge History of Africa*, 2:295–296, 3:472–473, 4:216–217.

18. This is the Slave Voyages Database (Slave Voyages: Trans-Atlantic Slave Trade— Database, www.slavevoyages.org), created by the Emory Center for Digital Scholarship,

which was established in 2013 at Emory University in Atlanta, Georgia. Work on the database is ongoing; therefore, figures change. These figures are based on accessing the website on 6 November 2020. They draw on extant information in libraries and archives around the Atlantic world. In the case of voyages that are known about but for which there are inadequate records, it is possible to compensate for incomplete information by estimating the likely sum of people on board. The author is grateful to K James Myers in the Department of History at Rice University for his expert assistance with these data and with the use of the Emory Center database, as well as with important contextual issues.

19. Slave Voyages: Trans-Atlantic Slave Trade—Estimates, Tables, www.slave voyages.org/assessment/estimates.

20. Eltis et al, 'Summary Statistics'; O'Malley, *Final Passages*; Borucki, Eltis, and Wheat, 'Atlantic History and the Slave Trade to Spanish America', pp 433–446.

21. 'Slavery and the British Transatlantic Slave Trade', a guide to the records held in the UK National Archives, accessed 6 November 2020, www.nationalarchives.gov.uk /help-with-your-research/research-guides/british-transatlantic-slave-trade-records/.

22. Slave Voyages: Trans-Atlantic Slave Trade—Estimates, Tables.

23. Because very little information is available regarding the earliest slave-trade voyages, it is impossible to establish which were the first ones to take place; it is largely a 'best guess' scenario. In contrast, the later voyages are much firmer in their details.

24. Slave Voyages: Trans-Atlantic Slave Trade—Estimates, Timeline, www.slave voyages.org/assessment/estimates.

25. Bernstein, *Thomas Jefferson*, p 34.

26. Goodwin, 'The Thirteenth Amendment', pp 899–990; Blackmon, *Slavery by Another Name*.

27. St Clair, *The Grand Slave Emporium*, pp 255–256.

28. Osei-Tutu, ed, *Forts, Castles and Society in West Africa*, p 11.

29. St Clair, *The Grand Slave Emporium*, pp 37 and 57.

30. Wright, *Black Power*, p 406.

31. *Ibid*, p 409.

32. *Ibid*, p 408.

33. Slave Voyages: Trans-Atlantic Slave Trade—Database, www.slavevoyages.org /voyage/database#searchId=rWziJb61.

34. This is based on the findings of Slave Voyages: Trans-Atlantic Slave Trade—Database, www.slavevoyages.org/voyage/database#searchId=rWziJb61.

35. Slave Voyages: Trans-Atlantic Slave Trade—Database, www.slavevoyages.org /voyages/1VqU4Wp9.

36. Slave Voyages: Trans-Atlantic Slave Trade—Database, www.slavevoyages .org/voyages/tQEpiVLw.

37. Powell, *Private Secretary*, p 117.

38. Raymond, *Black Star in the Wind*, p 278.

39. Powell, *Private Secretary*, p 117.

40. Hunton, *Alphaeus Hunton*, p 129.

41. Gaines, *American Africans in Ghana*, pp 6–9.

42. Angelou, *All God's Children Need Travelling Shoes*, pp 86–87.

43. *Ibid*, pp 222–227.

3. The Challenge of the Congo

1. Nkrumah, *Challenge of the Congo*, p 6.

2. Quoted in Nkrumah, *Challenge of the Congo*, p 4.

3. In French: *État Indépendant du Congo*; in Flemish: *Onafhankelijke Congostaat*.

4. Nzongola-Ntalaja, *The Congo from Leopold to Kabila*, p 22.

5. Hochschild, introduction to Marchal, *Lord Leverhulme's Ghosts*, p xiv.

6. *Ibid*, p xv.

7. Quoted in Gibbs, *The Political Economy of Third World Intervention*, p 45.

8. Jean Stengers, quoted in Gibbs, *The Political Economy of Third World Intervention*, p 46.

9. Hochschild, introduction to Marchal, *Lord Leverhulme's Ghosts*, p xviii.

10. Nzongola-Ntalaja, *The Congo from Leopold to Kabila*, p 22.

11. For an excellent account see Gibbs, *The Political Economy of Third World Intervention*, pp 51 ff.

12. Hochschild, introduction to Marchal, *Lord Leverhulme's Ghosts*, p xiv.

13. Renton et al, *The Congo: Plunder and Resistance*, p 66.

14. See Stanard, 'Revisiting Bula Matari and the Congo Crisis', pp 145–161.

15. Marchal, *Lord Leverhulme's Ghosts*, p 215.

16. Mwana Mboka, 'Leopoldville 1930s', *Kinshasa Then and Now*, blog, 12 February 2012, http://kosubaawate.blogspot.com/2012/02/leopoldville-1930s-leisure-in-time-of.html.

17. Huntington to Vanderbilt, 2 September 1942, NARA, RG 226, A1–210, Box 405.

18. Written in 1943; quoted in Price, *Anthropological Intelligence*, pp 42–43.

19. Laxalt, *A Private War*, p 57.

20. Groves, *Now It Can Be Told*, p 37, n 1.

21. Öhrström adds an analogy: 'It is relatively easy to construct a machine mechanically separating oranges from bananas. But if there are bananas, apples *and* oranges present, and only one orange for every ten apples, clearly it will be more tricky to get only the oranges'. Lars Öhrström to the author by email, 28 March 2021.

22. John R Ruhoff to L R Groves, 23 November 1943, NARA, RG 77, Entry 5, Box 68.

23. 'Damage by New Bomb', *The Times*, 8 August 1945.

24. George Padmore, 'Africa Holds Key to Atomic Future', *Chicago Defender*, 8 September 1945, p 5.

25. Bele, 'The Legacy of the Involvement of the Democratic Republic of the Congo in the Bombs Dropped on Hiroshima and Nagasaki'.

26. *FRUS*, 1951, vol 1, *National Security Affairs; Foreign Economic Policy*, document 249, https://history.state.gov/historicaldocuments/frus1951v01/d249.

27. Gheerbrant, *Congo Noir et Blanc*, p 92. The author is grateful to Robert Mpoyo for telling her about this book.

28. Borstelmann, *Apartheid's Reluctant Uncle*, p 198.

29. TNA, AB 16/1361. The equivalent sum on 11 December 2020 is US$236,794,171, using the conversion tool found here: https://fxtop.com/en/historical-currency-converter.php.

30. 'Shinkolobwe Development and Plant Expansion Programmes—Expansion as of June 30th 1956'. TNA, AB 16/1361.

31. United States Bureau of Mines, *Minerals Yearbook 1960*, pp 385–387.

32. Carlucci, interviewed by Charles Stuart Kennedy, 1 April 1997.

33. Quoted in Schechter et al, 'The CIA as an Equal Opportunity Employer', p 56.

34. Namikas, *Battleground Africa*, p 26.

35. Tweedy recalled the start date was 'somewhere around' the 15th or 18th of November 1959. SSCIA, Hearings, Bronson Tweedy, 9 October 1975, NARA Record Number 157-10014-10068.

36. Nkrumah, *Challenge of the Congo*, pp 243.

37. Nkrumah, *Neo-Colonialism*, pp 209–211.

38. Nkrumah, *Challenge of the Congo*, pp 235–237.

4. 'Hands off Africa!'

1. Conference of Independent African States, *Speeches Delivered at the Inaugural Session*, p 8.

2. Nkrumah, *Challenge of the Congo*, p xv.

3. *All African People's Conference* leaflet, 1958, W E B Du Bois Papers (MS 312), Special Collections and University Archives, University of Massachusetts Amherst Libraries, http://credo.library.umass.edu/view/pageturn/mums312-b148-i017/#page/1 /mode/1up.

4. Officials in some British government departments compiled lists of delegates; they do not match each other entirely but are largely similar. These can be found in the following files in the UK National Archives: TNA, FO 371/137938 and DO 35/9272 (the latter file has two separate, slightly different, lists).

5. 'All-African People's Conferences', *International Organization*, p 429.

6. Mphahlele, 'Accra Conference Diary', p 45.

7. Cameron Duodu, 'Frantz Fanon: Prophet of African Liberation', *Pambazuka News*, 5 December 2011.

8. Special Correspondent, 'Africa in Search of Its Own Voice', *Manchester Guardian*, 9 December 1958, p 3.

9. Hoskyns, 'Pan-Africanism at Accra', p 72.

10. Kyle, *The Politics of the Independence of Kenya*, p 89.

11. Richards, *Conversations with Maida Springer*, p 220.

12. Duodu, 'Frantz Fanon: Prophet of African Liberation'.

13. Cameron Duodu, 'Patrice Lumumba: The Rise and Assassination of an African Patriot', *Mashariaz*, 21 January 2011, http://mashariazgitonga.blogspot.co.uk/2011/01/.

14. Mboya, *Freedom and After*, p 13.

15. Kennett Love, 'Africa Is Warned of New Colonialism', *New York Times*, 9 December 1958, pp 1 and 15; the quotation is on p 15.

16. R A Lomotey, '"A Dream, Now Reality"—Mboya', *Daily Graphic*, 9 December 1958, p 3.

17. In fact, the number of states in the USA in December 1958 was forty-eight; it went up to fifty with the addition of Alaska and Hawaii in January and August of 1959, respectively. The author is grateful to Paul Broda for pointing this out.

18. Special Correspondent, 'Africa in Search of Its Own Voice'.

19. Speech by Prime Minister Nkrumah of Ghana at the opening session of the All-African People's Conference on Monday, 8 December 1958. The full speech is

given here: 'P M: Let Us Unite in the Fight to Free Africa', *Daily Graphic*, 9 December 1958, pp 1 and 13; and here: www.columbia.edu/itc/history/mann/w3005/nkrumba.html.

20. Nkomo, *Nkomo: The Story of My Life*, p 76.

21. Mphahlele, 'Accra Conference Diary', p 45.

22. See communications in TNA, FCO 141/461, and TNA, FCO 141/7064.

23. Gaines, *American Africans in Ghana*, p 95.

24. James, *George Padmore and Decolonization from Below*, p 179.

25. Duodu, 'Frantz Fanon: Prophet of African Liberation'.

26. J D Akumu, 'Mboya: Trade Unionist and a Great Son of Africa', reproduced in 'Tom Mboya: The Charismatic Pan-Africanist, Freedom Fighter and the Greatest President Kenya Never Had', *Trip Down Memory Lane*, 2 December 2013, https://kwekudee-tripdownmemorylane.blogspot.co.uk/2013/12/tom-mboya-charismatic-pan-africanist.html.

27. Thompson, *Ghana's Foreign Policy, 1957–1966*, p 58. The source given here is James Markham, Padmore's assistant at the time.

28. Richards, *Conversations with Maida Springer*, pp 219 and 218.

29. Makonnen, *Pan-Africanism from Within*, p 215.

30. Chiume, *Kwacha*, pp 101–102.

31. Ransby, *Eslanda*, pp 242–243.

32. Quoted in Clarke, 'Paul Robeson', p 229.

33. Quotations from the media relating to Paul Robeson, including the telegram to the AAPC, reported in *The Worker*, 18 January 1959, CIA, CREST, CIA-RDP 91-00965R000500120005-8, www.cia.gov/library/readingroom/docs/CIA-RDP91-00965 R000500120005-8.pdf.

34. Houser, *No One Can Stop the Rain*, p 71.

35. George M Houser, *A Report on the All African People's Conference, Accra, Ghana, December 8–13, 1958*, African Activist Archive, n.d., p 1, https://projects.kora.matrix.msu.edu/files/210-808-10390/PWACOAAAPC58opt.pdf.

36. Hoskyns, 'Pan-Africanism at Accra', p 72.

37. 'Race Relations in the United States and American Cultural and Informational Programs in Ghana, 1957–1966, Part 2', pp 2–3.

38. Shatz, 'Where Life is Seized'.

39. Burgess et al, 'A Tribute to A M Babu', p 339.

40. Houser, interviewed by Lisa Brock, 19 July 2004.

41. Nkomo, *Nkomo: The Story of My Life*, p 75.

42. Gewald, *Hands off Africa!!*, p 10.

43. Robeson, 'The Accra Conference', p 14.

44. Richards, *Conversations with Maida Springer*, pp 220–221.

45. 'JAD [John Aubrey Davis] to JTH [James Theodore Harris] Files', Report on Accra Conference (#2), 18 December 1958, AMSAC Papers, box 1.23, Moorland-Spingarn Center, Howard University.

46. Gaines, *American Africans in Ghana*, p 95.

47. Mphahlele, 'Accra Conference Diary', p 47.

48. Richards, *Conversations with Maida Springer*, p 219.

49. Mphahlele, 'Accra Conference Diary', p 47.

50. Burgess et al, 'A Tribute to A M Babu', p 326.

51. Gewald, *Hands off Africa!!*, p 11.

52. Quoted in George Loft, 'Report on All African People's Conference Held at Accra, Ghana, December 8–13, 1958', p 6, Sir Roy Welensky Papers, Mss Welensky, box 231/5, Bodleian Archives and Manuscripts, Oxford University.

53. Hutchinson, *The Other Side of the Road*, p 262.

54. Mphahlele, 'Accra Conference Diary', p 47.

55. *Ibid*, p 47.

56. *The Times*, 10 December 1958.

57. Special Correspondent, 'Cheers for the Mau Mau', *Manchester Guardian*, 12 December 1958, p 9.

58. Hoskyns, 'Pan-Africanism at Accra', p 73.

59. 'All of Lumumba's speeches were extemporaneous. Except during formal debates, when he would refer to documents in his possession, he never used notes when he spoke'. Introduction to Lumumba's speech at the AAPC in Accra, 11 December 1958, by Jean Van Lierde, in Van Lierde, ed., *Lumumba Speaks*, p 55.

60. Van Lierde, ed., *Lumumba Speaks*, p 58.

61. Gewald, *Hands off Africa!!*, p 17.

62. Duodu, 'Frantz Fanon: Prophet of African liberation'.

63. Quoted in Houser, *No One Can Stop the Rain*, p 73.

64. Quoted in Nesbitt, 'Race for Sanctions', p 35.

65. Hoskyns, 'Pan-Africanism at Accra', p 76.

66. Mphahlele, 'Accra Conference Diary', p 49.

67. Thompson, *Ghana's Foreign Policy, 1957–1966*, p 61.

68. Quoted in Burgess et al, 'A Tribute to A M Babu', pp 333–334.

69. Comment and quote in Macey, *Frantz Fanon*, p 365.

70. Nkrumah, *Challenge of the Congo*, p xv.

5. Infiltration into Africa

1. Gaines, *American Africans in Ghana*, p 96.

2. George M Houser, *A Report on the All African People's Conference, Accra, Ghana, December 8–13, 1958*, African Activist Archive, n.d., p 4, https://projects.kora.matrix.msu.edu/files/210-808-10390/PWACOAAAPC58opt.pdf.

3. Houser, *No One Can Stop the Rain*, p 72.

4. 'Council on African Affairs, 1937–1955', African Activist Archive, accessed 15 March 2021, https://africanactivist.msu.edu/organization.php?name=Council+on+African+Affairs.

5. Hunton, *Alphaeus Hunton*, p 130.

6. 'Council on African Affairs, 1937–1955'.

7. Hunton, *Alphaeus Hunton*, pp 81 ff.

8. Anthony, *Max Yergan*, p 239.

9. *Ibid*, p 275.

10. The articles published by the *New York Times* in February 1967 were: Neil Sheehan, 'A Student Group Concedes It Took Funds from C.I.A.', *New York Times*, 14 February 1967, pp 1, 7; Neil Sheehan, 'Foundations Linked to C.I.A. Are Found to

Subsidize 4 Other Youth Organizations', *New York Times*, 16 February 1967, p 26; Juan de Onis, 'Ramparts Says C.I.A. Received Student Report', *New York Times*, 16 February 1967, p 26; John Herbers, 'President Bars Agency Influence over Education', *New York Times*, 16 February 1967, pp 1, 26; Neil Sheehan, '5 New Groups Tied to C.I.A. Conduits', *New York Times*, 17 February 1967, pp 1, 16; Neil Sheehan, 'Aid by C.I.A. Put in Millions; Group Total Up', *New York Times*, 19 February 1967, p 1; Steven V Roberts, 'Students Opposing U.S.-Aided Regimes Got C.I.A. Subsidies', *New York Times*, 21 February 1967; E W Kenworthy, 'Hobby Foundation of Houston Affirms C.I.A. Tie', *New York Times*, 21 February 1967, p 32.

11. de Vries, 'The 1967 Central Intelligence Agency Scandal', p 1075.

12. Hunt, 'The CIA Exposures: End of an Affair', part I.

13. Rathbun, *The Point Man*, pp 114–115; Richard Harwood, '8 More Groups Linked to CIA's Fund Activities', *Washington Post*, 21 February 1967, p A6. See also Swanepoel, *Really Inside Boss*, pp 155–156.

14. Wilford, *The Mighty Wurlitzer*, p 302, n 18.

15. Quoted in Gewald, *Hands off Africa!!*, p 16.

16. 'AAI Remembers Life of Former Executive', Africa-America Institute, 28 October 2013, www.aaionline.org/aai-remembers-life-of-former-executive/.

17. Neil Sheehan, '5 New Groups Tied to C.I.A. Conduits', *New York Times*, 17 February 1967, pp 1, 16.

18. Cummings, *The Pied Piper*, p 178.

19. Kelley, *Africa Speaks, America Answers*, p 65; Urban, *Black Scholar*, p 163. This is discussed, with additional details, in Swanepoel, *Really Inside Boss*, pp 154–155.

20. Von Eschen, *Race Against Empire*, p 175.

21. Wilford, *The Mighty Wurlitzer*, p 206.

22. *Ibid*, p 210.

23. *Ibid*, p 208.

24. Cook, interviewed by Strutts Njiiri, 24 June 1981.

25. 'JAD [John Aubrey Davis] to JTH [James Theodore Harris] Files', Report on Accra Conference (#2), 18 December 1958, AMSAC Papers, box 1.23, Harris, James T, Moorland-Spingarn Center, Howard University.

26. Louis Menand, 'When the C.I.A. Duped College Students', *New Yorker*, 16 March 2013, www.newyorker.com/magazine/2015/03/23/a-friend-of-the-devil. Karen M Paget has provided a detailed exposé of the relationship between the National Student Association and the CIA in her book *Patriotic Betrayal*.

27. Hunt, 'The CIA Exposures: End of an Affair', part III.

28. Discussed and quoted in Wilford, *The Mighty Wurlitzer*, p 213.

29. Quoted in *ibid*, pp 213–214.

30. Urban, *Black Scholar*, pp 163–164; Wilford, 'The American Society of African Culture', p 29.

31. The American Committee for Cultural Freedom was formed in the 1950s as an affiliate of the International Congress for Cultural Freedom, and membership included prominent liberal and leftist artists and intellectuals across a broad political spectrum. The records of the organisation are held by the Tamiment Library and Robert F Wagner Labor Archive at New York University.

32. Stonor Saunders, *Who Paid the Piper?*, p 63.

33. Iber, *Neither Peace nor Freedom*, p 3.

34. Stonor Saunders, *Who Paid the Piper?*, p 91.

35. Iber, *Neither Peace nor Freedom*, p 6.

36. Arndt, *The First Resort of Kings*, p 222; the equivalent amount on 1 December 2020 is US$16,441,535.88, using the tool found here: https://fxtop.com/en/historical-currency-converter.php.

37. See final section, 'Magazine Got Funds', in *New York Times*, 27 April 1966, pp 1 and 28. The other articles published by the *New York Times* in April 1966 were: 'The C.I.A.: Maker of Policy, or Tool? Agency Raises Questions Around World; Survey Discloses Strict Controls But Reputation of Agency Is Found to Make It a Burden on U.S. Action', *New York Times*, 25 April 1966, p 1; 'How C.I.A Put an 'Instant Air Force' into Congo to Carry Out United States Policy', *New York Times*, 26 April 1966, p 30; 'C.I.A. Operations: A Plot Scuttled, or, How Kennedy in '62 Undid Sugar Sabotage', *New York Times*, 28 April 1966, p 28; 'C.I.A Operations: Man at Helm, Not the System, Viewed as Key to Control of Agency', *New York Times*, 29 April 1966, p 18.

38. Thomas W Braden, 'I'm Glad the CIA Is "Immoral"', *Saturday Evening Post*, 20 May 1967, pp 10–14.

39. Swanepoel, *Really Inside Boss*, pp 168–169.

40. Bird, *The Chairman*, pp 357–358, 412–413.

41. Price, 'The CIA Book Publishing Operations'.

42. Discussion and quotation in Iber, *Neither Peace nor Freedom*, pp 108–109.

43. Price, 'The CIA Book Publishing Operations', p 4.

44. Interview with Lawrence de Neufville by Stonor Saunders, 1997, quoted in Stonor Saunders, *Who Paid the Piper?*, p 357.

45. Interview with Tom Braden by Stonor Saunders, 1994, quoted in Stonor Saunders, *Who Paid the Piper?*, p 127.

46. Polsgrove, *Ending British Rule in Africa*, p 147.

47. Whitney, *Finks*, p 17 and 123.

48. Swanepoel, *Really Inside Boss*, p 101; Driver, *Patrick Duncan*, p 148.

49. Quoted and discussed in Driver, *Patrick Duncan*, p 158.

50. Quoted in *ibid*, p 203; this statement was made on 9 March 1961.

51. Herbstein, *White Lies*, p 57.

52. Stonor Saunders, *Who Paid the Piper?*, p 135.

53. Bird, *The Chairman*, pp 427–428.

54. Stonor Saunders, *Who Paid the Piper?*, p 142. US$7 million on 1 January 1960 is the equivalent of US$62.2 million in November 2020, using the tool found here: https://fxtop.com/en/historical-currency-converter.php.

55. Quoted in Stonor Saunders, *Who Paid the Piper?*, p 135; see also pp 138–139.

56. Soyinka, *You Must Set Forth at Dawn*, p 86.

57. As discussed in Davis, *African Literature and the CIA*, p 31. Soyinka responded to Davis's book in *Trumpism in Academe*, repudiating these suggestions.

58. Soyinka, *Trumpism in Academe*, pp 9–15.

59. *Ibid*, pp 17–19.

60. *Ibid*, pp 19–24.

61. Quotations from the media relating to Paul Robeson, including the telegram to the AAPC, reported in *The Worker*, 18 January 1959, CIA, CREST, CIA-RDP

91-00965R000500120005-8, www.cia.gov/library/readingroom/docs/CIA-RDP91-00965 R000500120005-8.pdf.

62. Eslanda Robeson, interview in *Blitz* (Bombay), 27 December 1958, in 'General CIA Records', released 12 August 2000, CIA-RDP91-00965R0005000120006-7, www.cia.gov/library/readingroom/document/cia-rdp91-00965r000500120006-7.

63. Ransby, *Eslanda*, p 245.

6. 'Africa Has Become the Real Battleground'

1. UK High Commissioner in Ghana to Commonwealth Secretary, London, 30 December 1958. Repeated in CRO print, 9 January 1959, TNA, DO 35/9272.

2. Biney, *The Political and Social Thought of Kwame Nkrumah*, p 137.

3. Houser, *No One Can Stop the Rain*, p 70.

4. Hutchinson, *The Other Side of the Road*, p 282.

5. Clément, 'Patrice Lumumba (Stanleyville 1952–53)', p 74.

6. Nkrumah, *Challenge of the Congo*, p 16.

7. Van Reybrouck, *Congo*, pp 215, 230–233.

8. Nzongola-Ntalaja notes in *Patrice Lumumba* that there are several narratives as to how Lumumba got to the conference in Accra (p 69). The narrative given here draws from the following: Burgess et al, 'A Tribute to A M Babu', contribution by Lionel Cliffe, p 322; Nzongola-Ntalaja, *Patrice Lumumba*, pp 69–70; Sutherland and Meyer, *Guns and Gandhi in Africa*, p 35; Plummer, *In Search of Power*, p 71.

9. Legum, *Congo Disaster*, p 56.

10. Van Lierde, ed, *Lumumba Speaks*, p 55.

11. Nkrumah, *Challenge of the Congo*, p 16.

12. Van Reybrouck, *Congo*, p 241.

13. Stockwell, *In Search of Enemies*, p 11.

14. *Ibid*, p 10.

15. For further discussion of the term *évolué*, see Stanard, *Selling the Congo*, p 275, n 84.

16. Zeilig, *Lumumba*, p 34.

17. Clément, 'Patrice Lumumba (Stanleyville 1952–53)', p 80.

18. Nzongola-Ntalaja, *Patrice Lumumba*, p 40.

19. See the analysis that is developed in Bouwer, *Gender and Decolonization in the Congo*.

20. Lemarchand, *Political Awakening in the Belgian Congo*, p 199.

21. An indication of the numbers of Congolese who visited Brussels between the end of World War II and the independence of the Congo can be inferred from an estimate that only ten did so in 1947. See Stanard, *Selling the Congo*, p 275, n 84.

22. Dayal, *Mission for Hammarskjöld*, p 290.

23. Lemarchand, *Political Awakening in the Belgian Congo*, p 200.

24. Nzongola-Ntalaja, *Patrice Lumumba*, pp 46–47.

25. *Ibid*, p 21.

26. Quoted in Lemarchand, *Political Awakening in the Belgian Congo*, p 161.

27. Van Reybrouck, *Congo*, p 241.

28. Quoted in Lemarchand, *Political Awakening in the Belgian Congo*, p 161.

29. Henry, *Ralph Bunche*, p 187.

30. Johnny Young, interviewed by Charles Stuart Kennedy, 21 October 2005.

31. Eric Pace, 'Ahmed Sékou Touré, A Radical Hero', *New York Times*, 28 March 1984.

32. Nelson, *Area Handbook for Guinea: 1961*, p 39. The equivalent sum on 19 December 2020 is US$253,317,325, using the conversion tool at https://fxtop.com/en/historical-currency-converter.php.

33. The man was Jean-Pierre Dericoyard, a businessman. S A Lockhart, British Consulate-General, Leopoldville, to J H A Watson, African Department, Foreign Office, 12 January 1959, TNA, FO 371/137937.

34. Woodrow Wilson International Center for Scholars, *The Congo Crisis, 1960–1961: A Critical Oral History Conference*, pp 48–49.

35. Kanza, *Conflict in the Congo*, p 50.

36. Marcum, *Conceiving Mozambique*, p xxii.

37. Hugh Wilford writes that the *New Leader* survived the 1950s 'only because the CIA wanted it kept alive, for intelligence and propaganda purposes' (*The Mighty Wurlitzer*, p 230).

38. *FRUS*, 1964–1968, vol 24, *Africa*, document 442, https://history.state.gov/historicaldocuments/frus1964-68v24/d442.

39. Cameron Duodu, 'An African Traitor', *The Guardian*, 14 August 2007.

40. Mahoney, *JFK: Ordeal in Africa*, p 270, n 129.

41. Kennett Love, 'All-Africa Body Weighing Tactics', *New York Times*, 10 December 1958, p 13.

42. Weiner, *Legacy of Ashes*, p 218.

43. Quoted in Rathbun, *The Point Man*, p 111.

44. Davies, *African Trade Unions*, p 201.

45. Quoted in Stoner, '"We Will Follow a Nationalist Policy; But We Will Never Be Neutral"', p 240.

46. Quoted in Meaney, 'Frantz Fanon and the CIA Man', pp 987–988.

47. *Ibid*, p 987.

48. Stoner, '"We Will Follow a Nationalist Policy; But We Will Never Be Neutral"', p 237.

49. Quoted in *ibid*, p 238.

50. *New York Post*, 24 February 1967, quoted in Cohen, 'The CIA and African Trade Unions', p 74.

51. Morgan, *A Covert Life*, p 304.

52. Richards, *Conversations with Maida Springer*, pp 1–3.

53. *Ibid*, p 220.

54. Quoted in *ibid*, p 219, n 15.

55. Morgan, *A Covert Life*, p 305.

56. Richards, *Conversations with Maida Springer*, p 213.

57. Quoted in Richards, *Maida Springer*, p 11.

58. Cohen, 'The CIA and African Trade Unions', p 75.

59. 'NSC Briefing: All-African People's Conference, 17 December 1958', CIA, CREST, CIA-RDP79R00890A001000080029-7, www.cia.gov/library/readingroom/document/cia-rdp79r00890a001000080029-7.

60. Von Eschen, *Race Against Empire*, p 143.

61. Quoted in Richards, *Conversations with Maida Springer*, p 202.

62. Cohen, 'The CIA and African Trade Unions', p 72.

63. Quoted in Stoner, '"We Will Follow a Nationalist Policy; But We Will Never Be Neutral"', p 243. The phrase 'confusion worse confounded' is a quote from Milton's *Paradise Lost*, book 2.

64. Rathbun, *The Point Man*, p 313.

65. Richards, *Conversations with Maida Springer*, pp 220, 218.

7. Atomium

1. Pluvinage, introduction, *Expo 58*, p 12.

2. Nilsen, *Projecting America, 1958*, p 88.

3. Pluvinage, introduction, *Expo 58*, p 11.

4. 'Expo 58', Atomium, accessed 15 March 2021, https://atomium.be/expo58; Laurenzo Arke, 'Expo 58: A Brief History of Belgium's World Fair Showcase', Culture Trip, 15 August 2017, https://theculturetrip.com/europe/belgium/articles /expo-58-a-brief-history-of-belgiums-world-fair-showcase/.

5. Quoted in Rika Devos, 'Building of the Month, December 2006—The American Pavilion of Expo 58', *Twentieth Century Society*, December 2006, https://c20 society.org.uk/building-of-the-month/the-american-pavilion-of-expo-58/.

6. Moreau and Brion, 'Business at the Service of Humanity?', pp 132–133; Tousignant, 'Geopolitics and Spatiality at Expo 58', pp 108–109.

7. Stanard, *Selling the Congo*, p 69.

8. Dunn, *Imagining the Congo*, p 67.

9. Tousignant, 'Geopolitics and Spatiality at Expo 58', p 111.

10. Stanard, *Selling the Congo*, p 47.

11. *Ibid*, pp 47–48.

12. *Ibid*, p 70.

13. Daniel Boffey, 'Belgium Comes to Terms with "Human Zoos" of Its Colonial Past', 16 April 2018, *The Guardian*, www.theguardian.com/world/2018/apr/16 /belgium-comes-to-terms-with-human-zoos-of-its-colonial-past.

14. Quoted in Stanard, *Selling the Congo*, p 73.

15. From *Le Soir pour les Enfants*, a weekly supplement to *Le Soir*, quoted in Stanard, *Selling the Congo*, p 72.

16. Tousignant, 'Geopolitics and Spatiality at Expo 58', pp 100–111.

17. Quoted in Van Reybrouck, *Congo*, p 239. Jamais Kolonga was the man at the centre of a famous song composed by the band known as African Jazz, led by Joseph Kabasele, as explained by Van Reybrouck in *Congo*, pp 219–221. African Jazz is discussed in Chapter 9 of this book.

18. Quoted in Van Reybrouck, *Congo*, p 240.

19. Young and Turner, *The Rise and Decline of the Zairian State*, pp 173–174.

20. Akyeampong and Gates, eds., *Dictionary of African Biography*, vol 4, p 237.

21. Nzongola-Ntalaja, *The Congo from Leopold to Kabila*, p 143.

22. Paul Masson, 'Visite avec un certain journaliste appelé Mobutu', *DH Les Sports*, 17 April 2008, www.dhnet.be/actu/societe/visite-avec-un-certain-journaliste -appele-mobutu-51b7bb1be4b0de6db98a7b02.

23. Footage of Mobutu being interviewed in Brussels is shown in the film *Mobutu*, by Michel Thierry.

24. Nzongola-Ntalaja, *The Congo from Leopold to Kabila*, p 144.

25. Nilsen, *Projecting America, 1958*, p 88.

26. Moreau and Brion, 'Business at the Service of Humanity?', p 138.

27. *Ibid*, p 138.

28. Helmreich, *Gathering Rare Ores*, p 247.

29. Fleckner and Avery, *Congo Uranium and the Tragedy of Hiroshima*, p 5.

30. Dwight D Eisenhower, 'Atoms for Peace Speech', address to the 470th Plenary Meeting of the United Nations General Assembly, 8 December 1953, www.iaea.org/about/history/atoms-for-peace-speech.

31. Quoted in Mian and Glas, 'A Frightening Nuclear Legacy', p 43.

32. 'History of Ghana Atomic Energy Commission', Ghana Atomic Energy Commission, accessed 15 March 2021, https://gaecgh.org/?page_id=4242.

33. Governor, Gold Coast, to Secretary of State, London, 20 June 1956, TNA, DO 35/8330.

34. 'History of Ghana Atomic Energy Commission'.

35. 'US and Belgium to Sign Contract for Sales of Uranium for Use by Belgian Congo', statement by US Atomic Energy Commission, 3 December 1958, TNA, AB 16/2744.

36. International Atomic Energy Agency, *Research Reactors in Africa*, p 8.

37. Tempelsman's visit to Expo 58 is recorded in McKeever, *Adlai Stevenson*, p 408. While in Brussels in 1958, Tempelsman met with Stevenson, who was also visiting Expo.

38. Heymann, *American Legacy*, pp 261–262.

39. *Ibid*, p 262.

40. Extract from a letter received from Mr John Russell in New York, attached to a letter from J H A Watson to T E Bromley, Foreign Office, 29 June 1955, TNA, FO 371/113462.

41. Martin, *Adlai Stevenson and the World*, p 414.

42. The letter was sent on 16 April 1957. Quoted in Johnson, ed, *The Papers of Adlai E Stevenson*, vol 6, p 515.

43. Office Memorandum, United States Government, C D DeLoach to Mr Tolson, 'Adlai Stevenson, Maurice Templesman [*sic*] and Company, Diamond Licenses in Ghana', 5 June 1959, in FBI, J Edgar Hoover Official and Confidential (O&C) Files, file 17, Jim Lesar private papers.

44. 'A Byte Out of History: J. Edgar Hoover's "Official & Confidential" Files', FBI website, 11 July 2005, https://archives.fbi.gov/archives/news/stories/2005/july/j.-edgar-hoovers-official-confidential-files.

45. Gibbs, *The Political Economy of Third World Intervention*, p 109.

46. Martin, *Adlai Stevenson and the World*, p 428; the sum is equivalent to over US$460,000 in 2020, using the conversion tool here: https://fxtop.com/en/historical-currency-converter.php.

47. *Fortune*, 15 November 1982, quoted in Gibbs, *The Political Economy of Third World Intervention*, p 108.

48. Heymann, *American Legacy*, pp 261–262.

49. Gina Faddis, 'George H Wittman: 1929–2020', *Washington Times*, 24 November 2020.

50. 'George Wittman, CIA Case Officer, Author, Consultant', AFIO Weekly Intelligence Notes #45-20, 1 December 2020, www.afio.com/sections/wins/2020/2020_45.htm#Wittman.

51. Wittman, *The Ghana Report*.

52. *Ibid*, p xi.

53. United States Department of State, Bureau of Intelligence and Research, *African Programs of US Organizations*, p 85.

54. Gibbs, *The Political Economy of Third World Intervention*, p 108.

55. This information and quotation are given by Janine Roberts, who interviewed Paul Baddo in 1991. *Glitter and Greed*, pp 176, 184, 203.

56. Faddis, 'George H Wittman'.

57. Wittman, *A Matter of Intelligence*, pp 132–133.

8. The Rise of Lumumba

1. Kanza, *Conflict in the Congo*, p 50; Van Lierde, ed., *Lumumba Speaks*, p 58.

2. Lumumba's speech at Leopoldville, 28 December 1958, in Van Lierde, ed., *Lumumba Speaks*, pp 59–68.

3. López Álvarez, *Lumumba*, p 17.

4. Nzongola-Ntalaja, *Patrice Lumumba*, p 72.

5. Robert Coughlan, 'Africa', *Life*, 2 February 1959.

6. López Álvarez, *Lumumba*, p 21.

7. 'Belgian Congo', January 7, 1959, CIA, CREST, NSC Briefing, CIA-RDP79R00890A001100010003-1, www.cia.gov/readingroom/docs/CIA-RDP79R00890A00110001003-1.pdf.

8. Underneath the date of 4-1-59 is written another that is not entirely legible but may be 2-2-59. 'Photo of Abako movement in January 1959; leader Kasavubu (hands up); just before Congo riots', 'Return to John Marcum', John Marcum Papers, M 1726, box 9, folder 2 (Misc photos—Africa), Special Collections Manuscripts Division, Stanford University Libraries.

9. Nzongola-Ntalaja, *The Congo from Leopold to Kabila*, p 87.

10. According to Adlai Stevenson, quoted by Mason (in Chicago) to J H A Watson, Chancery, British Embassy, Washington; copied by Watson in communication to T E Bromley, 27 June 1955, TNA, FO 371/113462.

11. Scott, *Tumbled House*, p 18.

12. Noted and discussed in Stanard, 'Revisiting Bula Matari and the Congo Crisis', p 156.

13. Nzongola-Ntalaja, *The Congo from Leopold to Kabila*, p 86.

14. Radio address by King Baudouin, 13 January 1959, translated into English here: https://en.wikipedia.org/wiki/King_Baudouin_speech_(13_January_1959)#cite_note-8.

15. Legum, *Congo Disaster*, p 87.

16. The conference took place from 16 to 22 March 1959.

17. 'De Lumumba à Laurent-Désiré Kabila, un demi-siècle pour un même combat', *Le Phare*, 28 June 2013, www.lephareonline.net/de-lumumba-a-laurent-desire-kabila-un-demi-siecle-pour-un-meme-combat/.

18. López Álvarez, *Lumumba: Ou l'Afrique frustrée*, p 32.

19. Nzongola-Ntalaja, *The Congo from Leopold to Kabila*, p 144.

20. K A B Jones-Quartey, introduction to Passin and Jones-Quartey, eds, *Africa: The Dynamics of Change*, p 1.

21. Scott-Smith and Lerg, eds, *Campaigning Culture and the Global Cold War*, p 248. See whole section of chapter pp 247–251.

22. *Ibid*, p 35.

23. Lumumba, 'African Unity and National Independence', 22 March 1959, reproduced in Van Lierde, ed, *Lumumba Speaks*, pp 69–75.

24. Passin and Jones-Quartey, eds., *Africa: The Dynamics of Change*, title page.

25. John C Hunt to Scott Charles, 16 October 1962, International Association for Cultural Freedom Records, box 171, folder 9, Special Collections Research Center, University of Chicago Library; Bernd Pulch, 'Cryptome Unveils CIA Proprietary Agencies & Agents Worldwide', 25 October 2012, https://berndpulch.org/2012/10/25/cryptome-unveils-cia-proprietary-agencies-agents-worldwide/.

26. 'The Institute of Congolese Studies' (with a marginal note on the front page: 'Fait pour Merrill'), n.d., International Association for Cultural Freedom Records, box 171, folder 9, Special Collections Research Center, University of Chicago Library.

27. 'Association "Institut d'Etudes Congolaises", Statuts', n.d., International Association for Cultural Freedom Records, box 171, folder 9, Special Collections Research Center, University of Chicago Library.

28. Namikas, *Battleground Africa*, p 43.

29. Nkrumah, *Challenge of the Congo*, pp 15–16.

30. See for example Cameron Duodu, 'Patrice Lumumba: The Rise and Assassination of an African Patriot', *Mashariaz*, 21 January 2011, http://mashariazgitonga.blogspot.co.uk/2011/01/.

31. These characterisations of Kalonji and Ileo are drawn by Dayal in *Mission for Hammarskjöld*, p 314.

32. Nkrumah, *Challenge of the Congo*, p 17.

33. Quoted in Lumumba, *May Our People Triumph*, p 208.

34. Discussed and quoted in Van Lierde, ed, *Lumumba Speaks*, pp 118, 148–149.

35. Hempstone, *Katanga Report*, p 57.

36. O'Brien, *To Katanga and Back*, p 73.

37. Calder, *Agony of the Congo*, p 134.

38. Smith Hempstone to Walter S Rogers, 3 February 1958, in Hempstone, *Letters from Africa to the Institute of Current World Affairs*.

39. Calder, *Agony of the Congo*, pp 134–137.

40. Hempstone to Rogers, 3 February 1958.

41. *New York Herald Tribune*, 26 October 1955, quoted in Giacometti, 'The Labor Movement in Tropical Africa III', p 101.

42. Van Nederveen, 'USAF Airlift into the Heart of Darkness', p 2.

43. *New York Herald Tribune*, 26 October 1955.

44. López Álvarez, *Lumumba*, p 51; Zeilig, *Lumumba*, p 87.

45. López Álvarez, *Lumumba*, pp 51–56; the lawyer was Maitre Jean Auburtin.

46. Namikas, *Battleground Africa*, p 43.

47. Lumumba to Luis López Álvarez, December 1959, www.luislopezalvarez.com /opiniones/sobre-su-accion/patrice-lumumba. The author is grateful to Emmanuel Barrault and Emile Goujon Garin for the translation.

9. 'Table Ronde'

1. Namikas, *Battleground Africa*, p 44.

2. Burden, interviewed by John Luter, 29 January 1968.

3. Van Lierde, ed, *Lumumba Speaks*, p 145.

4. Stewart, *Rumba on the River*, pp 84–86.

5. Young and Turner, *The Rise and Decline of the Zairian State*, p 175.

6. British Pathé, 'Belgium: I.C.F.T.U Congress, Brussels'.

7. 'The All Africa People's Conference in 1961', 1 November 1961, CIA, CREST, CIA-RDP78-00915R001300320009-3, www.cia.gov/readingroom/docs/CIA-RDP78 -00915R001300320009-3.pdf.

8. Goldsworthy, *Tom Mboya*, pp 158–159.

9. United States Department of the Army, *US Army Area Handbook for the Republic of the Congo (Leopoldville)*, June 1962, pp 478–479.

10. Van Lierde, ed, *Lumumba Speaks*, p 151.

11. Telegram from Lumumba to his attorneys, in Van Lierde, ed, *Lumumba Speaks*, pp 150–151.

12. Zeilig, *Voices of Liberation*, pp 20–21.

13. From Lumumba's Speech to the Amis de Présence Africaine in Brussels, 6 February 1960, in Van Lierde, ed, *Lumumba Speaks*, p 163.

14. Footage of Lumumba's welcome is shown in the film *Mobutu*, by Michel Thierry.

15. López Álvarez, *Lumumba: Ou l'Afrique frustrée*, p 64.

16. McKown, *Lumumba*, p 78.

17. López Álvarez, *Lumumba: Ou l'Afrique frustrée*, p 64.

18. *Ibid*, top photograph on p 3 of the image inset at the end of the book, ff p 228.

19. Legum, *Congo Disaster*, pp 76–77, 89, 95.

20. Zhukov, 'Such was Lumumba', p 163.

21. Stewart, *Rumba on the River*, pp 83–84.

22. For background information on African Jazz and OK Jazz, see Ndaywel è Nziem, *Histoire Générale du Congo*, p 487.

23. The journalist was Gilles Sala; quoted in Stewart, *Rumba on the River*, p 86.

24. Quoted in Stewart, *Rumba on the River*, p 88.

25. Stewart, *Rumba on the River*, pp 83–88.

26. *Ibid*, p 86.

27. *Ibid*, p 86.

28. Words in Lingala from Ndaywel è Nziem, *Histoire Générale du Congo*, p 549; translation into English from Tenaille, *Music Is the Weapon of the Future*, p 5.

29. 'All-African People's Conferences', p 431.

30. Legum, *Congo Disaster*, p 73.

31. Scott, *Tumbled House*, p 21.

32. Nzongola-Ntalaja, *Patrice Lumumba*, pp 82–83.

33. Kanza, *Conflict in the Congo*, p 81.

34. 'Democratic Republic of Congo'.

35. Lemarchand, *Political Awakening in the Belgian Congo*, pp 214–217.

36. Nzongola-Ntalaja, *Patrice Lumumba*, p 81.

37. Zeilig, *Voices of Liberation*, p 21.

38. Steigman, interviewed by Charles Stuart Kennedy, 29 April 1989.

10. Ambassador Burden

1. 'Belgian Congo: Bedlam in Brussels', *Time*, 22 February 1960, http://content
.time.com/time/subscriber/article/0,33009,939599,00.html.

2. The physical description is taken from Baker, *Baseless*, p 174.

3. Mahoney, *JFK*, p 52.

4. Burden, *Peggy and I*, pp 289–291.

5. Joyce Wadler, 'At Home with Wendy Burden: A Vanderbilt Descendant Laughs
Off Dysfunction', *New York Times*, March 24, 2010.

6. Burden, *Dead End Gene Pool*, p 233.

7. 'Civil Aviation', Mr Tree (Harborough), UK Parliament, House of Commons
Debate, 14 March 1944, vol 398, c 72, https://api.parliament.uk/historic-hansard
/commons/1944/mar/14/civil-aviation-1.

8. Burden, *Peggy and I*, between pp 244 and 245.

9. *Ibid*, pp 134, 169, 175 (with quotation).

10. *Ibid*, p 332.

11. Gibbs, *The Political Economy of Third World Intervention*, p 256, n 116.

12. Burden, interviewed by John Luter, 29 January 1968.

13. Gibbs, *The Political Economy of Third World Intervention*, p 100 and pp
245–246, n 159.

14. Borstelmann, *Apartheid's Reluctant Uncle*, p 163.

15. Murphy, *Diplomat Among Warriors*, p 402.

16. John Thompson to Nat Nakasa, 15 May 1962, Correspondence with Farfield
Foundation, Nathaniel Nakasa Papers, A2696, B3.2, University of the Witwatersrand, www.historicalpapers.wits.ac.za/index.php?inventory_enhanced/U/Collections
&c=264701/R/A2696-B3-2.

17. Eric Pace, 'William Burden, Ex-Museum President Dies', *New York Times*, 11
October 1984, p 26.

18. Michael R McBride, 'How Jackson Pollock and the CIA Teamed Up to
Win the Cold War: Unlikely Bedfellows, Ironic Subterfuge, and the American
Left', *Medium*, 15 October 2017, https://medium.com/@MichaelMcBride/how
-jackson-pollock-and-the-cia-teamed-up-to-win-the-cold-war-6734c40f5b14.

19. Alastair Sooke, 'Was Modern Art a Weapon of the CIA?', *BBC Culture*, 4
October 2016, www.bbc.com/culture/article/20161004-was-modern-art-a-weapon-of
-the-cia.

20. Burden, interviewed by John Luter, 29 January 1968.

21. Gibbs, *The Political Economy of Third World Intervention*, p 107.

22. Hochschild, *Half the Way Home*, pp 11–12.

23. For an insightful discussion, see Nesbitt, 'Race for Sanctions', p 60 ff; for quotation see *ibid*, p 61.

24. Hochschild, *Half the Way Home*, pp 105, 130.

25. 'Briefing of the Honorable William A. M. Burden', 25 September 1959, CIA, CREST, CIA-RDP80B01676R004300180009-9, www.cia.gov/readingroom/docs/CIA-RDP80B01676R004300180009-9.pdf.

26. Letter from Dulles to Burden, 27 November 1959; document release date: 14 August 2003, CIA, CREST, CIA-RDP80R01731R000200050062-1, www.cia.gov/readingroom/docs/CIA-RDP80R01731R000200050062-1.pdf.

27. Roberts, interviewed by Charles Stuart Kennedy; initial interview date 11 February 1991.

28. Devlin is not mentioned in any written account or official record that has been seen by the author of Ambassador Burden's trip to the Congo in March 1960. However, he himself referred to it in 2004, at a history conference at the Woodrow Wilson Center on the Congo in the early 1960s; the conference is referred to later in this chapter.

29. Devlin, *Chief of Station, Congo*, p xiii.

30. *Ibid*, p 47.

31. *Ibid*, p 48.

32. Marnham, *Snake Dance*, pp 217–218.

33. Burden, *Peggy and I*, p 300.

34. *Ibid*, p 307.

35. *Ibid*, pp 307–308.

36. Devlin, quoted in Woodrow Wilson International Center, *The Congo Crisis, 1960–1961*, p 15.

37. Namikas, *Battleground Africa*, p 52.

38. *FRUS*, 1958–1960, vol 14, *Africa*, document 97, https://history.state.gov/historicaldocuments/frus1958-60v14/d97.

39. Burden, *Peggy and I*, pp 296–297.

40. Carlucci, interviewed by Charles Stuart Kennedy, 1 April 1997.

41. Devlin, *Chief of Station, Congo*, p 98.

42. *Ibid*, p 72.

43. Devlin, quoted in Woodrow Wilson International Center, *The Congo Crisis, 1960–1961*, p 39.

44. Woodrow Wilson International Center, *The Congo Crisis, 1960–1961*, p 40.

45. Young and Turner, *The Rise and Decline of the Zairian State*, pp 438–439, n 20.

46. The conference, held on 23–24 September 2004, was one of a series of critical oral-history workshops sponsored by the Cold War International History Project (CWIHP); this one was cosponsored with the Africa Program.

47. Woodrow Wilson International Center, *The Congo Crisis, 1960–1961*, p 6.

48. Other participants at the conference included: Sergey Mazov, scholar at the Institute of World History, Russian Academy of Science; Jean Omasombo, professor at the University of Kinshasa, researcher at the Africa Museum, Tervuren, and

Congolese consultant for the Belgian Parliamentary Commission inquiry into Lumumba's assassination; Jean Muke, assistant of Cléophas Kamitatu; Tatiana Carayannis, of the UN International History Project at the City University of New York; and Lise Namikas, who helped to organise the conference. Representatives of the National Security Archive at George Washington University also attended.

49. Woodrow Wilson International Center, *The Congo Crisis, 1960– 1961,* p 41.

11. The Africa Division of the CIA

1. SSCIA, Hearings, Bronson Tweedy, 9 October 1975, NARA, Record Number 157-10014-10068.

2. United States Congress, Senate, *Final Report of the Select Committee to Study Governmental Operations with Respect to Intelligence Activities, United States Senate, Book IV,* p 68.

3. Prados, *Safe for Democracy,* p 275; Vic Socotra, 'Going Ashore', *Dailysocotra,* 6 November 2017, www.vicsocotra.com/wordpress/2017/11/going-ashore-2/.

4. Knightley, *A Hack's Progress,* p 1.

5. Streeter, 'Interpreting the 1954 U.S. Intervention in Guatemala', p 61.

6. 'The CIA Campus: The Story of Original Headquarters Building', CIA website, 22 May 2008, updated 30 April 2013, www.cia.gov/news-information/featured -story-archive/2008-featured-story-archive/original-headquarters-building.html.

7. Stockwell, *In Search of Enemies,* p 105.

8. *FRUS,* 1958–1960, vol 14, *Africa,* document 21, https://history.state.gov /historicaldocuments/frus1958-60v14/d21.

9. *FRUS,* 1964–1968, vol 23, *Congo, 1960–1968,* document 3, https://history.state .gov/historicaldocuments/frus1964-68v23/d3.

10. *Ibid,* document 4, https://history.state.gov/historicaldocuments/frus1964-68 v23/d4.

11. Quoted in Zeilig, *Lumumba,* pp 23–24.

12. This sum was worth over US\$1million dollars at the time and nearly US\$9 million on 15 November 2020; these conversions were achieved using the tool at https:// fxtop.com/en/historical-currency-converter.php.

13. Burden, interviewed by John Luter, 29 January 1968.

14. Quoted and discussed in Wise and Ross, *The Invisible Government,* p 206.

15. *Ibid,* p 209.

16. 'Reciprocal. McCone on USSR Atom Tour; Emelyanov Here Next Month', *Atomic Industry Reporter,* 14 October 1959, p 5:327.

17. Medvedev, 'Stalin and the Atomic Gulag'.

18. National Intelligence Estimate, Number 11-2A-58, 4 February 1958, 'The Soviet Atomic Energy Program', copy no 27, CIA, FOIA, document number 0000843183, www.cia.gov/library/readingroom/docs/DOC_0000843183.pdf.

19. Helmreich, *United States Relations with Belgium and the Congo, 1940–1960,* p 200.

20. The equivalent sum on 14 March 2021 is US\$235,446,971.88, using the tool at https://fxtop.com/en/historical-currency-converter.php.

21. McGrath, *Charles Kenneth Leith,* p 215.

22. Helmreich, *United States Relations with Belgium and the Congo, 1940–1960*, p 200.

23. Report on 'Highlights of Union Minière du Haut Katanga's Activities', sent by US Consulate, Elisabethville, to Department of State, Washington, 15 June 1961, NARA, RG 326, P85A, box 55, folder 2.

24. *Ibid*, pp 200–201.

25. 'The News in Nucleus', 'Uranium', *Atomic Industry Reporter*, 11 November 1959, p 5:353.

12. Voice of Africa

1. Polsgrove, *Ending British Rule in Africa*, p 159.

2. Letter from George Padmore to W E B Du Bois, 2 February 1958, Du Bois Papers (MS 312), Special Collections and University Archives, University of Massachusetts Amherst Libraries, https://credo.library.umass.edu/view/full/mums312-b161-i239.

3. Batsa, *The Spark*, p 16.

4. Makonnen, *Pan-Africanism from Within*, p 207.

5. Batsa, *The Spark*, p 29.

6. Ahlman, 'Road to Ghana', p 26.

7. Cameron Duodu, 'Frantz Fanon: Prophet of African Liberation', *Pambazuka News*, 5 December 2011.

8. Legum, *Pan-Africanism*, p 45.

9. 'Ghana: Convention People's Party Inaugurates New Ideological Week-end School', Information Report, CIA, 20 June 1959. This document was released by the CIA on 8 January 2020, in response to a FOIA submission to the CIA by Jeremy Bigwood on 9 March 2019, for records relating to George Padmore. Susan Williams Private Papers.

10. Quoted in Polsgrove, *Ending British Rule in Africa*, p 162.

11. Quoted in *ibid*, p 163.

12. Cablegrams, Bureau of African Affairs 1959, George Padmore Research Library on African Affairs, Bureau of African Affairs Collection, MSS/3.

13. Drake's 335-page FBI file, constructed between 1961 and 1971, is especially concerned with his African contacts. The file is available at the F B Eyes Digital Archives, http://omeka.wustl.edu/omeka/exhibits/show/fbeyes/drake.

14. Shepperson and Drake, 'The Fifth Pan African Conference, 1945 and the All African Peoples Congress, 1958', p 63.

15. Polsgrove, *Ending British Rule in Africa*, p 162; the article by Russell Warren Howe is 'George Padmore', *Encounter*, December 1959, pp 52–56.

16. Quoted in Polsgrove, *Ending British Rule in Africa*, p 151.

17. Grilli, *Nkrumaism and African Nationalism*, p 167. This book provides an excellent account of Pan-African institutions in Ghana between 1957 and 1966.

18. Gerits, '"When the Bull Elephants Fight"', p 956.

19. Dei-Anang, *The Administration of Ghana's Foreign Relations 1957–1965*, p 31.

20. *Ibid*, p 29.

21. Batsa, *The Spark*, p 14.

22. Barden to Agostino Lunga, 6 July 1960, Elizabeth Churchill Brown Papers, box 15, folder 28, Hoover Institution Archives.

23. Quoted in Grilli, *Nkrumaism and African Nationalism*, pp 192–193.

24. Barden to Agostino Lunga, 2 December 1960, Elizabeth Churchill Brown Papers, box 15, folder 28, Hoover Institution Archives.

25. The equivalent sum in December 2020 is US$746,449.24, using the tool at https://fxtop.com/en/historical-currency-converter.php.

26. Zukas, *Into Exile and Back*, p 121.

27. Ntumazah, *A Conversational Auto Biography*, p 378.

28. Mahoney, *JFK*, p 182.

29. '10.12.1662: The Royal African Company (RAC) Founded', African American Registry, 1 January 2021, https://aaregistry.org/story/the-royal-african-company -rac-founded/#:~:text=Records%20show%20that%20between%201662,English% 20colonies%20in%20North%20America.

30. Batsa, *The Spark*, p 13.

31. Marais, *Kwame Nkrumah*, p 23.

32. According to Batsa, one hundred thousand was 'the minimum print run' of *Voice of Africa* (Batsa, *The Spark*, p 13); this may have included all the copies that were printed, including the ones circulated outside Ghana. By contrast, Grilli reports that at the end of 1960, Barden raised the production from about ten thousand copies to at least twenty thousand (Grilli, *Nkrumaism and African Nationalism*, p 254).

33. Batsa, *The Spark*, pp 13–14.

34. Grilli, *Nkrumaism and African Nationalism*, p 186.

35. Gerits, '"When the Bull Elephants Fight"', p 956.

36. Quoted in *ibid*, p 955.

37. Speech by President Nkrumah on the Opening of the Ghana External Broadcasting Service, 27 October 1961, www.nkrumah.net/gov-pubs/gp-a917-61-62/gen .php?index=1.

38. Cameron Duodu to the author by email, 7 June 2019.

39. Simpson, *Science of Coercion*, pp 74–75.

40. Cameron Duodu to the author by email, 7 June 2019.

41. 'Secret: Ghanaian Subversion in Africa', attached to memorandum from L D Battle for Mr McGeorge Bundy, 12 February 1962, JFKL, NSF, box 99a.

13. American CIA Agent and Kenyan CIA Asset

1. Howard Imbrey Personnel File, OSS Personnel Files, NARA, RG 226, entry 224, box 362, location 230/86/33/05. See www.archives.gov/files/iwg/declassified -records/rg-226-oss/personnel-database.pdf.

2. Imbrey, interviewed by Charles Stuart Kennedy, 21 June 2001.

3. *Ibid*.

4. *Ibid*.

5. Scott Shane, 'Memories of a C.I.A. Officer Resonate in a New Era', *New York Times*, 24 February 2008.

6. Devlin, *Chief of Station, Congo*, p 273.

7. 'Obituaries: Howard Imbrey', *Washington Post*, 6 December 2002.

8. Louis Menand, 'A Friend of the Devil: Inside a Famous Cold War Deception', *New Yorker*, 23 March 2015.

9. Examples of such employees worked for the Canada mission, as set out in 'Permanent Missions to the United Nations' (New York: US Mission to the United Nations, December 1963), pp 4-5.

10. Price, *Cold War Anthropology*, table 7.3, pp 171–172; Don Irwin and Vincent J. Burke, '21 Foundations, Union Got Money from CIA', *Los Angeles Times*, 26 February 1967. Another address for the African Research Foundation in 1960 was 1050 Park Avenue, New York City (https://storage.rockarch.org/33c4a303-c707-4660-857f-46456af705ca-FCD001_002_00298.pdf); possibly the organisation moved to 333 East 46th Street in 1961 or had two addresses.

11. 'Two Young Americans Show How to Succeed in Business in Africa', *Negro Digest*, May 1962.

12. Okumu, *The African Renaissance*, pp 54–57.

13. Jacobs, 'The Awkward Biography of the Young Washington Okumu', p 228.

14. *Ibid*, p 229.

15. *Ibid*, p 228.

16. Paget, *Patriotic Betrayal*, pp 132–133.

17. Nick Roll, 'The CIA Within Academe', *Inside Higher Ed*, 3 October 2017 (a review of Golden, *Spy Schools*).

18. In *Chief of Station, Congo*, Devlin writes that after completing undergraduate studies, he went to 'Harvard's graduate International Relations program, a precursor to the Kennedy school'. He adds, 'I obtained my master's degree and had plans to continue with a doctorate' (p 1). Further details are available in the summary of an interview with Devlin in 1975, which was conducted for the Church Committee; the summary was declassified in April 2018 under the JFK Assassination Records Collection Act. It notes that Devlin 'went to Harvard where he studied in the Department of International Relations, working to a degree in political science, which he did not complete'. SSCIA, Miscellaneous Records of the Church Committee, 08/22/1975, NARA, record number 157-10014-10185.

19. Paget, *Patriotic Betrayal*, pp 133–134.

20. Quotes from and narrative about Okumu in this passage come from Jacobs, 'The Awkward Biography of the Young Washington Okumu', pp 226–237.

21. '"Traditional" Dictatorship: One Party State in KwaZulu Homeland Threatens Transition to Democracy', Human Rights Watch, South Africa, September 1993, accessed 14 February 2021, www.hrw.org/reports/1993/southafrica2/.

22. Sue Onslow and Martin Plaut, 'Archive Documents Reveal the US and UK's Role in the Dying Days of Apartheid', *The Conversation*, 18 July 2019, https://the conversation.com/archive-documents-reveal-the-us-and-uks-role-in-the-dying-days-of-apartheid-120507.

23. Jacobs and Bank, 'Biography in Post-Apartheid South Africa: A Call for Awkwardness', p 171.

24. *FRUS*, 1964–1968, vol 23, *Congo, 1960–1968*, document 5, https://history.state.gov/historicaldocuments/frus1964-68v23/d5.

25. *FRUS*, 1958–1960, vol 14, *Africa*, document 102, https://history.state.gov/historicaldocuments/frus1958-60v14/d102.

26. McIlvaine, interviewed by Charles Stuart Kennedy, 1 April 1988.

27. Steigman, interviewed by Charles Stuart Kennedy, 29 April 1989.

28. Imbrey, interviewed by Charles Stuart Kennedy, 21 June 2001.

29. Imbrey, interviewed by Curtis Ostle, 2 April 2001.

30. Imbrey, interviewed by Charles Stuart Kennedy, 21 June 2001. There is information on the Worldwide Information Services in Karlow, *Targeted by the CIA*, p 173, and in *Broadcasting Yearbook*, 1966, page D-10, https://worldradiohistory.com/Archive-BC-YB/1966/1966-BC-YB.pdf.

31. Imbrey, interviewed by Charles Stuart Kennedy, 21 June 2001.

32. Jacobs, 'The Awkward Biography of the Young Washington Okumu', p 232.

33. *Ibid*, p 230.

34. Okumu, *The African Renaissance*, p 61.

35. Imbrey, interviewed by Curtis Ostle, 2 April 2001.

36. Okumu, *The African Renaissance*, pp 23, 57.

37. Imbrey, interviewed by Charles Stuart Kennedy, 21 June 2001.

38. Quoted in 'In Memory of Prof. Washington Okumu', GoFundMe, created 7 November 2016, www.gofundme.com/f/in-memory-of-prof-washington-okumu.

39. Jacobs, 'The Awkward Biography of the Young Washington Okumu', p 238.

14. 'The Courageous Have Won'

1. Quoted in Stewart, *Rumba on the River*, p 87.

2. *Ibid*, p 87.

3. *Ibid*, p 90.

4. Blouin with MacKellar, *My Country, Africa*, p 203.

5. Quoted in Blouin, 'From Congo to Paris: The Story of "Black Passionaria"'.

6. Weiss, *Political Protest in the Congo*, p 178.

7. Imbrey, interviewed by Curtis Ostle, 2 April 2001.

8. Gizenga, *Ma Vie et Mes Luttes*, p 149.

9. *Ibid*, pp 149–150, 164.

10. Blouin's campaigning is described in *My Country, Africa*, a memoir by Blouin which was dictated to Jean MacKellar, an American writer, and published in 1983. Blouin was unhappy with the book and tried unsuccessfully to block it. The book needs to be read with care and sensitivity to Blouin's objections, but it is likely to be factually accurate. Bouwer gives a clear and helpful account of Blouin's conflict with MacKellar in *Gender and Decolonization in the Congo*, p 72. The publication of *My Country, Africa* is discussed further at the end of Chapter 24 of this book.

11. Blouin with MacKellar, *My Country, Africa*, p 214.

12. Martens, *Abo: Une Femme du Congo*, p 49.

13. Weiss, *Political Protest in the Congo*, p xix.

14. Quoted in Stuart A Reid, 'Overlooked No More: Andrée Blouin, Voice for Independence in Africa', *New York Times*, 14 February 2020.

15. Weiss to the author, 1 December 2020, by telephone.

16. Blouin with MacKellar, *My Country, Africa*, p 226.

17. *FRUS*, 1958–1960, vol 14, *Africa*, document 102, https://history.state.gov/historicaldocuments/frus1958-60v14/d102.

18. Quoted and discussed in Blouin with MacKellar, *My Country, Africa*, p 228.

19. Young and Turner, *The Rise and Decline of the Zairian State*, p 290. This is equivalent to US$5,574,843,256.64 on 11 December 2020, using the following tool: https://fxtop.com/en/historical-currency-converter.php.

20. James [illegible], British Embassy, Bogotá, to E B Boothby, 2 February 1960, TNA, FO 371/146630.

21. A G Evans to British Consul General, Léopoldville, 24 February 1960, TNA, FO 371/146631.

22. A clear table of the results can be found in T Lodge, D Kadima and D Pottie, eds, 'DRC: 1960 National Assembly Results', *Compendium of Elections in Southern Africa*, 2002, www.eisa.org/wep/drc1960results.htm.

23. 'Congo Leaders Fail to Agree', *Daily Graphic*, 22 June 1960, p 3.

24. Lumumba's press conference, published in *Indépendance*, 15 June 1960, reproduced in Van Lierde, ed, *Lumumba Speaks*, pp 199–203.

25. 'Top Posts for Lumumba', *Daily Graphic*, 23 June 1960, p 2.

26. Kanza, *Conflict in the Congo*, p 113.

27. 'Who Was the Woman Behind Lumumba?', *Africa Is a Country*, 17 January 2020, https://africasacountry.com/2020/01/who-was-the-woman-behind-lumumba.

28. Kashamura, *De Lumumba aux colonels*, p 54.

29. Imbrey, interviewed by Charles Stuart Kennedy, 21 June 2001.

30. *FRUS*, 1964–1968, vol 23, *Congo, 1960–1968*, document 6, https://history.state.gov/historicaldocuments/frus1964-68v23/d6.

31. 'Congo Is Now Independent', *Daily Graphic*, 1 July 1960, p 2.

32. For the series of photographs, see 'Le dessous des images: Le voleur de l'épée du roi belge', *Phototrend*, 19 September 2017, https://phototrend.fr/2017/09/le-dessous-des-images-le-voleur-de-lepee-du-roi-belge/. For newsreel reportage and a discussion of the significance of the event, see Nzwamba, '30 Juin 1960–30 Juin 2018: Ambroise Boimbo, un héros oublié'.

33. 'Congo Is Now Independent'.

34. Kinzer, *The Brothers*, p 260.

35. Eve Blouin, 'From Congo to Paris: The Story of "Black Passionaria"'.

36. Transcript of English translation of the speech by King Baudouin, 30 June 1960, in *Colonization and Independence in Africa*, pp 36–37, Choices Program, Brown University, accessed 4 April 2021, https://southwest.mpls.k12.mn.us/uploads/congo casestudy.pdf.

37. Harry Gilroy, 'Lumumba Assails Colonialism as Congo Is Freed', *New York Times*, 1 July 1960.

38. Photograph titled 'June 30, 1960—Baudouin's speech to Parliament. Kasavubu seated at his left', posted by Mwana Mboka, *Kinshasa Then and Now*, http://kosuba awate.blogspot.com/.

39. Lumumba's Speech at Proclamation of Independence, reproduced in Van Lierde, ed, *Lumumba Speaks*, pp 220–224.

40. Harry Gilroy, 'Congo Becomes Sovereign State', *New York Times*, 1 July 1960.

41. Murphy, *Diplomat Among Warriors*, pp 408–409.

42. Speech by Malcolm X at the Founding Rally of the Organization of Afro-American Unity, 28 June 1964, contributed by BlackPast, 15 October 2007, www

.blackpast.org/african-american-history/speeches-african-american-history/1964
-malcolm-x-s-speech-founding-rally-organization-afro-american-unity.

43. From a radio broadcast by Malcolm X on New York station WMCA, 28 November 1964, quoted in *Fire This Time*, vol 10, no 1, 2016, p 17, www.firethistime.net
/newspapers/FTTV10I1.pdf.

44. Speech by Malcolm X at the Founding Rally of the Organization of Afro-American Unity, 28 June 1964.

45. Ndaywel è Nziem, *Histoire Générale du Congo*, p 565.

46. Stewart, *Rumba on the River*, p 91.

47. Lukens, interviewed by Charles Stuart Kennedy, 17 November 1989.

48. López Álvarez, *Lumumba: Ou l'Afrique frustrée*, p 84. The author is grateful to Emmanuel Barrault for his translation.

15. Year of Africa

1. Dayal, *Mission for Hammarskjöld*, p 126.

2. Zeilig, ed and comp, *Voices of Liberation: Patrice Lumumba*, p 95.

3. Stonor Saunders, *Who Paid the Piper?*, p 102.

4. 'Guide to the International Association for Cultural Freedom Records 1941–1978', 2014, University of Chicago Library, Scope Note, Series VII, www.lib.uchi cago.edu/e/scrc/findingaids/view.php?eadid=ICU.SPCL.IACF.

5. Articles such as François Bondy, 'From the Belgian to the Balkanized Congo', Forum Service, Congress for Cultural Freedom, July 1960, press release, ACOA, box 174.

6. 'Worldwide Propaganda Network Built by the C.I.A.', *New York Times*, 26 December 1977, p 1.

7. Russell Warren Howe, 'Asset Unwitting: Covering the World for the CIA', *MORE* (New York), May 1978.

8. François Bondy, 'Lumumba Rose to Power from a Prison Cell', *Daily Graphic*, 30 June 1960, p 5.

9. *FRUS*, 1964-1968, vol 23, *Congo, 1960-1968*, document 4, https://history.state
.gov/historicaldocuments/frus1964-68v23/d4.

10. François Bondy, 'Lumumba Rose to Power from a Prison Cell'.

11. Stonor Saunders, *Who Paid the Piper?*, p 395.

12. Quoted in *ibid*, p 395.

13. Paul Hofmann, 'Bunche Says '60 Is Year of Africa', *New York Times*, 17 February 1960.

14. Adamafio, *By Nkrumah's Side*, p 91.

15. *Ibid*, pp 63–64.

16. 'Assessment by the Committee for Political Development', *Black World*, special edition: 'Kwame Nkrumah, 1909–1972', July 1972, pp 21–22.

17. Hadjor, *Nkrumah and Ghana*, p 75.

18. *Ibid*, p 81.

19. Quoted and discussed in Miescher and Tsikata, 'Hydro-Power and the Promise of Modernity and Development in Ghana', p 354.

20. Quoted in Nii Ardey Otoo, 'Nkrumah and the One Party State', *Pambazuka News*, 7 March 2007, www.pambazuka.org/pan-africanism/nkrumah-and-one-party-state.

21. Moxon, *Volta, Man's Greatest Lake*, p 275.

22. Miescher and Tsikata, 'Hydro-Power and the Promise of Modernity and Development in Ghana', p 354.

23. Maria Gkouma, 'Akosombo Dam', Institution of Civil Engineers, 2020, www.ice.org.uk/what-is-civil-engineering/what-do-civil-engineers-do/akosombo-dam.

24. Amamoo, *The Ghanaian Revolution*, chapters 1 and 2.

25. Amamoo, *Ghana: 50 Years of Independence*, pp 148, 144–145.

26. Bing, *Reap the Whirlwind*, pp 244–248, 265, 515. The large number of listings under 'Preventive Detention' in the index to Bing's memoir reveals the continuing importance he attached to the issue.

27. 'C.I.A. Denounced in Geneva', *New York Times*, 21 February 1967, p 32; Wilford, *The Mighty Wurlitzer*, p 258, n 17.

28. Tolley, *The International Commission of Jurists*, pp 64–65.

29. Azaransky, *The Dream Is Freedom*, p 51; Murray, *Song in a Weary Throat*, p 318.

30. Rahel Gebreyes, 'How "Respectability Politics" Muted the Legacy of Black LGBT Activist Pauli Murray', *HuffPost*, 10 February 2015, www.huffpost.com/entry/lgbt-activist-paulimurray_n_6647252.

31. The biographies drawn on here are: Bell-Scott, *The Firebrand and the First Lady*, and Rosenberg, *Jane Crow*. These are discussed in Kathryn Schulz, 'The Many Lives of Pauli Murray', *New Yorker*, 10 April 2017.

32. Azaransky, *The Dream Is Freedom*, pp 38–39.

33. *Ibid*, p 39.

34. Rosenberg, *Jane Crow*, pp 213–216.

35. The letters can be found in Pauli Murray Papers, MC412, folder 138, Schlesinger Library, Radcliffe Institute, Harvard University.

36. Rosenberg, *Jane Crow*, p 223.

37. Kirchwehm, 'Letter from Ghana', p 40.

38. Quoted in Richards, *Maida Springer*, p 207.

39. Pauli Murray journal, 18 September 1960, Pauli Murray Papers, MC412, folder 710; Murray to Barlow, undated fragment, marked 1960, Pauli Murray Papers, MC412, folder 138; Schlesinger Library, Radcliffe Institute, Harvard University.

40. Gaines, *American Africans in Ghana*, p 132.

41. Murray to Barlow, 9 August 1960, and Murray to Barlow, 6 October 1960, both in Pauli Murray Papers, MC412, folder 138, Schlesinger Library, Radcliffe Institute, Harvard University.

42. Marais, *Kwame Nkrumah*, p 67.

43. Murray, interviewed by Genna Rae McNeil, 13 February 1976.

44. Rosenberg, *Jane Crow*, p 230.

45. Analysis and quotation in Nwaubani, *The United States and Decolonization in West Africa 1950–1960*, p 143.

46. FRUS, 1958–1960, vol 14, *Africa*, document 27, https://history.state.gov/historicaldocuments/frus1958-60v14/d27.

47. For a trenchant discussion, see Nwaubani, *The United States and Decolonization in West Africa 1950–1960*, pp 144–146 and p 288 n 129.

48. Quoted in Postar, 'The Half-Lives of African Uranium', p 404.

49. IAEA List of Member States, giving year of membership: https://www.iaea
.org/about/governance/list-of-member-states, date accessed 16 May 2021.

50. Richard Stone, 'A Nuclear Revival in Ghana', Pulitzer Center, 31 August 2017,
https://pulitzercenter.org/reporting/nuclear-revival-ghana.

51. Speech delivered by Nkrumah when he laid the foundation stone for the
construction of the Ghana Atomic Reactor at Kwabenya on 25 November 1964. The
transcript is here: Linda Asante Agyei, 'Nkrumah Lays Foundation for Atomic Reactor', *GhanaWeb*, 11 April 2007, www.ghanaweb.com/GhanaHomePage/NewsArchive
/artikel.php?ID=122255.

16. Things Fall Apart

1. The author is grateful to Mwana Mboka for this and subsequent information about the residences of Lumumba and Kasavubu. Further information about
the residences can be found on Mwana Mboka's blog, *Kinshasa Then and Now*, http://
kosubaawate.blogspot.com/.

2. Scott, *Tumbled House*, p 43.

3. Nzongola-Ntalaja, *The Congo from Leopold to Kabila*, p 98.

4. Carlucci, interviewed by Charles Stuart Kennedy, 1 April 1997.

5. McKown, *Lumumba*, p 114.

6. Von Horn, *Soldiering for Peace*, pp 133–134.

7. Resolution adopted by the UN General Assembly, 1236 (XII), 14 December 1957,
https://undocs.org/en/A/RES/1236(XII).

8. Resolution adopted by the UN General Assembly, 290 (IV), 1 December 1949,
https://undocs.org/en/A/RES/290(IV).

9. The author thanks Georges Nzongola-Ntalaja for his insights on this matter.

10. Kanza, *Conflict in the Congo*, pp 201–203.

11. Administrative Remarks, *U.S.S. Wasp*, 17 July 1960, Reproduced on SoLant
Amity, accessed 22 March 2021, https://solantamity.com/Media/Images/LaMarr
AboardUSS_WaspCVS-18_GitmoToBelgianCongoSupportOfUs_Nationals
17July60.jpg.

12. Comments by Charlie La Marr, quoted on SoLant Amity, accessed 22 March
2021, http://solantamity.com/Extraneous/OtherSols.htm.

13. Ed Shea, 'Eligibility for the United Nations Medal for Service Rendered
in the Congo', n.d., accessed 22 March 2021, http://solantamity.com/Media/Docu
ments/UnitedNationsMedalEligibility.pdf.

14. McKown, *Lumumba*, p 132.

15. Brian Urquhart, 'Character Sketches: Patrice Lumumba', *UN News*, n.d.,
accessed 15 March 2021, https://news.un.org/en/spotlight/patrice-lumumba-brian
-urquhart.

16. McKown, *Lumumba*, p 116.

17. Nzongola-Ntalaja, *Patrice Lumumba*, p 93.

18. Gizenga, *Ma Vie et Mes Luttes*, pp 192–195.

19. *Ibid*, pp 192–194.

20. Baynham, *The Military and Politics in Nkrumah's Ghana*, p 93.

21. Mohan, 'Ghana, the Congo, and the United Nations', p 375.

22. 'World's Week: Some Talk by Alexander', *Topic*, 28 October 1961.

23. Rikhye, *Military Adviser to the Secretary-General*, p 50.

24. *Ibid*, pp 136–137.

25. Birmingham, *Kwame Nkrumah*, p 107.

26. *Ibid*, p 107.

27. Alexander, *African Tightrope*, p 38.

28. *FRUS*, 1958–1960, vol 14, *Africa*, document 127, https://history.state.gov /historicaldocuments/frus1958-60v14/d127.

29. Cameron Duodu, 'Patrice Lumumba: The Rise and Assassination of an African Patriot', *Mashariaz*, 21 January 2011, http://mashariazgitonga.blogspot.co.uk/2011/01/.

30. Alexander, *African Tightrope*, p 96.

31. Devlin, *Chief of Station, Congo*, p 39.

32. Rikhye, *Military Adviser to the Secretary-General*, pp 50 ff.

33. Sir Arthur Snelling, Accra, to D W S Hunt, n.d. [July 1960], TNA, FO 371/146640.

34. Lefever and Joshua, *United Nations Peacekeeping in the Congo: 1960–1964*, vol 2, p 301.

35. Dayal, *Mission for Hammarskjöld*, pp 13–14.

36. Quoted in von Horn, *Soldiering for Peace*, p 180.

37. Von Horn, *Soldiering for Peace*, p 147.

38. Nkrumah, *Challenge of the Congo*, p 41.

39. Alexander, *African Tightrope*, p 203.

40. *FRUS*, 1958–1960, vol 14, *Africa*, document 132, https://history.state.gov /historicaldocuments/frus1958-60v14/d132.

41. Kelly, *America's Tyrant*, p 33.

42. Blouin with MacKellar, *My Country, Africa*, p 263.

43. *Ibid*, p 264.

44. Kelly, *America's Tyrant*, p 34.

45. *FRUS*, 1958–1960, vol 14, *Africa*, document 136, https://history.state.gov /historicaldocuments/frus1958-60v14/d136.

46. Quoted in Kelly, *America's Tyrant*, p 34.

47. *FRUS*, 1958–1960, vol 14, *Africa*, document 140, https://history.state.gov /historicaldocuments/frus1958-60v14/d140.

48. Burden, *Peggy and I*, p 319.

17. Eisenhower Snubs Lumumba

1. McKown, *Lumumba*, pp 136–137.

2. Kanza, *Conflict in the Congo*, p 236.

3. 'News and Notes', *African Studies Bulletin*, October 1960, p 52.

4. '1960: Airlift Africa', an 'excerpt from a document prepared by Senator John F. Kennedy's office in August 1960', reproduced in *Kenya Democracy Project*, 19 August 2009, http://demokrasia-kenya.blogspot.com/search?q=airlift+africa.

5. Goldsworthy, *Tom Mboya*, p 167.

6. Kanza, *Conflict in the Congo*, p 236.

7. Urquhart, *Hammarskjöld*, p 407.

8. Kanza, *Conflict in the Congo*, p 232.

9. Gibbs, *The Political Economy of Third World Intervention*, p 92.

10. *FRUS*, 1958–1960, vol 14, *Africa*, document 148. https://history.state.gov /historicaldocuments/frus1958-60v14/d148.

11. *FRUS*, 1952–1954, vol 11, part 1, *Africa and South Asia*, document 113 (note 1), https://history.state.gov/historicaldocuments/frus1952-54v11p1/d113.

12. 'Congo Premier Flies to Accra on Way to U.S.', *Daily Graphic*, 23 July 1960, p 1.

13. *FRUS*, 1958–1960, vol 14, *Africa*, document 151. https://history.state.gov /historicaldocuments/frus1958-60v14/d151.

14. Woodrow Wilson International Center, *The Congo Crisis, 1960–1961*, p 52.

15. United States Congress, Senate, *Alleged Assassination Plots Involving Foreign Leaders*, p 53.

16. *FRUS*, 1958–1960, vol 14, *Africa*, document 140, https://history.state.gov /historicaldocuments/frus1958-60v14/d140.

17. *FRUS*, 1958–1960, vol 14, *Africa*, document 152, https://history.state.gov /historicaldocuments/frus1958-60v14/d152.

18. Kanza, *Conflict in the Congo*, p 237.

19. *Ibid*, p 241.

20. Woodrow Wilson International Center, *The Congo Crisis, 1960–1961*, p 50.

21. *FRUS*, 1958–1960, vol 14, *Africa*, document 142, https://history.state.gov /historicaldocuments/frus1958-60v14/d142.

22. McKown, *Lumumba*, p 140.

23. Quoted in Lumumba, *May Our People Triumph*, pp 200–201.

24. Alexander, *African Tightrope*, p 52.

25. Roberts, *Glitter and Greed*, p 177.

26. Lukens, interviewed by Charles Stuart Kennedy, 17 November 1989.

27. McKown, *Lumumba*, pp 140–141.

28. Statements given by Lumumba at Press Conference in Leopoldville, 9 August 1960, quoted in Van Lierde, ed, *Lumumba Speaks*, p 319.

29. Quoted in Nkrumah, *Challenge of the Congo*, p 29.

30. Baynham, *The Military and Politics in Nkrumah's Ghana*, p 93.

31. Milne, *Kwame Nkrumah: A Biography*, p 95.

18. Bribery, Bugging and Green Berets

1. Legum, *Congo Disaster*, p 146.

2. Thompson, *Ghana's Foreign Policy, 1957–1966*, p 144.

3. Cameron Duodu, 'Face to Face with the Congo (2)', *Modern Ghana*, 2 February 2019, www.modernghana.com/news/913022/face-to-face-with-the-congo.html; and Cameron Duodo to the author, 14 October 2020.

4. 'Our Men at Work in the Congo', *Daily Graphic*, 1 August 1960, p 5.

5. Dei-Anang, *The Administration of Ghana's Foreign Relations 1957–1965*, pp 24–25.

6. Kwaku Boateng's son, Paul Yaw Boateng, became the UK's first Black cabinet minister in 2002, when he was appointed chief secretary to the treasury. He was elevated to the peerage in 2010 as the Lord Boateng.

7. Dei-Anang, *The Administration of Ghana's Foreign Relations 1957–1965*, p 24.

8. Letter, Barden to Ondong (Uganda), 30 July 1960, George Padmore Research Library on African Affairs, Accra, BAA/348.

9. Grilli, *Nkrumaism and African Nationalism*, p 205.

10. Nwaubani, *The United States and Decolonization in West Africa 1950–1960*, p 150.

11. SSCIA, Miscellaneous Records of the Church Committee, 'Lumumba, Patrice, Assassination; CIA; Castro, Fidel', 00/00/1975 [*sic*], released 26 April 2018, NARA Record Number 157-10014-10178.

12. Devlin, *Chief of Station, Congo*, p 30.

13. The pseudonym used to refer to Devlin in cable traffic related to the Congo was Robert B Guthman (not to be confused with the pseudonym used by Devlin in the course of the 1975 Church Committee, which was Victor S Hedgeman). He reported to Bronson Tweedy, the head of the Africa Division, whose pseudonym was Thomas K Jadwin. The pseudonym of Tweedy's boss, Dick Bissell, in the Congo cables was John L Kane.

14. Devlin, *Chief of Station, Congo*, p 11.

15. Roberts, interviewed by Charles Stuart Kennedy, 11 February 1991.

16. Devlin, *Chief of Station, Congo*, p 139.

17. *Ibid*, pp 58, 63.

18. *Ibid*, p 68.

19. McKown, *Lumumba*, p 141.

20. Devlin, *Chief of Station, Congo*, p 59.

21. Steigman, interviewed by Charles Stuart Kennedy, 29 April 1989.

22. Herbert Weiss to the author, 14 October 2020.

23. Devlin, *Chief of Station, Congo*, p 30.

24. Nzongola-Ntalaja, *Patrice Lumumba*, p 100.

25. Weissman, 'Opening the Secret Files on Lumumba's Murder'.

26. SSCIA, Miscellaneous Records of the Church Committee, 'Lumumba, Patrice, Assassination; CIA; Castro, Fidel', 00/00/1975 [*sic*], released 26 April 2018, NARA Record Number 157-10014-10178.

27. Dayal, *Mission for Hammarskjöld*, p 66.

28. Gibbs, *The Political Economy of Third World Intervention*, p 96.

29. Robert D McFadden, 'Frank C. Carlucci, Diplomat and Defense Secretary to Reagan, Dies at 87', *New York Times*, 4 June 2018.

30. Carlucci, interviewed by Charles Stuart Kennedy, 1 April 1997.

31. Herbstein, *White Lies*, p 39.

32. Carlucci, interviewed by Charles Stuart Kennedy, 1 April 1997.

33. Devlin, *Chief of Station, Congo*, p 61.

34. Palmer, interviewed by Karen Lamoree, 14 June 1988.

35. Devlin, *Chief of Station, Congo*, p 66.

36. Liz Forgan, 'Our Woman at Somerville', *The Guardian*, 26 March 1979.

37. Quoted in Corera, *The Art of Betrayal*, p 112.

38. Pendennis, 'Table Talk', *Observer*, 7 August 1960.

39. Devlin, *Chief of Station, Congo*, p 132.

40. Quoted in Caroline Alexander, 'Vital Powers: A Profile of Daphne Park, O.B.E., C.M.G.', *New Yorker*, 30 January 1989.

41. Quoted in *ibid*.

42. 'On Her Majesty's Secret Service', *Panorama*, BBC, screened 22 November 1992.

43. Ray et al, eds, *Dirty Work 2*, p 351.

44. Doyle, *True Men and Traitors*, p 138.

45. *Ibid*, p 129.

46. Devlin, *Chief of Station, Congo*, p 52.

47. Doyle, *True Men and Traitors*, p 138.

48. Doyle, interviewed by Charles Southall, 19 June 2013, Susan Williams private papers; Doyle, *True Men and Traitors*, p 138.

49. Doyle, *True Men and Traitors*, p 129.

50. *Ibid*, pp 136–137.

51. *Ibid*, p 145.

52. Williams, *Spies in the Congo*, pp 141–142.

53. Gibbs, *The Political Economy of Third World Intervention*, p 111. Wittman's firm is listed in US State Department, *International Educational, Cultural and Related Activities for African Countries South of the Sahara*, August 1961, p 210.

54. Reports by George Wittman, 1960–1961, Archives Générales du Royaume de Belgique, Sibéka Papers, 536.

55. This set of reports is held in the archive of La Société Minière du Bécéca Papers (Sibéka), a mining company, which are held in the state archives of Belgium. They were sent to Tempelsman, who shared them with Alfred Moeller de Ladder-sous, a former Belgian colonial governor in the Congo, who was vice president of Sabena and in charge of the diamond sales of Forminière, which had a monopoly on diamond production in the province of Kasai. Tempelsman told Moeller that Tempelsman's mission was to establish contact with the US embassy in Leopoldville, with ONUC and with the Congolese government (Tempelsman to Governor A Moeller de Laddersous, 18 October 1960, Archives Générales du Royaume de Belgique, Sibéka Papers, 536). Moeller in turn shared the reports with Edgar Van der Straeten, the vice governor of Société Générale (A Moeller de Laddersous to E Van der Straeten, 7 November 1960, Sibéka Papers, 536). It was through this route that the reports ended up in the Sibéka archive. The communications are one-sided; although references are made to incoming cables, these are not in the file.

56. GW-2, Leopoldville, 22 September 1960, Archives Générales du Royaume de Belgique, Sibéka Papers, 536.

57. Alumni of '51, *Trinity Alumni Magazine*, January 1961, p 23. The story appeared in a wide range of US newspapers, for example the *Waxahachie Daily Light*, 16 October 1960.

58. Discussion and quotation from State Department in Gibbs, *The Political Economy of Third World Intervention*, pp 109–110.

59. GW-4, Leopoldville, 4 October 1960, Archives Générales du Royaume de Belgique, Sibéka Papers, 536.

60. GW-2, Leopoldville, 22 September 1960, Archives Générales du Royaume de Belgique, Sibéka Papers, 536. (Wittman sent two reports from Leopoldville dated 22 September 1960 and also one from Accra with the same date.)

61. GW-2, Leopoldville, 22 September 1960, Archives Générales du Royaume de Belgique, Sibéka Papers, 536.

62. Emphasis added. Quoted and discussed in Williams, *Spies in the Congo*, p 95 ff.

63. Gibbs, *The Political Economy of Third World Intervention*, p 110. Gibbs attributes the quotation (n 43, p 250) to Mahoney in 'The Kennedy Policy in the Congo', who cites a 'leading U.S. diplomat as his source' (n 36, p 264).

64. GW-2, Leopoldville, 22 September 1960, Archives Générales du Royaume de Belgique, Sibéka Papers, 536.

65. GW-6, Leopoldville, 12 October 1960, Archives Générales du Royaume de Belgique, Sibéka Papers, 536.

66. The presentations of Sully deFontaine's family name are various: for example, de Fontaine in the literature of the Special Forces Regiment (www.soc.mil/SWCS /RegimentalHonors/_pdf/sf_defontaine.pdf); DeFontaine; and De Fontaine. This book follows Jack Lawson's *The Slaver's Wheel*, which uses deFontaine.

67. Lawson, *The Slaver's Wheel*, p 126. The author is grateful to Herbert Weiss for telling her about this book.

68. *Ibid*, pp 348, 131.

69. '10th SFG (A) History', United States Army Special Operations Command, US Army website, accessed 16 March 2021, www.soc.mil/USASFC/Groups/10th /history.html.

70. Lawson, *The Slaver's Wheel*, p 85.

71. *Ibid*, pp 129–131, 133.

72. *Ibid*, pp 147–148.

73. *Ibid*, pp 213-214, 230–231.

74. *Ibid*, p 234.

75. Quoted in Peter Beaumont, 'Mercenary "Mad Mike" Hoare Dies in South Africa Aged 100', *The Guardian*, 3 February 2020.

76. SSCIA, Miscellaneous Records of the Church Committee, 08/22/1975, NARA Record Number 157-10014-10185.

77. See, for example, 'CIA Provided Mad Mike Hoare "Logistic Support and Air Cover" in the Congo', *Soldier of Fortune*, 11 February 2020.

78. Devlin, *Chief of Station, Congo*, p 46.

19. The Road to Calvary

1. *FRUS*, 1958–1960, vol 14, *Africa*, document 179, https://history.state.gov/his toricaldocuments/frus1958-60v14/d179.

2. *Ibid*, document 178, https://history.state.gov/historicaldocuments/frus1958-60 v14/d178.

3. *Ibid*, document 180, https://history.state.gov/historicaldocuments/frus1958-60 v14/d180.

4. *FRUS*, 1964–1968, vol 23, *Congo, 1960–1968*, document 10, https://history.state .gov/historicaldocuments/frus1964-68v23/d10.

5. United States Congress, Senate, *Alleged Assassination Plots Involving Foreign Leaders*, pp 13–15.

6. SSCIA, Miscellaneous Records of the Church Committee, 'Lumumba, Patrice, Assassination; CIA; Castro, Fidel', 00/00/75 [*sic*], NARA Record Number 157-10014-10178.

7. *Ibid.*

8. Grose, *Gentleman Spy*, p 506.

9. *FRUS*, 1964–1968, vol 23, *Congo, 1960–1968*, document 14, https://history.state
.gov/historicaldocuments/frus1964-68v23/d14.

10. Analysis by Borstelmann, *The Cold War and the Color Line*, p 314, n 96.

11. *FRUS*, 1958–1960, vol 14, *Africa*, document 180, https://history.state.gov
/historicaldocuments/frus1958-60v14/d180.

12. Devlin, *Chief of Station, Congo*, p 63.

13. Burden, *Peggy and I*, p 319.

14. Prados, *Safe for Democracy*, p 275.

15. Eisenhower, *Waging Peace 1956–1961*, p 575.

16. *Ibid*, p 99.

17. Carlucci, interview by Charles Stuart Kennedy, 1 April 1997.

18. United States Congress, Senate, *Alleged Assassination Plots Involving Foreign Leaders*, p 18; emphasis added.

19. Nwaubani, *The United States and Decolonization in West Africa 1950–1960*, p 150.

20. The author is grateful to Georges Nzongola-Ntalaja for sharing his insights on this conference with the author, 26 September 2020, by email.

21. Zhukov, 'Such Was Lumumba', p 163.

22. Lumumba, speech at the opening of the All-African Conference in Leopold-ville, 25 August 1960, reproduced in Lumumba, *May Our People Triumph*, pp 21–31.

23. Devlin, *Chief of Station, Congo*, p 66.

24. British Pathé, 'Mr. Lumumba Opens the Pan-African Co-Operation Conference'.

25. Zhukov, 'Such Was Lumumba', pp 165–166; also here: www.marxists.org/subject/africa/lumumba/reminiscences/zhukov/suchwas.htm.

26. Jacobs, 'The Awkward Biography of the Young Washington Okumu', p 230.

27. Devlin, *Chief of Station, Congo*, p 71.

28. Blouin with MacKellar, *My Country, Africa*, pp 225, 228.

29. Jacobs, 'The Awkward Biography of the Young Washington Okumu', pp 229–230.

30. Blouin with MacKellar, *My Country, Africa*, p 265.

31. Devlin, *Chief of Station, Congo*, p 63.

32. Van Lierde, ed, *Lumumba Speaks*, pp 353–354.

33. Cameron Duodu, 'A Look Back into History', *Ghanaian Times*, 17 August 2010, www.s158663955.websitehome.co.uk/ghanaculture/mod_print.php?archiveid=1634.

34. Blouin with MacKellar, *My Country, Africa*, p 266.

35. United Nations General Assembly, *Items in Peace Keeping Operations—United Nations Operations in the Congo—Lumumba—Reports on His Death*, p 12.

36. Gizenga, *Ma Vie et Mes Luttes*, p 205.

37. Kashamura, *De Lumumba aux colonels*, pp 147–150.

38. Reproduced in Nkrumah, *Challenge of the Congo*, p 39.

39. Nkrumah, *Challenge of the Congo*, p 41.

40. Reproduced in *ibid*, pp 43–46.

41. The letter from Djin to Nkrumah is reproduced in *ibid*, pp 48–54.

42. SSCIA, Miscellaneous Records of the Church Committee, 08/22/1975, NARA Record Number 157-10014-10185.

43. Weissman, 'Opening the Secret Files on Lumumba's Murder'.

44. Devlin, *Chief of Station, Congo*, p 86.

45. Palmer, interviewed by Karen Lamoree, 14 June 1988.

46. Devlin, *Chief of Station, Congo*, p 85.

47. Blouin with MacKellar, *My Country, Africa*, p 268.

48. *Ibid*, pp 268–270.

49. *Ibid*, p 268.

50. Ntumazah, *A Conversational Auto Biography*, p 380.

51. Atangana, *The End of French Rule in Cameroon*, p 125.

52. Burden, *Peggy and I*, p 319.

53. Carlucci, interviewed by Charles Stuart Kennedy, 1 April 1997.

54. Nkrumah, *Challenge of the Congo*, p 63.

20. The Poison Plot

1. Blouin with MacKellar, *My Country, Africa*, p 270.

2. The Church Committee report refers to 'Joe', as does Larry Devlin in *Congo, Chief of Station*, but the removal of the redaction in the transcript of Bronson Tweedy's testimony reveals that the name used was actually 'Sid': SSCIA, Hearings, Bronson Tweedy, 9 October 1975, NARA Record Number 157-10014-10068.

3. SSCIA, Report, 'Select Committee—Assassination Report (Updated Oct 16, 1975)', 09/01/1975, NARA Record Number 157-10005-10297.

4. SSCIA, Hearings, Bronson Tweedy, 9 October 1975, NARA Record Number 157-10014-10068.

5. *Ibid*, NARA Record Number 157-10014-10089.

6. *FRUS*, 1958–1960, vol 14, *Africa*, document 223, https://history.state.gov /historicaldocuments/frus1958-60v14/d223.

7. Corera, *The Art of Betrayal*, p 123.

8. Kinzer, *Poisoner in Chief*, pp 176–177.

9. Richelson, *The Wizards of Langley*, p 11.

10. United States Congress, Senate, *Project MKUltra*, p 69.

11. *Ibid*, p 30.

12. *Ibid*, p 5.

13. Rupert Cornwell, 'Obituary: Sidney Gottlieb', *Independent*, 16 March 1999.

14. In the course of the Church Committee investigation, Gottlieb was given the pseudonym of Joseph Scheider.

15. The transcripts of the following testimonies are missing: 'Joseph Scheider' (alias for Sidney Gottlieb), 10/7/75 (21 pp); 'Joseph Scheider', 10/9/75 (21 pp). For a discussion, see Rex Bradford, 'Missing Church Committee Transcripts', Mary Ferrell Foundation, 2016, www.maryferrell.org/pages/Featured_Missing_Church_Committee_Transcripts.html.

16. Rex Bradford to the author, 22 October 2020, by email.

17. Quoted in United States Congress, Senate, *Alleged Assassination Plots Involving Foreign Leaders*, pp 20–21.

18. United States Congress, Senate, *Final Report of the Select Committee to Study Governmental Operations*, vol 1, p 391.

19. The reference to MKDelta is as follows: 'I talked with Jack Earman about the Inspector General's report on TSD [Technical Services Division] insofar as the MKDELTA programme is concerned. He read to me a few pages of his draft which I think set forth Dr Tietjen's position fairly well. However, he had not made any specific recommendations. He assured me that he would do so, and I assume that I will be able to find out what they are'. 'DAIRY [*sic*] NOTES', 27 September 1963, CIA, CREST, CIA-RDP76-00183R000400060047-5.

20. A Freedom of Information Act (FOIA) request was submitted to the CIA for an unredacted record, but this was unsuccessful. It was a Mandatory Declassification Review Request, submitted by Jeremy Bigwood to CIA, 1 March 2019. The response from CIA was sent on 23 October 2020, nearly eighteen months later, from the Information and Privacy Coordinator to Jeremy Bigwood; Reference EOM-2019-00452. The document was provided but remained heavily redacted (with some additional but minimal disclosures).

21. United States Congress, Senate, *Project MKUltra*, pp 71–72.

22. United States Congress, Senate, *Final Report of the Select Committee to Study Governmental Operations*, vol 1, p 392.

23. CIA, JFK, Meeting with Mr. Burt Wides (Senate Staff Members), 06/20/75, NARA Record Number 104-10059-10236.

24. David Wise, 'The CIA—Licensed to Kill for Decades', *Los Angeles Times*, 22 July 2000. The report is available on the website of the National Security Archive at George Washington University in Washington, DC: https://nsarchive2.gwu.edu /NSAEBB/NSAEBB4/ciaguat2.html.

25. Observation by science historian Ed Regis, quoted in Kinzer, *Poisoner in Chief*, p 177.

26. Quoted in Kinzer, *Poisoner in Chief*, p 184.

27. Stockwell, *In Search of Enemies*, p 172.

28. Kinzer, *Poisoner in Chief*, pp 175–180; quotation from *Alleged Assassination Plots Involving Foreign Leaders*, p 25.

29. United States Congress, Senate, *Alleged Assassination Plots Involving Foreign Leaders*, p 68.

30. Stockwell, *In Search of Enemies*, p 10.

31. *Ibid*, p 172.

32. Lemarchand, 'The CIA in Africa: How Central? How Intelligent?', p 15.

33. GW-3, Leopoldville, 30 September 1960, Archives Générales du Royaume de Belgique, Sibéka Papers, 536.

34. GW-4, Leopoldville, 4 October 1960, Archives Générales du Royaume de Belgique, Sibéka Papers, 536.

35. GW-3, Leopoldville, 30 September 1960, Archives Générales du Royaume de Belgique, Sibéka Papers, 536.

36. GW-6, Leopoldville, 12 October 1960, Archives Générales du Royaume de Belgique, Sibéka Papers, 536.

37. GW-10, Leopoldville, 20 October 1960, Archives Générales du Royaume de Belgique, Sibéka Papers, 536.

38. Haynes, interviewed by Charles Stuart Kennedy, 20 April 2011.

39. Lawson, *Slaver's Wheel*, pp 270–271.

40. *Ibid*, p xx.

41. *Ibid*, p 324.

42. The author is grateful to Mwana Mboka for providing information about Lumumba's movements between his private home on Boulevard Albert 1er and his official residence, as prime minister, on Avenue Tilkens.

43. Blouin with MacKellar, *My Country, Africa*, p 269.

44. Fursenko and Naftali, *Khrushchev's Cold War*, p 319.

45. 'A Man of Supreme Patience: Rajeshwar Dayal, Hammarskjöld's Envoy', *New York Times*, September 1960, quoted in Swapna Kona Nayudu, '"A Man of Supreme Patience": Rajeshwar Dayal, Hammarskjöld's Envoy', Wilson Center, History and Public Policy Program, 23 April 2018, www.wilsoncenter.org/blog-post /man-supreme-patience-rajeshwar-dayal-hammarskjolds-envoy.

46. United Nations General Assembly, *Items in Peace Keeping Operations—United Nations Operations in the Congo—Lumumba—Reports on His Death*, p 14.

47. *Ibid*, p 15.

48. GW-3, Leopoldville, 30 September 1960, Archives Générales du Royaume de Belgique, Sibéka Papers, 536.

49. Dayal, *Mission for Hammarskjöld*, p 86.

50. *Ibid*, p 88.

51. GW-11, Leopoldville, 24 October 1960, Archives Générales du Royaume de Belgique, Sibéka Papers, 536.

52. Marcum, *The Angolan Revolution*, vol 1, p 68.

53. SSCIA, Hearings, Bronson Tweedy, 9 October 1975, NARA Record Number 157-10014-10089.

54. Dayal, *Mission for Hammarskjöld*, p 88.

55. GW-3, Leopoldville, 30 September 1960, Archives Générales du Royaume de Belgique, Sibéka Papers, 536.

56. *Ibid*, p 89.

57. Legum, *Congo Disaster*, p 153.

21. Africa at the United Nations

1. Dahomey, Upper Volta, Cameroon, Central African Republic, Chad, Republic of the Congo (Leopoldville), Republic of the Congo (Brazzaville), Côte d'Ivoire, Gabon, Madagascar, Niger, Somalia, Togo, Mali and Senegal; Nigeria would join in October 1960.

2. Dayal, *Mission for Hammarskjöld*, p 91.

3. *Ibid*, pp 103, 92.

4. Evan Andrews, 'Fidel Castro's Wild New York Visit'.

5. Meriwether, *Proudly We Can Be Africans*, p 200.

6. Angelou, *The Heart of a Woman*, p 120.

7. *Ibid*, pp 119–120.

8. 'Address by President Dwight Eisenhower to the UN General Assembly', Archived Content, US Department of State, 22 September 1960, accessed 5 April 2021, https://2009-2017.state.gov/p/io/potusunga/207330.htm.

9. *FRUS*, 1958–1960, vol 14, *Africa*, document 221, editorial note, https://history .state.gov/historicaldocuments/frus1958-60v14/d221.

10. 'Address by President Dwight Eisenhower to the UN General Assembly'.

11. Simon Hall, 'Fidel Castro Stayed in Harlem 60 Years Ago to Highlight Racial Injustice in the U.S.', *Smithsonian Magazine*, 18 September 2020.

12. 'Aid to Africa as a World Challenge', *The Times*, 23 September 1960, p 14.

13. Quoted and discussed in Mahoney, *JFK*, p 50.

14. Powell, *Private Secretary*, p 137.

15. Marais, *Kwame Nkrumah*, pp 57–59.

16. Price, *The Social Basis of Administrative Behavior in a Transitional Polity*, p 393.

17. Powell, *Private Secretary*, p 137.

18. Meriwether, *Proudly We Can Be Africans*, p 198.

19. Dayal, *Mission for Hammarskjöld*, p 92.

20. Kwame Nkrumah, 'Dawn of a New Era', speech to the UN General Assembly, 23 September 1960, *Africa Renewal*, August 2010, www.un.org/africarenewal/magazine/august-2010/visions-independence-then-and-now.

21. Meriwether, *Proudly We Can Be Africans*, p 198.

22. Powell, *Private Secretary*, p 137.

23. Nwaubani, *The United States and Decolonization in West Africa 1950–1960*, p 153.

24. Mahoney, *JFK*, p 50.

25. Nwaubani, *The United States and Decolonization in West Africa 1950–1960*, p 153.

26. *Ibid*, p 146.

27. Eisenhower, *Waging Peace 1956–1961*, p 583.

28. Quoted in Nwaubani, *The United States and Decolonization in West Africa 1950–1960*, p 154.

29. *Ibid*, p 156.

30. GW-11, Accra, 22 September 1960, Archives Générales du Royaume de Belgique, Sibéka Papers, 536. (Wittman also sent a report from Leopoldville on 22 September 1960, likely because that was the day the pouch was sent from the US embassy.)

31. Speech by Mr Khrushchev, Chairman of the Council of Ministers of the Union of Soviet Socialist Republics, at the 869th Plenary Meeting of the 15th Session of the UN General Assembly, 23 September 1960, History and Public Policy Program Digital Archive, UN Document A/PV.869: 65–84, http://digitalarchive.wilsoncenter.org/document/155185.

32. Dayal, *Mission for Hammarskjöld*, pp 92–93.

33. *Ibid*, p 93.

34. Paul DeBenedetto, "FLASHBACK: Fidel Castro's Controversial 1960 Trip to NYC," *DNA Info*, updated 28 November 2016, www.dnainfo.com/new-york/20161126/turtle-bay/flashback-fidel-castros-controversial-1960-nyc-trip/.

35. Powell, *Private Secretary*, p 139.

36. Dayal, *Mission for Hammarskjöld*, pp 95–96.

37. Eisenhower, *Waging Peace 1956–1961*, p 585.

38. Hayes, *Queen of Spies*, p 167.

39. Foreign Office minutes by HFT Smith, ADM Ross and Sir R Stevens, 28–29 September 1960, TNA, FO 371/146650/401.

40. GW-3, Leopoldville, 30 September 1960, Archives Générales du Royaume de Belgique, Sibéka Papers, 536.

41. Eisenhower, *Waging Peace 1956–1961*, pp 586–588.

42. Powell, *Private Secretary*, p 138.

22. Spying on the UN

1. Kashamura, *De Lumumba aux colonels*, p 157.

2. Wise and Ross, *The Invisible Government*, p 218.

3. Roberts, interviewed by Charles Stuart Kennedy, 11 February 1991.

4. The equivalent figure on 7 December 2020 is US$1,778,267,520.80, using the tool at https://fxtop.com/en/historical-currency-converter.php.

5. Buchanan, interviewed by Charles Stuart Kennedy, 15 March 1996.

6. Roberts, interviewed by Charles Stuart Kennedy, 11 February 1991.

7. Convention on the Privileges and Immunities of the United Nations, New York, Article II, Section 3, 13 February 1946, https://treaties.un.org/doc/Treaties /1946/12/19461214%2010-17%20PM/Ch_III_1p.pdf.

8. 'United Nations and United States of America, Agreement Regarding the Headquarters of the United Nations', signed at Lake Success, 26 June 1947, https:// treaties.un.org/doc/Publication/UNTS/Volume%2011/volume-11-I-147-English.pdf.

9. 'African Studies in America: The Extended Family', Africa Research Group, 1969, p 38, https://africanactivist.msu.edu/document_metadata.php?objectid=210-808-8942.

10. Imbrey, interviewed by Charles Stuart Kennedy, 21 June 2001.

11. Jacobs, 'The Awkward Biography of the Young Washington Okumu', p 232.

12. When the practice was codified by the UN Economic and Social Council (ECOSOC) into a statute, it was explicitly stated that an NGO concerned with ECOSOC's work on 'questions of human rights' could be granted consultative status. (ECOSOC Resolution 288(B), para 2, adopted on 27 February 1950.) For a broad overview of the history of consultative status and its application throughout the UN system, see chapter 2 of Willetts, *Non-Governmental Organizations in World Politics*.

13. Peter Willetts to the author by email, 23 March 2021.

14. See Chapter 5, endnote 10, for a list of the articles published in February 1967 by the *New York Times*.

15. International Commission of Jurists: Tolley, *The International Commission of Jurists*, p xvi; World Assembly of Youth: Stonor Saunders, *Who Paid the Piper?*, p 142.

16. Madsen, *The Almost Classified Guide*, pp 161–162, 404.

17. 'Any financial contribution or other support, direct or indirect, from a Government . . . shall be openly declared . . . and fully recorded in the financial and other records of the organisation'. UN Economic and Social Council, Resolution 1296 (XLIV), para 8, adopted on 23 May 1968.

18. Human rights NGOs had to have 'a general international concern' and not be restricted to 'the situation in a single State' (Resolution 1296, para 17).

19. Willetts, 'Consultative Status for NGOs at the UN', pp 41–42.

20. Peter Willetts to the author by email, 23 March 2021.

21. Hazzard, *Countenance of Truth*, pp 8–9.

22. Singer, interviewed by Richard Jolly, 2 January 2000.

23. Hazzard, *Countenance of Truth*, pp 9–11.

24. Singer, interviewed by Richard Jolly, 2 January 2000.

25. Hazzard, *Countenance of Truth*, p 22.

26. Urquhart, *Hammarskjöld*, p 59.

27. *Ibid*, p 63.

28. Urquhart, *Ralph Bunche*, pp 247–253.

29. Urquhart, *Hammarskjöld*, pp 63–64.

30. The author is grateful to Sixten Svensson, Boris Hagelin's brother-in-law, for sharing information and insights on this topic.

31. Greg Miller, 'The Intelligence Coup of the Century', *Washington Post*, 11 February 2020.

32. The African nations listed are: Algeria, Angola, Egypt, Gabon, Ghana, Guinea, Ivory Coast, Libya, Mauritius, Morocco, Nigeria, Republic of the Congo (Brazzaville), South Africa, Sudan, Tanzania, Tunisia, Democratic Republic of the Congo, Zimbabwe. Miller, 'The Intelligence Coup of the Century'.

33. Smith, *Economic Democracy*, p 138.

34. Williams, *Who Killed Hammarskjöld?*, pp 119–120.

35. *Ibid*, p 4.

36. United Nations General Assembly, *Investigation into the Conditions and Circumstances Resulting in the Tragic Death of Dag Hammarskjöld and of the Members of the Party Accompanying Him*, A/71/1042, 5 September 2017, p 40.

37. Quoted in *ibid*, p 40.

38. *Ibid*, p 12.

39. *Ibid*, p 9.

40. Miller, 'How the CIA Used Crypto AG Encryption Devices to Spy on Countries for Decades'.

41. Smith, *Economic Democracy*, p 138.

42. Preamble, Charter of the United Nations, UN website, 24 October 1945, www.un.org/en/sections/un-charter/preamble/index.html.

23. 'Lumumba Assails US on Uranium'

1. 'Rapport présenté par Monsieur Kahamba, Représentant du Gouvernement de la République du Congo, et par le Docteur L. P. Gillon du Centre Nucléaire TRICO', n.d., ARMS, United Nations Archives, S-0739-28-1.

2. U L Soswani to Sture Linner, 30 October 1961, ARMS, United Nations Archives, S-0739- 28-1.

3. The course was organised by the Commission for Technical Co-operation in Africa South of the Sahara, along with the World Health Organisation. IAEA, *Annual Report of the Board of Governors to the General Conference, 1 July 1959–30 June 1960*.

4. Professor Broda was demonstrably in Leopoldville in May 1960, since he wrote to his son from there on 10 May 1960. Paul Broda Private Papers.

5. See TNA, KV 2/2349.

6. Haynes et al, *Spies*, pp 64–69.

7. Broda, *Scientist Spies*, p xi.

8. Broda's shift in concerns is explained in a book by his son: Paul Broda, *Scientists Spies*, for example in pp 244 and 262–263.

9. 'A list of members of the Staff of the Vienna Technische Hochschule, who have Communist affiliations and sympathies. These persons listed below are mentioned in the following U.S.A.F.A. Bi-Weekly Reports', n.d., CIA, CREST, CIA-RDP79 -01203A000200400011-8, www.cia.gov/readingroom/docs/CIA-RDP79-01203A0002 00400011-8.pdf.

10. For example: Scientific Abstracts, CIA, CREST, CIA-RDP86-00513R000 307130009-8; Consolidated Translations, CIA, CREST, CIA-RDP91-00929R000 200580006-1 (no release date given); Scientific Abstracts, CIA, CREST, CIA-RDP86 -00513R000204210019-2; Consolidated Translations, CIA CREST, CIA-RDP84 -00581R000100450017-0.

11. Gillon, *Servir*, p 147.

12. Details of the fissionable material in the reactor are given here: International Atomic Energy Agency, 'The Texts of the Instruments Connected with the Agency's Assistance to the Congo (Leopoldville) in Continuing a Research Reactor Project', INF/CIRC37, 15 February 1963, www.iaea.org/sites/default/files/infcirc37.pdf.

13. Lars Öhrström to the author, 26 February 2021, by email.

14. Devlin, *Chief of Station, Congo*, pp 27–28.

15. 'Lumumba Assails U.S. on Uranium: Ousted Congo Premier Says Katanga Gets U.N. Aid Because of Its Mines', *New York Times*, 10 October 1960.

16. Burden, *Peggy and I*, p 325.

17. *FRUS*, 1958–1960, vol 14, *Africa*, document 236, https://history.state.gov /historicaldocuments/frus1958-60v14/d236.

18. McCone to Dillon, 7 October 1960, NARA, RG 326, Entry P14-B, Box 61.

19. Dillon to McCone, 10 October 1960, NARA, RG 326, Entry P14-B, Box 61. Relevant material, including the specified memorandum, was withdrawn from this file. The 'Withdrawal Notice' in the file describes one of the classified documents as a two-page 'Memo' on 10 October 1960 from McCone to 'Dillon, et al'; it was withdrawn in 2001 'because access to it is restricted'. A letter from McCone to Dillon, presumably the letter to which the memorandum is attached, was withdrawn in 2005. A third document withdrawn from the same file is a five-page telegram from Leopoldville to the secretary of state; it was withdrawn in 2001.

20. McCone to Gray, 7 October 1960, NARA, RG 326, P85A, box 55, folder 2.

21. McCone to Gray, 7 October 1960, NARA, RG 326, P85A, box 55, folder 2; McCone to Dillon, 7 October 1960, NARA, RG 326, Entry P14-B, box 61.

22. Agee, *Inside the Company*, p 36.

23. 'Summary of Facts: Investigation of CIA Involvement in Plans to Assassinate Foreign Leaders', 5 June 1975, in Gerald R. Ford Presidential Library, Richard B. Cheney Files, box 7, folder 'Intelligence—Report on CIA Assassination Plots (1)', www.fordlibrarymuseum.gov/library/document/0005/7324009.pdf.

24. Harr to McCone, 14 October 1960, NARA, RG 326, Entry P14-B, box 61.

25. A submission was made in April 2020 to the US National Archives and Records Administration (NARA), under the Mandatory Declassification Review, to obtain a copy of these documents (Jeremy Bigwood to the US National Archives and Records Administration, 13 April 2020). However, NARA responded to say that it is not able to release any of these documents at this stage, on the grounds of sensitivities relating to national security information. (NARA said it is consulting the appropriate

agencies for further review. Its response reads, 'NARA has limited authority to release national security information and other sensitive information. Under Executive Order 13256, Section 3.6(b), we must send copies of the remaining documents which you requested to the appropriate agencies for further review'.) In fact, the response did include a copy of one document, which it claimed had been declassified; however, this document had a different date from the one requested and in any case was already in the public domain (Don McIlwaine to Jeremy Bigwood, 7 October 2020, NARA Case Number: NW 64105). Susan Williams Private Papers.

26. Marnham, *Snake Dance*, pp 217–218.

27. Statement by USAEC Commissioner L K Olson on 13 October 1960, quoted in R D J Walker, Metals Branch, to S H U Bowie, Geological Survey of Great Britain, 4 October 1961, TNA, AB 16/2480. This file has been withdrawn from public access since it was studied in the course of research for this book. A Freedom of Information request for the reopening of the file has been submitted to the UK National Archives (Carole Steers to TNA, 2 October 2019). The response by TNA explained that the file had been withdrawn as part of a security review by the UK Nuclear Decommissioning Authority, which has withdrawn a collection of records relating to the early development of military and civil nuclear technology. TNA stated that it is not yet in a position to decide if the record can be reopened (TNA to Carole Steers, Call reference number F0059337, 22 October 2019).

28. Memorandum, 'Congo Uranium', sent by R D J Walker, Metals Branch, to Mr Prichard, Overseas Relations, 29 September 1961, TNA, AB 16/2480.

29. Hempstone, *Katanga Report*, p 54.

30. Verbatim record, Informal Restricted Meeting of the Standing Group with the Belgian Military Representative, 18 July 1960, in Conference Room B, the Pentagon, 19 July 1960, pp 7–9, NATO Record, SG 18076, RECORD-SG-180760_INF _RESTR_ENG_PDP.

31. Kashamura, *De Lumumba aux colonels*, p 191.

32. Omasombo, quoted in Woodrow Wilson International Center, *The Congo Crisis, 1960–1961*, p 78.

24. Third-Country Agent QJWIN

1. Mahoney, *JFK*, p 52.

2. Quoted in United States Congress, Senate, *Alleged Assassination Plots Involving Foreign Leaders*, p 42, footnote.

3. Report by Military Information, S/A/3-8, 8 July 1961, ARMS, S 0805-0013-10, United Nations Archives.

4. McKown, *Lumumba*, pp 158–159.

5. United States Congress, Senate, *Alleged Assassination Plots Involving Foreign Leaders*, p 32.

6. GW-11, Leopoldville, 24 October 1960, Archives Générales du Royaume de Belgique, Sibéka Papers, 536.

7. Weissman, 'Opening the Secret Files on Lumumba's Murder'.

8. Devlin, *Chief of Station, Congo*, p 114.

9. United States Congress, Senate, *Alleged Assassination Plots Involving Foreign Leaders*, p 39.

10. For the purpose of the Church Committee investigations, Justin O'Donnell was given the pseudonym of Michael Mulroney.

11. Quoted in United States Congress, Senate, *Alleged Assassination Plots Involving Foreign Leaders*, p 39.

12. The transcripts of the following testimonies are missing: "Michael Mulroney" (alias for Justin O'Donnell), 6/9/75 (p 38); "Michael Mulroney", 9/9/75 (p 38; note: this possibly is a typo and refers to 6/9/75); "Michael Mulroney", 9/11/75 (p 38). For a discussion, see Rex Bradford, 'Missing Church Committee Transcripts', Mary Ferrell Foundation, 2016, www.maryferrell.org/pages/Featured_Missing_Church _Committee_Transcripts.html.

13. SSCIA, Miscellaneous Records of the Church Committee, 06/09/1975, NARA Record Number 157-10014-10106.

14. United States Congress, Senate, *Alleged Assassination Plots Involving Foreign Leaders*, pp 42, 39, 37.

15. *Ibid*, pp 40–42.

16. *Ibid*, p 43.

17. He had a history of different aliases, including Moise Morris Shexlak and Jacques Berger. HSCA, CIA Segregated Collection, 11/22/78, NARA Record Number 180-10143-10212.

18. Quoted in United States Congress, Senate, *Alleged Assassination Plots Involving Foreign Leaders*, p 43.

19. CIA, JFK, Journal—Office of Legislative Counsel, Thursday, 2 March 1978, NARA Record Number 104-10146-10221.

20. CIA, JFK, Memo on QJWIN, oo/oo/ [*sic*], NARA Record Number 104-10103-10291.

21. Weissman, 'Opening the Secret Files on Lumumba's Murder'.

22. United States Congress, Senate, *Alleged Assassination Plots Involving Foreign Leaders*, p 44. A number of RYBAT cables between the CIA station in Leopoldville and headquarters in Washington are slugged 'LAURICLE ZRACORN'. 'LAURI-CLE' is an action indicator for the operations of Division D—the unit in charge of signals and communications intelligence, which worked with the National Security Agency. In the case of 'ZRACORN', it has been assumed that this slug refers to the project to assassinate Lumumba. However, there is no clear evidence to support this assumption. Furthermore, Devlin asserted—both to the Church Committee and in his later memoir—that cable traffic relating to the assassination operation was slugged not 'ZRACORN' but 'PROP' (he did not use the digraph 'YQ' as a prefix to 'PROP' in the memoir, which is consistent with the redactions in Church Committee documentation).

23. CIA, JFK, 'CABLE—QJWIN HAS CULTIVATED CLOSE PER-SONAL RELATIONSHIP WITH IDEN A WHO AGREED SMUGGLE IN-DUSTRIAL DIAMONDS FOR HIM TO ITALY', 12/08/1960, NARA Record Number 104-10185-10060.

24. Burden, *Peggy and I*, pp 314–315.

25. *FRUS*, 1964–1968, vol 23, *Congo, 1960–1968*, document 46, https://history.state .gov/historicaldocuments/frus1964-68v23/d46.

26. Talbot, *The Devil's Chessboard*, pp 468–469.

27. SSCIA, 'EXCERPT OF INTERVIEW WITH WILLIAM HARVEY', 00/00/1976 [*sic*], NARA Record Number157-10004-10138.

28. United States Congress, Senate, *Alleged Assassination Plots Involving Foreign Leaders*, p 43, n 1.

29. SSCIA, Memorandum, 'PROJECT ZRRIFLE AND QJWIN', 05/30/1975, NARA Record Number 157-10003-10490.

30. CIA, JFK, 'DOCUMENT RE QJWIN', NARA Record Number 104-10059 -10223.

31. Mpisi, *Antoine Gizenga*, p 224.

32. Blouin with MacKellar, *My Country, Africa*, p 105.

33. *Ibid*, p 274.

34. Quoted in *FRUS*, 1958–1960, vol 14, *Africa*, document 242, https://history.state .gov/historicaldocuments/frus1958-60v14/d242.

35. 'Praeger Discusses CIA Book Ties', *Publisher's Weekly*, 6 March 1967, CIA, CREST, CIA-RDP88-01350R000200320012-6.

36. Price, 'The CIA Book Publishing Operations'.

37. Bouwer, *Gender and Decolonization in the Congo*, p 72.

38. Quoted in Whitney, *Finks*, p 123.

39. Rowley, *Richard Wright*, p 516.

40. *Ibid*, pp 517, 525.

25. 'The Big American Stick'

1. Dayal, *Mission for Hammarskjöld*, p 116.

2. Kanza, *Conflict in the Congo*, p 307.

3. *Ibid*, p 307.

4. Dayal, *Mission for Hammarskjöld*, p 117.

5. Quoted in *ibid*, p 117.

6. Quoted in *ibid*, p 117.

7. UPI, 'Valerian A. Zorin, Soviet Envoy, Dies', *New York Times*, 19 January 1986.

8. The elected chairman of the Conciliation Commission was Jaja Wachuku of Nigeria. UN document A/4592, Report of 24 November 1960 by Advisory Committee on Congo for consideration at the UN General Assembly 15th Session, 1960–1961, https://digitallibrary.un.org/record/1304848.

9. 'Ghana's Voice at U.N.; Alex Quaison-Sackey', *New York Times*, 9 November 1960.

10. Dayal, *Mission for Hammarskjöld*, p 119.

11. Imbrey, interviewed by Charles Stuart Kennedy, 21 June 2001.

12. Imbrey, interviewed by Curtis Ostle, 2 April 2001.

13. Russell, interviewed by William W Moss, 24 January 1973.

14. Resolution adopted on the report of the credentials committee, 1498 (XV), Credentials of the Representatives of the Republic of the Congo (Leopoldville), 924th Plenary Meeting, 22 November 1960, Resolution A/RES/1498 (XV), UN General Assembly 15th Session, 1960–1961, https://digitallibrary.un.org/record/205863?ln=en.

15. Nkrumah, *Challenge of the Congo*, p 84.

16. Dayal, *Mission for Hammarskjöld*, p 119.

17. *Ibid*, p 120.

18. 'M. Kasavubu a gagné la bataille de l'O.N.U.', *Le Monde*, 24 November 1960.

19. Quoted in transcript of meeting of US Senate Committee on Foreign Relations, 28 February 1961, made public April 1984, vol 13 (Washington: US Government Printing Office, 1984), p 216.

20. Mahoney, *JFK*, p 53.

21. Kanza, *Conflict in the Congo*, pp 308–309.

22. Dayal, *Mission for Hammarskjöld*, pp 110–125.

23. Imbrey, interviewed by Charles Stuart Kennedy, 21 June 2001.

26. Ambassador Satch

1. The six members of the All Stars that went with him were Trummy Young (trombone), Williams Kyle (piano), Mort Herbert (bass), Velma Middleton (vocalist), Danny Barcelona (drums) and Barney Bigard (clarinet).

2. See the exchange of correspondence in Louis Armstrong House Museum Collection, 1068329.

3. Quoted in Von Eschen, *Satchmo Blows Up the World*, p 63.

4. Telegram from Louis Armstrong to Lucille Preston, 25 May 1956, Georgetown University Library website, accessed 20 February 2021, www.library.georgetown.edu /exhibition/jazz-ambassador-louis-armstrong-ghana-1956.

5. 'Advertising: Akwaaba to Satchmo in Ghana', *New York Times*, 14 October 1960, p 44.

6. 'Pepsi Brings You "Satchmo" 6 P.M.: Accra Stadium 15th & 17th Oct.', *Daily Graphic*, 26 September 1960, p 4.

7. Advertising: Akwaaba to Satchmo in Ghana'.

8. Dillon to Timberlake, 12 October 1960, Louis Armstrong House Museum Collection, 1068388.

9. US Embassy Leopoldville to Department of State, 17 November 1960, Louis Armstrong House Museum Collection, 1068352.

10. 'Satchmo Swings in Congo', Universal-International News, 1960, www.you tube.com/watch?v=TgItFk9q2bQ.

11. The lyrics are here: 'Kalle Chanting Satchmo: A Warm Breeze in a Cold War', *Planet Ilunga*, 2 October 2014, https://planetilunga.com/2014/10/02 /kalle-chanting-satchmo-a-warm-breeze-in-a-cold-war/.

12. Quoted in Ade Daramy, 'Musical Ambassador, Louis Armstrong and Africa: The Triumph and Tragedy', African Postmark, updated 27 April 2018, https://africanpost mark.com/musical-ambassador-louis-armstrong-and-africa-the-triumph-and-tragedy.

13. Fitzhugh Green, US Embassy Leopoldville, to Department of State, 17 November 1960, Louis Armstrong House Museum Collection, 1068352.

14. Harrison Golden, 'Cool Cats of the Congo', *Bachelor*, September 1961, p 67, Louis Armstrong House Museum Collection, 1069882.

15. Quoted in 'I Always Say a Note Is a Note in Any Language', *The Nation*, 5 January 2012, https://nation.africa/kenya/life-and-style/dn2/-i-always-say-a-note -is-a-note-in-any-language-795390.

16. Devlin, *Chief of Station, Congo*, p 119.

17. Doyle, *True Men and Traitors*, p 153.

18. 'Program for Visits to Elisabethville of Ambassador and Mrs. Timberlake and Louis Armstrong and His Troupe, November 20–23 1960', Louis Armstrong House Museum Collection, 1067836.

19. In Subject Files of the Office of the Force Commander, Military Information Branch, 405/5/2, ARMS, S-0805-12-3, United Nations Archives.

20. Sha to Charles, 24 June 1961, ARMS, S-0805-12-3, United Nations Archives.

21. This was identified by the artist Amanda Rice.

22. Fitzhugh Green, Public Affairs, US Embassy Leopoldville, to State Department, 17 November 1961, Louis Armstrong House Museum Collection, 1068352.

23. Timberlake to Secretary of State, 15 November 1960, Louis Armstrong House Museum Collection, 1068388.

24. Devlin, *Chief of Station, Congo*, p 126.

25. 'Satchmo Blows Up the World', *Jam Session*, Meridian International Center and Institute of Jazz Studies, Rutgers University, accessed 16 March 2021, www.meridian.org/jazzambassadors/louis_armstrong/louis_armstrong.php.

26. Reiner, Freetown, to Secretary of State, 15 June 1960, Louis Armstrong House Museum Collection, 1068324.

27. Withers, Nairobi, to Secretary of State, 24 August 1960, Louis Armstrong House Museum Collection, 1068326.

28. 'Satchmo Goes to Paris', *New York Times*, 6 December 1960, p 53.

29. Von Eschen, *Satchmo Blows Up the World*, p 88.

30. Lehren, 'Jazz and the FBI'. A copy of the FBI file on Armstrong is here: Louis Armstrong House Museum Collection, 1068982.

27. Trick or Escape?

1. McKown, *Lumumba*, p 161.

2. Gizenga, *Ma Vie et Mes Luttes*, p 271.

3. United States Congress, Senate, *Alleged Assassination Plots Involving Foreign Leaders*, p 48.

4. *FRUS*, 1964–1968, vol 23, *Congo 1960–1968*, document 46, https://history.state.gov/historicaldocuments/frus1964-68v23/d46.

5. *Ibid.*

6. Lawson, *The Slaver's Wheel*, pp 322–325.

7. Devlin, *Chief of Station, Congo*, p 114.

8. Dayal, *Mission for Hammarskjöld*, p 142.

9. United Nations General Assembly, *Items in Peace Keeping Operations—United Nations Operations in the Congo—Lumumba—Reports on His Death*, p 17.

10. *Ibid*, p 17.

11. Dayal, *Mission for Hammarskjöld*, p 143.

12. Devlin, *Chief of Station, Congo*, p 114.

13. *Ibid*, p 114.

14. United States Congress, Senate, *Alleged Assassination Plots Involving Foreign Leaders*, p 42.

15. Mensah, *In the Shadows of Politics*, pp 4–5; *Chicago Tribune*, November 17, 1960.

16. 'Aloof Ghanaian in Congo; Nathaniel Azarco Welbeck', *New York Times*, 22 November 1960, p 8.

17. Devlin, *Chief of Station, Congo*, p 123.

18. 'Welbeck Comes Back to Ghana', *Daily Graphic*, 23 November 1960, p 1.

19. Dayal, *Mission for Hammarskjöld*, p 130; Mensah, *In the Shadows of Politics*, p 1.

20. The welcome at Accra airport on 22 November is reported in 'Welbeck Comes Back to Ghana'.

21. Mensah, *In the Shadows of Politics*, p 14.

22. Nkrumah, *Challenge of the Congo*, pp 86–87.

23. Alexander, *African Tightrope*, pp 131–136.

24. Reported by Alexander in *ibid*, p 59.

25. *FRUS*, 1958–1960, vol 14, *Africa*, document 132, https://history.state.gov /historicaldocuments/frus1958-60v14/d132.

26. Dayal, *Mission for Hammarskjöld*, pp 130–131.

27. Nkrumah, *Challenge of the Congo*, p 89.

28. Gizenga, *Ma Vie et Mes Luttes*, p 272.

29. Dayal, *Mission for Hammarskjöld*, pp 142 (emphasis added) and 143.

30. *Ibid*, p 142.

31. Hayes, *Queen of Spies*, p 170.

32. Kashamura, *De Lumumba aux colonels*, p 166.

33. *Ibid*, pp 164–165.

34. *Ibid*, p 164–167.

35. Devlin, *Chief of Station, Congo*, p 115.

36. *Ibid*, p 116.

28. Manhunt for Lumumba

1. United Nations General Assembly, *Items in Peace Keeping Operations—United Nations Operations in the Congo—Lumumba—Reports on His Death*, p 18.

2. Report by Dayal to Hammarskjöld, quoted in Dayal, *Mission for Hammarskjöld*, p 144.

3. Kashamura, *De Lumumba aux colonels*, p 168.

4. McKown, *Lumumba*, p 164.

5. *Ibid*, p 164.

6. Lumumba, *May Our People Triumph*, p 139. In this section of *May Our People Triumph*, a Soviet journalist, Lev Volodin, repeats an account given to him by Jacques N, who had been in the convoy of people with Lumumba.

7. McKown, *Lumumba*, p 166.

8. Marchal, *Lord Leverhulme's Ghosts*, pp 88–92.

9. Alexander, *African Tightrope*, p 61.

10. Volodin, 'Last Days of Freedom', p 135.

11. Lumumba, *May Our People Triumph*, pp 135–144.

12. McKown, *Lumumba*, p 169.

13. Quoted in Lumumba, *May Our People Triumph*, pp 135–144.

14. Central Intelligence Bulletin, 31 August 1961, p 3, www.zerohora.com.br /pdf/23048138.pdf.

15. Mohan, 'Ghana, the Congo, and the United Nations', p 390.

16. Quoted in United States Congress, Senate, *Alleged Assassination Plots Involving Foreign Leaders*, pp 49, 48.

17. Quoted in *ibid*, p 44.

18. Quoted in *ibid*, p 44.

19. CIA, JFK, 'Cable: Please expedite dispatch KUTUBE/D only with all details and results QJWIN trip', 02/23/61, NARA, Record Number 104-10185-10053.

20. US$1,000 on 1 January 1960 is the equivalent of US$8,891 in November 2020, using the tool at https://fxtop.com/en/historical-currency-converter.php.

21. Quoted in United States Congress, Senate, *Alleged Assassination Plots Involving Foreign Leaders*, p 44.

22. SSCIA, Memorandum, 'PROJECT ZRRIFLE AND QJWIN', 05/30/1975, NARA, Record Number,157-10003-10490.

23. McKown, *Lumumba*, pp 170–171.

24. Carlucci, interviewed by Charles Stuart Kennedy, 1 April 1997.

25. McKown, *Lumumba*, p 171.

26. Dayal, *Mission for Hammarskjöld*, pp 146–147; McKown, *Lumumba*, p 171.

27. Quoted and comments in Nkrumah, *Challenge of the Congo*, p 90; McKown, *Lumumba*, pp 171–172.

28. Dayal, *Mission for Hammarskjöld*, p 146.

29. Quoted in McKown, *Lumumba*, p 172.

30. From a report by Hammarskjöld to the UN Security Council, 5 December 1960, quoted in United Nations General Assembly, *Items in Peace Keeping Operations— United Nations Operations in the Congo—Lumumba—Reports on His Death*, p 19.

31. Lumumba's Last Recorded Message, in Van Lierde, ed, *Lumumba Speaks*, pp 426–431.

32. Talbot, *The Devil's Chessboard*, pp 361–362.

33. Nwaubani, *The United States and Decolonization in West Africa 1950–1960*, pp 44–45.

34. Quoted in Talbot, *The Devil's Chessboard*, pp 361–362.

35. The task force sailed under the command of Admiral A L Reed, COMSO-LANT for Operation SOLANT AMITY, later designated SoLant Amity I.

36. William C Daley Jr, in 'Biographies [of] the Members of 3rd Platoon "G" Company, 2nd Battalion, 6th Marine Regiment of the 2nd Marine Division's Fleet Marine Force at Camp LeJeune, North Carolina Taking Part in the U.S. Navy's SoLant Amity I Cruise to South America and Africa, from November 1960 Through April of 1961', SoLant Amity, accessed 22 March 2021, http://solantamity.com /Personnel/Biographies_3rdA-F.htm.

37. Ed Shea, 'Eligibility for the United Nations Medal for Service Rendered in the Congo', n.d., accessed 22 March 2021, http://solantamity.com/Media /Documents/UnitedNationsMedalEligibility.pdf.

38. Scott Drummond, USCG Veteran, 'Solant Amity', *Towns County Herald*, 27 April 2016.

39. Daley, 'Biographies [of] the Members of 3rd Platoon "G" Company'.

40. Thomas DeLange, quoted in 'USS Vogelgesang DD-862', n.d., accessed 22 March 2021, http://solantamity.com/Extraneous/Comments.htm#Vogel.

41. Stockwell, *In Search of Enemies*, p 125.

42. Gullion, interviewed by Samuel E Belk, 17 January 1964.

43. George Jones, 'USS Gearing 1957', Gearing Historical Site, n.d., accessed 22 March 2021, https://dd710.com/GJ/gear57.pdf.

44. Shea, 'Eligibility for the United Nations Medal for Service Rendered in the Congo'.

29. Deep Cover Agent WIROGUE

1. Nyangoni, *Africa in the United Nations System*, pp 95–97.

2. Nkrumah, *Neo-colonialism*, p ix.

3. Nkrumah, *Challenge of the Congo*, pp 111–112.

4. Kanza, *Conflict in the Congo*, pp 313–314.

5. 'Bi-weekly Propaganda Guidance', 16 January 1961, CIA Electronic Reading Room, Document CIA-RDP78-03061A000100030003-6.pdf.

6. Church, *A Lifelong Affair*, pp 132–135.

7. Frank Church, draft of speech, 'Emerging Africa: A New Dimension in World Affairs Kiwanis-Rotary Idaho Falls, ID', 1961/03/01, p 2, Frank Church Papers, box 7, folder 40.

8. Central Intelligence Bulletin, 20 December 1960, www.cia.gov/readingroom/docs/CENTRAL%20INTELLIGENCE%20BULL%5B15798791%5D.pdf.

9. Namikas, 'History Through Documents and Memory', p 539; Mazov, 'Soviet Aid to the Gizenga Government in the Former Belgian Congo (1960–61) as Reflected in Russian Archives', pp 425–437.

10. Kanza, *Conflict in the Congo*, pp 219–230.

11. Imobighe, 'An African High Command', pp 241–242.

12. Nkrumah, *Challenge of the Congo*, pp 115–118.

13. CIA, JFK, DOCUMENT RE QJWIN, NARA, Record Number 104-10059-10223.

14. CIA, JFK, 'WIROGUE' (VOL 3), NARA, Record Number 104-10182-10057.

15. Quoted in United States Congress, Senate, *Alleged Assassination Plots Involving Foreign Leaders*, Africa Division to Leopoldville, 10/27/60, p 46.

16. CIA, JFK, 'WIROGUE' (VOL 3), NARA, Record Number 104-10182-10057.

17. *Ibid.*

18. *Ibid.*

19. 'PROJECT WIZARD' has been used by a number of commentators as the cryptonym for the plot to kill Patrice Lumumba. It is not included here because these commentators do not appear to have provided an original primary source; efforts have been made to find a reference to such a cryptonym in a document produced by the CIA, but without success thus far. Nor is 'PROJECT WIZARD' mentioned in the reports of official investigations into Lumumba's murder—not in the 1961 UN report, nor in the Church Committee report of 1975, nor in the report of the Belgian parliamentary committee in 2001.

The fruitless search for this alleged cryptonym included relevant records released in 2017 and 2018 under the JFK Assassination Records Collection Act (1992). However, these records *do* show that individuals who were seen as belonging to one group were given the cryptonyms WIZARD/1, WIZARD/2, WIZARD/3 and so forth, from around mid-August 1961. The following excerpt from a cable dated 28 August 1961 illustrates this use of WIZARD, along with other cryptonyms using the WI digraph: 'WIROGUE/1 knew every little re station activities. . . . Aware Guthman [Devlin] in contact with WIZARD/4. Was used pass money to WIBOTTLE in hospital. Station using apartment W/1 rented as safe apartment and has post office box under W/1 name'.

In a different sphere of activity in the US in the mid-twentieth century, the term 'Project Wizard' was used to describe a project contracted by the US Army Air Forces in 1946 to develop a ballistic missile system; it was cancelled in 1959. See Baucom, 'Eisenhower and Ballistic Missile Defense', pp 8, 12, 13, 16.

20. Stockwell, *In Search of Enemies*, p 46, footnote.

21. CIA, JFK, CIA File on WIROGUE, NARA, Record Number 104-10182-10052.

22. Devlin, *Chief of Station, Congo*, p 113.

23. CIA, JFK, Document Re QJWIN, NARA, Record Number 104-10059-10223.

24. 'Subject: David. Dates of Interview 8, 9, 10 Jan', CIA, JFK, 'WIROGUE' (VOL 3), NARA, Record Number 104-10182-10057.

25. United States Congress, Senate, *Alleged Assassination Plots Involving Foreign Leaders*, p 46.

26. CIA, JFK, Memorandum: WIROGUE/1 Mission to Kinshasa, December 1960, NARA, Record Number 104-10310-10016.

27. US$300 on 1 January 1960 is the equivalent of US$667 in November 2020, using the tool at https://fxtop.com/en/historical-currency-converter.php.

28. CIA, JFK, 'WIROGUE' (Vol 3), NARA, Record Number 104-10182-10057.

29. CIA, JFK, Document Re QJWIN, NARA, Record Number 104-10059-10223.

30. CIA, JFK, Meeting with Mr. Burt Wides (Senate Staff Members), 06/20/75, NARA, Record Number 104-10059-10236.

31. Briefing by Allen Dulles, recorded in memorandum by Marion W Boggs, *FRUS*, 1958–1960, vol 14, *Africa*, document 236, https://history.state.gov/historicaldocuments/frus1958-60v14/d236.

32. See the discussion in Deininger and Meier, 'Sabotage of Public Water Supply Systems'.

33. CIA, JFK, Document Re QJWIN, NARA, Record Number 104-10059-10223.

34. Quoted in Gerard and Kuklick, *Death in the Congo*, pp 188–189.

35. *FRUS*, 1964–1968, vol 23, *Congo, 1960–1968*, document 50, https://history.state.gov/historicaldocuments/frus1964-68v23/d50.

36. *Ibid*, document 53, https://history.state.gov/historicaldocuments/frus1964-68v23/d53.

37. *FRUS*, 1958–1960, vol 14, *Africa*, document 292, https://history.state.gov/historicaldocuments/frus1958-60v14/d292.

38. Devlin, *Chief of Station, Congo*, p 117–118.

39. Dayal, *Mission for Hammarskjöld*, p 158.

40. 'The Widening Gulf Between African Radicals and the West', 7 February 1961, CIA, CREST, CIA-RDP85T00875R002000190003-3.

41. 'The Last Letter of Patrice Lumumba' (La dernière lettre de Patrice Lumumba), *MROnline*, posted 18 January 2008, https://mronline.org/2008/01/18 /lumumba180108-html/. The French text is from the website of the Mouvement des indigènes de la république; the English translation is from Nkrumah, *Challenge of the Congo*, pp 128–129.

30. Baking a Snake

1. Teresa Kerr, 'Morocco Commemorates 60th Anniversary of the Death of King Mohammed V'.

2. Buyout Footage Historic Film Archive, 'HD Stock Footage 1960's African Summit Meeting in Casablanca'.

3. McKeon, 'The African States and the OAU'.

4. Namikas, *Battleground Africa*, p 123.

5. Buyout Footage Historic Film Archive, 'HD Stock Footage 1960's African Summit Meeting in Casablanca'.

6. Quoted in Milne, *Kwame Nkrumah: A Biography*, p 92.

7. Dayal, *A Life of Our Times*, p 441.

8. Kelly, *America's Tyrant*, p 70.

9. *Ibid*, p 50.

10. Kashamura, *De Lumumba aux colonels*, pp 172–173.

11. Commentary by Van Lierde in Van Lierde, ed, *Lumumba Speaks*, p 431.

12. *Ibid*, p 432.

13. United Nations General Assembly, *Items in Peace Keeping Operations—United Nations Operations in the Congo—Lumumba—Reports on His Death*, p 27.

14. Namikas, 'Review of *FRUS, 1964–1968, Volume XXIII, Congo, 1960–1968*'.

15. Gerard and Kuklick, *Death in the Congo*, pp 200 ff.

16. *Ibid*, p 205; De Witte, *The Assassination of Lumumba*, pp 119-210.

17. Gerard and Kuklick, *Death in the Congo*, p 208.

18. Jason Burke, 'Belgium Must Return Tooth of Murdered Congolese Leader, Judge Rules', *The Guardian*, 10 September 2020, www.theguardian.com/world /2020/sep/10/judge-orders-return-of-tooth-said-to-be-from-assassinated-congolese -icon.

19. The letter was published in the *Washington Post* and reproduced in Stockwell, *In Search of Enemies*, p 273.

20. Stockwell, *In Search of Enemies*, p 105.

21. *Ibid*, p 13.

22. Gerard and Kuklick, *Death in the Congo*, p 208.

23. *Ibid*, p 208.

24. United States Congress, Senate, *Alleged Assassination Plots Involving Foreign Leaders*, p 51.

25. *Ibid*, p 51.

26. *FRUS*, 1964–1968, vol 23, *Congo, 1960–1968*, document 68, https://history.state .gov/historicaldocuments/frus1964-68v23/d68.

27. United States Congress, Senate, *Alleged Assassination Plots Involving Foreign Leaders*, p 51.

28. SSCIA, Hearings, 'Hedgman, Victor' [Larry Devlin], 08/25/75, NARA, Record Number 157-10014-10076.

29. SSCIA, Hearings, Tweedy, Bronson, 09/09/1975, NARA, Record Number 157-10014-10067.

30. United States Congress, Senate, *Alleged Assassination Plots Involving Foreign Leaders*, p 51, n 2.

31. SSCIA, Miscellaneous Records of the Church Committee, 06/09/1975, NARA, Record Number 157-10014-10106; italics in the original.

32. SSCIA, Miscellaneous Records of the Church Committee, 06/09/1975.

33. The version is headed 'Draft: October 6, 1975 Frederick D. Baron', SSCIA, Report, 'Select Committee—Assassination Report (Updated Oct 16, 1975)', 09/01/1975, NARA, Record Number 157-10005-10297.

34. SSCIA, Report, 'Select Committee—Assassination Report (Updated Oct 16, 1975)'.

35. Devlin, *Chief of Station, Congo*, p 126.

36. Doyle, *True Men and Traitors*, p 150.

37. CIA, JFK, CIA File on WIROGUE, NARA, Record Number 104-10182-10052; CIA, JFK, 'Nonrelated. WIROGUE', NARA, Record Number 104-10291-10003.

38. United Nations General Assembly, *Items in Peace Keeping Operations—United Nations Operations in the Congo—Lumumba—Reports on His Death*, p 118.

39. *FRUS*, 1961–1963, vol 20, *Congo Crisis*, document 6, https://history.state.gov/historicaldocuments/frus1961-63v20/d6.

40. Belgian House of Representatives, *Enquête Parlementaire visant à déterminer les circonstances exactes de l'assassinat de Patrice Lumumba*.

41. 'La CIA minimise son rôle dans le repérage et l'arrestation de Lumumba. . . En fait, cette version repose sur des témoignages d'agents de la CIA qui—l'arrestation de Lumumba leur ayant été confirmée—n'avaient aucun intérêt à être trop précis sur leur rôle exact. La seule collaboration CIA évoquée concerne une collaboration « avec le gouvernement congolais » pour la surveillance et le blocage de certaines voies possibles que tenteraient d'utiliser Lumumba et ses compagnons. Encore, Lawrence Devlin précise-t-il, ce ne fut pas une assistance majeure que la CIA put apporter en la matière, aux autorités congolaises'. Belgian House of Representatives, *Enquête Parlementaire visant à déterminer les circonstances exactes de l'assassinat de Patrice Lumumba*, pp 219–220.

42. Weissman, 'Opening the Secret Files on Lumumba's Murder', *Washington Post*, 21 July 2002.

43. Quoted in United States Congress, Senate, *Alleged Assassination Plots Involving Foreign Leaders*, p 49.

44. Newton, *Eisenhower*, p 347.

45. Transcript of the Inaugural Address of John F Kennedy, 20 January 1961, Avalon Project, https://avalon.law.yale.edu/20th_century/kennedy.asp.

31. Sunk Hope

1. United Nations General Assembly, *Items in Peace Keeping Operations—United Nations Operations in the Congo—Lumumba—Reports on His Death*, pp 39–40.

2. 'Lumumba Killed—Official', *Daily Graphic*, 14 February 1961, p 1.

3. 'Widow of Lumumba Marches in Mourning to Ask U.N. Help', *New York Times*, 15 February 1961, p 16.

4. Mpisi, *Antoine Gizenga*, pp 280–281.

5. Pauline Opangu Lumumba to Colette Braeckman, quoted in Misser, 'Mrs Lumumba Speaks'.

6. Gizenga, *Ma Vie et Mes Luttes*, p 276. The author is grateful to Emmanuel Barrault for his translation.

7. Musica, 'Franco Luambo and Mobutu Sese Seko: AStrange Relationship', *Africa Music News*, 8 November 2015, http://kenyapage.net/commentary/afromusic /franco-luambo-and-mobutu-sese-seko-a-strange-relationship/.

8. Radar, 'Rumba Lumumba', Bozar, accessed 22 February 2021, www.bozar.be/en /magazine/149084-rumba-lumumba.

9. Milne, *Kwame Nkrumah: A Biography*, p 148.

10. Nkrumah, *Challenge of the Congo*, pp 129–133.

11. 'Lumumba Killed—Official'.

12. Gerits, '"When the Bull Elephants Fight"', pp 958–959.

13. George Padmore Research Library on African Affairs, Bureau of African Affairs Collection (BAA), 303.

14. Cameron Duodu, 'Face to Face with the Congo (2)', *Modern Ghana*, 2 February 2019, www.modernghana.com/news/913022/face-to-face-with-the-congo.html.

15. Quoted in Gerits, '"When the Bull Elephants Fight"', p 959.

16. Weissman, *American Foreign Policy in the Congo, 1960–1964*, p 141.

17. Fanon, 'La mort de Lumumba: Pouvions-nous faire autrement?', in *Pour la révolution Africaine*, http://frantz-fanon.blogspot.com/2011/04/la-mort-de-lumumba -pouvions-nous-faire.html. The author is grateful to Emmanuel Barrault for his translation.

18. Kelley and Tuck, eds, *The Other Special Relationship*, p xxx.

19. López Álvarez, *Lumumba: Ou l'Afrique frustrée*, p 124. The author is grateful to Emmanuel Barrault for his translation.

20. Prosser, *An Ethic for Survival*, p 270 ff.

21. Angelou, *The Heart of a Woman*, pp 198–200.

22. Herbert Weiss, unpublished text, 2011; Herbert Weiss to the author, 15 October 2020, by email.

23. Richards, *Conversations with Maida Springer*, p 216; italics in the original.

24. Jacobs, 'The Awkward Biography of the Young Washington Okumu', p 230.

25. Burden, *Peggy and I*, p 319.

26. 'The Congo: Death of Lumumba—& After', *Time*, 24 February 1961.

27. Kinzer, *Poisoner in Chief*, p 179.

28. Devlin, *Chief of Station, Congo*, p 131.

29. Caroline Alexander, 'A Profile of Daphne Park', *New Yorker*, 30 January 1989.

30. Lea, letter to the editor.

31. Hayes, *Queen of Spies*, p 180.

32. The photograph, taken by Jacques Lowe, appears on the cover of the hardback edition of Mahoney, *JFK*.

33. *FRUS*, 1958–1960, vol 14, *Africa*, document 204, n 1, https://history.state.gov/historicaldocuments/frus1958-60v14/d204.

34. Quoted in Gerard and Kuklick, *Death in the Congo*, p 190.

35. Memo from Harriman to Kennedy, President's Office Files, box 114, folder 5a, quoted in Ritchie, 'A Familiar Frontier', p 26.

36. Haynes, interviewed by Charles Stuart Kennedy, 20 April 2011.

37. Doyle, *True Men and Traitors*, p 145.

38. United States Congress, Senate, *Alleged Assassination Plots Involving Foreign Leaders*, p 118.

39. *Ibid*, p 117.

40. The victims were Finant, Fataki, Yangara, Muzungu, Elengesa and Nzizi.

41. '6 More Leaders Murdered in Congo', *Daily Graphic*, 21 February 1961, p 1.

42. Nkrumah, *Challenge of the Congo*, p 138.

43. '400/1—Investigation into Lumumba's Death—Project "Sunk Hope"' (title of folder), 28 November 1960–26 May 1962, ARMS, S-0805-0011-04, United Nations Archives, https://search.archives.un.org/400-1-investigation-into-lumumbas-death-project-sunk-hope.

32. Arming the Skies

1. Governor, Malta, to Chapelries [Secretary of State for the Colonies], London, 18 February 1961, TNA, FCO 141/11581.

2. *Ibid*.

3. Mahoney, *JFK*, pp 80–81.

4. The Lincoln Building became known as One Grand Central Place in 2009.

5. 'Briefings', *Flying Magazine*, January 1961, p 106.

6. 'Intercontinental and Interocean', *FLIGHT International*, 1 November 1962, p 698.

7. Jan Knippers Black, 'I Was Sitting in this Bar in Luxembourg . . .', *Washington Monthly*, July/August 1980. This open source article was collected and filed by the CIA; it was approved for release on 22 March 2007 under the CIA CREST system and is available in the online CIA Reading Room: www.cia.gov/readingroom/docs/CIA-RDP99-00498R000200010169-6.pdf.

8. 'Caribbean and Congo Role Is Laid to C.I.A.'s Airline', *New York Times*, 1 September 1973.

9. Madsen, *The Almost Classified Guide to CIA Front Companies, Proprietaries and Contractors*, pp 343–344.

10. *Ibid*, pp 158–159.

11. Michael Hathorn, 'To Ghana 1961', chapter 17, p 6, Michael Hathorn Private Papers.

12. The message was repeated in a telegram from Secretary of State, Colonial Office, London, to Governor Malta, 18 February 1961, TNA FCO 141/11581.

13. *Ibid*, 2 February 1961.

14. UK Parliament, House of Commons, Written Answers, 1 February 1962, vol 652, c 109: Question by H Wilson and Answer by R Maudling, https://api .parliament.uk/historic-hansard/written-answers/1962/feb/01/aircraft. For background see: 'Aircraft for Katanga. Parl. Question: "Seven Seas Firm"', TNA FCO 141/ 11581.

15. Doyle, *True Men and Traitors*, pp 149–150; Southall interviewed by Sir Stephen Sedley, 21 September 2012.

16. Doyle, *True Men and Traitors*, p 150.

17. Secretary of State, Colonial Office, London, to Governor Malta, 2 February 1961, TNA, FCO 141/11581.

18. Assigned as N9540C with De Long Corp, USAF Serial Number Search Results, accessed 27 February 2021, http://cgibin.rcn.com/jeremy.k/cgi-bin/gzUsaf Search.pl?target=&content=C-97.

19. Secretary of State, Colonial Office, London to Governor Malta, 18 February 1961, TNA, FCO 141/11581.

20. Quoted in full here: US Ambassador Russell, Accra, to Secretary of State, Washington, 21 February 1961, JFKL, President's Office Files, 117b.

21. Mahoney, *JFK*, p 81.

22. The message from the Foreign Office was addressed on 17 February 1961 to the UK Mission in New York; it was then repeated in a telegram from the Secretary of State, Colonial Office, London, to Governor Malta, 18 February 1961, TNA, FCO 141/11581.

23. The information from Luxembourg was addressed on 27 February 1961 to the Foreign Office in London; it was then repeated in a telegram from the Secretary of State, Colonial Office, London, to Governor Malta, 3 March 1961, TNA, FCO 141/11581.

24. Dorn, 'The UN's First "Air Force"', p 1403.

25. Bob Williams, 'The Love of Flying', *Frontier News*, July 2014, pp 24–25, http:// fal-1.tripod.com/FL_News2014-56Summer.pdf.

26. Commando 42-3679, Aircraft Identification, The Curtiss Commando Page, accessed 27 February 2021, http://curtisscommando.e-monsite.com/pages/aircraft/s -n-42-3578-to-42-3683-curtiss-c-46a-35-cu-c-46a-36-cu-commando/commando-42 -3679.html.

27. United Nations General Assembly, *Investigation into the Conditions and Circumstances Resulting in the Tragic Death of Dag Hammarskjöld and of the Members of the Party Accompanying Him*, A/73/973, 12 September 2019, p 31 and passim.

28. The author is grateful to Hans Kristian Simensen for his analysis and contribution to this account.

29. Southall interviewed by Sir Stephen Sedley, 21 September 2012.

30. United Nations General Assembly, *Investigation into the Conditions and Circumstances*, pp 65–69. For a full account of the SAIMR documents, see chapter 16 of Williams, *Who Killed Hammarskjöld?*

31. Joseph Majerle III and Matthew Stevenson, 'Who or What Brought Down Dag Hammarskjöld?', *CounterPunch*, 11 January 2019, www.counterpunch .org/2019/01/11/who-or-what-brought-down-dag-hammarskjold/.

32. This tactic is the subject of the chapter 'Rat Catching' in Clostermann, *The Big Show*, pp 248–253.

33. Majerle to the author, 25 February 2021, by email.

34. Craig Bowman, 'Military Funeral for WWII Fighter Ace', War History Online, 23 December 2013, www.warhistoryonline.com/war-articles/military-funeral -wwii-fighter-ace.html.

35. 'Urban L Drew', List of P-47 pilots, P-47 Thunderbolts Association, accessed 18 March 2021, http://p47pilots.com/P47-Pilots.cfm?c=incP47BiographyHome.cfm &vm=BIO&pilotid=134&p=Urban%20L.%20Drew.

36. Bowman, 'Military Funeral for WWII Fighter Ace'.

37. Gerdan, *Dossier A... Comme Armes*, pp 248–252.

38. 'Cloak and Dagger Story', *The Citizen*, 21 February 2014.

39. Julian Borger, 'Dag Hammarskjöld's Plane May Have Been Shot Down, Ambassador Warned', *The Guardian*, 4 April 2015.

40. The author is grateful to Matthew Stevenson for this idea and sharing it with her.

41. Williams, *Who Killed Hammarskjöld?*, pp 188–191.

42. Justia US Law, *Johnson v Drew*, 25 July 1963, https://law.justia.com/cases /california/court-of-appeal/2d/218/614.html.

43. Rudd Leeuw, 'Propliners Around Johannesburg, 2004', *Aviation History and Photography*, 3 September 2015, www.ruudleeuw.com/sa04.htm.

44. Witness statement by Colonel Ben M Matlick to Rhodesian Federation Board of Investigation into the death of Dag Hammarskjöld, n.d. [1961], for the Air Accident report of November 1961, chaired by Lieutenant Colonel Maurice Barber, Federal Director of Civil Aviation, Bo Virving Private Papers.

45. Baker, *Historical Highlights of Andrews AFB, 1942–1989*, pp 421–422.

46. Witness statement by Colonel Ben M Matlick to Rhodesian Federation Board of Investigation into the death of Dag Hammarskjöld.

47. Hellström, *Fredsflygarna: FN-flyget i Kongo*, pp 162–163. The author is grateful to Hans Kristian Simensen for his translation.

48. Witness statement by Colonel Ben M Matlick to Rhodesian Federation Board of Investigation into the Death of Dag Hammarskjöld.

49. CIA, JFK, 'MEMORANDUM: WIROGUE/1 MISSION TO KINSHASA, DECEMBER 1960', 00/00/75 [*sic*], NARA, Record Number 104-10310-10016.

50. CIA, JFK, 'CIA FILE ON WIROGUE', 01/01/0000 [*sic*], NARA, Record Number 104-10182-10052.

51. CIA, JFK, 'MEMORANDUM: WIROGUE/1 MISSION TO KINSHASA, DECEMBER 1960'.

52. CIA, JFK, 'CIA FILE ON WIROGUE'.

53. CIA, JFK, 'CIA FILE ON WIROGUE'.

54. CIA, JFK, 'SUBJECT: WIROGUE/1', 03/14/1975, NARA, Record Number 104-10182-10059.

55. CIA, JFK, NARA, Record Numbers 104-10182-10003 (186 pp), 104-10182 -10004 (177 pp) and 104-10182-10002 (144 pp).

56. National Archives (NARA), 'JFK Assassination Records, CIA Miscellaneous Files', 15 August 2016, www.archives.gov/research/jfk/finding-aids/cia-files.html.

33. 'A Bride Everybody Wants'

1. Gerard and Kuklick, *Death in the Congo*, p 192.

2. *Ibid*, p 192.

3. Dayal, *Mission for Hammarskjöld*, pp 240–241.

4. Mahoney, *JFK*, p 73.

5. Russell, Accra, to Secretary of State, Washington, 16 and 17 February 1961, JFKL, President's Office Files, 117b.

6. Mahoney, *JFK*, p 73.

7. Jack Raymond, 'US Navy Ready for Congo Role', *New York Times*, 20 February 1961.

8. Gibbs, *The Political Economy of Third World Intervention*, p 110.

9. Mahoney, 'The Kennedy Policy in the Congo, 1961–1963', pp 262, 259. US$54 million on 1 January 1961 is equivalent to US$480,979,331 on 29 March 2021, using the tool at https://fxtop.com/en/historical-currency-converter.php.

10. The file is in an archive of documents relating to Edouard Pilaet, a Belgian who had been a resistance fighter in World War II and was a secret agent for Belgium in the Congo after its independence: CegeSoma, Collection Edouard Pilaet, PP 13/823 (AA 823).

11. 'Dossier propositions Tempelsman', n.d., CegeSoma, Collection Edouard Pilaet, PP 13/823 (AA 823), Dossier III.

12. Telex on the subject of the interview of Kennedy and Tempelsman; there is also a French translation of the telex, n.d. [start of August 1961], n.d., CegeSoma, Collection Edouard Pilaet, PP 13/823 (AA 823), Dossier III.

13. 'Dossier propositions Tempelsman', n.d., CegeSoma, Collection Edouard Pilaet, PP 13/823 (AA 823), Dossier III.

14. Gibbs, *The Political Economy of Third World Intervention*, p 110.

15. A separate report of 1965 by the US government—located in a file relating to 'Barter Acquisition Procedures for Stockpile Materials' and titled 'Report to the Secretary of Agriculture by the Ad Hoc Interagency Committee on Barter Acquisition Methods'—refers to a plan to convert to barter a cash contract for uranium concentrates produced in South Africa, involving also the acquisition of industrial diamonds from the Congo. Tempelsman does not identify the country to which he was referring in his memorandum of 19 October 1961, and it is not possible to exclude altogether that Tempelsman was writing as early as 1961 about South African uranium. However, the balance of evidence is that Tempelsman was referring to Congolese uranium. Also, the US government was less guarded in its references to South African uranium than to Congolese uranium, about which it was always very secretive (hence frequently using the cover of industrial diamonds). NARA, 16 e 17, box 4250.

16. Maurice Tempelsman to the President, 19 October 1961, JFKL, POF, 1961: TA-TU, Digital Identifier JFKPOF-005-010-p0031.

17. *FRUS*, 1961–1963, volume 9, *Foreign Economic Policy*, document 335, https://history.state.gov/historicaldocuments/frus1961-63v09/d335.

18. Maurice Tempelsman to the President, 19 October 1961.

19. Mahoney, 'The Kennedy Policy in the Congo, 1961–1963', p 265.

20. Quoted in Gibbs, *The Political Economy of Third World Intervention*, p 110 and p 249, n 37.

21. Alumni of '51, *Trinity Alumni Magazine*, Winter 1966, p 32, https://issuu.com /tcdigitalrepository/docs/winter1966.

22. Kahamba and Gillon, '10150: Report on the Development of the Trico Nuclear Centre', p 1308.

23. IAEA, Official Record of the 48th Plenary Meeting, 26 September 1961, GC(V)/OR.48, 20 November 1961, https://inis.iaea.org/collection/NCLCollection Store/_Public/41/123/41123503.pdf.

24. Robert K Mpoyo, 'Mining (Shinko), Militaries (Mura), Missionaries (Mulungwishi)', Robert K Mpoyo Private Papers.

25. Calder, *Agony of the Congo*, p 130.

26. Williams, *Africa for the Africans*, p 86.

34. Made in America

1. Nkrumah to Reba Lewis, 28 April 1969, in Milne, comp, *Kwame Nkrumah: The Conakry Years*, p 305.

2. Roger Lipsey to the author by email, 30 October 2020. The friend is Sture Linnér; his words are quoted in Lipsey, *Dag Hammarskjöld*, p 109.

3. Narrative in this passage of the events in Ghana comes from Nkrumah, *Challenge of the Congo*, pp 138–140, 152–154, 158.

4. Central Intelligence Bulletin, 17 April 1961, www.cia.gov/readingroom/docs /CENTRAL%20INTELLIGENCE%20BULL%5B15815746%5D.pdf.

5. Gullion, interviewed by Samuel E Belk, 17 January 1964.

6. *FRUS*, 1961–1963, vol 20, *Congo Crisis*, document 43, https://history.state.gov /historicaldocuments/frus1961-63v20/d43.

7. Ed Shea, 'Eligibility for the United Nations Medal for Service Rendered in the Congo', n.d., accessed 22 March 2021, http://solantamity.com/Media/Documents /UnitedNationsMedalEligibility.pdf.

8. Dayal, *Mission for Hammarskjöld*, p 297.

9. Devlin, *Chief of Station, Congo*, p 103.

10. Dayal, *Mission for Hammarskjöld*, pp 259–261.

11. *FRUS*, 1958–1960, vol 20, *Congo Crisis*, document 67, https://history.state.gov /historicaldocuments/frus1961-63v20/d67.

12. The statement was made on 25 May 1961. 'U.N. Statement on Dayal', *New York Times*, 26 May 1961, p 2.

13. Question asked in September 1961, quoted in Ostrower, *The United Nations and the United States*, p 105.

14. C-1, Leopoldville, 27 June 1961, Archives Générales du Royaume de Belgique, Sibéka Papers, 536.

15. Weissman, 'CIA Covert Action in Zaire and Angola', p 270.

16. Namikas, 'Review of Foreign Relations of the United States, *1964–1968, Volume XXIII, Congo, 1960–1968*', p 4. US$23,000 on 1 January 1960 is the equivalent of US$201,739 in November 2020, using the tool at https://fxtop.com/en/historical -currency-converter.php.

17. 'How C.I.A. Put "Instant Air Force" into Congo', *New York Times*, 26 April 1966.

18. C-1, Leopoldville, 27 June 1961, Archives Générales du Royaume de Belgique, Sibéka Papers, 536.

19. *FRUS, 1958–1960*, vol 20, *Congo Crisis*, document 93, https://history.state.gov/historicaldocuments/frus1961-63v20/d93.

20. Quoted in Weissman, 'CIA Covert Action in Zaire and Angola', p 270.

21. Weissman, *American Foreign Policy in the Congo*, 1960–1964, p 106.

22. Weissman, 'CIA Covert Action in Zaire and Angola', p 270.

23. United States Department of Justice, Report of the Attorney General to the Congress of the United States on the Administration of the Foreign Agents Registration Act of 1938, as Amended for the Calendar Year 1961; and in subsequent reports for 1962 and 1963.

24. Imbrey, interviewed by Curtis Ostle, 2 April 2001.

25. Nzongola-Ntalaja, *The Congo from Leopold to Kabila*, pp 122–124.

35. Hands off Ghana!

1. Helmer Reenberg, 'President John F. Kennedy's Remarks of Welcome to President Nkrumah of Ghana'.

2. Summary record of meeting, described in Mahoney, *JFK*, p 167.

3. Quoted and discussed in *ibid*, p 167.

4. *FRUS*, 1961–1963, vol 21, *Africa*, document 224, https://history.state.gov/historicaldocuments/frus1961-63v21/d224.

5. Munger, *Touched by Africa*, p 255.

6. *Ibid*, p 288.

7. Price, *Cold War Anthropology*, p 285.

8. Bing, *Reap the Whirlwind*, p 409.

9. *Ibid*, p 152.

10. Powell, *Private Secretary*, p 110.

11. Bing, *Reap the Whirlwind*, p 153.

12. Kaba, *Kwame Nkrumah and the Dream of African Unity*, p 77.

13. Russell to Secretary of State, 25 September (received 26) 1961, Section One, JFKL, NSF, box 099.

14. Russell, interviewed by William W Moss, 24 January 1973.

15. Michael Hathorn, interview by the author, 27 November 2018.

16. Michael Hathorn, 'To Ghana 1961', chapter 18, p 11, Michael Hathorn Private Papers.

17. John M. Goshko, 'Fund Tightly Controlled by Founder', *Washington Post*, 3 August 1977.

18. United States Congress, Senate, *Human Drug Testing by the CIA, 1977*, pp 91, 90.

19. These figures on 19 November 2020 are equivalent to over US$4.5million and close to US$9.5million, using the following tool: https://fxtop.com/en/historical-currency converter.php.

20. United States Congress, Senate, *Human Drug Testing by the CIA, 1977*, p 84.

21. *Ibid*, pp 44–45, 88, 90.

22. 'Dawn Broadcast 1, Accra, April 8, 1961', Edward A. Ulzen Memorial Foundation, 8 April 2018, www.eaumf.org/ejm-blog/2018/4/8/april-8-1961-nkrumahs-dawn-broadcast-condemns-corruption-in-the-cpp-and-government.

23. Quoted in Hadjor, *Nkrumah and Ghana*, p 86.

24. Joseph Amamoo to the author by email, 13 December 2020.

25. Bing, *Reap the Whirlwind*, p 405.

26. Biney, *The Political and Social Thought of Kwame Nkrumah*, p 90.

27. 'The Truth about Komla Gbedemah', by a 'Non-Ghanaian Intellectual', December 1964, CIA, CREST, CIA-RDP75-00001R000300210022-8, www.cia.gov/library/readingroom/docs/CIA-RDP75-00001R000300210022-8.pdf.

28. Powell, *Private Secretary*, p 184.

29. Intelligence Note from Roger Hilsman, INR, to the Secretary of State, Internal Dissension in Ghana, 6 September 1961, JFKL, NSF, box 099.

30. Russell, interviewed by William W Moss, 24 January 1973.

31. Russell to Secretary of State, 7 September 1961, JKFL, NSF, box 099. Destoolment refers in Ghana to the removal of a leader from power.

32. Russell, interviewed by William W Moss, 24 January 1973.

33. *FRUS*, 1961–1963, vol 21, *Africa*, document 232, https://history.state.gov/historicaldocuments/frus1961-63v21/d232.

34. Quoted and discussed in Mahoney, *JFK*, p 173.

35. *FRUS*, 1961–1963, vol 21, *Africa*, document 232, https://history.state.gov/historicaldocuments/frus1961-63v21/d232.

36. Quoted and discussed in Mahoney, *JFK*, p 173.

37. The surname 'Grosse' does not appear in the Accra telephone directory for the relevant years. The closest match that has been found is Solomon Joseph Gros (with no terminal 'e'), who was the UK deputy high commissioner in Accra in 1966 and 1967 and was closely involved in the High Commission's response to the overthrow of Nkrumah in 1966.

38. Reports by George Wittman, Archives Générales du Royaume de Belgique, Sibéka Papers, 536.

39. Quoted and discussed in Mahoney, *JFK*, p 174.

40. *Ibid*, p 174.

41. Russell to Secretary of State, 22 September 1961, JFKL, NSF, box 099.

42. Powell, *Private Secretary*, p 187.

43. *Ibid*, p 187.

44. Letter of Dismissal from President Nkrumah, 22 September 1961, reproduced as Annex E in Alexander, *African Tightrope*, p 149.

45. Nkrumah, *Challenge of the Congo*, p 167.

46. US Department of State to US Embassy London, copied to US Embassy Accra, 24 September 1961, JFKL, NSF, box 099.

47. Mahoney, *JFK*, p 171.

48. Intelligence Note from Roger Hilsman, INR, to the Secretary of State, 'Internal Dissension in Ghana', 14 September 1961.

49. 'World's Week: Some Talk by Alexander', *Topic*, 28 October 1961.

50. Russell to Secretary of State, 25 September (received 26) 1961, Section Two, JFKL, NSF, box 099.

51. Russell to Secretary of State, 25 September (received 26) 1961, Section One, JFKL, NSF, box 099.

52. Russell to Secretary of State, 28 September 1961, 8.55 pm, JFKL, NSF, box 099.

53. Russell to Secretary of State, 28 September 1961, 9 pm, JFKL, NSF, box 099.

54. Russell to State Department, 28 September 1961, JFKL, NSF, box 099.

55. Russell to Secretary of State, 28 September 1961, JFKL, NSF, box 099.

56. Rabinowitz, *Coups, Rivals and the Modern State*, p 120.

57. Akyeampong, *Between the Sea and the Lagoon*, p 202.

58. Russell, interviewed by William W Moss, 24 January 1973.

59. Telcon, Black/Ball, 11/1/61, JFKL, Ball Papers, box 4, file 'Ghana-Volta Project 2/24/61–4/9/63'.

60. Telcon, Black/Ball, 11/22/61, JFKL, Ball Papers, box 4, file 'Ghana-Volta Project 2/24/61–4/9/63'.

61. Baynham, *The Military and Politics in Nkrumah's Ghana*, p 131.

62. Powell, *Private Secretary*, p 184.

63. Ghana Government: 'Statement by the Government on the Recent Conspiracy', 11 December 1961, Accra, Ghana, WP No 7/61, Jay Lovestone papers, box 73, folder 'Ghana—Statement by the Government on the Recent Conspiracy', Hoover Institution Archives.

64. Mahoney, *JFK*, pp 184–185.

65. Telcon, Ball/Bundy, 11/4/61, quoted in Mahoney, 'The Kennedy Policy in the Congo, 1961–1963', p 266.

66. Telcon, Ball/The President, 11/13/61, quoted in *ibid*, pp 265–266.

36. 'America's Angolan'

1. Marcum, *The Angolan Revolution*, vol 1, p 65.

2. Weissman, 'CIA Covert Action in Zaire and Angola', p 278.

3. SSCIA, Hearings, 'Tweedy, Bronson', 9 October 1975, NARA, Record Number 157-10014-10089.

4. Houser, *No One Can Stop the Rain*, p 152.

5. Weissman, 'CIA Covert Action in Zaire and Angola', p 278.

6. By Agence France-Presse, 'Holden Roberto Dies at 84; Fought to Free Angola from Portuguese Rule', *New York Times*, 4 August 2007.

7. Weissman, 'CIA Covert Action in Zaire and Angola', p 276.

8. Paget, *Patriotic Betrayal*, p 263.

9. This was against the background of the US voting in favour of resolutions opposing Portuguese colonialism in the United Nations General Assembly (April 1961, December 1961 and January 1962) and Security Council (June 1961).

10. Marino, 'America's War in Angola, 1961–1976', p 45.

11. *Ibid*, p 3.

12. Paget, *Patriotic Betrayal*, p 266.

13. Quoted in Anyaso, ed, *Fifty Years of U.S. Africa Policy*, p 114.

14. Victoria Brittain, 'Holden Roberto', *The Guardian*, 8 August 2007.

15. Swanepoel, *Really Inside Boss*, p 101.

16. Driver, *Patrick Duncan*, pp 200–201.

17. Marcum, *Conceiving Mozambique*, p xxii.

18. Blackmer, *The MIT Center for International Studies*.

19. Marcum, *The Angolan Revolution*, vol 1, p viii.

20. *FRUS*, 1961–1963, vol 21, *Africa*, document 355, https://history.state.gov/historicaldocuments/frus1961-63v21/d355.

21. Quoted in Gerald J Bender, 'Angola: A Story of Stupidity', *New York Review*, 21 December 1978, www.nybooks.com/articles/1978/12/21/angola-a-story-of-stupidity/.

22. John Stockwell, 'The Secret Wars of the CIA', Libcom.org, speech given October 1987, posted 11 December 2012, https://libcom.org/history/secret-wars-cia-john-stockwell.

23. Cameron Duodu, 'An African Traitor', *The Guardian*, 14 August 2007.

37. 'The CIA Reptilian Coils'

1. 'Foreign News', *Jet*, 23 March 1961, p 22.

2. Wilford, *The Mighty Wurlitzer*, p 214.

3. Swanepoel, *Really Inside Boss*, pp 155–156.

4. Barnes, interviewed by Charles Stuart Kennedy, 2004, p 13.

5. Monaville, 'Decolonizing the University', p 375.

6. 'The Institute of Congolese Studies [with a marginal note on the front page: "Fait pour Merrill"], Annex A, Budget Project for 1961–62', International Association for Cultural Freedom, Records, box 171, folder 9. US$37,180 on 1 January 1962 is the equivalent of US$323,945 in November 2020, using the tool at https://fxtop.com/en/historical-currency-converter.php.

7. 'The Institute of Congolese Studies, Annex B, Testimonials', International Association for Cultural Freedom, Records, box 171, folder 9. The funding of the ICJ by the CIA is discussed in Chapter 15 of this book.

8. Suhr-Sytsma, *Poetry, Print, and the Making of Postcolonial Literature*, p 64.

9. Quoted in *ibid*, p 60.

10. Mphahlele, *Afrika My Music*, p 23.

11. Suhr-Sytsma, *Poetry, Print, and the Making of Postcolonial Literature*, pp 62–63, 66–67.

12. Moore, 'The Transcription Centre in the Sixties', p 171.

13. Mphahlele, *Afrika My Music*, pp 30–33.

14. Quoted in Swanepoel, *Really Inside Boss*, pp 180–181.

15. Mphahlele, *Afrika My Music*, p 46.

16. Mphahlele, 'Chemchemi Creative Centre, Nairobi', p 115.

17. Quoted in Moore, 'The Transcription Centre in the Sixties', p 169.

18. *Ibid*, p 180.

19. Mphahlele, letter to the editor, *Transition* 7, no 34 (1968): 5.

20. Mphahlele, *Afrika My Music*, pp 90–91.

21. Soyinka, *You Must Set Forth at Dawn*, p 86.

22. Quoted in Swanepoel, *Really Inside Boss*, p 145.

23. 'Correspondence with Farfield Foundation, New York, 1962–1963', Nathaniel Nakasa Papers, Item A2696.B3.2.

24. Daniel Massey, 'After Decades in Exile, a South African Writer's Remains Will Head Home', *New York Times*, 8 August 2014.

25. Brown, *A Native of Nowhere*, p 167.

26. David Wise, 'The CIA—Licensed to Kill for Decades', *Los Angeles Times*, 22 July 2000. The manual is available on the website of the National Security Archive at George Washington University, accessed 1 March 2021, https://nsarchive2.gwu.edu /NSAEBB/NSAEBB4/ciaguat2.html.

27. 'From Mind Control to Murder? How a Deadly Fall Revealed the CIA's Darkest Secrets', *The Guardian*, 6 September 2019.

28. Quoted in *Mother Jones*, February 1988, p 16.

38. Closing In on Nkrumah

1. Macey, *Frantz Fanon*, pp 483–487.

2. Quoted and discussed in Meaney, 'Frantz Fanon and the CIA Man', pp 988–990.

3. Ntumazah, *A Conversational Auto Biography*, p 381.

4. Milne, *Kwame Nkrumah: A Biography*, p 267.

5. Adamafio, *By Nkrumah's Side*, pp 103–107.

6. 'Nkrumah's Address to Freedom Fighters: Now is the Time to Win!', *New Age*, 14 June 1962.

7. Adamafio, *By Nkrumah's Side*, p 108.

8. 'August 1, 1962: Nkrumah Is Injured by an Attempt on His Life from a Bomb in Kulungugu', Ghana History Moments, Edward A Ulzen Memorial Foundation, 1 August 2017, www.eaumf.org/ejm-blog/2017/8/1/august-1st-1962-nkrumah-is -injured-by-an-attempt-on-his-life-from-a-bomb-in-kulungugu.

9. Christenson, ed, *Political Trials in History*, pp 3–5; Milne, *Kwame Nkrumah*, p 172.

10. Montgomery, 'The Eyes of the World Were Watching', p 181.

11. Lloyd Garrison, 'Portrait of Nkrumah as Dictator', *New York Times*, 3 May 1964.

12. Angelou, *All God's Children Need Travelling Shoes*, pp 86–90.

13. Biney, 'Kwame Nkrumah', p 174.

14. Mahoney, interviewed by William W Moss, 14 May 1975.

15. Gerard and Kuklick, *Death in the Congo*, p 91.

16. Marais, *Kwame Nkrumah*, p 92.

17. A W Snelling, 'Another Anti-Nkrumah Plot', 25 March 1965, TNA, PREM 13/2677.

18. Frederick, *Ten First Ladies of the World*, p 135.

19. Marais, *Kwame Nkrumah*, pp 91–92.

20. Powell, *Private Secretary*, p 194.

21. Margaret Monyani, 'One Party State: Is It Good or Bad for Governance?', E-International Relations, 25 May 2018, p 1, www.e-ir.info/2018/05/25/one -party-state-is-it-good-or-bad-for-governance/.

22. Quaidoo, 'The United States and the Overthrow of Kwame Nkrumah', p 70.

23. Amamoo, *Ghana: 50 Years of Independence*, p 146.

24. 'Special Report: The Leftward Trend in Ghana', 17 January 1964, CIA, CREST, CIA Office of Current Intelligence, CIA-RDP79-00927A004300080004-5.

25. 'Letters to *The Times*', 'Dodd Evaluates Nkrumah', *New York Times*, 24 July 1963.

26. Broda, *Scientist Spies*, pp xvi–xvii, 295.

27. 'Atom Spy to Be Professor in Ghana', *New York Times*, 10 January 1962.

28. Broda, *Scientist Spies*, p 288.

29. Minute, R T Reed (14/10/53), TNA, KV/2/2222; discussed in Brown, 'The Viennese Connection', p 187.

30. Narrative and quotations in this passage about Paul Robeson come from Robeson Jr, *The Undiscovered Paul Robeson: Quest for Freedom 1939–1976*, pp 327, 308, 311–312, 321.

31. Information about the experiments at the Allan Memorial Institute of McGill University in Montreal has since emerged, provoking strong condemnation for their cruelty and dishonesty. See for example Kwabena Oduro, 'Survivors of the Montreal Experiments at Allan Memorial Institute Rally for Justice', *Global News*, 19 September 2020. https://globalnews.ca/news/7346181/montreal-experiments-allen-memorial-institute/.

32. Tom Rhodes, 'US Poisoned Paul Robeson with Mind-Bending Drug', *Sunday Times*, 14 March 1999.

33. Quoted in Robeson Jr, *The Undiscovered Paul Robeson: Quest for Freedom 1939–1976*, p 309.

34. Rhodes, 'US Poisoned Paul Robeson with Mind-Bending Drug'.

35. Mahoney, *JFK*, p 235.

36. 'A Cry from the Heart', Alexander to Ankrah, 22 September 1961, reproduced as Annex D in Alexander, *African Tightrope*, pp 147–148.

37. *FRUS*, 1958–1960, vol 24, *Africa*, document 236, https://history.state.gov/historicaldocuments/frus1964-68v24/d236.

38. Garrison, 'Portrait of Nkrumah as Dictator'.

39. Lasky, *Africa for Beginners*, pp 110–111, 64, 103; Gary Gappert, 'Review of *Africa for Beginners*', *Saturday Review*, 30 March 1963.

40. *FRUS*, 1964–1968, vol 24, *Africa*, document 237, https://history.state.gov/historicaldocuments/frus1964-68v24/d237.

41. Minute by [illegible signature], 22 September [1964], TNA, DO 195/416.

42. Sanchia Berg, '"Fake News" Sent Out by Government Department', *BBC News*, 18 March 2019, www.bbc.co.uk/news/uk-politics-47571253.

43. Minute by C Duke, 15 July 1964, TNA, DO 195/416.

44. As discussed and quoted in Marable, *Malcolm X*, pp 315–317. The speech is given in full here: 'Malcolm X at University of Ghana (May 13, 1964)', *Malcolm X* (blog), accessed 7 April 2021, http://malcolmxfiles.blogspot.com/2013/07/university-of-ghana-may-13-1964_1.html.

45. Malcolm X, *The Autobiography*, p 405.

46. *Ibid*, p 406.

47. The name of the deputy chief of the CIA's Africa Division is redacted from the memorandum: '[name not declassified]'. *FRUS*, 1964–1968, vol 24, *Africa*, document 251, https://history.state.gov/historicaldocuments/frus1964-68v24/d251.

48. A W Snelling, Minute, 25 March 1965, TNA, PREM 13/2677.

49. *FRUS*, 1964–1968, vol 24, *Africa*, document 253, https://history.state.gov/historicaldocuments/frus1964-68v24/d253.

50. Marais, *Kwame Nkrumah*, p 92.

51. 'Proposed Coup Against President Nkrumah', n.d. [1965], TNA, PREM 13/2677.

52. Snelling, Minute, 25 March 1965.

53. Marais, *Kwame Nkrumah*, p 92.

54. Nkrumah, *Neo-colonialism*, pp 89 and 104.

55. Robert P Smith, interviewed by Charles Stuart Kennedy, 28 February 1989.

56. *FRUS*, 1964–1968, vol 24, *Africa*, document 256, https://history.state.gov /historicaldocuments/frus1964-68v24/d256.

39. 'One Step Backward. We Shall Take Two Forward'

1. Amuzu, 'Nuclear Option for Ghana', pp 282–283.

2. Nkrumah, *Dark Days in Ghana*, p 49.

3. Robert P Smith, interviewed by Charles Stuart Kennedy, 28 February 1989.

4. 'Genoveva Esther Marais: The Woman Rumoured to be Nkrumah's Secret Lover', *Braperucci*, 29 April 2020, https://braperucci.africa/about-us/.

5. Milne, *Kwame Nkrumah: A Biography*, pp 180–181.

6. *FRUS*, 1964–1968, vol 24, *Africa*, document 260, https://history.state.gov /historicaldocuments/frus1964-68v24/d260.

7. Stockwell, *In Search of Enemies*, p 201, footnote.

8. Seymour Hersh, 'CIA Said to Have Aided Plotters Who Overthrew Nkrumah in Ghana', *New York Times*, 9 May 1978.

9. Kessler, *Inside the CIA*, p 14.

10. Discussed and quoted in Milne, *Kwame Nkrumah: A Biography*, pp 187-188; Nkrumah, *Dark Days in Ghana*, p 19; and quoted in Milne, comp, *Kwame Nkrumah: The Conakry Years*, pp 135, 121.

11. Quoted in *ibid*, pp 19, 147–149.

12. Marais, *Kwame Nkrumah*, p 126.

13. Biney, *The Political and Social Thought of Kwame Nkrumah*, p 160; the correspondence between Fathia Nkrumah and Kwame Nkrumah quoted in Milne, comp, *Kwame Nkrumah: The Conakry Years*, reveal their affection and concerns for each other and the children.

14. Milne, *Kwame Nkrumah: A Biography*, p 248.

15. 'JM's Notebook: 27 February–19 March 1967', in Milne, comp, *Kwame Nkrumah: The Conakry Years*, p 126.

16. Letter from June Milne to Nkrumah, 12 May 1968, quoted in *ibid*, p 233.

17. Milne, *Kwame Nkrumah: A Biography*, p 244.

18. Quoted in Kim Yi Dionne, 'Amílcar Cabral's Life as a Pan-Africanist, Anti-Colonial Revolutionary Still Inspires', *Washington Post*, 21 June 2019, www .washingtonpost.com/politics/2019/06/21/amlcar-cabrals-life-pan-africanist-anti -colonial-revolutionary-still-inspires-today/.

19. Quoted in Milne, comp, *Kwame Nkrumah: The Conakry Years*, p 135.

20. Nkrumah, Author's Note, 1 June 1969, p ix, *Challenge of the Congo*, 1969 ed.

21. Nkrumah, *Dark Days in Ghana*, p 156.

22. Quoted in Milne, comp, *Kwame Nkrumah: The Conakry Years*, p 381.

23. Milne, *Kwame Nkrumah: A Biography*, p 257.

24. *Ibid*, pp 255–262.

25. *Ibid*, pp 259 and 262.

26. 'Watch Nkrumah's Funerals in Guinea and Ghana Which Have Been Wiped from History', *GhanaWeb*, 27 April 2020, www.ghanaweb.com/GhanaHomePage /NewsArchive/Watch-Nkrumah-s-funerals-in-Guinea-and-Ghana-which-have -been-wiped-from-history-935716.

27. Milne, *Kwame Nkrumah: A Biography*, p 267.

28. *Ibid*, p 245.

29. Ntumazah, *A Conversational Auto Biography*, p 382.

30. Quoted in Inusah Mohammed, 'Nkrumah, Ghana and Its Independence in the Words of the Greats', *MyJoy Online*, 14 March 2017, www.myjoyonline.com /opinion/nkrumah-ghana-and-its-independence-in-the-words-of-the-greats/.

40. The Dead Hand

1. Nkrumah, *Dark Days in Ghana*, p 50.

2. Stockwell, *In Search of Enemies*, p 168.

3. Quoted in United States Congress, Senate, *Alleged Assassination Plots Involving Foreign Leaders*, p 39.

4. The version is headed 'Draft: October 6, 1975 Frederick D. Baron', SSCIA, Report, 'Select Committee—Assassination Report (Updated Oct 16, 1975)', 09/01/1975, NARA, Record Number 157-10005-10297.

5. Georges Nzongola-Ntalaja to the UK First Tier Tribunal (Information Rights), 29 August 2010, in support of an appeal by Susan Williams. Williams was appealing a decision by the UK information commissioner that it was lawful for the UK National Archives to withhold specific information relating to the Congo in 1960. The appeal against the commissioner's decision was taken up by the UK Freedom of Information Campaign in 2010 with a submission to the tribunal under the heading 'Does the public interest test include the benefit to the public overseas?' See www.cfoi.org.uk/pdf/cfoiEA20100100.pdf.

6. 'In 1996, historian David Gibbs questioned the accuracy of Volume XX which "virtually excludes" any mention of covert operations in the Congo. Stephen Weissman cast further doubt on the integrity of the public record with his article on the CIA's role in the "extraordinary rendition" of Lumumba, turning him over to those known to have wanted him dead'. Namikas, 'Review of *Foreign Relations of the United States, 1964–1968, Volume XXIII, Congo, 1960–1968*'.

7. *Ibid*.

8. Quoted in United States Congress, Senate, *Alleged Assassination Plots Involving Foreign Leaders*, pp 20–21.

9. 'DOCUMENT RE QJWIN', CIA, JFK, NARA, Record Number 104-10059 -10223.

10. Rex Bradford, 'Missing Church Committee Transcripts', Mary Ferrell Foundation, 2016, www.maryferrell.org/pages/Featured_Missing_Church_Committee _Transcripts.html.

11. Agency Release Panel, CIA, Washington to Jeremy Bigwood, 22 September 2020, Susan Williams Private Papers. The quotation is taken from the following

paragraph: 'In accordance with Section 3.6(a) of Executive Order 13526, the CIA can neither confirm nor deny the existence or nonexistence of records responsive to your request. The fact of the existence or nonexistence of such records is itself currently and properly classified and is [*sic*] intelligence sources and methods information protected from disclosure by Section 6 of the CIA Act of 1949, as amended, and Section 102A(i) (l) of the National Security Act of 1947, as amended. Therefore, your request is denied pursuant to FOIA exemptions (b)(1) and (b)(3)'.

12. Namikas, 'Review of *Foreign Relations of the United States, 1964–1968, Volume XXIII, Congo, 1960–1968*'.

13. Weissman, 'What Really Happened in the Congo'.

14. Bissell, *Reflections of a Cold Warrior*, p 142.

15. Whipple, *The Spymasters*, p 8.

16. Agee, *Inside the Company*, p 10.

17. Amamoo, *My African Journey*, pp 268–270 and 104.

18. Devlin took over from Mark Garsin, who held the position from 1961 until 1975, when he was expelled from the Congo by Mobutu. Susan Mazur, 'Tempelsman's Man Weighs In on the Murder of Patrice Lumumba', *CounterPunch*, 29 January 2005, www.counterpunch.org/2005/01/29/tempelsman-s-man-weighs-in -on-the-murder-of-patrice-lumumba.

19. Stockwell, *In Search of Enemies*, p 137.

20. Dayal, *Mission for Hammarskjöld*, p 297.

21. Asante, *The History of Africa*, p xiii.

22. Obama, *Dreams from My Father*, p 300.

23. The speech is here: Grayzone, 'Ex-CIA Director Pompeo: "We Lied, We Cheated, We Stole"'. The author is grateful to Jeremy Bigwood for alerting her to this statement by Pompeo.

24. Nzongola-Ntalaja, 'Revisiting the 1958 All-African People's Conference: The Unfinished Business of Liberation and Transformation', University of Ghana in Accra, 5–8 December 2018, p 3. The text of the address was shared by Professor Nzongola-Ntalaja with the author on 29 September 2020 by email.

25. *All African People's Conference*, leaflet, 1958, W E B Du Bois Papers (MS 312), http://credo.library.umass.edu/view/pageturn/mums312-b148-i017/#page/1/mode/1up.

26. Nzongola-Ntalaja, 'Revisiting the 1958 All-African People's Conference', pp 3–4.

27. Cameron Duodu, 'Patrice Lumumba: The Rise and Assassination of an African Patriot', *Pambazuka News*, 20 January 2011, www.pambazuka.org/governance /patrice-lumumba-rise-and-assassination-african-patriot.

28. Mutombo Nkulu-N'Sengha to the author by telephone interview in a discussion of his essay, 'African Traditional Religions', 14 November 2020.

29. Bissell, *Reflections of a Cold Warrior*, p 142; emphasis added.

30. Nzongola-Ntalaja, *The Congo from Leopold to Kabila*, p 139.

31. Kisangani and Bobb, *Historical Dictionary of the Democratic Republic of the Congo*, Third Edition, pp lxvi, 81; Weiss, quoted in Woodrow Wilson International Center, *The Congo Crisis, 1960–1961*, p 118.

32. Ewens, *Congo Colossus*, p 102.

33. Ikambana, *Mobutu's Totalitarian Political System*, p 56.

34. Van Reybrouck, *Congo*, pp 335–340.

SELECTED BIBLIOGRAPHY

Books and Reports

Adamafio, Tawia. *By Nkrumah's Side: The Labour and the Wounds*. Accra: Westcoast Publishing House, in association with Rex Collings, London, 1982.

Africa Research Group. *African Studies in America: The Extended Family*. Cambridge, Massachusetts: Africa Research Group, 1969.

Agee, Philip. *Inside the Company: CIA Diary*. 1975; Harmondsworth, UK: Penguin, 1976.

Ahlman, Jeffrey S. *Living with Nkrumahism: Nation, State, and Pan-Africanism in Ghana*. Athens: Ohio University Press, 2017.

Akyeampong, Emmanuel Kwaku. *Between the Sea and the Lagoon: An Eco-social History of the Anlo of Southeastern Ghana c.1850 to Recent Times*. Oxford, UK: James Currey, 2001.

Akyeampong, Emmanuel K, and Henry Louis Gates Jr, eds. *Dictionary of African Biography, Vols* 1–6. London: Oxford University Press, 2011.

Albright, David E. *Communism in Africa*. Bloomington: Indiana University Press, 1980.

Alexander, Henry Templer. *African Tightrope: My Two Years as Nkrumah's Chief of Staff*. London: Pall Mall Press, 1965.

Amamoo, Joseph Godson. *Ghana: 50 Years of Independence*. Bloomington, Indiana: Xlibris, 2013.

———. *The Ghanaian Revolution*. London: Jafint Co., 1988.

———. *My African Journey*. Bloomington, Indiana: Xlibris, 2014.

———. *The New Ghana: The Birth of a Nation*. 1958; Lincoln, Nebraska: Authors Choice Press, 2000.

Ampiah, Kweku. *The Political and Moral Imperatives of the Bandung Conference of 1955: The Reactions of the US, UK and Japan*. Folkestone, UK: Global Oriental, 2007.

Amuzu, Josef K A. *First World, Third World: A Collection of Essays on Science, the Nuclear Threat and Energy in the Third World*. Accra: Ghana Universities Press, 1988.

Anderson, David, and David Killingray, eds. *Policing and Decolonisation: Politics, Nationalism, and the Police, 1917–65*. Manchester, UK: Manchester University Press, 1992.

Andrew, Christopher M, and Vasili Mitrokhin. *The Mitrokhin Archive II: The KGB and the World*. London: Allen Lane, 2005.

Angelou, Maya. *All God's Children Need Travelling Shoes*. 1986; London: Virago Press, 2008.

———. *The Heart of a Woman*. 1981; London: Virago Press, 2008.

———. *A Song Flung Up to Heaven*. 2002; London: Virago Press, 2008.

Anthony, David Henry, III. *Max Yergan: Race Man, Internationalist, Cold Warrior.* New York: New York University Press, 2006.

Anyaso Claudia E, ed. *Fifty Years of U.S. Africa Policy: Reflections of Assistant Secretaries of African Affairs and U.S. Embassy Officials.* Arlington, Virginia: Xlibris, 2011.

Apter, David E. *Ghana in Transition.* 1963; 2nd rev ed, Princeton, New Jersey: Princeton University Press, 1972.

Arkhurst, Frederick S, ed. *U.S. Policy Toward Africa.* New York: Praeger Publishers, 1974.

Armah, Kwesi. *Peace Without Power: Ghana's Foreign Policy 1957–1966.* Accra: Ghana Universities Press, 2004.

Arndt, Richard T. *The First Resort of Kings: American Cultural Diplomacy in the Twentieth Century.* Washington, DC: Potomac Books, 2005.

Asante, Molefi Kete. *The History of Africa: The Quest for Eternal Harmony.* London: Routledge, 2007.

Atangana, Martin. *The End of French Rule in Cameroon.* Lanham, Maryland: University Press of America, 2010.

Attwood, William. *The Reds and the Blacks: A Personal Adventure.* London: Hutchinson, 1967.

Austin, Dennis, and Robin Luckham, eds. *Politicians and Soldiers in Ghana, 1966–1972.* London: Frank Cass, 1975.

Azaransky, Sarah. *The Dream Is Freedom: Pauli Murray and American Democratic Faith.* New York: Oxford University Press, 2011.

Baker, Colin. *Chipembere: The Missing Years.* Zomba, Malawi: Kachere Series, 2006.

———. *State of Emergency: Crisis in Central Africa, Nyasaland 1959–1960.* London: Tauris Academic Studies, I B Tauris Publishers, 1997.

Baker, Nicholson. *Baseless: My Search for Secrets in the Ruins of the Freedom of Information Act.* New York: Penguin Press, 2020.

Baker, Raymond D. *Historical Highlights of Andrews AFB, 1942–1989.* Andrews AFB, Maryland: Office of History, 1776th Air Base Wing, 1990.

Barbé, Luc. *België En de Bom: De Rol van België in de Proliferatie van Kernwapens.* N.p., 2012.

Batsa, Kofi. *The Spark: From Kwame Nkrumah to Hilla Limann.* London: Rex Collings, 1985.

Baynham, Simon. *The Military and Politics in Nkrumah's Ghana.* Boulder, Colorado: Westview Press, 1988.

Belgian House of Representatives. *Enquête Parlementaire visant à déterminer les circonstances exactes de l'assassinat de Patrice Lumumba et l'implication éventuelle des responsables politiques belges dans celui-ci', Rapport Fait au Nom de la Commission d'Enquête par Mm. Daniel Bacquelaine et Ferdy Willems et Mme Marie-Thérèse Coenen.* Doc 50 0312/006, 16 November 2001. www.lachambre.be/FLWB/PDF/50/0312/50K0312006.pdf.

Belgian Information Center. *Belgian Congo at War.* New York: Belgian Information Center, 1942.

Bell-Scott, Patricia. *The Firebrand and the First Lady.* New York: Knopf, 2016.

Benson, Peter. *Black Orpheus, Transition, and Modern Cultural Awakening in Africa.* Berkeley: University of California Press, 1986.

Bernstein, Richard B. *Thomas Jefferson*. Oxford: Oxford University Press, 2003.

Biney, Ama. *The Political and Social Thought of Kwame Nkrumah*. New York: Palgrave Macmillan, 2011.

Bing, Geoffrey. *Reap the Whirlwind: An Account of Kwame Nkrumah's Ghana from 1950 to 1966*. London: MacGibbon and Kee, 1968.

Bird, Kai. *The Chairman: John J. McCloy: The Making of the American Establishment*. New York: Simon and Schuster, 1992.

Birmingham, David. *Kwame Nkrumah*. London: Sphere Books, 1990.

Bissell, Richard M, Jr, with Jonathan E Lewis and Frances T Pudlo. *Reflections of a Cold Warrior: From Yalta to the Bay of Pigs*. New Haven, Connecticut: Yale University Press, 1996.

Black, Conrad. *Richard Milhous Nixon: The Invincible Quest*. London: Quercus, 2007.

Blackmer, Donald L M. *The MIT Center for International Studies: The Founding Years, 1951–1969*. Cambridge, Massachusetts: MIT Press, 2002.

Blackmon, Douglas A. *Slavery by Another Name: The Re-Enslavement of Black Americans from the Civil War to World War Two*. New York: Anchor Books, 2008.

Blouin, Andrée, in collaboration with Jean MacKellar. *My Country, Africa: Autobiography of the Black Pasionaria*. New York: Praeger Publishers, 1983.

Blum, William. *Killing Hope: US Military and CIA Interventions since World War II*. London: Zed Books, 2003.

Borstelmann, Thomas. *Apartheid's Reluctant Uncle: The United States and Southern Africa in the Early Cold War*. Oxford: Oxford University Press, 1993.

———. *The Cold War and the Color Line: American Race Relations in the Global Arena*. Cambridge, Massachusetts: Harvard University Press, 2003.

Botwe-Asamoah, Kwame. *Kwame Nkrumah's Politico-Cultural Thought and Policies: An African-Centered Paradigm for the Second Phase of the African Revolution*. New York: Routledge, 2005.

Bouwer, Karen. *Gender and Decolonization in the Congo: The Legacy of Patrice Lumumba*. New York: Palgrave Macmillan, 2010.

Brion, René, and Jean-Louis Moreau. *De La Mine à Mars: La Genèse d'Umicore*. Tielt, Belgium: Umicore et Editions Lannoo, 2006.

Broda, Paul. *Scientist Spies: A Memoir of My Three Parents and the Atom Bomb*. Kibworth Beauchamp, UK: Matador, 2011.

Brown, Ryan. *A Native of Nowhere: The Life of Nat Nakasa*. Sunnyside, Auckland Park, South Africa: Jacana, 2013.

Burden, Wendy. *Dead End Gene Pool: A Memoir*. 2010; New York: Gotham Books, 2011.

Burden, William A M. *Peggy and I: A Life Too Busy for a Dull Moment*. 1982; New York: n.p., 1983.

Buser, Hans. *In Ghana at Independence: Stories of a Swiss Salesman*. Basel, Switzerland: Basler Afrika Bibliographien, 2010.

Byrnes, James F. *Speaking Frankly*. London: Heinemann, 1945.

Calder, Ritchie. *Agony of the Congo*. London: Victor Gollancz, 1961.

Campbell, Alexander. *The Heart of Africa*. London: Longmans, Green, 1954.

Carew, Anthony, Michel Dreyfus, Geert Van Goethem, Rebecca Gumbrell-McCormick, Marcel van der Linden, eds. *The International Confederation of Free Trade Unions*. Bern, Switzerland: Peter Lang, 2000.

Cartlan, Jean. *Barbara Ward*. London: Continuum UK, 2010.

Castro, Fidel. *My Life*. Edited by Ignacio Ramonet. Translated by Andrew Hurley. London: Penguin, 2007.

Cervenka, Zdenek, and Barbara Rogers. *The Nuclear Axis: Secret Collaboration Between West Germany and South Africa*. London: Julian Friedmann Books, 1978.

Chafe, William H. *Never Stop Running: Allard Lowenstein and the Struggle to Save American Liberalism*. New York: Basic Books, 1993.

Chiume, M W Kanyama. *Kwacha: An Autobiography*. Nairobi: East African Publishing House, 1975.

Christenson, Ron, ed. *Political Trials in History: From Antiquity to the Present*. New Brunswick, New Jersey: Transaction Publishers, 1991.

Church, Bethine. *A Lifelong Affair: My Passion for People and Politics*. Washington, DC: Francis Press, 2003.

Clostermann, Pierre. *The Big Show: The Greatest Pilot's Story of World War II*. 1951; London: Cassell Military Paperbacks, 2004.

Coates, Kenneth S, ed. *'Collateral Damage' or Unlawful Killings? The Amnesty Report*. Nottingham, UK: Spokesman, 2000.

Colby, Gerard, with Charlotte Dennett. *Thy Will Be Done: The Conquest of the Amazon: Nelson Rockefeller and Evangelism in the Age of Oil*. New York: HarperCollins, 1995.

Colvin, Ian. *The Rise and Fall of Moise Tshombe: A Biography*. London: Leslie Frewin, 1968.

Conference of Independent African States. *Speeches Delivered at the Inaugural Session*. Accra: Government Printer, 1958.

Corera, Gordon. *The Art of Betrayal: The Secret History of MI6*. London: Weidenfeld and Nicolson, 2012.

Couch, William T. *Collier's 1956 Year Book: An Encyclopaedic Supplement and Review of National and International Events 1955*. New York: P F Collier and Son, 1956.

Cowan, E A. *Evolution of Trade Unionism in Ghana*. Accra, Ghana: Trades Union Congress, n.d.

Cummings, Richard. *The Pied Piper: Allard K. Lowenstein and the Liberal Dream*. New York: Grove Press, 1985.

Daly, Sara, John Parachini, and William Rosenau. *Aum Shinrikyo, Al Qaeda, and the Kinshasa Reactor: Implications of Three Case Studies for Combating Nuclear Terrorism*. Santa Monica, California: RAND Corporation, 2005.

Danquah, Joseph Boakye. *You Always Reap What You Sow: Dr Danquah's Last Letter to K A Gbedemah*. Accra: George Boakie Publishing, 1969.

Davidson, Basil. *Black Star: A View of the Life and Times of Kwame Nkrumah*. London: Allen Lane, 1973.

Davies, Ioan. *African Trade Unions*. Harmondsworth, UK: Penguin, 1966.

Davies, Philip H J, and Kristian C Gustafson, eds. *Intelligence Elsewhere*. Washington, DC: Georgetown University Press, 2013.

Davis, Caroline. *African Literature and the CIA: Networks of Authorship and Publishing*. Cambridge, UK: Cambridge University Press, 2020.

Dayal, Rajeshwar. *A Life of Our Times*. London: Sangam, 1998.

———. *Mission for Hammarskjöld: The Congo Crisis*. London: Oxford University Press, 1976.

Dean, William Patrick. *The ATL-98 Carvair: A Comprehensive History of the Aircraft and All 21 Airframes*. Jefferson, North Carolina: McFarland and Company, 2008.

Dei-Anang, Michael. *The Administration of Ghana's Foreign Relations 1957–1965: A Personal Memoir*. London, published for the Institute of Commonwealth Studies: Athlone Press, 1975.

de la Torre, Miguel A, ed. *The Hope of Liberation in World Religions*. Waco, Texas: Baylor University Press, 2008.

Deubel, Tara F, Scott M Youngstedt, and Helen Tissieres, eds. *Saharan Crossroads: Exploring Historical, Cultural, and Artistic Linkages Between North and West Africa*. Newcastle upon Tyne, UK: Cambridge Scholars Publishing, 2014.

Devlin, Larry. *Chief of Station, Congo: Fighting the Cold War in a Hot Zone*. New York: PublicAffairs, 2007.

De Witte, Ludo. *L'ascension de Mobutu: Comment la Belgique et les USA ont fabriqué un dictateur*. Brussels: Investig'Action, 2017.

———. *The Assassination of Lumumba*. Translated by Ann Wright and Renée Fenby. 1999 (*De Moord op Lumumba*); London: Verso, 2001.

Doyle, David W. *True Men and Traitors: From the OSS to the CIA, My Life in the Shadows*. Chichester, UK: John Wiley and Sons, 2001.

Driver, C J. *Patrick Duncan*. London: Heinemann, 1980.

Duberman, Martin Bauml. *Paul Robeson*. London: Bodley Head, 1989.

Dunn, Kevin C. *Imagining the Congo: The International Relations of Identity*. New York: Palgrave Macmillan, 2003.

Dworkin, Ira. *Congo Love Song: African American Culture and the Crisis of the Colonial State*. Chapel Hill: University of North Carolina Press, 2017.

Eckes, Alfred E, Jr. *The United States and the Global Struggle for Minerals*. Austin: University of Texas Press, 1979.

Eisenberg, Dennis, Eli Landau, and Menahem Portugali. *Operation Uranium Ship*. London: Corgi, 1978.

Eisenhower, Dwight D. *Waging Peace 1956–1961: The White House Years*, Vol 2. New York: Doubleday, 1965.

Escalante, Fabian. *The Cuba Project: CIA Covert Operations 1959–1962*. Translated by Maxine Shaw. Melbourne: Ocean Press, 2004.

Ewens, Graeme. *Africa O-Ye!* New York: Da Capo, 1991.

———. *Congo Colossus: The Life and Legacy of Franco and OK Jazz*. North Walsham, UK: Buku Press, 1994.

Fage, John Donnelly, and Roland Oliver, eds. *The Cambridge History of Africa*, vols 1–8. Cambridge, UK: Cambridge University Press, 1975–1986.

Fanon, Frantz. *Pour la révolution africaine: Écrits politiques*. Paris: François Maspero, 1964.

Fleckner, Mads, and John Avery. *Congo Uranium and the Tragedy of Hiroshima*. 55th Pugwash Conference, Hiroshima, Japan. July 2005. http://s2.e-monsite.com/2010/05/31/82250333congo-uranium-pdf.pdf.

Frederick, Pauline. *Ten First Ladies of the World*. New York: Meredith Press, 1967.

Freemantle, Brian. *CIA*. London: Michael Joseph, 1983.

Friedman, Norman. *The Fifty-Year War: Conflict and Strategy in the Cold War*. Annapolis, Maryland: Naval Institute Press, 2000.

FRUS (Foreign Relations of the United States). 1951, vol 1, *National Security Affairs; Foreign Economic Policy*. Eds Neal H Petersen, Harriet D Schwar, Carl N Raether, John A Bernbaum and Ralph R Goodwin. 1979.

FRUS. 1952–1954, vol 11, *Africa and South Asia*, part 1. Eds Paul Claussen, Joan M Lee, David W Mabon, Nina J Noring, Carl N Raether, William F Sanford, Stanley Shaloff, William Z Slany, Louis J Smith. General ed John P Glennon. 1983.

FRUS. 1958–1960, vol 14, *Africa*. Eds Harriet Dashiell Schwar and Stanley Shaloff. 1992.

FRUS. 1961–1963, vol 9, *Foreign Economic Policy*. Eds Evans Gerakas, David S Patterson, William F Sanford Jr, Carolyn B Yee. General ed Glenn W LaFantasie. 1995.

FRUS. 1961–1963, vol 20, *Congo Crisis*. Ed Harriet Dashiell Schwar. 1994.

FRUS. 1961–1963, vol 21, *Africa*. Eds Nina D Howland, Glen W LaFantasie. 1995.

FRUS. 1964–1968, vol 23, *Congo, 1960–1968*. Eds Nina D Howald, David C Humphrey and Harriet D Schwar. 2013.

FRUS. 1964–1968, vol 24, *Africa*. Eds Nina D Howland. 1999.

Fursenko, A A, and Timothy J Naftali. *Khrushchev's Cold War: The Inside Story of an American Adversary*. New York: Norton, 2007.

Gaines, Kevin Kelly. *American Africans in Ghana: Black Expatriates and the Civil Rights Era*. Chapel Hill: University of North Carolina Press, 2008.

Garrow, David J. *Bearing the Cross: Martin Luther King, Jr., and the Southern Christian Leadership Conference*. New York: William Morrow, 1986.

George, Edward. *The Cuban Intervention in Angola, 1965–1991: From Che Guevara to Cuito Cuanavale*. London: Frank Cass, 2012.

Gerard, Emmanuel, and Bruce Kuklick. *Death in the Congo: Murdering Patrice Lumumba*. Cambridge, Massachusetts: Harvard University Press, 2015.

Gerard-Libois, J. *Sécession au Katanga*. Bruxelles: Centre de Recherche e d'Information Socio-Politiques CRISP, n.d.

Gerdan, Eric. *Dossier A . . . Comme Armes*. Paris: Alain Moreau, 1975.

Gewald, J B. *Hands off Africa!!: An Overview and Analysis of the Ideological, Political and Socio-Economic Approaches to African Unity Expressed at the First All-African People's Conference Held in Accra, Ghana, in December 1958*. Leiden, Netherlands: African Studies Centre Library, 1990.

Gheerbrant, Alain. *Congo Noir et Blanc*. Paris: Gallimard, 1955.

Ghose, Sankar. *Jawaharlal Nehru: A Biography*. New Delhi: Allied Publishers, 1993.

Gibbs, David N. *The Political Economy of Third World Intervention: Mines, Money, and US Policy in the Congo Crisis*. Chicago: University of Chicago Press, 1991.

Gillon, Monseigneur Luc. *Servir: En actes et en vérité*. Paris: Editions Duculot, 1988.

Gizenga, Antoine. *Ma Vie et Mes Luttes*. Paris: L'Harmattan, 2011.

Gleijeses, Piero. *Conflicting Missions: Havana, Washington, and Africa, 1959–1976: Envisioning Cuba*. Chapel Hill: University of North Carolina Press, 2002.

———. *Visions of Freedom: Havana, Washington, Pretoria, and the Struggle for Southern Africa, 1976–1991*. Chapel Hill: University of North Carolina Press, 2013.

Golden, Daniel. *Spy Schools: How the CIA, FBI and Foreign Intelligence Secretly Exploit America's Universities*. New York: Henry Holt, 2017.

Goldsworthy, David. *Tom Mboya: The Man Kenya Wanted to Forget*. London: Heinemann, 1982.

Goodman, Michael S. *Spying on the Nuclear Bear: Anglo-American Intelligence and the Soviet Bomb*. Stanford Nuclear Age Series. Stanford, California: Stanford University Press, 2007.

Gordin, Michael D, Helen Tilley, and Gyan Prakash, eds. *Utopia/Dystopia: Conditions of Historical Possibility*. Princeton, New Jersey: Princeton University Press, 2010.

Graham, Thomas, Jr, and Keith A Hansen. *Preventing Catastrophe: The Use and Misuse of Intelligence in Efforts to Halt the Proliferation of Weapons of Mass Destruction*. Stanford, California: Stanford Security Studies, 2009.

Grilli, Matteo. *Nkrumaism and African Nationalism: Ghana's Pan-African Foreign Policy in the Age of Decolonization*. Cham, Switzerland: Palgrave Macmillan, 2018.

Grose, Peter. *Gentleman Spy: The Life of Allen Dulles*. 1994; London: André Deutsch, 1995.

Groves, Leslie Richard. *Now It Can Be Told: The Story of the Manhattan Project*. London: André Deutsch, 1963.

Gunther, John. *Inside Africa*. London: Hamish Hamilton, 1955.

Hadjor, Kofi Buenor. *Africa in an Era of Crisis*. Trenton, New Jersey: Africa World Press, 1990.

———. *Nkrumah and Ghana: The Dilemma of Post-Colonial Power*. 1988; Trenton, New Jersey: Africa World Press, 2003.

Hamrell, Sven, and Carl Gösta, eds. *The Soviet Bloc, China and Africa*. London: Pall Mall Press for the Scandinavian Institute of African Studies, 1964.

Hancock, Larry. *Nexus: The CIA and Political Assassination*. Southlake, Texas: JFK Lancer Productions and Publications, 2012.

Hayes, Paddy. *Queen of Spies: Daphne Park, Britain's Cold War Spy Master*. London: Duckworth Overlook, 2015.

Haynes, John Earl, Harvey Klehr and Alexander Vassiliev. *Spies: The Rise and Fall of the KGB in America*. New Haven, Connecticut: Yale University Press, 2009.

Hazzard, Shirley. *Countenance of Truth: The United Nations and the Waldheim Case*. 1990; London: Chatto and Windus, 1991.

Hecht, Gabrielle. *Being Nuclear: Africans and the Global Uranium Trade*. Cambridge, Massachusetts: MIT Press, 2012.

———, ed. *Entangled Geographies: Empire and Technopolitics in the Global Cold War*. Cambridge, Massachusetts: MIT Press, 2011.

———. *The Radiance of France: Nuclear Power and National Identity After World War II*. Cambridge, Massachusetts: MIT Press, 1998.

Hellström, Leif. *Fredsflygarna: FN-flyget i Kongo 1960–1964*. Stockholm: Freddy Stenboms Förlag, 2002.

Helmreich, Jonathan E. *Gathering Rare Ores: The Diplomacy of Uranium Acquisition, 1943–1954*. Princeton, New Jersey: Princeton University Press, 1986.

———. *United States Relations with Belgium and the Congo, 1940–1960*. Newark: University of Delaware Press, 1998.

Helms, Richard, and William Hood. *A Look over My Shoulder: A Life in the Central Intelligence Agency*. New York: Ballantine Books, 2004.

Hempstone, Smith. *Katanga Report*. London: Faber and Faber, 1962.

———. *Letters from Africa to the Institute of Current World Affairs, New York*. Vol 1, no 1-118: 6 November 1956 to 1 December 1958. Athens: The Association, 1956–1961.

———. *The New Africa*. London: Faber and Faber, 1961.

Henry, Charles P. *Ralph Bunche: Model Negro or American Other?* New York: New York University Press, 1999.

Herbstein, Denis. *White Lies: Canon Collins and the Secret War Against Apartheid*. Cape Town: HSRC Press, 2004.

Heymann, C David. *American Legacy: The Story of John and Caroline Kennedy*. New York: Atria Books, 2007.

Higginson, John. *A Working Class in the Making: Belgian Colonial Labor Policy, Private Enterprise, and the African Mineworker, 1907–1951*. Madison: University of Wisconsin Press, 1989.

Hochschild, Adam. *Half the Way Home: A Memoir of Father and Son*. London: Viking, 1996.

———. *King Leopold's Ghost: A Story of Greed, Terror and Heroism in Colonial Africa*. 1998; London: Macmillan, 1999.

Holden, Philip. *Autobiography and Decolonization: Modernity, Masculinity, and the Nation-State*. Madison: University of Wisconsin Press, 2008.

Holland, Robert, ed. *Emergencies and Disorder in the European Empires After 1945*. London: F Cass, 1994.

Holm, Richard L. *The American Agent: My Life in the CIA*. London: St Ermin's Press, 2003.

Horne, Gerald. *Black and Red: W. E. B. Du Bois and the Afro-American Response to the Cold War, 1944–1963*. New York: State University of New York Press, 1986.

———. *Race Woman: The Lives of Shirley Graham Du Bois*. New York: New York University Press, 2000.

Hoskyns, Catherine. *The Congo Since Independence: January 1960–December 1961*. London: Oxford University Press, 1965.

Houser, George M. *No One Can Stop the Rain: Glimpses of Africa's Freedom Struggle*. New York: Pilgrim Press, 1989.

Hughes, Langston, ed. *An African Treasury*. London: Victor Gollancz, 1961.

Hunton, Dorothy. *Alphaeus Hunton: The Unsung Valiant*. D K Hunton, 1986.

Hunton, W Alphaeus. *Decision in Africa: Sources of Current Conflict*. 1957; London: John Calder, 1959.

Hutchinson, Alfred. *Road to Ghana*. London: Victor Gollancz, 1960.

Hutchinson, Hazel. *The Other Side of the Road*. Guildford, UK: Grosvenor House Publishing, 2010.

Iber, Patrick. *Neither Peace nor Freedom: The Cultural Cold War in Latin America*. Cambridge, Massachusetts: Harvard University Press, 2015.

Ignat'ev, Oleg Konstantinovich. *Secret Weapon in Africa*. Translated by David Fidlon. Moscow: Progress Publishers, 1977.

Ikambana, Peta. *Mobutu's Totalitarian Political System: An Afrocentric Analysis*. London: Routledge, 2007.

International Atomic Energy Agency (IAEA). *Annual Report of the Board of Governors to the General Conference, 1 July 1959–30 June 1960*. Vienna: IAEA, July 1960. www.iaea.org/sites/default/files/gc/gc04-114_en.pdf.

———. *Research Reactors in Africa*. Vienna: IAEA, November 2011. www.iaea.org/sites/default/files/18/09/research-reactors-in-africa.pdf.

James, C L R. *Nkrumah and the Ghana Revolution*. London: Allison and Busby, 1977.

James, Leslie. *George Padmore and Decolonization from Below: Pan-Africanism, the Cold War, and the End of Empire*. London: Palgrave Macmillan, 2015.

Jeffreys-Jones, Rhodri. *The CIA and American Democracy*. 3rd ed. New Haven, Connecticut: Yale University Press, 1989.

Johnson, Loch K, ed. *Strategic Intelligence 1: Understanding the Hidden Side of Government*. Westport, Connecticut: Praeger Security International, 2007.

Johnson, Walter, ed. *The Papers of Adlai E. Stevenson*. Vol 6. Boston: Little, Brown, 1976.

Jolis, Albert. *A Clutch of Reds and Diamonds: A Twentieth Century Odyssey*. Boulder, Colorado: East European Monographs, dist. by Columbia University Press, New York, 1996.

July, Robert W. *An African Voice: The Role of the Humanities in African Independence*. Durham, North Carolina: Duke University Press, 1987.

Kaba, Lansiné. *Kwame Nkrumah and the Dream of African Unity*. Translation from French. 1991; Brooklyn, New York: Diasporic Africa Press, 2017.

Kamitatu, Cleophas. *La Grande Mystification du Congo-Kinshasa, Les Crimes de Mobutu*. Paris: François Maspero, 1971.

Kanza, Thomas. *Conflict in the Congo: The Rise and Fall of Lumumba*. Harmondsworth, UK: Penguin, 1972.

Karlow, S Peter. *Targeted by the CIA: An Intelligence Professional Speaks Out on the Scandal That Turned the CIA Upside Down*. Nashville, Tennessee: Turner Publishing Company, 2001.

Kashamura, Anicet. *De Lumumba aux colonels*. Paris: Buchet-Chastel, 1966.

Kay, Sean. *Global Security in the Twenty-First Century: The Quest for Power and the Search for Peace*. Oxford, UK: Rowman and Littlefield, 2006.

Kelley, Robin D G. *Africa Speaks, America Answers: Modern Jazz in Revolutionary Times*. Cambridge, Massachusetts: Harvard University Press, 2012.

Kelley, Robin D G, and Stephen Tuck, eds. *The Other Special Relationship: Race, Rights, and Riots in Britain and the United States*. Abingdon, UK: Palgrave Macmillan, 2015.

Kelly, Sean. *America's Tyrant: The CIA and Mobutu of Zaire*. Washington, DC: American University Press, 1993.

Kessler, Ronald. *Inside the CIA*. New York: Pocket Books, 2014.

Kgosana, Philip Ata. *Lest We Forget*. Braamfontein, South Africa: Skotaville Publishers, 1988.

Khazanov, A M. *Agostinho Neto*. Translated by Cynthia Carlile. Moscow: Progress Publishers, 1986.

Killingray, David, ed. *Africans in Britain*. London: Frank Cass, 1994.

King, Martin Luther, Jr. Edited by Clayborne Carson, Susan Carson, Adrienne Clay, Virginia Shadron, Kieran Taylor. *The Papers of Martin Luther King, Jr.* Vol 4, *Symbol of the Movement, January 1957–December 1958*. London: University of California Press, 2000.

Kinzer, Stephen. *The Brothers: John Foster Dulles, Allen Dulles, and Their Secret World War*. New York: Henry Holt, 2013.

———. *Poisoner in Chief: Sidney Gottlieb and the CIA Search for Mind Control*. New York: Henry Holt, 2019.

Kisangani, Emizet François, and F Scott Bobb, *Historical Dictionary of the Democratic Republic of the Congo*, 3rd ed. *Historical Dictionaries of Africa*, no 112. Lanham, Maryland: Scarecrow Press, 2010.

Knightley, Phillip. *A Hack's Progress*. London: Jonathan Cape, 1997

Konadu, Kwasi, and Clifford C Campbell. *The Ghana Reader: History, Culture, Politics*. London: Duke University Press, 2016.

Kondlo, Kwandiwe. *In the Twilight of the Revolution: The Pan Africanist Congress of Azania (South Africa) 1959–1994*. Basel, Switzerland: Basler Afrika Bibliographien, 2009.

Kwitny, Jonathan. *Endless Enemies: The Making of an Unfriendly World*. New York: Congdon and Weed, 1984.

Kyle, Keith. *The Politics of the Independence of Kenya*. London: Palgrave Macmillan, 1999.

Lasch, Christopher. *The Agony of the American Left: One Hundred Years of Radicalism*. 1969; London: André Deutsch, 1970.

Lasky, Melvin J. *Africa for Beginners: A Traveler's Notebook*. London: Weidenfeld and Nicolson, 1962.

Lauer, Helen, ed. *Ghana: Changing Values/Changing Technologies*. Ghanaian Philosophical Studies, II. Washington, DC: Council for Research in Values and Philosophy, 2000.

Lawson, Jack, from the memoirs of Sully deFontaine. *The Slaver's Wheel: Sully in the Congo—A Green Beret's True Story of His Classified Mission in the Congo*. Prescott, Arizona: JNM Media, 2009.

Laxalt, Robert. *A Private War: An American Code Officer in the Belgian Congo*. Reno: University of Nevada Press, 1998.

Lefever, Ernest W, and Wynfred Joshua. *United Nations Peacekeeping in the Congo: 1960–1964: An Analysis of Political, Executive and Military Control*. Vol 2. Washington, DC: Brookings Institution, 1966. https://apps.dtic.mil/dtic/tr/fulltext/u2/711935.pdf.

Legum, Colin. *Congo Disaster*. Harmondsworth, UK: Penguin, 1961.

———. *Pan-Africanism: A Short Political Guide*. New York: Frederick A Praeger, 1962.

Lemarchand, René. *Political Awakening in the Belgian Congo*. Berkeley: University of California Press, 1964.

Lipsey, Roger. *Dag Hammarskjöld: A Life*. Ann Arbor: University of Michigan Press, 2013.

Livingstone, Fay. *The Love Story of Kwame Nkrumah and Helena Fathia*. 2nd ed. Accra: Blue Savana, n.d. [2007].

Lodge, Tom. *Black Politics in South Africa Since 1945*. London: Longman, 1983.

Lodge, Tom, Denis Kadmia, and David Pottie, eds. *Compendium of Elections in Southern Africa*. Johannesburg: Electoral Institute of South Africa, 2002.

López Álvarez, Luis. *Lumumba: Ou l'Afrique frustrée*. Paris: Editions Cujas, 1964.

Lowenstein, Allard K. *Brutal Mandate: A Journey to South West Africa*. New York: Macmillan, 1962.

Ludi, Gerard. *The Communistisation of the ANC*. Alberton, South Africa: Galago Books, 2011.

Lumumba, Patrice. *Congo, My Country*. 1962 (*Le Congo, terre d'avenir-est-il menacé?*); London: Frederick A Praeger, 1969.

————. *Fighter for Africa's Freedom*. Moscow: Progress Publishers, 1961.

————. *May Our People Triumph: Poem, Speeches, Letters and Interview of Congo's Revolutionary Prime Minister*. Prepared for publication by Paul Daniel Aravinth. CreateSpace Independent Publishing, n.d. [2016].

————. *Panaf Great Lives*. Bedford, UK: Panaf Books, 1973.

————. *The Truth About a Monstrous Crime of the Colonialists*. Moscow: Foreign Languages Publishing House, 1961.

Macey, David. *Frantz Fanon: A Biography*. 2000; London: Verso, 2012.

Madsen, Wayne. *The Almost Classified Guide to CIA Front Companies, Proprietaries and Contractors*. 2017; Milton Keynes, UK: self-published, 2018.

Mahoney, Richard D. *JFK: Ordeal in Africa*. New York: Oxford University Press, 1983.

Makonnen, Ras. *Pan-Africanism from Within*. As recorded and edited by Kenneth King. London: Oxford University Press, 1973.

Manby, Bronwen. *'Traditional' Dictatorship: One Party State in KwaZulu Homeland Threatens Transition to Democracy*. Edited by Abdullahi An-Na'im. Human Rights Watch, September 1993. www.hrw.org/reports/1993/southafrica2/.

Mandela, Nelson. *Long Walk to Freedom*. 1994; London: Abacus, 2002.

Marable, Manning. *Malcolm X: A Life of Reinvention*. 2011; London: Penguin, 2012.

Marais [later Kanu], Genoveva. *Kwame Nkrumah: As I Knew Him*. Chichester, UK: Janay Publishing, 1972.

Marchal, Jules. *Lord Leverhulme's Ghosts: Colonial Exploitation in the Congo*. Translated from the French by Martin Thom. 2001; London: Verso, 2017.

Marchetti, Victor, and John D Marks. *The CIA and the Cult of Intelligence*. 1974; London: Coronet Books, n.d.

Marcum, John A. *The Angolan Revolution*. Vol 1, *The Anatomy of an Explosion (1950–1962)*. Cambridge, Massachusetts: MIT Press, 1969.

————. *The Angolan Revolution*. Vol 2, *Exile Politics and Guerrilla Warfare (1962–1976)*. Cambridge, Massachusetts: MIT Press, 1979.

————. *Conceiving Mozambique*. Edited by Edmund Burke III and Michael W Clough. Cham, Switzerland: Palgrave Macmillan, 2017.

Marnham, Patrick. *Snake Dance: Journeys Beneath a Nuclear Sky*. London: Chatto and Windus, 2013.

Martens, Ludo. *Abo: Une Femme du Congo*. Brussels: Editions EPO, 1991.

Martin, John Bartlow. *Adlai Stevenson and the World: The Life of Adlai E. Stevenson*. New York: Doubleday, 1977.

Mazov, Sergey. *A Distant Front in the Cold War: The USSR in West Africa and the Congo, 1956–1964*. Washington, DC: Woodrow Wilson Center Press, 2010.

Mazuzan, George T, and J Samuel Walker. *Controlling the Atom: The Beginnings of Nuclear Regulation 1946–1962*. London: University of California Press, 1984.

Mboya, Tom. *Freedom and After*. London: André Deutsch, 1963.

McGrath, Sylvia Wallace. *Charles Kenneth Leith: Scientific Adviser*. Madison: University of Wisconsin Press, 1971.

McKeever, Porter. *Adlai Stevenson: His Life and Legacy*. New York: William Morrow, 1989.

McKown, Robin. *Lumumba: A Biography*. New York: Doubleday, 1969.

Mendiaux, Edouard. *Moscou, Accra et le Congo*. Bruxelles: Charles Dessart, 1960.

Mensah, Sylvester A. *In the Shadows of Politics: Reflections from My Mirror*. Blooming-ton, Indiana: AuthorHouse, 2013.

Meriwether, James H. *Proudly We Can Be Africans: Black Americans and Africa, 1935–61*. Chapel Hill: University of North Carolina Press, 2002.

Merriam, Alan P. *Congo: Background of Conflict*. Evanston, Illinois: Northwestern University Press, 1961.

Meyer, Cord. *Facing Reality: From World Federalism to the CIA*. New York: Harper and Row, 1980.

Michel, Serge. *Nour le voilé: De la casbah au Congo, du Congo au désert, la révolution*. Paris: Editions du Seuil, 1982.

———. *Uhuru Lumumba*. Paris: René Julliard, 1962.

Milne, June. *Kwame Nkrumah: A Biography*. London: Panaf Books, 1999.

———, comp. *Kwame Nkrumah: The Conakry Years: His Life and Letters*. London: Panaf Books, 1990.

Minter, William, Gaily Hovey, and Charles Cobb Jr, eds. *No Easy Victories: African Liberation and American Activists over a Half Century, 1950–2000*. Trenton, New Jersey: African World Press Books, 2004.

Mitchell, Nancy. *Jimmy Carter in Africa: Race and the Cold War*. Washington, DC: Woodrow Wilson Center Press, 2016.

Mokoena, Kenneth, ed. *South Africa and the United States: The Declassified History*. New York: New Press, 1993.

Moody, Roger. *Rocks and Hard Places: The Globalization of Mining*. London: Zed Books, 2007.

Moore, Gerald, ed. *African Literature and the Universities*. Ibadan, Nigeria: Published for the Congress of Cultura Freedom by the University of Ibadan, 1965.

Moore, Gerald, and Ulli Beier, eds. *Modern Poetry from Africa*. Harmondsworth, UK: Penguin, 1963. Revised in 1984 as *The Penguin Book of Modern African Poetry*.

Moore, Robin. *The Green Berets*. 1965; New York: Crown Publishers, 1969.

Morgan, Ted. *A Covert Life: Jay Lovestone: Communist, Anti-Communist, and Spymas-ter*. New York: Random House, 1999.

Mosley, Leonard. *Dulles: A Biography of Eleanor, Allen, and John Foster Dulles and Their Family Network*. London: Hodder and Stoughton, 1978.

Moss, Norman. *The Politics of Uranium*. London: André Deutsch, 1981.

Moxon, John. *Volta, Man's Greatest Lake: The Story of Ghana's Akosombo Dam*. London: André Deutsch, 1984.

Mphahlele, Es'kia. *Afrika My Music: An Autobiography 1957–1983*. Johannesburg: Ra-van Press, 1984.

Mpisi, Jean. *Antoine Gizenga: Le Combat de l'héritier de P. Lumumba*. Paris: L'Harmat-tan, 2007.

Muehlenbeck, Philip E. *Betting on the Africans: John F. Kennedy's Courting of African Nationalist Leaders*. Oxford: Oxford University Press, 2012.

———. *Czechoslovakia in Africa, 1945–1968*. London: Palgrave Macmillan, 2016.

Munger, Edwin S. *African Field Reports 1952–1961*. Cape Town: C Struik, 1961.

Munger, Ned. *Touched by Africa*. Pasadena, California: Castle Press, 1983.

Murphy, Robert. *Diplomat Among Warriors*. London: Collins, 1964.

Murray, Pauli. *Proud Shoes: The Story of an American Family.* 1956; Boston: Beacon Press, 1999.

———. *Song in a Weary Throat: An American Pilgrimage.* London: HarperCollins, 1987. Reprinted as *The Autobiography of a Black Activist, Feminist, Lawyer, Priest, and Poet.* 1989; Knoxville: University of Tennessee Press, 1990.

Mwakikagile, Godfrey. *Western Involvement in Nkrumah's Downfall.* Dar es Salaam, Tanzania: New Africa Press, 2015.

Nagel, Stuart S, ed. *Handbook of Global International Policy.* New York: Marcel Dekker, 2000.

Namikas, Lise. *Battleground Africa: Cold War in the Congo 1960–1965.* Washington, DC: Woodrow Wilson Center Press, 2013.

Ndaywel è Nziem, Isidore. *Histoire Générale du Congo.* Brussels: De Boeckand Larcier, 1998.

Nelson, Harold D. *Area Handbook for Guinea:* 1961. 2nd ed. Washington, DC: US Government Printing Office, 1975.

Newton, Jim. *Eisenhower: The White House Years.* New York: Doubleday, 2011.

Nilsen, Sarah. *Projecting America, 1958: Film and Cultural Diplomacy at the Brussels World's Fair.* Jefferson, North Carolina: McFarland, 2011.

Njubi Nesbitt, Francis. *Race for Sanctions: The Movement Against Apartheid, 1946–1994.* Bloomington: Indiana University Press, 2004.

Nkomo, Joshua. *Nkomo: The Story of My Life.* London: Methuen, 1984.

Nkrumah, Arhin. *The Life and Work of Kwame Nkrumah: Papers of a Symposium Organized by the Institute of African Studies, University of Ghana, Legon.* Trenton, New Jersey: Africa World Press, 1993.

Nkrumah, Kwame. *Africa Must Unite.* 1964; London: Panaf Books, 2007.

———. *The Autobiography of Kwame Nkrumah.* Edinburgh: Thomas Nelson and Sons, 1957.

———. *Challenge of the Congo: A Case Study of Foreign Pressures in an Independent State.* 1967; London: Panaf, 2002.

———. *Class Struggle in Africa.* 1970; London: Panaf Books, 1980.

———. *Consciencism.* London: Heinemann, 1964.

———. *Dark Days in Ghana.* 1968; London: Panaf Books, 2001.

———. *Handbook of Revolutionary Warfare: A Guide to the Armed Phase of the African Revolution.* 1968; New York: International Publishers, 1969.

———. *I Speak of Freedom: A Statement of African Ideology.* London: Mercury Books, 1961.

———. *Neo-colonialism: The Last Stage of Imperialism.* London: Nelson, 1965.

———. *Revolutionary Path.* London: Panaf Books, 1973.

———. *Rhodesia File.* 1974; London: Panaf Books, 2005.

———. *The Struggle Continues.* 1969; London: Panaf Books, 2006.

———. *Towards Colonial Freedom.* 1957; London: Heinemann, 1962.

———. *Voice from Conakry.* 1967; London: Panaf Books, 2006.

Ntloedibe, Elias L. *Here Is a Tree: Political Biography of Robert Mangaliso Sobukwe.* Mogoditshane, Botswana: Century-Turn Publishers (PTY), 1995.

Ntumazah, Ndeh. *A Conversational Auto Biography.* Edited by Linus T. Asong and Simon Ndeh Chi. Mankon, Bamenda, Cameroon: Langaa Research and Publishing, 2001.

Nwaubani, Ebere. *The United States and Decolonization in West Africa* 1950–1960. Rochester, New York: University of Rochester Press, 2001.

Nyangoni, Wellington Winter. *Africa in the United Nations System*. London: Associated University Presses, 1985.

Nzongola-Ntalaja, Georges. *The Congo from Leopold to Kabila: A People's History*. 2002; London: Zed Books, 2007.

———. *Patrice Lumumba*. Athens: Ohio University Press, 2014.

Obama, Barack. *Dreams from My Father: A Story of Race and Inheritance*. 1995; Edinburgh: Canongate, 2007.

O'Brien, Conor Cruise. *Memoir: My Life and Themes*. London: Profile Books, 1998.

———. *To Katanga and Back: A UN Case History*. London: Hutchinson, 1962.

O'Donoghue, David. *The Irish Army in the Congo* 1960–1964 : *The Far Battalions*. Dublin: Irish Academy Press, 2006.

Öhrström, Lars. *Curious Tales from Chemistry: The Last Alchemist in Paris, and Other Episodes*. 2013; rpt. Oxford, UK: Oxford University Press, 2015.

Okumu, WAJ. *The African Renaissance: History, Significance and Strategy*. Trenton, New Jersey: Africa World Press, 2002.

———. *Lumumba's Congo: Roots of Conflict*. New York: Obolensky, 1962.

O'Malley, Gregory E. *Final Passages: The Intercolonial Slave Trade of British America*, 1619–1807. Chapel Hill: Omohundro Institute and University of North Carolina Press, 2016.

O'Neill, John Terence, and Nicholas Rees. *United Nations Peacekeeping in the Post–Cold War Era*. London: Routledge, 2005.

Osei-Tutu, John Kwadwo, ed. *Forts, Castles and Society in West Africa: Gold Coast and Dahomey*, 1450–1960. Vol 7 of *African History*. Boston: Brill, 2018.

Osgood, Kenneth Alan. *Total Cold War: Eisenhower's Secret Propaganda Battle at Home and Abroad*. Lawrence: University of Kansas Press, 2006.

Osseo-Asare, Abena Dove. *Atomic Junction: Nuclear Power in Africa After Independence*. Cambridge, UK: Cambridge University Press, 2019.

Ostrower, Gary B. *The United Nations and the United States*. New York: Twayne Publishers, 1998.

Paget, Karen M. *Patriotic Betrayal:The Inside Story of the CIA's Secret Campaign to Enroll American Students in the Crusade Against Communism*. New Haven, Connecticut: Yale University Press, 2015.

Park, Baroness Daphne. *Difficult Places: Some Reflections on the Future Relationship with the Former Soviet Union*. Liverpool: Liverpool University Press, 1993.

Passemiers, Lazlo. *Decolonization and Regional Politics: South Africa and the Congo Crisis*, 1960–1965. Abingdon, UK: Routledge, 2019.

Passin, H, and K A B Jones-Quartey, eds. *Africa: The Dynamics of Change*. Ibadan, Nigeria: Ibadan University Press, published for the Congress for Cultural Freedom, 1963.

Pateman, Roy. *Residual Uncertainty: Trying to Avoid Intelligence and Policy Mistakes in the Modern World*. Lanham, Maryland: University Press of America, 2003.

Perkovich, George. *India's Nuclear Bomb: The Impact on Global Proliferation*. New Delhi: Oxford University Press, 2002.

Perrings, Charles. *Black Mineworkers in Central Africa: Industrial Strategies and the Evolution of an African Proletariat in the Copperbelt, 1911–41*. London: Heinemann Educational, 1979.

Picard, Maurin. *Ils ont tué Monsieur H.: Congo, 1961 : Le complot des mercenaires français contre l'ONU*. Paris: Seuil, 2019.

Plummer, Brenda Gayle. *In Search of Power: African Americans in the Era of Decolonization, 1956–1974*. Cambridge, UK: Cambridge University Press, 2013.

Pluvinage, Gonzague, ed. *Expo 58: Between Utopia and Reality*. Brussels: Brussels City Archives and State Archives, Editions Racine, 2008.

Poe, D. Zizwe. *Kwame Nkrumah's Contribution to Pan-Africanism: An Afrocentric Analysis*. London: Routledge, 2003.

Polsgrove, Carol. *Ending British Rule in Africa: Writers in a Common Cause*. Manchester, UK: Manchester University Press, 2009.

Powell, Erica. *Private Secretary (Female)/Gold Coast*. London: C Hurst, 1984.

Prados, John. *Safe for Democracy: The Secret Wars of the CIA*. Chicago: Ivan R Dee, 2006.

Price, David H. *Anthropological Intelligence: The Deployment and Neglect of American Anthropology in the Second World War*. Durham, NC: Duke University Press, 2008.

———. *Cold War Anthropology: The CIA, the Pentagon, and the Growth of Dual Use Anthropology*. London: Duke University Press, 2016.

Price, Robert M. *The Social Basis of Administrative Behavior in a Transitional Polity: The Case of Ghana*. Berkeley: University of California Press, 1971.

Prosser, Michael H, ed. *An Ethic for Survival: Adlai Stevenson Speaks on International Affairs 1936–1965*. New York: William Morrow, 1969.

Quaison-Sackey, Alex. *Africa Unbound: Reflections of an African Statesman*. London: André Deutsch, 1963.

Quarm, S E. *Diplomatic Offensive: An Overview of Ghana's Diplomacy under Dr Kwame Nkrumah*. Accra: Afram Publications, 1997.

Rabinowitz, Beth S. *Coups, Rivals and the Modern State: Why Rural Coalitions Matter in Sub-Saharan Africa*. Cambridge, UK: Cambridge University Press, 2018.

Rahman, A. *The Regime Change of Kwame Nkrumah: Epic Heroism in Africa and the Diaspora*. London: Palgrave Macmillan, 2015.

Ramondy, Karine. *Leaders Assassinés en Afrique Centrale 1958–1961: Entre construction nationale et régulation des relations internationales*. Paris: Editions l'Harmattan, 2020.

Ranelagh, John. *The Agency: The Rise and Decline of the CIA: From Wild Bill Donovan to William Casey*. New York: Cambridge Publishing, 1986.

Ransby, Barbara. *Eslanda: The Large and Unconventional Life of Mrs Paul Robeson*. New Haven, Connecticut: Yale University Press, 2013.

Rathbone, Richard. *Nkrumah and the Chiefs: The Politics of Chieftaincy in Ghana, 1951–60*. Oxford, UK: James Currey, 2000.

Rathbun, Ben. *The Point Man: Irving Brown and the Deadly Post-1945 Struggle for Europe and Africa*. London: Minerva Press, 1996.

Ray, Carina E. *Crossing the Color Line: Race, Sex, and the Contested Politics of Colonialism in Ghana*. Athens: Ohio University Press, 2015.

Ray, Ellen, William Schaap, Karl Van Meter, and Louis Wolf, eds. *Dirty Work 2: The CIA in Africa*. London: Zed Books, 1980.

Raymond, Robert. *Black Star in the Wind*. London: MacGibbon and Kee, 1960.

Renton, David, David Seddon, and Leo Zeilig. *The Congo: Plunder and Resistance*. London: Zed Books, 2007.

Richards, Yevette. *Conversations with Maida Springer: A Personal History of Labor, Race, and International Relations*. Pittsburgh: University of Pittsburgh Press, 2004.

———. *Maida Springer: Pan-Africanist and International Labor Leader*. Pittsburgh: University of Pittsburgh Press, 2000.

Richelson, Jeffrey T. *Spying on the Bomb: American Nuclear Intelligence from Nazi Germany to Iran and North Korea*. New York: Norton, 2006.

———. *The Wizards of Langley: Inside the CIA's Directorate of Science and Technology*. Boulder, Colorado: Westview Press, 2001.

Rikhye, Indar Jit. *Military Adviser to the Secretary-General: UN Peacekeeping and the Congo Crisis*. London: Hurst, 1993.

———. *Trumpets and Tumults: The Memoirs of a Peacekeeper*. New Delhi: Manohar, 2002.

Rizzo, John. *Company Man: Thirty Years of Controversy and Crisis in the CIA*. London: Scribe, 2014.

Roberts, Janine. *Glitter and Greed: The Secret World of the Diamond Cartel*. 2003; New York: Disinformation Company, 2007.

Robeson, Paul, Jr. *The Undiscovered Paul Robeson: An Artist's Journey, 1898–1939*. New York: Wiley, 2001.

———. *The Undiscovered Paul Robeson: Quest for Freedom, 1939–1976*. Hoboken, NJ: John Wiley and Sons, 2010.

Rooney, David. *Kwame Nkrumah: Vision and Tragedy*. Accra: Sub-Saharan Publishers, 1988.

Rosenberg, Rosalind. *Jane Crow: The Life of Pauli Murray*. New York: Oxford University Press, 2017.

Rowley, Hazel. *Richard Wright: The Life and Times*. 2001; Chicago: University of Chicago Press, 2008.

Rubin, Andrew N. *Archives of Authority: Empire, Culture, and the Cold War*. Princeton, New Jersey: Princeton University Press, 2012.

Sander, Alfred Dick. *Eisenhower's Executive Office*. Contributions in Political Science, Number 386. Westport, Connecticut: Greenwood Press, 1999.

Schatzberg, Michael G. *Mobutu or Chaos? The United States and Zaire, 1960–1990*. Lanham, Maryland: University Press of America, 1991.

Scholz, Sally J, and Shannon M Mussett, eds. *The Contradictions of Freedom: Philosophical Essays on Simone de Beauvoir's* The Mandarins. Albany: State University of New York Press, 2005.

Schorr, Daniel, Matthew Passmore, and Chip Robertson. *Forgive Us Our Press Passes: Selected Works by Daniel Schorr, 1972–1998*. San Francisco: University of California, Hastings College of Law, 1998.

Scott, Anne Firor. *Pauli Murray and Caroline Ware: Forty Years of Letters in Black and White*. Chapel Hill: University of North Carolina Press, 2006.

Scott, Ian. *Tumbled House: The Congo at Independence*. London: Oxford University Press, 1969.

Scott-Smith, Giles, and Charlotte A. Lerg, eds. *Campaigning Culture and the Global Cold War: The Journals of the Congress for Cultural Freedom*. London: Palgrave Macmillan, 2017.

Sherwood, Marika. *Kwame Nkrumah: The Years Abroad 1935–1947*. Legon, Ghana: Freedom Publications, 1996.

Shubin, Vladimir Grennadevich. *The Hot 'Cold War': The USSR in Southern Africa*. London: Pluto Press, 2008.

Simelane, Thokozani, and Mohamed Abdel-Rahman, eds. *Energy Transition in Africa*. Pretoria: Africa Institute of South Africa, 2011.

Simpson, Christopher. *Science of Coercion: Communication Research and Psychological Warfare 1945–1960*. Oxford, UK: Oxford University Press, 1994.

Simpson, Thula. *Umkhonto We Sizwe: The ANC's Armed Struggle*. Cape Town: Penguin Books, 2016.

Smith, J W. *Economic Democracy: The Political Struggle of the 21st Century*. New York: Routledge, 2007.

Smith, Jean Edward. *Eisenhower in War and Peace*. New York: Random House, 2012.

Smith, John H. *Alan Nunn May: The Atom Spy and MI5*. Malvern, UK: Aspect Design, 2012.

Socialist Forum of Ghana, ed. *The Great Deception*. Accra: Socialist Forum of Ghana, 2012.

Soyinka, Wole. *Trumpism in Academe: The Example of Caroline Davis and Spahring Partners*. Ibadan, Nigeria: Bookcraft, 2021.

———. *You Must Set Forth at Dawn: A Memoir*. 2006; London: Methuen, in association with Ibadan: Bookcraft, 2007.

Spaak, Paul Henri. *The Continuing Battle: Memoirs of a European, 1936–1966*. Translated by Henry Fox. London: Weidenfeld and Nicolson, 1971.

Spahr, Juliana. *Du Bois's Telegram: Literary Resistance and State Containment*. Cambridge, Massachusetts: Harvard University Press, 2017.

Stanard, Matthew G. *Selling the Congo: A History of European Pro-Empire Propaganda and the Making of Belgian Imperialism*. Lincoln: University of Nebraska Press, 2011.

St Clair, William. *The Grand Slave Emporium: Cape Coast Castle and the British Slave Trade*. London: Profile Books, 2006.

Stearns, Jason K. *Dancing in the Glory of Monsters: The Collapse of the Congo and the Great War of Africa*. New York: PublicAffairs, 2011.

Stewart, Gary. *Rumba on the River: A History of the Popular Music of the Two Congos*. London: Verso, 2000.

Stockwell, John. *In Search of Enemies: A CIA Story*. New York: Norton, 1978.

Stonor Saunders, Frances. *Who Paid the Piper? The CIA and the Cultural Cold War*. London: Granta, 1999.

Suhr-Sytsma, Nathan. *Poetry, Print, and the Making of Postcolonial Literature*. Cambridge, UK: Cambridge University Press, 2017.

Sutherland, Bill, and Matt Meyer. *Guns and Gandhi in Africa: Pan African Insights on Nonviolence, Armed Struggle and Liberation in Africa*. Trenton, New Jersey: Africa World Press, 2000.

Swanepoel, P C. *Really Inside Boss: A Tale of South Africa's Late Intelligence Service (and Something About the CIA)*. Pretoria: self-published, 2007.

Talbot, David. *The Devil's Chessboard: Allen Dulles, the CIA, and the Rise of America's Secret Government*. 2015; London: William Collins, 2016.

Tenaille, Frank. *Music Is the Weapon of the Future: Fifty Years of African Popular Music*. Translated by Stephen Toussaint and Hope Sandrine. Photographs by Akwa Betote. 2000; Chicago: Lawrence Hill Books, 2002.

Thompson, Willard Scott. *Ghana's Foreign Policy, 1957–1966: Diplomacy, Ideology, and the New State*. Princeton, New Jersey: Princeton University Press, 1969.

Timothy, Bankole. *Kwame Nkrumah from Cradle to Grave*. 2nd ed. Dorchester, UK: Gavin Press, 1981.

Tolley, Howard B, Jr. *The International Commission of Jurists: Global Advocates for Human Rights*. Philadelphia: University of Pennsylvania Press, 2010.

Tully, Andrew. *CIA: The Inside Story*. London: Arthur Barker, 1962.

———. *The Secret Spies: More Secret, More Powerful than the CIA*. London: Arthur Barker, 1969.

Turner, Thomas. *The Congo Wars: Conflict, Myth and Reality*. London: Zed Books, 2007.

Twigge, Stephen Robert, and Len Scott. *Planning Armageddon: Britain, the United States and the Command of Western Nuclear Forces 1945–1964*. Vol 8 of Studies in the History of Science, Technology and Medicine. Amsterdam: Harwood Academic Publishers, 2000.

United Nations General Assembly. *Investigation into the Conditions and Circumstances Resulting in the Tragic Death of Dag Hammarskjöld and of the Members of the Party Accompanying Him*. New York: UN Headquarters. A/71/1042, 5 September 2017; and A/71/973, 12 September 2019.

———. *Items in Peace Keeping Operations—United Nations Operations in the Congo—Lumumba—Reports on His Death*. United Nations Archives, S-0875-0007-05-00001. 11 November 1961.

United Nations Operations in the Congo. *Investigation into Lumumba's Death: Project Sunk Hope*. United Nations Archives, S-0805-0011-04. 28 November 1960–26 May 1962.

United States Bureau of Mines. *Minerals Yearbook 1960*. Washington, DC: US Government Printing Office, 1961.

United States Congress, Senate. *Alleged Assassination Plots Involving Foreign Leaders: An Interim Report of the Select Committee to Study Governmental Operations with Respect to Intelligence Activities*. 94th Congress, 1st session. November 1975.

———. *Final Report of the Select Committee to Study Governmental Operations with Respect to Intelligence Activities, Book IV, Supplementary Detailed Staff Reports on Foreign and Military Intelligence*. Washington: US Government Printing Office, 1976. www.intelligence.senate.gov/sites/default/files/94755_IV.pdf.

———. *Human Drug Testing by the CIA, 1977: Hearings Before the Subcommittee on Scientific Research of the Committee on Human Resources*. 95th Congress, 1st session, to amend the Public Health Service Act to establish the president's commission for the protection of human subjects of biomedical and behavioral research, and for other purposes. 20 and 21 September 1977.

————. *Project MKUltra, the CIA's Program of Research in Behavioral Modification: Joint Hearing Before the Select Committee on Intelligence and the Subcommittee on Health and Scientific Research of the Committee on Human Resources.* 95th Congress, 1st session. 3 August 1977.

United States Department of the Army. *US Army Area Handbook for the Republic of the Congo (Leopoldville).* 1962.

United States Department of Justice. *Report of the Attorney General to the Congress of the United States on the Administration of the Foreign Agents Registration Act of 1938, as Amended for the Calendar Year* 1961. October 1962. www.justice.gov/nsd-fara /page/file/991886.

United States Department of State, Bureau of Intelligence and Research. Comp. Jacqueline S Mithun. *African Programs of U.S. Organizations.* May 1965.

United States President's Materials Policy Commission. *Resources for Freedom.* Vol 1, *Foundations for Growth and Security.* 1952.

United States, Threat Reduction Agency, Department of Defense. *Defense's Nuclear Agency,* 1947–1997. Washington, DC: US Government Printing Office, 2002.

Urban, Wayne J. *Black Scholar: Horace Mann Bond* 1904–1972. Athens: University of Georgia Press, 1992.

Urquhart, Brian. *Hammarskjöld.* London: Bodley Head, 1972.

————. *Ralph Bunche: An American Life.* London: Norton, 1993.

Valentine, Douglas. *The Strength of the Wolf: The Secret History of America's War on Drugs.* London: Verso, 2004.

Van Bilsen, Jef. *Congo* 1945–1965: *La fin d'unecolonie.* Translated by Serge Govaert. 1993; Brussels: CRISP, 1994.

Van Dongen, Luc, Stéphanie Roulinand, and Giles Scott-Smith, eds. *Transnational Anti-Communism and the Cold War: Agents, Activities, and Networks.* Houndmills, UK: Palgrave Macmillan, 2014.

Van Lierde, Jean, ed. *Lumumba Speaks: The Speeches and Writings of Patrice Lumumba,* 1958–1961. Introduction by Jean-Paul Sartre. Translated by Helen R Lane. 1963; Boston: Little, Brown and Company, 1972.

Van Reybrouck, David. *Congo: The Epic History of a People.* Translated by Sam Garrett. 2010; London: Fourth Estate, 2014.

Vansina, Jan. *Paths in the Rainforests: Toward a History of Political Tradition in Equatorial Africa.* London: Currey, 1990.

Villafaña, Frank. *Cold War in the Congo: The Confrontation of Cuban Military Forces,* 1960–1967. New Brunswick, New Jersey: Transaction Publishers, 2009.

Vitalis, Robert. *White World Order, Black Power Politics: The Birth of American International Relations.* Ithaca, New York: Cornell University Press, 2015.

Von Eschen, Penny M. *Race Against Empire: Black Americans and Anticolonialism,* 1937–1957. Ithaca, New York: Cornell University Press, 1997.

————. *Satchmo Blows Up the World: Jazz Ambassadors Play the Cold War.* Cambridge, Massachusetts: Harvard University Press, 2004.

von Horn, Carl. *Soldiering for Peace.* London: Camelot, 1966.

Waggitt, Peter. *Radiological Report on an Inter-Agency Mission to the Shinkolobwe Mine Site, DRC,* 24 *October to* 4 *November* 2004. Vienna: IAEA, 16 November 2004.

Walker, John R. *Britain and Disarmament: The UK and Nuclear, Biological and Chemical Weapons Arms Control and Programmes 1956–1975*. Farnham, UK: Ashgate, 2012.

———. *Foreign and Commonwealth Office, UK, British Nuclear Weapons and the Test Ban 1954–1973: Britain, the United States, Weapons Policies and Nuclear Testing: Tensions and Contradictions*. Farnham, UK: Ashgate, 2010.

Walker, Margaret. *Richard Wright, Daemonic Genius: A Portrait of the Man, a Critical Look at His Work*. New York: Warner Books, 1988.

Walton, Calder. *Empire of Secrets: British Intelligence, the Cold War and the Twilight of Empire*. London: Harper Press, 2013.

Waters, Mary-Alice, ed. *Cuba and Angola: Fighting for Africa's Freedom and Our Own*. New York: Pathfinder Press, 2013.

Waters, Robert Anthony, Jr, and Geert Van Goethem. *American Labor's Global Ambassadors: The International History of the AFL-CIO During the Cold War*. New York: Palgrave Macmillan, 2013.

Weart, Spencer R. *The Rise of Nuclear Fear*. Cambridge, Massachusetts: Harvard University Press, 2012.

Weiner, Tim. *Legacy of Ashes: The History of the CIA*. London: Allen Lane, 2007.

Weinstein, Allen, and Alexander Vassiliev. *The Haunted Wood: Soviet Espionage in America—the Stalin Era*. New York: Random House, 1999.

Weiss, Herbert F. *Political Protest in the Congo: The Parti Solidaire Africain During the Independence Struggle*. Princeton, New Jersey: Princeton University Press, 1967.

Weiss, Herbert, and Benoit Verhaegen. *Parti Solidaire Africain (PSA): Documents 1959–1960*. Brussels: CRISP, 1963.

Weissman, Stephen R. *American Foreign Policy in the Congo, 1960–1964*. Ithaca, New York: Cornell University Press, 1974.

White, George. *Holding the Line: Race, Racism, and American Foreign Policy Toward Africa, 1953–1961*. New York: Rowman and Littlefield, 2005.

Whitney, Joel. *Finks: How the C.I.A. Tricked the World's Best Writers*. New York: OR Books, 2016.

Whipple, Chris. *The Spymasters*. New York: Simon and Schuster, 2020.

Wilford, Hugh. *The CIA, the British Left and the Cold War: Calling the Tune?* London: Frank Cass, 2003.

———. *The Mighty Wurlitzer: How the CIA Played America*. Cambridge, Massachusetts: Harvard University Press, 2008.

Willetts, Peter, ed. *'The Conscience of the World': The Influence of Non-Governmental Organisations in the UN System*. Washington, DC: Brookings Institution, 1996.

———. *Non-Governmental Organizations in World Politics. The Construction of Global Governance*. Routledge Global Institutions Series. London: Routledge, 2011.

Williams, G Mennen. *Africa for the Africans*. Grand Rapids, MI: William Eerdmans Publishing Company, 1969.

Williams, Susan. *Spies in the Congo: America's Atomic Mission in World War II*. New York: PublicAffairs, 2016.

———. *Who Killed Hammarskjöld? The UN, the Cold War and White Supremacy in Africa*. London: Hurst, 2011.

Winter, Gordon. *Inside BOSS: South Africa's Secret Police*. London: Allen Lane, 1981.

Wise, David, and Thomas B Ross. *The Invisible Government*. New York: Jonathan Cape, 1965.

Wittman, George. *The Ghana Report: Economic Development and Investment Opportunities, Legal Problems Relative to Investment, Sociological Factors Relative to General Economic Development*. New York: G H Wittman, 1959.

———. *A Matter of Intelligence*. New York: Macmillan Publishing, 1975.

Wolfers, Michael. *Thomas Hodgkin: Wandering Scholar: A Biography*. London: Merlin Press, 2007.

Woodrow Wilson International Center for Scholars' History and Public Policy Program and Africa Program. *The Congo Crisis, 1960–1961: A Critical Oral History Conference*. Washington, DC: Wilson Center, 23–24 September 2004.

Wright, George. *The Destruction of a Nation: United States' Policy Towards Angola Since 1945*. London: Pluto Press, 1997.

Wright, Richard. *Black Power*. London: Dennis Dobson, 1954. Reprinted in *Three Books from Exile: Black Power, the Color Curtain, and White Man, Listen!* New York: Harper Perennial, 2008.

———. *White Man, Listen!* New York: Anchor Books, 1964.

Wrong, Michela. *In the Footsteps of Mr Kurtz: Living on the Brink of Disaster in Mobutu's Congo*. 2000; London: Perennial, 2002.

X, Malcolm. *The Autobiography of Malcolm X*. As told to Alex Haley. 1964; New York: Random House, 1965.

Yadav, RK. *Mission R&AW*. New Delhi: Manas Publications, 2014.

Yordanov, Radoslav A. *The Soviet Union and the Horn of Africa During the Cold War: Between Ideology and Pragmatism*. Lanham, Maryland: Lexington Books, 2017.

Young, Crawford, and Thomas Turner. *The Rise and Decline of the Zairian State*. Madison: University of Wisconsin Press, 1985.

Zeilig, Leo. *Lumumba: Africa's Lost Leader*. London: Haus Publishing, 2008.

———, ed and comp. *Voices of Liberation: Patrice Lumumba*. Cape Town: HSRC Press, 2013.

Ziegler, Charles A, and David Jacobson. *Spying Without Spies: Origins of America's Secret Nuclear Surveillance System*. London: Praeger, 1995.

Zoellner, Tom. *Uranium: War, Energy, and the Rock That Shaped the World*. London: Penguin, 2009.

Zukas, Simon. *Into Exile and Back*. Lusaka, Zambia: Bookworld Publishers, 2002.

Articles and Book Chapters

Ahlman, Jeffrey S. 'Road to Ghana: Nkrumah, Southern Africa and the Eclipse of a Decolonizing Africa'. *Kronos* 37, no 1 (January 2011): 23–40.

'All-African People's Conferences'. *International Organization* 16, no 2 (1962): 429–434.

Allman, Jean. 'Nuclear Imperialism and the Pan-African Struggle for Peace and Freedom Ghana, 1959–1962'. *Souls* 10, no 2 (April–June 2008): 83–102.

Amuzu, Josef K A. 'Nuclear Option for Ghana'. In *Ghana: Changing Values/Changing Technologies*. Ghanaian Philosophical Studies, II, edited by Helen Lauer, 281–291.

Andrews, Evan. 'Fidel Castro's Wild New York Visit'. *History*, 18 September 2015. Updated 31 August 2018.

Aning, Emmanuel Kwesi, Emma Birinkorang, and Ernest Ansha Lartey. 'The Process and Mechanisms of Developing Intelligence Culture in Ghana'. In *Intelligence Elsewhere*, edited by Philip H J Davies and Kristian C Gustafson, 199–217.

Baucom, Donald R. 'Eisenhower and Ballistic Missile Defense: The Formative Years, 1944–1961'. *Air Power History* 51, no 4 (Winter 2004): 4–17.

Bele, Jean. 'The Legacy of the Involvement of the Democratic Republic of the Congo in the Bombs Dropped on Hiroshima and Nagasaki'. *MIT Faculty Newsletter*, January–February 2021.

Blouin, Eve. 'From Congo to Paris: The Story of "Black Passionaria" and the Fight for Freedom'. *Chime*, 7 November 2019.

Borucki, Alex, David Eltis, and David Wheat. 'Atlantic History and the Slave Trade to Spanish America'. *American Historical Review* 120 (April 2015): 433–446.

Brown, Andrew. 'The Viennese Connection: Engelbert Broda, Alan Nunn May and Atomic Espionage'. *Intelligence and National Security* 24, no 2 (April 2009): 173–193.

Burgess, Jan, et al. 'A Tribute to A M Babu'. *Review of African Political Economy* 23, no 69 (September 1996): 321–348.

Clark, John F. 'What Price Empire? A Study of the Costs and Benefits of American Involvement in Zaire'. In *Handbook of Global International Policy*, edited by Stuart Nagel, 21–41.

Clarke, John Henrik. 'Paul Robeson: The Artist as Activist and Social Thinker'. *Présence Africaine* no 107 (1978): 223–241.

Clément, Pierre. 'Patrice Lumumba (Stanleyville 1952–53)'. *Présence Africaine* 12, no 40 (1962): 57–78.

Cohen, Barry. 'The CIA and African Trade Unions'. In *Dirty Work 2: The CIA in Africa*, edited by Ellen Ray et al, 70–80.

Deininger R A and Meier P G. 'Sabotage of Public Water Supply Systems'. In *Security of Public Water Supplies*, edited by R A Deininger, P Literally, and J Bartram, 241–248. NATO Science Series, Environmental Security, vol 66. Dordrecht, Netherlands: Springer, 2000.

'Democratic Republic of Congo'. In *Compendium of Elections in Southern Africa*, edited by Tom Lodge, Denis Kadmia, and David Pottie, 63–65.

De Vries, Tity. 'The 1967 Central Intelligence Agency Scandal: Catalyst in a Transforming Relationship between State and People'. *The Journal of American History* 98, no 4 (March 2012): 1075–1092.

Dorn, A Walter, and David J H Bell. 'Intelligence and Peacekeeping: The UN Operation in the Congo 1960–64'. *International Peacekeeping* 2, no 1 (Spring 1995): 11–33.

Dorn, Walter. 'The UN's First "Air Force": Peacekeepers in Combat, Congo 1960–64'. *Journal of Military History* 77 (October 2013): 1399–1425.

Eltis, David, et al. 'Summary Statistics'. Voyages: The Intra-American Slave Trade Database, accessed 6 November 2020. www.slavevoyages.org/american/database#statistics.

Gerits, Frank. '"When the Bull Elephants Fight": Kwame Nkrumah, Non-Alignment, and Pan-Africanism as an Interventionist Ideology in the Global Cold War (1957–66)'. *International History Review* 37, no 5 (August 2015): 951–969.

Giacometti, A. 'The Labor Movement in Tropical Africa III: Concluding a Study of the African Working Class (March 1956)'. *New International* 23, no 2 (Spring 1957): 94–101.

Gibbs, David N. 'International Influences on Third World Development: The Case of Mobutu's Zaire'. *Nytt fan Nordiska Afrikainstitutet* 29 (1992): 12–22.

Goodwin, Michele. 'The Thirteenth Amendment: Modern Slavery, Capitalism, and Mass Incarceration'. *Cornell Law Review* 104 (2019): 899–990.

Grilli, Matteo. 'Nkrumah, Nationalism, and Pan-Africanism: The Bureau of African Affairs Collection'. *History in Africa: African Studies Association* 44 (June 2017): 295–307.

Hoskyns, Catherine. 'Pan-Africanism at Accra'. *Africa South* 3, no 3 (April–June 1959): 71–76.

Hunt, Richard M. 'The CIA Exposures: End of an Affair'. *Virginia Quarterly Review* 45, no 2 (Spring 1969): 211–229.

Imobighe, T A. 'An African High Command: The Search for a Feasible Strategy of Continental Defence'. *African Affairs* 79, no 315 (April 1980): 241–254.

Jack, Homer A. 'The Belgrade Conference'. *Bulletin of the Atomic Scientists* 17, no 9 (November 1961): 390–392.

Jacobs, Nancy J. 'The Awkward Biography of the Young Washington Okumu: CIA Asset (?) and the Prayer Breakfast's Man in Africa'. *African Studies* 78, no 2 (2019): 225–245.

Jacobs, Nancy J, and Andrew Bank. 'Biography in Post-Apartheid South Africa: A Call for Awkwardness'. *African Studies* 28, no 2 (2019): 165–182.

Kahamba, J, and L P Gillon. '10150: Report on the Development of the Trico Nuclear Centre'. *Nuclear Science Abstracts* 17, no 5 (15 March 1963): 1308.

Kerr, Teresa. 'Morocco Commemorates 60th Anniversary of the Death of King Mohammed V'. *Morocco World News*, 15 May 2019.

Kesman, Czeslaw. 'Africa at Brussels: A Focus of Attention'. *The Tablet*, 24 May 1958, 486.

Killingray, David. 'Soldiers, Ex-Servicemen, and Politics in the Gold Coast, 1939–50'. *Journal of Modern African Studies* 21, no 3 (September 1983): 523–534.

Kirchwehm, Maria. 'Letter from Ghana', *Foreign Service Journal* 36, no 9 (September 1959): 40–42.

Krige, John. 'The Peaceful Atom as Political Weapon: Euratom and American Foreign Policy in the Late 1950s'. *Historical Studies in the Natural Sciences* 38, no 1 (Winter 2008): 5–44.

———. 'Techno-Utopian Dreams, Techno-Political Realities: The Education of Desire for the Peaceful Atom'. In *Utopia/Dystopia: Conditions of Historical Possibility*, edited by Michael D Gordin, Helen Tilley, and Gyan Prakash, 151–175.

Lea, David. Letter to the editor, *London Review of Books*, 11 April 2013.

Legum, Colin. 'Pan-Africanism and Communism'. In *The Soviet Bloc, China and Africa*, edited by Sven Hamrell and Carl Gösta, 9–29.

Lehren, Andrew W. 'Jazz and the FBI: Guilty Until Proven Innocent'. *Jazz Times*, 25 April 2019.

Lemarchand, René. 'The CIA in Africa: How Central? How Intelligent?' In *Dirty Work 2: The CIA in Africa*, edited by Ellen Ray et al, 9–23.

Mazov, Sergei. 'Soviet Aid to the Gizenga Government in the Former Belgian Congo (1960–61) as Reflected in Russian Archives'. *Cold War History* 7, no 3 (2007): 425–437.

McKeon, Nora. 'The African States and the OAU'. *International Affairs (Royal Institute of International Affairs)* vol 42, no 3 (1966): 390–409.

Meaney, Thomas. 'Frantz Fanon and the CIA Man'. *American Historical Review* 124, no 3 (June 2019): 983–995.

Medvedev, A Zhores. 'Stalin and the Atomic Gulag'. In *'Collateral Damage' or Unlawful Killings?*, edited by Kenneth S. Coates, 91–111.

Mensah, Sylvester A. 'In the Shadow of Politics'. *Chicago Tribune*, 17 November 1960.

Mian, Zia, and Alexander Glas. 'A Frightening Nuclear Legacy'. *Bulletin of the Atomic Scientists* 64, no 4 (September/October 2008): 42–47.

Miescher, Stephen F, and Dzodzi Tsikata. 'Hydro-Power and the Promise of Modernity and Development in Ghana'. In *The Ghana Reader: History, Culture, Politics*, edited by Kwasi Konadu and Clifford C. Campbell, 15–53.

Miller, Greg. 'How the CIA Used Crypto AG Encryption Devices to Spy on Countries for Decades'. *Washington Post*, 11 February 2020.

Misser, François. 'Mrs Lumumba Speaks (Cover Story 1: Great Lives)'. *New African*, April 2002.

Mohan, Jitendra. 'Ghana, the Congo, and the United Nations'. *Journal of Modern African Studies* 7, no 3 (October 1969): 369–406.

Moore, Gerald. 'The Transcription Centre in the Sixties: Navigating in Narrow Seas'. *Research in African Literatures* 33, no 3 (Fall 2002): 167–181.

Moreau, Jean-Louis, and René Brion. 'Business at the Service of Humanity? The Belgian Section at Expo 58'. In *Expo 58: Between Utopia and Reality*, edited by Gonzague Pluvinage, 119–142.

Mostefaoui, Aziz. 'The Ghanaian Leadership and the Colonial Situation in Algeria (with Special Reference to the Late 1950s–Early 1960s)'. In *Saharan Crossroads: Exploring Historical, Cultural, and Artistic Linkages Between North and West Africa*, edited by Tara F. Deubel, Scott M Youngstedt, and Helen Tissieres, 27–36.

Mphahlele, Ezekiel. 'Accra Conference Diary'. In *An African Treasury*, edited by Langston Hughes, 45–49.

———. 'Chemchemi Creative Centre, Nairobi'. *Journal of Modern African Studies* 3, no 1 (1965): 115–117.

———. Letter to the editor. *Transition* 7, no 34 (1968): 5.

Murphy, Mojalefa. 'Africa's Nuclear Power Potential: Its Rise, Recession, Opportunities and Constraints'. In *Energy Transition in Africa*, edited by Thokozani Simelane and Mohamed Abdel-Rahman, 21–54.

Namikas, Lise. 'History Through Documents and Memory: Report on a CWIHP Critical Oral History Conference on the Congo Crisis, 1960–1961'. *Cold War International History Project*, bulletin 16 (Fall 2007/Winter 2008): 537–539.

———. 'Review of *Foreign Relations of the United States, 1964–1968, Volume XXIII, Congo, 1960–1968*'. *FRUS Review*, no 33 (October 2017). https://networks.h-net.org/system/files/contributed-files/frus33.pdf.

Nkulu-N'Sengha, Mutombo. 'African Traditional Religions'. In *The Hope of Liberation in World Religions*, edited by Miguel A de la Torre, 217–238.

Nyameko, B S. 'Fight U.S. Subversion of Trade Union Movement in Africa!' *African Communist* 87 (Fourth Quarter 1981): 56–57.

Nzongola-Ntalaja, Georges. 'Patrice Lumumba and the Unfinished Business of Liberation'. *ROAPE*, 15 January 2021. https://roape.net/2021/01/15/patrice-lumumba-and-the-unfinished-business-of-liberation/.

Obuobi, Patrick Peprah. 'Evaluating Ghana's Intelligence Oversight Regime'. *International Journal of Intelligence and Counterintelligence* 31, no 2 (2018): 312–341.

Osseo-Asare, Abena Dove. '"Atomic Lands": Understanding Land Disputes near Ghana's Nuclear Reactor'. *African Affairs* 115, no 460 (July 2016): 443–465.

Postar, Stephanie. 'The Half-Lives of African Uranium: A Historical Review'. *Extractive Industries and Society* 4, no 2 (April 2017): 398–409.

Potekhin, Ivan. 'Problems of Economic Independence of African Countries'. In *First International Congress of Africanists, 11th–18th December* 1962. Accra: University of Ghana, 1962.

Price, David. 'The CIA Book Publishing Operations: Fragments of Sol Chaneles' Lost Manuscript'. *CounterPunch*, 13 September 2020.

Rabinowitch, Eugene, and Ruth Adams, eds. *Bulletin of the Atomic Scientists* 20, no 10 (December 1964).

'Race Relations in the United States and American Cultural and Informational Programs in Ghana, 1957–1966, Part 2'. *Prologue* 31, no 4 (Winter 1999).

Rathbone, Richard. 'Police Intelligence in Ghana in the Late 1940s and 1950s'. In *Emergencies and Disorder in the European Empires After 1945*, edited by Robert Holland, 107–128.

Robeson, Eslanda. 'The Accra Conference'. *New World Review*, February 1959.

Rogers, Asha. '*Black Orpheus* and the African Magazines on the Congress for Cultural Freedom'. In *Campaigning Culture and the Global Cold War*, edited by Giles Scott-Smith and Charlotte A. Lerg, 243–259.

Schecter, Dan, Michael Ansara, and David Kolodney. 'The CIA as an Equal Opportunity Employer'. In *Dirty Work 2: The CIA in Africa*, edited by Ellen Ray et al, 50–69.

Schorr, Daniel. 'Forgive Us Our Press Passes'. *Hastings Communications and Entertainment Law Journal* 20, no 2 (1998): 269–273.

Shatz, Adam. 'Where Life Is Seized'. *London Review of Books*, 19 January 2017.

Shepperson, George, and St Clare Drake. 'The Fifth Pan-African Conference, 1945 and the All African Peoples Congress, 1958'. *Contributions in Black Studies: A Journal of African and Afro-American Studies* 8 (September 2008): 34–66.

Sherwood, Marika. 'Kwame Nkrumah: The London Years, 1945–47'. In *Africans in Britain*, edited by David Killingray, 164–194.

Stanard, Matthew G. 'Revisiting Bula Matari and the Congo Crisis: Successes and Anxieties in Belgium's Late Colonial State'. *Journal of Imperial and Commonwealth History* 48, no 1 (2018): 144–168.

Stelzl-Marx, Barbara. 'Death to Spies! Austrian Informants for Western Intelligence Services and Soviet Capital Punishment During the Occupation of Austria'. *Journal of Cold War Studies* 14, no 4 (Fall 2012): 167–196.

Stoner, John C. '"We Will Follow a Nationalist Policy; but We Will Never Be Neutral": American Labor and Neutralism in Cold War Africa, 1957–1962'. In *American Labor's Global Ambassadors: The International History of the AFL-CIO During the Cold War*, edited by Robert Anthony Waters Jr and Geert Van Goethem, 237–251.

Streeter, Stephen M. 'Interpreting the 1954 U.S. Intervention in Guatemala: Realist, Revisionist, and Postrevisionist Perspectives'. *History Teacher* 34, no 1 (2000): 61–74.

Tousignant, Nathalie. 'Geopolitics and Spatiality at Expo 58: The International, Foreign and Belgian Colonial Sections'. In *Expo 58: Between Utopia and Reality*, edited by Gonzague Pluvinage, 95–118.

Van Den Bosch, Jean. 'Document 1: Memoire de M. l'Ambassadeur Jean Van Den Bosch Relatif aux événements des 6 and 7 juillet 1960, à Leopoldville'. *Chronique De Politique Étrangère* 14, no 5/6 (1961): 597–603.

Van Goethem, Geert. 'From Dollars to Deeds: Exploring the Sources of Active Interventionism, 1934–1945'. In *American Labor's Global Ambassadors: The International History of the AFL-CIO During the Cold War*, edited by Robert Anthony Waters Jr and Geert Van Goethem, 9–22.

Volodin, Lev. 'Last Days of Freedom'. In *May Our People Triumph*, by Patrice Lumumba, 135–144.

Von Bülow, Mathilde. 'Irving Brown and ICFTU Labor Diplomacy During Algeria's Struggle for Independence, 1954–1962'. In *American Labor's Global Ambassadors: The International History of the AFL-CIO During the Cold War*, edited by Robert Anthony Waters Jr and Geert Van Goethem, 217–236.

Weissman, Stephen R. 'CIA Covert Action in Zaire and Angola: Patterns and Consequences'. *Political Science Quarterly* 94, no. 2 (Summer, 1979): 263–286.

———. 'An Extraordinary Rendition'. In *Intelligence and National Security* 25, no 2 (April 2010): 198–222.

———. 'Opening the Secret Files on Lumumba's Murder'. *Washington Post*, 21 July 2002.

———. 'What Really Happened in the Congo: The CIA, the Murder of Lumumba, and the Rise of Mobutu'. *Foreign Affairs*, July–August 2014.

Wilford, Hugh. 'The American Society of African Culture: The CIA and Transnational Networks of African Diaspora Intellectuals in the Cold War'. In *Transnational Anti-Communism and the Cold War*, edited by Luc van Dongen, Stéphanie Roulinand, and Giles Scott-Smith, 23–34.

Willetts, Peter. 'Consultative Status for NGOs at the UN'. In *'The Conscience of the World': The Influence of Non-Governmental Organisations in the UN System*, edited by Peter Willetts, 31–62.

Zhukov, Yuri. 'Such Was Lumumba'. In *May Our People Triumph*, by Patrice Lumumba, 161–177.

Theses and Dissertations

Biney, Ama Barbara. 'Kwame Nkrumah: An Intellectual Biography'. Doctoral thesis, SOAS, University of London, 2007.

Grice, Carter. '"Happy Are Those Who Sing and Dance": Mobutu, Franco, and the Struggle for Zairian Identity'. Master's thesis, University of the Graduate School of Western Carolina University, November 2011.

Grilli, Matteo. 'African Liberation and Unity in Nkrumah's Ghana: A Study of the Role of "Pan African Institutions" in the Making of Ghana's Foreign Policy, 1957–1966'. Doctoral thesis, Leiden University, November 2015.

James, Leslie Elaine. '"What We Put in Black and White": George Padmore and the Practice of Anti-Imperial Politics'. Doctoral thesis, London School of Economics, April 2012.

Mahoney, Richard D. 'The Kennedy Policy in the Congo, 1961–1963'. Doctoral thesis, Johns Hopkins University School of Advanced International Studies, 1979.

Marino, Alexander Joseph. 'America's War in Angola, 1961–1976'. Master's thesis, University of Arkansas, 2015.

Monaville, Pedro A G. 'Decolonizing the University: Postal Politics, the Student Movement, and Global 1968 in the Congo'. Doctoral thesis, University of Michigan, 2013.

Montgomery, Mary E. 'The Eyes of the World Were Watching: Ghana, Great Britain, and the United States, 1957–1966'. Doctoral thesis, University of Maryland, 2004.

Nesbitt, Francis Njubi. 'Race for Sanctions: The Movement Against Apartheid, 1946–1994'. Doctoral thesis, University of Massachusetts Amherst, 2002.

Quaidoo, Eric. 'The United States and the Overthrow of Kwame Nkrumah'. Master's thesis, Fort Hays State University, Fall 2010. https://scholars.fhsu.edu/cgi/view content.cgi?article=1177&context=theses.

Ritchie, Tyler. 'A Familiar Frontier: The Kennedy Administration in the Congo'. Master's thesis, Brandeis University, 2012. https://bir.brandeis.edu/bitstream /handle/10192/49/Thesis.pdf?sequence=3.

Van Nederveen, Captain Gilles K. 'USAF Airlift into the Heart of Darkness, the Congo 1960–1978: Implications for Modern Air Mobility Planners'. Research Paper 2001-04, College of Aerospace Doctrine, Research and Education, Airpower Research Institute, Air University, September 2001.

Wellerstein, Alex. 'Knowledge and the Bomb: Nuclear Secrecy in the United States, 1939–2008'. Doctoral thesis, Harvard University, 2010.

Yoon, Duncan McEachern. 'Cold War Africa and China: The Afro-Asian Writers' Bureau and the Rise of Postcolonial Literature'. Doctoral thesis, UCLA, 2014.

Films/Videos

British Pathé. 'Belgium: ICFTU Congress, Brussels'. 12 December 1959. www.british pathe.com/video/VLVABMNEKU6XNCX02RIUL69V5KOU1-BELGIUM -ICFTU-CONGRESS-BRUSSELS/query/Belgium.

———. 'Mr. Lumumba Opens the Pan-African Co-Operation Conference'. 1960. www.britishpathe.com/video/mr-lumumba-opens-the-pan-african-co-operation -conf.

Buyout Footage Historic Film Archive. 'HD Stock Footage 1960's African Summit Meeting in Casablanca'. 9 January 1961, uploaded 10 February 2013. https://youtu .be/YhsBbaq_kLQ.

Grayzone. 'Ex-CIA Director Pompeo: "We Lied, We Cheated, We Stole"'. 24 April 2019. https://youtu.be/DPt-zXno5ac.

Nzwamba. '30 Juin 1960–30 Juin 2018: Ambroise Boimbo, un héros oublié'. 30 June 2018. https://youtu.be/Lz1g3VKI0ZU.

Reenberg, Helmer. 'President John F Kennedy's Remarks of Welcome to President Nkrumah of Ghana'. 8 March 1961, uploaded 6 August 2013. https://youtu .be/1OzMa79TXTM.

Thierry, Michael. *Mobutu, King of Zaire—Congo—VostEn—Belgique*. 1999, uploaded 30 April 2019, by AfricaShows. https://youtu.be/OpCb_Yg_qJA.

'Watch Nkrumah's Funerals in Guinea and Ghana Which Have Been Wiped from History'. *GhanaWeb*, 27 April 2020. www.ghanaweb.com/GhanaHomePage /NewsArchive/Watch-Nkrumah-s-funerals-in-Guinea-and-Ghana-which -have-been-wiped-from-history-935716.

Interviews

Interviews Conducted for the US Association for Diplomatic Studies and Training (ADST)

Barnes, Shirley Elizabeth. Interview by Charles Stuart Kennedy. 2004. *Country Reader: Series Republic of the Congo*, 11–17. https://adst.org/wp-content/uploads/2012/09 /Republic-of-the-Congo.pdf.

Buchanan, Thompson R. Interview by Charles Stuart Kennedy. Initial interview 15 March 1996. https://www.loc.gov/item/mfdipbib000162/.

Carlucci, Frank, III. Interview by Charles Stuart Kennedy. 1 April 1997, continuation of an interview that began 31 December 1996. www.adst.org/OH%20TOCs /Carlucci,%20Frank%20Charles%20III%20_April%201,%201997_.pdf.

Cook, Mercer. Interview by Ruth Strutts Njiiri. 24 June 1981. ADST, Ralph J. Bunche Legacy: Minority Officers. www.adst.org/OH%20TOCs/Cook,%20Mercer.toc .pdf.

Freeman, Phyllis. Interview by Hope Meyers. 10 October 1986. ADST Foreign Service Spouse Series. www.adst.org/OH%20TOCs/Freeman,%20Phyllis.toc.pdf.

Haynes, Ulric, Jr. Interview by Charles Stuart Kennedy. 20 April 2011. www.adst.org /OH%20TOCs/Haynes,%20Ulric,%20Jr.%20toc.pdf.

Imbrey, Howard. Interview by Charles Stuart Kennedy. 21 June 2001. https://collec tions.digitalmaryland.org/digital/collection/saac/id/12759/rec/1.

Lukens, Alan W. Interview by Charles Stuart Kennedy. Initial interview 17 November 1989. www.adst.org/OH%20TOCs/Lukens,%20Alan%20W%20.toc.pdf.

McIlvaine, Robinson. Interview by Charles Stuart Kennedy. Initial interview 1 April 1988. www.adst.org/OH%20TOCs/Mcilvaine,%20Robinson.toc.pdf.

Roberts, Owen W. Interview by Charles Stuart Kennedy. Initial interview 11 February 1991. www.adst.org/OH%20TOCs/Roberts,%20Owen%20W.toc.pdf.

Smith, Robert P. Interview by Charles Stuart Kennedy. Initial interview 28 February 1989. https://tile.loc.gov/storage-services/service/mss/mfdip/2004/2004smi 09/2004smi09.pdf.

Steigman, Andrew L. Interview by Charles Stuart Kennedy. 29 April 1989. https:// tile.loc.gov/storage-services/service/mss/mfdip/2004/2004ste05/2004ste05.pdf.

Young, Johnny. Interview by Charles Stuart Kennedy. 21 October 2005. https://tile .loc.gov/storage-services/service/mss/mfdip/2010/2010youo1/2010youo1.pdf.

Other Interviews

Burden, William A M. Interview by John Luter. 29 January 1968. Eisenhower Administration Project, Columbia Center for Oral History, Columbia University

Libraries. https://oralhistoryportal.library.columbia.edu/document.php?id=ldpd
_13752420.

Doyle, David W. Interview by Charles M Southall. 19 June 2013. Honolulu. Susan
Williams Private Papers.

Gullion, Edmund A. Interview by Samuel E Belk III. 17 July 1964. Washington, DC.
John F Kennedy Library Oral History Program. www.jfklibrary.org/sites/default
/files/archives/JFKOH/Gullion%2C%20Edmund%20A/JFKOH-EDAG-01
/JFKOH-EDAG-01-TR.pdf.

Helms, Richard M. Interview by David Frost. 22–23 May 1978. Washington, DC.
www.cia.gov/library/center-for-the-study-of-intelligence/kent-csi/vol44no4
/html/v44i4a07p_0001.htm.

Houser, George M. Interview by Lisa Brock. 19 July 2004. Rockland County, New
York. www.noeasyvictories.org/interviews/into2_houser.php.

Imbrey, Howard. Interview by Curtis Ostle. 2 April 2001. 'The Congo: An Indirect
Fight Against Communism'. St Andrew's Episcopal School, Potomac, Maryland.
https://collections.digitalmaryland.org/digital/collection/saac/id/12759/rec/1.

Mahoney, William P. Interview by William W Moss. 14 May 1975. Waltham, Massachusetts. John F Kennedy Library Oral History Program.www.jfklibrary.org
/sites/default/files/archives/JFKOH/Mahoney%2C%20William%20P/JFKOH
-WPM-01/JFKOH-WPM-01-TR.pdf.

Murray, Pauli. Interview by Genna Rae McNeil. 13 February 1976. Interview G-0044.
Southern Oral History Program Collection. #4007. https://docsouth.unc.edu
/sohp/G-0044/G-0044.html.

Nichols, Kenneth. Interview in three parts; part 3 by Stephane Groueff. 4 January
1965. Voices of the Manhattan Project in partnership with the National Museum
of Nuclear Science and History. Oral Histories. www.manhattanprojectvoices.org
/oral-histories/general-kenneth-nicholss-interview-part-2.

Palmer, Alison. Interview by Karen Lamoree. 14 June 1988. Cape Cod, Massachusetts. Pembroke Center Oral History Project, Brown University. www.brown.edu
/initiatives/pembroke-oral-histories/sites/brown.edu.initiatives.pembroke-oral
-histories/files/transcripts/pemb000125.pdf.

Russell, Francis H. Interview by William W Moss. 24 January 1973. Medford, Massachusetts. John F Kennedy Library Oral History Program.www.jfklibrary.org
/sites/default/files/archives/JFKOH/Russell%2C%20Francis%20H/JFKOH
-FHR-02/JFKOH-FHR-02-TR.pdf.

Singer, Hans W. Interview by Richard Jolly. 2 January 2000. Sussex, UK. United Nations
Intellectual History Project. https://clio.columbia.edu/catalog/9145424?counter=1.

Southall, Charles M. Interview by Sir Stephen Sedley, Chair of the Hammarskjöld Commission. 21 September 2012. London. Hans Kristian Simensen Private
Papers.

INDEX

DR. SUSAN WILLIAMS is a senior research fellow in the School of Advanced Study, University of London. Her pathbreaking books include *Who Killed Hammarskjöld?*, which in 2015 triggered a new, ongoing UN investigation into the death of the UN Secretary General in 1961; *Spies in the Congo*, which spotlights the link between US espionage in the Congo and the atomic bombs dropped on Japan in 1945; *Colour Bar*, the story of Botswana's founding president, which was made into the major 2016 film *A United Kingdom*; and *The People's King*, which presents an original perspective on the abdication of Edward VIII and his marriage to Wallis Simpson.

PublicAffairs is a publishing house founded in 1997. It is a tribute to the standards, values, and flair of three persons who have served as mentors to countless reporters, writers, editors, and book people of all kinds, including me.

I. F. STONE, proprietor of *I. F. Stone's Weekly*, combined a commitment to the First Amendment with entrepreneurial zeal and reporting skill and became one of the great independent journalists in American history. At the age of eighty, Izzy published *The Trial of Socrates*, which was a national bestseller. He wrote the book after he taught himself ancient Greek.

BENJAMIN C. BRADLEE was for nearly thirty years the charismatic editorial leader of *The Washington Post*. It was Ben who gave the *Post* the range and courage to pursue such historic issues as Watergate. He supported his reporters with a tenacity that made them fearless and it is no accident that so many became authors of influential, best-selling books.

ROBERT L. BERNSTEIN, the chief executive of Random House for more than a quarter century, guided one of the nation's premier publishing houses. Bob was personally responsible for many books of political dissent and argument that challenged tyranny around the globe. He is also the founder and longtime chair of Human Rights Watch, one of the most respected human rights organizations in the world.

·   ·   ·

For fifty years, the banner of Public Affairs Press was carried by its owner Morris B. Schnapper, who published Gandhi, Nasser, Toynbee, Truman, and about 1,500 other authors. In 1983, Schnapper was described by *The Washington Post* as "a redoubtable gadfly." His legacy will endure in the books to come.

Peter Osnos, *Founder*